Children's
Literature
Review

Guide to Gale Literary Criticism Series

For criticism on	Consult these Gale series
Authors now living or who died after December 31, 1959	*CONTEMPORARY LITERARY CRITICISM (CLC)*
Authors who died between 1900 and 1959	*TWENTIETH-CENTURY LITERARY CRITICISM (TCLC)*
Authors who died between 1800 and 1899	*NINETEENTH-CENTURY LITERATURE CRITICISM (NCLC)*
Authors who died between 1400 and 1799	*LITERATURE CRITICISM FROM 1400 TO 1800 (LC)* *SHAKESPEAREAN CRITICISM (SC)*
Authors who died before 1400	*CLASSICAL AND MEDIEVAL LITERATURE CRITICISM (CMLC)*
Black writers of the past two hundred years	*BLACK LITERATURE CRITICISM (BLC)*
Authors of books for children and young adults	*CHILDREN'S LITERATURE REVIEW (CLR)*
Dramatists	*DRAMA CRITICISM (DC)*
Hispanic writers of the late nineteenth and twentieth centuries	*HISPANIC LITERATURE CRITICISM (HLC)*
Native North American writers and orators of the eighteenth, nineteenth, and twentieth centuries	*NATIVE NORTH AMERICAN LITERATURE (NNAL)*
Poets	*POETRY CRITICISM (PC)*
Short story writers	*SHORT STORY CRITICISM (SSC)*
Major authors from the Renaissance to the present	*WORLD LITERATURE CRITICISM, 1500 TO THE PRESENT (WLC)*

ISSN 0362-4145

volume 46

Children's Literature Review

Excerpts from Reviews,
Criticism, and Commentary
on Books for Children
and Young People

Linda R. Andres
Editor

GALE

DETROIT • NEW YORK • TORONTO • LONDON

The paper used in this publication meets the minimum requirements of American National Standard for Information Sciences—Permanence Paper for Printed Library Materials, ANSI Z39.48-1984.

Library of Congress Catalog Card Number 76-643301
ISBN 0-7876-1140-9
ISSN 0362-4145
Printed in the United States of America

10   9   8   7   6   5   4   3   2   1

Contents

Preface

Literature for children and young adults has evolved into both a respected branch of creative writing and a successful industry. Currently, books for young readers are considered among the most popular segments of publishing. Criticism of juvenile literature is instrumental in recording the literary or artistic development of the creators of children's books as well as the trends and controversies that result from changing values or attitudes about young people and their literature. Designed to provide a permanent, accessible record of this ongoing scholarship, *Children's Literature Review (CLR)* presents parents, teachers, and librarians—those responsible for bringing children and books together—with the opportunity to make informed choices when selecting reading materials for the young. In addition, *CLR* provides researchers of children's literature with easy access to a wide variety of critical information from English-language sources in the field. Users will find balanced overviews of the careers of the authors and illustrators of the books that children and young adults are reading; these entries, which contain excerpts from published criticism in books and periodicals, assist users by sparking ideas for papers and assignments and suggesting supplementary and classroom reading. Ann L. Kalkhoff, president and editor of *Children's Book Review Service Inc.,* writes that "*CLR* has filled a gap in the field of children's books, and it is one series that will never lose its validity or importance."

Scope of the Series

Each volume of *CLR* profiles the careers of a selection of authors and illustrators of books for children and young adults from preschool through high school. Author lists in each volume reflect:

- an international scope.

- representation of authors of all eras.

- the variety of genres covered by children's and/or YA literature: picture books, fiction, nonfiction, poetry, folklore, and drama.

Although the focus of the series is on authors new to *CLR*, entries will be updated as the need arises.

Organization of This Book

An entry consists of the following elements: author heading, author portrait, author introduction, excerpts of criticism (each preceded by a bibliographical citation), and illustrations, when available.

- The **Author Heading** consists of the author's name followed by birth and death dates. The portion of the name outside the parentheses denotes the form under which the author is most frequently published. If the majority of the author's works for children were written under a pseudonym, the pseudonym will be listed in the author heading and the real name given on the first line of the author introduction. Also located at the beginning of the introduction are any other pseudonyms used by the author in writing for children and any name variations, including transliterated forms for authors whose languages use nonroman alphabets. Uncertainty as to a birth or death date is indicated by question marks.

- An **Author Portrait** is included when available.

- The **Author Introduction** contains information designed to introduce an author to *CLR* users by presenting an overview of the author's themes and styles, biographical facts that relate to the author's literary career or critical responses to the author's works, and information about major awards and prizes the author has received. The introduction begins by identifying the nationality of the author and by listing the genres in which s/he has written for children and young adults. Introductions also list a group of representative titles for which the author or illustrator being profiled is best known; this section, which begins with the words "major works include," follows the genre line of the introduction. For seminal figures, a listing of major works about the author follows when appropriate, highlighting important biographies about the author or illustrator that are not excerpted in the entry. The centered heading "Introduction" announces the body of the text.

- **Criticism** is located in three sections: **Author's Commentary** (when available), **General Commentary** (when available), and **Title Commentary** (commentary on specific titles).

  - The **Author's Commentary** presents background material written by the author or by an interviewer. This commentary may cover a specific work or several works. Author's commentary on more than one work appears after the author introduction, while commentary on an individual book follows the title entry heading.

  - The **General Commentary** consists of critical excerpts that consider more than one work by the author or illustrator being profiled. General commentary is preceded by the critic's name in boldface type or, in the case of unsigned criticism, by the title of the journal. *CLR* also features entries that emphasize general criticism on the oeuvre of an author or illustrator. When appropriate, a selection of reviews is included to supplement the general commentary.

  - The **Title Commentary** begins with the title entry headings, which precede the criticism on a title and cite publication information on the work being reviewed. Title headings list the title of the work as it appeared in its first English-language edition. The first English-language publication date of each work (unless otherwise noted) is listed in parentheses following the title. Differing U.S. and British titles follow the publication date within the parentheses. When a work is written by an individual other than the one being profiled, as is the case when illustrators are featured, the parenthetical material following the title cites the author of the work before listing its publication date.

    Entries in each title commentary section consist of critical excerpts on the author's individual works, arranged chronologically by publication date. The entries generally contain two to seven reviews per title, depending on the stature of the book and the amount of criticism it has generated. The editors select titles that reflect the entire scope of the author's literary contribution, covering each genre and subject. An effort is made to reprint criticism that represents the full range of each title's reception, from the year of its initial publication to current assessments. Thus, the reader is provided with a record of the author's critical history. Publication information (such as publisher names and book prices) and parenthetical numerical references (such as footnotes or page and line references to specific editions of works) have been deleted at the discretion of the editors to provide smoother reading of the text.

- Centered headings introduce each section, in which criticism is arranged chronologically; beginning with Volume 35, each excerpt is preceded by a boldface source heading for easier access by readers. Within the text, titles by authors being profiled are also highlighted in boldface type.

- Selected excerpts are preceded by **Explanatory Annotations,** which provide information on the critic or work of criticism to enhance the reader's understanding of the excerpt.

- A complete **Bibliographical Citation** designed to facilitate the location of the original book or article precedes each piece of criticism.

- Numerous **Illustrations** are featured in *CLR.* For entries on illustrators, an effort has been made to include illustrations that reflect the characteristics discussed in the criticism. Entries on authors who do not illustrate their own works may also include photographs and other illustrative material pertinent to their careers.

Special Features: Entries on Illustrators

Entries on authors who are also illustrators will occasionally feature commentary on selected works illustrated but not written by the author being profiled. These works are strongly associated with the illustrator and have received critical acclaim for their art. By including critical comment on works of this type, the editors wish to provide a more complete representation of the artist's career. Criticism on these works has been chosen to stress artistic, rather than literary, contributions. Title entry headings for works illustrated by the author being profiled are arranged chronologically within the entry by date of publication and include notes identifying the author of the illustrated work. In order to provide easier access for users, all titles illustrated by the subject of the entry are boldfaced.

CLR also includes entries on prominent illustrators who have contributed to the field of children's literature. These entries are designed to represent the development of the illustrator as an artist rather than as a literary stylist. The illustrator's section is organized like that of an author, with two exceptions: the introduction presents an overview of the illustrator's styles and techniques rather than outlining his or her literary background, and the commentary written by the illustrator on his or her works is called "illustrator's commentary" rather than "author's commentary." All titles of books containing illustrations by the artist being profiled are highlighted in boldface type.

Other Features: Acknowledgments, Indexes

- The **Acknowledgments** section, which immediately follows the preface, lists the sources from which material has been reprinted in the volume. It does not, however, list every book or periodical consulted for the volume.

- The **Cumulative Index to Authors** lists all of the authors who have appeared in *CLR* with cross-references to the biographical, autobiographical, and literary criticism series published by Gale Research. A full listing of the series titles appears before the first page of the indexes of this volume.

- The **Cumulative Index to Nationalities** lists authors alphabetically under their respective nationalities. Author names are followed by the volume number(s) in which they appear.

- The **Cumulative Index to Titles** lists titles covered in *CLR* followed by the volume and page number where criticism begins.

A Note to the Reader

CLR is one of several critical references sources in the Literature Criticism Series published by Gale Research. When writing papers, students who quote directly from any volume in the Literature Criticism Series may use the following general forms to footnote reprinted criticism. The first example pertains to material drawn from periodicals, the second to material reprinted from books.

[1]T. S. Eliot, "John Donne," *The Nation and the Athenaeum,* 33 (9 June 1923), 321-32; excerpted and reprinted in *Literature Criticism from 1400 to 1800,* Vol. 10, ed. James E. Person, Jr. (Detroit: Gale Research, 1989), pp. 28-9.

[1]Henry Brooke, *Leslie Brooke and Johnny Crow* (Frederick Warne, 1982); excerpted and reprinted in *Children's Literature Review,* Vol. 20, ed. Gerard J. Senick (Detroit: Gale Research, 1990), p. 47.

Suggestions Are Welcome

In response to various suggestions, several features have been added to *CLR* since the beginning of the series, including author entries on retellers of traditional literature as well as those who have been the first to record oral tales and other folklore; entries on prominent illustrators featuring commentary on their styles and techniques; entries on authors whose works are considered controversial; occasional entries devoted to criticism on a single work or a series of works; sections in author introductions that list major works by and about the author or illustrator being profiled; explanatory notes that provide information on the critic or work of criticism to enhance the usefulness of the excerpt; more extensive illustrative material, such as holographs of manuscript pages and photographs of people and places pertinent to the careers of the authors and artists; a cumulative nationality index for easy access to authors by nationality; and occasional guest essays written specifically for *CLR* by prominent critics on subjects of their choice.

Readers who wish to suggest authors to appear in future volumes, or who have other suggestions, are cordially invited to contact the editor. By mail: Editor, *Children's Literature Review,* Gale Research, 835 Penobscot Bldg., 645 Griswold St., Detroit, MI 48226-4094; by telephone: (800) 347-GALE; by fax: (313) 961-6599; by E-mail: CYA@Gale.com.

Acknowledgments

The editors wish to thank the copyright holders of the excerpted criticism included in this volume and the permissions managers of many book and magazine publishing companies for assisting us in securing reproduction rights. We are also grateful to the staffs of the Detroit Public Library, the Library of Congress, the University of Detroit Mercy Library, Wayne State University Purdy/Kresge Library Complex, and the University of Michigan Libraries for making their resources available to us. Following is a list of the copyright holders who have granted us permission to reproduce material in this volume of *CLR*. Every effort has been made to trace copyright, but if omissions have been made, please let us know.

COPYRIGHTED EXCERPTS IN *CLR*, VOLUME 46, WERE REPRINTED FROM THE FOLLOWING PERIODICALS AND BOOKS:

The ALAN Review, v. 10, Winter, 1983; v. 30, May, 1994; v. 24, Winter, 1997. Copyright © 1983, 1994, 1997 by The Alan Review. All reproduced by permission.—*Best Sellers*, v. 26, December 1, 1966; v. 35, June, 1975; v. 35, December, 1975; v. 37, December, 1977; v. 38, July, 1978; v. 42, June, 1982; v. 43, December, 1983; v. 45, September, 1985. Copyright 1966, 1975, 1977, 1978, 1982, 1983, 1985 by the University of Scranton. All reproduced by permission of the publisher.—*The Bloomsbury Review*, v. 13, May-June, 1993 for "Testimonies of Native American Life" by Carl L. Bankston III. Reproduced by permission of the author.—*The Book Report*, v. 14, May-June, 1995. Copyright © 1995 by Linworth Publishing, Inc., Worthington, Ohio. Reproduced with permission.—*Bookbird*, n. 2, 1984. Reproduced by permission.—*Booklist*, v. 73, September 15, 1976; v. 73, April 15, 1977; v. 74, October 1, 1977; v. 74, May 15, 1978; v. 75, September 1, 1978; v. 75, March 15, 1979; v. 75, April 1, 1979; v. 76, September 15, 1979; v. 76, December 1, 1979; v. 76, February 1, 1980; v. 76, March 15, 1980; v. 77, April 1, 1981; v. 78, September 15, 1981; v. 78, January 15, 1982; v. 78, April 15, 1982; v. 79, March 1, 1983; v. 79, April 15, 1983; v. 80, September 1, 1983; v. 80, September 15, 1983; v. 80, June 15, 1984; v. 81, January 15, 1985; v. 81, July, 1985; v. 82, October 1, 1985; v. 82, October 15, 1985; v. 82, November 1, 1985; v. 82, May 1, 1986; v. 82, July, 1986; v. 83, October 1, 1986; v. 83, December 15, 1986; v. 83, August, 1987; v. 84, September 1, 1987; v. 84, November 1, 1987; v. 84, January 15, 1988; v. 84, June 1, 1988; v. 85, September 1, 1988; v. 85, October 1, 1988; v. 85, December 1, 1988; v. 85, March 1, 1989; v. 85, May 1, 1989; v. 86, September 1, 1989; v. 86, November 15, 1989; v. 86, February 15, 1990; v. 86, March 1, 1990; v. 86, April 1, 1990; v. 87, September 1, 1990; v. 87, September 15, 1990; v. 87, December 15, 1990; v. 87, January 15, 1991; v. 87, February 1, 1991; v. 87, February 11, 1991; v. 87, March 15, 1991; v. 87, April 1, 1991; v. 87, August, 1991; v. 88, September 1, 1991; v. 88, October 1, 1991; v. 88, November 1, 1991; v. 88, December 15, 1991; v. 88, March 1, 1992; v. 88, April 15, 1992; v. 89, September 1, 1992; v. 89, November 15, 1992; v. 89, February 15, 1993; v. 89, March 1, 1993; v. 90, September 1, 1993; v. 90, October 1, 1993; v. 90, December 15, 1993; v. 90, January 15, 1994; v. 90, March 1, 1994; v. 90, April 1, 1994; v. 90, June 1 & June 15, 1994; v. 91, September 15, 1994; v. 91, October 1, 1994; v. 91, November 15, 1994; v. 91, January 1, 1995; v. 91, March 15, 1995; v. 91, May 1, 1995; v. 92, September 15, 1995; v. 92, November 15, 1995; v. 92, December 1, 1995; v. 92, February 1, 1996; v. 92, March 15, 1996; v. 92, April 1, 1996; v. 92, April 15, 1996; v. 92, May 1, 1996; v. 93, November 1, 1996; v. 93, February 15, 1997. Copyright © 1976, 1977, 1978, 1979, 1980, 1981, 1982, 1983, 1984, 1985, 1986, 1987, 1988, 1989, 1990, 1991, 1992, 1993, 1994, 1995, 1996, 1997 by the American Library Association. All reproduced by permission of the publisher.—*The Booklist*, v. 68, January 1, 1972; v. 70, December 15, 1973, v. 70, March 15, 1974; v. 71, June 15, 1975; v. 72, November 1, 1975, v. 72, March 1, 1976; v. 74, April 1, 1978 . Copyright © 1972, 1973, 1974, 1975, 1976, 1978 by the American Library Association. All reproduced by permission of the publisher.—*Books for Keeps*, n. 42, January, 1987; n. 51, July, 1988; n. 52, September, 1988; n. 63, July, 1990; n. 71, November, 1991; n. 75, July, 1992; n. 76, September, 1992; n. 83, November, 1993; n. 87, July, 1994; n. 95, November, 1995. Copyright © 1987, 1988, 1990, 1991, 1992, 1993, 1994, 1995 by School Bookshop Association. All reproduced by permission of the publisher.—*Books in Canada*, v. XXIV, April, 1995 for a review of "Keepers of Life: Discovering Plants through Native Stories and Earth Activities for Children" by Donna Nurse. Reproduced by permission of the author.—*British Book News Children's Books*, June, 1987. Copyright © 1987 by The British

ILLUSTRATIONS APPEARING IN *CLR*, VOLUME 46, WERE REPRODUCED FROM THE FOLLOWING SOURCES:

PHOTOGRAPHS APPEARING IN *CLR,* VOLUME 46, WERE REPRODUCED FROM THE FOLLOWING SOURCES:

Children's
Literature
Review

Joseph Bruchac III
1942-

Native American storyteller, poet, songwriter, and novelist for young adults.

Major works include *Keepers of the Earth* (1988), *Turtle Meat and Other Stories* (1992), *Dawn Land* (1993), *A Boy Called Slow* (1995), *The Boy Who Lived with the Bears and Other Iroquois Stories* (1995).

INTRODUCTION

Widely respected as one of the foremost Native American storytellers in the United States, Bruchac is best known to young readers for his folktales that vividly depict the life and lore of many Indian cultures. Praised for his ability to evoke a wide range of characters and situations, Bruchac uses an engaging variety of viewpoints, dialects, and writing techniques to explore such themes as the bond between the Earth and its creatures, the sacredness of the natural world, and the inevitable links between legend and life. Although his stories frequently appeal to people of all ages, they are often recommended for middle school students. Bruchac hopes that his readers will understand that "Native American folklore is based on deep understandings of the natural world and human nature." According to the author, he likes to share traditional stories because "they have messages, sometimes very subtle, which can help show young people the good paths to follow."

Biographical Information

Born in Saratoga Springs, New York, Bruchac was raised by his grandparents in the foothills of the Adirondack Mountains. Although he is of Abenaki Indian, Slovak, and English heritage, it was not until his teens that Bruchac began to learn about his Native American heritage and the rich folklore of his ancestors. After receiving a Bachelor of Arts degree from Cornell University in 1965 and a Master of Arts degree from Syracuse University in 1966, Bruchac taught English and literature in Ghana for three years. He returned to the United States in 1969 to teach African and African-American literature in New York State, later earning his Ph.D. from Union Graduate School. Author or co-author of more than fifty books, Bruchac has been the publisher and editor of *Greenfield Review* since 1969 and director of Greenfield Review Literary Center since 1981. In 1970, Bruchac and his wife founded the Greenfield Review Press, which publishes multicultural literature. Bruchac also writes and performs music, often about American Indian themes. He plays the guitar, the Native American flute, and Native American drum, and performs as part of a family group (with his two sons, Jesse and Jim, and his sister, Marge) called the

Dawn Land Singers. Bruchac believes that even his non-writing activities—hiking, canoeing, gardening, martial arts—contribute to his storytelling: "When we recognize that life is a circle, we see how things are related and our lives can be much fuller and more interesting."

Major Works

Bruchac's experience as a teacher is evident in *Keepers of the Earth,* the first of three books dealing with Native-centered science—followed later by *Keepers of Animals* and *Keepers of Light* (plants)—that are appropriate for students from elementary through late middle school grades. Co-authored by Michael Caduto, the book interweaves Native American legends, scientific explanations, and hands-on activities as a tool for the holistic study of the Earth, its creatures, and the interactions that tie them together. *Turtle Meat and Other Stories* is a more traditional collection of original stories, all set in the Adirondack region, where Indian and European heritages are entwined, reflecting the author's heritage. Combining legend, memories, history, humor, realism, and magic, the stories span a time frame from the Viking invasion to contemporary Native America. Many of the tales focus on conflicts between Native Americans and Caucasians, while other stories involve animals and the special relationship that develops between humans, animals, and the land.

Bruchac's first novel, *Dawn Land,* has a special appeal for young adults. Set 10,000 years in the past, it is the story of Young Hunter, an Abenaki (the name means "People of the Dawn Land") who is sent on a journey through what are now called the Adirondack Mountains to save his tribe from beings called the "Ancient Ones," a fearsome race of giants. As the young hero encounters one adventure after another in the defense of his people, the author weaves into the narrative the world view of the Abenaki and their relation with the Earth. Critics praise the lyrical circle of legends and natural history that makes up the novel, the work of a master storyteller. In *The Boy Who Lived with the Bears and Other Iroquois Stories,* Bruchac presents a collection of traditional Iroquois tales in which animals learn about the importance of caring and responsibility and the dangers of selfishness and pride. Turning to a dramatic true story in *A Boy Called Slow,* Bruchac portrays a Lakota Sioux child so deliberate and methodical that he was nicknamed Slow, until the day when a group of Lakotas meets a Crow war party, and Slow earns a new name—Sitting Bull. Reviewers commend the book as a dignified and poignant picture of a young boy becoming a man and the greatest Lakota hero.

Awards

The Boy Who Lived with the Bears and *A Boy Called Slow* were selected as American Library Association Notable Children's Books in 1996. *The Boy Who Lived with the Bears* was also named a 1996 *Boston Globe-Horn Book.*

GENERAL COMMENTARY

Carl L. Bankston III

SOURCE: "Telling the Truth in Tales," in *The San Francisco Review of Books,* Vol. 18, No. 3, May-June, 1993, pp. 8-9.

During our hour-long morning phone conversation, Joseph Bruchac is remarkably alert and cheerful, considering that just the evening before he returned to his home in the Adirondacks from Florida, where he had been trapped for three days by the freak blizzard that had hit the east coast. The last twenty-four hours of his unexpectedly long and cold stay had been spent standing in line at the airport. "It was an adventure," he laughs good naturedly.

Bruchac's readers might not be surprised by this optimistic resilience. For over twenty years, he has been an in-

defatigable collector and editor of Native American writings and folklore. He regards his work as the tending of vital oral traditions. "Someone once asked me the difference between a 'revivalist storyteller' and a 'tradition bearer'," he says. "Well, a revivalist is someone who just gets stories out of books."

In becoming a novelist, Bruchac has not abandoned his dedication to other people's words. *Dawn Land,* his first full-length novel, is a narrative woven from the ancient, living tales of the Abenaki and Iroquois tribes. It tells the tale of a young Abenaki warrior in the area now known as New England and his defeat of a race of gigantic cannibals, the "Ancient Ones" or the "Stone Giants" threatening to destroy his people.

As the hunter travels from his home by the Connecticut or Long River to the Adirondack Mountains where he confronts the giants, he hears and remembers the stories that enable him to make sense of his life. Like *A Thousand and One Nights,* *Dawn Land* is a tale that holds a collection of tales. This wealth of folklore is set against a background of beautifully clear, detailed descriptions of the primordial North American natural environment. The result is an exquisite book that succeeds both as a novel and as a re-telling of old legends.

Bruchac downplays his role in the creation of this book: "It was a novel that was in many ways given to me, rather than constructed by me . . . It was given to me by the stories; it was given to me by the strange and wonderful process by which a book begins to write itself and all you can do is follow along with the tale and see where it takes you."

He stresses the importance of remaining true to the spirit of the original Iroquois and Abenaki stories. "At each stage as I was writing the book I would send chapters to Stephen Laurent, an Abenaki elder and linguist, whose father was the principal chief of the Canadian Abenaki nation. Steve would critique every page I wrote." Bruchac also sought the advice of others knowledgeable about Native American folklore. "By having those people respond to it and critique it, I was able to be very accurate and detailed."

"The Stone Giants," he explains, "occur in both Iroquois and Abenaki traditions. The place called Onondaga means 'the place among the hills'. It's at Onondaga that they say the Stone Giants were destroyed by being tricked into entering a cavern where a boulder was rolled down on them. So, in a sense, I've recapitulated that destruction of the Stone Giants."

The stories, Bruchac emphasizes, are creations of the New England Native American people who are both the source and first audience of *Dawn Land.* As soon as he had finished the book, he sought the opinion of friends in the Abenaki tribe. "When I sent them the preliminary copy, they made photocopies and passed them around to everyone. They wanted to share it and their approval made me feel very good about it."

Traditional storytelling, of course, does not mean preserving legends as museum pieces. Tribal narrators draw upon a pool of inherited narratives and adapt them to present needs. In an oral culture, myths change and take a variety of forms over millennia of recounting. In giving his own version of the ancient tales, Bruchac is simply doing what storytellers have always done. There is, however, a significant difference: Bruchac's medium is print.

When asked about the relationship between written literature and oral traditions, he adamantly insists that there is not necessarily a conflict between the two. "A lot of people say that if you write something down, you destroy the oral tradition. I think that it's quite the other way, that writing can be a way of making a bridge."

Bruchac's lifelong commitment to bringing Native American oral literature to a wider audience stems from his relationship to his homeland and to his family. Growing up in the Adirondacks, he was especially close to his maternal grandparents. His grandfather was an Abenaki and a great talker, who instilled in Bruchac a love of nature. Although the grandfather was "a dark-skinned, very Indian-looking man," he was not at all active in tribal affairs and did not discuss his native background. "There had been a lot of pain in our family because of that background. My grandfather was trying to pass and be like everyone else." Nevertheless, Bruchac's attachment to his mother's father, "really planted the seed in me that would continue as an adult, wanting to be close to nature, and wanting to find out more about that heritage that I knew was there, but that I hadn't been given directly."

The author's grandmother, the second major influence on his life, was of Czechoslovakian descent. "The ironic thing is, I knew even less about that side of my family. Ethnicity was kind of a family secret; no one talked about it." While Bruchac traces his love of storytelling and folklore to his grandfather, he credits his grandmother with nourishing the other side of his work, his passion for the written word. "My grandmother was well-educated and her house was always full of books," he remembers. In early adulthood, Bruchac determined to learn more about his grandfather's heritage. "I sought out Abenaki people," he explained. "Even though there was no blood relationship there, the way they looked and the way they talked, they were so much like my grandfather." At the same time, he began to work seriously on his writing. His first published poem appeared in 1966, in a book entitled *New College Writing*.

From 1966 to 1969, Bruchac lived and taught in Ghana under the auspices of the Teachers in West Africa Program. He learned the language of the area well enough to do some translating and was impressed by some of the similarities between Native American and African tribal cultures. This was a fallow period in his writing, though, since teaching required most of his attention.

On returning to the U.S., he moved into the house built by his grandfather a half-century before in the small vil-

lage of Greenfield Center in the foothills of the Adirondacks. He also plunged into a flurry of literary activity. In the early 1970's, Bruchac founded and edited *The Greenfield Review,* published several books of poems and two novellas, wrote essays for *The Nickel Review* and other periodicals, edited a special issue of *The Small Press Review* on the small presses of Africa, and co-edited a volume of prison writings. Through these activities, and through his involvement in the anti-war movement, he became friends with some of the best-known figures in contemporary American literature, including Ishmael Reed ("Ishmael is one of the great gadflies of our time; he always knows the right button to push to get people upset") and Robert Bly ("I think Robert's another example of someone who's often wonderfully wrong, but really gets things stirred up, which is what we need. I suppose you could say that in some ways Robert is one of my models.")

Despite his energy, ability, and contacts, Bruchac has remained, for the most part, behind the scenes. He has directed most of his efforts toward bringing Native American writers and folklore to the attention of the reading public. "I think that's part of my responsibility," he explained. "One thing I've learned is expressed by an African proverb, 'no person dislikes good things, but first they have to know about them.'"

Through his editing, Bruchac feels that he has made a contribution to the increasing ethnic diversity of the American literary scene, one of the most important developments of the past quarter century: "American literature has come a long way in the last twenty years. There was a lot of what I would call 'sterility' in the emphasis on 'English literature' as the real literature of America, which I thought totally misrepresented what we now call the 'multicultural' nature of the United States. The awareness and the strengthening of multiculturalism has been one of the best things to happen to literature in this country. We have a much more vital literature today as a result of it."

A former teacher at several universities, including Columbia University, Hamilton College, and Skidmore College, he left the university setting over a decade ago to concentrate even more on his family and his craft. At last, it appears that he is beginning to focus his attention on publishing his own work. In 1992, he published a book of short stories, ***Turtle Meat and Other Stories,*** and two of the stories in this book are part of a novel in progress. I asked him why, after so many years in the writing trade, he has now started to use the longer fictional form of the novel. "Part of it is technology, having a word processor, because I'm very meticulous about revision and it takes a long time to revise and retype a novel. It's ironic," he muses, "using modern technology to do traditional storytelling."

Kit Alderdice

SOURCE: "Joseph Bruchac: Sharing a Native-American

Heritage," in *Publishers Weekly,* Vol. 243, No. 8, February 19, 1996, pp. 191-92.

"It wasn't really a matter of choice. It was a matter of finding what road I was supposed to be on and then staying on it" is Joseph Bruchac's characteristically down-to-earth description of his work as poet, editor, professional storyteller and scholar of Native American culture. The most recent bend in his career path has led the multitalented Bruchac to the publication of more than a dozen children's books revolving around Native American themes.

Though merely one part of an already impressive career, this latest development is surely worthy of note: since 1988, Bruchac's books for children have been published by such major houses as Philomel, Bridgewater, Fulcrum, Harcourt Brace, Dutton and Dial. Among the honors he has garnered are the American Book Award, the Cherokee Nation Prose Award and the *Scientific American* Award for Young Readers. Most recently, his telling of the story of Sitting Bull, *A Boy Called Slow,* issued by Philomel, won the Mountains & Plains Booksellers Association's 1996 Regional Book Award for children's literature.

PW's interview with Joseph Bruchac starts off with a tour of his home in Greenfield Center, N.Y., several miles outside Saratoga Springs. Filled with books, mementos and a profound sense of personal history, the Bruchac family residence was originally two separate buildings: the house where the author was raised, and his grandparents' gas station/general store. Clever renovation joined the two structures in a single space which serves not only as home, but also as office and warehouse for The Greenfield Review Press, the independent publishing house founded by Bruchac and his wife, Carol. As our house tour evolves into an animated conversation, the lanky, ponytailed author returns repeatedly to the themes of nature, storytelling and Native American culture—the interconnected passions that have given form to so much of his career and life.

Certainly Bruchac—who is of Abenaki, English and Slovakian descent—has found his own Native American heritage to be a great source of inspiration. Raised by his maternal grandparents (his lawyer grandmother and his grandfather, who was "visibly Indian but wouldn't talk about it"), Bruchac grew up hoping to become "something like a park ranger, or one of those interpretive naturalists who goes and gives tours in national parks and explains what things are." But as a young adult, he gravitated toward literature and, intrigued in part by his grandfather's reticence, felt drawn to his Native American roots. "Even when I was in college [at Cornell University], my first poems . . . were about American Indian themes," he observes.

In the mid-1960s, after completing a master's degree in creative writing at Syracuse University, Bruchac set off with his wife for Africa, where for three years they taught in a secondary school in Keta, Ghana. At the end of this stint, the Bruchacs returned to upstate New York and moved in with Bruchac's grandfather, settling in Bruchac's childhood home.

It was in 1971 that Joseph and Carol Bruchac started the *Greenfield Review,* a multicultural literary magazine devoted to publishing what he describes as "an equal blend of established and lesser-known writers." Though the magazine ceased publication six years ago, its book publishing arm, The Greenfield Review Press, and a spinoff project, the North American Native Authors Catalog, are still going strong. Given his strong sense of responsibility to his heritage, it's not surprising that Bruchac continued his commitment to education as well. After four years of teaching ethnic literature at Skidmore College, he founded—and for eight years directed—the school's program at the Great Meadow Correctional Facility, a maximum-security prison in Comstock, N.Y.

Bruchac was known as a poet before he branched into other genres. His first book was a volume called *Indian Mountain and Other Poems,* issued by Ithaca Press in 1971, and he has been prolific ever since. "I think I've been published now in 500 different poetry magazines," he says. He was one of the judges for the poetry panel of the National Book Awards in 1995.

Bruchac's close relationship with his two sons, Jim and Jesse, now in their mid-20s, was the catalyst for his work both as a professional storyteller and as a children's author. "When the boys were very little, I started telling them stories," he recalls. "And the stories I chose to tell were the traditional stories that I had grown up with, read in books and then, as an adult, been hearing from elders. I began seeking out more stories, so I could share them with the kids."

This private pursuit gained a wider audience thanks to Bruchac's friends John and Elaine Gill of Crossing Press, who asked the poet to write down some of the tales he told his sons. The end result was Bruchac's first book for children, *Turkey Brother and Other Iroquois Stories,* first published in 1976 and in print ever since.

Publication led in turn to Bruchac's now flourishing career as a professional storyteller. An invitation to read from *Turkey Brother* at an elementary school precipitated Bruchac's first storytelling performance, when, he recalls, "I got out in front of a group of kids with a book in my hand." Spontaneously, he remembers, "I just put the book down and said, 'Let me *tell* you these stories.'"

The transition from reader to storyteller is easy enough to imagine: even in casual conversation, Bruchac's gently resonant voice is persuasive, and he seems to possess an intuitive notion of the internal formation of even the smallest anecdote.

Propelled as he has been from one accomplishment to the next by a happy combination of good fortune and hard work, it's small wonder, Bruchac says, that he is a "strong believer in things occurring when they're meant to happen. That it's very different if you try to force things . . . but if you follow a sort of natural flow, the results are usually much better—for yourself, and for other people, too."

Certainly this idea of a natural flow is borne out as Bruchac describes how he started writing picture books. Familiar with Bruchac's work as a poet, Paula Wiseman, then senior editor at Philomel, had contacted the writer with the idea of a future project. Meanwhile, author Jonathan London, the writer's longtime friend and correspondent, asked Bruchac to collaborate with him on a collection of Native American-inspired poems and stories about the seasons. When London pitched this idea to Wiseman, the project became *Thirteen Moons on Turtle's Back,* illustrated by painter Thomas Locker, with whom Bruchac has continued to work.

Bruchac's work with London is just one of several occasions on which collaboration has led to publication. A fruitful association with Dial Books for Young Readers (three picture books published to date, with a middle-grade novel, *Children of the Longhouse,* in the works for this spring) began when a mutual acquaintance introduced Bruchac to the illustrator Anna Vojtech, who told Bruchac she was interested in illustrating a Native American story involving flowers. Bruchac recalls that he wrote down a version of a Cherokee tale. As he remembers it, Vojtech "did a few illustrations and showed them to me, and I thought, 'Those are really nice.' And then more than a year went by, and she called and said, 'Joe, our book is accepted!' and I said, 'What book?' I had no idea that she was sending it out. I'm sure she mentioned it to me, but it just didn't register." Dial published the book, titled *The First Strawberries,* in 1993.

Serendipitous encounters of this sort notwithstanding, not all Bruchac's efforts have met with such stress-free success. *Keepers of the Earth,* written in collaboration with storyteller and naturalist Michael Caduto, "was rejected by more than 40 publishers" before being accepted by Fulcrum. An ambitious collection of Native American stories and environmental activities related to each tale, *Keepers of the Earth* (first released in 1988) and its sequels are all still in print, having sold more than 80,000 copies.

These days, Bruchac is much sought after. As he readily admits, "Virtually everything I do tends to be an idea that's been suggested to me by a publisher, rather than something I've come up with. I really don't have a lot of time to spend thinking up ideas and pitching them to people."

With his various talents very much in demand, Bruchac has the luxury of being able to pick and choose his projects. "I honestly don't want to do anything unless I can put myself into it fully: intellectually and spiritually," he says. This attitude enables him, he says, to promote other Native American writers. "Although I continue to do a lot of books, I'm constantly referring projects to other people. I can think of probably a dozen different books I could

have done, over the last two years, or the next few years, that are being done by other Native writers whom I've recommended for those books. Which makes me feel very good."

A Deeply Appreciative Audience

Writing for children is exceptionally satisfying, Bruchac says. "It's an audience who really, deeply appreciate what you do. They're not just reading you because you're the latest bestseller and everybody else is buying the book. And then there's the whole aspect of what I think writing should do. I think writing, like storytelling, has a dual purpose. At *least* a dual purpose.

"The first is to entertain. Because if it entertains, then people will really pay attention to it. The second is to teach. To provide lessons. And not to do so in an overly preachy way, or in a way which is forced, but to do it within the flow and the rhythm of the tale itself."

One lesson that seems to crop up in all Bruchac's books is a reverence for nature. "Unless we become part of the land, the land will reject us. It will continue without us, but it will reject us," he says. "No one will convince me that this is not the case. It's as clear as the fact that breathing in gives you life. And when you cut off the breath, the body dies."

Nowhere is this message more evident than in *Between Earth and Sky,* his latest collaboration with Thomas Locker, due out from Harcourt Brace this April. Beautifully designed, and filled with luminous paintings and haunting poetry, this picture book explores 10 places in North America that are sacred to Native peoples.

Powerful though his vision of the natural world is, it is not for this reason alone that Bruchac's work has captured a wide audience. Describing his success, he says, "I don't think it is just because, as some people have said, Indians are 'hot' right now. I really think that what people are seeing are those basic values: of family, of environment and community and storytelling. Values that all come together so clearly in the Native American traditions. But these are basic human values. And you don't have to be an Indian, or even interested, per se, in American Indian culture, to appreciate a book like *Between Earth and Sky*."

Despite the time and energy Bruchac has dedicated to making Native voices and visions better known to the world at large, he gently shrugs off any suggestion that he might be seen as a spokesperson for the Native American community. "There are more than 400 different living American Indian cultures in North America," he points out. "No one knows them all. And what I can say is that I know a bit, to some detail, about a couple of them."

Rather than assume the lofty title of spokesperson, Bruchac has a simple vision of his role. "I want to be able to speak clearly and well," he says, "and to say things in a way that I hope people will listen to." Given the receptiveness of his audience, the eagerness of his editors and the volume and quality of his writing, Bruchac is well on his way to achieving his goal.

TITLE COMMENTARY

TURKEY BROTHER AND OTHER TALES: IROQUOIS FOLK STORIES (1976)

Marily Richards

SOURCE: A review of *Turkey Brother and Other Tales: Iroquois Folk Stories*, in *School Library Journal*, Vol. 22, No. 7, March, 1976, p. 89.

A collection of Seneca folk tales, many of which emphasize the Indian principle of kindness to animals. The title story tells of two brothers who leave their uncle and return to their parents' land. Three stories are about Turtle, a trickster who uses his brains to overcome his slow speed and small size. Other selections tell why something came to be, e.g., why the Iroquois have a Porcupine Clan or why the bear has a short tail. Enhanced by Kahonhes' black-and-white line drawings, the stories are well paced and make their point without condescension or moralizing. Characterizations are especially good in the animal tales, and these particularly should appeal to slow readers in the sixth and seventh grades.

Denise M. Wilms

SOURCE: A review of *Turkey Brother and Other Tales: Iroquois Folk Stories*, in *The Booklist*, Vol. 72, No. 13, March 1, 1976, p. 974.

This judicious sampling of short Iroquois tales, retold by a part-Abenaki poet and novelist who heard the stories as a child, provides a neat resource for storytellers; the first three tales feature Turtle, a trickster not unlike the Ashanti Anansi figure. Turtle emerges a crafty winner in two of the stories: his undoing in **"Turtle Makes War on Men"** cautions that wit can outdo itself. The remaining five stories also offer entertaining lessons or explanations of one sort or another. A foolish bear succumbs to a coyote's trick and loses his tail, accounting for the reason bears have short tails; a sadistic man causes rattlesnakes to make war against humans. **"Two Feathers and Turkey Brother"** fits the hero tale mold, while **"The Boy Who Lived with the Bears"** and **"The Porcupine Clan"** explain the significance of each animal to the Iroquois people. The prose is smooth, simple, and written to be read aloud; the preface, coupled with a vignette explaining how legends came about, makes an effective prelude to the stories. Illustrated with simple pen-and-ink drawings on gray paper by Kahonhes, an Akwesasne Indian artist.

Kirkus Reviews

SOURCE: A review of *Turkey Brother and Other Iroquois Folk Stories*, in *Kirkus Reviews*, Vol. XLIV, No. 6, March 15, 1976, p. 326.

Workmanlike retellings of nine tales from the Iroquois, most of them only two or three pages long. The title story—strongest in the collection and, at ten pages, the longest—contains a satisfying twist on a familiar motif (the traveling hero disobeys his uncle's cautionary prohibitions without disaster, easily overcoming the monsters who emerge at the forbidden spots) and a strong ending when the same hero impresses his new father-in-law, a chief, by spitting wampum but an impostor challenged to do the same can only come up with dead worms and lizards.

STONE GIANTS & FLYING HEADS: MORE IROQUOIS FOLK TALES (1978; republished as *Stone Giants and Flying Heads: Adventure Stories of the Iroquois*, 1979)

James F. Hamburg

SOURCE: A review of *Stone Giants & Flying Heads: Adventure Stories of the Iroquois*, in *Children's Book Service*, Vol. 7, No. 8, March, 1979, p. 73.

Nine authentic Iroquois legends about several aspects of Indian life and mythology are told in this beautifully written book. The Native American author has used contemporary American Indian English in his text, and the Iroquois illustrators have done an outstanding job. This very readable book will appeal to persons interested in Native American mythology, whether they are five or one hundred and five.

Gale Eaton

SOURCE: A review of *Stone Giants & Flying Heads: Adventure Stories of the Iroquois*, in *School Library Journal*, Vol. 25, No. 8, April, 1979, p. 53.

Joseph Bruchac, part Abenaki, has been hearing these stories since his childhood and has often retold them for his own children. In print, on handsome stock, they lie a little flat, but storytellers will find lively material here—the tricky braggart Skunny-Wundy, the brave mother running steadily from the Flying Head, and the girl who was not satisfied with simple things but fell into the power of a handsome shapeshifter. Several of the pieces are laid out in short lines, as if they were poetry, and should be quite accessible to reluctant readers.

Denise M. Wilms

SOURCE: A review of *Stone Giants & Flying Heads:*

Adventure Stories of the Iroquois, in *Booklist,* Vol. 75, No. 15, April 1, 1979, p. 1217.

A companion volume to **Turkey Brother, and Other Tales,** this offers eight more selections in a mix of prose and free verse. A creation story tells how the wife of an ancient chief brought the first plants to earth; a related tale accounts for good and evil. One Skunny-Wundy trickster story injects a humorous note, while the remaining tales highlight virtues such as bravery, obedience, or goodness rewarded.

📖 KEEPERS OF THE EARTH: NATIVE AMERI-CAN STORIES AND ENVIRONMENTAL ACTIVITIES FOR CHILDREN (cowritten with Michael J. Caduto, 1988; paperback edition published as *Native American Stories*)

Robert E. Yager

SOURCE: "Bubbles and Dinosaurs Highlight Science Materials," in *Instructor,* Vol. XCVIII, No. 7, March, 1989, p. 53.

Keepers of the Earth: Native American Stories and Environmental Activities for Children by Michael J. Caduto and Joseph Bruchac relates stories from Native Americans, some of the keenest observers of the natural world. Designed to inspire children aged 5 through 12, these tales help them feel part of their natural surroundings. Hands-on activities help children understand the influence they can have on the environment. The book is a valuable resource for integrating science with social studies in the classroom.

Anne Fuller

SOURCE: A review of *Keepers of the Earth: Native American Stories and Environmental Activities for Children,* in *Science Books & Films,* Vol. 24, No. 5, May-June, 1989, p. 296.

The rich text of this book relates myths and fables, and the evocative line drawings complement the narrative. An introductory 15-page orientation guides a teacher or parent in how to share the book with children to teach them science, specifically ecology. Activities are also included. The myths and fables are translated from different native American languages into English, but they are not distorted. The patterns and phrasings of the tales are distinctly different from one another as well as from most elementary school readings. The sections providing background are succinct but lack scientific names or references. Also, some of the suggested activities are complex; for example, a heated room is baffled from a cooler one to create wind. This is a grand idea, but it would be physically impossible for many groups to demonstrate. There is no mention of land use policy, not even of parks. The book also assumes that natural surroundings are available to its users for exploration and study. Finally, although research

skills are listed among desired goals, the suggested activities are mostly demonstrations and reenactments; this criticism shows that the book has both the strengths and weaknesses of holistic storytelling education. I recommend this book as spice for a science program, but it cannot stand alone as a complete ecology curriculum.

📖 KEEPERS OF THE ANIMALS: NATIVE AMERICAN STORIES AND WILDLIFE ACTIVITIES FOR CHILDREN (cowritten with Michael J. Caduto, 1991)

Ilene Cooper

SOURCE: A review of *Keepers of the Animals: Native American Stories and Wildlife Activities for Children,* in *Booklist,* Vol. 88, No. 3, October 1, 1991, p. 340.

Schools with native American units—i.e., all schools—will be interested in the stories and activities that this book provides for kids to enjoy. The focus is on the special relationship between native peoples and wildlife, and the authors show great respect for both, as well as for the young people who are the book's secondary audience. A useful opening chapter gives tips and techniques for conducting outdoor activities, staging puppet shows, and catching and caring for animals (insects, frogs, snakes, turtles). The rest of the book consists of more than 20 stories that come from Indian nations across the U.S., each bolstered by discussion topics and activities. Librarians, scout leaders, and others who work with children will appreciate this volume, too. A glossary and pronunciation guide are appended.

Joan McGrath

SOURCE: A review of *Keepers of the Animals: Native Stories & Wildlife Activities for Children,* in *Quill and Quire,* Vol. 58, No. 2, February, 1992, p. 33.

Two subjects of vital interest to current school programming are the presentation of a true picture of native Canadians, who have been so often misrepresented in school curricula and library collections; and encouraging an ecologically-conscious, conservationist approach to the wildlife of this and other countries. These two topics are successfully combined in this new addition to the "Keepers" Series.

The traditional approach of native hunters to their prey was that of respect. If the fish, birds, and mammals on whom their lives depended were treated properly, as fellow creatures under the protection of the Great Spirit, they would agree to let themselves be taken; but if proper rites were not observed, they would refuse to make the sacrifice, and the hunters remained empty-handed.

Keepers of the Animals, a volume of imposing size and weight, provides teachers with a methodology for encouraging this respect for the creatures of the wild. Each section opens with one or two traditional tales, drawn from the mythology of native peoples from all parts of North America. All are centred on the animal world, its interactions with people, and the lessons those people learn by this close contact.

Each of the 27 stories or pairs of stories are followed by quite sophisticated natural history notes on the animal featured, including descriptions of habitat, breeding, identification of threatened species, etc. There are suggested topics for discussion to further extend the learning; finally there are activities and projects that emphasize co-operation and group participation.

With two of the three members of the creative team from native groups and the third an ecologist, the authenticity of this volume seems assured. The work is illustrated with black and white drawings by native artists, and includes a glossary, index of activities, and a general index for easy reference.

Peter Croskery

SOURCE: A review of *Keepers of the Animals: Native Stories and Wildlife Activities for Children,* in *CM: A Reviewing Journal of Canadian Materials for Young People,* Vol. XX, No. 2, March, 1992, p. 59.

According to its press release, ***Keepers of the Animals***

> provides a complete program of study in the importance of wildlife ecology and environmental issues concerning animals. The activities . . . involve children in creative arts, theatre, reading, writing, science, social studies, mathematics and sensory awareness. They engage a child's whole self, while emphasizing creative thinking and synthesis of knowledge and experience.

For the most part, these claims are a valid representation of the book.

Keepers of the Animals: Native Stories and Wildlife Activities for Children uses a native North American approach as its dominant theme. The authors believe that "Native North Americans emphasize a close relationship with nature versus control of the natural world." Through an understanding of the native North American's approach to wildlife, children can "learn to live in a healing relationship with the animals."

The book is divided into three parts. Parts I and II are included in ***Keepers of the Animals,*** while the third part is a separate teacher's guide to ***Keepers of the Animals*** (which was not reviewed).

Part I is a teaching guide to assist an adult to use this book effectively. A small part of the book (twenty-one pages), it contains a wealth of good advice including a guide to the layout of the material. One nice aspect of the book that appears throughout is the strong emphasis placed on teaching respect for all animals.

Part I also explains the native attitude to wildlife: "the cycle of giving and receiving—maintaining the circle of life—is fundamental to Native North American culture." Unlike the Europeans, who for most Canadians are our forefathers, native people lived responsively with wildlife. Their culture and traditions have a strong basis in the reality of wildlife. Much of their culture and tradition was passed from generation to generation through legends or stories. Part II includes samples of these stories.

Within Part II, each chapter starts with one or two traditional native North American stories. These stories establish the chapter's theme. Then follows an explanation of the story and its meaning and/or message. This opens the door for the biological study of the individual animal or group of animals "introduced" by the story.

Now that children (or adults) are equipped with the background, a series of activities are presented that help reinforce, demonstrate or "implant" the information.

The native North American stories are all very short, usually not longer than a page. (In Part I there is a brief section, "Telling the Stories," that reminds us how important the delivery of the story is to the impact on the audience.) The stories are great, but many are complex and will require some guidance in order to be understood by children. They are not the bedtime stories that parents would like to read to their children. However, in a teaching setting they will make a child want to learn more.

The biological sections of the book are not well done. As I wandered through the book I found a number of inaccuracies and a lack of clarity in some of its content. These deficiencies do not short change the effectiveness of the book, but a better technical editing of the book would have greatly improved its overall quality. For example, phytoplankton are characterized as "these green plants," but not all phytoplankton are green plants. "Minnow" is referred to as a freshwater fish where in fact it is a group of fishes, Cyprinidae, that includes some of the other "species" listed. The explanation of growth rings, or annuli, on the scales of the fish is inaccurate, leaving the reader with the impression that a "ring" is deposited each summer, which is not the case. In explaining parasitism, the authors confuse social behaviour with parasitism. True parasitism involves a relationship whereby the parasite does little or no harm to its host, since its ultimate survival largely depends on the well-being of its host.

But a really nice feature of the book is having the technical/biological information included with the teaching material.

Many of the activities are great! All are good, simple and strong learning opportunities for children. A number of activities create the opportunity for children to exercise controlled imagination. The native North American story "kick-starts" the child's imagination and the activity encourages the child to "go beyond" according to simple guidelines. "Circle of the Sea," an activity in the chapter "Salmon Boy," sits children on a seashore facing and listening to the water and asks them to think of a gift they have received from the sea. (This activity would work on any inland shoreline equally well.)

"Beauty in the Beast" asks children to rewrite an animal story depicting the animal in a more realistic way.

Keepers of the Animals is designed for educators. Included are an index of all the book's activities and a glossary of native North American terms. Although the book would be most effective for educators working exclusively with native children, this should not be considered a limitation. The materials of this book will be effective with all children. We are simply using the experience of native North Americans to help children understand and respect our wildlife.

I highly recommend this book. I can foresee myself using some of these materials with adult groups wishing to learn more about the environment.

Jack DeForest

SOURCE: A review of *Keepers of the Animals: Native American Stories and Wildlife Activities for Children,* in *Science Books & Films,* Vol. 28, No. 2, March, 1992, p. 49.

This book is a companion to the authors' popular *Keepers of the Earth*. The text and format serve well in conveying a much needed message about the type of behavior that is required for protecting global ecosystems and their inhabitants from destructive industrial technology and human population pressures. A stewardship philosophy must be developed that insures the maintenance of life-sustaining environments. The many individuals who contributed to the creation of this book deserve praise for providing a much needed public service; namely, the structuring of baseline information for educating youth in ways that will impact intergenerational behavior. While the book's target audience is children (aged 5 to 12), it is obvious that the overall message warrants the serious attention of everyone. [Michael J.] Caduto and Bruchac are experienced hands-on educators who understand the ethical standards required for maintaining sustainable ecosystems. They articulate persuasively the historic relationships of various Amerindian tribes with the natural world. Their training strategy highlights a scientific and mythological understanding of the natural world and the need for having operational environmental ethics. Traditional native cultures are focused with mystic storytelling that embodies a rich cultural heritage. Tribal tales of human-animal links are followed by illuminating discussions, questions, and suggested demonstration projects. While some activities are rather complex and may be difficult to implement, a teacher's guide is available. The instructive goal is to educate youth about the imperative for stewardship behavior of the type followed by Native Americans. This worthwhile mission is needed in an era dominated by the anthropocentric philosophy embodied in nearly all organized religions. The time has come, in an era of increased human-generated environmental destruction, to recognize the impact of irresponsible behavior on all species. In order to encourage the development of remedial ethics and behavior, one should incorporate elements of cultural mythology into existing hard science in order to form a rewarding and sustainable lifestyle. It is necessary to inform open-minded people about this imperative. The interdisciplinary studies promoted in these "Keeper" books should inspire people of all ages to evaluate and modify their personal impact on the planet earth and the "right to life" status of *all* species.

NATIVE AMERICAN ANIMAL STORIES (cowritten with Michael J. Caduto, 1992)

[*Native American Animal Stories* consists of selections from *Keepers of the Earth: Native American Stories and Environmental Activities for Children.*]

Hazel Rochman

SOURCE: A review of *Native American Animal Stories,* in *Booklist,* Vol. 89, No. 1, September 1, 1992, p. 43.

Abenaki writer Bruchac and Mohawk illustrator [John Kahionhes] Fadden have collected animal stories from native American tribes across North America. The tales have a directness and rhythm that's great for reading aloud and storytelling, as in the lyrical Cherokee tale **"The Lake of the Wounded,"** the dramatic Apache tale **"The Boy and the Rattle Snake,"** or the Zuni story **"Eagle Boy,"** which is both soaring and pragmatic. The extensive descriptive notes at the back on tribal nations are an added bonus, as is the foreword by [Vine] Deloria about the unobtrusive teaching role of these stories in many native cultures. The design is clear and attractive, with black-and-white drawings that capture the mystery as well as the physicalness of these tales of "feathers and fur, scales and skin."

Lisa Mitten

SOURCE: A review of *Native American Animals Stories,* in *School Library Journal,* Vol. 38, No. 11, November, 1992, p. 83.

Twenty-four stories, organized by theme, excerpted from Bruchac and Michael Caduto's *Keepers of the Animals*. Excellent introductions by Bruchac and Vine Deloria, Jr., set the proper tone; they will be of particular use to those planning readalouds, and are important for understanding the messages of the tales. The pieces come from tribes across North America, each illustrated with a full-page line drawing and appropriate border designs. Bonuses are the superb glossary of words and names and the descriptions of tribal nations. Providing an insider's knowledge and insight, Bruchac gives information about the people today and cites sources for additional versions of the stories. There are many similar collections and retellings available, some by well-meaning people who do not truly understand the tales' importance. Storytellers can feel secure in knowing that these selections will not cause offense to listeners with Bruchac's work, which presents the stories with respect for readers of all ages. Public, school, and tribal libraries should purchase this one.

📖 THIRTEEN MOONS ON TURTLE'S BACK: A NATIVE AMERICAN YEAR OF MOONS (cowritten with Jonathan London, 1992)

Karen Hutt

SOURCE: A review of *Thirteen Moons on Turtle's Back: A Native American Year of Moons,* in *Booklist,* Vol. 88, No. 13, March 1, 1992, p. 1281.

In many native American cultures, each of the 13 moon cycles in a year has a specific name and a story. Drawing on his Abenaki heritage, storyteller Bruchac has collaborated with author [Jonathan] London to present stories from 13 different tribes. Explaining that the 13 scales on the turtle's back represent the 13 moons of the year, a young Abenaki boy's grandfather introduces the chronologically arranged stories. [Thomas] Locker, well known for his landscapes, has created a dramatic oil painting for each short tale. His artwork portrays seasonal changes in the land as well as the specific seasonal activities of humans and animals. The large format with minimal text will appeal to younger children, while the alternative calendar, based on changes in nature, will interest middle readers. An unusual, easy-to-use resource for librarians, teachers, and others wishing to incorporate multicultural activities throughout the year.

Kay E. Vandergrift

SOURCE: A review of *Thirteen Moons on Turtle's Back: A Native American Year of Moons,* in *School Library Journal,* Vol. 38, No. 7, July, 1992, p. 67.

The book opens with an Abenaki storyteller explaining to his grandson that just as there are always 13 scales on "Old Turtle's back," there are 13 moons in a year, each of which has a name and a story. The poetic tales and corresponding paintings that follow represent myths or legends of different Native American tribes. Although the language of these poems is not particularly memorable or childlike, it does evoke images and passes on some of the traditions of the native people and their closeness to the natural world. The cadence is that of an adult explaining things to a child. Both text and illustrations have a distancing effect on readers. [Thomas] Locker's large, dark paintings stand parallel to or in tandem with the poems but are not integral to them. They create a mood and capture portions of the text, encouraging viewers to look "at" rather than "into" these images. There is a sense of vastness in these paintings, and sometimes a harshness, but little of the lushness or the warmth of the land. Although the cover illustration of the turtle is inviting and the large format attractive, these are poems that will prob-

ably not entice most youngsters on their own. They can be appreciated, however, when presented by an adult and will be a welcome addition to units on Native American cultures.

📖 TURTLE MEAT AND OTHER STORIES (1992)

Kirkus Reviews

SOURCE: A review of *Turtle Meat and Other Stories,* in *Kirkus Reviews,* Vol. LX, No. 19, October 1, 1992, p. 1201.

Native American eco-consciousness expressed through retellings of legend and myth, tales of the supernatural and of revenge, celebrations of nature and wit all rooted in the often overlooked Northeastern Woodlands cultures. Editor/writer/storyteller Bruchac draws on his Abenaki heritage and brings the eye of poet and naturalist to his first collection.

These 17 stories span centuries of Indian/white relations in the Adirondack foothills region of New York State: first contact with **"The Ice-Hearts"** (Vikings); a war of wits between a Mohican and the mayor of 19th-century Albany; conflict with Prohibition-era bootleggers; the WW II service of two Indians who find themselves living out their commanding officer's Hollywood-inspired vision; a present day when Indians officially don't exist and people of Native blood—avoiding deadly prejudice—allow themselves to be identified as "Canadian" or "French." The collection is rounded out with some fine, seemingly autobiographical pieces that explore man's relationship to the natural world. Throughout, Bruchac questions the boundaries between animals and men, remembering the distant past when Iroquois women nursed orphaned beaver kits at the breast and, more recently, when farm people kept wild animals as pets. Sometimes people and animals magically change places, but even when boundaries remain, men take life-lessons from wolves, fish, bears, etc. Much of the charm here is in the writing (swallows dart, "stitching the face of the sky") and in the slyly laconic, self-aware humor of Indian conversation.

Style, humor, and grace enliven familiar themes; atypical for folkloric writing, most characters emerge three-dimensional and real.

Gilbert Taylor

SOURCE: A review of *Turtle Meat and Other Stories,* in *Booklist,* Vol. 89, No. 6, November 15, 1992, p. 578.

With this, his fifteenth volume of woodland Indian lore, Bruchac gathers momentum as a voice worth listening to. He usually speaks to young adults, but here pitches his dozen-plus stories to the older generation. Most are set in the Adirondack Mountains, and feature an encounter between a native American's inherited values (e.g., no ownership of land, respect for animist spirits in living things) and the selfishness of white culture. A caricature can result, as in **"Wolves,"** in which a beer-swilling, gun-toting yahoo destroys the sylvan serenity and himself as well. A more effective theme is the intrusion of externals (such as the influence of the city or of ancestors) upon the mystical thoughts of a solitary character who fishes or hunts. Enjoyable both as story and as metaphor, Bruchac's short stories exalt their rustic settings.

Debbie Bogenschutz

SOURCE: A review of *Turtle Meat and Other Stories,* in *Library Journal,* Vol. 117, No. 19, December 15, 1992, p. 103.

Abenaki storyteller Bruchac here presents a beautiful collection of vignettes of contemporary Native life. These stories celebrate the strengths and differences of the Native American people without being the least bit sentimental. Bruchac's images are fresh and his language poetic. For instance, in **"Notes from a Morning of Fishing,"** his narrator reports that after a heavy rain "the grasses and flowers are still slicked down and just starting to stand—like the protesting cowlick of a boy." In **"Bears,"** a young lawyer talks the older Foxy into helping him kidnap a bear from the zoo, since bears and Indians are closely related and the older man speaks the animal's language. In the title story, a loving portrait of an older couple, the man's struggle with a turtle is used as a metaphor for the woman's struggle to control her own destiny. Enthusiastically recommended for short story collections.

Carl L. Bankston III

SOURCE: "Testimonies of Native American Life," in *The Bloomsbury Review,* Vol. 13, No. 3, May-June, 1993, p. 5.

Some writers have a single story they tell over and over again, in the same voice, renaming the characters and rearranging the events. The variations on the story are only vehicles for that one obsessive autobiographical confession, political message, or philosophical meditation. Others, the true storytellers, change constantly, adopting a new tone for each tale, submerging themselves in their characters, producing the unexpected in each new narrative. Joseph Bruchac is one of the true storytellers.

This collection of 18 short stories shows an impressive range of styles and forms. Several common themes run through these fictions: the past and present of Native American peoples, the sacredness of the natural world, and humanity's ruptured relations with untamed animals. But in exploring these themes, Bruchac adopts the points of view of a variety of protagonists and refracts his interests through a prism of techniques. Some of the stories present themselves as folklore; others employ the old device of the ironic ending in a manner reminiscent of the classic short stories of de Maupassant or O. Henry; still others blend naturalism and fantasy after the fashion of the subversive narrative strategy known as magical realism.

The first story begins where the Mad Hatter suggested stories should begin: at the beginning. **"The Ice Hearts"** tells of the appearance of the first whites in the North American woodland, from the perspective of those who were there before them. The narrator, Fox-Looking-Around, recounts how the people he calls Ice-Hearts, with hard clothing the color of flint, "long knives and big axes shiny as ice," and "the coldness of ice in their sky-colored eyes," came to his village, killed, stole food, and then vanished into the storm that had given them birth. Two of these fierce creatures are captured by the tribe. After some debate, the tribal people agree to adopt and "humanize" the invaders.

The story depends on the tension between two times and two sets of knowledge. Even though the events are presented to the reader through a first-person narration located 300 or 400 years in the past, the ominous but economical symbolism of the whites' stormy invasion and the description given by one of the tamed whites of his people's hunger for land never allow the reader to escape from the historical present. In this way, all the tragic history of the Native American is implied in a few wryly humorous pages. The Ice-Hearts are captured when one of the Indians interrupts the fighting with a fart and the combatants are figuratively and literally disarmed by laughter. One of the captives is adopted by the widow of a man murdered by the white leader; the murdered man's name was Goes In The Corner, because he constantly soiled a corner of the longhouse to avoid going outside in winter. We look back on the tragedy of history and see that its pathos is partially abated by its comic absurdity.

The other stories begin where Fox-Looking-Around's tale ends. Sometimes these stories take the form of jokes, as in **"Peter Schuyler and the Mohican: A Story of Old Albany."** **"Jed's Grandfather"** adopts the literary convention of the childhood reminiscence. **"All Dishonest Men"** is an adventure tale. **"How Mink Stole Time"** is an adaptation of the traditional Native American trickster myth. But through all of these transformations runs the conflict between past and present, between our ties to nature and our violation of nature.

Bruchac is capable of the simplicity of a storyteller seated before a campfire. When appropriate, though, he can express himself in startling imagery. In **"Code Talker,"** a TV movie reminds an elderly Native American in a nursing home of his exploits in World War II: "They've got it [the TV] up perched on a shelf on the wall, like an eagle on a cliff up where it can look down at its prey and swoop for the kill." The direct, precise prose style achieves its greatest intensity in passages on the woodlands and its creatures, as in the description of the autumn battles of the bull moose in **"The White Moose"** or the account of the protagonist's meeting with a fox in **"The Fox Den."**

The characters, Native Americans, mixedbloods, and rural whites, take on life through the author's sharp ear for dialect and his ability to use actions to suggest personalities. In the title story, Homer LaWare's struggle with a huge turtle on the end of a fishing line establishes him as a tenacious man in a long struggle with life. Homer is a loser; he owns nothing and, in the end, loses even the roof over his head. But his tenacity and willingness to walk away constitute a stoic victory. "It's the Indian in me don't want to own no land," he says. Outsiders, the characters in these tales are heroes because they manage to remain themselves.

Occasionally the work in this book seems unfinished or directionless. **"Notes From a Morning of Fishing"** is less of a short story than a series of well-written journal entries. It would be excellent material for fiction, but it seems like a mistake to include it in this collection in its present form. **"Going Home"** appears to be a story about two Native American escaped convicts, but their circumstances, background, and motivations are all so enigmatic that it leaves the reader a little baffled and unsatisfied.

Despite these minor lapses, ***Turtle Meat and Other Stories*** will appeal to nearly all readers. Joseph Bruchac possesses a voice both distinctive and capable of a wide range of expression. He finds the mythical in the real, the survival of the past in the present, and an indigenous soul in a land conquered by Europeans. This is a voice we will want to hear again.

DAWN LAND (1993)

Debbie Bogenschutz

SOURCE: A review of *Dawn Land,* in *Library Journal,* Vol. 118, No. 8, May 1, 1993, p. 114.

With his first novel, Abenaki storyteller Bruchac has joined the multitude who spin out prehistoric coming-of-age stories, but he's done so with a difference and with great skill. . . . Bruchac focuses on the male rite of passage. On a quest to bring meat to his people, Young Hunter is bitten by a snake. Returning to his village, he relates his experiences to the oldest Talker, who sees that Young Hunter was chosen by the snake to protect the Only People from approaching danger. Bruchac seamlessly weaves ancient myths into his compelling tale of the young boy and his encounters with an earlier form of being, thought to be extinct, that threatens the survival of the human race. An outstanding work in its genre, *Dawn Land* should be popular with both general and young adult readers.

Judy Sokoll

SOURCE: A review of *Dawn Land,* in *School Library Journal,* Vol. 39, No. 8, August, 1993, p. 205.

Ten thousand years ago, the Abenaki (People of the Dawn Land) and the Iroquois (People of the Long Lodges) lived in the Adirondack and Green Mountains, along the St. Lawrence and Connecticut Rivers. Young Hunter is chosen to follow a noble quest to prevent unseen and presently unknown forces from destroying the world and its peoples. Elders with the power to foresee and foretell the future prepare the young man for the perilous adventure in which his strength of mind, body, and soul will be tested repeatedly. Here is a classic hero in a classic myth, replete with flesh-eating giants, wise counselors, friends, and enemies. Suspense builds as the presence of evil comes steadily closer. Told in the cadence of a storyteller's voice, the tale weaves together Native American history, traditions, values, and beliefs, central to which is the sacredness and interrelation of all things. Bruchac writes in a rich, precise, gentle, yet powerful descriptive style. Often he tells a story within a story, but YAs who like historical fiction will eagerly follow the multiple threads.

Carl L. Bankston III

SOURCE: A review of *Dawn Land,* in *Parabola,* Vol. XVIII, No. 4, November, 1993, pp. 106, 108, 110.

During his long literary career, Joseph Bruchac has filled many roles: teacher, poet, anthologist, founder and editor of the *Greenfield Review,* storyteller. Perhaps he is best known to the reading public, though, as a folklorist. In books for young people and adults, Bruchac's retelling of traditional Native American tales has been invaluable for preserving and passing on an endangered heritage in oral literature.

With ***Dawn Land,*** Bruchac takes on a new role, that of novelist. In this book, which is both historical novel and myth, he combines intimate knowledge of legends of the Abenaki and Iroquois tribes, carefully cultivated skill in the craft of storytelling, and meticulous care for narrative and descriptive prose to create an epic that is at once modern and neolithic. In ***Dawn Land*** Bruchac attempts to recreate the world and the spirit of pre-Columbian North America.

The central character, a prehistoric Abenaki warrior named Young Hunter, learns, through a series of dreams, of the impending return of the Ancient Ones, a race of gigantic, stone-like cannibals who will hunt and destroy his people. Following the counsel of tribal shamans and accompanied by his dogs, Young Hunter travels from his Abenaki homeland near the Connecticut River through the territories of the Iroquois to the Adirondack Mountains, where he must confront the giants. The geographical journey mirrors a spiritual journey. As he traverses the landscape of the primordial northeast, the hero also crosses a mindscape of stories. He hears and recalls the traditional tales of his people and these enable him to reach an understanding of his world and of his place in it.

This is a novel that can be read at a number of levels simultaneously. Bruchac's strategy of weaving his plot around old stories makes it a fine collection of Native American myths. The sharply-drawn characters and limpid descriptions of natural surroundings and village life enable it to succeed as a reconstruction of an ancient world. Intended as an ecological parable, with the destructive Ancient Ones offered as an example of a society out of balance with the surrounding environment, *Dawn Land* also works remarkably well as an adventure story.

Some readers may feel that Bruchac's Abenaki and Iroquois tribespeople, portrayed as egalitarian, non-sexist, and ecologically conscious, represent an attempt to read modern values into an overly idealized past. Anticipating this criticism, in his introduction the author cites anthropological and historical evidence to support his admittedly favorable view of prehistoric tribal society. However, the question of just how "politically correct" these hunters and gatherers really were is, ultimately, as irrelevant as it is unresolvable. Storytellers have always reworked the past to address the concerns of the present and each storyteller's version of the past must be judged on the basis of its internal logic, in terms of whether the story itself convinces us and compels us to read on and reflect. Anyone compiling a reading list should put *Dawn Land* at the top.

THE FIRST STRAWBERRIES: A CHEROKEE STORY (1993)

Kirkus Reviews

SOURCE: A review of *The First Strawberries: A Cherokee Story,* in *Kirkus Reviews,* Vol. LXI, No. 14, July 15, 1993, p. 931.

A gentle story of the Sun's healing of marital discord by a gift of ripe strawberries that magically grow at the feet of an angry woman as she flees her husband's harsh words, thus halting her departure long enough for him to catch up and make amends. Thereafter, the story concludes, whenever the Cherokee eat strawberries, they are reminded to be kind to one another. Quietly luminous watercolors [by Anna Vojtech] capture details of dress, dwelling, implements, flora, and fauna against an open landscape of rolling hills. Small touches dramatize the story's moods: a bouquet of brown-eyed Susans flung to the ground in anger; an empty nest in a pine tree as the woman disappears behind the western hills; the glimmer of a single firefly as man and wife are reconciled. Complete harmony of text and pictures: altogether lovely.

Betsy Hearne

SOURCE: A review of *The First Strawberries: A Cherokee Story,* in *Bulletin of the Center for Children's Books,* Vol. 47, No. 1, September, 1993, p. 6.

In a folktale especially well chosen for its accessibility to younger listeners, the first man and woman ("made at the same time so that neither would be lonesome") live happily until their first quarrel. He is angry to find her picking flowers instead of preparing food; she walks away

from his hurtful words. In response to the man's vain attempts to overtake her, the sun intervenes with four creations to slow her down—raspberries, blueberries, blackberries, and strawberries—the last, successful. "'Forgive me for my hard words,' he said to her. And she answered him by sharing the sweetness of the strawberries." The moral here is so delectable ("to remember that friendship and respect are as sweet as the taste of ripe, red berries") and so richly couched in simple story terms that those first learning to resolve their differences will glean as much from it as their elders who have, theoretically, learned the lesson. Equally palatable are [Anna] Vojtech's paintings, also kept simple in scale, composition, and coloration so that listeners in a group can see and absorb the idyllic mountain landscapes emphasized as context for the story. It's too bad Bruchac doesn't name the elderly Cherokee friend whom he mentions as having passed the story to him many years ago, but his own telling is skillfully rendered.

Lauralyn Persson

SOURCE: A review of *The First Strawberries: A Cherokee Story,* in *School Library Journal,* Vol. 39, No. 9, September, 1993, p. 222.

This Cherokee *pourquoi* tale begins, "Long ago when the world was new. . . ." The first two people live in an Eden-like paradise. One day, the man scolds his wife for picking flowers rather than preparing dinner. She gets angry and leaves. The sun takes pity on the remorseful man, and causes berries to grow in the woman's path, hoping that they will cause her to slow down enough for her husband to catch up and apologize. Raspberries don't do it, nor do blackberries or blueberries; but "At last the Sun tried its hardest. It shone its light down in the grass right in front of the woman's feet, and strawberries appeared." These strike her fancy and she stops to taste one. She remembers the sweetness she has shared in her marriage, and the story ends with the couple's reconciliation. This retelling (rather casually documented with a note saying only that Bruchac first heard it from a Cherokee friend) is simply and clearly written, and as sweet as the berries the woman stops to taste. The attractive watercolor and colored-pencil illustrations show an idealized pastoral world. Sometimes the writing is a bit more vivid than the artwork (the strawberries "glowed like fire," yet they appear on the page as a nice gentle red). Not especially dramatic or exciting, this story does have something to say about the glories of nature, and how insignificant by comparison petty human emotions can be. It is as pleasant (and as wispy) as a soft breeze on a June day.

FLYING WITH THE EAGLE, RACING THE GREAT BEAR: STORIES FROM NATIVE NORTH AMERICA (1993)

Publishers Weekly

SOURCE: A review of *Flying with the Eagle, Racing the*

Great Bear, in *Publishers Weekly,* Vol. 240, No. 29, July 19, 1993, p. 255.

In Native American cultures the passage of a boy into manhood is a highly significant event marked by a variety of rituals. "One powerful way in which the meanings of this transition have been taught for thousands of years is through traditional stories," remarks storyteller/author Bruchac in the introduction to this selection of coming-of-age tales. Organized according to the region of North America from which they originate, these brief fables have the moral structure and pungent immediacy found in the more widely known European folktales. In the title story, from the Iroquois, Swift Runner—a small, underestimated boy—becomes a man when he hunts and kills a bear that has murdered members of his tribe. A Caddo story, **"The Wild Boy,"** links the origin of thunder and lightning to two brothers' quest. Ignored by his father, the Pueblo hero of **"The Bear Boy"** is raised alongside a mother bear's cubs. Words and phrases from various Native American languages liberally stud the well-cadenced text, enhancing the already authentic atmosphere.

Kirkus Reviews

SOURCE: A review of *Flying with the Eagle, Racing with the Great Bear,* in *Kirkus Reviews,* Vol. LXI, No. 16, August 15, 1993, pp. 1070-71.

Sixteen stories with similar themes, gathered from various Native American traditions. Boys—sometimes with names like "Bad Young Man" or "Boy Who Grew Up Wild"—pass into manhood after they undertake vision quests, heroically slay monsters, or are transformed into animals. Several have magic helpers or receive good advice from elders; strength is displayed by sparing life as well as taking it. In the Navajo **"How the Hero Twins Found Their Father,"** Monster Slayer deliberately allows Hunger, Cold, Poverty and Old Age to go free; the Muskogee Blue Fox makes peace with Cherokee attackers rather than slaughtering them. Though the flavor of Bruchac's spare, formal language is more literary than oral, he has drawn few (if any) of these stories from printed sources; thus, he offers readers new insight into a range of Native American cultures—and into history, too, since he includes a description of Crazy Horse's vision quest, and a subarctic hunter's reminiscence of his first whale hunt. The tales in each regional section are prefigured by [Murv] Jacob's handsome, white-on-black medallions. Brief reading list; foreword and afterword on the value of oral and cultural transmission.

Yvonne Frey

SOURCE: A review of *Flying with the Eagle, Racing the Great Bear: Stories from Native North America,* in *School Library Journal,* Vol. 39, No. 9, September, 1993, p. 238.

These 16 rich, thought-provoking Native American tales associated with rites of passage come from a variety of

tribal nations. The stories are meant "not only to help the boy find his way to full manhood, but also to help the man remember the boy within himself," and hence are for sons both young and old. Despite the fact that the selections come from different peoples, they share many of the same motifs: dream visions, ordeals, quests, transformations, magical powers and gifts, animal helpers, monsters, rejuvenation, man's closeness to nature, and community and family devotion. Between each of the four sections, Bruchac comments briefly on the relationship between the tales and the tribe that tells them. In the Iroquois **"Racing the Great Bear,"** a boy is mocked by others but volunteers for a dangerous mission and succeeds, using his newly gained power to help his people. Other tales warn of the misuse of nature, such as the Tlingit **"Salmon Boy,"** or tell of the importance of parental love, as in the Pueblo **"The Bear Child."** Others explain natural phenomena, like the Navajo **"How the Hero Twins Found Their Father,"** or relate a true story, as in the Lakota tale of Crazy Horse's vision. All show the reverence for nature; all are full of magic and adventure. A volume that will be useful to students of multicultural folklore as well as to those interested in good storytelling.

Karen Hutt

SOURCE: A review of *Flying with the Eagle, Racing the Great Bear: Stories from Native North America,* in *Booklist,* Vol. 90, No. 8, December 15, 1993, p. 749.

Bruchac introduces his collection of male rites-of-passage stories by explaining that Native American cultures used stories both to instruct and to entertain. Because of the significance of the number four in many tribes, he's arranged the stories, which he's drawn from tales he shared with his sons, into four geographically organized sections, each containing four stories. Some are tales of courage, some are pourquoi tales, and some show the impact of disobedience or disrespect. The tales are easy to follow and to envision, but they can be understood and interpreted on many levels. Striking black-and-white illustrations, with decorated borders, introduce each of the sections, which begin with information about the significance of the tales to their tribes. Unfortunately, Bruchac fails to provide source notes, though he does suggest a few additional resources for stories and information about storytelling in American Indian cultures. A useful collection for middle-school readers as well as classroom teachers.

FOX SONG (1993)

Betsy Hearne

SOURCE: A review of *Fox Songs,* in *Bulletin of the Center for Children's Books,* Vol. 47, No. 2, October, 1993, p. 40.

Jamie lies in bed remembering her Abenaki great-grandmother, who spent time in the woods showing her the ways of wildlife, telling her stories, and teaching her traditions of Native American craft and reverence for nature. With the potential for becoming nostalgic, this is instead carried by the weight of emotional intensity and action once-removed, as Jamie comes full circle to see the fox her grandmother had promised would appear to remind her of their time together. [Paul] Morin's woods scenes are painted with the same concentration of color with which Bruchac writes, though the human figures seem photographically stiff compared with the fluidity in the drafting of flora and fauna. Story and art together, however, make a rich combination that will move the adults reading this aloud as much as it does the children who hear it. Mourning, as Jamie's parents realize, is a very private experience, and it will be important to leave listeners some time and space with their own reactions to the book.

Patricia Fry

SOURCE: A review of *Fox Song*, in *CM: A Reviewing Journal of Canadian Materials for Young People*, Vol. XXI, No. 5, October, 1993, pp. 186-87.

Fox Song is a sensitive story about a young native girl coming to terms with the death of her great-grandmother. The hours that the two spent together have resulted in a potpourri of memories for the child, and these memories forge the link between past and present, between death and life.

The book is exquisitely illustrated by Paul Morin, an award-winning Canadian artist well known for his illustrations in both *The Orphan Boy* and *The Dragon's Pearl*. The stunningly detailed and colourful paintings in this book, one on every page, capture the spirit of the story. The special bond between the child and her great-grandmother is evident in their happy faces as the old woman passes on her wisdom to the girl.

"Grama Bowman," an Abenaki, is more than ninety years old and has lived with Jamie and her parents for six years, most of Jamie's life. The two discuss native beliefs and ways of living as they gather berries together, make birchbark baskets, and tramp through the snow studying animal tracks.

The fox is Grama's favourite animal and she tells Jamie that someday, when she is gone, Jamie may see a fox and think of her. Near the end of her life, Grama teaches Jamie a welcoming song of the Abenaki people and explains that when she sings it, she will not be alone. For Jamie, this song becomes the "fox song," and when she sings it at the end of the story as she thinks of her great grandmother, a fox steps into the meadow and pauses to listen. A gentle connection between death and life is made.

In a note about the story, author Joseph Bruchac explains that it is based on several events in his life as well as traditions among the Abenaki people. . . .

Although *Fox Song* is aimed at children ages six to ten,

its striking illustrations and gentle story will be appreciated by children and adults alike.

Highly recommended.

📖 *THE GREAT BALL GAME: A MUSKOGEE STORY* (1994)

Elizabeth Bush

SOURCE: A review of *The Great Ball Game: A Muskogee Story*, in *Bulletin of the Center for Children's Books*, Vol. 48, No. 1, September, 1994, p. 7.

Animals and sports, two winning themes among the primary set, make this title valuable for classroom and home readalouds, and among early independent readers. Birds and Animals agree to settle a quarrel over the relative merits of wings and teeth by a ball game rather than by a war, but Bat, with both teeth and wings, can't decide which team to join. Rejected by the Birds because of his small size, Bat is finally invited onto the Animal side on the condition that he must "hold back and let the bigger Animals play first." In a game of stickball the airborne Birds have the advantage, and as twilight approaches the Animals are all but worn out defending their goal when Bat, easily navigating across the darkened field, steals the ball from Crane to score the decisive point. He names the Birds' penalty—they must leave the land for half of each year—and he still comes out daily at dusk "to see if the Animals need him to play ball." Straightforward telling that moves swiftly through the game's action is just right for young listeners, and the paper-collage critters, limbs and wings waving wildly, capture the energy of the contest. In a children's-book market rapidly flooding with cut-paper illustration, [Susan L.] Roth's array of carefully selected papers stands out, as she coaxes her medium into yielding fur and feathers, grainy earth, deep shadows, and bright, blue-streaked sky. In a succinct introductory essay which will be welcomed by teachers, Bruchac cites his sources and comments on the role of ball games in Native American cultures.

Carolyn Polese

SOURCE: A review of *The Great Ball Game: A Muskogee Story*, in *School Library Journal*, Vol. 40, No. 12, December, 1994, p. 96.

In this traditional Muskogee story, the birds and the animals quarrel over which group is better, those with wings or those with teeth. The argument threatens to turn into all-out war, so the creatures decide to settle it by playing a ball game instead. When the game (which resembles lacrosse) starts, no one wants little, weak Bat to play on their side. But in the end it is Bat—with both teeth and wings—who wins the match for the animals. As a result the birds are banished to the south each winter. This *pourquoi* tale is told in clean, spare sentences with the emphasis on action and character. In a foreword, Bruchac briefly discusses ball games in traditional Native American life, including the role of sports in conflict management. He mentions two other written versions of the story, as well as Louis Littlecoon Oliver's, which he cites as his source.

📖 THE GIRL WHO MARRIED THE MOON: STORIES FROM NATIVE NORTH AMERICA (cowritten with Gayle Ross, 1994)

Karen Hutt

SOURCE: A review of *The Girl Who Married the Moon: Tales from Native North America,* in *Booklist,* Vol. 91, No. 3, October 1, 1994, p. 315.

A companion volume to Bruchac's *Flying with the Eagle, Racing with the Great Bear* this anthology focuses on the role of women in traditional Indian cultures. The 16 stories, collected from tribes representing all areas of North America, range from female rites of passage to cautionary and *pourquoi* tales. Utilizing the significance of the number four to native cultures, each of the four sections represents a different region and contains four stories. [Gayle] Ross introduces the collection by noting that the role of women in traditional native cultures is "perhaps the most falsely portrayed," and indeed these tales bring a perspective that is little known outside the communities they represent. Striking black-and-white stylized drawings [by S. S. Burrus] as well as background information about the region and the stories introduce each section. Acknowledgments for some of the stories are appended, as is a general source list. An excellent addition for storytelling collections.

Patricia (Dooley) Lothrop Green

SOURCE: A review of *The Girl Who Married the Moon: Tales from Native North America,* in *School Library Journal,* Vol. 40, No. 11, November, 1994, p. 112.

What sets this book apart from other collections of Native American tales is its focus on women. Of the 16 stories (4 from each corner of the U. S.), most are relatively unknown. In one Pandora-like tale, the heroine's curiosity is rewarded, not punished. A Cinderella variant, on the other hand, ends unhappily. Several selections involve abduction; there is a bit of cruelty and gore; and one romantic story ends tragically. Edging toward nonfiction, two pieces reflect actual coming-of-age ceremonies, and another celebrates the courage of a woman during the historical battle of Rosebud Creek. Although none of the retellings has the individual power of some Native-heroine tales available in picture-book form, e.g., Rafe Martin's *Rough-Face Girl,* the volume as a whole is valuable and, as its introduction points out, will balance the popular image of the passive "squaw."

Betsy Hearne

SOURCE: A review of *The Girl Who Married the Moon: Tales from Native North America,* in *Bulletin of the Center for Children's Books,* Vol. 48, No. 5, January, 1995, p. 160.

Two veteran storytellers have collaborated to produce a collection of sixteen Native American tales dominated by themes of strong women and organized into four sections to represent groups from the northeastern, southeastern, southwestern, and northwestern United States. A general description of cultural settings precedes each section, and the stories themselves show unusual variety, from myths ("The Girl Who Married the Moon") and *pourquoi* tales ("Chipmunk Girl and Owl Woman") to traditional coming-of-age rites ("The Beauty Way—The Ceremony of White-Painted Woman") and legendary historical incidents ("Where the Girl Rescued Her Brother"). There's also a broad tonal range, including some great scary tales and eerie encounters with the supernatural. Although a few are commonly anthologized ("The Poor Turkey Girl," for instance), a number of others would be hard or impossible to come by. It's perhaps unfair of the authors to compare these female characters to "such European heroines as Sleeping Beauty or Little Red Riding Hood, who need strong men to rescue them"—the selection here is more akin to Molly Whuppie and company in [Rosemary] Minard's *Womenfolk and Fairy Tales,* [Alison] Lurie's *Clever Gretchen,* [Ethel Johnston] Phelps' *Maid of the North,* or [James] Riordan's *Woman in the Moon*—but this will certainly find a comfortable place alongside those volumes. The adaptations are clean, and the sources respected in an afterword, acknowledgments, and bibliography. Intricate and stylized black-and-white line drawings head up each section.

Carmen Oyenque

SOURCE: A review of *The Girl Who Married the Moon,* in *Voice of Youth Advocates,* Vol. 17, No. 6, February, 1995, p. 354.

Bruchac has collaborated with Cherokee storyteller [Gayle] Ross in a sequel to *Flying With the Eagle, Racing the Great Bear* which is listed in the *Junior High Catalog.* This collection of sixteen stories celebrates the passage from girlhood to womanhood. The tales represent tribes throughout the U.S. Tales are arranged into four geographic sections with a brief historical note and black ink drawings by award-winning Cherokee artist S. S. Burrus. Tribes are listed with each title on the table of contents page. The cover has a wonderful mystical color drawing by Burrus to illustrate the title tale. "Afterword" by Ross and "Acknowledgments" by Bruchac give credit to others for the tales told. "Sources" lists titles for further reading. The tales are brief, interestingly written and will be enjoyed by students of folktales and multicultural stories, and women's studies.

KEEPERS OF LIFE: DISCOVERING PLANTS THROUGH NATIVE AMERICAN STORIES AND EARTH ACTIVITIES FOR CHILDREN (cowritten with Michael J. Caduto, 1994)

George Cohen

SOURCE: A review of *Keepers of Life: Discovering Plants through Native American Stories and Earth Activities for Children,* in *Booklist,* Vol. 91, No. 4, October 15, 1994, p. 377.

This is the third volume in Fulcrum's Keepers series of books teaching children environmental awareness. Presented here are 18 Native American stories from such tribes as the Huron, Seneca, Cheyenne, Cherokee, Mandan, Inuit, Pueblo, and Osage, covering such topics as botany, plant ecology, and the natural history of North American plants and plantlike organisms. Following each story is advice for parents, teachers, naturalists, or camp counselors on holding a discussion, asking questions, doing related activities, and extending the experience (reading, growing plants, writing and acting out a story, establishing a compost heap, taking a field trip, etc.). There is also a guide for using the book and a glossary and pronunciation key to Native American words and proper names.

Donna Nurse

SOURCE: A review of *Keepers of Life: Discovering Plants through Native Stories and Earth Activities for Children,* in *Books in Canada,* Vol. XXIV, No. 3, April, 1995, p. 58.

Like the earlier books in this uniquely conceived series (*Keepers of the Earth* and *Keepers of the Animals*) this volume offers a Native North American approach suitable for children five to twelve. [Michael] Caduto and Bruchac brilliantly link traditional Native myths to lessons in nature. In doing so they tie storytelling to its original purpose—the passing along of wisdom from generation to generation. In addition, *Keepers of Life* contains an entire section that guides parents and educators on how to use the book and offers dozens of age-appropriate activities. The entire series encourages readers of all ages to adopt a reverence towards nature; let's hope that reverence will translate into improved stewardship of the earth.

 KEEPERS OF THE NIGHT: NATIVE AMERICAN STORIES AND NOCTURNAL ACTIVITIES FOR CHILDREN (cowritten with Michael J. Caduto, 1995)

Jack DeForest

SOURCE: A review of *Keepers of the Night: Native American Stories and Nocturnal Activities for Children,* in *Science Books & Films,* Vol. 30, No. 4, May, 1994, p. 111.

Anyone who understands that training our youth to comprehend and appreciate the value of the natural world must realize the need for stimulating textbooks in the field for both teachers and parents. This addition to the author's *Keepers of the Earth* and *Keepers of the Animals* is another valuable volume for helping to develop a stewardship philosophy that encourages the "right to life" prospects for all species. The authors are Native American storytellers with a solid scientific and cultural knowledge base who know how to articulate elements of the human linkage to the natural world in a format and style seldom encountered in publications. The nocturnal substance of this volume covers a range of environmental issues that will enlighten readers about natural habitats and wildlife species little known or understood in the global community. Following a foreword by Merlin Tuttle, the founder and director of Bat Conservation International, who highlights the value of the diverse bat population, a preface titled "The Birth of Light" explains elements of the Great Circle and Universal Balance embodied in Amerindian cultures. The first, unique, chapter, "Tips and Techniques . . . ," suggests the best way to use the book—from field activities to how to tell a story—a great teacher guideline. The well-written chapters include discussions with illuminating scientific information, a series of questions designed to ensure student understanding, and recommendations for night venture activities, with "extending the experience" projects to highlight further the natural subjects addressed. Bibliographical notes listing additional supplemental material are included. The book begins with an examination of nocturnal animals in terrestrial and aquatic environments and then moves on to insects, stars, and campfires, and Amerindian games and dances and their impressive link to bears. Indeed, many interesting nocturnal subjects are discussed. Although targeted for children, the extensive subject matter with field-tested activities will affect the emotions, senses, and environmental thinking of any naturalist. Whether looking at animals or plants or stargazing after a sunset, the reader of this book will have his or her mind opened to a fascinating nocturnal vision seldom encountered by today's human population.

Patricia Fry

SOURCE: A review of *Keepers of the Night: Native Stories and Nocturnal Activities for Children,* in *CM: A Reviewing Journal of Canadian Materials for Young People,* Vol. XXII, No. 6, November-December, 1994, pp. 225-26.

Keepers of the Night provides an integrated approach to teaching the mystery and fascination of the animals, plants, insects and planets that inhabit the world of night. Continuing the tradition established by *Keepers of the Earth* and *Keepers of the Animals,* this newest book in the series combines traditional native stories with excellent environmental activities to teach about the Earth.

Night-time is experienced as more than a period of time between sunset and sunrise. The reader is taught the native North American concept that night is a crucial part of the balance that is the root of the harmonious workings of the universe. Like all the dualities of life—winter and summer, male and female—the night and the day complement one another and maintain the natural balance.

The book itself is an excellent teaching tool. A preface and a twenty-page section introduce techniques to use this book, covering several peripheral issues such as native philosophy, preparation for story-telling, and safety during field trips. There are five units based on the following topics: nocturnal animals, nocturnal insects and plants, astronomy and night-time weather, campfires and campsites, and the connectedness of all life. Each unit introduces its topic with a native legend, suggests areas for discussion with questions, and provides several activities that range from those with a literary focus to scientific experiments. Each activity has detailed teaching instructions with goal, age-appropriate levels, materials required, and procedure. Finally, the experience can be extended with other abbreviated activity ideas. There are also notes, which provide sources and additional factual information.

The book provides a map of native North America showing cultural areas and tribal locations as they appeared around 1600. There is also a glossary of native words, names and cultures, as well as a general index.

Fear of the dark is as old as humankind and it is understandable because, at night, only the light of the stars and moon and the light of fire stand between life on Earth and utter blackness. After participating in some of the activities described in *Keepers of the Night,* a person would have a new appreciation of this "nearest frontier." Infused with native lore and wisdom, the stories and activities provide valuable lessons about nature and also help dispel common fears about the night-time world.

The ideas in this book would be very useful for any environmental program, especially those school activities that involve an overnight field trip to wilderness areas.

Highly recommended.

Lisa A. Mitten

SOURCE: "After Dark," in *School Library Journal,* Vol. 41, No. 9, September, 1995, p. 132.

This latest entry in the acclaimed "Keepers" series (*Keepers of the Earth; Keepers of the Animals*) brings the nocturnal world alive for young readers. Educator [Michael J.] Caduto and Abenaki storyteller Bruchac present a wealth of activities to help the teacher, parent, scout leader, or camp counselor open up the wonders of the night-time world and its residents. As with the other "Keepers" titles, the authors set a theme for each chapter with a story from one of the many Native traditions. They discuss the concepts illustrated in the stories and follow up by suggesting questions to ask the children, numerous activities to illustrate the concepts, ideas for further ex-

ploration, and notes. The excellent glossary and pronunciation guide go far beyond the usual reference functions. Abundant and appropriate drawings and an index round out this third winner from a wonderful team. Highly recommended.

GLUSKABE AND THE FOUR WISHES (1995)

Donna L. Scanlon

SOURCE: A review of *Gluskabe and the Four Wishes,* in *School Library Journal,* Vol. 41, No. 2, February, 1995, pp. 104-05.

Bruchac is a master storyteller, and his talent is amply displayed in this retelling of an Abenaki tale. Four men travel to the island where the legendary Gluskabe has concealed himself, each hoping to have a wish granted. One hopes for fine possessions while another, already tall, wants to be even taller. The third man wants to live forever, and the fourth wants to be a better hunter so that he can provide for his people. Gluskabe promises to grant their wishes and gives each a pouch, cautioning them not to look inside until they are home. Three succumb to temptation, and their wishes are granted in unexpected ways—the first man's canoe sinks beneath the weight of the things that pour out of his pouch; the second man is transformed into a tall tree; and the third changes into a boulder. The hunter does as he is asked, and the animals reveal their secrets to him. The text is lean and elegant, without an extraneous word, and the gentle, easy cadence lends itself to reading aloud; even the source note sings. The full-and double-page, muted, misty watercolors complement the text perfectly. [Christine Nyburg] Shrader gives each of the nameless men individuality, hinting in their features at the outcome. A worthy addition to any collection.

Kirkus Reviews

SOURCE: A review of *Gluskabe and the Four Wishes,* in *Kirkus Reviews,* Vol. LXIII, No. 4, February 15, 1995, p. 222.

Gluskabe, a cultural hero of the Western Abenaki, is busy improving the world: ensuring fresh water for humans, making big animals smaller and therefore less dangerous. While resting on a far island, Gluskabe receives four visitors, each of whom wants one wish granted. One man wishes to live longer than anyone else, another to be the tallest man, a third to possess fine things, and the fourth to be a better hunter and thus better provider for his people. Gluskabe hands each man a pouch to be opened upon his return home; curiosity overwhelms the first three while the fourth gains tremendous insight.

Bruchac wonderfully recrafts this traditional story; the lesson has a strong undercurrent of entertainment, vastly increasing its effectiveness. [Christine Nyburg] Shrader's oil paintings convey an appropriately dreamy sense of magic and timelessness. Rarely do the virtues of patience, humility, and generosity get such pleasurable handling.

A BOY CALLED SLOW: THE TRUE STORY OF SITTING BULL (1995)

Elizabeth Bush

SOURCE: A review of *A Boy Called Slow: The True Story of Sitting Bull,* in *Bulletin of the Center for Children's Books,* Vol. 48, No. 8, April, 1995, pp. 265-66.

In this undocumented chronicle, Bruchac recounts the early years of the young Lakota boy who grows from an unprepossessing child named "Slow," to a youth whose careful and deliberate actions bring honor to the name, to a young warrior whose courage in defeating the Crow earns him his father's vision name Tatan'ka Iyota'ke—Sitting Bull. The narration, at first formal and restrained, marks time with the boy's measured development; then, with a startling cry of "Hiyu'wo!" Slow springs into battle, and both hero and tale rush headlong into the climactic victory scene. Bruchac does not reveal the English translation of Tatan'ka Iyota'ke's celebrated name until the end, a dramatic effect that may be lost on younger listeners yet unacquainted with Sitting Bull. [Rocco] Baviera's illustrations—cunningly brushed onto rough canvas to resemble painted hides—are often too darkly atmospheric to be shared in a group and the text initially moves as slowly as its subject. Still, this title will be especially welcome in classrooms as an introduction to the Lakota leader.

Ellen Fader

SOURCE: A review of *A Boy Called Slow: The True Story of Sitting Bull,* in *The Horn Book Magazine,* Vol. LXXI, No. 4, September-October, 1995, pp. 616-17.

In 1831 the man who became known as the great warrior Sitting Bull is born to a family of the Hunkpapa band of the Lakota Sioux. Because he does everything in a careful and deliberate manner, he earns the childhood name of Slow. He is inspired by stories that establish the reputation of his father, Returns Again to Strike the Enemy, and by tribal wisdom that his elders relate to him about the early days of the Lakota. Like many of the other boys, he dislikes his name. He yearns for the opportunity to prove himself to his people and therefore earn a new name. He spends his childhood developing his strength and courage and earning the respect of the other young boys. Finally, the opportunity to demonstrate his bravery comes during an encounter with Crow warriors. Fourteen-year-old Slow rides in front of the assembled Lakota, counts coup on a Crow warrior, and turns back the rest of the Crow. Because of his son's determination in battle, Slow's father proudly bestows on Slow one of his many names—*Tatan'ka Iyota'ke*—or Sitting Bull. Although Bruchac does not include any sources for the episode, his sensitive and respectful account of this segment of Sitting Bull's life echoes that of other respected writers. This picture book

coming-of-age story's important message—that success comes through hard work and determination rather than as a right of one's birth—comes through clearly. The story also demonstrates the importance of family and community among the Lakota people. [Rocco] Baviera's darkly atmospheric, dramatic paintings frequently feature startling bits of bright color, as in the setting sun or a piece of sky visible through the smoke hole of a family's tipi. The pictures evoke a sense of timelessness and distance, possessing an almost mythic quality that befits this glimpse into history.

Carolyn Polese

SOURCE: A review of *A Boy Called Slow,* in *School Library Journal,* Vol. 41, No. 10, October, 1995, p. 145.

This picture-book biography recounts the boyhood of a real Lakota Sioux named Slow, who grew up in the 1830s. Today's children of any background can empathize with his efforts to outgrow his childhood name and take his place as an adult among his people. The illustrations [by Rocco Baviera], oils that are rich and somber, convey details of traditional Lakota life, from the warm, close interiors of the family home to a pre-dawn assembly of warriors about to raid their Crow neighbors. The text creates an equally subtle portrayal of Plains Indian life. Many stereotypes of Native American culture are gently corrected, as when the author acknowledges that "women are the heart of the nation." The traditional Lakota explanation for the advent of horses is given alongside mention of their historical introduction by European explorers. Dialogue in the Native language helps to convey the richness of the culture. By the time Slow earns his new name, young readers will feel they know a real person—the man who was to become Sitting Bull, one of the great Sioux warriors and a hero at the Battle of Little Bighorn. This book works beautifully as historical fiction; it is less successful as biography as none of the dialogue is documented. An inspiring story.

LONG RIVER (1995)

Publishers Weekly

SOURCE: A review of *Long River,* in *Publishers Weekly,* Vol. 242, No. 31, July 31, 1995, p. 68.

Young Hunter, the hero of Native American storyteller Bruchac's first novel, **Dawn Land,** returns in this slightly disappointing sequel. It is two years since the young warrior saved his tribe, the Only People, by defeating the Ancient Ones, evil giants who crave human flesh. The intervening moons have been so idyllic for Young Hunter and his people that he has begun to forget details of the encounter with the monsters and, indeed, has doubts that it ever happened at all. Now, however, new evil from a dimly remembered past approaches to threaten the Only People once again. Walking Hill, a woolly mammoth wounded by humans as the last Ice Age retreated, has sworn revenge for the loss of his family and for his painful spear wounds. Worse yet, the only Ancient One not killed by Young Hunter revives, determined to avenge the death of his kind. Warned by dreams, the brave young Native must once more defend the Only People. Meanwhile, taking impassive note of the conflict is the river Kwanitewk (aka Connecticut). The story is at its best when it incorporates actual myths from the oral tradition of the Abenaki (from whom Bruchac is descended). The narrative lacks the momentum of *Dawn Land,* however, so readers familiar with that novel may feel let down, while those new to the series may be confused by allusions to earlier events.

📖 *THE STORY OF THE MILKY WAY: A CHEROKEE TALE* (cowritten with Gayle Ross, 1995)

Kirkus Reviews

SOURCE: A review of *The Story of the Milky Way: A Cherokee Tale,* in *Kirkus Reviews,* Vol. LXIII, No. 16, August 15, 1995, p. 1185.

A charming look at the time when the world was new. An old couple in the village notices that someone has been stealing their cornmeal during the night. Their grandson discovers that the thief is a giant spirit dog, which the villagers frighten away with drums and rattles; the dog jets across the sky, spilling cornmeal from its mouth that becomes the Milky Way. A simple, well-phrased text introduces ideas of respect for elders, cooperation, and reverence for the spirit world, without ever veering from the storyline. The acrylic illustrations show the villagers dressed up in clothes that were fashionable among the Cherokee in the early 1800s, and the scenes themselves have delicate patterns, especially apparent in the pictures of the women seen through the stalks of corn. The mouthless faces are deliberately uniform, but it means that young readers have only hair color—black, gray, or white—to find the characters featured in the story. Bruchac, [Gayle] Ross and [illustrator Virginia A.] Stroud each provides notes.

Donna L. Scanlon

SOURCE: A review of *The Story of the Milky Way: A Cherokee Tale,* in *School Library Journal,* Vol. 41, No. 9, September, 1995, pp. 190, 192.

Bruchac and [Gayle] Ross retell a Cherokee tale with simplicity and respect. Back when there were few stars in the sky, people depended on corn for their food. An elderly couple finds that someone—or something—is stealing their cornmeal, and their grandson discovers that the thief is a large spirit dog. The villagers catch the dog in the act, and he runs away. As he leaps into the sky, the cornmeal in his mouth spills out, each grain becoming a star in the Milky Way. The story is told in a clear, straightforward style, with careful attention to the cadence of the

language. It is accessible on many levels; it will hold the attention of young listeners, yet remain interesting to older readers. Both Bruchac and Ross provide source notes. The acrylic illustrations depict stylized figures and resemble fabric art. [Virginia A.] Stroud sets the story in the early 1800s, a time when clothing was made of cloth rather than buckskin, and the colors and textures heighten the applique effect, especially the sprigged calicoes worn by the women. The text and illustrations work well together, and the layout makes the book an especially good choice for story time.

Ellen Fader

SOURCE: A review of *The Story of the Milky Way: A Cherokee Tale,* in *The Horn Book Magazine,* Vol. LXXI, No. 4, September-October, 1995, pp. 611-12.

Storytellers Bruchac and [Gayle] Ross retell a traditional tale from Ross's Cherokee heritage. In the time when the world was young and there were few stars in the sky, cornmeal begins to disappear from a family's bin. Their young grandson sets out to find the thief. He discovers that the culprit is a group of stars in the shape of a dog. Wise and respected Beloved Woman predicts that the dog is a spirit being, worthy of great caution. The following evening, the Cherokee people come together to use their drums and rattles to chase the spirit dog away. Frightened, the dog runs off and, from the top of a hill, jumps right into the sky. As it goes, it spills the white cornmeal it had in its mouth; it remains "behind as a great band of light across the night sky. Each grain of cornmeal that fell became a star." Thus the Milky Way comes into being. [Virginia A.] Stroud illustrates this gracefully told story with her trademark acrylic paintings full of the rich blues of the night and the green grass of the fields. She includes many details that make her work worth close examination—flowery patterns on young girls' dresses, intricate drawings of baskets and containers, and, of course, the stars that make up the visiting spirit dog. The authors and illustrator include notes on the story's origin and on the choice of the story's historical setting.

📖 *THE EARTH UNDER SKY BEAR'S FEET* (1995)

Kirkus Reviews

SOURCE: A review of *The Earth Under Sky Bear's Feet,* in *Kirkus Reviews,* Vol. LXIII, No. 20, October 15, 1995, p. 1487.

Thirteen poems and songs gathered from as many traditions, mostly about—despite the subtitle "Native American Poems of the Land"—stars, spirits, and the sky. Many of the selections contain references to the Sky Bear, a constellation also known as the Big Dipper that, Bruchac claims, has been seen as a bear by cultures on three continents. [Thomas] Locker's awesome landscape technique has seldom worked to better effect: Skies flame at dawn or sunset over dramatic vistas that seem more real than the indistinct, turned-away human figures, while shadows and rich blends of blue and purple give the evening scenes an air of mystery. An engrossing companion to *Thirteen Moons On Turtle's Back.*

Karen Hutt

SOURCE: A review of *The Earth Under Sky Bear's Feet: Native American Poems of the Land,* in *Booklist,* Vol. 92, No. 11, February 1, 1996, p. 927.

To quiet her granddaughter's fear of the approaching darkness, Grandmother shares what Sky Bear (also known as the Big Dipper) sees and hears through the night. This companion volume to Bruchac's *Thirteen Moons on Turtle's Back: A Native American Year of Moons* presents 12 nature stories, each from a different North American Indian tribe, about summer fireflies, blooming cacti, the northern lights, and an old wolf's predawn song. [Thomas] Locker's richly colored paintings capture the mood of each story, from the midnight sun of the Inuit to the seven stars sparkling against a blue-black sky. Similar in format to the earlier book, this offers easily accessible folklore that will appeal to young listeners and readers. Source notes appended.

THE BOY WHO LIVED WITH THE BEARS AND OTHER IROQUOIS STORIES (1995)

Margaret A. Bush

SOURCE: A review of *The Boy Who Lived with the Bears: And Other Iroquois Stories,* in *The Horn Book Magazine,* Vol. LXXI, No. 6, November-December, 1995, p. 750.

Expert storyteller Joseph Bruchac presents six well-polished Iroquois tales threaded through with bits of humor and wisdom. When Turtle wages war on humans with the help of Skunk and Snake, each of the warriors receives a sound blow which gives him a distinctive physical characteristic. Pussy willows remind us of Rabbit's greed, as he is stranded in a tree from which he then tumbles, leaving behind his once-bushy tail. "If you look up at the top of certain trees . . . you will see little rabbit tails still hanging there to remind you to be satisfied with enough of a good thing." The title story is the most somber and complex, dealing with a theme common to the folklore of many cultures. A boy whose parents have died is living with his uncle. "But this boy's uncle did not have a straight mind." After treating the boy cruelly, the uncle tricks him into entering the cave of a bear and then blockades the entrance. Children will love the boy's careful strategy and the care he then receives from the animals. In their subject matter and in their finely crafted phrasing and pacing, the stories are inviting fare for storytellers and pleasurable for personal reading. The presentation is further enhanced by lovely paintings [by Murv Jacob], one for each story, which are bold in hue and delicate in detail. Each picture is framed in its own folk art design, and a

vine motif borders each page of text. Bruchac's introduction explains a bit of Iroquois history and storytelling tradition. An elegant and inviting production.

Janice Del Negro

SOURCE: A review of *The Boy Who Lived with the Bears and Other Iroquois Stories,* in *Booklist,* Vol. 92, No. 7, December 1, 1995, p. 624.

An orphan abused by his guardian uncle finds refuge as a member of a bear family in the title story of this collection of six Iroquois teaching tales, which spring from Bruchac's close association with Iroquois elders and are sourced in tales he heard while growing up. An introduction that doesn't overwhelm puts the tales into historical and cultural context. Bruchac's style is clean and spare. His direct, immediate language makes the book accessible to a wide range of children; including reluctant and new readers, and the humor and inherent drama make the tales ideal for reading and telling aloud. The seven full-page color paintings by Murv Jacob are brightly framed with floral and other patterns that enhance the vibrant compositions, and, whether animal or human, the characters are nicely individualized and energetically executed. A gray flowered border surrounds each page of text, the type is large, the design is spacious, and the detailing is attractive. This is a fine example of good book-making, which combines quality of content with quality of craft.

DOG PEOPLE: NATIVE DOG STORIES (1995)

Kathleen McCabe

SOURCE: A review of *Dog People: Native Dog Stories,* in *School Library Journal,* Vol. 42, No. 1, January, 1996, pp. 114-15.

Five highly readable, engaging tales of Abenaki Indian children and their dogs. Long ago, canines were thought of not just as animals, but as important members of the family, and were given names that epitomized their value and loyalty to their owners. As in *Flying with Eagle, Racing the Great Bear* and *Native American Animal Stories,* Bruchac fills these short stories with details of daily life and symbolic explanations, but the bonds between dogs and humans will be familiar to today's young people. The homes he describes are welcoming and warm and readers will identify with the people. A full-page pen-and-ink drawing [by Murv Jacob] accompanies each selection.

BETWEEN EARTH AND SKY: LEGENDS OF NATIVE AMERICAN SACRED PLACES (1996)

Kirkus Reviews

SOURCE: A review of *Between Earth and Sky,* in

Kirkus Reviews, Vol. LXIV, No. 6, March 15, 1996, p. 445.

From the creators of *The Earth Under Sky Bear's Feet,* philosophical free-verse legends about (and portraits of) places across the US and the native people who hold them sacred.

Little Turtle asks his uncle, Old Bear, about the existence and meaning of sacred places; Old Bear's answer is a procession of legends, each accompanied by a full-page painting. Each tale is colorful, if stiff; each contains an ethical point; each represents a direction or an aspect of direction by which people locate themselves in physical and spiritual landscapes: east, west, north, south, center, above, below, balance lost, and balance held. The superfluous framework of the uncle and nephew's conversation includes a throwaway reference to a powwow they'll be attending later that day; much of what Old Bear conveys in these scenes is also covered by Bruchac in an author's note that precedes them. In fact, the frame (and Old Bear's overarching first-person presence in the legends) distances readers, creating a gap that the real beckoning treasures of this book—the tales themselves and [Thomas] Locker's monumental oil landscapes—cannot bridge.

Karen Hutt

SOURCE: A review of *Between Earth and Sky: Legends of Native American Sacred Places,* in *Booklist,* Vol. 92, No. 15, April 1, 1996, p. 1358.

In response to Little Turtle's questions about places sacred to the Delaware Indians, Old Bear explains that all people have sacred places and shares 10 legends from different tribes. Each legend explains how a particular place came to be, noting its ongoing significance to its tribal people. The picture-book format is similar to that of *Thirteen Moons on Turtle's Back.* Here, short, easy-to-understand legends are accompanied by full-page oil paintings in [Thomas] Locker's dramatic signature style. Pairing places familiar to many students, such as Niagara Falls and the Grand Canyon, with legends offers readers new perspectives on the natural world and an excellent curricular connection. A solid addition for school and public libraries. A map and pronunciation guide are appended.

Ellen Fader

SOURCE: A review of *Between Earth and Sky: Legends of Native American Sacred Places,* in *The Horn Book Magazine,* Vol. LXXII, No. 3, May-June, 1996, pp. 341-42.

A brief introduction explains that this book is concerned with where and how to look for the places that are sacred to Native people, thereby ensuring that "we will not miss seeing the beauty that is around us and within us as we walk between Earth and Sky." Old Bear brings his nephew Little Turtle to the place where their Delaware ancestors once lived. After he explains the Seven Directions, which encompass the obvious East, North, South, and West, as well as Above, Below, and the place Within, Old Bear spins stories, from ten Native American tribes, that are set in each direction. From the Navajo: when the Hero Twins push an ogre over a cliff, he becomes the mountain El Capitan, which "stands there to this day, a sacred symbol of how good can overcome evil." Bruchac also includes legends from Above (a story about how people came to wear the sacred feathers of Falcon and Eagle) and from Below (a Hopi tale about how people lived in worlds beneath this one). At the end of his storytelling lesson, Little Turtle comes to understand that all places are sacred if "we always carry the teachings with us," thus emphasizing the importance of the place Within. Each of these spare tales is a model of economy, gracefully distilling its message, while [Thomas] Locker's dynamic, evocative landscapes capture the mysticism inherent in each story's setting. A map of North America identifies the location of each legend, and the book includes suggested pronunciations of many Native words. An excellent choice that will provoke both introspection and discussion.

FOUR ANCESTORS (1996)

Publishers Weekly

SOURCE: A review of *Four Ancestors: Stories, Songs, and Poems from Native North America,* in *Publishers Weekly,* Vol. 243, No. 14, April 1, 1996, pp. 76-7.

Representing more than 20 tribes, these stories, songs and poems of this collection are in good hands. As usual, Bruchac tells the tales with opacity, allowing each story's inherent beauty and meaning to shine through. And since the illustrators are either tribal members or Native American descendants, their closeness to the subject nets a medley of styles that reflect both tradition and modern, personal perspectives. The selections are grouped around the themes of Fire, Earth, Water and Air—the "ancestors" of all creation. In the Fire section, for example, the selections relate to fire or to things that reflect "the light of fire," such as sun, moon, stars and fireflies. The sheer breadth of this collection and Bruchac's consistently gifted storytelling merit attention and respect.

Connie C. Rockman

SOURCE: A review of *Four Ancestors: Stories Songs, and Poems from Native North America,* in *School Library Journal,* Vol. 42, No. 5, May, 1996, pp. 120-21.

In the traditions of the many native peoples of North America, earth, air, fire, and water are viewed as living beings. According to Bruchac, we can think of these elements as our four ancestors. The tales and poems in this book are grouped around the elements they reflect; for example, the "Water" section includes **"The Cloud-Swal-**

lower Giant" from the Zuni, **"Raven and the Tides"** from the Tshimshian people of the Pacific Northwest, and a Papago rain song from the Southwest desert dwellers. Bruchac is an accomplished and energetic storyteller, and his versions of these stories are easily told or read aloud. The songs and poems interspersed throughout add a change of pace with their richly lyrical language. Background notes on each selection are included. Four artists of Cherokee, Ojibway, and San Carlos/Yavapai Apache heritage perfectly complement the text with evocative, full-page paintings and accent pieces. An especially effective design feature is the vertical border on each page that defines the element for that section. This handsome volume will enhance any folklore collection and enliven programs and lessons on Native American lore and ecology.

CHILDREN OF THE LONGHOUSE (1996)

Karen Hutt

SOURCE: A review of *Children of the Longhouse,* in *Booklist,* Vol. 92, No. 17, May 1, 1996, p. 1506.

Eleven-year-old Ohkwa'ri overhears Grabber and his friends planning to raid a neighboring village and warns the tribal elders, preventing the raid but gaining the wrath of the older boys. When the village decides to hold a game of Tekwaarathon (lacrosse) in an attempt to restore elderly Thunder's Voice to health, Ohkwa'ri realizes he must face those enemies on the playing field. Set in a Mohawk village in the late 1490s, the story offers a detailed look at the traditional Mohawk way of life. Through Ohkwa'ri and his twin sister, Otsi:stia, Bruchac explores the roles of men and women, teaching practices, family relationships, and social life and customs before contact with European explorers and traders. Although the information overshadows the story at times, middle readers interested in traditional practices will find this clear and easy to understand. An afterword describes the efforts of the Mohawk people to return to their traditional lands. A reading list and a glossary are appended.

Publishers Weekly

SOURCE: A review of *Children of the Longhouse,* in *Publishers Weekly,* Vol. 243, No. 24, June 10, 1996, p. 100.

Told from the alternating points of view of Native American Ohkwa'ri and his twin sister Otsi:stia, this historic novel shows a Mohawk village during the best of times: after the Great League of Peace is formed and before European settlers rob the tribe of its land. The story revolves around 11-year-old Ohkwa'ri's conflicts with a pompous bully, but the plot is less essential than the painstakingly wrought details about the tribe's daily rituals, legends and annual celebrations. Bruchac, who states in an afterword that his book is "the result of a lifetime of learning from my Mohawk friends and neighbors," eloquently conveys how democracy, respect and justice

are integral components of the Native Americans' religion and government. Besides learning the origins of modern-day lacrosse and certain kinds of tool-making, readers will come away from this novel with a broadened awareness of a nearly vanished culture.

EAGLE SONG (1997)

Elizabeth Bush

SOURCE: A review of *Eagle Song,* in *Bulletin of the Center for Children's Books,* Vol. 50, No. 7, March, 1997, p. 242.

Danny's mother and father have relocated the family from their Iroquois "rez" to Brooklyn to take up offers of better jobs. But while Richard Bigtree makes good money at dangerous high steel work and wife Salli is settling in well at the American Indian Community House, Danny catches the taunting of his classmates: "Hey, Chief, going home to your teepee?" Dad makes a visit to Danny's fourth-grade class in the hope that a little pride and education will mitigate the class's prejudice, but it's only after Mr. Bigtree is injured at the jobsite that Danny is able to discern just how appropriate his father's myth about Iroquois peacemaker Aionwahta had been. Bruchac limns a close, loving family that doesn't take itself too seriously—teasing, cavorting around the living room, and mimicking matinee Indian-speak ("'You know what it is, Dancing Eagle, my son?' 'No, my father, what is it?' 'We Iroquois men always listen to women because if we don't, they will beat us up!'") The book is heavily message-driven throughout, however, and the parallel between Dad's story of Aionwahta and Danny's reconciliation with the class bully is heavily overdrawn, leaving readers with the medicinal aftertaste of a tale that has been good for them. Full-page black-and-white illustrations [by Dan Andreasen] and a glossary and pronunciation guide are included.

Lenore Rosenthal

SOURCE: A review of *Eagle Song,* in *Children's Book Service,* Vol. 25, No. 11, June, 1997, p. 126.

Daniel has recently moved to Brooklyn and still longs for the Mohawk reservation. The only kids who will talk to him tease him about his heritage. His father tells him a long Indian story from the Iroquois Nation. After his father tells the same story to Dan's class, Dan's life begins to change. The text is quiet, nice, and instructive, but not captivating.

TELL ME A TALE: A BOOK ABOUT STORY-TELLING (1997)

Maxine Kamin

SOURCE: A review of *Tell Me a Tale: A Book about*

Storytelling, in *Children's Book Service,* Vol. 25, No. 11, June, 1997, p. 129.

Joseph Bruchac is a talented and well-respected storyteller. He draws upon his wealth of experience to write this comprehensive how-to book of storytelling. Bruchac divides the process into four parts: listening, observing, remembering and sharing. Throughout the book he uses examples from his own life and stories from many cultures to make his point. Each chapter ends with suggested activities for young people that will sharpen the four skills that are needed to write or tell a story. Though there are a few flaws in the book, such as the incredibly small diagram of the family tree, there are many helpful suggestions for remembering stories and telling them to a group.

> **Additional coverage of Bruchac's life and career is contained in the following sources published by Gale Research:** *Authors and Artists for Young Adults,* **Vol. 19;** *Contemporary Authors New Revision Series,* **Vol. 47;** *DISCovering Authors: Multicultural Authors Module* **(CD-ROM);** *Junior DISCovering Authors* **(CD-ROM);** *Native North American Literature;* **and** *Something about the Author,* **Vol. 89.**

Lois Lowry

1937-

American author of fiction and nonfiction for children and young adults.

Major works include *A Summer to Die* (1977), *Anastasia Krupnik* (1979), *Rabble Starkey* (1987), *Number the Stars* (1989), *The Giver* (1993).

For information on Lowry's career prior to 1984, see *CLR,* Vol. 6.

INTRODUCTION

Lois Lowry has gained a loyal following among young readers and critics for her sensitive, humorous, and realistic portrayals of modern preadolescents and teenagers and the dilemmas and choices they face. Probably best known for her lighthearted and imaginatively plotted Anastasia books, Lowry has also explored in other books, such as her two Newbery Medal-winners *Number the Stars* and *The Giver,* the darker issues that fascinate so many children as they attempt to understand the complex, morally challenging, and sometimes sinister adult world they are poised to enter. Both styles of writing have garnered universal praise for Lowry as a creator of lively, tight-knit plots, dialogue as witty as it gets, and intelligent and likable protagonists with whom readers can readily identify. Her books convey her fascination with "the general continuity of life, the beginnings and ends, transitions, people's adjustments to change"—themes that she explores in a wide range of settings. Sometimes poignantly, sometimes hilariously, she shows her young readers that knowing when to laugh, especially at themselves, is a powerful way to prevail over whatever problems they encounter. Adults in her fictional worlds may have acquired some wisdom and compassion, but none of them pretend to have all the answers. Indeed, Lowry measures the success of each of her books by how well it helps her readers "answer their own questions about life, identity, and human relationships."

Biographical Information

Born into the peripatetic life of a "military brat" (her father was an army dentist), Lowry moved as a small child from her birthplace in Hawaii to her grandparents' home in Pennsylvania for the duration of World War II. After the war her family was reunited with her father in Japan, where he was stationed for two years. She returned to the United States in her early teens, at the outbreak of the Korean War, to attend boarding school and Pembroke College. In 1956, as was common for young women in the fifties, she left college after only two years to be married. Her husband, Donald Grey Lowry, attended Har-

vard Law School while she worked part-time; after a few years of marriage, he was an attorney and she had four children under the age of five. She had wanted to be a writer since childhood, but having married at nineteen, "there were children to raise, education to complete, experience to learn from, and losses to mourn." By the time her youngest child was in high school, she was finally writing professionally—two textbooks and magazine articles and stories—and had also become a photographer. She wrote her first novel after a Houghton Mifflin editor noticed one of her stories and asked whether she'd ever thought of writing for children. *A Summer to Die,* inspired by her own experience with the death of her sister Helen from cancer in her twenties, was published in 1977—the same year she was divorced, after twenty-one years of marriage. Since then Lowry has written more than two dozen books for middle-grade readers and others, all of them shaped by her own memories of childhood and experiences raising two sons and two daughters.

Major Works

Anastasia Krupnik is Lowry's most popular creation. Over

the course of the series that began in 1979 with the publication of *Anastasia Krupnick,* this intelligent and high-spirited girl has aged from ten to thirteen. In the first book, Anastasia is naturally anxious about the eminent arrival of her first sibling. Her sympathetic parents give her the honor of naming the baby, and after considering various horrible possibilities over the course of the book, she finally chooses "Sam," also the name of her grandfather. In *Anastasia Again!* (1981) the family moves to a suburb of Boston. Anastasia is reluctant to leave her beloved Cambridge neighborhood but soon makes new friends, including the recurring character Gertrude Stein, her elderly neighbor. This book illustrates the often conflicting needs of twelve-year-olds to be independent on the one hand but still intimately involved in family decisions on the other. Summertime finds Anastasia bored and dreaming of financial independence in *Anastasia at Your Service* (1982). Setting out to become a rich lady's companion, she ends up her maid instead. In *Anastasia, Ask Your Analyst* (1984), the normal turmoil of early adolescence has our heroine, now a seventh-grader, convinced that she needs a psychiatrist. Her exceptionally forbearing parents explain that her problem is "hormones," and so Anastasia settles for private sessions with a plaster bust of Freud to help her through a difficult time. The fifth Anastasia book, *Anastasia on Her Own* (1985), chronicles the wonderful misadventures of an overconfident girl who thinks it should be "ridiculously easy" to help her father run the house when her mother is away on business for ten days. Since 1986 Lowry has published four more books in the series—*Anastasia Has the Answers* (1986), the aspiring journalist answers the "who, what, where, when, and why" questions; *Anastasia's Chosen Career* (1987), the aspiring bookstore owner takes a modeling course in downtown Boston; *Anastasia at This Address* (1991), now thirteen, Anastasia tries on womanhood by answering a personals ad; and *Anastasia Absolutely* (1995) our heroine's adventures in ethics. "Each . . . sequel seems to be better than the previous one," according to Laura Zaidman, writing in the *Dictionary of Literary Biography.* "Lowry maintains her high standards for plot, characterization, and dialogue to reinforce the central theme of understanding adolescence." Lowry has also published three books in a series focusing on Anastasia's little brother Sam—*All About Sam* (1988), *Attaboy Sam!* (1992), and *See You Around, Sam* (1996). That series, the Anastasia books, and the Tate novels—another Lowry series on the complications and adventures of modern adolescence—are set in a time and culture very familiar to Lowry herself (and many of her readers).

By contrast, most of her serious fiction takes place much further afield. At a time when she was hearing a lot about teenage pregnancy, she happened to be paying visits to her brother at his home in the mountains of West Virginia. The two influences came together in *Rabble Starkey.* "Often in writing," Lowry has said, "it works better when you reverse the obvious. So I [wrote] the book from the point of view of a kid who has been born to a kid." Rabble's mother Sweet Hosanna was fourteen when she gave birth to Rabble, who is now twelve. The two live with the Bigelow family, taking care of the house and

baby Gunther and becoming particularly close to Mr. Bigelow and twelve-year-old Veronica after Mrs. Bigelow is hospitalized for depression. It is a warm and poignant tale whose message about "broken" families and love may have particular appeal to children coping with less than ideal circumstances in their own lives. As Laura Zaidman commented in *Twentieth-Century Children's Writers,* "Lowry's fictional families are not perfect—they would not be realistic if they were—but they provide unconditional love and support when calamity strikes."

Number the Stars takes place in Denmark during World War II. Inspired by the recollections of a close Danish friend of Lowry's, the novel centers on the Johansen family, who shelter a Jewish friend of ten-year-old Annemarie's when the occupying German army tries to round up Danish Jews. Eventually the Johansens smuggle the entire family out of the country and to safety in Sweden—as did so many brave Danes at this time, following the example of their gentle, heroic monarch. Newbery Committee chair Caroline Ward remarked, "Lowry creates suspense and tension without wavering from the viewpoint of Annemarie, a child who shows the true meaning of courage."

The Giver is in many ways Lowry's most ambitious novel to date—and most successful in the view of many critics. It is set in a future society in which all choice and conflict have been eliminated in favor of the reigning value of Sameness. When twelve-year-old Jonas is selected to receive from the Giver the burden of all the community's memories, he begins to learn the very high price that has been paid for living "without color, pain, or past." As Ilene Cooper pointed out in *Booklist, The Giver* "makes an especially good introduction to the genre [of anti-Utopian novels] because it doesn't load the dice by presenting the idea of a community structured around safety as totally negative. There's a distinctly appealing comfort in sameness that kids—especially junior high kids—will recognize."

Awards

International Reading Association award, 1978, for *A Summer to Die;* ALA Notable Book citation, 1980, for *Autumn Street;* American Book Award nomination, 1983, for *Anastasia Again!;* several awards, including the *Boston Globe-Horn Book* award, all 1987, for *Rabble Starkey;* Christopher Award, 1988; several awards, including the Newbery Medal, all 1990, for *Number the Stars;* Newbery Medal, 1994, for *The Giver.*

GENERAL COMMENTARY

Walter Lorraine

SOURCE: "Lois Lowry," in *The Horn Book Magazine,* Vol. LXX, No. 4, July-August, 1994, pp. 423-26.

I first met Lois in a short story many years ago. As I recall, it was about a young girl who goes to the big city alone for the first time. She buys what she has been led to believe is a magic box. In a few simple but immensely effective passages, the reader learns that life is not as nice as it seems, that reality can disillusion the strongest faith. Yet an impression is left, whatever the harshness of reality, that it's good to believe in magic. The writing had many levels. Here obviously was a writer, but, more important, a writer who really had something to say.

At least that is how I interpreted the story. Other readers likely came away with different impressions. There is a quality in Lois's writing that encourages this. She invites each reader to bring his or her personal experience to the story. In one sense her writing becomes more complete with the reader's participation—a true Gestalt in which the whole is greater than the sum of its parts. Often provocative contradictions result, sometimes to the extent that the protagonist dies or lives happily ever, each reader being convinced of a different interpretation.

Lois's writing is always accessible to a very broad audience. Young readers can accept most complicated concepts as long as they do not need adult experience to understand them. A successful poet that I once knew used references to Greek mythology to make his points about love and hate. Such writing is accessible to those people who know Greek mythology. On the other hand, love and hate can be expressed without those Greeks. The references in Lois's work are simple to understand, yet she is able to organize them to express most important concepts whether the work is as humorous as *Anastasia Krupnik*— or as serious as *Autumn Street*. . . .

Early in her career, when she lived in Maine, we exchanged voluminous correspondence. Or perhaps more accurately, Lois wrote many entertaining letters to my occasional lumbering note. There was a sound to those letters, a rhythm that made them comfortable to the eye and mind. All of her writing has that quality. There is a meter to the relationship of the words which makes it uniquely accessible. With many writers, it takes the reader, at least a clumsy reader like me, half a chapter or so before he becomes comfortable with the style. I'd say half a book for Conrad. With Lois one sentence draws you immediately into the world of the story. There is an instinctive feel for the way all those word sounds are woven into a rhythmic whole. . . .

Lois is a risk taker and a just plain good guy in an often cynical world. She has always taken chances. *Rabble Starkey* and *Autumn Street* are powerful and individual statements. The Anastasia stories are very funny, but woven into that humor is far more worldly insight than is usual for such popular fiction. In an age of conformity Lois is a unique and important voice. She is an author who truly has something to say and is willing to risk saying it. Which is Lois's best book? Certainly *The Giver* is an exceptional book. Still, I am absolutely convinced that Lois's best book is yet to come. I am looking forward to it.

Michael Cart

SOURCE: A review of *Anastasia, Absolutely*, in *The New York Times Book Review*, January 14, 1996, p. 23.

Librarians and critics have been speaking ill of series books for children since the turn of the century, when the Stratemeyer Literary Syndicate began spewing out its endless adventures of the Rover Boys and Tom Swift, all distinguished by a faithful adherence to formula, shallow characterization and reader-comforting predictability. Today we would call the Stratemeyer Syndicate a "packager," and Tom Swift has made way for R. L. Stine's "Goosebumps" books, not to mention a zillion "Sweet Valley High" spin-offs (and knockoffs), but the critical disdain remains the same. And usually with good reason.

But not always. Consider some notable exceptions: the enduringly popular Ramona Quimby books by Beverly Cleary, the Alice series by Phyllis Reynolds Naylor, the ebullient Blossom Family novels by Betsy Byars and— my personal favorite—Lois Lowry's continuing story of the days and doings of the irrepressible Anastasia Krupnik.

Anastasia Krupnik first appeared in 1979 in the book of the same name. She was 10 then and doubly distressed: about her conflicted feelings for her nonagenarian grandmother and about the impending birth of a baby brother, since her parents ("the rats!") hadn't bothered to consult her on this. A decade and a half later she's still going strong in *Anastasia, Absolutely*. In the seven titles separating this latest from the first, Anastasia has been growing up—she's now a 13-year-old eighth grader—and along the way she has confronted, with varying degrees of aplomb, a number of age-appropriate rites of passage: family deaths, romance, career choices, the creation of the Krupnik Family Nonsexist Housekeeping Schedule (don't ask). Now, as befits someone facing the moral quandaries and complex issues posed in a Values class, that rite of passage at the end of middle school, an indecisive Anastasia feels like the wishiest of the wishy-washy.

The hypothetical assumes real-life relevance, and controls the fragile plot, when, walking her new dog at the crack of dawn, a sleepy Anastasia confuses the bag in which she's placed his daily—uh—deposit with a package her mother had asked her to mail and she drops Sleuth's parcel into a corner mailbox.

Realizing her mistake, she concludes that she's committed a Federal offense and agonizes endlessly—and amusingly—over whether she should do the right thing and confess. When she finally does ("Doing the right thing is something you can't ever be wishy-washy about"), Anastasia becomes an inadvertent heroine. It seems that a bomb, placed inside the mailbox by a disgruntled postal worker, was defused by the bag she dropped on it.

This is funny in a subversively Freudian way; needless to say, Anastasia's 3-year-old brother, Sam, thinks the subject is hilarious, and I imagine readers of the *Boston Globe*,

Anastasia's hometown newspaper, will be amused to learn that the plastic bag containing the plot-driving dog deposit is the very one in which the Krupniks' *New York Times* was delivered. But as a plot device it's pretty pale when compared with earlier Anastasia adventures. Frankly, though, it's not plot that principally distinguishes this series.

Lois Lowry is a two-time Newbery Medal winner—for *Number the Stars,* a World War II novel about the rescue of 7,000 Jews by the Danish resistance, and *The Giver,* a novel about an authoritarian cult that was a radical departure from the realistic fiction that established her reputation. Artistic integrity shines from the pages of her serious fiction, but it didn't necessarily follow that Ms. Lowry would bring similar literary strengths to her comic stories of Anastasia. Before she began writing books for young readers, she was a photographer and journalist, and some of the skills she developed in those years are on display in this light fiction, too. She presents multidimensional characters, closely observed settings, bright and believable dialogue, and an artfully easy style. It's also wonderfully obvious that Ms. Lowry appreciates the power that a humorous view of life lends her readers in their dealings with adversity—even if it's as benign and plausible an adversity as dropping the wrong parcel into a mailbox by accident.

But perhaps the greatest of Ms. Lowry's successes in this series is to have created, with no hint of the holier-than-thou, a believably flourishing functional family. Equally agreeable is the author's subtle celebration of intelligence and the work of the creative mind: consider that Anastasia's father, Myron, is a celebrated poet and Harvard professor; her mother, Katherine, is a Caldecott Honor-winning children's book illustrator; and her brother, too young for a career, is nevertheless superbly gifted at using the food on his dinner plate to build things. Give this lad enough mashed potatoes and I'll bet he could create the Empire State Building!

As for Anastasia: despite her endearing self-doubts, she is reassured by her teacher that her answers to the questions posed in the Values class are "terrific." Some of the questions—Would you donate a kidney to save the life of a sibling? If you see someone shoplifting, would you tell the store manager? If you could save the life of an American baby who you know will grow up to be a violent criminal by giving up a day of your own, would you do it?—and her thoughtful answers are printed at the end of each chapter so readers can judge for themselves.

The author's light touch saves all this from tendentiousness and is mightily helped by her characters' own self-deprecating humor. In other words, readers are invited to take this lightly because the characters take themselves so lightly.

The irony is that earnest committees that present awards have also taken the books lightly. No Newberys or medallion acclaim for Anastasia, alas. But Ms. Lowry is in good company in the realm of critical oversight. Her

companions in the creation of artful series—Cleary, Naylor and Byars—all earned their Newberys for serious, nonseries books, too.

But no matter. Anastasia is a winner. Long may her series flourish.

TITLE COMMENTARY

📖   *THE ONE HUNDREDTH THING ABOUT CAROLINE* (1983)

Kathleen Brachmann

SOURCE: A review of *The One Hundredth Thing About Caroline,* in *School Library Journal,* Vol. 30, No. 2, October, 1983, p. 160.

Eleven-year-old Caroline is pretty much your average child; she has a mother who persists in serving weird vegetables at dinner and an obnoxious older brother, J. P., who is a self-proclaimed genius. What *isn't* average about Caroline is that Frederick Fiske, the mysterious man who lives upstairs, is plotting to kill both her and J. P.—at least, that's what Caroline and her chum Stacy think. While Stacy, a would-be investigative reporter who speaks in headlines ("Slayer Stalks Tots"), keeps herself busy gathering clues, Caroline frantically tries to squelch her mother's growing friendship with Fiske, and even J. P. gets into the act as he plans a high-voltage defense. The real explanation behind all this may be obvious to some, but many young readers will be kept in suspense right up to the climactic scene at a dinner party, which is both tense and humorous. As demonstrated in her "Anastasia" books, Lowry's style is bright, fast-paced and funny, with skillfully-drawn, believable characters.

Ethel L. Heins

SOURCE: A review of *The One Hundredth Thing About Caroline,* in *The Horn Book Magazine,* Vol. LIX, No. 6, December, 1983, p. 711.

The author has previously demonstrated her ability as a humorist and now writes a contemporary farce set in New York City. At eleven Caroline Tate has a membership in the Museum of Natural History and an ambition to become a vertebrate paleontologist—like her hero Gregor Keretsky, the dinosaur expert. Much to the chagrin of her hard-working divorced mother, a state of perpetual war exists between Caroline and her older brother, whose electrical tinkering often disrupts the entire household. Egged on by her best friend Stacy, who believes herself to be a budding investigative reporter, Caroline puts together some specious clues and concocts an elaborate theory that Frederick Fiske, the new man in the top-floor apartment, is an incipient murderer. For Caroline's own "Tate Theory of Evolution" makes her believe that the sinister Mr. Fiske is actually "little more than an unevolved Tyrannosaurus Rex. The Great Killer." When the mystery man becomes interested in their mother and takes her out to dinner, brother and sister—feuding temporarily forgotten—decide that a raid on Mr. Fiske's apartment will produce the incriminating evidence they seek. The last scene in the book—their mother's dinner party reduced to a shambles—is like the grand finale in an old-fashioned slapstick movie. Crackling dialogue, plenty of action, a couple of nimble-witted youngsters, and their long-suffering mother almost guarantee an entertaining story.

Zena Sutherland

SOURCE: A review of *The One Hundredth Thing About Caroline,* in *Bulletin of the Center for Children's Books,* Vol. 37, No. 6, February, 1984, p. 112.

Caroline is eleven, the brother with whom she squabbles is thirteen, and they live in Manhattan with their divorced mother. The two are happily adjusted: this is not a story about divorce, but a humorous tale of a child's mistaken suspicions about a neighbor. Caroline has found a discarded letter to the man who lives in the apartment above hers, and it says "The woman's terrific. . . . Eliminate the kids. You can find a way." She's convinced her life is threatened; the man proves to be an author, his correspondent a literary agent, but even readers who spot this probability should enjoy the antics of Caroline and her best friend as they play detective. This has less depth than most Lowry books, but it's just as clever, just as smoothly structured.

Victor Watson

SOURCE: "Quests for All Ages," in *Times Educational Supplement,* No. 3970, July 31, 1992, p. 21.

Now is a good time for young readers to discover Lois Lowry. In *The 100th Thing About Caroline,* three children discover a letter to a neighbour containing the sinister instruction: "Eliminate the kids". They set about a murder investigation, with entertaining consequences. The children combine ingenuity with daftness; if the book is ever televised, the characters will be insufferable, but the story is easy to read, fast-moving and funny. There are other books about the same children (and some readers might go on to discover Lois Lowry's more famous Anastasia Krupnik series).

📖 *ANASTASIA, ASK YOUR ANALYST* (1984)

Zena Sutherland

SOURCE: A review of *Anastasia, Ask Your Analyst,* in *Bulletin of the Center for Children's Books,* Vol. 37, No. 9, May, 1984, p. 169.

In this sequel to earlier books about Anastasia, the redoubtable heroine is now thirteen, and the accumulation of adolescent woes (her hormones, her relationship with her parents, who have suddenly developed awful faults, and her feelings about her younger brother) convinces her she needs therapy. Her problems are perfectly normal for her age, her father says, and refuses. Anastasia buys a bust of Freud and talks to it, often answering her own questions quite rationally. "I don't hate you and Dad anymore," Anastasia tells her mother at the close of the book, "I think my hormones are gone." This is up-beat, funny, and sophisticatedly witty, like Lowry's other Anastasia stories; the characters are solidly conceived, the writing style and dialogue both polished and effervescent.

Carolyn Noah

SOURCE: A review of *Anastasia, Ask Your Analyst,* in *School Library Journal,* Vol. 30, No. 9, May, 1984, p. 82.

"How do you know I don't have symptoms of necrosis?" Anastasia, 13 and exhibiting all the emotional signs of adolescence, is sure she needs an analyst. She's also sure that she needs gerbils, over her mother's objections. Being Anastasia, she gets both. The gerbils are ostensibly for her science project; her analyst a plaster Freud. Anastasia's sessions with Freud provide a humorous vehicle for internal monologues, and the 11 gerbils' escape provides outright comedy. As always, Lowry's dialogue captures the spirit of her subjects, and the pace is fast enough to snare most young readers. However, there is a problem with this book. Anastasia spends the bulk of the novel bemoaning the "hormones" that come with being 13. Conveniently, on the next-to-last page, Anastasia declares that her "hormones" are gone, along with all her other problems. It's a rare teen who recovers in a season, and we have come to expect more effective character resolution from this author. Despite this hitch, *Anastasia* . . . is still readable, basically credible and will be enjoyable to those who already belong to her following.

Kate M. Flanagan

SOURCE: A review of *Anastasia, Ask Your Analyst,* in *The Horn Book Magazine,* Vol. LX, No. 3, June, 1984, pp. 330-31.

The fourth book about Anastasia and the Krupnik family has many of the same admirable qualities as the earlier ones. The dialogue is snappy and humorous, and the author is skillful at depicting her heroine's unique point of view. Now thirteen, Anastasia was experiencing a common phenomenon of adolescence: Her family had suddenly become an embarrassment to her. She wished her mother was an ordinary housewife instead of an artist and that her father sold insurance. And her precocious brother Sam, three years old with "an IQ of about a billion," was a "huge humongous humiliation" to her. Anastasia was convinced that she needed a psychiatrist to handle her problems but had to settle for a plaster bust of Sigmund

Freud and a volume of his works. In the meantime she was engrossed in a science fair project that consisted of watching two gerbils and recording her observations in a journal. Anastasia's journal entries are often amusing as they document her problems with the rapidly multiplying gerbils, her thoughts about her family, and her interpretations of Freud. Unfortunately, the author chose to repeat each previous entry whenever the girl added a new one, and the effect is tiresome. Another problem in the book is the author's inclusion of several references to ethnic groups and to the handicapped which might well be disturbing to some people. In any case, they make the Krupnik family seem just a little less likable than before.

Adrian Jackson

SOURCE: A review of *Anastasia, Ask Your Analyst,* in *Books for Keeps,* No. 51, July, 1988, p. 10.

There seems to be something wrong with parents and child, or so the child thinks. No it's not her name, it's adolescence. Anastasia begins a Science Project on gerbils (extracts of which are repeated annoyingly at intervals through the book) but ends up analysing herself. Lois Lowry has a gentle and sometimes sharp touch and the best parts are the conversations with Freud—in bust form—the escape of the gerbils and the attempts to help younger brother Sam cope with the dreaded Nicky Coletti. It's all good fun and sometimes thoughtful too.

US AND UNCLE FRAUD (1984)

Maria Salvadore

SOURCE: A review of *Us and Uncle Fraud,* in *School Library Journal,* Vol. 31, No. 3, November, 1984, pp. 133-34.

For the first time in three years, Claude Cunningham visits his sister, her husband and their four children. Stephanie is a typical two-and-a-half-year-old, lively and growing. Fourteen-year-old Tom emulates his father, taking responsibility seriously. Though liked by both the eldest and youngest, Claude captures the imaginations of both middle children, Marcus and Louise, who are naively eager for adventure. Louise thought at first that "Uncle Claude was a real disappointment," with his bland face and shabby clothes. Claude's brief visit, however, changes their opinion. His talk of exotic places, the promise of hidden treasure and a cryptic note send the children on a treasure hunt that ultimately leads to some important discoveries about themselves and their family. The credible quick-paced plot, plausible characters and satisfactory resolution realistically evolve as the Cunningham's story is told by Louise. She describes their town as indistinguishable from most others; yet in this small town dramatic and some less dramatic events—a burglary, a flood, a family trying to cope with a son in a coma—create conflict, ten-

sion and mystery as Marcus and Louise attempt to sort fantasy from reality, fraud from dreams. Although there are light, even humorous moments, the more serious tone and sometimes adult point of view is reminiscent of Lowry's *Autumn Street*. As in Lowry's other novels, there is a strong female protagonist and the family portrayed is a basically solid one.

Ethel R. Twitchell

SOURCE: A review of *Us and Uncle Fraud,* in *The Horn Book Magazine,* Vol. LX, No. 6, November-December, 1984, pp. 759-60.

Just what is Uncle Claude up to, anyway? Full of whimsical banter and silly teasing during his short visit, he convinces Louise and her younger brother Marcus that he has left them a hidden treasure; but after his sudden departure they find only a strange message, which they are unable to decipher. At first, they are baffled and cross but are quickly distracted when a major flood hits their small town. Amid the dark, swirling water the two children discover that they have a deep-seated bond with their overbearing older brother Tom, when he attempts to rescue Marcus and all three are almost swept away. The conclusion unravels a few mysteries about Uncle Claude, the identity of a town thief, and the real meaning of Claude's message. Like other books by the author, the story exudes a warm family feeling, although it does not have the acerbic humor or smart-aleck zest of the "Anastasia" books. The excitement of the flood offers some dramatic moments as does the family's agonizing wait for the injured Tom to awaken from a deep coma. At best, Uncle Claude is a shadowy, fey character as the story shifts from him to the children's frightening experience during the nearly fatal disaster.

Zena Sutherland

SOURCE: A review of *Us and Uncle Fraud,* in *Bulletin of the Center for Children's Books,* Vol. 38, No. 4, December, 1984, p. 71.

Uncle Claude is, according to Father, a cadger and a layabout; according to Mother, her brother Claude is a sweet, gentle dreamer. According to Louise, the narrator, and her brother Marcus, Uncle Claude is fun, an exciting visitor who goes off abruptly leaving them the promise of a treasure hidden in the house—Faberge eggs, they have been led to believe. But they find no treasure, suspect that Claude's a fraud and—even worse—that he's a thief. They know (but can't tell) that Claude knew where there was a hidden key to a house where a robbery had been committed. The story has Lowry's usual wit, humor, and polish; it also has more drama than some of her other books, because of the combination of the excitement of a flood, suspense about the robbery, and tension about an older brother who is swept away in the flood and is for a long time in a coma before he recovers.

Lyn Littlefield Hoopes

SOURCE: "Children's Books: The Cream of the Crop," in *The Christian Science Monitor,* March 1, 1985, p. 65.

In *Us and Uncle Fraud*, Lois Lowry introduces us to Uncle Claude, the baffling maverick, and with him a mystery, and a story of family love. Uncle Claude blows in at Easter, turning the world of Marcus and Louise inside out with his reckless dreaming. He comes bearing a gift, a "priceless and fragile secret." Then, just as suddenly he is gone, leaving Marcus and Louise the order to "search hard, my comrades," and this one puzzling clue: "YA TEBYA LYUBLYU."

Lowry creates a superb companionship between brother and sister in their search for treasure, their promised secrets and in their bond against their grandiose older brother, Tom. The search is soon put on hold with the advent of a mysterious robbery, and the dangerous flooding of their river valley. It is Tom's accident as he bravely saves Marcus from the surging river that brings the family together and the mysteries to light.

Determined to see Tom live, Marcus and Louise talk to him in his deep coma, telling him anything, everything, to draw him out, even their prized secrets: "YA TEBYA LYUBLYU," they sing, "YA TEBYA LYUBLYU." This sharing of their valued secret coincides with Tom's revival, and true to Lowry's sense of irony, unlocks the meaning of the mysterious phrase—"I LOVE YOU" in Russian—which is itself the "priceless and fragile" gift.

Lowry's telling shines with her singular wit and humor, and her uncanny sense of children. Although the story's meaning surfaces a bit suddenly at the end, the idea of family unity and what can be accomplished through love is compellingly brought forth.

ANASTASIA ON HER OWN (1985)

Zena Sutherland

SOURCE: A review of *Anastasia on Her Own,* in *Bulletin of the Center for Children's Books,* Vol. 38, No. 9, May, 1985, p. 170.

Often preoccupied with her work as an illustrator, Anastasia's mother is a careless housekeeper; she bemoans the fact that she forgets, almost every day, to thaw meat for dinner. Her husband and daughter set up a housekeeping schedule, but when Mom is called away on a business trip, it's Anastasia who's in charge of the housekeeping and her three-year-old brother. Hampered by little Sam's chicken pox (they don't tell Mom when she calls) Anastasia has to stay home from school (they don't tell Mom) and then is faced with making a gourmet dinner when Mr. Krupnik's old flame invites herself for a meal (they certainly don't tell Mom). This doesn't have a strong story line, but it is breezy and funny in the *Egg and I* tradition of housekeeping disaster literature.

Kathryn M. Weisman

SOURCE: A review of *Anastasia on Her Own,* in *School Library Journal,* Vol. 31, No. 10, August, 1985, p. 68.

Anastasia is back again—in her fifth and perhaps best adventure yet. This time Mrs. Krupnik is called away to California for a ten-day consulting job, leaving Dr. Krupnik and Anastasia in charge. Anastasia and her father are both certain that keeping up with household duties will be a simple task—"Any moron could do it. All you need is a schedule." They create the Krupnik Family Nonsexist Housekeeping Schedule—which goes through a variety of versions and revisions as the week progresses. Naturally disasters strike—younger brother Sam develops chicken pox, Dr. Krupnik's old girl-friend pops in for a surprise visit, and Anastasia is asked out for her first real date. Actually, Anastasia copes quite well—and quite realistically—in the face of these disasters. In the end, however, even she is forced to admit that she needs reinforcements—and Mrs. Krupnik is only too happy to return home early from California. A thoroughly enjoyable and believable book which will have wide appeal.

JoEllen Broome

SOURCE: A review of *Anastasia on Her Own,* in *Voice of Youth Advocates,* Vol. 8, No. 3, August, 1985, p. 186.

Anastasia Krupnik is off and running again performing feats this time as an efficiency expert right in her own home. Crisis levels have been reached when playful, artsy mom regularly forgets to defrost meat for the family dinner. An outbreak of list making for mom's benefit occurs daily. While Mrs. Krupnik attends to her illustrating business in Los Angeles, Anastasia is forced to practice what she herself preached in mom's absence. The fun begins when little Sam catches chicken pox, dad's old girlfriend shows up, and Anastasia arranges a formal dinner party to chaperone her father and to impress her boorish boyfriend. A hilarious account of Murphy's Law working at the teenage level. Engaging dialogue. Delightfully honest and upbeat look at the little upheavals of family life.

Ann A. Flowers

SOURCE: A review of *Anastasia on Her Own,* in *The Horn Book Magazine,* Vol. LXI, No. 5, September-October, 1985, pp. 556-57.

Lois Lowry is fast becoming the Beverly Cleary for the upper middle grades. Her Anastasia Krupnik books furnish the solid, funny, staple reading that the Ramona stories give to younger readers. The Anastasia books are a little more sophisticated and urban, clearly more advanced, have realistic but not overpowering family problems, and have a likable central character who is easy to identify with and has equally affectionate and sensible parents. This sequel shows Anastasia dealing with the household during her mother's unprecedented absence on a business trip. Naturally, the careful arrangements disintegrate: Sam develops chicken pox, salesmen solicit the inexperienced Anastasia over the phone, and the state of the house degenerates with remarkable rapidity. Even Anastasia's normally competent father trembles with trepidation when his old girl friend proposes to come to dinner. The pictures of Anastasia giving Sam baths in baking powder (rather than baking soda), struggling with *haute cuisine,* and dyeing the tablecloth purple because she has read that purple is the color of passion, are wildly funny. Scattered throughout the book are more of Anastasia's justifiably famous lists—this time continually revised and simplified housekeeping schedules. The family solidarity is obvious, however, and Anastasia's troubles are merely temporary. Warm, witty, and realistic, this fine addition to the Anastasia books is the best sequel yet.

📖 *SWITCHAROUND* (1985)

Publishers Weekly

SOURCE: A review of *Switcharound,* in *Publishers Weekly,* Vol. 228, No. 19, November 8, 1985, p. 60.

Rating another A+ for the latest in an unbroken list of superb novels, Lowry regales us with the second adventures of Caroline and J. P. Tate, who won readers' hearts in **The One Hundredth Thing About Caroline**. "We're in a nightmare," says J. P. "Wrong," says his sister. "We're in Des Moines." Their father Herb sends for his son and daughter, nine years after the divorce from their mother, and they arrive from New York with plans to get even for banishment to the boonies. It's even worse than the siblings had imagined. J. P., the electronics genius, is compelled to coach a kids' sandlot team, "Taters' Chips," sponsored by their father's store. Caroline's fate is being sidetracked from boning up on paleontology in preparation for her future career. She has to take care of her stepsisters, infant twins, and pathetic David (Poochie), a six-year-old loser on the baseball team. The tender, funny story moves rapidly to an auspicious event where the title proves to have more than one meaning. Caroline's last letter to her mother goes, "Now that everything is switched around, J. P. and I actually like Des Moines quite a bit."

Kemie Nix

SOURCE: "A Trio to Tickle the Funny Bone," in *The Christian Science Monitor,* November 11, 1985, p. 64.

In **Switcharound,** by Lois Lowry, J. P. and his sister, Caroline, are both subjected to and the instigators of onerous switches. When their divorced father legally forces them to come to Des Moines for the summer, these young, happy New Yorkers are subjected to a series of unpleasant culture shocks.

Interested in computers and chess, J. P. is compelled by his father, who owns a sporting goods store, to coach a baseball team of six-year-olds. One of the members of

this team is also his roommate, his half brother Poochie. Caroline finds herself not only rooming with twin baby girls but baby-sitting for them while their mother (her stepmother) takes a real estate course.

With a summer of misery stretching out before them, J. P. and Caroline commiserate and decide to seek revenge. Because they are both extremely intelligent, their revenges are diabolically clever. Because they are both extremely young, their revenges, although partially successful, also backfire—as revenges are wont to do.

Through a light, witty story, Lois Lowry teaches that hasty judgments can be wrong, and even *relatives* deserve to be given the benefit of the doubt.

Zena Sutherland

SOURCE: A review of *Switcharound,* in *Bulletin of the Center for Children's Books,* Vol. 39, No. 5, January, 1986, p. 90.

Whether or not readers remember siblings J. P. and Caroline, they should enjoy this story of the united front the two achieve when faced with what seems to them not just adversity but catastrophe. Their father, remarried and now also the father of a boy of six, Poochie, and twin female infants, has decided after some years of ignoring them, to have J. P. and Caroline visit for the summer. They don't want to leave New York to come to Des Moines and they certainly don't want to spend the summer as Dad has planned: babysitting for Caroline (babies bore her) while her stepmother takes a course, and baseball coaching of Poochie's team for J. P., who hates baseball. There is a bit too convenient an all-ends-tied final chapter, but the strong characterization, the humorous style and yeasty dialogue, and the change and development (including some shaking of stereotypical sex roles) in the two main characters give the story both substance and appeal.

Maria B. Salvadore

SOURCE: A review of *Switcharound,* in *School Library Journal,* Vol. 32, No. 6, February, 1986, p. 87.

Caroline Tate and her brother rarely agree on anything, but when their father asks them to spend the summer in Des Moines, they suddenly sound like the "Mormon Tabernacle Choir." Leaving New York means that Caroline won't have the Museum of Natural History, and J. P.'s summer computer project will have to be postponed. It also means that J. P. will have to play baseball and they'll both have to put up with their father's three kids, Poochie and twin baby girls. The summer starts out badly: Caroline takes care of the messy twins, while J. P. is expected to coach Poochie's baseball team of clumsy six year olds, the Tater Chips. Both plan revenge, but a surprising revelation concerning their father and the opportunity for Caroline and J. P. to use their own special talents reverses the situation. Everyone gains a new perspective, and all ends well. Readers will recognize the feuding siblings from Lowry's *One Hundredth Thing About Caroline,* although this may be enjoyed independently. Again, Lowry has created realistic, likable characters in plausible, humorous situations. Lowry retains her ear for dialogue; the conversations are snappy and often funny (as is the entire text). Lowry fans will not be disappointed with the *Switcharound.*

ANASTASIA HAS THE ANSWERS (1986)

Kirkus Reviews

SOURCE: A review of *Anastasia Has the Answers,* in *Kirkus Reviews,* Vol. LIV, No. 7, April 1, 1986, pp. 546-47.

Anastasia Krupnik and her family return in a sixth witty and perceptive novel.

Anastasia, now 13, is studying to become a journalist. But even applying journalistic techniques and asking the proper questions doesn't solve all the problems in her life. She's concerned about her friend Daphne's situation, with a father who's left the family and a mother who now hates men. How can Anastasia reinterest Daphne's mother in a social life? And Anastasia wonders why she is the only one who can't climb the ropes in gym class—especially when her gym teacher is, in Anastasia's eyes, the worst possible person to witness her humiliation. With her customary zest, Anastasia tackles these problems head-on, and surprises even herself with the success in solving them.

Lowry's deft portrayal of the emotional ups and downs of being 13 is right on target. Readers will identify with Anastasia and enjoy her methods of coping with problems and feelings. Some readers may be offended by the flip attitude toward the death of Anastasia's Aunt Rose. The blasé reactions of Anastasia and her little brother Sam may be true to life, but at least the recently bereaved Uncle George could show a little feeling. This quibble aside, Anastasia will win new fans and delight her old ones with this addition.

Carolyn Noah

SOURCE: A review of *Anastasia Has the Answers,* in *School Library Journal,* Vol. 32, No. 9, May, 1986, p. 94.

Humiliated by her inability to climb a rope in gym class, 13-year-old Anastasia schemes to overcome the obstacle and impress her beautiful lady gym teacher, on whom she has a crush. Counterpoints to the plot are Anastasia's matchmaking efforts on behalf of a newly widowed uncle and a friend's mother, her struggle to make a smarmy recitation come alive and her attempt to view life as a journalist. In fact, each chapter begins humorously with Anastasia's efforts to make the day's events fit into "WHO WHAT WHEN WHERE WHY," somehow, nonetheless,

reading in the style of the *National Enquirer.* The language in Lowry's stories about Anastasia is always natural, but . . . *Answers* also benefits from this stylistic variation. The surrounding characters, from baby brother Sam playing funeral on the floor to bereaved "Clark Gablish" Uncle George are colorful and quirky and distinct. Anastasia manages, with some help from her mother, to resolve the rope conflict. The story's other elements fall, quite literally, into their own likely and lively places. Not only does Anastasia have the answers, but she's also at the top of her form.

Mary M. Burns

SOURCE: A review of *Anastasia Has the Answers,* in *The Horn Book Magazine,* Vol. LXII, No. 3, May-June, 1986, pp. 327-28.

Once again, Anastasia Krupnik proves herself a true original among the galaxy of memorable characters in children's literature. As indestructible and irrepressible at thirteen as she was at eight, she has become a durable creation with whom her fans can empathize. Like the earlier stories, this latest chronicle follows an episodic pattern in which various vignettes are connected by a central problem, scaled to preadolescent understanding. This time the problem is self-image: Anastasia just can't seem to master the art of rope climbing in gym class. Humiliation in front of her peers would be bad enough; appearing as a constant failure to her favorite teacher, Ms. Wilhelmina Willoughby—tall, slender, fashionably dressed, with distinctively handsome black features—is unbearable. Yet, while Anastasia may be down, she is never quite out. Her fondness for lists has evolved logically into a passion for journalism. She believes all problems and situations can be resolved by neatly subsuming their disparate elements under the reporter's canons of who, what, when, where, and why. But life, she learns, is not that simple, and this discovery leads, in true Anastasia fashion, to a variety of complications—from finding a suitable second wife for her Clark Gable look-alike uncle to impressing the visitors from the International Commission for Educational Excellence with a memorable gymnastic performance. As always, the descriptions of Anastasia's antics are witty and urbane—as befits a not-so-typical suburban family. And the end of the chapter excerpts, representing Anastasia's efforts to translate events into an investigative reporter's style, are both funny and revealing. While not quite up to the sustained high comedy of *Anastasia on Her Own,* this sequel is certainly an entertaining interlude between major phases in Anastasia's life.

Carrie Carmichael

SOURCE: A review of *Anastasia Has the Answers,* in *The New York Times Book Review,* September 14, 1986, p. 37.

Anastasia Krupnik is still hopeless with her feet. She walks just fine, but she could not cope with ballet and now she cannot climb the ropes in her seventh grade gym class. That humiliates and embarrasses her in front of the person she admires more than any other in the whole world, her tall, lanky physical education teacher Wilhelmina Willoughby. In *Anastasia Has the Answers* the title character comes to grips with her problems.

In this sixth Anastasia book featuring the now 13-year-old daughter of a Harvard University English professor and poet, and a painter living in a Boston suburb, Lois Lowry addresses every teen-ager's fear: being weird. Anastasia is afraid she will be the only girl who never climbs the ropes. She is also fearful that her feelings for her gym teacher are "gross" and "sick," because the gym teacher is female. At a time when homosexuality is discussed openly—from television talk shows to the painfully public arena of health classes in school—Anastasia worries about what her feelings for the gym teacher may mean for her own future. Confiding to her mother that a "friend" has a crush on a female teacher, Anastasia discovers that as a 13-year-old, her very own mother, Katherine Krupnik, had a crush on her pretty piano teacher and went on to turn out perfectly O.K.

In addition to worrying about being weird, teen-agers are terrified at the thought of being invisible, not recognized as special. When her school is selected as the New England host for an international team of educators, Anastasia ponders what would happen if, when the far-flung educators return home and someone asked, "'What about Anastasia Krupnik? . . . They would furrow their brows. They would say, finally, 'WHO?' Anastasia couldn't bear it. The worst thing in the world, she decided, was to be on the receiving end of a brow-furrowed WHO.'"

A reader new to the series may have a little trouble sorting out the cast of characters at first. Early on, Anastasia and her parents talk after "Sam was in bed." Starting without the previous episodes, you don't know if Sam is a pet snake, elderly boarder, juvenile-delinquent brother, or none of the above. Actually, Sam is Anastasia's brother, a decade younger, precious and precocious. The same kind of mystery extends to Mrs. Stein. It takes chapters for the new reader to grasp her role. She is a neighbor, surrogate grandmother and feisty senior citizen. I am glad to see Mrs. Stein back. Her absence from a few books had me worried, and Mrs. Stein is getting on in years.

Anastasia Has the Answers follows the tradition of the other books in the series. The characters and their situations are not just plausible, they have the sound of real authenticity. Although Anastasia's father does the dishes twice a week, one uncle never washed a dish in 30 years of marriage. The real middle-class American world is present. The Krupnik family's favorite entertainment is quoting dialogue from classic movies, and their young teen-ager is a modern mixture of sophistication and naïveté. She may know Rhett Butler lines she would love to hear spoken to her, but in real life affairs

of the heart and in her inexperienced attempts at matchmaking, Anastasia turns to the bible of contemporary relationships between women and men. She quotes *Cosmopolitan.*

RABBLE STARKEY (1987; British edition as *The Road Ahead*, 1990)

[The following excerpt is from Lowry's acceptance speech for the 1987 Boston Globe-Horn Book Award for fiction.]

Lois Lowry

SOURCE: "Rabble Starkey," in *The Horn Book Magazine,* Vol. LXIV, No. 1, January-February, 1988, pp. 29-31.

In the same way that the readers of *The Red Pony* could, with Mr. Steinbeck's help, create a picture of a dog built out of his words and also out of every dog they had ever known, I hoped that readers of *Rabble Starkey* would create a picture of a place and that into their picture might go all the small towns they had ever known.

I needed that sense of place to be very true and very sure. If a thirteen-year-old girl in Anastasia Krupnik's neighborhood ran off with a boy in a blue pickup truck—and came home a year later with a newborn baby—things would be quite different. The baby would go to a day-care center. Its mother would go to a therapist. A book about them would be a book about problems more than a book about people.

When Sweet Hosanna ran off at thirteen, it had to be in a place where a boy in a blue pickup truck seemed a truly many-splendored thing. And it had to be a place where, when she came home with her baby a year later, they would both be welcome. Then I could write about their lives, not their troubles.

Rabble Starkey is a book which describes one school year: Rabble's sixth-grade year, when she is twelve and her mother twenty-six. Not much happens. No one is murdered, no one has an affair, no one is abused, no one succumbs to drink or drugs. Rabble and her mother simply live and grow and change and move on. That they do so with success and confidence is, I think, because of their geography, their landscape, their community: because they live in a place where neighbors appear at the kitchen door with a chicken casserole and a hug when things go badly. And, come to think of it, the neighbors do exactly the same when things go well. Rabble and Sweet Hosanna live in a place where love has no conditions imposed upon it.

It appears to me, from the Boston Globe-Horn Book Award, that my trust in the reader was justified: that all of you have places like that in your own memory or dreams and that they are comfortable places to be. Thank you for that.

Kirkus Reviews

SOURCE: A review of *Rabble Starkey,* in *Kirkus Reviews,* Vol. LV, No. 5, March 1, 1987, p. 374.

For Parable Ann (Rabble) and her mother, Sweet Hosanna, her sixth-grade year is a time of growth and change.

Sweet-Ho was 14 when she ran off with Ginger Starkey; he left her the next year, when Rabble was a month old. Now she's been caring for the Bigelows for four years, and it seems like a first true home. Veronica Bigelow, also 12, is Rabble's best friend, almost a sister. Then Mrs. Bigelow, deeply depressed since four-year-old Gunther's birth, erupts into frightening, bizarre behavior and is institutionalized; while she's away, the little family that's left enjoys peaceful, joyous times; Phil Bigelow reads aloud in the evening and treats the two girls as though they were both his daughters. As the year progresses, the girls take responsibility for helping the cantankerous old woman who lives alone next door; the obnoxious local bully shows signs of blossoming into Veronica's first beau; Sweet-Ho goes back to school and does so well she decides to get a college degree, and narrator Rabble decides to tidy up her own grammar (a neat stylistic transition on Lowry's part). But although Rabble has surprised Phil and Sweet-Ho in a tender kiss, when Mrs. Bigelow is able to come home, Sweet-Ho decides to move on—both she and Rabble have more growing to do, more things in store.

Lowry, with six "Anastasias" and several other fine books to her credit, is adept at portraying the nuances of relationships and emotions. Here she presents a lively cast of characters in an unusual plot, skillfully handled.

Kathleen Brachmann

SOURCE: A review of *Rabble Starkey,* in *School Library Journal,* Vol. 33, No. 7, April, 1987, p. 99.

Twelve-year-old Parable Ann ("Rabble") and her mother, Sweet Hosanna, live over the Bigelows' garage. Sweet-Ho is the hired help for the Bigelows, while Rabble is best friends with their daughter, Veronica. As the story opens, the two girls are working on a family tree assignment, and this somewhat worn device serves to introduce the characters. After a slow start, the pace picks up, but while Rabble's life is eventful enough, nothing much seems to *happen*—possibly because the narrative is so low-key as to be almost soporific. Rabble and Veronica reluctantly befriend elderly, grumpy Millie Bellows; Veronica begins to show an interest in boys; Veronica's mentally unstable mother is institutionalized after nearly drowning her young son; and the beginnings of romance spring up between Sweet-Ho and Veronica's father. But while all this is going on, readers learn more about the secondary characters than about Rabble herself, despite the fact that she is the narrator. Although she has the potential to be a strong character, she never comes to life. The narration is littered with vernacular—"So we was

friends," "Without no exceptions"—which is annoying, although it lends a touch of realism to the story. Lowry's fans will read this despite its flaws, but it's a disappointing effort.

Betsy Hearne

SOURCE: "Families Shaped by Love, Not Convention," in *The Christian Science Monitor,* May 1, 1987, pp. B3-B4.

Family is a fundamental concern of children. The absence of family, no less than its presence, shapes a child's character and decisions. Recently, several veteran writers for children have focused on protagonists struggling to create families where none exist.

The most exciting of these new books is Lois Lowry's novel, **Rabble Starkey**. Lowry has created an intelligent heroine longing for a traditional family. Named Parable (to ward off trouble) by the Bible-loving grandmother who raised her, Rabble was born when her mother, Sweet Hosanna, was 14 years old and abandoned by the child's father. Sweet-Ho has made the best of her life and is caring for two children whose mother, Mrs. Bigelow, is hospitalized for mental illness.

Moving in with the Bigelows suits Rabble just fine. Veronica Bigelow is her best friend, little Gunther Bigelow is her favorite kid, and Mr. Bigelow is both wise and generous. In fact, Rabble begins to feel this is the family she never had, until Mrs. Bigelow's recovery forces her to confront, and accept change as courageously as Sweet-Ho does in leaving the Bigelows, setting up an independent household with Rabble, and starting a college education. Rabble discovers it is love, not convention, that shapes a family, and love can come from many directions and take many forms.

Lowry's main cast is memorably individualized, but so are her secondary characters, including a cranky old neighbor and a local juvenile delinquent who, thanks to Rabble, briefly become a kind of family for each other. The Appalachian dialect is natural and the point of view carefully consistent with the development of a maturing sixth-grade observer. The scenes are realistic but varied in tone, from Mrs. Bigelow's wrenchingly depicted nervous breakdown to the quiet mother-daughter conversations between Sweet-Ho and Rabble.

Ann A. Flowers

SOURCE: A review of *Rabble Starkey,* in *The Horn Book Magazine,* Vol. LXIII, No. 4, July-August, 1987, pp. 463-65.

In Rabble Starkey Lois Lowry has a winner, a surprising and invigorating change from her usual, but always admirable, suburban, middle-class protagonists. Rabble—short for Parable—is the daughter of Ginger Starkey, long since disappeared, and his fourteen-year-old wife, Sweet Ho-sanna, known as Sweet-Ho. In spite of these difficulties, Rabble has turned out exceptionally well. She lives with her mother in West Virginia, where Sweet-Ho works as a housekeeper and babysitter for the Bigelows. Rabble and Sweet-Ho are very happy with the Bigelows. Mr. Bigelow is a fine man, kind and generous; twelve-year-old Veronica is Rabble's best friend; and the baby, Gunther, is a loving, sweet, although exceptionally homely child. But Mrs. Bigelow is a pathetic case, severely depressed after the birth of Gunther, and after a harrowing scene in which she nearly drowns Gunther trying to baptize him in a river, she is sent to a mental hospital. The little household is warm and supportive. Sweet-Ho is a good surrogate mother and particularly adept at caring for Gunther, who suffers from an inordinate number of minor but tiresome medical problems. Rabble and Veronica are always together, attending sixth grade and doing their homework, discussing boys, trick-or-treating, playing with Gunther, and helping out the crabby old lady down the street. But eventually Mrs. Bigelow recovers, and Rabble and Sweet-Ho move on. The action is slight, but the small-town, down-home ambiance feels authentic; the rhythm of the local speech throughout is enjoyable but understandable; the humor is low-key; and the characterization is splendid. Sweet-Ho has developed from a teenage mother into a responsible young woman determined to get an education; Rabble and Veronica's arch-enemy turns into a human being; and the crabby old lady remains crabby to the day of her death. Rabble is an interested and understanding observer of life, truthful but compassionate, hardworking and unresentful of her problems, an agreeable and distinct personality. In fact, we feel that we know all the characters immediately and intimately—a tribute to Lois Lowry's skill as a novelist.

📖 *ANASTASIA'S CHOSEN CAREER* (1987)

Dudley B. Carlson

SOURCE: A review of *Anastasia's Chosen Career,* in *School Library Journal,* Vol. 34, No. 1, September, 1987, p. 180.

Back for her seventh appearance, Anastasia Krupnik is feeling all the gawky awkwardness of her seventh-grade height. A winter vacation assignment to write about "My Chosen Career" prompts her to sign up for a week-long modeling course on the strength of an ad promising increased poise, confidence, and maturity. The modeling school provides her with a new friend, feisty Henry Peabody ("Call me Henrietta and you die"); a new view of nerdy Robert Giannini, who rises to the occasion when a hero is called for; and some fresh insights into her own resourcefulness. Lowry, a skilled observer of adolescence, knows Anastasia to be both generous and realistic. In Henry Peabody Lowry adds another to her list of unforgettable characters, and Henry is responsible for a good part of Anastasia's education during this vacation week. It is she who insists, "You quit planning on a rich husband, Anastasia. You're gonna get rich on your own. You

and me, if we *want* husbands, fine. But we won't *need* them." Lowry gives readers a fine mixture of wit and wisdom, offering funny adolescent dialogue that is true to their interests and language, and the insight of an affectionate and perceptive observer of the human scene. It is a mixture far too scarce in contemporary literature for early adolescents, who respond to the thoughtful, reflective side of Anastasia as well as the flip side.

Denise M. Wilms

SOURCE: A review of *Anastasia's Chosen Career,* in *Booklist,* Vol. 84, No. 1, September 1, 1987, pp. 66-7.

In a funk about her looks ("a tall, skinny, bony, gross-haired, slump-shouldered, nearsighted, big-nosed freak of a person"), 13-year-old Anastasia decides that "charm" school is in order. Getting her parents' permission is a little tricky, though, for they're reluctant to let Anastasia travel alone to downtown Boston, where the school is located. Coupling self-improvement with research for a school assignment tips the balance in Anastasia's favor; she can interview the owner of the nearby Pages bookstore for her "My Chosen Career" report on the way. Barbara Page turns out to be a warm friend whose obvious love of books and reading appeals to Anastasia; the problem is that Pages isn't making money, partly because of the owner's overly casual management. Charm school, meanwhile, is full of surprises. It certainly is *not* the glamorous beehive of modeling activity that Anastasia had imagined, and when she first lays eyes on the place, she is tempted to ask for a refund. But tacky as the school's surroundings are, the couple who run it *do* provide their five students with positive experiences. Anastasia gets a flattering new haircut and watches as two of her ho-hum-looking classmates are transformed into real beauties. Most importantly, she makes a friend in classmate Henrietta and gains respect for the class' only boy, who initially had seemed a perfect nerd. The currents of humor through the story are strong, and Lowry's savvy hand with dialogue makes the story flow briskly. This is light popular reading at its very best.

Lucinda Deatsman

SOURCE: A review of *Anastasia's Chosen Career,* in *Voice of Youth Advocates,* Vol. 11, No. 1, April, 1988, p. 26.

Anastasia Krupnik is back again, this time investigating careers for a school assignment. She decides she wants to be a bookstore owner, and signs up to take a modeling course in order to gain the necessary confidence and poise. Also taking the course are a black girl named Henry and Anastasia's old friend, Robert Giannini. The course is full of funny situations, as are Anastasia's interviews with a real bookstore owner and her family's responses to what she's learning, but some of the humor is more contrived and less spontaneous than some of the previous Anastasia books. Still, it is a well written book sure to be popular with readers of the series, and could be used in conjunction with career education units.

ALL ABOUT SAM (1988)

Trev Jones

SOURCE: A review of *All About Sam,* in *School Library Journal,* Vol. 34, No. 11, August, 1988, p. 96.

Once again Lowry shows that she knows exactly how children think and feel and what they find funny—no small feat here, since she begins her story just as Anastasia's brother emerges into the world, wondering "Who am I." By the end, Sam knows exactly who he is, and so do readers. The humor is supplied through childhood misconceptions and/ or misunderstandings (of course Anastasia's pet goldfish would love to be flushed down the toilet), Sam's frustrations when he knows exactly what he wants to say but all that comes out is "Waaaahhh" or "Phhlllt," his ways of educating his family to his needs and wants, and the logical explanations behind his actions. Many events of childhood are incorporated, including fear of nursery school, refusal to be toilet trained, the tremendous guilt after stealing something, and the relief after confessing. Sam and his loving family are sure to be a hit with anyone who has a younger sibling or has ever wanted one. The book also has sure-fire appeal to Anastasia's many fans, but it's too funny not to be shared with a class as a read-aloud.

Roger Sutton

SOURCE: A review of *All About Sam,* in *Bulletin of the Center for Children's Books,* Vol. 42, No. 2, October, 1988, pp. 46-7.

Given what we've seen of Sam in Lowry's "Anastasia Krupnik" books, it should come as no surprise that Sam, from birth, has given new meaning to the word *precocious.* When the Krupniks first bring him home to his pantry-nursery, Sam thinks "*Pan-tree.* Rock-a-bye baby in the pan tree. Okay. Whatever it means I'm all for it, because she said 'sleep.' And I am very, very sleepy." Roughly paralleling the time span from *Anastasia Krupnik* to Sam first learning to "flash" (see *Anastasia Again!*), this is a good mix of fabled moments from the other books (Sam, at four months, saying "thank you" to strained apricots) and new material, such as Sam bringing Myron's pipe to nursery school show-and-tell. (One might not have thought it possible to score some wicked points off nursery school mores, but Lowry does, right here.) The conceit grows thin every once in a while, and there isn't much of a plot, but Anastasia's fans will find here a welcome and enlightening subtext.

Denise M. Wilms

SOURCE: A review of *All About Sam,* in *Booklist,* Vol. 85, No. 3, October 1, 1988, pp. 322-23.

Anastasia's brother Sam is center stage here, and fans of the precocious Anastasia will recognize some of the incidents that appear, this time from Sam's point of view. Beginning with Sam's birth and carrying through to when he is approximately two-and-a-half, the story evolves in an episodic manner with the two-year-old's naiveté thoroughly mined for humor: almost all of Sam's mischief stems from his literal interpretation of conversations and meanings. For example, after his mother explains where water goes after it comes out of the faucet, Sam flushes Anastasia's goldfish Frank down the toilet, because doing so, Sam thinks, will connect Frank to one big watery adventure. Sam's other pranks include shoplifting a package of gum, cutting his hair (with disastrous results), and bringing his father's pipe and lighter for show-and-tell at nursery school. Though Lowry is adept at creating solid scenes, the humor here is sometimes too predictable. Genuine laughs surface to delight old fans and capture new ones, but this novel lacks the easy spontaneity and overall punch of the Anastasia books.

Cathryn A. Camper

SOURCE: A review of *All About Sam,* in *The Five Owls,* Vol. III, No. 4, April, 1989, pp. 59-60.

This book chronicles the major events in the Krupnik family—the arrival of a new baby and their move to a new house—through the eyes of someone other than the omnipresent Anastasia. This is her little brother Sam's story, from the minute he first saw his family as a baby up through his experiences in nursery school.

In the same way that the Ramona books parallel the other Beverly Cleary books, this book complements its predecessors; though it's written for a slightly younger audience, it will certainly hold the attention of older Anastasia fans. Lowry's sense of humor twinkles here bright as ever, and readers of all ages will be giggling sympathetically with Sam as he tries to puzzle out the adult mysteries of "the Terrible Twos" and the "Pled Jelly-juntz to the flag." The section in which Sam flushes Anastasia's goldfish down the toilet (so he can see it rain fish) is a classic both in understanding children's logic and in writing for children.

Since each chapter here works as a story on its own, this is a perfect read-aloud choice, one that will elicit laughter from everyone from kindergartners to grandparents.

NUMBER THE STARS (1989)

[The following is an excerpt from Lowry's 1990 Newbery Medal acceptance speech for Number the Stars.*]*

Lois Lowry

SOURCE: "Newbery Medal Acceptance," in *The Horn*

Book Magazine, Vol. LXVI, No. 4, July-August, 1990, pp. 412-21.

During the same years that I was a child growing up in a small Pennsylvania town—the years of World War II—Annelise was a child growing up in Copenhagen. I didn't know her then, of course. My entire knowledge of cultural geography in those years came from the books by Lucy Fitch Perkins. I probably thought that all children in foreign countries were twins. I read about the Belgian Twins, and the Scottish Twins, and the Dutch Twins, and if there were Danish Twins in that series—I no longer remember—then I read about the Danish Twins as well.

Certainly as I became older, I read about the roles of various nations during that war, and I read about the Danish people and how they saved their Jewish population.

But when Annelise and I became friends, some twenty years ago, when she was living in the United States, it never occurred to me to ask her about what I thought of in some vague way as "history." I asked her, instead, as I ask all my friends (and an occasional startled stranger on an airplane), about her childhood. And Annelise—a good storyteller, like all Danes—told me a lot of details of her growing-up years, so I began to know about her family, their home in Copenhagen, her school days, the clothes she wore, the games she played with friends. I feel, still, as if I know her mother's little garden as well as I do my own.

Our talk wasn't always light-hearted talk of gardens and games, but it was always personal memories. We had each, when we were young, lost a greatly loved older sister. We talked a lot about that, Annelise and I; and about the effect on an entire family when the oldest child dies too soon, too young.

Two years ago, in the spring of 1988, Annelise and I took a vacation together. Always, before, our times together had been interrupted by jobs or friends or children. But now we stayed, just the two of us, for a week in a little guest house in Bermuda, and it was the first time we had, for an extended, uninterrupted period, talked and talked and talked.

This time, for the first time, talking of the past, I became truly aware of the way her childhood was colored by war. Not just colored by the concept of war in a broad and abstract sense, the way my own childhood had been; but war through the perceptions of a child in a conquered country: humorous perceptions, sometimes; frightened ones, occasionally; uncomprehending, often.

For the first time—why did it take me so long?—I really understood that historic events and day-to-day life are not separate things.

We all know that the events that happened under the regime of the Third Reich were the most huge and horrible events in the history of mankind.

But when I asked Annelise to describe her childhood then, she didn't describe anything huge and horrible. She said things like: "I remember being cold."

And: "I remember wearing mittens to bed."

Those were exactly the kinds of things—the small, almost inconsequential details of a child's life, from day to day, that I realized, quite suddenly, would tell a larger story.

I would be a terrible newspaper reporter because I can't write well about huge events. They use the verb *cover* in newsrooms. They send reporters out to "cover" things. But if they sent me out to "cover" some catastrophe, I would stand there watching while flood water carried away houses, and flames spurted into the sky, and buildings toppled, and victims were extricated by the hundreds. I would watch it all, and I would *see* it all. But I would write about a broken lunch box lying shattered in a puddle.

As a writer, I find that I can only cover the small and the ordinary—the mittens on a shivering child—and hope that they evoke the larger events. The huge and horrible are beyond my powers. . . .

My friend Annelise gave me the glimpses I needed of that child. She told me what a little girl would have worn to school, and how she would have carried her schoolbooks in a stiff leather knapsack.

I put those things into the book.

She told me what the family dog, in a Danish family, would have been named. I put the dog in, and gave him that name.

And she corrected me when I had written apple pie into the manuscript. "Haven't you ever heard the phrase, 'as *American* as apple pie'?" she asked me. And so the apple pie—which the Danes would never have heard of—turned into applesauce (a much less satisfying dessert, in my opinion, but a more realistic one) in the final revision.

She introduced me to a woman in Copenhagen named Kirsten Krogh, an older woman who was a young bride at the time of the German occupation. It was Kirsten Krogh—who with her husband had been involved in the Resistance movement—who told me what novel a young mother would have read, and loved, during those years. It surprised me. *Gone with the Wind?* An American novel about a feisty Southerner named Scarlett who pushed and shoved her way around Atlanta as it burned?

But I shouldn't have been surprised, because it connected with something else that Kirsten Krogh told me. When I asked her what was the worst single thing she remembered from those years, she thought about her answer for a long time. Then she said: "the powerlessness."

Of *course* they loved Scarlett O'Hara. I put *Gone with the Wind* in the book, too.

And it was Kirsten Krogh who told me what flowers would be in bloom along the Danish coast in autumn, and, in telling me, reminded me that flowers continue to bloom in terrible times, and that children still play with kittens.

I put in the flowers, and a kitten.

In Denmark I collected countless details to add to those that Annelise and Kirsten told me of their own lives during the war years. In Copenhagen I saw a pair of shoes made from fish skin. It was true, of course, that during the occupation the Danes couldn't import anything, so there was no leather for shoes. And surely it was a marvel of ingenuity that they figured out how to make shoes from the skin of fish.

But when I saw the shoes, I didn't think about the economic consequences of war. I couldn't even marvel at the craftsmanship or the cleverness, because I was living, by then, completely in the consciousness of a little girl: a little girl who wouldn't know—or care—about imports or economics. All I could think was what that child would think, on being given such a pair of shoes: Oh, they're so *ugly*.

And I put the ugly shoes, and the child's reaction, into the book.

When I asked Annelise to describe, through the eyes of her own childhood, the German soldiers themselves, she said: "I remember the high shiny boots."

As all writers do, I had to sift and sort through the details and select what to use. There were some that I had to discard, though I didn't want to. The image of wearing mittens to bed was one of those that eventually I had to let go of. The events about which I wrote took place entirely in October—it simply wasn't mitten weather yet. But I would ask you all tonight, sitting here as we are in great comfort and luxury, to remember that in the winter of 1943 a little girl wore mittens to bed because she was cold.

I certainly did use—and use and use—those high shiny boots. Annelise had mentioned them first; and then, when I pored over the old photographs, I saw them myself, again and again.

When I had delivered the completed manuscript to my editor, he called it to my attention. Walter Lorraine has been my editor—and friend—for seventeen books. I listen to what he says with great respect, and though we occasionally argue, he is almost always right.

This time he said that there were too many references in the book to the shiny boots. And I listened. I listened with respect. But I looked at the photographs again, and I tried to place myself within the visual awareness of a child. Sometimes we forget that their vantage point is lower than ours. They don't look into adult faces. Certainly a frightened child would not look into the faces of enemy soldiers. As Annelise did, the child would see—and notice, more than an adult—those terrifying boots. I asked Walter to give me a little time to make that decision, and he agreed.

That fall, the fall of 1988, when this book had been written and was still in the late stages of editing, I was sent by my British publisher on a tour of Australia and New Zealand. I had just seen the first preliminary design for the cover of *Number the Stars,* the first time I had seen the art director's—Sue Sherman's—plan to use that beautiful gold necklace, with the Star of David, embossed against the haunting face of the young girl.

When I was in Brisbane, Australia, I met a woman, slightly younger than I, who was wearing an identical necklace. It is not an unusual necklace—indeed, its simplicity is what makes it so beautiful. But when I saw it around her neck, I described the book, and its cover, to the woman. And she told me her story. I think she would not mind my retelling it, to you.

She had been born in Holland, to a Jewish mother and a Christian father. That mixed parentage made her a potential victim, of course, of the Nazis. So her parents had created a hiding place under the floorboards of their Amsterdam apartment—a place to hide a tiny child, if the moment should come when it was needed.

As we know, those terrible moments did come; they came all too often. When the Nazis banged on the door of that Amsterdam apartment, as they did on the door of the Copenhagen apartment in my book, this little girl, no more than a toddler, was quickly lifted into the hiding place. She huddled there and watched through a crack in the boards while they took her mother away.

She told me that she wears the necklace in memory of the mother she never saw again.

I asked her, as we sat there talking, if she remembered any of it.

She said that the memory was very vague, because she had been so very young. There was only one thing, she told me, that she recalled clearly from that day when she had peeked out through a crack in the floor.

She said: "I remember the high shiny boots."

So when I went back to the United States, back to Walter, I asked him to leave the boots there in the book—every reference—again and again and again. I decided that if any reviewer should call attention to the overuse of that image—none ever has—I would simply tell them that those high shiny boots had trampled on several million childhoods and I was sorry I hadn't had several million more pages on which to mention that.

Louise L. Sherman

SOURCE: A review of *Number the Stars,* in *School Library Journal,* Vol. 35, No. 7, March, 1989, p. 177.

A moving and satisfying story of heroism in war time which is totally accessible to young readers. Annemarie's life in occupied Copenhagen in 1943 seemingly is not much changed by the war—until the Nazi persecution of Danish Jews begins. Annemarie's family becomes involved in the Resistance effort, helping a Jewish friend by having her pose as Annemarie's dead sister Lise. When an important packet must be taken to the captain of one of the ships smuggling Jews to neutral Sweden, Annemarie finds the courage needed to deliver it despite grave danger to herself. Later her Uncle Henrik tells her that *brave* means "not thinking about the dangers. Just thinking about what you must do." Lowry's story is not just of Annemarie; it is also of Denmark and the Danish people, whose Resistance was so effective in saving their Jews. Annemarie is not just a symbol, however. She is a very real child who is equally involved in playing with a new kitten and running races at school as in the dangers of the occupation. *Number the Stars* brings the war to a child's level of understanding, suggesting but not detailing its horrors. It is well plotted, and period and place are convincingly recreated. An afterword answers the questions that readers will have and reiterates the inspirational idealism of the young people whose courage helped win the war.

Denise Wilms

SOURCE: A review of *Number the Stars,* in *Booklist,* Vol. 85, No. 13, March 1, 1989, p. 1194.

Denmark is occupied by Germany, and when best friends Annemarie Johansen and Ellen Rosen are confronted by a pair of patrolling soldiers, they find the experience unnerving. More frightening, however, is news that Jews are being rounded up. The Rosens flee, quickly and silently, leaving Ellen in the care of the Johansen family, who shield her when the Nazis raid the Johansen apartment in the middle of the night. Afterward, Annemarie's mother moves the children to her childhood home, where Sweden can be seen in the distance and where Annemarie's uncle carries on his fishing business. The rural seaside is far from tranquil, however, for German soldiers patrol here as well. Unbeknownst to Annemarie, Uncle Henrik is involved in smuggling Jews out of Denmark; arrangements have been made for Ellen to be reunited with her parents and for the Rosens to be transported to Sweden. Lowry tells her story well, fashioning a tense climax and following the narrative with a lengthy author's note that fills readers in on the sometimes-surprising truths behind the story's fictional events. While the novel has an absorbing plot, its real strength lies in its evocation of deep friendship between two girls and of a caring family who make a profoundly moral choice to protect others during wartime. Permeated with clear elements of popular appeal as well as rich substance, this novel will also be an ideal support for classroom units on World War II.

Edith Milton

SOURCE: "Escape from Copenhagen," in *The New York Times Book Review,* May 21, 1989, p. 32.

Number the Stars, by the American popular-fiction writer Lois Lowry, author of the "Anastasia Krupnik" series, tells it from the point of view of a 10-year-old Christian, Annemarie Johansen, whose best friend, Ellen Rosen, is Jewish. At the news of the Germans' planned onslaught, the Johansens take Ellen in and pretend she is Annemarie's sister. They go on "holiday" to Uncle Henrik, who has a fishing boat and will bring the Rosens, and many other Jews, to safety. Some of the details in *Number the Stars* are very telling: the Germans' brutal search for hidden Jews, the ruse of a "funeral" to explain why so many people have gathered at Uncle Henrik's house, the handkerchief treated with rabbit's blood and cocaine to put the guard dogs off their scent, the mutual pride between good King Christian and his people during this worst of times.

What the book fails to offer is any sense of the horror that is the alternative if the Johansens' efforts to save Ellen and her family fail. Aimed at children aged 8 to 12, the story has a sort of homey quality to it that necessarily fights with the historical facts until the very end. The German occupation seems little more than an invasion of bad-tempered bores with no respect for the country they are occupying. Annemarie is, after all, a Danish Christian citizen in good standing, and her innocent viewpoint keeps us at too great a distance to see clearly either the scale of the evil or the magnitude of the courage from which this story springs.

Mary M. Burns

SOURCE: A review of *Number the Stars,* in *The Horn Book Magazine,* Vol. LXV, No. 3, May-June, 1989, p. 371.

The setting is Copenhagen in 1943; Denmark, now under the domination of Hitler's Third Reich, is faced with the "relocation" of its Jewish citizenry. The Danes rally around their neighbors, eventually smuggling nearly the entire Jewish population of Denmark to Sweden—and safety. The heroism of these ordinary folk is commemorated in a noteworthy novel, scaled to the comprehension of elementary school readers without sacrificing elements of style. Lois Lowry belongs to the select group that has mastered the art of writing for this audience, perhaps because she has never quite forgotten what it is like to be teetering on the brink of adolescence. In this re-creation of times past, the protagonist is ten-year-old Annemarie Johansen, who, with her best friend, Ellen Rosen, remembers life before the war when there were no food shortages or Nazi soldiers standing on every corner and her older sister was still alive. In contrast, Annemarie's five-year-old sister serves as an effective foil, heightening tension with the unpredictability typical of her age. Then the Rosens learn of their imminent danger from the Nazis, and the Johansen family, through resistance contacts, hastily conspire to help them escape. The elder Rosens are spirited away while Ellen joins the Johansens as their daughter, something which the Nazis are reluctantly forced to accept. Annemarie is not only entrusted with details of the operation but must also exhibit remarkable courage in demonstrating friendship and concern for her neighbors' welfare. The appended author's note details the historical incidents upon which Lowry bases her plot. By employing the limited omniscient third-person perspective, she draws the reader into the intensity of the situation as a child of Annemarie's age might perceive it. The message is so closely woven into the carefully honed narrative that the whole work is seamless, compelling, and memorable—impossible to put down; difficult to forget.

📖 *YOUR MOVE, J. P.!* (1990)

Ruth Ann Smith

SOURCE: A review of *Your Move, J. P.!,* in *Bulletin of the Center for Children's Books,* Vol. 43, No. 7, March, 1990, p. 169.

"James Priestley Tate, age twelve, had an overwhelming urge for the first time in his life, to use deodorant" in this third book about J. P. and his sister Caroline. J. P.'s sudden fascination with personal hygiene is sparked by his crush on Angela Galsworthy, newly arrived at his private school from London, England. Suddenly, J. P. finds chess (his former passion) a bore, starts walking into walls, tripping over his own feet, and confiding in a total stranger. It *must* be love! Anxious to sustain Angela's interest, J. P. tells her that he is suffering from triple framosis, a rare but fatal disease. Angela believes him and J. P. is stuck with his lie. Lowry's brand of comic realism combines a keen sense of the absurd with a sympathetic understanding of early adolescent angst. This fast-paced plot contains only one implausible element: J. P.'s conversation with a stranger in the park who acts as his conscience and sounding board. J. P.'s ardency makes him seem a cousin to Byars' Bingo Brown. Like Byars, Lowry articulates her hapless hero's thoughts in words more witty than he could imagine (or appreciate); at the same time she keeps the narrative and dialogue spontaneous, natural, and humorous.

Ilene Cooper

SOURCE: A review of *Your Move, J. P.!,* in *Booklist,* Vol. 86, No. 13, March 1, 1990, p. 1345.

Move over Bingo Brown. Here's a kid that's just as funny, even more real, and totally enmeshed in adolescent angst. Readers will remember J. P. Tate as the older brother in ***The One Hundredth Thing About Caroline***. Now he steps center stage, only to trip over his own emotions— J. P. is hopelessly, desperately in love. The object of the seventh grader's affections is Angela Galsworthy, who has transferred to the Burke-Thaxter school from London. Suddenly, J. P. finds himself using similies: "her teeth were straight and white, and they looked like . . . pearls. . . . Her skin! . . . her skin was like porcelain." J. P. also finds himself using deodorant, even if the only kind his mother owns is something called Sunny Meadow. Though "Love" is almost the story's leading character, that doesn't

preclude a wonderful supporting cast including a homeless hypochondriac, who knows that character flaws are more easily dealt with than halitosis, and J. P.'s chess-playing gal pal, who's ready to be more. Like an episode of television's "Wonder Years," which this resembles in both voice and plot, Lowry's story is awash in real emotion yet able to make fun of itself at the same time. As J. P. might say, here's a book that makes you laugh a lot and cry a little . . . like life.

Ethel R. Twitchell

SOURCE: A review of *Your Move, J. P.!,* in *The Horn Book Magazine,* Vol. LXVI, No. 2, March-April, 1990, pp. 201-02.

Love for Angela Patricia Galsworthy reduces J. P. Tate to jelly—and worse. The beautiful newcomer from England has only to sit next to him in his seventh-grade math class to cause J. P.—never one to notice girls, much less their hair or voices—to think in terms of teeth like pearls and skin like porcelain. But even worse is the progression of small fibs leading to the larger lies he tells in order to win her attention and sympathy. Like many liars, J. P. becomes hopelessly enmeshed in his own web of deceit. His pretense of being subject to a rare, nonexistent illness leads to a wonderfully ridiculous situation when Angela, in turn, tells him that her father might be just the one doctor who could cure him. All this nonsensical brew is spiced up further with J. P.'s encounters in the park with an old derelict with whom he exchanges, in alphabetical order, a list of physical ailments and with his hilariously impractical idea of outfitting himself and Angela as golf bags for the school's Spring Fling. The author makes the most of the humor in J. P.'s antics but maintains a rueful sympathy throughout for his plight and for his eventual admission of truth. A sequel to ***The One Hundredth Thing About Caroline*** and ***Switcharound,*** the book presents a good case for the dangers of mixing lies and love and is just as lively and entertaining as the earlier two.

📖 *ANASTASIA AT THIS ADDRESS* (1991)

Zena Sutherland

SOURCE: A review of *Anastasia at This Address,* in *Bulletin of the Center for Children's Books,* Vol. 44, No. 7, March, 1991, p. 169.

Anastasia Krupnik is now thirteen and is intrigued by a magazine entry: "SWM, 28, boyish charm, inherited wealth, looking for tall young woman, nonsmoker, to share Caribbean vacations, reruns of *Casablanca,* and romance." Deciding that she is certainly tall and young, as well as a nonsmoker, Anastasia begins a fervid if deceptive correspondence, sending an old snapshot of her mother when SWM asks for a photograph. Most of the book has to do with Anastasia's ingenuous interpretations of her pen-pal's remarks, some of these seeming naïve even for a thirteen-year-old. The book has the component of humorous skirmishes with a younger brother and lively conversations with parents that fans have enjoyed in earlier books about Anastasia. To some extent, therefore, the appeal of this story will be in the comfort of a format that's expectable; as is usual in the series, Lowry provides a twist-of-plot that should amuse most readers.

Kirkus Reviews

SOURCE: A review of *Anastasia at This Address,* in *Kirkus Reviews,* Vol. LIX, No. 6, March 15, 1991, p. 396.

More on-target predicaments and laugh-aloud funny dialogue from Lowry, who now takes her articulate protagonist through some seminal exchanges with the opposite sex. Anastasia has a pen pal, Septimus Smith, a 28-year-old SWM she's contacted through a personals column; meanwhile, she and her three best friends have sworn off boys (seventh-graders have little to offer, even to the girls' lively imagination)—until the four are drafted as "junior bridesmaids" to one friend's sister and wangle invitations for the boys, too. At the same time, the pen-pal correspondence flourishes; Septimus is convinced that (despite the candid 13-year-old voice of Anastasia's letters) she is the 22-year-old pictured in the snapshot of her mother that Anastasia has sent him, and that she has a sloop (Anastasia never lies: the sloop is brother Sam's bath toy).

This is Anastasia in her farcical mode: credibility is stretched when Septimus turns out to be the bride's Uncle Tim, but that's part of the fun. No great insights here, but all the splendidly realized characters continue to grow. Fine entertainment; a must for fans.

Stephanie Zvirin

SOURCE: A review of *Anastasia at This Address,* in *Booklist,* Vol. 87, No. 15, April 1, 1991, p. 1564.

When Anastasia Krupnik skims through the *New York Review of Books,* it isn't because she likes to read. She's intrigued by the "personals." In fact, she's so intrigued that she answers one, spinning all kinds of fantasies about Septimus Smith, the person ("28, boyish charm, inherited wealth . . . ") who wants "a tall young woman . . . to share Caribbean vacations, reruns of *Casablanca,* and romance." Of course she fudges a bit in describing herself, forgetting to mention that she's only in seventh grade and sending her mother's picture instead of her own. But who would expect Septimus Smith to want to come for a visit, and who would expect him to turn out to be the uncle of one of her very best friends? Anastasia is thoroughly delightful here as a pen-wielding, romance-crazy teen, caught up in plans for a friend's sister's wedding; her family, as usual, is warm and winning; and the story's humor, whether it comes from Anastasia's own mischief or straight from the mouth of her independent-minded three-year-old brother, will leave readers chuckling out loud. A delightful, funny book.

ATTABOY, SAM! (1992)

Publishers Weekly

SOURCE: A review of *Attaboy, Sam!,* in *Publishers Weekly,* Vol. 239, No. 6, January 27, 1992, p. 97.

In this high-spirited and generally funny novel, Anastasia Krupnik's younger brother displays her enterprising spirit—and her propensity for disaster. For his mother's birthday, Sam determines to concoct a special perfume by combining her favorite smells: his father's pipe, chicken soup and freshly washed hair, to name a few. The resulting hideous brew is uncorked in a waggish scene that resists the obvious moral ("It's the thought that counts") and concentrates instead on the value of enjoying a good chuckle at oneself. Sam's generosity and naïveté, along with his relationship with Anastasia, add palpable warmth. The book's humor, however, is not consistently focused. On the whole, it seems geared to readers at the lower end of the age range, those young enough to identify with a preschooler's mistakes. But other elements—in particular, a subplot concerning an awkward poem Anastasia is writing—are better suited to older readers.

Kirkus Reviews

SOURCE: A review of *Attaboy, Sam!,* in *Kirkus Reviews,* Vol. LX, No. 5, March 1, 1992, p. 326.

Anastasia's little brother, whose infant point of view was explored in ***All About Sam,*** is now a preschooler whose wit and persistence mark him as precocious, but who is still winningly typical in such details as the messy results of mixing mustard and ketchup on his hotdog. Mom's birthday is coming up; she's outspokenly devastated by being 38 and wants only homemade presents. No problem: hearing that her favorite perfume is no longer available, Sam manufactures a substitute in a not-quite-empty grape-juice bottle from the recycling bin. Ever-alert to what Mom says smells good, he keeps Ziplock bags at the ready and manages to add to his brew a bit of sea water, one of Dad's old pipes, chicken soup, tissues that have been used for cleaning up a baby (both ends), and some yeast—his concern over the increasingly noxious odor competing with his truly childlike hope that somehow it will all come right. It doesn't—but the concoction's explosion is only the most spectacular of three resounding failures: Dad has clumsily touched up a portrait photo, and Anastasia has written a notably tactless poem (Sam's offhand help with this proves that he's inherited a lot more of poet Dad's talent than his sister; unfortunately, she tinkers with her effort after Sam's last suggestions). Still, in the end, Sam saves the day, in a tidy but thoroughly satisfying conclusion. Warm, lively, true to children's real inner lives, and laugh-aloud funny all the way.

Roger Sutton

SOURCE: A review of *Attaboy, Sam!,* in *Bulletin of the*

Center for Children's Books, Vol. 45, No. 8, April, 1992, pp. 213-14.

Sam and Anastasia Krupnik are a team that has displayed an astonishing degree of talents and precocity; unfortunately, this latest installment in their saga shows both at a far more generalized level. Sam Krupnik, who knew Morse code at two, here gets kudos for tapping out S*A*M on the typewriter. His big sister Anastasia, who gave her teacher poetry when she only wanted verse, is churning out doggerel. In honor of her mother's birthday, she writes: "I'm glad that you are 38. / I'm glad you're Katherine, not just Kate. / I'm glad our father is your mate. / Your size and shape are really great." Okay, it's supposed to be bad, but why is Anastasia writing bad verse? The attenuated plot follows Sam as he collects his mother's favorite smells to concoct a homemade perfume for her birthday: his father's pipe, some hair, baby poop and spit-up ("I've always loved the smell of new babies," says an unsuspecting Katherine), chicken soup, sea water . . . and yeast. A similar plot, more gracefully handled, can be found in one chapter of Judith Caseley's *Hurricane Harry.* While Lowry's latest has little of the fresh detailing of others in the series and veteran fans may be dismayed to see two well-loved characters played a little lazily, the broad humor will probably find a broad audience.

Marcia Hupp

SOURCE: A review of *Attaboy, Sam!*, in *School Library Journal,* Vol. 38, No. 5, May, 1992, p. 114.

Mrs. Krupnik insists she wants only homemade gifts for her birthday—except for a new bottle of her favorite perfume. When it turns out the fragrance is no longer available, Sam rises to the occasion with a concoction of his own invention. After all, he knows all his mother's favorite smells and has all of a week to collect them. By week's end, Sam's surprise is bubbling and brewing—and fouling the air of his bedroom—and his enthusiasm wanes. Meanwhile, Anastasia and her father are having second thoughts about their own offerings. Can this birthday be saved? Yes, hilariously, as Lowry succeeds where others might fail in taking each carefully contrived scenario one step beyond its predictable outcome. Readers may well anticipate the results of Sam's attempts to collect that "new baby" aroma, but it's the essence of baking bread that proves the salient ingredient of the noxious brew. And readers all know that the boy will somehow manage to keep the gray kitten his father is allergic to, but it's serendipity and not the relenting of adoring parents that allows it to happen. While Lowry snags readers with her teasing style, exaggeration, and gimmickery, she holds them with an unerring sense of humor and a sure sense of her audience. Attagirl, Lois!

📖 *THE GIVER* (1993)

[The following essay is Lowry's acceptance speech for the 1993 Newbery Medal which she delivered at the American Library Association's annual meeting on June 26, 1994, in Miami, Florida.]

Lois Lowry

SOURCE: "Newbery Medal Acceptance," in *The Horn Book Magazine,* Vol. LXX, No. 4, July-August, 1994, pp. 414-22.

"How do you know where to start?" a child asked me once, in a schoolroom where I'd been speaking to her class about the writing of books. I shrugged and smiled and told her that I just start wherever it feels right.

This evening it feels right to start by quoting a passage from *The Giver,* a scene set during the days in which the boy, Jonas, is beginning to look more deeply into the life that has been very superficial, beginning to see that his own past goes back further than he had ever known and has greater implications than he had ever suspected.

> Now he saw the familiar wide river beside the path differently. He saw all of the light and color and history it contained and carried in its slow-moving water; and he knew that there was an Elsewhere from which it came, and an Elsewhere to which it was going.

Every author is asked again and again the question we probably each have come to dread the most: How did you get this idea?

We give glib, quick answers because there are other hands raised, other kids in the audience waiting.

I'd like, tonight, to dispense with my usual flippancy and glibness and try to tell you the origins of this book. It is a little like Jonas looking into the river and realizing that it carries with it everything that has come from an Elsewhere. A spring, perhaps, at the beginning, bubbling up from the earth; then a trickle from a glacier; a mountain stream entering farther along; and each tributary bringing with it the collected bits and pieces from the past, from the distant, from the countless Elsewheres: all of it moving, mingled, in the current.

For me, the tributaries are memories, and I've selected only a few. I'll tell them to you chronologically. I have to go way back. I'm starting forty-six years ago.

In 1948 I am eleven years old. I have gone with my mother, sister, and brother to join my father, who has been in Tokyo for two years and will be there for several more.

We live there, in the center of that huge Japanese city, in a small American enclave with a very American name: Washington Heights. We live in an American-style house, with American neighbors, and our little community has its own movie theater, which shows American movies, and a small church, a tiny library, and an elementary school; and in many ways it is an odd replica of a United States village.

(In later, adult years I was to ask my mother why we had lived there instead of taking advantage of the opportunity to live within the Japanese community and to learn and experience a different way of life. But she seemed surprised by my question. She said that we lived where we did because it was comfortable. It was familiar. It was safe.)

At eleven years old I am not a particularly adventurous child, nor am I a rebellious one. But I have always been *curious*.

I have a bicycle. Again and again—countless times—without my parents' knowledge, I ride my bicycle out the back gate of the fence that surrounds our comfortable, familiar, safe American community. I ride down a hill because I am curious, and I enter, riding down that hill, an unfamiliar, slightly uncomfortable, perhaps even unsafe—though I never feel it to be—area of Tokyo that throbs with life.

It is a district called Shibuya. It is crowded with shops and people and theaters and street vendors and the day-to-day bustle of Japanese life.

I remember, still, after all these years, the smells: fish and fertilizer and charcoal; the sounds: music and shouting and the clatter of wooden shoes and wooden sticks and wooden wheels; and the colors: I remember the babies and toddlers dressed in bright pink and orange and red, most of all; but I remember, too, the dark blue uniforms of the schoolchildren—the strangers who are my own age.

I wander through Shibuya day after day during those years when I am eleven, twelve, and thirteen. I love the feel of it, the vigor and the garish brightness and the noise: all such a contrast to my own life.

But I never talk to anyone. I am not frightened of the people, who are so different from me, but I am shy. I watch the children shouting and playing around a school, and they are children my age, and they watch me in return; but we never speak to one another.

One afternoon I am standing on a street corner when a woman near me reaches out, touches my hair, and says something. I back away, startled, because my knowledge of the language is poor and I misunderstand her words. I think she has said *"kirai-desu,"* meaning that she dislikes me; and I am embarrassed, and confused, wondering what I have done wrong: how I have disgraced myself.

Then, after a moment, I realize my mistake. She has said, actually, *"kirei-desu."* She has called me pretty. And I look for her, in the crowd, at least to smile, perhaps to say thank you if I can overcome my shyness enough to speak. But she is gone.

I remember this moment—this instant of communication gone awry—again and again over the years. Perhaps this is where the river starts.

In 1954 and 1955 I am a college freshman, living in a very small dormitory, actually a converted private home, with a group of perhaps fourteen other girls. We are very much alike. We wear the same sort of clothes: cashmere sweaters and plaid wool skirts, knee socks and loafers. We all smoke Marlboro cigarettes, and we knit—usually argyle socks for our boyfriends—and play bridge. Sometimes we study; and we get good grades because we are all the cream of the crop, the valedictorians and class presidents from our high schools all over the United States.

One of the girls in our dorm is not like the rest of us. She doesn't wear our uniform. She wears blue jeans instead of skirts, and she doesn't curl her hair or knit or play bridge. She doesn't date or go to fraternity parties and dances.

She's a smart girl, a good student, a pleasant enough person, but she is different, somehow alien, and that makes us uncomfortable. We react with a kind of mindless cruelty. We don't tease or torment her, but we do something worse: we ignore her. We pretend that she doesn't exist. In a small house of fourteen young women, we make one invisible.

Somehow, by shutting her out, we make ourselves feel comfortable. Familiar. Safe.

I think of her now and then as the years pass. Those thoughts—fleeting, but profoundly remorseful—enter the current of the river.

In the summer of 1979, I am sent by a magazine I am working for to an island off the coast of Maine to write an article about a painter who lives there alone. I spend a good deal of time with this man, and we talk a lot about color. It is clear to me that although I am a highly visual person—a person who sees and appreciates form and composition and color—this man's capacity for seeing color goes far beyond mine.

I photograph him while I am there, and I keep a copy of his photograph for myself because there is something about his face—his eyes—which haunts me.

Later I hear that he has become blind.

I think about him—his name is Carl Nelson—from time to time. His photograph hangs over my desk. I wonder what it was like for him to lose the colors about which he was so impassioned.

I wish, in a whimsical way, that he could have somehow magically given me the capacity to see the way he did.

A little bubble begins, a little spurt, which will trickle into the river.

In 1989 I go to a small village in Germany to attend the wedding of one of my sons. In an ancient church, he marries his Margret in a ceremony conducted in a language I do not speak and cannot understand.

But one section of the service is in English. A woman stands in the balcony of that old stone church and sings the words from the Bible: *Where you go, I will go. Your people will be my people.*

How small the world has become, I think, looking around the church at the many people who sit there wishing happiness to my son and his new wife, wishing it in their own language as I am wishing it in mine. *We are all each other's people now,* I find myself thinking.

Can you feel that this memory is a stream that is now entering the river?

Another fragment. My father, nearing ninety, is in a nursing home. My brother and I have hung family pictures on the walls of his room. During a visit, he and I are talking about the people in the pictures. One is my sister, my parents' first child, who died young of cancer. My father smiles, looking at her picture. "That's your sister," he says happily. "That's Helen."

Then he comments, a little puzzled, but not at all sad, "I can't remember exactly what happened to her."

We can forget pain, I thought. And it is comfortable to do so.

But I also wonder briefly: is it safe to do that, to forget?

That uncertainty pours itself into the river of thought which will become the book.

1991. I am in an auditorium somewhere. I have spoken at length about my book *Number the Stars,* which has been honored with the 1990 Newbery Medal. A woman raises her hand. When the time for her question comes, she sighs very loudly, and says, "Why do we have to tell this Holocaust thing over and over? Is it really *necessary?*"

I answer her as well as I can, quoting, in fact, my German daughter-in-law, who has said to me, "No one knows better than we Germans that we must tell this again and again."

But I think about her question—and my answer—a great deal.

Wouldn't it, I think, playing devil's advocate to myself, make for a more comfortable world to *forget* the Holocaust? And I remember once again how comfortable, familiar, and safe my parents had sought to make my childhood by shielding me from Elsewhere. But I remember, too, that my response had been to open the gate again and again. My instinct had been a child's attempt to see for myself what lay beyond the wall.

The thinking becomes another tributary into the river of thought that will create *The Giver*.

Here's another memory. I am sitting in a booth with my daughter in a little Beacon Hill pub where she and I often have lunch together. The television is on in the back-ground, behind the bar, as it always is. She and I are talking. Suddenly I gesture to her. I say, "Shhh," because I have heard a fragment of the news and I am startled, anxious, and want to hear the rest.

Someone has walked into a fast-food place with an automatic weapon and randomly killed a number of people. My daughter stops talking and waits while I listen to the rest.

Then I relax. I say to her, in a relieved voice, "It's all right. It was in Oklahoma." (Or perhaps it was Alabama. Or Indiana.)

She stares at me in amazement that I have said such a hideous thing.

How comfortable I made myself feel for a moment, by reducing my own realm of caring to my own familiar neighborhood. How safe I deluded myself into feeling.

I think about that, and it becomes a torrent that enters the flow of a river turbulent by now, and clogged with memories and thoughts and ideas that begin to mesh and intertwine. The river begins to seek a place to spill over.

When Jonas meets The Giver for the first time, and tries to comprehend what lies before him, he says, in confusion, "I thought there was only us. I thought there was only now."

In beginning to write *The Giver,* I created, as I always do, in every book, a world that existed only in my imagination—the world of "only us, only now." I tried to make Jonas's world seem familiar, comfortable, and safe, and I tried to seduce the reader. I seduced myself along the way. It did feel good, that world. I got rid of all the things I fear and dislike: all the violence, prejudice, poverty, and injustice; and I even threw in good manners as a way of life because I liked the idea of it.

One child has pointed out, in a letter, that the people in Jonas's world didn't even have to do dishes.

It was very, very tempting to leave it at that.

But I've never been a writer of fairy tales. And if I've learned anything through that river of memories, it is that we can't live in a walled world, in an "only us, only now" world, where we are all the same and feel safe. We would have to sacrifice too much. The richness of color would disappear. Feelings for other humans would no longer be necessary. Choice would be obsolete.

And besides, I had ridden my bike Elsewhere as a child, and liked it there, but had never been brave enough to tell anyone about it. So it was time.

A letter that I've kept for a very long time is from a child who has read my book *Anastasia Krupnik*. Her letter—she's a little girl named Paula from Louisville, Kentucky—says:

"I really like the book you wrote about Anastasia and her family because it made me laugh every time I read it. I especially liked when it said she didn't want to have a baby brother in the house because she had to clean up after him every time and change his diaper when her mother and father aren't home and she doesn't like to give him a bath and watch him all the time and put him to sleep every night while her mother goes to work . . ."

Here's the fascinating thing: *Nothing that the child describes actually happens in the book.* The child—as we all do—has brought her own life to a book. She has found a place, a place in the pages of a book, that shares her own frustrations and feelings.

And the same thing is happening—as I hoped it would happen—with *The Giver.*

Those of you who hoped that I would stand here tonight and reveal the "true" ending, the "right" interpretation of the ending, will be disappointed. There isn't one. There's a right one for each of us, and it depends on our own beliefs, our own hopes.

Let me tell you a few endings which are the right endings for a few children out of the many who have written to me.

From a sixth grader: "I think that when they were traveling they were traveling in a circle. When they came to 'Elsewhere' it was their old community, but they had accepted the memories and all the feelings that go along with it."

From another: "Jonas was kind of like Jesus because he took the pain for everyone else in the community so they wouldn't have to suffer. And, at the very end of the book, when Jonas and Gabe reached the place that they knew as Elsewhere, you described Elsewhere as if it were Heaven."

And one more: "A lot of people I know would hate that ending, but not me. I loved it. Mainly because I got to make the book happy. I decided they made it. They made it to the past. I decided the past was our world, and the future was their world. It was parallel worlds."

Finally, from one seventh-grade boy: "I was really surprised that they just died at the end. That was a bummer. You could of made them stay alive, I thought."

Very few find it a bummer. Most of the young readers who have written to me have perceived the magic of the circular journey. The truth that we go out and come back, and that what we come back to is changed, and so are we. Perhaps I have been traveling in a circle, too. Things come together and become complete.

Here is what I've come back to:

The daughter who was with me and looked at me in horror

the day I fell victim to thinking we were "only us, only now" (and that what happened in Oklahoma, or Alabama, or Indiana didn't matter) was the first person to read the manuscript of *The Giver*.

The college classmate who was "different" lives, last I heard, very happily in New Jersey with another woman who shares her life. I can only hope that she has forgiven those of us who were young in a more frightened and less enlightened time.

My son, and Margret, his German wife—the one who reminded me how important it is to tell our stories again and again, painful though they often are—now have a little girl who will be the receiver of all of their memories. Their daughter had crossed the Atlantic three times before she was six months old. Presumably my granddaughter will never be fearful of Elsewhere.

Carl Nelson, the man who lost colors but not the memory of them, is the face on the cover of the book. He died in 1989 but left a vibrant legacy of paintings. One hangs now in my home.

And I am especially happy to stand here tonight on this platform with Allen Say because it truly brings my journey full circle. Allen was twelve years old when I was. He lived in Shibuya, that alien Elsewhere that I went to as a child on a bicycle. He was one of the Other, the Different, the dark-eyed children in blue school uniforms, and I was too timid then to do more than stand at the edge of their schoolyard, smile shyly, and wonder what their lives were like.

Now I can say to Allen what I wish I could have said then: *Watashi-no tomodachi desu.* Greetings, my friend.

I have been asked whether the Newbery Medal is, actually, an odd sort of burden in terms of the greater responsibility one feels. Whether one is paralyzed by it, fearful of being able to live up to the standards it represents.

For me the opposite has been true. I think the 1990 Newbery freed me to risk failure.

Other people took that risk with me, of course. One was my editor, Walter Lorraine, who has never to my knowledge been afraid to take a chance. Walter cares more about what a book has to say than he does about whether he can turn it into a stuffed animal or a calendar or a movie.

The Newbery Committee was gutsy, too. There would have been safer books. More comfortable books. More familiar books. They took a trip beyond the realm of sameness, with this one, and I think they should be very proud of that.

And all of you, as well. Let me say something to those of you here who do such dangerous work.

The man that I named The Giver passed along to the boy

knowledge, history, memories, color, pain, laughter, love, and truth. Every time you place a book in the hands of a child, you do the same thing.

It is very risky.

But each time a child opens a book, he pushes open the gate that separates him from Elsewhere. It gives him choices. It gives him freedom.

Those are magnificent, wonderfully *unsafe* things.

I have been greatly honored by you now, two times. It is impossible to express my gratitude for that. Perhaps the only way, really, is to return to Boston, to my office, to my desk, and to go back to work in hopes that whatever I do next will justify the faith in me that this medal represents.

There are other rivers flowing.

Gary D. Schmidt

SOURCE: A review of *The Giver,* in *The Five Owls,* Vol. VIII, No. 1, September-October, 1993, pp. 14-15.

Jonas lives in a world with no poverty, no disease, no pain, no inequality. It is a perfect society where everyone knows his or her place, where there are no hard questions to ask. When Jonas is given his life assignment—the task he will perform for his society for the rest of his life—he is astonished to find he is not to have one of the expected tasks. He is to be the next Giver, the one who holds the collective memory of the society. When he meets the present Giver, he begins to understand why his world is so perfect. There is no great pain or sadness, but neither is there real pleasure and joy. Every family is a perfect model, but there is no love. When he discovers the darkest secrets beneath this world, Jonas must decide if a perfectly safe life is worth the loss of his own humanity.

The novel is written in a simple and straightforward style, as though everything is visible on the surface. The characters too are simple and one-dimensional, for theirs is a society where there are no complexities. However, once Jonas begins to sense the cost of a perfectly secure life where differences are all rigorously discouraged, his character begins to grow in complexity, as does the narrative style of the book. The ending, when Jonas has escaped from his community, is ambiguous enough to allow for a series of different readings. In fact, the reader must do what Jonas must now do for the first time: make a choice.

This is a fantasy novel that does what fantasy at its best can do: make us see reality all the more clearly. The questions it asks about the costs of love, the structure of the family, the role of painful memories, the nature of the perfect society are all timely. But most of all, the novel examines what it is that makes us human. Jonas's world is one built on euphemism and denial, on the quick fix, on the evasion of responsibility. Lowry suggests the costs

of such a mentality, while at the same time writing a suspenseful page-turner that will not be easily forgotten.

M. Jean Greenlaw

SOURCE: A review of *The Giver,* in *The New Advocate,* Vol. 6, No. 4, Fall, 1993, p. 305

If you could design an ideal world, what would it look like? How would you control the behaviors of the people who inhabit that world? Lowry has given us such a world, a Utopia, free from pain and poverty, racism and riots. But, at what price? With meticulous plotting, Lowry leads the reader on an inexorable march from comfort to horror, from Utopia to dystopia, revealing the ramifications of an ideal world through the eyes of one boy. Seemingly innocent statements make the hackles stand up on the nape of one's neck, if one values privacy and individualism. Readers will be forced to confront their beliefs, and the book's contents and implications will echo in the mind for days. Lowry continues to extend her oeuvre, revealing her excellence in many genres. Writers of science fiction have considered this theme before, but none that I have read has handled it in such a compelling and masterful manner. I have deliberately refrained from discussing the plot in detail, as it would spoil the unfolding for the reader.

Patty Campbell

SOURCE: "The Sand in the Oyster," in *The Horn Book Magazine,* Vol. LXIX, No. 6, November-December, 1993, pp. 717-21.

Once in a long while a book comes along that takes hardened young-adult reviewers by surprise, a book so unlike what has gone before, so rich in levels of meaning, so daring in complexity of symbol and metaphor, so challenging in the ambiguity of its conclusion, that we are left with all our neat little everyday categories and judgments hanging useless. Books like Robert Cormier's *I Am the Cheese* or Terry Davis's *Mysterious Ways* are examples of these rare treasures. But after the smoke of our personal enthusiasm has cleared, we are left with uneasy thoughts: Will young adults understand it? Will the intricate subtleties that so delight us as adult critics go right over their heads? Will the questions posed by the ending leave them puzzled and annoyed, rather than thoughtful and intrigued? It all depends—on the maturity of the particular young adult, on how well we introduce the book and follow up with discussion, and on certain qualities in the book itself. In the past year young-adult literature has been blessed with two such extraordinary works: *The Giver* by Lois Lowry and *You Must Kiss a Whale* by David Skinner.

The Giver is particularly surprising because it is a major departure from the style and type of book we have come to expect from Lois Lowry, as *Horn Book* Editor Anita Silvey pointed out in her July/August 1993 editorial. Up until now, much of Lowry's work has consisted of "contemporary novels with engaging characters that explore something very rare—a functional family." But *The Giver* is a dystopia, "driven by plot and philosophy—not by character and dialogue," and the picture of the functional family turns disturbingly awry as the story proceeds. Indeed, it is Lowry's skill at depicting cheerful, ordinary reality that makes the revelation of the sinister difference in this alternate reality so chilling.

Most surprising of all is the leap forward Lowry has made in mastering the creation of a subtext by innuendo, foreshadowing, and resonance. Take, for example, the opening sentence. "It was almost December, and Jonas was beginning to be frightened." The word *December* is loaded with resonance: the darkness of the solstice, endings, Christmas, cold. *Almost* and *beginning* pull forward to the future source of his fear, "that deep, sickening feeling of something terrible about to happen." The name Jonas, too, is evocative—of the biblical Jonah, he who is sent by God to cry against the wickedness of Nineveh, an unwilling lone messenger with a mission that will be received with hostility. In one seemingly simple sentence Lowry sets the mood and direction of her story, foreshadows its outcome, and plants an irresistible narrative pull.

The fascinating gradual revelation of a world and its interlocking rationale as explained by a protagonist immersed in the culture is reminiscent of Margaret Atwood's *Handmaid's Tale*. Lowry plays with our perceptions and our emotions, creating tension by presenting details of this community that win our approval, and then hinting at something terribly wrong. The family, for instance, seems ideal: a gentle, caring father and mother and the one child of each gender that tells us that this community has solved the population problem; the scenes of their warm, bantering conversations around the dinner table; their formal sharing (as required by the Rules) of feelings from their day and dreams from their night; the comfort and support they offer one another. But then we hear of Birthmothers and applications for children and spouses; we begin to wonder why there are no grandparents and to suspect what lies behind the parents' talk of "release."

Lowry has structured the intriguing details of this planned community with meticulous care, focusing particularly, through Jonas's eyes, on the education system that produces a society which functions by internalized values. At first it seems to be an autocratic state—an impression that is given credence by Orwellian images such as the rasping voices that chastise from ubiquitous speakers. But soon it is revealed that the community is ruled by an elected Committee of Elders and that the citizens long ago chose this controlled life. Each peer group of fifty children is called by their ages—Fives, Elevenses—and is distinguished by certain clothes, haircuts, and required behaviors that are appropriate for their stage of development. At eight they begin to spend their afterschool hours volunteering in the various work of the community, and at twelve they are each given an Assignment, based on the careful observation of the Committee of Elders, which will be their job for life.

When the fateful December ceremony comes, Jonas is stunned to learn that he has been appointed the new Receiver of Memory, the highest position in the community. Each day he goes to the rooms of the old Receiver of Memory, a reclusive elderly man whom he comes to call the Giver. There his innocence is gradually transformed as the old man transmits to him, often with great pain for Jonas, the memories of experiences and emotions that the people have chosen to banish from their minds so that they might sustain the illusion of social order and success. Jonas's first memory-lesson is a sled ride that teaches him the concepts of cold and snow and of "downhill"—ideas that are new to him because the community has abolished weather and irregular terrain in the interests of efficiency. As the days wear on, Jonas experiences war and pain and love, and begins to understand how his society has given up choice and freedom for control and predictability.

And then one day he asks to view a videotape of a "release" that his father has that morning performed on an unwanted baby at the community nursery, and learns to his horror that the euphemism covers engineered death—for the old, for rule-breakers, and for surplus or difficult infants. Watching his father sweetly wave bye-bye to the small corpse as it slides down the disposal chute, Jonas realizes with cold shock that his nurturing family is a sham, held together by trained reactions, not love, and that there is only hollowness at the heart of the society's life. He and the Giver hatch a plot to force the community to change. Jonas will flee, so that the memories he has assimilated will return to the people, forcing them to suffer and grow. But that night Jonas's father announces that Gabriel, the difficult toddler who has been temporarily sharing their home and whom Jonas loves, will be "released" the next morning. There is no time to carry out the plot; in the night, Jonas and Gabriel bicycle away.

And now we come to the inherent difficulty of every dystopia story—how to end. Basically, there are three possibilities. The protagonist escapes as the society collapses; the protagonist escapes with the intention of returning with the seeds of change; or the protagonist escapes, but it turns out to be an illusion. Lowry opts for elements of all three. Jonas journeys for days and days and, finally, at the end of his strength, comes to a place where there is snow, and a hill, and a sled. Here the story, which up till now has been readable as an adventure tale, becomes symbolic and ambiguous as Jonas and the dying baby begin the sled ride toward the faint distant Christmas lights which are part of his memory of love. Is it a dream? Are they already dead? Or will they find a new life? Will the community they left behind reshape itself in a more human mold? Lowry refuses to provide a tidy ending. The challenge of the ambiguity is appropriate for the stature of this intricately constructed masterwork.

Jane Inglis

SOURCE: A review of *The Giver,* in *The School Librarian,* Vol. 43, No. 1, February, 1995, pp. 31-2.

This is a strangely disturbing tale set in a future when communities live by rigidly conformist rules, avoiding the major challenges and rewards of life as we know it. One of Lois Lowry's most interesting achievements is to hint at so much without feeling compelled to spell it out. Only one community features in her tale: others lie just beyond the scope of her narrative. People take pills throughout adult life from the first stirrings of puberty: the implications of repressing sexuality are not explored. What hideous catastrophes have driven human beings to refuse the experience of colour in their lives, and what has brought them to abolish pain?

Only the Giver retains the history of humanity in his memory, but he is old and tired. Jonas awaits the ceremony at which he and his age group will be assigned to their future careers. He is puzzled and dismayed when he is sent to the Giver and appointed his successor. Over the weeks that follow Jonas experiences pain. He gradually shares the burden of memory which the old man carries, and comes to understand some of the mystery surrounding the community. In the course of his initiation he has to face the duplicity and cruelty of his parents and comes gradually to reject the values by which his community exists. The ending brings a dramatic bid for freedom and self-determination, without exploring too deeply into unknown territory.

This novel is both stimulating and controlled. Some able readers will be frustrated by the strict limits imposed by the author on her creative imagination, but this very control will make the story accessible to less confident readers. Told in clear, fast-paced prose with realistic dialogue, this would be an admirable early venture into fictional dystopias, with lots of follow-up material available for the reader who craves for more.

📖 *ANASTASIA, ABSOLUTELY* (1995)

Deborah Stevenson

SOURCE: A review of *Anastasia, Absolutely*, in *Bulletin of the Center for Children's Books*, Vol. 49, No. 1, September, 1995, pp. 20-1.

Anastasia is in eighth grade now, and she's finally got the dog for which she's so long wished. In her attempt to be a responsible dog owner, however, she accidentally makes a terrible mistake, slipping the bag of doggie-do into the mailbox and throwing her mother's illustrations into the trash—instead of the other way around. She's wracked with guilt, which she examines through assignments for her Values class and discussions with her father, who is currently serving on a jury. Eventually she confesses, and she finds she's a heroine: a bomber had dropped a bomb in that mailbox and Anastasia's misplaced package had kept the device from exploding. Anastasia's still funny, but this is a shallow sitcom plot without a shred of plausibility to it; unlike her original incarnation, Anastasia here is amusing not because she's believable but because she does such stupid things, which both thins and cheap-

ens the book. The class-assigned values questions and the conversations with Mr. Krupnik are more stimulating, but they don't blend well with the main story or provide it with any weight. Fans will still enjoy the familial warmth and comforting goofiness of the Krupniks, and they won't mind that this isn't one of their more notable outings.

Claudia Cooper

SOURCE: A review of *Anastasia, Absolutely*, in *School Library Journal*, Vol. 41, No. 10, October, 1995, p. 136.

Another Anastasia adventure, this time adding a new dog and a Values class for the modern 13-year-old's coping skills. During an early morning walk with Sleuth, Anastasia inadvertently deposits a bag of dog poop into the corner mailbox instead of her mother's envelope of illustrations intended for her publisher. When she later tries to correct her mistake, she discovers the mailbox has been removed. Anastasia assumes she is to blame and that she has become a federal felon. Finally gathering the courage to call the post office to admit her mistake, she learns that she not only has the information that leads to the arrest of a mail bomber, but also that the poop parcel had actually prevented the explosion of a bomb planted right before her "deposit." This effort falls short of the guffaws found in Lowry's earlier titles. The plot is pretty far-fetched and the dog-doo dilemma packs only so much humor. The Values class assignments tagged to the end of each chapter—scenarios drawn from modern life—are also a letdown. The "wishy-washy" responses from Anastasia and her family reveal neither humor nor depth of thought and are out of character from the Krupniks we have come to know. While children have come to expect more from this very talented author, the book is packed with believable dialogue and references to current groups and situations.

Sandra M. Lee

SOURCE: A review of *Anastasia, Absolutely*, in *Voice of Youth Advocates*, Vol. 18, No. 5, December, 1995, p. 304.

The latest installment in the "Anastasia" series, and another quest for a non-allergenic pet for the Krupnik household also has a bit of mystery and a message about making the right decisions in the face of difficult choices. Anastasia's dilemmas include homework questions for her "Values Class" at school—hypothetical and compromising scenarios, like deciding whether you would kill a pesky animal in a garden that would feed an undernourished family for a year. Anastasia struggles with this speculative soul searching but her most difficult decision is whether to admit to her parents, and the police that she inadvertently dropped her bag of dog poop in the mailbox. It is a stressful confession, because Anastasia is well aware that tampering with U.S. mail is a major felony. A mystery develops with the subplot of a disgruntled man setting explosives in the same neighborhood mailboxes. Anastasia then becomes a suspect of a very serious crime.

The book has a sitcom style plot but the pat ending is a satisfying resolution.

The "Anastasia" series, while not being as pulpish as some series, suffers from the unfortunate inevitability that as series evolve, they become episodic. Perhaps because we are acquainted with the idiosyncrasies of the lovable Anastasia and the Krupnik family, the further chronicles have little character development remaining. Anastasia's self-consciousness nears tiresome but it ties in nicely with the sub-plot of her homework for "Values Class" at school, making the book a cohesive personal look at a favorite thirteen-year-old. The book is definitely a crowd pleaser, an easy booktalk and a must buy because of the overall quality of the series. Just the mention of dog poop will have them lining up for the book. Besides, everyone loves a good mystery.

📖 *SEE YOU AROUND, SAM!* (1996)

Janice M. Del Negro

SOURCE: A review of *See Your Around, Sam!,* in *Bulletin of the Center for Children's Books,* Vol. 50, No. 3, November, 1996, p. 105.

Sam is truly irritated with his mother's "fangphobia" (she won't let him wear the fake fangs he traded his Etch-A-Sketch for) so he decides to run away—to Alaska, where animals with "fangs" lie around in furry piles and eat blubber. Visits with neighborhood friends convince him this is not a good idea, but it's not until big sister Anastasia shows up and offers him an alternative course of action that all ends well. Lowry gives a remarkably credible depiction of Sam's mounting anxiety as no one comes forth to keep him from running off to the frozen North. Of course, all the neighbors are on the phone to Sam's mother before and after each visit, and Anastasia certainly isn't going to let him waltz off into the night—still, there is a certain amount of baby suspense, as Sam tries to figure out how to get out of the situation he put himself in in the first place.

Additional coverage of Lowry's life and career is contained in the following sources published by Gale Research: *Authors and Artists for Young Adults,* Vol. 5; *Contemporary Authors New Revision Series,* Vol. 43; *Dictionary of Literary Biography,* Vol. 52; *Junior DISCovering Authors* (CD-ROM); *Major Authors and Illustrators for Children and Young Adults; Something about the Author,* Vol. 70; and *Something about the Author Autobiography Series,* Vol. 3.

Emily Arnold McCully

1939-

American illustrator and author of children's books and adult fiction.

Major works include *MA nDA LA* (1971, written by Arnold Adoff), *Picnic* (1984), *Mirette on the High Wire* (1992), *Little Kit: Or, the Industrious Flea Circus Girl* (1995), *The Bobbin Girl* (1996).

INTRODUCTION

An award-winning illustrator and author of children's books, McCully has illustrated over one hundred books by other authors and has created several of her own picture books. Her earlier children's books are noted for their minimal use of words and highly expressive watercolor paintings. Her first solo book, *Picnic,* does not contain any words and yet clearly relates the story about a young mouse that gets separated from its family on the way to a picnic. Many of her later books spotlight a similar theme of separation, chiefly, a lone, heroic child in a historic setting, as in her Caldecott-winning title, *Mirette on the High Wire.* In a review of *Mirette,* Jean Van Leeuwen wrote that McCully "has captured, in admirably few words matched with expressive watercolor paintings, the excitement and stubborn determination of the budding artist."

Biographical Information

Born in Galesburg, Illinois, on July 1, 1939, McCully displayed an early talent for drawing. As a young girl she spent time writing and illustrating adventure stories. Her mother, intent on her daughters developing skills that would support them, became McCully's first critic and encouraged McCully to practice and develop her craft. McCully spent her formative years in Long Island, New York, and her proximity to New York City's art scene profoundly influenced her own artistic ambitions. McCully studied theater and art history at Brown University in Rhode Island and received a master's degree in art history from Columbia University in New York. McCully worked as an illustrator for various magazines and other freelance projects. A New York editor saw her drawings for a radio station's advertisement and asked her if she would be interested in illustrating a children's book. McCully illustrated other authors' children's books for almost twenty years, then in 1984, she produced her first solo work, *Picnic.* Since then McCully has written and illustrated numerous titles for children, including her Caldecott Medal winner, *Mirette on the High Wire,* a story of a heroic young girl set in nineteenth-century Paris. McCully has also received critical praise for her adult fiction. Her first novel, *A Craving,* won an American Book Award nomination in 1982. McCully continues to illus-

trate and write for both children and adults as well as pursue her other artistic love, the theater.

Major Works

McCully began her career illustrating other authors' works. Her colorful drawings, portraying the joy of family life, accompanied and added meaning to Arnold Adoff's song-like, monosyllabic text in *MA nDA LA.* She then decided to create books on her own, and her first attempts were wordless stories about a young mouse first introduced in *Picnic.* She incorporated more and more text as she created picture books with such humorous characters as a shy sheep and competitive grandmothers. McCully challenged herself yet again with *Mirette on the High Wire,* the story of a young girl who, through her determination to learn the dangerous skill of walking the high-wire, manages to save the self-respect of her renowned but aging mentor. Not only did she choose a subject that was more serious than what she was accustomed to, she also substituted her usual pen line style for painting. The resulting post-impressionist pictures were lauded for their portrayal of French architecture and culture and for their unique perspectives, including the image of Mirette and the great Bellini on the high wire. Continuing to experiment with more serious subject matter, McCully addressed the topic of child labor in the period piece, *Little Kit, Or: the Industrious Flea Circus Girl,* which tells the story of orphan Kit, who is induced to work for the unscrupulous Professor Malefetta in nineteenth-century London. Another historical fiction story for children that McCully wrote is *The Bobbin Girl,* which examines the lives of female mill workers in nineteenth-century Lowell, Massachusetts, through the eyes of ten-year-old Rebecca Putney. Once again her watercolor paintings capture the historic period and bring it to life for her readers.

Awards

McCully has received numerous state and regional awards. *A Craving* earned an American Book Award nomination in 1982; *Picnic* won the Christopher Award in 1985; and *Mirette on the High Wire* was awarded the Caldecott Medal and the *New York Times* One of Ten Best Illustrated Books in 1993.

AUTHOR'S COMMENTARY

Emily Arnold McCully

SOURCE: "Caldecott Medal Acceptance," in *The Horn Book Magazine,* Vol. LXIX, No. 4, July-August, 1993, pp. 424-29.

[*The following is Emily Arnold's acceptance speech for the Caldecott Medal, which she delivered at the American Library Association meeting in New Orleans, Louisiana, on June 27, 1993.*]

The glow from this splendid honor has illuminated a certain continuity in my life and restored some lost fragments. Out of the misty past, for example, came an exuberant note of congratulation from a librarian who remembered being at camp with me in 1948. "Those counselors had heart failure when you used to hang from the rafters in the old barn," she recalled. I had forgotten entirely, but it fits. In fact, *Mirette on the High Wire* for all it owes to fin-de-siècle Paris, is an intensely personal book. Of this I was not immediately conscious. Rather, I felt emotionally detached from the story—curiously detached. It took a friend to point out that I had rummaged in my own past for both matter and metaphor.

The wonderful reception accorded *Mirette* kept me thinking about the book long after I'd ordinarily have put it aside. There it was, forcing me to dwell not only on all the ways I might have made the pictures better, but also on the parts of myself I'd unwittingly invested. I see now that I was not so much detached as defended. The story and the artistic challenges it presented forced me to step

out on a wire, throw off my cloaks of irony, humor, and sketchiness, and embrace Mirette's desire without reservation. For you to understand how perilous and finally how liberating it was, I will have to provide some history.

Most of my life I've subscribed to a rule that can be found in the Chinese book of wisdom *I Ching:* perseverance furthers. I absorbed it at an early age (although not from the *I Ching* and phrased more often at home as "that's not good enough yet"). At three I learned to read and began to draw. Observing that I drew what I could see, my mother decided to improve the impulse. She stood over me while I worked at accuracy with regard to ears, or the drape of a jacket, guided not by convention, but the actual thing. There never was a period of stick figures and happy suns for me, but instead the discipline of daily practice, the elusive goal, the pain of failure, and the end product. This wasn't a grim ordeal; I did it because I was fascinated and fulfilled. The complicated yet instinctive act seemed to use my whole being and link me with the external world. Drawing sharpens the eye and the hand and also the affections. It isn't possible to draw something without feeling it.

My mother did not draw; her authority lay in the realm of criticism. But that didn't squash my maverick tendencies. I started drawing grotesques, much encouraged by a traveling show of Leonardo's notebooks, and grim, urban scenes inspired by my beloved Ashcan School. "Why can't you draw things people will like?" Mother complained. But I persisted with "expressive" faces and male figures in action. I loved the rugged, the startling, the dynamic. I wrote stories about lone child heroes, then illustrated and bound them. My attachment to text was so great that nearly everything I drew was an illustration.

I have a photograph of my first-grade class posing before a mural that depicts a countryside at Easter time. It covers one whole wall, and I conceived it all by myself. I turned out posters, scenery, illustrated reports, greeting cards, house portraits, and copies of old masters (which I peddled from a stand like lemonade). On Memorial Day, when the town celebrated with a parade and fair, I drew dozens of "two-minute" portraits at twenty-five cents a head.

My father worked in radio, and I had seen from the control room how stories were delivered by actors and sound effects simulated with props and voices. But still, alone in my room with my imagination, I surrendered to illusion, and the broadcasts came vividly to life. I illustrated them, too, and learned the trick of dramatizing through suggestion.

My sister and I were active and resourceful children, and we improvised all sorts of play and playthings. We also dared each other to climb to a higher branch, go all the way to the roof—hand over hand up the cornerstones—leap off on a bet, and in general risk life and limb. Our mother, whose frustrated talents were for music and drama, compounded the pain of a failed marriage with endless domestic labor. My sister and I did a great deal of chopping and scrubbing and digging, and we ate a few kidney stews. Our Sisyphean routine was spiced with memories and phrases in French from Mother's student year abroad. We had the strong feeling that she was last truly happy in Paris, her unrealized promise forsaken there. It gave the place a potent, already bittersweet allure. A *jolie tristesse,* we would have said.

Pretty soon, wanting to please adults as well as to satisfy the impossible standards I was starting to set for myself, I told everyone I was going to be an illustrator when I grew up. My mother was determined that my sister and I be independent and self-supporting. Commercial art was the answer, in my case—certainly not precarious Art. My father had wanted to be a playwright, but earned his living writing radio dramas. I was aware of the ambivalence behind his pride in his achievements. His work, calling for cleverness and style, drew me inexorably, but it depended on the sufferance of the network. For protection, I tried not to take myself too seriously, and I trusted criticism more than praise.

By adolescence, writing and drawing served different purposes. My drawing had been almost a performance, certainly very public. Writing was a solitary search for the comprehending narrative that would later hold up to the light. When I set out to earn a living, my focus was still divided between commercial art assignments and closet fiction writing.

But how lucky I have been! In 1966 or so, Ellen Rudin, then an editor at Harper, noticed a poster I had done for an advertising campaign and asked if I'd like to illustrate a children's book. For a long time afterward, illustrating and writing remained separate. But over the last decade I've hearkened back to the time when I made up my own stories and illustrated them. This offered such safety that I found myself, without any experience to go on, creating large happy families. Emotional truthfulness became more important than representational art. Generous, astute people and luck had steered me into the only medium that unites the two halves of myself, the one who writes and the other who draws.

I've been in the children's book field for nearly thirty years. With the recent sweeping changes and big profits in the publishing industry, many books are taken out of print before they can find an audience. I saw a few of my own dismissed with what seemed like undue haste, and, in the months before I began *Mirette,* gravity was weighing heavily on me. If I were not to succumb to discouragement, I needed to soar above perseverance, somehow to recapture the free spirit, passion for life, defiance, and inexhaustible enthusiasm of a nine-year-old daredevil. The story of *Mirette* became both a metaphor for artistic transformation and an actual artistic leap for me.

First, there were the ingredients from my past: refigured memories of work; persistence; aspiration; Paris; and an elusive and uneasy adult male whose artistry beckoned but posed dangers as well. There was also nostalgia, the volatile ingredient that separates us from children and drives us to tell them stories. After having written about the childhood I never knew, it was time to deal obliquely with the one I had.

Next came collaboration. Every published work is a joint effort. One doesn't step out on a wire without perceptive encouragement. *Mirette* began in an unprecedented way when the brilliant young editor Arthur Levine asked if I had any ideas for picture books that we might work on together. I submitted six or so, and he liked them all, but he was most struck by the one about the little girl and the high-wire walker in Paris. Over lunch we determined that the man would have a failure of nerve and somehow be revived by the girl. Usually I write the text first and then square it with the editor, but Arthur made no such requirement, so I went right to the dummy, doing text and pictures simultaneously. This was followed by color sketches. They were going to have to be very different from my usual loosely drawn pastorals to suggest Paris in the 1890s. I was entering a new realm that had already been thoroughly interpreted by my idols of painting. Rather than look at those paintings for guidance, I kept a book of Atget photographs open on my desk. I was also stirred by my recent emotional return to Paris after twenty years.

Mirette's characterization came about with the help of photographs of Colette as a child. Her little sailor dress and gravity of mien were inspiration enough, but they vibrate with portent. What happened to Colette when she grew up made for an undercurrent of excitement in my own little girl's life. Mirette is by forceful design a heroine like Colette. When I was young and aspiring, it was a disadvantage to be female. Girls still need encouragement to see themselves as actors, not acted upon. Mirette is intrepid in her quest for poise and equality on the wire.

I presented my sketches to Nanette Stevenson, Putnam's superb art director, and she saw at once that since my book was a period piece and the period was post-impressionist, it would benefit from a more painterly approach. "Why don't you try dropping your line?" she suggested.

But I had never made illustrations without line! I had no idea how to proceed without line! And what an irony, to embark on a book about tightrope walkers without my own tightrope. Ahead lay weeks of despair and futile regret that I'd never been trained at art school. But perseverance does further, especially when risk is high. I kept trying to make pictures that were like paintings, asking more of my little watercolor set, certainly more of my brushes, than ever before, adding pastel for the first time—failing, then failing less, and finally getting to a point where I was comfortable enough to go on with the book.

I should say that as an evolving illustrator, I always struggle. My technique never seems quite up to the job of reproducing the images that will carry a story. And even after multiple revisions, I want the picture to seem spontaneous, for nothing to be still. My wastebasket fills with false tries. I'm not drawing from life anymore, and the stuff of my imagination emerges in spasms. But the result is fully felt; whatever I've managed to capture is still wriggling. I hope that authenticates it in a way that a knockout graphic might not. Furthering the narrative with emotional verisimilitude is not the same as painting a masterful picture.

As an author of children's books, I am the adult version of a child who learned about the world in libraries. That often illicit thrill may be forever denied children today, who know everything before they know anything. But children do still pay attention to books, even as the hard-core adult readership dwindles drastically.

The current boom in children's books will be a boomerang if access, diversity, and guidance are not given all young readers. Many gorgeous and expensive books are being produced these days. As we all know, several hundred specialized bookstores have sprung up to sell these beautiful books to parents and grandparents. Many are set up like libraries, for comfortable browsing. They serve the affluent well. Poorer children end up at warehouse-like stores in malls, buying formulaic books. I am always overwhelmed by respect and gratitude for the many teachers and librarians who buy worthy books for their classes with their own money and line up to have them autographed. They are attempting to make readers out of all their children, without bias. The cultural inequity between the affluent and the disadvantaged can sabotage our democracy. The problem is the same one posed by the public schools: as we grow old in this country we can expect to become dependent on succeeding generations who are impoverished intellectually, as well as by the deficit, unless we find a solution. The institution designed to serve everyone equally is, of course, the library. Libraries must be adequately funded and esteemed or our future is compromised.

Thank you, Jane Botham and the Caldecott committee, for commending *Mirette* and for taking my books into your library havens for so many years. Thank you, Elizabeth Diggs, a brilliant critic and champion, who sees my work before anyone else does. I am so grateful to Harriet Wasserman, who hoped I was writing a novel, but has given boundless support to everything else. Thank you, Margaret Frith—my relationship with Putnam could not have been more gratifying, and you were all extremely good to me even before things started to happen. I am ever indebted to Doreen Rappaport for generously sharing Arthur Levine. Arthur, Nanette Stevenson, Colleen Flis, and all the designers, you know what this has meant. It's our book, and it was immensely satisfying to work on it with you.

Mirette on the High Wire changed everything for me. But since perseverance still furthers, I say, "On to the next!"

Emily McCully

SOURCE: In an interview in *The Reading Teacher*, Vol. 47, No. 5, February, 1994, pp. 358-61.

[The Reading Teacher *interviewed Emily Arnold McCully.*]

THE READING TEACHER: *How did the idea for* Mirette on the High Wire, *the book for which you received the Caldecott Medal, emerge?*

McCULLY: Several years ago, I thought about doing a biographical picture book about Blondin, a predecessor of the fictional Bellini, who was a world famous high wire walker in the 1860s. It was the notion of pictures such as those of Bellini's exploits that first interested me.

Then a friend introduced me to an editor, who asked me to submit a few ideas for picture books that we might work on. This was very unusual. I'd never before approached an editor with just an idea. So I sent him a letter with about six. They were maybe one sentence long; I no longer have this document, but I think I said a little girl in Paris who meets a high wire walker. The editor and I met, and at the end of the conversation it was clear that the man would lose his nerve and that the girl would help him somehow.

The story was new to me because it was not a humorous one. I had never approached a story that seemed to be quite sentimental. And for the first time, I worked on text and pictures together. Usually editors want to have a finished manuscript before they're interested in seeing a dummy. In this case I did them simultaneously. So I did the whole thing very differently—in one large gesture—but I was a bit hesitant about it because I couldn't cloak it in my usual humorous approach.

RT: *Can you describe the historical and artistic influences on* Mirette on the High Wire? *Had you lived in Paris?*

McCULLY: I did not try to reproduce actual images of Paris because I'm a rather careless artist. It would not be like me to do a representational work. I did use photographs as a kind of inspiration because I thought paintings would influence my actual style too much. I wanted to invent things. I wanted simply to create an atmosphere.

I do love Paris. When I was a graduate student, I lived in Brussels and spent quite a bit of time in Paris. I was brought up to love Paris. A year before I began *Mirette,* I went back to Paris for the first time in almost 20 years. I don't remember thinking, "I must set a book in Paris," but once I decided to do that, the period came naturally. I think of this time as the sort of heyday of the Paris that we all recognize.

RT: *What about artistic influence? A number of our colleagues have commented on having a feeling of Toulouse-Lautrec. Others have commented on the genuineness of the body movements, stances, and poses.*

McCULLY: The quotations from Lautrec are there to lend color and authenticity to the setting. I simply put in people with the same kinds of hairdos, for example. I didn't go to a lot of trouble with that; I just grabbed a book to get a couple of things I liked, just to give it that feeling.

I did research with a book by Philipe Petit, who is a contemporary high wire walker. Several years ago, he wrote a rather mystical description of his art and his approach to it, and it was illustrated with photographs. So the actual walking on the wire and the point where Bellini sits on the wire are adapted from that book about Philipe Petit, who is currently an artist in residence at St. John the Divine in New York.

RT: *Emily, you've written and illustrated many other picture books.* **Mirette** *is certainly contrasting in style and topic. Was this a conscious turning point?*

McCULLY: Yes. I wanted to do something more ambitious. A lot of the approach to painting I owe to my art director at Putnam. This was the first time that I'd consulted an art director at length or in any detail before beginning to work. She looked at sketches that were done with a pen line. The characters and everything else were the same except I'd used a pen line, as I had always done. She suggested that I not do that, which threw me into something of a panic, because it meant painting instead of drawing and I had no training in either one. But I did have a habit of drawing. So it took a huge amount of practicing and rejecting my terrible efforts until I got to the point where I could actually do the book. In the end, the pictures looked more like post-Impressionist paintings than they would have if I had proceeded as usual.

RT: *Tell us a little bit about the interaction between yourself and the art director.*

McCULLY: First of all, the art director has to be good at what she does and to have a feeling for the book. She has to have respect for the artist. I didn't feel that she was telling me what to do; we had a good relationship and still do. At once, I realized that what she was suggesting-was right, even though it was going to mean much harder work for me. So I was very grateful.

RT: *It sounds like you worked very hard at this transition. I think that might come as a surprise to people who don't understand the process.*

McCULLY: As I prepared **Mirette** and all the books I've done since where I've tried to hold to this new technique, it has become more familiar and a little easier. My main notion is to make it look gestural. I really want the focus to be lively. I want characterization and emotion and action to be what you experience when you look at the book. I don't want it to look as though it were hard work. I think sometimes picture books can be so gorgeous that the surface actually discourages you from entering into the world of the story. I'm after the story and the emotions that you are invited to feel in sympathy with the characters, rather than some artistic look that may be more gorgeous.

RT: *Is there a difference in the depth of performance as an artist when the book characters are yours as opposed to those of another author?*

McCULLY: Depth of performance can mean several dif-

ferent things. My own enjoyment is superior when the characters are mine. I find that the challenge of enlarging or interpreting or bringing a different understanding to somebody else's characters can be great. Sometimes I worry that I'm not going to get it right or please the other people and that can add a dimension that makes it seem a greater effort. Sometimes doing my own seems easier; I think the results are more interesting, because the text and illustrations are completely integrated.

RT: *It removes all the worry of trying to walk in step with another mind.*

McCULLY: Although editors don't really encourage one to walk in step. It's fun in a way. I'm on a schedule where I turn in something that I've written and illustrated myself, say, early in the summer. For the rest of the summer, there's usually something else for me to illustrate. It's kind of relaxing. It's completely different. The thinking is entirely visual, although the way I write and the way I illustrate are very similar. In both I try very hard not to use conventions and not to rely on easy choices. I want to feel that I'm inventing, that I'm hacking a new path. And so that's true for making up pictures for both my stories and other texts, because that's the only real satisfaction.

People have such a misconception about children's books—how easy they are to do and of what they can consist. I've published two adult novels; the process, especially doing a picture book like **Mirette,** is almost exactly the same as writing a novel. It's just much shorter. I have to figure out how to tell the story using two media in 32 pages. But I do not think before I begin, "Well, this is only for children." It has to interest me, or I can't sustain the effort. It has to amuse me. It has to move me enough to be complex and yet then distilled so that it will work in 32 pages.

RT: *Do you find that a particular challenge?*

McCULLY: Oh, sure. Doing something longer is always easier than something shorter.

RT: *That brings to mind another question: How do you know when your piece is finished?*

McCULLY: It's kind of hard to say. It's a matter of making choices and eliminating things. I'm used to it now. I just wrote a first draft of a new book last week; it's a very complex story, but it was easier to think of it in terms of 32 pages than it had been in the past.

I had written children's books for years and years while illustrating other people's texts. All my manuscripts were rejected. The breakthrough was my first wordless book. I just worked out the story with 32 little squares and a little sketch in each square on one sheet of paper. As I looked it over, I realized I didn't need words, so I developed it that way. I still think in those terms, not just about the text but about how many pictures it will take. Because I do the pictures, I know exactly which images will convey the things I don't therefore need to write. It is harder for someone who isn't going to illustrate the story herself to realize that so much doesn't need to be said in words.

RT: *How does the story reflect real life? Was there something special you hoped to achieve with* **Mirette?**

McCULLY: The idea of having a feisty little girl is sort of an obvious and simple notion and one that has appeal just in itself. After I completed the book, I was a little bit worried that people might take it to be sentimental. I really didn't know how it was going to be received. When no one complained about a girl getting up on a high wire and walking toward this old guy, I was really astounded and relieved.

Then friends, in particular those who know me very well, began to point out all the things in my life that were in the book. My father was a rather remote figure in my childhood. He was a gifted writer but didn't realize his highest ambitions. Yet in a way, he and his life beckoned to me and inspired me as I was growing up, warts and all. And in a very sweet way, this is kind of a resolution of my relationship with him. As a child, I frequently helped my mother out. My sister and I did a lot of chores around the house. We both harbored ambitions and practiced our skills all the time, drawing in my case, but lots of others too. So it really came from deep inside me, from a period when it was truly a disadvantage to be a girl. I was keenly aware that girls were not expected to do the things I wanted to do. I believe that this is still often true to varying degrees, that there is still a subtle message to girls not to make the most of themselves and be all they can be. So, anyway, that is the strongest inspiration that I felt.

RT: *So Mirette is you, really.*

McCULLY: Well, I think so.

RT: *What are some elements of story and illustration that you consider when creating for your audience?*

McCULLY: I really do these to entertain myself. I think it would be folly to try to please some unknown reader, to try to "psyche out" the market. That's one of the things that's so amazing and fantastic about the reception that *Mirette* has gotten. I never would have predicted this in a million years. It's really wonderful.

I try to maintain the energy and the look of spontaneity that I think will draw people in and move them along. That's what I want. Ironically, I have to do pictures over and over and over, but I try to do them so that the final result looks as if it hasn't been labored over too much.

Emotional truth is the thing that interests me the most— the characterization and how the people feel. I would do that in adult illustrations as well, but I think it is especially important for children. Story is so important. Picture books these days often look so amazing that they invite wonder. You look at them, but it's a little hard to get past that and get into them and into the story and into the

narrative. But that's something that I like the best, and I'm going to keep trying to tell stories.

RT: *What can we expect from you in the future?*

McCULLY: There's going to be a great variety. I'm trying now to write a new story for the Grandmas series about two wacky Grandmas. The pictures are sort of cartoonish. *The Amazing Felix* will be out at the end of the summer or in early fall. It's set in the 1920s; it's a very elegant-looking book about a boy and a girl named Felix and Fanny, who are the children of a world famous concert pianist. They are sailing on a great oceanliner to England. They end up in an English castle, and a magician and magic tricks are involved.

I just finished doing the paintings for yet another book, called *Crossing the New Bridge,* which will be ready in a year. It's set in middle Europe in the 16th century and it's sort of a comic fable. And there's another, *My Real Family,* which is a continuation of a series about a family of bears that runs a theater. It's about one of the kids in the family who imagines that she's adopted.

RT: *How many pieces do you work on simultaneously?*

McCULLY: I'm working on yet another one now about a little girl in Dickens's London who is a homeless orphan and ends up working for a flea circus operator. All of these have been going at once, but in vastly different stages of development.

RT: *Winning the Caldecott medal is certainly synonymous with prestige in a public sense. How do you measure the success of a work?*

McCULLY: Ordinarily, I measure the success of a work as soon as I have finished the pictures, because I pour the most intense energy and emotion into them. Doing the finished pictures for a book usually takes 4 to 6 weeks of very intense effort. I'm basically an untrained and rather sloppy artist. Trying to finish the pictures and get them just right can be truly agonizing, so when I've finished, that's when I'm most attached to the book. That's when I judge it. Usually I've worked hard enough to give myself some measure of satisfaction.

GENERAL COMMENTARY

Arthur Levine

SOURCE: "Emily Arnold McCully," in *The Horn Book Magazine,* Vol. LXIX, No. 4, July-August, 1993, pp. 430-32.

The key to understanding the work of Emily McCully is one word: drama. I imagine that those who know Emily may find that a strange assertion, because she herself is not outwardly, obviously "dramatic." In fact when I first met her, I was struck by how normal she seemed: Emily Arnold McCully—the woman who illustrated the first children's book to win a National Book Award! Someone of her stature might well have appeared at my office swathed in scarves, sporting oversize dangly earrings. Perhaps I expected her to have a poodle in one hand and a cigarette holder in another, which she would wave at the tall, silent chauffeur-type who would be carrying her portfolio. Instead she appeared—as she has every time that we've met since—by herself: a petite woman in softly tailored clothes, with a generous smile and a calm, self-possessed manner. True, her voice has a musical quality. And if you look closely, her eyes shine in the manner of a person about to play a joke on you. But I didn't find her intimidating until *after* we'd begun working together. And that is because Emily McCully reserves the lion's share of her "drama" for her work.

Of course, drama can take many forms. And through three decades of illustration, Emily has expressed just about all of them. Take, for instance, a typically understated picture in *That Mean Man,* by Liesel Moak Skorpen, showing the perfectly horrid man of the title and his scowling, needle-nosed wife sourly rocking in a rowboat, as piranhas frolic beneath the waves. The text reads simply, "They honeymooned at sea." But the energy of the picture comes from the delightfully exaggerated characters and the implication of their impending doom.

Even in benign or fantastical situations, such as the ones posed by Sylvia Plath's text for *The Bed Book,* Emily is capable of suggesting layers of story and underlying conflict. Typical, I think, is the picture illustrating the concept of a "Jet-Propelled Bed / for visiting Mars." Certainly, in this picture, you have your requisite night sky over a bucolic rural backyard. But driving the rocketing crib in question is a baby who looks as apprehensive as he is excited. Some nighttime toys tumble from the "rocket," and the baby's brother and sister wave good-bye enthusiastically from the window, clearly as thrilled by the prospect of getting rid of their little sibling as they are with the miraculous bed! What could be truer both to the fantasy text and to the real relationships and emotions of children?

For Emily McCully, drama can also emerge from the absurd. If you doubt this, open up *The Twenty-Elephant Restaurant* by Russell Hoban and turn to the illustration of a line of impatient elephants waiting for a pay phone that is being hogged by a temperamental pachyderm in a chef's hat. Only a New Yorker who has waited for an occupied pay phone could appreciate the truly incendiary potential of such a situation—elephants or no elephants.

From 1966 to 1984 Emily brought this unique sensibility and skill exclusively to the illustration of other writers' texts. As a writer of adult fiction, she was nominated for an American Book Award—for the novel *A Craving*—but had never been the author of a picture book. Ironically, her first such venture eschewed words entirely: the exuberant *Picnic,* winner of the 1985 Christopher Award.

Picnic is an example of pure, unbridled action, deepened by characterization and emotional truthfulness. In the first few pages a family of mice sets out for a picnic, leaving behind their youngest child. What follows is a brilliantly worked out sequence that has the spontaneous feeling of improvisation. Without such a clear sense of plot and drama, I believe Emily could never have made a wordless picture book so perfectly clear to follow—and so much fun.

Four more books chronicled the adventures of the mouse family. Then picture-book readers began to experience the treat of Emily McCully the writer as well as the illustrator. Not surprisingly, these newer efforts occasionally brought her even closer to a "dramatic" base, notably her charming series of books about a theatrical family of bears.

In the latest of these, *Speak Up, Blanche!,* a stagestruck sheep becomes apprenticed to the bear family by a pushy stage-aunt. Blanche (the sheep) fails miserably at all things thespian—she is simply too shy—until she gets a chance to paint the scenery. And here she shines, expressing all the things as an artist that she could not do as an actress.

Emily McCully, it turns out, is more than comfortable with both disciplines. Recently I saw her act in an off-Broadway play. I was impressed with how good she was. But not surprised. She has after all done so many things well: co-authored a musical in college, published wonderful picture books and novels, raised two children, earned a master's degree—not necessarily in that order. But what fills me with admiration is not only that she's done these things but that she continues to push herself to explore, to risk.

There is a scene in *Mirette on the High Wire* in which Mirette, having learned the true identity of her mentor, Bellini, bursts into the room to confront him. It was the first piece of finished art Emily sent in, and I vividly remember opening up the package. I suspect most editors have a moment of held breath at this point in a project—when the early stages have been so thrilling, so promising, that you almost can't let yourself hope that the finished art will live up to that promise.

But when I opened up the piece, there it was: all the characterization and drama that was so typically McCully. The innocent, breathless excitement of the young girl punctuated by the sweep of her dress, the flush of her cheeks; and the counterpoint of Bellini at the moment of his greatest despair at having to disappoint his pupil. All of it in a style that we had never seen Emily McCully produce!

Who could have guessed that she'd illustrate a story about courage and risk with a technique that for her took so much of both? But I've come to expect nothing less from this exceptional artist—this exceptional person—than gutsiness, skill, truthfulness. And drama.

———————

TITLE COMMENTARY

📖 *MA NDA LA* (written by Arnold Adoff, 1971)

Zena Sutherland

SOURCE: A review of *MA nDA LA,* in *Bulletin of the Center for Children's Books,* Vol. 25, No. 3, November, 1971, p. 37.

Pictures that are suffused with sunshine and love echo the triumphant poem of the story, told in rhyming syllables. The jacket explains (the book does not) that MA is mother, DA father, HA laughing, RA cheering, LA is singing, NA sighing, and AH feeling good. A family goes out to sow, to see the seedlings come up, to gather the tall corn, grind it, cook it; and in each picture the ritual is celebrated "MA nDA LA, MA nDA HA, MA nDA LA LA LA . . ." It must be read aloud to get the full effect of a child's blithe crooning, it must be seen for the full effect of the dark figures (silhouette save for the brilliantly patterned clothing) against the colors of the tropical foliage. Not suitable for group use, but right for reading aloud to an individual child.

Gertrude B. Herman

SOURCE: A review of *MA nDA LA,* in *Library Journal,* Vol. 96, No. 20, November 15, 1971, p. 3888.

A praise song to the earth, the African earth which produces corn for the family: planted by "MA" and ("n") "DA," nourished by rain and sun, watched over by all, sighed for ("NA"), laughed at ("HA"), sung about ("LA"), cheered ("RA"), and inspiring happy feelings ("AH"). All this without words as such; rather, the song is sung in the above-mentioned lilting sounds, the meaning conveyed by the sequence of sounds and by the stunning watercolor paintings, themselves a glowing celebration in color and pattern. This is a unique book to be shared intimately with very young children, who will sing and interpret it as an experience never twice the same.

Lisa Hammel

SOURCE: "A Sound Way of Learning," in *The New York Times Book Review,* January 23, 1972, p. 8.

MA nDA LA is a curious experiment with sound—seven monosyllables to be exact. Each of the syllables stands for a word or an idea—MA is mother, DA is father, LA is singing (although in what language, if any, we are never told), and Arnold Adoff has simply arranged and rearranged the monosyllables on each page. It is also never clear what relation Emily McCully's sunny illustrations of family life—apparently set in Africa—bear to the singsong syllables. But maybe it would be fun to shout it all out.

Ethel L. Heins

SOURCE: A review of *MA nDA LA,* in *The Horn Book Magazine,* Vol. XLVIII, No. 1, February, 1972, p. 38.

A beautiful but imperfect picture book which leaves a feeling of imbalance between text and illustrations. Actually the warm, energetic paintings, vibrant with tropical color, are almost self-sufficient in their telling of a black family's way of life—how together they find joy in the continuous process of tilling the earth, caring for the crops, and reaping the harvest. The recurring monosyllables of the text may be sounded or sung, emphasized or accented in any way. "MA nDA LA / MA nDA HA / MA n DA / LA LA LA / Ma nDA / HA HA HA." Now the adult scarcely requires the explanation—printed only on the dust jacket—but, for clarity, children might need to be told that "MA is mother; DA is father; LA is singing; HA is laughing." Again it is a note on the dust jacket, rather than in the book itself, that reveals the author's intent in his "story-poem that celebrates the circle of family and the cycle of life." For there is the obvious *double-entendre* in the title; since the word *mandala,* with its circular connotation, is a term used in psychology and art.

📖 ***THE BLACK DOG WHO WENT INTO THE WOODS*** (written by Edith Thacher Hurd, 1980)

Zena Sutherland

SOURCE: A review of *The Black Dog Who Went into the Woods,* in *Bulletin of the Center for Children's Books,* Vol. 33, No. 11, July-August, 1980, p. 215.

The youngest of three children, Benjamin, dolefully reports that their old dog has disappeared; he is sure that she has gone off to the woods to die. For days the members of the family search for Black Dog, and finally they admit that Benjamin is probably right. One night each member of the family has a dream about Black Dog, a dream in which each remembers some incident. At breakfast they talk about the way Black Dog had come in the night to say farewell to them and, the book ends, "Benjamin did not say anything more about Black Dog after that." The illustrations, line and wash, softly echo the quiet poignancy of the story; while the fact that each member of the family had a dream about the dog on the same night, after she had been missing for days, is not quite credible, this is a sensitive handling of adjustment to a pet's death, written with direct simplicity and restraint.

From Picnic, *by Emily Arnold McCully.*

📖 *PICNIC* (1984)

Zena Sutherland

SOURCE: A review of *Picnic,* in *Bulletin of the Center for Children's Books,* Vol. 37, No. 8, April, 1984, p. 151.

Young children may need a little help in understanding that the scene of action shifts in this wordless picture book, but they won't have any problem understanding the plight of the very small mouse who's jolted off the back of a truck and tearfully watches her family riding on for their picnic. The scene shifts between the small mouse (who consoles herself with picking raspberries) and the myriad activities of the picnic. Eventually the loss is discovered, there's a frantic hunt, the truck returns to pick up the little mouse, and the picnic basket is brought out once again. The paintings are cozily detailed, light and bright, and appropriately vernal for a story that is likely to appeal to children both because of the drama and because of the engaging, if tearful, protagonist.

Ann A. Flowers

SOURCE: A review of *Picnic,* in *The Horn Book Magazine,* Vol. LX, No. 2, April, 1984, p. 185.

In a wordless picture book a large family of mice prepares to go on a picnic in a rickety truck. On the way to the chosen spot the smallest mouse—always shown carrying her mouse dolly—falls, unnoticed, off the back of the truck. The family drives on and gaily begins the standard activities of a picnic—swimming, baseball, tree climbing. After a few tears the small one finds some luscious berries to console herself with; meanwhile, the picnickers discover her absence, also shed a few tears, and immediately set out to find her. Distress, jubilation, and carefree activity are affectionately rendered in paintings showing a cozy countryside in fresh, summery green.

Kenneth Marantz

SOURCE: A review of *Picnic,* in *School Library Journal,* Vol. 30, No. 8, April, 1984, p. 106.

A very large family of anthropomorphic mice pack a picnic basket, get in their red pick-up truck and head out to a swimming hole for some group fun. One of the youngest, who carries a pink stuffed animal, falls off the truck and is eventually picked up when the loss is finally noticed. There is no text, but the sequence of naturalistic (a bit like Steig) pictures "tells" it all. Transparent watercolors and black ink lines create an appealing summer's day with light green foliage, assorted flowers and pale blue sky. The premise that one child can be so easily lost is both frightening and yet reassuringly unreasonable, even for so large a family. Yet the mice do all the things we do at family picnics. They are very simply drawn but project vitality, puzzlement, consternation and other behaviors. Without the artist's fine sense of design and her light-handed use of her media, this would be a rather dull affair. But the simplicity of the narrative is made much more complex by her aesthetic insights.

FIRST SNOW (1985)

Publishers Weekly

SOURCE: A review of *First Snow,* in *Publishers Weekly,* Vol. 227, No. 29, July 19, 1985, p. 52.

In the sequel to McCully's award-winning *Picnic,* the dear toddler mouse faces another intimidating aspect of life. Again, no words are needed to tell the tale that unfolds in pictures with colors that sparkle like the sun on the wintry New England hills. With her venturesome brothers and sisters, the tiny girl is visiting Grandpa and Grandma. Off they drive to a frozen lake for skating, then to the top of a steep hill where the older mice whiz down on sleds, leaving the little one too frightened to take the plunge. Finally, she gains the courage to take off, zipping down so fast she sends siblings and grandparents scattering. And now they have to wait for the beginner to perform her feat over and over again. By the time the bunch is back in Grandma's cozy kitchen, they're almost too tired to sip their naptime hot chocolate.

Cathy Woodward

SOURCE: A review of *First Snow,* in *School Library Journal,* Vol. 32, No. 2, October, 1985, p. 158.

From the moment children see the littlest mouse from *Picnic* peering out her window into the cool, clean freshness of the snow to the last look at her sound asleep at the supper table, they will be entranced by the mouse family's activities in the first snow of the season. Loaded into the old red truck, the mice children set out for a day of wintering with their grandparents. After climbing, ice skating, making angels and a snowmouse, the young mice line up their sleds for the descent. Finally, only the littlest mouse, clad in her hot pink hat and muffler, is left at the top of the hill. Using alternating visual perspectives from the little mouse's view from the top of the hill to the beckoning grandparent's view from the bottom of the hill, the mouse's quandary is felt. Once the initial swoosh to the bottom is achieved, the pages burst with hot pink as the little mouse climbs and rides up and down the slopes. A wordless story filled with subtleties of mood and dynamics of action. An excellent book to share with children, and they will also appreciate the flow of the line, mood and action independently.

THE SHOW MUST GO ON (1987)

Publishers Weekly

SOURCE: A review of *The Show Must Go On,* in *Publishers Weekly,* Vol. 231, No. 14, April 10, 1987, p. 93.

Bruno and Sophie met on stage, and their children Edwin, Sarah and Zaza were born to it—they sleep in steamer trunks or on stage props. Being traveling actors was "a hard life, but it was in their blood." When Sophie's Great-uncle Max leaves them a farm, they are all—except Bruno—thrilled. They'd been wanting a quieter life. Quiet? It's a little too peaceful, so they open the Farm Theater in their barn. Advance ticket sales are discouraging, until a wealthy benefactress/former actress helps out. After that, it's encore after encore. This surely is the "Seven Little Foys" of the picture-book set—McCully shows her family doing vaudeville, Shakespeare and juggling acts. Bruno grumps amiably, Sophie is given to wearing wild scarves, the children cheer up all of them—this ebullient bunch of bears makes McCully's book a grand matinee.

SCHOOL (1987)

Denise M. Wilms

SOURCE: A review of *School,* in *Booklist,* Vol. 84, No. 1, September 1, 1987, p. 67.

The mouse family of *Picnic* and *First Snow* is featured against an autumn backdrop involving another adventure for the youngest family member. Watching her siblings ready themselves for school, the littlest mouse is intrigued; while her mother relaxes with a book, the curious baby decides to follow their footsteps down the path to see what a day at school is like. An accommodating teacher makes her welcome but also calls her mother, who shows up to claim the errant offspring, who has just enjoyed a story hour and snack. The wordless action is easy to follow in McCully's quick line-and-watercolor drawings. The story's comfortable warmth will appeal to preschoolers, who may enjoy the vicarious peek at school as much as the protagonist does.

Pamela Miller Ness

SOURCE: A review of *School,* in *School Library Journal,* Vol. 34, No. 2, October, 1987, p. 116.

This companion to McCully's *Picnic* and *First Snow* illustrates with humor and affection the bustling activities of the mouse children as they prepare for school on a brilliant fall morning. The action begins on the title page of this wordless picture book as both parents prepare breakfast for their nine offspring in a homey kitchen cluttered with backpacks, notebooks, and sports equipment. After waving good-bye to father and the eight older children, mother mouse settles down in a comfortable armchair with a book. Insatiable curiosity, however, gets the better of her youngest child, who sets off down the path to discover for himself what school is all about. McCully's full-page pen-and-ink drawings, softly shaded with translucent washes of watercolor in primary hues and earth tones, clearly establish the sequential action of the story, carefully delineate the personalities of the individual mice, and completely involve children in the unfolding drama. Preschoolers should identify with the eager curiosity of the youngest mouse and his obvious pleasure as the sensitive teacher involves him in the class activities; kindergartners will recognize the activities, accoutrements, and antics of their own classrooms. This is a warm, wise, and humorous book about a special experience irrevocably linked with autumn, a story for parent and child to "read" together or for children to savor on their own.

Zena Sutherland

SOURCE: A review of *School,* in *Bulletin of the Center for Children's Books,* Vol. 41, No. 4, December, 1987, p. 71.

This might be subtitled, "Small Mouse Makes Good," and most of the read-aloud audience should enjoy the accomplishment, the adventure that leads to it, and the cheerful pictures that show cozy interiors and glowing autumn colors outdoors. When older siblings go off on the first day of school, the youngest mouse sneaks off in their wake, slips into the classroom, wins distinction by prowess at the blackboard, and enjoys snack time and story hour. The wordless plot ends with the appearance of a worried mother, who reclaims her perfectly happy child. There are some pages in which the action is not as clear as this genre demands, but it's a book children can "read" with amused empathy.

📖 NEW BABY (1988)

Kirkus Reviews

SOURCE: A review of *New Baby,* in *Kirkus Reviews,* Vol. LV, No. 24, December 15, 1987, p. 1735.

Charming watercolor illustrations in soft colors tell a familiar story in this fourth wordless tale about little mouse and her large family at home in the country. Displaced by a new baby, little mouse exhibits some of the classic symptoms of sibling rivalry. As children and relatives crowd around, she sucks her thumb, cries, sulks, takes the baby's bottle, and crawls into the carriage with baby. At last, mother hugs her, gives her a special job to do (pushing the baby carriage), and shows her there is enough lap for both.

The mice live in a pleasant cottage with floral wallpaper, strawberry curtains, and soft fluffy quilts, set in a picturesque garden with white wrought-iron furniture. The doctor mouse drives a truck, but no one wears clothes. Why a mother with nine children would be so unaware of the feelings of her former youngest is not explained; but young children, especially those displaced by siblings, will know just how little mouse feels.

Publishers Weekly

SOURCE: A review of *New Baby,* in *Publishers Weekly,* Vol. 232, No. 26, December 25, 1987, p. 73.

McCully's fourth wordless picture book about the mouse family both celebrates the excitement of a baby's arrival and acknowledges the confusion such an event can prompt for the newly usurped youngest sibling. While its brothers and sisters crowd 'round to see the baby, the littlest mouse hangs back. In a bid for attention, it reverts to babyish behavior—which includes hopping into the carriage and curling up beside the newborn. This last action sparks understanding and a cuddle from mother; there is love enough for all. Once again, McCully captures the complex, delicate interplay of family emotions. The little mouse's sudden, temporary loneliness is balanced by the happy fuss made by both visiting grandmothers and by the background antics—tag, headstands, bubble-blowing and others—of the older mouse siblings. Pastel pinks and greens create the freshly washed sparkle of spring throughout.

Marianne Pilla

SOURCE: A review of *New Baby,* in *School Library Journal,* Vol. 35, No. 9, June-July, 1988, pp. 92-3.

Another delightful companion to McCully's **School, First Snow** and **Picnic** featuring the mouse family. This one is remarkable in telling, without words, yet with humor and realism, the mixed emotional effect that a new sibling has on a young one. Three generations of the family welcome a new baby in a beautiful springtime setting—indoors and out. Everyone is happy but the youngest mouse, who tries to veer attention from the infant by sulking, screaming, thumb-sucking—even drinking the baby's bottle and climbing into the carriage. But then the mother finds a solution, and the final page shows acceptance of the new baby while in its mother's arms. What makes this so special, when compared with other new baby books, is the universal appeal of the wordless format. Even those who cannot read (or read English) will be able to appreciate the cleverness, the subtlety, and the warm cozy feelings that exude from page to page. The watercolor illustrations, so bright and detailed, fill the book—except for the spotlight shots used adroitly to feature select episodes. This colorful, reassuring, and timely work belongs in every library collection.

📖 THE BOSTON COFFEE PARTY (written by Doreen Rappaport, 1988)

Elisabeth Griffith

SOURCE: A review of *The Boston Coffee Party,* in *The New York Times Book Review,* April 10, 1988, p. 39.

At a gathering to make shirts for Revolutionary soldiers, Sarah's mother complains that the prices charged by Merchant Thomas are outrageous. A "greedy man," Mr. Thomas hoards products like coffee and sugar until he can make greater profits. As the women consider how to protest, Sarah shouts, "Let's have a party!" Not now, is the reply, until the girl explains that she means a party "like the men had" when they tossed British tea into Boston harbor. *The Boston Coffee Party,* based on an episode described by Abigail Adams in a letter to her husband, away in Philadelphia creating a new Government, tells the story of what the women did next. It is Revolutionary history, on several levels.

Told from a child's perspective, in straightforward, big-print, early-reader prose, Doreen Rappaport's narrative moves along briskly, with charm, brevity and humor. The illustrations, by Emily Arnold McCully, are ample and accurately capture the details of the Revolutionary era from cobblestones to mobcaps. The reality of sugar sold in bulk, of jam made from scratch, of clothes cut and stitched by hand, of war shortages and absent fathers is understated but significant.

What is also both historically accurate and culturally revolutionary is the picture of women and girls in active roles. Women head households, keep shops, organize protests and take action; girls run, shout, work and think.

Their sewing circle is not a passive occupation but a Revolutionary cabal—indeed, the sewing circle may be the prototype for female organizations ranging from quilting bees to ladies' auxiliaries to the consciousness-raising groups of the 1970s.

Working together in informal networks, women volunteers have reformed American society. From consumer protests like Sarah's coffee party during the Revolution to the efforts to abolish slavery, educate women, win suffrage, protect workers, prohibit drinking, stop lynching and end the arms race, women have changed American society.

Children who read this book will, one hopes, grow up expecting congruent coverage in their history textbooks. They will not be surprised to learn that "Molly Pitcher," the mythical camp follower, was not carrying water to thirsty soldiers but to swab out and cool down cannon before they could be fired again; or that Betsy Ross was hired to make the first flag not because she was nimble-fingered, but because she owned the upholstery business that had covered the chairs on which the Founders sat in Carpenters Hall in Philadelphia.

Like the changes in children's fictional heroines from sleeping beauties to practical princesses, the expansion of history to include the reality of women's lives breaks a paradigm and influences the way children see themselves and one another. In *The Boston Coffee Party,* women and girls act "like men," like intelligent, take-charge people. Such historical revision can be revolutionary.

Sylvia S. Marantz

SOURCE: A review of *The Boston Coffee Party,* in *School Library Journal,* Vol. 35, No. 8, May, 1988, p. 87.

There really was a "Boston Coffee Party" during the American Revolution in which women punished a selfish merchant who was hoarding his coffee bean stock during the wartime shortage until the price was high enough for profit. Rappaport tells a story based on this historic detail from the point of view of two young sisters of that time, in words that are easy to read but convey the feelings of the time and the action of the plot. Greedy merchant Thomas has already held back sugar; when they find him doing the same with coffee, the women of the sewing circle plan their "party" for revenge. Although their knowledge of history and of the original Boston Tea Party may be vague, young readers and listeners have probably seen and heard enough about the American Revolutionary period and its costumes to enjoy and appreciate the story, which can stand on its own. McCully's competent line drawings with watercolor and charcoal create a sense of time and place while they convey the action through movement and gesture.

YOU LUCKY DUCK! (1988)

Publishers Weekly

SOURCE: A review of *You Lucky Duck!,* in *Publishers Weekly,* Vol. 233, No. 17, April 29, 1988, pp. 73-4.

Zaza and her family (*The Show Must Go On*) of theatrical bears are back, and she is harboring doubts about the lives they lead. Her father writes plays like *King Bear,* which the family troupe then performs. "Why can't we just be normal?" Zaza wonders, a sentiment reinforced whenever she visits her friend Shirl. Shirl's family—a bevy of ducks—spends time on activities like mowing the lawn and cooking dinner, which look blissfully ordinary to Zaza's eyes. Although Zaza is careful to conceal her family's eccentricities, one day Shirl drops in on a rehearsal. "You're all in a play! You lucky duck!" she exclaims—and Zaza begins to see that, indeed, she is. This good-humored story aptly speaks to children who have ever felt embarrassed by their family. McCully masterfully expresses the story through pictures; they are effectively combined with a low-key, straightforward text. Her simple lines, overlaid with watercolor wash, convey a wealth of humor and affection.

THE GRANDMA MIX-UP (1988)

Publishers Weekly

SOURCE: A review of *The Grandma Mix-Up,* in *Publishers Weekly,* Vol. 234, No. 7, August 12, 1988, p. 456.

From an accomplished author/illustrator comes a sweetly child-centered I Can Read. Pip's parents are going on a trip and there's a mix-up. Mom asked Grandma Nan to baby-sit while Dad asked Grandma Sal. The grandmothers arrive, and agree that they'll *both* stay. Active and stylish, Grandma Nan demands a neat room and strictly nutritious meals. Laid-back and cozy Grandma Sal would rather watch the ball game with her feet up, or offer Gummy Bears before lunch. Pip is uncomfortable with the opposing forces. "I want to do things OUR way, like everyday when Mom and Dad are home," he asserts. Chastened, Grandma Nan and Grandma Sal agree on this sensible course. McCully has once again focused her wry humor on a situation of genuine concern to children: the security of family routines. She illustrates this charmer with warmly humorous watercolors, with all the droll details for which she is known.

Denise M. Wilms

SOURCE: A review of *The Grandma Mix-Up,* in *Booklist,* Vol. 85, No. 7, December 1, 1988, pp. 656-57.

When Pip's parents go away for a brief trip, both of his grandmothers arrive to stay with their grandchild. "No matter," says one, "We can both baby-sit." However, the grandmothers' styles are drastically different: Grandma Sal is relaxed and easygoing, while Grandma Nan is an organizer and rule maker. Caught between the two, Pip finally rebels and declares that he wants things done "our way, like everyday when Mom and Dad are home." The grandmas take the message to heart, and peace is restored. McCully's two-color, line-and-wash drawings emphasize the personality differences by consciously flouting stereotypes: Pip's laid-back Grandma Sal has white hair and glasses, while his strict Grandma Nan dresses like a teenager. Choice of words and sentence length will make the sly humor easy for beginning readers to grasp.

THE CHRISTMAS GIFT (1988)

Denise M. Wilms

SOURCE: A review of *The Christmas Gift,* in *Booklist,* Vol. 85, No. 1, September 1, 1988, p. 81.

It's Christmas for McCully's mouse family, and their household is as chaotic as one might expect on Christmas morning with children, toys, and wrapping paper everywhere. Later, when they all visit Grandmother and Grandfather, one little mouse inadvertently breaks the mechanical airplane that has seemed so special to her. Grandfather compensates by taking her up to the attic and pulling out his old train set, which he gives to her to keep. An air of affection pervades this mouse family, making McCully's wordless story, decked out in soft colors and fluid lines, most appealing. The warmth of Grandfather's gesture won't be lost on viewers, who will find it a fine expression of the holiday season. A nice cap on the series.

Susan Hepler

SOURCE: A review of *The Christmas Gift,* in *School Library Journal,* Vol. 35, No. 2, October, 1988, pp. 35-6.

A delight. The mouse family is back for its fifth adventure in wordless picture book format. It is a tribute to McCully's watercolor artistry that the strong narrative "line" never falters. The mouse family members prepare for Christmas and exchange gifts (ones any child would covet—soccer ball, trumpet, beads, rocking horse, and a remote-controlled airplane). Then it's off to the grandparents' house. But readers will have begun to notice the mouse with the airplane: he just can't leave it behind. The plane's crash into Grandpa's wall ends his happiness. No one can seem to comfort him until Grandpa has an idea. Up in the attic, they open up a box of toys Grandpa had as a boy and both shed tears, sentimental and happy. The two set up a train downstairs, and Grandpa joyfully shows his grandson how it works. Readers are set to consider the airplane "The Christmas Gift," but it is really the old train and the sense of family love and continuity that are the true gifts, as the final picture shows the mouse children back home all gathered around their brother and the wonderful train.

DINAH'S MAD, BAD WISHES (written by Barbara M. Joose, 1989)

Ellen Dibner

SOURCE: A review of *Dinah's Mad, Bad Wishes,* in *School Library Journal,* Vol. 35, No. 11, July, 1989, p. 67.

Mama is furious at Dinah for drawing on the newly painted walls. Dinah is furious at Mama for yelling at her. From upstairs to downstairs and back again, readers see how each character vents her anger. Mama gets on her Exercycle and whizzes the pedals around and around. Dinah, meanwhile, slams the door to her room, barricades it with a chair, and then plops herself in her rocker. As she bangs back and forth, she fantasizes about all of the horrid things that should happen to her mean mother to make her sorry for yelling at her. Mama remembers how angry her mother was when she cut up the curtains, while Dinah worries that her wishes might come true. Together Mama and Dinah meet lovingly at the bedroom door for a warm reconciliation. McCully's expressive illustrations in pen and colored wash capture the humorous side to this recognizable, common experience. As with *The Thinking Place* and *Jam Day,* Joosse sets a non-threatening tone for a group discussion on feelings.

Lois F. Anderson

SOURCE: A review of *Dinah's Mad, Bad Wishes,* in *The Horn Book Magazine,* Vol. LXV, No. 5, September-October, 1989, p. 612.

Dinah has made her mother angry by drawing on the wall, and Dinah is mad at her mother for yelling at her. Mama vents her anger by scrubbing the wall very hard and riding an exercise bicycle. Dinah slams her door and, bumping around in her rocking chair, thinks very angry thoughts about her mother. It's a typical family impasse. Eventually, Mama recalls one of her childhood capers that had upset her own mother and is now able to forgive Dinah. At the same time, Dinah begins to worry that, because of her angry thoughts, something might really happen to her mother and is ready to forgive also. "They had whizzed and bumped and wished their angry feelings away." Emily Arnold McCully's full-color drawings are full of movement and capture the poignancy of the family dilemma as well as the humor of the situation. Facial expressions are priceless. For parents of young children the book is perfect to share on those days when things are less than perfect in the mother-child relationship.

📖 THE TAKE-ALONG DOG (written by Barbara Ann Porte, 1989)

Elizabeth S. Watson

SOURCE: A review of *The Take-Along Dog,* in *The Horn Book Magazine,* Vol. LXV, No. 3, May-June, 1989, pp. 362-63.

Starring Benton, the bravest small dog in the world, the amusing story of a dog-shy mom has lots to say about give-and-take in family relations. The household members accommodate Mom's canine aversion by toting the adopted pup with them—to the pool, the library, and even the movie theater—rather than leaving him home with her. The inevitable difficulties that Benton causes provide meat for a lively and humorous tale, yet all is resolved nicely when Benton shows his loyalty to Mom and wins her admiration. The bright watercolor illustrations outlined in black ink portray Benton and his family with an appropriate amount of detail for the story. Benton is not only the bravest but also one of the cutest dog characters to be drawn recently, and many a reader will wish for just such a pup to take along.

Pamela Miller Ness

SOURCE: A review of *The Take-Along Dog,* in *School Library Journal,* Vol. 35, No. 10, June, 1989, p. 91.

Because of their mother's fear of dogs, Sam and Abigail must take their new dog Benton to all their summer activities: swimming lessons, reading club at the library, and the movies. They break the "no dogs" rule wherever they go, and are banished from one activity after another. Finally, during a family picnic at the park, Benton is left sleeping on the blanket with Mother. When a large dog races towards them, he bravely protects territory and family, thus assuaging Mother's fears and winning her friendship. Despite the mundane plot and simple language, *The*

Take-Along Dog subtly emphasizes important human values: acknowledgement of a parent's fear, unusual sensitivity of children toward siblings and parents, and the negation of gender stereotypes (Sam takes ballet lessons and Abigail assumes major responsibilities). Moreover, McCully's delicate and affectionate watercolors people the children's urban world with characters of all races. A thoughtful story with underlying values to share with preschoolers and for beginning readers to enjoy independently.

📖 ZAZA'S BIG BREAK (1989)

Publishers Weekly

SOURCE: A review of *Zaza's Big Break,* in *Publishers Weekly,* Vol. 236, No. 4, July 28, 1989, p. 220.

Last seen in *The Show Must Go On,* Zaza, Edwin and Sarah are part of a family of theater bears; their father writes the plays, their mother directs and all of them perform. Then Zaza is invited to Hollywood to try out for a TV show. Edwin and Sarah are rather subdued about the news, but Zaza is extremely happy. On the plane ride out, Zaza's parents hope that TV won't make Zaza grow up too fast; Zaza dreams of life as a star. But while acting in front of the camera, Zaza begins to have doubts. And after a day of filming, she has to admit she doesn't like TV acting, and knows she must face the director with her news. McCully (*New Baby* and *The Christmas Gift*) has created a secure, loving story about Zaza and her close-knit family. The pictures express the many emotional moments of each member, as well as the contrasts between the snug theater world and the false glamour of Hollywood.

Julie Corsaro

SOURCE: A review of *Zaza's Big Break,* in *Booklist,* Vol. 86, No. 1, September 1, 1989, p. 79.

The struggle to achieve competence is chronicled in an amusing story with an unusual setting. The bear Zaza is satisfied with life in a successful theatrical family until Hollywood beckons with a screen test. Accompanied by her parents, who fear Tinseltown's jading influence, she experiences life on the backlot with caution. Finally, homesickness and isolation cause her to soundly declare, "Television is not my cup of tea." The warmth, sensitivity, and humor of the text are echoed in vibrant watercolor paintings that are memorably strong in character, action, and detail. References to the longstanding rivalry between stage and screen, along with other sophisticated tidbits, will engage adults who read this to children. Young listeners will not only relate to Zaza, but also to her annoying siblings. (When they see their sister for the first time in her Shirley Temple curls, Edwin and Sarah are reduced to hysterical laughter.) Zaza may have rejected tabloid headlines, but she's a star in the picture-book firmament.

Barbara S. McGinn

SOURCE: A review of *Zaza's Big Break,* in *School Library Journal,* Vol. 35, No. 16, December, 1989, p. 85.

Zaza is a young bear who, along with her brother and sister, acts in the family theater productions written by her father and directed by her mother. One day Zaza is called to try out for a part in a TV sitcom, and the whole family, somewhat reluctantly, travels to Hollywood for the audition. Zaza garners the part but has difficulty "being herself" when she reads her lines, for what she enjoys most about acting is "being someone else." The director is understanding, and tells Zaza, "If the theater is in your blood, you should go back to it." Zaza and her family happily return to their hometown, where Zaza's best friend is overjoyed. The story is a little too predictable, but the last page makes up for some of that when readers realize that, although the heroine is back on familiar turf, she has changed as a result of her Hollywood experiences. McCully's colorful watercolors greatly enhance the text. Careful attention to detail and facial expressions add another dimension to the story line. All in all, a pleasing story with a gentle moral and a conclusion which carries the story above the ordinary.

📖 *GRANDMAS AT THE LAKE* (1990)

Denise Wilms

SOURCE: A review of *Grandmas at the Lake,* in *Booklist,* Vol. 86, No. 15, April 1, 1990, p. 1562.

Nan and Sal, those grandmas with opposite personalities from *The Grandma Mix-Up,* are back again, this time sharing a lakeside cabin with Pip and her friend, Ski. The kids find it hard to put up with the grandmas' contradictory advice and a general tendency to oversupervise, so they go rowing by themselves to teach the two a lesson: "Promise to let us have fun! . . . Promise to let us play by ourselves," they call from afar. The Grandmas comply, and peace is restored, sort of. A humorous account in easy-to-read style that beginning readers will find easy to master. The adult-child negotiations get a lift from McCully's visual interpretation of these two extremely disparate personalities.

Zena Sutherland

SOURCE: A review of *Grandmas at the Lake,* in *Bulletin of the Center for Children's Books,* Vol. 43, No. 9, May, 1990, pp. 221-22.

In a sequel to *The Grandma Mix-Up,* Pip's two grandmothers and his friend Ski are his companions at a lakeside cabin, rented by Grandma Nan, who has invited Grandma Sal and the boys. The hostess is rigid and highly organized, while plump Grandma Sal is easy-going. Pip and Ski get tired of being told what to do by the

Grandmas, especially when the directives contradict each other. They are even more weary of never being allowed to do anything by themselves. While the women are napping, the boys go off in a rowboat. At first alarmed, the grandmothers concede that the boys are doing a good job and come for a ride, promising to let Pip and Ski play by themselves. The paintings are bright, casual, and funny in cartoon style; the story is nicely gauged for the beginning-to-read audience, with appropriate length and vocabulary. While not outstanding in conception or development, it should please readers who sympathize with the boys' desire for independence and enjoy, vicariously, the pleasure of having achievement recognized.

Joan McGrath

SOURCE: A review of *Grandmas at the Lake,* in *School Library Journal,* Vol. 36, No. 6, June, 1990, p. 104.

Pip has two grandmas: fuss-budget Grandma Nan and easygoing Grandma Sal, both of whom first appeared in *The Grandma Mix-Up.* If one of them says "yes," the other immediately says "no"; so when Pip and his buddy Ski go for a holiday in the country with both the grandmas, the ceaseless tug-of-war between uptight Nan and laidback Sal spoils all the fun. The boys explain their feelings, and a compromise that all can live with is reached. The bright cartoon illustrations are sure to appeal to young readers. While the story line is slight and insubstantial, it fulfills its purpose as another of the dependable controlled-vocabulary stories for beginning independent readers.

📖 *THE EVIL SPELL* (1990)

Mary Lou Budd

SOURCE: A review of *The Evil Spell,* in *School Library Journal,* Vol. 36, No. 9, September, 1990, p. 207.

The theatrical bear family introduced in *Zaza's Big Break* is staging a new production, with Edwin, the youngest, in his first starring role. He is full of excitement and confidence—that is, until he steps out on stage. Mortified when his mind goes blank, he runs into the woods to hide in shame. His family lovingly explains that he has a simple case of stage fright and Father encourages, "It's just like any fear . . . you mustn't run away. You must try again." With newfound faith in himself, Edwin does succeed in the following performance. The storyline flows smoothly through its manageable text, and readers will empathize with the moods of anticipation, preparation, heart-thumping horror, and final triumph. Father's wise words say it all and provide the impetus for the story's satisfying conclusion. McCully's soft watercolor cartoons visually complement this well-structured story on every page, showing a full spectrum of emotions. The text is geared toward older readers, but young audiences will enjoy this read-aloud spellbinder.

Carolyn K. Jenks

SOURCE: A review of *The Evil Spell,* in *The Horn Book Magazine,* Vol. LXVI, No. 6, November-December, 1990, p. 731.

Edwin, the middle member of a bear family of actors, finally gets his long-awaited chance to play an important part: he will be the king who says the magic words that break an evil spell. He is honored and excited until the first night of the performance, when he is frozen with fear and runs off the stage. The subsequent warm support of the other bears, both as family members and fellow actors, is beautiful to see. Edwin asks, "'How do you get rid of stage fright?' 'It's just like any fear,' said Bruno. 'You mustn't run away. You must try again. We know you're a good actor. You must believe it too. You are the king. The king will do what he is supposed to do.'" And Edwin does, breaking his own "evil spell." The grand excitement of life in the bear family theater troupe is everything an actor could hope for: good drama, parts for everyone, cooperation, and a lightness of spirit that inspires everyone to do his or her best. The pictures are full of action, giving the reader a view of both on-stage and backstage events. Droll imagination combines with a worrisome problem to make an appealing story. The circumstances of Edwin's fear will be unknown to many readers, but the essence of it will be vividly recognizable.

MEATBALL (written by Phyllis Hoffman, 1991)

Zena Sutherland

SOURCE: A review of *Meatball,* in *Bulletin of the Center for Children's Books,* Vol. 44, No. 7, March, 1991, p. 166.

Marilyn, chronicler of the activities at a preschool daycare center, is called "Meatball" by her affectionate teacher because she's "round and yummy." This is preschool as it really is, presented in faithful detail from the joys of the block corner and the felicity of friendship to occasional squabbles or the indignity (tactfully handled by the teacher) of pants-wetting. The drawings are bright, clean-lined, and sprightly, with plenty of space to set off both print and watercolors. This should encourage the child who's ready for playschool and appeal to the child who's a seasoned participant.

John Philbrook

SOURCE: A review of *Meatball,* in *School Library Journal,* Vol. 37, No. 8, August, 1991, p. 150.

Marilyn, who is called Meatball by her preschool teacher, details daily life in her class. The story is written in simple, dull sentences, in which verbalization and conceptualization do not always ring true for this age level. Much of the first-person narrative is taken up with Meatball's friendship with Lu, her Chinese classmate. Incidents, such as Lu's acclimatizing by Meatball plopping a fireman's hat over Lu's head to the mirth of all, are more apt to cause trauma than acceptance at this age. An argument between Meatball and Lu and another girl while playing doctor is never resolved, leaving a rather unsettling impression. During a counting game, English and Spanish numbers are used, and then Chinese numbers are given in what is supposed to be Cantonese; they are so poorly transcribed that two of the numbers are in Mandarin and one is in Northern Min dialect—no child would count like this. The repetition of one child whining for his mother may be intended as humor, but its impact is closer to annoyance. Jacket illustration notwithstanding, illustrations are lively and colorful, portraying a broad multicultural group of children and adults, although the teacher is remarkably reminiscent of Little Orphan Annie. In sum, this is an attempt at a much needed multicultural interaction book for small children, laudable in its intentions but a bit inept in its execution.

SPEAK UP, BLANCHE! (1991)

Liza Bliss

SOURCE: A review of *Speak Up, Blanche!,* in *School Library Journal,* Vol. 37, No. 9, September, 1991, p. 237.

Blanche, a shy lamb, joins the theatrical bear family of *Zaza's Big Break* and *The Evil Spell,* for dramatic coaching. Eclipsed by the extroverted energy all around her, Blanche is a pathetic failure onstage, unable to raise her voice above a whisper. Finally frustration drives her to assert herself; she insists on a job creating sets, which takes advantage of her artistic talents in an appropriate way. As in Rosemary Wells's *Shy Charles,* readers see that shyness does not deserve to be equated with ineptitude. Consistent with the earlier titles, McCully effectively evokes readers' empathy by focusing on a single, common trait and avoids other distractions. Obvious clues pointing to Blanche's ability with painting are dropped frequently, so that even the youngest readers will feel involved in the resolution. The text's pleasing humor is reflected in the details of the watercolor illustrations. While not a must-buy sort of book, this one will be appreciated by "Farm Theater" fans. In addition, it will be a useful acquisition for libraries in which there are never enough titles such as *Shy Charles* to go around.

Ilene Cooper

SOURCE: A review of *Speak Up, Blanche!,* in *Booklist,* Vol. 88, No. 1, September 1, 1991, p. 57.

McCully's theatrical bears get a new addition to their troupe when an old friend, Eva the sheep, drops her granddaughter Blanche off to apprentice at the theater. Blanche is eager to be a part of the next production, *The Strange Pudding,* but she is on the shy side, to say the least. In fact, she barely speaks above a whisper. Zaza tries to coach her, but Blanche quite clearly "stinks." She's not much better at selling tickets or collecting props. Blanche's career in the theater seems doomed until she learns the bears are sending her home. Then she booms, "YOU WANT ME TO SHOW MY FEELINGS? WELL, HERE THEY ARE!" Her other failures aside, Blanche informs the astonished troupe that she can draw, and she wants to paint the sets. On opening night, she receives accolades. The book's messages about overcoming shyness and finding your niche never overpower the story, which is wittily and cleverly told. The book even uses teeny-tiny print while Blanche is speaking—until she turns bold, of course. Then the print does, too. McCully's spirited artwork does her story justice as she combines just the right picture with the text. In a hilarious moment, Sarah, another bear, tries to teach Blanche *acting*. "'Show us your feelings!' cried Sarah. 'Watch how I do it.' Sarah took a bite of the pudding. '*Blaaaaahhhhp!* See? Now the audience knows the pudding is strange.'" Sarah's funny, contorted, throwing-up face in the small accompanying drawing lets the picture book viewer know it, too.

📖 *MIRETTE ON THE HIGH WIRE* (1992)

Mary M. Burns

SOURCE: A review of *Mirette on the High Wire,* in *The Horn Book Magazine,* Vol. LXVIII, No. 5, September-October, 1992, p. 577.

McCully has created an independent female protagonist—one with panache and a soupçon of something out of the ordinary. In a wonderfully exuberant picture book set in late nineteenth-century Paris, Mirette is the daughter of the hardworking widow Gâteau. Madame Gâteau runs a boarding house for the traveling players from all over the world who come to perform in the theaters and music halls of Paris. One evening, a handsome stranger who introduces himself as Bellini, a retired high-wire walker, asks for a room. Unlike the usual gregarious boarders, he keeps to himself, practicing his routines in the back courtyard—to the delight of Mirette, who is fascinated with his skill and longs to learn the art. Despite his refusal to become her mentor, she stubbornly proceeds to teach herself, thus inveigling him into acknowledging that she might have talent. Inadvertently, she learns that her friend, once an internationally famous daredevil, has retired because he had become fearful—a fatal emotion for one in his profession. How she salvages his self-respect and earns a place of her own in the limelight is the climactic moment in a well-conceived tale with the charm of an Offenbach score and the brilliance of a poster by Toulouse-Lautrec. McCully is thoroughly comfortable with the watercolor medium, exploiting its potential to achieve remarkable effects in creating interior and characters. A bravura performance.

Deborah Stevenson

SOURCE: A review of *Mirette on the High Wire,* in

From Mirette on the High Wire, *written and illustrated by Emily Arnold McCully.*

Bulletin of the Center for Children's Books, Vol. 46, No. 2, October, 1992, p. 49.

Young Mirette, daughter of the Widow Gâteau, helps her mother run a theatrical boardinghouse in *fin de siècle* Paris, where she meets the famous high-wire walker Bellini. Bellini warns her that "once you start, your feet are never happy again on the ground," but Mirette loves walking the tightrope; she grows so proficient under Bellini's tutelage that she is able to save him and his performance when his nerve fails during his big comeback. The illustrations are effectively reminiscent of the period, with a lively Toulouse-Lautrec flavor in the scenes of Parisian life; McCully uses some creative perspectives (Mirette, her mouth open with concentration, seen from underneath the wire on which she balances) and a varied palette that is most effective in the somber interiors and luminous night scenes, where Mirette's orange hair shines out in contrast. She makes an enviable and plucky heroine, darting among the theatrical crowd and doggedly practicing her difficult skill; young readers will want to pull on their own high-button boots and join her as she dances between the rooftops.

Ruth K. MacDonald

SOURCE: A review of *Mirette on the High Wire,* in *School Library Journal,* Vol. 38, No. 10, October, 1992, p. 92.

Mirette's mother keeps a boardinghouse that attracts traveling performers. The girl is intrigued by one silent visitor, Bellini, who has come for a rest. She finds him next morning walking a high wire strung across the backyard. Immediately, she is drawn to it, practicing on it herself until she finds her balance and can walk its distance. But she finds the man unusually secretive about his identity; he was a famous high-wire artist, but has lost his courage. He is lured by an agent to make a comeback, but freezes on the wire. Seeing Mirette at the end of it restores his nerve; after the performance the two set off on a new career together. As improbable as the story is, its theatrical setting at some historical distance, replete with European architecture and exotic settings and people, helps lend credibility to this circus tale. Mirette, through determination and perhaps talent, trains herself, overcoming countless falls on cobblestone, vaunting pride that goes before a fall, and lack of encouragement from Bellini. The impressionistic paintings, full of mottled, rough edges and bright colors, capture both the detail and the general milieu of Paris in the last century. The colors are reminiscent of Toulouse-Lautrec, the daubing technique of Seurat. A satisfying, high-spirited adventure.

Publishers Weekly

SOURCE: A review of *Mirette on the High Wire,* in *Publishers Weekly,* Vol. 239, No. 47, October 25, 1992, p. 70.

In this picture book set in 19th-century Paris, a child helps a daredevil who has lost his edge to regain his confidence. Many traveling performers stay at Madame Gateaux's boarding house, but Mme.'s daughter Mirette is particularly taken with one guest—the quiet gentleman who can walk along the clothesline without falling off. Mirette implores the boarder to teach her his craft, not knowing that her instructor is the "Great Bellini" of high wire fame. After much practice the girl joins Bellini on the wire as he conquers his fear and demonstrates to all of Paris that he is still the best. McCully's story has an exciting premise and starting point, but unfortunately ends up as a missed opportunity. Bellini's anxiety may be a bit sophisticated for the intended audience and, surprisingly, the scenes featuring Mirette and Bellini on the high wire lack drama and intensity. McCully's rich palette and skillful renderings of shadow and light sources make this an inviting postcard from the Old World.

Jean Van Leeuwen

SOURCE: "Walking on Air," in *The New York Times Book Review,* November 8, 1992, p. 38.

Here is a spunky heroine with whom young children will be able to identify. Mirette is the daughter of the widow Gateau, who runs a boardinghouse where all the traveling theatrical players come to stay when they perform in Paris. One day a mysterious stranger arrives and takes a room. He is the great Bellini, a world-famous high-wire walker, now retired. Mirette comes upon him "crossing the court-

yard on air" and is entranced. She begs him to teach her the art of wire-walking. But Bellini refuses. It seems that Bellini—who once crossed Niagara Falls on a thousand-foot wire, stopping in the middle to cook an omelet, and who once fired a cannon on a high wire over the bullring in Barcelona—has fallen victim to fear.

Mirette practices in secret until at last she can walk the length of the wire in the courtyard. When she demonstrates her skill to Bellini, he sees the perseverance of a committed artist and agrees to take her on as a pupil. As Mirette's balancing skills grow, she longs to become a performer. In the end it is the pupil who teaches the master an important lesson about the need to face one's demons. And, in a tension-filled climax, the two perform a dramatic pas de deux on the high wire over the rooftops of Paris.

The appealing heroine of *Mirette on the High Wire* is a down-to-earth child who works hard scrubbing floors, peeling potatoes and serving guests, yet who dares to dream soaring dreams. Emily Arnold McCully has captured, in admirably few words matched with expressive watercolor paintings, the excitement and stubborn determination of the budding artist. When Mirette first watches the great Bellini perform, she thinks: "Of all the things a person could do, this must be the most magical. Her feet tingled, as if they wanted to jump up on the wire beside Bellini." And when she realizes her wire-walking dreams at the end, "she stepped onto the wire, and with the most intense pleasure, as she had always imagined it might be, she started to cross the sky."

With a rich palette of deep colors, the artist immerses the reader in 19th-century Paris. Colorful theatrical personalities—acrobats and jugglers, actors and agents and mimes—fill the glowing interiors with robust life. And the exterior scenes, with their rooftop backgrounds, are filled with the magic of a Paris night when anything can happen, even a young girl and an old master wire-walker taking a stroll across the sky. *Mirette on the High Wire* is an exuberant and uplifting picture book.

GRANDMAS AT BAT (1993)

Carolyn Phelan

SOURCE: A review of *Grandmas at Bat,* in *Booklist,* Vol. 89, No. 13, March 1, 1993, p. 1240.

When Pip's baseball coach comes down with chicken pox, a replacement coach must be found or the team, the Stings, will have to forfeit Saturday's game. Pip's two grandmothers, high in enthusiasm and low in expertise, come to the rescue, though their team soon benches them for squabbling at practice. At the game, the weirdly dressed grandmothers begin to lead cheers for their losing team. Initially embarrassed, the Stings start to believe in themselves and soon rally to win. Illustrated with McCully's expressive ink drawings washed in bright colors, this unusual, and admittedly improbable, baseball tale will entertain beginning readers as well as slightly younger sluggers who like to hear sports stories read aloud.

Kirkus Reviews

SOURCE: A review of *Grandmas at Bat,* in *Kirkus Reviews,* Vol. LXI, No. 6, March 15, 1993, p. 374.

From the new Caldecott medalist, a third "I Can Read" book about Pip and her squabbling grandmas. The Stings' coach has chicken pox—and unless Pip and her team come up with a substitute, they won't be allowed to play. Both grandmas volunteer; their constant bickering and mutual competing almost prevents the Stings from practicing, until one kid complains, "Your Grandmas are driving us bananas!" and another points out that "The coaches are hogging the field!" Finally leaving the team in peace, the grandmas find another way to help: at the big game, it's their cheerleading that spurs the Stings to victory. Baseball action and the amusingly caricatured grandmas are deftly drawn; best, the funny, true-to-life dialogue is sure to entertain beginning readers.

Luann Toth

SOURCE: A review of *Grandmas at Bat,* in *School Library Journal,* Vol. 39, No. 6, June, 1993, p. 83.

The squabbling grandmothers who appeared in McCully's **The Grandma Mix-Up** and **Grandmas at the Lake** here agree to fill in as substitute coaches for Pip's Little League team. The pair have plenty of ideas about conducting a practice, but are both disappointed when the Stings strongly suggest that they sit on the bench and watch. At the big game the following Saturday, the Grandmas figure out how to get a piece of the action—as cheerleaders. They yell and wave pom-poms and their confidence in the team inspires a comeback victory as the Stings win the game "for the grandmas." The illustrations present humorous images of two very different women; Grandma Sal is cozy and homespun, while Grandma Nan is slim and stylish. The only thing this unlikely duo ever agree upon is their unflagging affection for their granddaughter. An easy-reading sports story with bright, appealing artwork and a lot of spirit.

📖 THE AMAZING FELIX (1993)

Publishers Weekly

SOURCE: A review of *The Amazing Felix,* in *Publishers Weekly,* Vol. 240, No. 33, August 16, 1993, p. 102.

Caldecott winner McCully captures the elegance of the 1920s with sprightly prose and effervescent illustrations. Felix's famous pianist father departs for a world tour, leaving behind the instructions "You must practice." Sister Fanny throws herself into a Bach fugue while Felix doubts his talents and feels "a surge of joy—and a clap of dread!" at the thought of seeing his father again. Aboard a fancy ocean liner, however, he discovers a new pastime and hopes to impress his father with a magic trick or two. As it happens, he saves Fanny from the cold clutches of a castle tower and wins hearts with his sure-handed magic performance. The story is weakened by a single ill-defined but pivotal moment, yet is otherwise well paced and filled with snatches of warm humor and insight. With McCully's subtle but expert use of color, water shimmers aqua, ladies' gowns rustle. Finely tuned for the most part, it is unfortunate that the female characters are less than inspiring. Mother barely features and Fanny gets nothing for all her practice and perseverance.

Kirkus Reviews

SOURCE: A review of *The Amazing Felix,* in *Kirkus Reviews,* Vol. LXI, No. 17, September 1, 1993, p. 1148.

An old-fashioned tale of kids making their not-so-ordinary way among the rich and famous. En route to Europe in the 20's, Felix—enjoined by his concert-pianist Papa to "Practice, practice"—despairs of ever playing as well as sister Fanny; but he does learn some prestidigitation from a magician aboard ship. In England, while Papa plays a command performance, Fanny and three other children ("cousins of a duchess") get trapped in a castle tower. Following the sound of music, Felix runs for help; then, while Papa interrupts his playing to rescue the frightened children, Felix mollifies and amuses his audience, finally making the delightful discovery that Papa wants to learn to palm a coin, too ("With your fingers, it ought to be a cinch," Felix allows). It's an unlikely but satisfying fantasy, with handsome pictures of the elegant ocean liner and country house, and lush impressionistic settings accented with the dramatic black of pianos and tuxedos—while Felix's chance to advise Papa to "practice, practice" makes the perfect denouement.

Carolyn Phelan

SOURCE: A review of *The Amazing Felix,* in *Booklist,* Vol. 90, No. 3, October 1, 1993, p. 342.

Felix and his sister, Fanny, board an ocean liner with their mother for the voyage to England, where the family will be reunited with the father, a concert pianist on a world tour. Admonished by the father to "practice, practice, practice" until he sees them again, Fanny dutifully practices piano for hours, but Felix's imagination is caught by a shipboard magician, who teaches him a magic trick and offers the same advice his father gave. "Practice, practice, practice." Later, when the lack of piano practice puts Felix on the spot, his skill as a magician saves him from revealing his ineptness as a musician. As in her Caldecott-winning **Mirette on the Highwire,** McCully handled watercolors with facility and panache, using impressionistic dapples of color to delineate forms. The 1920s settings on board ship and in an English castle lend themselves to a variety of intriguing illustrations, but even more impressive are her subtle characterizations of adults and children. McCully's original story, with its involving pictures and sense of childhood concerns, is an especially fine choice for reading aloud.

Joanne Schott

SOURCE: A review of *The Amazing Felix,* in *Quill and Quire,* Vol. 59, No. 12, December, 1993, p. 36.

Felix wants to please his father, a famous pianist, but hates to practice and knows he can never measure up to his older sister, Fanny. En route by sea to meet his father, who is performing in London, Felix dreads facing him. But his fear is forgotten as he watches, fascinated, while a magician entertains the ship's passengers. The man teaches him to palm a coin and tells him to practice. *This* practice comes easily.

While their father gives a recital at a nobleman's estate, Felix and Fanny go exploring with some other children. A door in the tower slams shut and locks. Only Felix, lagging behind, is free to go for help, breaking in on the recital. Father goes to the rescue, leaving his son to continue the entertainment, saying, "He practiced . . . he will perform for you." Felix *has* practiced, and he removes coins from guests' ears with professional aplomb. He quickly gains his father's approval, and envy.

As in *Mirette on the High Wire,* McCully again successfully recreates a specific setting. Here it is a 1920s world of leisure and affluence aboard a luxury liner and in a stately home. Vibrant colour and expressive drawing bring both the scenes and the drama to life. Every line of Felix's body reveals his response to his predicament. Father seems a bit too good to be true, but no one will quarrel with his sincere praise for Felix, who has had the reader's sympathy all the way.

MY REAL FAMILY (1994)

Publishers Weekly

SOURCE: A review of *My Real Family,* in *Publishers Weekly,* Vol. 241, No. 13, March 28, 1994, p. 96.

The thespian Bear Family makes a welcome return in this warm story, which opens as the curtain closes on one of the Bears' hit plays. Praise abounds for the writing, directing, acting—and especially for the sets painted by Blanche, an orphaned sheep who is visiting the Bears. But no one compliments Sarah for her work on the props and costumes. Blanche continues to command the attention to which Sarah feels entitled. Then comes the last straw: father Bruno offers to adopt Blanche—and gives her Sarah's bedroom. Infuriated, Sarah imagines that she doesn't really belong to this family; rather, her true parents are heroic forest rangers who have long missed her. She sets off into the woods to find them, but instead stumbles upon her "real family." At last, Sarah concedes that

Blanche (who masterminded the search for her) is an okay addition to the clan. McCully masterfully combines ink, watercolors and pastels to create fetching illustrations for this buoyant tale, which will help soothe that common childhood malady of feeling neglected.

Ilene Cooper

SOURCE: A review of *My Real Family,* in *Booklist,* Vol. 90, No. 15, April 1, 1994, p. 1461.

McCully's latest story about her troupe of performing bears begins where the last one left off. In *Speak Up, Blanche!,* a timid orphan sheep, Blanche, couldn't properly play her role in the troupe's latest drama, but she was a hit at drawing and painting the sets. Now, as the applause is dying down, youngest bear Sarah realizes she is anxious for Blanche's grandmother to pick Blanche up and get her out: she's getting far too much attention. But Blanche's moment in the sun is just beginning, and when it culminates with the bears asking to adopt Blanche, Sarah decides to take a hike. She figures she's the one who's adopted and runs away to find her *real* parents waiting for her in the forest. But Sarah only gets lost. It's not until she hears her family searching for her, and praising her as well, that Sarah understands how much her *really real* family loves her. The strength of this series is McCully's ability to capture with precision the emotions children feel; this will certainly resonate with any little one who's felt unloved and underappreciated. The picture-perfect ending is a bit too sugary, but the sweetness is cut by the watercolor artwork, which is far more subtle than the text. Adults who want to do more than read will find this offers a lot to discuss as well.

Anna Biagioni Hart

SOURCE: A review of *My Real Family,* in *School Library Journal,* Vol. 40, No. 6, June, 1994, p. 110.

The theatrical Bear Family (*The Evil Spell* and *Speak Up, Blanche!*) is back, this time with an offstage adventure. Sarah, the youngest, is pleased with herself for doing such a good job as props manager and costume mistress in the latest Farm Theater production, but no one in her family pays much attention to her. Instead, they praise Blanche, an orphaned lamb who is visiting. And, worst of all, instead of sending Blanche home, Sarah's parents invite her to stay with them. They even announce that they would like to adopt her. Sarah seems close to losing everything— her parents' love, her room, her place in the universe. She decides that she was adopted, and runs away into the woods to find her birth parents. Of course, the heartsick Bruno and Sophie pursue her. In the end, Sarah gains a greater understanding of the unshakable place she holds in her family. The enormously appealing, almost impressionistic illustrations are done in pen and ink, watercolor, and pastels. With economy of line and marvelous use of accent and shadow, they capture, in turn, the friendly and fearsome ambiance of the forest, and explore the full range of ursine emotions. These charming and expressive creatures draw readers into Sarah's world. A book that will be of comfort to all youngsters, especially those who think they deserve more attention than they get.

CROSSING THE NEW BRIDGE (1994)

Elizabeth Bush

SOURCE: A review of *Crossing the New Bridge,* in *Bulletin of the Center for Children's Books,* Vol. 48, No. 1, September, 1994, p. 18.

"The old bridge suddenly creaked, cracked, and fell into the water." Luckily, the Jubilattis are quick to arrive at the scene, and the four sunny-tempered medieval workaholics immediately set to the task of rebuilding, leaving the crusty old Mayor to search for the town's happiest person, who must cross the bridge first and ward off a traditional curse. The rich banker, the beautiful baker, the soulful poet, and the mother of many healthy children all have their private woes, and it looks as if the bridge will indeed be cursed. But daughter Jubilatti, standing at the foot of their completed masterpiece, lays worry to rest: the Jubilattis themselves, who are overjoyed to have built the best bridge of their lives, have in fact already crossed the bridge. This gentle lesson about finding happiness in accomplishment is delivered in a smoothly paced narration with plenty of lively, clipped dialogue. Although this is not McCully's finest artwork—the bright watercolors have a certain uniformity of tone and composition that grows a bit tiresome—such comic details as the Mayor's absurd hat and elongated feet, and the bespectacled Scribe who shadows his every move, enliven the scenes. Glimpses of medieval town life, considerably freshened and romanticized, and of bridge construction, discernible in the background, extend the audience's interest beyond the plot of the story.

Lisa S. Murphy

SOURCE: A review of *Crossing the New Bridge,* in *School Library Journal,* Vol. 40, No. 9, September, 1994, p. 190.

In this "original folktale," an ancient bridge collapses into the river, and the town hires the Jubilattis to build a new one. As the family construction crew sets to work with gusto, an old woman reminds the mayor of the tradition that the first person to cross the bridge must be the happiest in the town. To do otherwise would bring a curse on all of them. The bumbling mayor and his scribe begin their search, but find everyone harried by the small details of life. One afternoon, a cheer of "WE DID IT" rises as the Jubilattis come rushing into town, celebrating the completion of their best work ever. Their spirits are temporarily dampened when they hear of the mayor's failed efforts, until their wise child makes an observation that changes everything. Caldecott-award winner McCully has created a picture book that glows. All of the paintings are diffused with light, with shimmering lines and brilliant colors

that bring the medieval seaside community to life. Just as the town's people dance joyfully across their new bridge, readers are sure to take pleasure in this job well done.

Publishers Weekly

SOURCE: A review of *Crossing the New Bridge,* in *Publishers Weekly,* Vol. 241, No. 36, September 5, 1994, p. 109.

When the Old Bridge crumbles into the river, the townspeople immediately commission the Jubilatti family to construct a replacement. As the relieved mayor begins to plan his ceremonial strut across the new bridge, an elderly woman reminds him of an ancient tradition: the first to cross a new bridge must be the happiest person in town, or a curse will fall on everyone. The mayor searches the cobbled, gabled village for its most joyful citizen, but one by one the likeliest candidates disqualify themselves from the honor. Caldecott Medalist McCully's text ripples with gentle laughter as she catalogues the roots of people's unhappiness: blisters, wrinkles, a lost sovereign, misplaced shoes. Her story moves toward an obvious but satisfying conclusion as the Jubilattis live up to their name. Soft watercolors depict a quaint town in a picturesque Old World full of life and merriment, if not true happiness; the worrywart mayor, meanwhile, is the picture of genial inefficiency. This agreeable picture book lightly conveys the pleasures of a job well done.

LITTLE KIT; OR, THE INDUSTRIOUS FLEA CIRCUS GIRL (1995)

Publishers Weekly

SOURCE: A review of *Little Kit; or, The Industrious Flea Circus Girl,* in *Publishers Weekly,* Vol. 241, No. 50, December 12, 1994, p. 62.

Like a female Oliver Twist, Kit is plucked from the streets of 19th-century London to labor for a ne'er-do-well. Her harsh taskmaster is one Professor Malefetta, manager of a traveling flea circus, who unwittingly takes her for a boy. Expecting a life of adventure, Kit instead finds herself as poorly treated as her charges, the professor's overworked fleas. When a pickpocket at a countryside fair discovers her true identity and threatens to reveal it to the professor, Kit liberates the fleas and finds safe haven with a wholesome rural family. McCully, who came across references to flea circuses while researching *Mirette on the High Wire,* provides a historical note to explain how fleas "performed." Expansively illustrated with bustling watercolors, her scrumptious period piece balances treachery with poetic justice in as cozy a manner as any of Dickens's peers.

Carolyn Phelan

SOURCE: A review of *Little Kit; or, the Industrious Flea*

Circus Girl, in *Booklist,* Vol. 91, No. 9, January 1, 1995, p. 821.

A full-bodied Dickensian tale about Little Kit, a ragamuffin who sells flowers in Victorian London. Mistaking her for a lad, Professor Malefetta offers Kit a position helping with his Industrious Flea Circus, so Kit disguises herself as a boy and travels with the cruel professor and his oppressed performing fleas. At a country fair, Kit befriends little Nell, whose parents adopt Kit, outwit Malefetta, and even free the fleas. The colorful artwork, lively in composition and impressionistic in style, gracefully interprets the setting, the characters, and the story. Although most children will have no knowledge of the era, Little Kit is such a sympathetic character and the flea circus so intriguing, they'll be caught up in the adventure immediately. A particularly appealing choice because there's as much in the text as there is in the art.

Susan Dove Lempke

SOURCE: A review of *Little Kit; or, The Industrious Flea Circus Girl,* in *Bulletin of the Center for Children's Books,* Vol. 48, No. 6, February, 1995, p. 208.

Kit is a young girl who sells flowers to keep herself alive in Victorian London. When "Professor" Malefetta comes offering "a bed, meals, a few pence for hard work—and the company of artists," she leaps at the chance, taking advantage of the fact that Malefetta thinks she is a boy. At first she is disappointed that the "artists" turn out to be costumed fleas, but they amaze her with their act, and she begins to sympathize with the "poor, exhausted little creatures" and eventually runs away, taking the fleas with her. Readers will need to take this for the Victorian melodrama it is and to accept melodramatic conventions in plot and pictures to properly enjoy it. McCully's good people have lovely faces and beautiful hair, and the evil characters have twisted faces and missing teeth. For heroes and villains alike, her watercolors are lushly glowing; pastel highlights burnish Kit's golden hair. Each illustration holds meticulous historical detail without ever being busy. McCully's notes on the verso of the title page give background information on flea circuses, which one might otherwise be tempted to disbelieve. This makes a fine companion to McCully's previous costume dramas such as the Caldecott winner *Mirette on the High Wire.*

Kay E. Vandergrift

SOURCE: A review of *Little Kit; or, The Industrious Flea Circus Girl,* in *School Library Journal,* Vol. 41, No. 10, October, 1995, p. 108.

Little Kit, an orphan, lives with her extended street-family in mid-19th-century London. Offered a job by Professor Malefetta, who has mistaken her for a boy, she leaves to work with his traveling flea circus and develops a fondness for the cruelly treated insects. Finally, after personally enduring the professor's abuse throughout their

tour of the countryside, Kit makes a new friend, Nell, and escapes to find a home with a loving farm family. McCully is not completely successful in blending the three major events into a whole, as there is not enough development of the first part to evoke empathy for Kit. The illustrations of the fleas are few but, in one, their size is overly large and their costumes are more visually elaborate than would have been possible with the pasted papers ordinarily used to "dress" these insects. The illustrations are watercolors with pastel highlights and have a darker tone than is usual with this medium but somehow convey a gentleness, in spite of the characterization of Malefetta and his evil ways. McCully is obviously concerned about the horrors of child labor in Victorian England but somehow she fails to convince readers to care as passionately. As a story, this seems too romanticized to carry such weighty content.

📖 THE PIRATE QUEEN (1995)

Susan Dove Lempke

SOURCE: A review of *The Pirate Queen,* in *Bulletin of the Center for Children's Books,* Vol. 49, No. 2, October, 1995, p. 62.

Despite the similarity in titles, McCully's work differs entirely in subject and approach from Jane Yolen's recent book *The Pirate Queens.* McCully's attention to historical fiction (as shown in **Mirette on the High Wire,** and **Little Kit,**) turns now to fictionalized history in this portrait of real female pirate Grania O'Malley. Born to a powerful seafaring and pirating family, Grania shows her strong will and ferocity from an early age, and by sixteen she has married and taken charge of her husband's family fleet. Battles, imprisonment, the deaths of two husbands and a son, and the theft of her riches by the British follow, until the "old sea queen" petitions "another woman warrior," Elizabeth I, for justice. Although the writing is somewhat desultory, the story's richness is vividly translated in McCully's paintings, which vary from the serenity of the Irish landscape and quiet seas to the raging turbulence of a wild ocean and swirling battle scenes: one particularly noteworthy pairing shows an angelic Grania nursing her newborn son below deck and then coming up to fight Turkish pirates with great fierceness. McCully masterfully ages Grania from childhood to maturity, and if she has chosen a historic figure who is the modern day equivalent of a mob kingpin, Grania O'Malley certainly is a gripping one.

Publishers Weekly

SOURCE: A review of *The Pirate Queen,* in *Publishers Weekly,* Vol. 242, No. 41, October 9, 1995, p. 85.

Gifted at breathing life into a remote past, Caldecott Medalist McCully once again reaches into the grab bag of history—and unabashedly embroidered legend—emerging with this swashbuckling tale of Grania O'Malley, Ireland's famed lady pirate. Her larger-than-life career is chronicled here from birth in 1530 (her mother reputedly noted that the babe had "the light of the sea in her eyes") and early days sailing and marauding with her father, through marriage and childbirth (on the high seas of course), building and losing an empire (half a dozen castles), imprisonment and, finally, meeting her worthy contemporary, Elizabeth I of England, to whom she pleaded her case and won her bold gamble to return to the high seas. McCully writes with great flair, and her sweeping watercolors capitalize on the historical drama. Whether depicting the misty Irish seas or an exciting shipboard melee, her artwork bestows on Grania's life the big-screen effect it deserves. What a woman, what a tale. Hollywood, are you listening?

Kirkus Reviews

SOURCE: A review of *The Pirate Queen*, in *Kirkus Reviews*, Vol. LXIII, No. 20, October 15, 1995, p. 1496.

Many male pirates have fared less well in stories than Grania O'Malley, 16th-century female swashbuckler, who is presented in a consistently glamorous, if not outright admiring, light. Although she is depicted as robber and murderer, these aren't shown to be negative traits; McCully merely concedes that O'Malley "sided with the power of the moment, English or Irish, as long as it furthered her own purpose." Ireland's travails at the hands of England are downplayed; without this background, readers may not comprehend O'Malley's political motives, only her marauding ones. The sweeping, entertaining narrative is accompanied by McCully's characteristically bold, beautiful paintings. In other words, readers old enough to grapple with the moral issues will love it.

Wendy Lukehart

SOURCE: A review of *The Pirate Queen*, in *School Library Journal*, Vol. 41, No. 11, November, 1995, pp. 91-2.

This story of Irish swashbuckler Grania O'Malley is culled from both legend and history (an author's note provides clarification). McCully introduces a 16th-century heroine who will intrigue youngsters and who will offer educators an alternative to what is traditionally presented as a male "occupation." Grania's unique mixture of brains and brawn was revealed at an early age through her fluent Latin, her ability to outdance and outgamble any of the sailors, and through a courageous act that saved her father's life. Nothing deterred her. A day after her son was born at sea, Grania "exchanged the babe for a blunderbuss . . . and burst onto the deck" in the midst of a Turkish raid. At the pinnacle of her success, the fearless marauder met her match in an English governor, hired to subdue the Irish. The climax poses the pirate queen in a face-off with Queen Elizabeth I. Windswept hair, leaping figures, blurred outlines, and a liberal use of white highlights pack the paint-

ings with motion and energy that propel the adventures. It is interesting to note that the title appears in the same year as Jane Yolen's *The Ballad of the Pirate Queens*. While the two books differ in specific subject, in literary form, and in artistic style, they certainly invite comparison and pairing. Brave students and teachers will want to read both.

Carolyn Phelan

SOURCE: A review of *The Pirate Queen*, in *Booklist*, Vol. 42, No. 6, November 15, 1995, p. 562.

This handsome picture book introduces a colorful figure in Irish history. Born in 1530, Grania O'Malley took to the sea as a child, learning her father's trade of seafaring (and piracy) and saving his life in a battle with English buccaneers. She later married, had children, led her own ships, and built her own kingdom in Clew Bay. Captured and released by the English, she traveled to London, met Queen Elizabeth, and formed an alliance that granted Grania the right to her lands and "to defend the Crown with fire and sword." Rich with color and the effects of light on seascapes, landscapes, and people, the artwork makes the most of the story's dramatic content. Children intrigued by pirates will enjoy McCully's unusual picture book, which offers some insight into the history behind the legend and illuminates more than the life of Grania O'Malley.

THE BOBBIN GIRL (1996)

Kirkus Reviews

SOURCE: A review of *The Bobbin Girl*, in *Kirkus Reviews*, Vol. LXIV, No. 3, February 1, 1996, p. 230.

Rebecca Putney, "Bobbin Girl," gazes out from the cover of this exceptional work and draws readers into the fascinating lives of the young women who were part of the unique social and industrial milieu of the mills in 19th-century Lowell, Massachusetts.

Rebecca, ten, works at the mill to help her mother's finances. The excitement of employment—of young, independent women living, working, and learning together—is effectively contrasted with the need, ultimately, to strike. Judith, an older girl whom Rebecca admires, inspires the work stoppage; Rebecca decides for herself whether she, too, will struggle for better working conditions. Exquisite watercolors are perfectly integrated into the text, extending it and amplifying it. Many marvelous spreads—workers filing into the imposing factory, girls gathered in a boardinghouse parlor, an outdoor rally, and, especially, a tumble of girls rushing down stairs and out of the factory into the light—beckon readers into another era. A careful author's note offers background; this is a perfect classroom companion to Katherine Paterson's *Lyddie*. Some will say McCully has surpassed herself.

Carolyn Noah

SOURCE: A review of *The Bobbin Girl,* in *School Library Journal,* Vol. 42, No. 4, April, 1996, p. 114.

This tale of child labor, early efforts to organize against unfair employers, and human courage is based on the true story of Harriet Hanson Robinson, whose mother ran a mill boardinghouse in 19th-century Lowell, MA. It tells of Rebecca Putney, a 10-year-old bobbin girl who follows the lead of an older firebrand and walks out of the textile mill in protest of a pay cut. The house provides the context to move the plot because it's there that the women talk about their goals and conditions. McCully's straightforward narrative is told in the third person with substantial dialogue. The artwork, realistic watercolors, supports the narrative but does little to move the story forward. Though crowd scenes offer opportunities for drama, the composition is somewhat static. Not all of the human figures are well-rendered. Some spreads are compelling, as in the after-dinner hours when the women sit around the fire, one wearily soaking her feet. Another striking scene shows one woman's collapse in the hazy spinning room. Despite Rebecca's central position in the narrative, she is primarily an observer and reporter and never really comes to life. Though this entry offers a valuable slice of history and will be useful for curriculum support, it lacks vitality of its own.

Carolyn Phelan

SOURCE: A review of *The Bobbin Girl,* in *Booklist,* Vol. 92, No. 16, April 15, 1996, p. 1439.

When her mother's income from the boarding-house no longer covers their expenses, 10-year-old Rebecca helps out by working as a bobbin girl at the local textile mill. The young women who board with Mrs. Putney endure the mill's bad air, loud machinery, high injury rate, and low wages in the hope of improving their lot, but when the mill owners threaten to lower their wages, the mill workers stage a "turnout," refusing to work. Although the protest fails, young Rebecca is proud of doing the right thing and vows to carry on the struggle. A Lowell, Massachusetts, textile mill in the 1830s may be an unlikely setting for a picture book, even one for older readers, but McCully weaves historical facts and fictional characters into an intriguing story. The author's note details the background, incidents, and people who inspired the book. Beautifully composed watercolor paintings give a vivid impression of America in the 1830s and bring the period to life. A useful book for history units.

Publishers Weekly

SOURCE: A review of *The Bobbin Girl,* in *Publishers Weekly,* Vol. 243, No. 23, June 3, 1996, p. 83.

Caldecott Medalist McCully spins an engrossing, fact-based tale with feminism and fair labor practices at its heart. Ten-year-old Rebecca supplements her family's meager income by toiling as a "bobbin girl" in 1830s New England. She is one of the thousands of girls and women who endure 13½-hour days in the stuffy textile mills of Lowell, Mass., the City of Spindles. Rebecca sees first-hand the courage of her co-workers, who all share a dream of building a better life with the money they earn. She also observes the illnesses, injuries and anxiety caused by the harsh conditions and callous mill owners. When a decrease in wages is announced, the mill girls rally to stage a "turn out" (strike) and protest their predicament. McCully deftly weaves feminist themes into her spirited text, and her meaty author's note places her story in context. Her characters speak of self-reliance and education; they read and attend lectures whenever possible. The courage and ambition these role models inspire in Rebecca are palpable. Rough-edged watercolors, frequently awash in gray light, convey the often oppressive mood of an industrial town of the time. The shawled and bonneted women and an abundance of other period details add further historical depth.

Additional coverage of McCully's life and career is contained in the following sources published by Gale Research: *Major Authors and Illustrators for Children and Young Adults; Something about the Author,* Vol. 76; and *Something about the Author Autobiography Series,* Vol. 7.

Ann Rinaldi

1934-

(Born Ann Feis) American author of historical fiction for young people.

Major works include *Wolf by the Ears* (1991), *A Break with Charity: A Story of the Salem Witch Trials* (1992), the "Quilt" trilogy, *Hang a Thousand Trees with Ribbons: The Story of Phillis Wheatley* (1996), *The Second Bend in the River* (1997).

INTRODUCTION

Rinaldi, the author of twenty novels for young adults, sixteen of which are historical, is best known for weaving engaging fictional narratives into factual events of American Colonial and Civil War history. Praised for both literary soundness and painstakingly researched historical settings, her fiction is at once an inquiry into themes discussed in high school classrooms as well as those in history. Rinaldi's novels, often characterized as "coming of age," follow an intricate plot in which the protagonist—usually a female teenager—must make a consequential and personal decision relating to a public issue of history. Rinaldi's characters are unique and spirited; she creates imaginative and authentic first-person witnesses to legendary events. Rinaldi's historical research is thorough—she provides extensive bibliographies of her sources and carefully notes what fiction she has added to the facts, which according to Kay Weisman "strengthens the credibility of the story without diminishing any of its appeal."

Biographical Information

Rinaldi's mother died soon after Ann was born and, after a few happy years living with her aunt and uncle, Rinaldi's father abruptly took Ann to live with her siblings and new stepmother in New Jersey. Perhaps one can get a glimpse of the young writer in the characters which populate her novels. Nicki, the protagonist in her first two novels, is "always observant. [She] should be a writer. [She] gets vibes about people." But Rinaldi's creative inclinations would only percolate during her adolescent years, as she spent her high school and post high school years working as a secretary. In 1960, Ann married Ronald P. Rinaldi and by 1969 had a son and a daughter.

Rinaldi's professional writing career began in 1969 when she landed positions as a columnist and feature writer, first for the *Somerset Messenger Gazette,* and then in 1970 for the *Trentonian.* During these years as a working mother of two, Rinaldi wrote award-winning journalism and found the time to hone her fiction-writing skills, composing several novels. However, not until 1980 did she find suc-

cess in the fiction market, when her short story-turned-novella, *Term Paper,* was published. A sequel, *Promises Are for Keeping,* and *But in the Fall I'm Leaving* appeared soon after, continuing Rinaldi's exploration into the uniquely complex conflicts facing contemporary teens. When her journalism assignments required she cover bicentennial events in Trenton and Princeton and her son began to express a strong interest in military history, Rinaldi was inspired to write her first historical novel, *Time Enough for Drums.* Her literary agent and ten publishers refused to publish it, saying they couldn't give history to young people, but Rinaldi persevered and Holiday House published *Time Enough for Drums* in 1986. Since then, many publishers have created sources of historical fiction for young people and have even established series in the genre for girls. Rinaldi continues to bring history to life for young readers through her writing. She is prolific, publishing two novels a year, and her works have been translated into four languages.

Major Works

Rinaldi candidly presents young people with the topic of

slavery in *Wolf by the Ears,* the story of a light-skinned slave named Harriet Hemings, who may be the daughter of Thomas Jefferson. Promised freedom when she turns twenty-one, Harriet struggles with the decision of whether to remain home or to pass herself off as white and marry a white man. Rinaldi's thorough research for *Wolf by the Ears* is evident by the inclusion of a bibliography and through her portrayal of both her black and white characters' perceptions of slavery and the moral dilemmas it raises. Sister Mary Veronica wrote, "Settings, characters, dialogue, clothing, and actions are all true to the time of Thomas Jefferson." In *A Break with Charity,* Rinaldi effectively addresses the issue of peer pressure, still a prominant concern among young people today, in the context of seventeenth-century Salem, Massachusetts. The story is told in retrospect by Susanna Hawthorne, who longs to be a part of a group of village girls until she learns that they are accusing innocent people of being witches. Afraid to tell lest her own parents be named, Susanna struggles with her feelings of guilt. Rinaldi uses Puritan grammar and diction to impart the restrictiveness of the Puritan culture against which the girls were rebelling. She is also careful to present a large cast of characters to prevent stereotyping: for instance, she portrays ministers who try to stop the trials to counterbalance the ones who encourage the girls to condemn more citizens. Rinaldi also set her "Quilt" trilogy in Massachusetts. The first novel, *A Stitch in Time,* introduces teenager Hannah, who has looked after her family ever since her mother died several years earlier. Even as Hannah worries about her father and wayward siblings, she and her two sisters, Abby and Thankful, work on a quilt whose theme is trust. In the second novel, entitled *Broken Days,* Hannah is an adult living with her teenage niece, Ebie. War between the United States and Great Britain threatens, and Hannah and Ebie's lives are further impacted when a half-Indian girl arrives on their doorstep and claims to be Thankful's daughter. The trilogy, *The Blue Door,* concludes with Abby's granddaughter, Amanda, who travels to visit her great-grandfather. The three books work well as a series but can also stand on their own. The issue of the poor working conditions in the cotton mills is threaded through all three novels, as well as the unifying theme of the quilt.

Rinaldi imparts what life in Boston was like just prior to the Revolutionary War while she tells African-American poet Phillis Wheatley's story in *Hang a Thousand Trees with Ribbons.* The novel covers Phillis Wheatley's life from the age of seven until she is about twenty-one. Rinaldi compares Phillis Wheatley's African family and life there as a free person, with her American one and her status as a literate slave, allowing readers to note the cultural differences. The romance of teenage settler Rebecca Galloway with Shawnee chief Tecumseh is the focus of *The Second Bend in the River.* Rebecca narrates the novel which covers fifteen years, beginning when she first met the diplomatic leader at the age of seven and concluding when she learns of Tecumseh's death. Through her characters' use of vocabulary from the pioneer times, her description of such details as colonial wedding traditions, and her inclusion of the events that led to the War of 1812, Rinaldi portrays a clear view of frontier life.

Awards

Rinaldi received first place New Jersey Press awards from the New Jersey Press Association in 1978 and 1989, and several second place awards in subsequent years for her newspaper columns. She has also won a National History Award from the Daughters of the American Revolution for her historical novels which "bring history to life." *But in the Fall I'm Leaving* was selected as a Notable Children's Trade Book in the Field of Social Studies by the joint committee of the National Council for Social Studies and the Children's Book Coucil. *Time Enough for Drums* was selected one of the American Library Association's Best Books for Young Adults in 1986 and was named a Junior Literary Guild selection. Most of her historical novels have been named Notable American Library Association's Best Books for Young Adults. *Wolf by the Ears* was cited as an American Library Association's "Best of the Best" in Young Adult literature, as well as given the Best Book Award, senior division, from the Pacific Northwest Library Association in 1994 and the M. Jerry Weiss Book award for 1998.

TITLE COMMENTARY

📖 *TERM PAPER* (1980)

Zena Sutherland

SOURCE: A review of *Term Paper,* in *Bulletin of the Center for Children's Books,* Vol. 34, No. 2, October, 1980, p. 39.

Nicki is a high school freshman who's dismayed, when her teacher is hospitalized, to find that her much-older brother Tony, also on the faculty, is taking over her English class. The story she writes is Tony's assignment: her term paper is to be an attempt to get Nicki to face her father's death, which she's refused to talk about. What emerges is not just Nicki's viewpoint of family affairs and relationships, but a tender story of the loving care and sacrifice that Tony, his wife, and another brother have made for the little sister they've raised (their mother died at Nicki's birth, their father took little responsibility) and of the way in which Nicki matures as she comes to understand the stresses on her family. The characterization and dialogue are strong, the writing style and plot development consistently structured and paced.

Publishers Weekly

SOURCE: A review of *Term Paper,* in *Publishers Weekly,* Vol. 218, No. 18, October 13, 1980, p. 86.

For orphaned Nicki DeBonis, living with her brother Tony

and his wife Carol is fine. She loves them both but finds it hard to accept another situation, Tony's assignment as teacher of her freshman English class. Aware of his young sister's hangups, Tony orders her—on pain of failing the semester—to write a term paper venting her feelings. Nicki pours into the composition revelations about her father: his callous treatment of his children, including drug-dependent Larry, the older DeBonis son; the mistress the father had carried on with for years; the immediate cause of the man's death, a quarrel with Nicki; etc. Rinaldi's first novel is impressive, although she tends to make the good guys' hats improbably white and to resolve the family's knotty troubles a bit too easily.

Patt Parsells Kent

SOURCE: A review of *Term Paper*, in *Children's Book Review Service*, Vol. 9, No. 6, Winter, 1981, p. 49.

Term Paper is the story of Nicki DeBonis, a sad thirteen-year-old whose family feelings are turning to guilt. Her mother is dead, and her father seems to be indifferent to her tremendous need to be loved. Whenever she tries to explain this, an argument always ensues. During one of these arguments, her father suffers a fatal heart attack. Nicki believes herself responsible. Her dilemma, who to turn to and how to deal with such deep-seated guilt, makes for a tender and meaningful book. The other people in her life—an older brother and his alcoholic wife, an eccentric aunt, and her busy medical-student brother— are not easy obstacles to overcome. Forcing someone to listen to her is Nicki's biggest task, and she gives it her all.

Mary K. Chelton

SOURCE: A review of *Term Paper*, in *Voice of Youth Advocates*, Vol. 3, No. 6, February, 1981, pp. 32-3.

Teenage Nicki writes her feelings about her father's death in a "term paper" for her brother who is her substitute English teacher for a semester. Many of her problems have to do with being torn between disliking her real father and resisting her brother's surrogate, strict parenting. There are a variety of family problems which seem preposterous listed in a review—a mistress revealed at graveside, another brother popping pills from the hospital where he's a doctor, an eccentric aunt who undermines Nicki's affection for her brother and her acceptance of her father, etc. but which work in the story. The writing has some minor awkwardness common in first novels, but the sense of a family trying to cope and accept each other is very strong. Sex role attitudes are traditional but logical in context, and the reader is delighted when poor Nicki finally throws the cathartic tantrum which clears the air. Since the relationships are more well-rounded than most, this novel may avoid the trap of being labelled merely "a death book," and future efforts from the author will be worth waiting for if this is an indication of her talent.

PROMISES ARE FOR KEEPING (1982)

Jennifer Brown

SOURCE: A review of *Promises Are for Keeping*, in *Children's Book Review Service*, Vol. 10, No. 12, Spring, 1982, p. 119.

Nicki has an unusually bad case of adolescence. Her older brothers, who are her legal guardians and appear to have given her a loving upbringing, are suddenly her enemies, she feels. The fact that she sneaks out of the house for a date, steals birth-control pills for a friend from her brother, a doctor, and takes part in a good many other irresponsible acts, could make enemies out of anyone. I found Nicki an unsympathetic, spoiled character, yet she does share other teenagers' problems and the book is well written. Recommended if your collection needs this type of fiction.

Will Manley

SOURCE: A review of *Promises Are for Keeping*, in *School Library Journal*, Vol. 28, No. 8, April, 1982, p. 84.

This is a continuation of the story of Nicki DeBonis, to whom readers were introduced in *Term Paper*. Fifteen-year-old Nicki seems a nice enough kid, but for some reason she has constant bad luck. She's continually getting into trouble and raising the ire of her two brother-guardians, Tony, a record-breaking high-school football coach, and Larry, a sort of small-town version of Dr. Ben Casey. The book contains the usual formula of drugs, death, crime, sex, abortion and growing pains that are found in the plots of many YA novels today, and so at first glance would seem to be nothing special. However, the characters, especially the adults, are more interesting and much better developed than in most books of this type. Also, the author is particularly adept at dealing with the perennial teen problem of peer pressure. In addition to these strengths the book has a well-crafted ending that ties together all the loose ends of a helter-skelter plot in a most satisfying way.

Zena Sutherland

SOURCE: A review of *Promises Are for Keeping*, in *Bulletin of the Center for Children's Books*, Vol. 35, No. 10, June, 1982, p. 196.

In a sequel to *Term Paper* Nicki is in trouble because of her lack of responsibility; Larry, a doctor who is one of the two older brothers who are her guardians, is already irate because a silly friend has made a prankish telephone call, resulting in a tapped line—and when he discovers that Nicki has taken some birth control pills from his office, Larry is both angry and heartsick. (They're for a friend, but Nicki can't tell him that.) As a corrective to her rebellious behaviour, Nicki is ordered to begin working as a hospital volunteer. From that and other experiences Nicki begins to understand that in the complexities of human relationships there cannot be abuse, there must be forgiveness, and one must take responsibility for one's behavior. This is written with consistency in characterization and a fluent style with natural dialogue, but it is a bit overcrowded in plot: the friend for whom Nicki has taken the pills becomes pregnant, has an abortion, and becomes ill; Larry and his girl break up; a friend who is on probation breaks his parole at Nicki's instigation, and Nicki overhears some criminals threatening Larry, a sequence that ends with the police shooting the man who has a gun in Larry's ribs.

Mary K. Chelton

SOURCE: A review of *Promises Are for Keeping,* in *Voice of Youth Advocates,* Vol. 5, No. 3, August, 1982, p. 36.

In this sequel to **Term Paper,** Nicki is now 15 but not much smarter. Parenting is now shared by her two older brothers, Tony the school coach, and Larry now practicing medicine. Through a sequence of stupid actions, Nicki loses her brother Larry's trust, only to realize how much he really loves her when she saves him by calling the police when he is being robbed. Until then, she exhibits amazingly thoughtless, although typical, adolescent behavior. She steals birth control pills from Larry's office for a friend; believes rumors that her boyfriend was secretly fathered by Tony, and is generally obnoxious and resentful of attempts to control her. The sequel stands well on its own merit without belaboring the plot of the first book, and Rinaldi is extremely skilled at depicting a much more typical kid than many in teen novels, not to mention the ethnic and class setting of a New Jersey Italian family of a certain type. The real problem is whether Nicki's reality makes her unbearable for 187 pages, in the midst of a somewhat crowded plot. For me, she got a little stale; for readers like her, she may not. I hope so, because, despite its structural flaws, Rinaldi still has a freshness some of the more prolific authors of the genre now achieve only rarely. Nicki sounds like a real kid, not an imitation.

BUT IN THE FALL I'M LEAVING (1985)

Publishers Weekly

SOURCE: A review of *But in the Fall I'm Leaving,* in *Publishers Weekly,* Vol. 227, No. 23, June 7, 1985, p. 81.

Having written such outstanding novels as **Term Paper** and **Promises Are for Keeping,** Rinaldi seems to have let her new story get out of hand. Rebellious Brieanna (Brie) McQuade is the narrator of numbingly convoluted happenings, mostly unbelievable. Brie wants to leave her stern father and fly to California to live with the mother who had deserted the family when the girl was two. In the meantime, she has to work for civic-minded Miss Emily whose house Brie had spray-painted on a dare. Mr. Mc-

Quade agrees with the judge who decides Brie's punishment, but it's obvious that her father worries about the result of the girl's connection with Miss Emily. Brie depends on her brother Kevin, a priest, for moral support, although he tries to make her understand that their father loves her, and that going to stay with their mother would be a mistake. Feeling there is a secret about Miss Emily's effects on her father, Brie begs Kevin to tell her what it is, but he refuses. Why she doesn't figure it out, as any reader will easily, is the real mystery. There are also talky subplots, deplorable usages like, "I'm as good as her" (as her what? one wonders) and other disappointments in the book.

Kathryn M. Weisman

SOURCE: A review of *But in the Fall I'm Leaving,* in *School Library Journal,* Vol. 31, No. 10, August, 1985, pp. 80-1.

Arrested for spray painting an elderly woman's house, 14-year-old Brie McQuade is sentenced to spend her free time working for Miss Emily. Brie's father is upset, not so much because of the deed itself, but because of the compromising position it has placed him in as owner of the town's newspaper. Older brother Kevin, a priest in the slums of Newark, is afraid that Brie will be influenced and corrupted by Miss Emily and her "wasteful middle class preoccupations." Brie, for her part, is sorry about the vandalism, depressed because her mother does not have time for her and upset that her father is pre-occupied with his work (especially his latest project, exposing and closing up the local red light district, which causes a classmate's father's suicide). She decides that all her problems will be solved, however, in the fall, when she will leave her father to live with her mother in California. Brie is basically a good kid who succumbs occasionally to peer pressure and all too frequently to her own temper. She is frequently abrasive with adults, and on several occasions, she is both arrogant and rude. She feels that her father manipulates her with his "soft words," but she in turn manipulates him and Kevin with her own words and actions. The most blatant (and perhaps most unbelievable) manipulation, however, is of Brie herself—nearly everyone in the story is involved in a conspiracy to keep Brie from finding out that Miss Emily is really her maternal grandmother. Some of the characters lack development; Brie's mother is known only through her letters and long distance calls, and Miss Emily does not come to life. However, the other characters are multidimensional. True, this is the stuff of which soap operas are made. But Rinaldi spins a good yarn—and while adults may be too embarrassed to admit that they enjoy such stuff, teens will unabashedly keep turning the pages for more.

Diane C. Donovan

SOURCE: A review of *But in the Fall I'm Leaving,* in *Best Sellers,* Vol. 45, No. 6 September, 1985, p. 240.

The theme may be familiar and even overused: a teenager's dissatisfaction with the father she lives with leads her to idolize her long-absent, long-distance mother; but as with any book, it's the handling and presentation that count, and Rinaldi's ability to turn an ordinary theme into an engrossing, refreshing story makes this title anything but trite.

When Brienna's spray-painting prank attracts the attention and anger of a juvenile judge, who sentences her to months of part-time work for a rich matron whom her father despises, newspaper editor's daughter Brienna incurs her father's wrath.

Her priest-brother Kevin, who has taken a vow of poverty and lives in a slum, is a strong force in her life; but despite his efforts Brie's increasing tension and conflicts with her father lead to her determination to leave home to stay with her mother in California.

Her father's involvement with another woman whom Brie dislikes, his tensions over her (spoiled) behavior and actions, and his creation of an exposé which renews her conflicts with her school friends heighten into a situation in which Brie cannot avoid her personal 'black pit of depression'; and when her mother calls with shocking news at a time when Brie's world is crumbling, even her concerned brother cannot help.

This story's protagonist is unusually realistic in a period when themes of parental separation and children's conflicts are so common that readers may initially groan upon seeing yet another title on the topic.

Superior craftsmanship can elevate a mundane theme to a blockbuster: could *Gone With the Wind,* for example, be categorized as "just another romance" despite its soap opera-type passions? No; and neither can *But In the Fall I'm Leaving* be dismissed as "just another story of a youth's broken home."

TIME ENOUGH FOR DRUMS (1986)

Kirkus Reviews

SOURCE: A review of *Time Enough for Drums,* in *Kirkus Reviews,* Vol. LIV, No. 7, April 1, 1986, p. 552.

Between 1775 and 1781 Jemima Emerson grew from a rebellious child to a courageous young woman. Set in Trenton, NJ, during the American Revolution, her story tells how the war touched life around her.

At 15, spirited and independent Jemima is eager to be involved in what is going on—too eager in the minds of her father and her tutor, John Reid. As war clouds gather, Jemima takes her place as a patriot with her family. Slowly Jemima learns just how deep the family's involvement is: her mother writes essays urging support for the Colonial cause, and her father will not sell anything British in his shop. But why are they so close to John Reid, a Tory? Jemima resents his firmness with her and even more his

politics, but comes to realize two things: that John is a spy for the Colonies and that they love each other. Jemima's life is filled with pain: her father is killed, her mother withdraws from the world, she worries about her brothers and John, and through it all she must manage the house and shop. But after much travail, all ends well; Jemima is ready to begin anew with John.

A stirring book which brings history to life accurately. Rinaldi's enthusiasm for her subject is catching.

Therese Bigelow

SOURCE: A review of *Time Enough for Drums,* in *School Library Journal,* Vol. 32, No. 9, May, 1986, pp. 108-09.

Jemima Emerson witnesses the events of the Revolutionary War as they affect her family and home town of Trenton, N.J. She is a feisty young lady whose family represents the differing positions of the colonies' fight for independence. Her older sister is married to a British officer, her paternal grandfather works for Indian justice and the cause of independence, her maternal grandfather is a Tory, her older brother an officer in Washington's army, and her mother writes pseudonymous patriotic letters to the newspaper. Jemima is tutored by John Reid, a supposed Tory who is really a spy for Washington, with whom she clashes as he tries to make her a proper young lady. Gradually her feelings for Reid change from animosity to love. The book is a good introduction to the causes and effects of the war but does not have the ring of veracity as does *My Brother Sam Is Dead* by James and Christopher Collier. Problems arise with the use of first person in providing Jemima with information to report to readers. Lucy the house slave knows that the Hessian grenadiers had killed more American soldiers than any other Hessian unit on American soil. How Lucy became privy to this evaluation is not explained. Another issue that does not sit well is Reid's manipulation of Jemima. This might have been standard treatment for the period or an element borrowed from paperback historical romances, but it lessens the appeal of Jemima as the heroine of the story. Twentieth century prejudice aside, readers will share the events of the war and be rewarded with a better understanding of the War for Independence.

Hazel Rochman

SOURCE: A review of *Time Enough for Drums,* in *Booklist,* Vol. 82, No. 17, May 1, 1986, p. 1304.

Jemima Emerson grows from a spoiled 15-year-old girl to a mature woman during the revolutionary war. As her brothers go off to fight for the Americans and her unpleasant sister marries a British officer, Jemima must stay home in Trenton, New Jersey, smarting under the discipline of her stern tutor, John Reid, and attracted to him despite her contempt for his pro-British sympathies. But of course John is not really a Tory; he's a spy for the Americans, and he and Jemima declare their love as the war comes closer. The characters have little depth; and, despite Rinaldi's meticulous research (discussed in a note at the end), most of the historical events seem to happen far in the background. Even when Jemima's father is killed, her mother breaks down, and enemy soldiers are quartered in her home, the focus is on Jemima's relationship with John. A light, enjoyable historical romance, complete with a masterful, handsome hero taming the spirited young girl into submission for her own good.

Publishers Weekly

SOURCE: A review of *Time Enough for Drums,* in *Publishers Weekly,* Vol. 229, No. 22, May 30, 1986, p. 69.

Set in Trenton, N.J. during the American Revolution, this well-plotted historical romance has been written with an excellent feel for the period. Jemima (Jem) Emerson, 15, is constantly at loggerheads with her handsome, strict, Tory tutor, John Reid. In a town of divided loyalties, the Emersons are avid patriots. During the war, they endure death, privation, Hessians and Redcoats. Jem grows up and falls in love with Reid, who is not *quite* the stuffy Royalist he appears. The Emersons are an intelligent, loving and likable family. But as Jem's childish feistiness mellows into womanly demureness, it almost seems as if Reid has tutored her solely to prepare her to be a good wife for him. Readers will find their romance involving, but may wish that Jem had a bit more substance.

THE GOOD SIDE OF MY HEART (1987)

Zena Sutherland

SOURCE: A review of *The Good Side of My Heart,* in *Bulletin of the Center for Children's Books,* Vol. 40, No. 10, June, 1987, p. 195.

Sturm und Drang in the life of a 16-year-old is revealed by the protagonist, Brie, as she wrestles with the problems of a) having fallen in love with a handsome senior who proves to be a homosexual (readers will probably guess this although Brie does not) and b) being involved in knowledge of a peer drug pusher and his stash. (She knows but can't tell because others—as innocent as she—would suffer.) There's also the up/down relationship with strict Daddy, and the anguished relationship with Kevin, an older brother who is a priest and is thinking of leaving the priesthood. These all give rise to a series of tediously repetitive scenes of introspection or confrontation, at the end of which all problems seem to be solved: purged by confessing, Brie in turn (although not in the confessional) gives Kevin solace and hope; Brie and her quondam love become friends; the pusher calls Brie and says he'll keep her out of it; Brie accepts Daddy's marriage to a woman with whom he has long had an affair. The quality of characterization is variable, the plot is turgid, and the writing style, less controlled than it has been in earlier books by Rinaldi, is unfortunately larded with "wanna," "gonna," "Hadda," and similar phonetic spellings, obtrusive and not always used with consistency.

Cynthia K. Leibold

SOURCE: A review of *The Good Side of My Heart,* in *School Library Journal,* Vol. 33, No. 11, August, 1987, p. 98.

Rinaldi again writes of Brieanna McQuade, the spirited female protagonist introduced in *But in the Fall I'm Leaving.* In this new episode Brie, now 16, begins dating Joshua Falcone, her best friend's brother. While he seems thoughtful and charming, he has a bad reputation—a sex scandal resulting in his expulsion from a military school. Forbidden by her father to see Josh outside of school, Brie meets him secretly, hoping that the relationship will progress beyond friendship. Meanwhile her older brother and confidante Kevin is experiencing doubts about remaining in the priesthood. Brie presses Josh for romantic attention, forcing him to reveal that the scandal had involved him and the colonel's son, not his daughter. Feeling both abandoned and betrayed, Brie confronts the issue of Josh's homosexuality in a lengthy confessional with Kevin. Subsequently, she seeks to reestablish her friendship with Josh and then offers strength to Kevin when he needs it most. Brie's submission to peer pressure, her uncontrolled temper, and her defiance of parental discipline remain intact from the first book. There is nothing fresh, creative, or unique here, but the story line moves quickly and reads easily—except for the lengthy confessional dialogue. This novel will appeal most to readers already familiar with the McQuade family; however, it can stand alone.

Clara G. Hoover

SOURCE: A review of *The Good Side of My Heart,* in *Voice of Youth Advocates,* Vol. 10, No. 3, August, 1987, pp. 122-23.

Despite her father's disapproval and her best friend Gina's warnings, Brie McQuade (from Rinaldi's earlier book *But in the Fall I'm Leaving*) dates Gina's brother, Josh Falcone. On an outing with Josh and several other seniors, 16 year old Brie drinks several beers to prove that she's not too straight-laced just because her older brother Kev is a priest. Brie has always been able to talk openly with her father, but can't tell him about a boy who is selling drugs and stashing them on her family's property. Even though her father grounds her, Brie sneaks out of the house to be with Josh.

Brie is troubled that despite her growing physical attraction for Josh, he never kisses her or seems to have any sexual attraction for her. When she asks Josh to kiss her, he's forced to tell her that he's a homosexual. He wants her to be his friend, but not in a romantic way. Brie can't handle this. She feels betrayed and is unwilling to forgive him. She finally confesses to her brother. As a result Brie better understands herself and Josh. She accepts him as a close friend. She also develops a deeper understanding of Kev who has his own self-doubts about being a priest.

The theme of this well written novel is commitment after disillusionment. The author's style is conversational and introspective. The characters are well developed. YAs will easily identify with the conflict, self-doubt, and resolution. The tone is positive. Despite their age differences and conflicting roles, it's refreshing to observe Brie, Kev, Josh, and Mr. McQuade work out their individual and collective problems, and through open discussion develop deeper understanding of, and love for, each other.

Like Kerr's *Night Kites* and Scoppettone's *Trying Hard to Hear You*, this book depicts attitudes towards homosexuality, but its tone is not tragic. Rinaldi expresses more hope.

📖 *THE LAST SILK DRESS* (1988)

Kirkus Reviews

SOURCE: A review of *The Last Silk Dress,* in *Kirkus Reviews,* Vol. LVI, No. 4, February 15, 1988, p. 283.

The horrors of the Civil War come alive in this intense, intricate story of the consciousness-raising of a young girl.

Susan Chilmark is the daughter of a prominent Richmond iron merchant and a hysterical, obsessive mother who upholds the nobility of the Southern cause with every breath. Susan, whose father has told her to be true to herself, finds her own ways of being patriotic—including gathering silk dresses to be made into an observation balloon. But after reuniting with a black-sheep brother and helping to nurse the wounded, she begins to have strong doubts about the "Cause," and eventually betrays her "own" balloon to the Yankees to express her loathing for the South's hypocrisy. Her actions endanger people she loves and completely estrange her from her home and mother; her brother helps her escape to the North.

Susan's transition from girl to thinking young woman is well developed, although her betrayal of the balloon is disturbingly treasonous. Many other ethical issues are also raised in this lengthy adventure, including adultery, prostitution, and the social stratification of the South; it is the issue of miscegenation that finally disillusions Susan. The Civil War background is exceptionally well portrayed.

Zena Sutherland

SOURCE: A review of *The Last Silk Dress,* in *The New York Times Book Review,* April 10, 1988, p. 38.

At the beginning of 1861, the year covered by this historical novel, Susan Chilmark is 14, and as ardent a Confederate supporter as any other girl of "good" family in Rich-

mond. Susan adores her father and has a love/hate relationship with her neurotic, abusive mother, who calls her only daughter a "Yankee brat." She is comforted by the family's black slave, Rhody, and is deeply curious about her older brother, Lucien, who has long been banished from the family. Lucien, who has a rakish Rhett Butler aura, is spurned by Richmond society because he will not enlist, although he considers himself a true Southerner and hopes to help rebuild the South at the end of a war he considers lost.

In *The Last Silk Dress* Ann Rinaldi, a novelist and newspaper columnist, uses Susan, the innocent adolescent, to convey a message about corruption and discrimination in Southern society. Shortly after her father's death Susan learns that he was not her natural father. Her mother had had a brief affair with a Yankee professor to spite her husband after learning that he had had a child by a slave woman in the household.

As she talks and listens to Lucien, Susan feels increasing repugnance for the Southern way of life. This rather slowly emerging theme carries the burden of the tale, along with a contrapuntal indictment of war. There is a plot, based on some historical evidence, about the fashioning of a Confederate surveillance balloon from silk dresses donated by patriotic Confederate women (a prefatory note tells readers what is factual and what is fictional in the novel), as well as a secondary story of a budding romance between Susan and a Yankee artist who is a friend of Lucien's.

The development of Susan's awareness of the racial double standard is strong stuff, not often considered in historical or fictional material for young people, and Ms. Rinaldi allows her protagonist's dismay and anger to develop convincingly. The writing is not without flaws—the Yankee artist, a college graduate, often uses bad grammar, Southern accents are indicated erratically and the pace and plot development are uneven. Still, the structure and characterization are strong. *The Last Silk Dress* is interesting not only for its theme and story, but also for the evidence it gives of Ms. Rinaldi's respect for her adolescent audience.

Elizabeth M. Reardon

SOURCE: A review of *The Last Silk Dress,* in *School Library Journal,* Vol. 35, No. 8, May, 1988, pp. 112-13.

This historical novel takes place during the Civil War, in the confederate capital of Richmond. Fourteen-year-old Susan Dobson Chilmark is abused by her mother, who suffers from severe mood swings. Her father is off fighting—and is eventually killed. Her brother, Lucien, is estranged from the family for mysterious reasons. As the novel unfolds, Susan befriends her brother, falls in love with his Yankee friend, tries to sort out her feelings about the war and the "cause," and learns that her beloved father was not really her father. Rinaldi's south is not romanticized—readers see the corruption of the society and its unfair treatment of blacks. Through it all, Susan tries to live by her father's last words to her—do what is right even if it might hurt someone you love. At times, this theme is too obvious; one almost gets tired of hearing Susan recite it. The book is part romance, part historical fiction, and it is more involving as a coming-of-age story set in the past than as historical fiction. It drags a little toward the end, but it should appeal to historical romance buffs, especially those who long to settle down with a big story.

Zena Sutherland

SOURCE: A review of *The Last Silk Dress,* in *Bulletin of the Center for Children's Books,* Vol. 41, No. 11, July-August, 1988, p. 237.

Susan is fourteen, as ardent a supporter of the Confederate cause as were other citizens of Richmond at the time of the Civil War. She adores her father; despairs of ever pleasing the mother who unaccountably calls her a "Yankee brat"; confides in Rhody, the black housekeeper; wonders why there has been a breach between her parents and her older brother Lucien; and conceives the idea of asking women to donate their silk dresses so that the Cause can have an observation balloon as the Yankees do. Rinaldi does a good job of interweaving these elements, a modest love story, and historical details. Although the writing has some flaws (chiefly in the uneven use of phonetically-manifested dialect) it is on the whole stylistically competent, with good pace and momentum, smooth integration of fact and fiction, consistent characterization (including tyrannical behavior by Lucien), and a particularly strong development of the theme. What Rinaldi is concerned with is the relationship between white slave-owners and their abuse and exploitation of black slaves. Susan discovers that her adored father is not her natural father; she is a scorned "Yankee brat" because her mother (emotionally disturbed after the death of a child) had an affair with a Yankee to take revenge on her husband because he fathered a child by a slave. As Susan learns about the prevalence of the latter practice in Southern society, she becomes heartsick and angry. That so serious a theme is adequately treated but does not overbalance the narrative is very impressive. A prefatory note gives information about those parts of the book that are based on fact; a bibliography provides access to the author's sources.

Cynthia L. Beatty

SOURCE: A review of *The Last Silk Dress,* in *Voice of Youth Advocates,* Vol. 11, No. 5, December, 1988, pp. 241-42.

An excellent historical novel based on a little-known incident said to have occurred during the Civil War. The South, according to General James Longstreet, lost a hot air balloon to the North and with it, "the last silk dress in the Confederacy" from which it was made. The author explains in a note how she came to learn of this and ultimately write this fictionalized account of how it may have happened. Included is a three-page bibliography of other books covering the time period of the novel, 1861-1862. Told in the first person by Susan Chilmark, the reader will learn quite a bit of history of the period and what it must have been like to be living then. A modern topic—child abuse—figures quite prominently in Susan's story. As she grows from a naive 14 year old to a knowledgeable young woman, Susan copes with her mother's illness, the death of her beloved father, disclosure of the family secrets, and falling in love with a Yankee. Her life is given direction by one of the last things her father said to her—that sometimes you have to do what you feel is right, even if it hurts someone you love.

WOLF BY THE EARS (1991)

Ilene Cooper

SOURCE: A review of *Wolf by the Ears,* in *Booklist,* Vol. 87, No. 11, February 1, 1991, p. 1125.

Thomas Jefferson once said that in slavery, "we have a wolf by the ears, and we can neither hold him, nor safely let him go. Justice is on one scale, and self-preservation the other." This dichotomy is evident in Jefferson's life: though he disavowed slavery, his home was filled with slaves, including some rumored to be his own children. Rinaldi uses Harriet Hemings, daughter of Jefferson's longtime mistress, Sally, and purportedly his child, as her heroine. Harriet loves her life at Monticello, where she is more servant than slave, but she also anxiously wonders about who her father is. Sally has extracted a promise from Jefferson that all her children will go free at age 21, but Harriet is unsure about taking this liberty and is even more frightened about the possibility that she will have to pass as white to make her way in the world, though in fact because of her ancestry, she is more white than black. The novel is written in diary form, and readers will be not only engrossed by Harriet's decisions, but also caught up in the moral dilemmas facing most of the characters. It is unfortunate that the confused genealogy of the Jefferson family intrudes on the story, at times stopping readers short as they try to remember who's who (though Rinaldi makes a game effort to keep explaining it). Some may also be offended by a statement made by Harriet's betrothed, a white man who is ready to help her pass, in part, because of her lighter skin color: "I'm not saying that because your skin is almost white you should be free while others around here remain slaves. I am saying that when one comes face to face with a person who is almost white and that person is a slave, it underscores the awfulness of the practice we have allowed to come to pass in this country." For the most part, though, Rinaldi writes moving historical fiction, getting inside her characters, both black and white, and showing how slavery distorted their perceptions of themselves and each other. Harriet, her brothers, even Thomas Jefferson cannot really examine themselves as long as they are locked in the dark box of slavery.

Bruce Anne Shook

SOURCE: A review of *Wolf by the Ears,* in *School Library Journal,* Vol. 37, No. 4, April, 1991, pp. 142-43.

This historical novel explores the life of Harriet Hemings, one of Jefferson's household slaves and possibly his daughter. While the character of Harriet is largely fictional, her story is set firmly within an authentic historical context. The plot is revealed through Harriet's diary, a device that occasionally seems forced. A very light-skinned slave, she is favored in the Monticello household where she feels secure and protected. Other less fortunate members of the slave community urge her to make plans to take her freedom when she turns 21, a freedom that Jefferson has promised to all of the children of his supposed mistress, Sally Hemings. It is not until she is almost raped by the drunken husband of Jefferson's granddaughter that Harriet begins to contemplate what life might be like at Monticello after Jefferson dies. Thus, she makes the decision to move to Washington, D.C., and to pass as white. Knowing that this is her best hope for a decent life does not prevent her from feeling guilt over abandoning her race or grief over leaving behind all that she knows and loves. The moral dilemmas Harriet faces are played out against the backdrop of Jefferson's own ambivalence about the institution of slavery. The most telling observation in the novel is that the whites find slavery most repugnant when those enslaved look almost white themselves. Harriet's plight is poignant, and she is a finely drawn, believable character. The racism inherent in the enslavement of Africans is clearly exposed. The evils of slavery appear in a stark light even in the relatively benign environment of Monticello. Exploring the thoughts and feelings of both blacks and whites, this book should provide readers with insights into one of the most significant moral problems in American history.

Publishers Weekly

SOURCE: A review of *Wolf by the Ears,* in *Publishers Weekly,* Vol. 238, No. 16, April 5, 1991, p. 146.

". . . And we can neither hold him, nor safely let him go." Thomas Jefferson's metaphor for slavery is dramatically brought to life through his illegitimate daughter (Rinaldi suggests) by a slave woman. In this thoughtful fictionalization, 19-year-old Harriet Hemings is one of many "nigra servants" on Jefferson's estate. Light-skinned, with red hair, Harriet knows she is different; and although the master has granted the servants' freedom when they reach 21, no one ever suggests that he is their father. Now Harriet must choose between the place and the people she loves and the frightening, often deceitful world of freedom. The subtly crafted style of Harriet's journal entries grows with her as she becomes more aware of the "velvet trap" of her life at Monticello. This is an intelligent yet earthy history that lends insight into the complex feelings surrounding race relations.

Zena Sutherland

SOURCE: A review of *Wolf by the Ears,* in *Bulletin of the Center for Children's Books,* Vol. 44, No. 10, June 1991, pp. 247-48.

The title phrase is taken from a remark by Thomas Jefferson, speaking of slavery: " . . . we have the wolf by the ears, and we can neither hold him, nor safely let him go." Harriet, the narrator, understands very well: she's a favored slave who is approaching the age (of twenty-one) when she will be freed by Jefferson, whom she adores and calls "Master." She believes that she and her brothers are his children. Her mother convinces Harriet that she should agree to make use of her impending freedom and her education by passing as a white woman and marrying a white man, a Northerner who has been smitten by Harriet's charm. Rinaldi presents an issue seldom faced with candor in books for young people, and she deals capably with the facets of the problem through discussions among both black and white characters. There is a trace of contrivance occasionally, but for the most part the novel deals convincingly (if occasionally slowly) with changes in Harriet's attitudes about leaving Monticello and about passing as white. A provocative story.

Sister Mary Veronica

SOURCE: A review of *Wolf by the Ears,* in *Voice of Youth Advocates,* Vol. 14, No. 2, June, 1991, p. 101.

Harriet Hemings, young woman and slave on Monticello at the time of Thomas Jefferson, is living with a mystery. Who is her father? Her mother is a slave, but Harriet's white skin and red hair point to a white father. Various signs seem to indicate that Thomas Jefferson is probably her father. Why has he promised freedom to the Hemings children when they reach age 21? Why does he seem to find their light skin an embarrassment? Why does Jefferson see that a more complete education is given to the Hemings children than to the other slaves at Monticello? Why has he never sold the Hemings when he's sold other slaves? What does it all mean? Harriet's mother won't tell.

Harriet's diary vividly portrays life at Monticello from her privileged point of view. Harriet lives in the "nigra" world and learns its customs and beliefs. After a white man, a guest of Thomas Jefferson, attempts to rape her, she realizes she must leave Monticello as soon as she is able to take her freedom. She makes the hard decision to pass as white. When Jefferson learns of Harriet's decision to "pass," he arranges for her to learn French and other skills which will make her a cultured white woman. Leaving Monticello, Harriet bids farewell to her past, and taking a new name, goes out into the world and passes into it.

A Wolf by the Ears is meditative at times, yet filled with swift and steady action. A long-distance romance adds to the final mystery of the book: What happened to Harriet

Hemings? The wraparound cover art is eye catching, beautifully done, and true to the story. Rinaldi has thoroughly researched her topic and includes a bibliography. The high quality of the author's preparation is evident throughout the book: setting, characters, dialogue, clothing, and actions are all true to the time of Thomas Jefferson. This is a tantalizing book. It is history brought to life by a skillful and imaginative author.

A RIDE INTO MORNING: THE STORY OF TEMPE WICK (1991)

Kirkus Reviews

SOURCE: A review of *A Ride into Morning: The Story of Tempe Wick,* in *Kirkus Reviews,* Vol. LIX, No. 7, April 1, 1991, p. 475.

Written to order for the "Great Episodes" series, a novelization of a legend with as little authenticity as the one about Washington and the cherry tree: how a young woman near Morristown, N.J., hid her horse in her house in order to prevent his being commandeered by mutinous Revolutionary soldiers.

Best here are the author's background notes, scrupulously distinguishing fact from fiction: with minor exceptions, all the characters are historical, but some of their histories have been changed. Most significantly, 14-year-old Mary, Tempe's cousin, has been imported to provide a young narrator since Tempe herself was 22 at the time of the incident. But the novel itself, though crammed with authentic detail, is much less satisfactory. The major characters are inconsistently drawn: Tempe's irascibility and coldness are rationally explained, but sit oddly with her compassion for the hungry crowding her doorstep; Mary is a pastiche of actions contrived to make her a convenient observer. The language is accessible but often clumsy, an uncomfortable blend of period phrases ("must needs") and conspicuous anachronisms. Worst, the philosophical underpinnings are muddled and inadequately developed; e.g., Tempe spends most of the book learning that compromise is morally suspect, but Mary's mentor-brother concludes by explaining that it is a "necessary commodity." Despite the exemplary documentation, second-rate.

Zena Sutherland

SOURCE: A review of *A Ride into Morning: The Story of Tempe Wick,* in *Bulletin of the Center for Children's Books,* Vol. 44, No. 9, May, 1991, p. 225.

The narrator is Mary Cooper, who has been sent by her Tory family to stay with her older cousin Tempe Wick. Since both young women are ardent Patriots, Mary had expected to be welcomed. Tempe, however, is hostile and critical, especially when Mary befriends Tempe's estranged brother Henry. Believed to be mentally ill, Henry is actually helping the cause of independence, his pretended

affliction making him free to wander anywhere. That is important because a Pennsylvania regiment is camped on the Wick property, a New Jersey farm. Rinaldi has done a good job of meshing fictional and historical elements, and her writing style is competent. The pace of the story is uneven, however, and the plot is laded with cumbersome intricacies. An author's note and a bibliography of sources are provided.

Candace Smith

SOURCE: A review of *A Ride into Morning: The Story of Tempe Wick,* in *Booklist,* Vol. 87, No. 22, August, 1991, p. 2141.

The winter of 1781 was bitter for patriot troops camped on the Wick farm in New Jersey. Supplies were scarce, and many of the soldiers and their families were dying of hunger and exposure. Mary Cooper, 14, sent to the farm of her favorite cousin Tempe Wick when she protested her brother's dealings with the British, is thrilled to be in a home so near the action. But the war has changed 22-year-old Tempe. She's still spirited and beautiful, but she's tired of people begging for food, bitter about the death of her father, oppressed by endless farm chores, and weary of the constant compromises needed to stay out of the war. It's only when some discontented soldiers try to commandeer her horse to lead a mutiny that she is forced to take a stand. Feisty Mary Cooper narrates the story, based on the legend of Tempe Wick, who hid her horse inside her house to keep it from rebellious soldiers. With historically grounded characters, such as charismatic General Anthony Wayne, and conflicts between cousins to add tension, the book is a suspenseful read with enough everyday detail to make it realistic and enough adventure to make it exciting. The civilian perspective reminds readers that war is also fought by those at home.

A BREAK WITH CHARITY: A STORY ABOUT THE SALEM WITCH TRIALS (1992)

Kirkus Reviews

SOURCE: A review of *A Break with Charity: A Story about the Salem Witch Trials,* in *Kirkus Reviews,* Vol. LX, No. 14, July 15, 1992, p. 924.

Why, in 1692, did Salem execute 22 citizens accused by hysterical girls? Various causes—political, economic, scientific—have been advanced; Rinaldi makes a plausible case for a combination of these with the repression of a society with few amusements, late marriages, and young adults treated as children. As a wise old woman says here, " . . . the spirit it took to tame this wilderness is so strong it would not bow to the authority of the Puritan covenant . . . They see this . . . as a failure of their vision. So they seek to lay blame."

Rinaldi chooses as narrator Susanna English, ancestor of Nathaniel Hawthorne, fictionalizing her role of a fascinated, horrified observer who's told, early on, by ringleader Ann Putnam that the girls are deliberately seeking attention and power; Susanna keeps silent lest her own family be accused. The device works well as Susanna tries to negotiate with Ann; sees her parents accused despite her promise; falls in love with Magistrate Hathorne's son and persuades him of the "witches'" innocence; is taken in by Joseph Putnam, who is secretly encouraging opposition; and finally shares her knowledge, only to have her certainty challenged by prophecies that, amazingly, come true: " . . . the line is thin between what is fanciful and what is real."

Rinaldi's characterizations aren't subtle, but she has done her research well and fashioned an enthralling, authentic story that makes the results of compounding malicious lies with false confessions of terrified victims tragically believable. Fine historical fiction; Rinaldi at her best. Bibliography; excellent note sorting out fact and fiction.

Carolyn Noah

SOURCE: A review of *A Break with Charity: A Story about the Salem Witch Trials,* in *School Library Journal,* Vol. 38, No. 9, September, 1992, p. 279.

Well researched, this story of the Salem witch trials is told 14 years later from the perspective of a young woman who lingered on the fringes of the bewitched girls' circle in 1692. Susanna English, daughter of a free-thinking Salem family, is both attracted to and frightened by what she sees brewing in Tituba's kitchen. When the group begins to "cry out" on townspeople, one girl admits to Susanna that they are playing a game, seeking freedom from the harsh Puritan code of conduct. As the game gains momentum, the circle begins to believe in its own power. One young woman warns Susanna that if she betrays them, the bewitched girls will accuse her family. In fact, Susanna's family is torn apart, and so is all of Salem. The plot is rich with details and names that will be familiar to those who have read about the trials. However, despite the tumultuous events, the characters remain rigid. Contributing to the formality of the text is the author's use of Puritan diction and grammar. Even Susanna's anguish, as she is torn between her fear of revealing her secret and her sense of responsibility because she is silent, is muted. Nevertheless, *A Break with Charity* portrays an excruciating era in American history from a unique perspective, and it will be enjoyed by readers who enjoy psychology, the supernatural, and history. An excellent companion volume is Ann Petry's *Tituba of Salem Village.*

Margaret M. Bush

SOURCE: A review of *A Break with Charity: A Story about the Salem Witch Trials,* in *The Horn Book Magazine,* Vol. LXVIII, No. 6, November-December, 1992, p. 730.

New facets are revealed in this plausible rendering of the deceit and hysteria that gripped Salem for those few fate-

ful months of 1692. Ann Rinaldi tells the story from the viewpoint of a teenager outside the circle of accusers. Susanna English at first longs to be part of the group flocking around the parson's slave Tituba for the forbidden pleasures of stories and predictions of the future, but she is shunned by the village girls for her status as the daughter of a wealthy merchant. Eventually, her own respected parents are rejected for their independence of mind and are named as witches. During their imprisonment, Susanna is cared for by relatives of malicious young Ann Putnam, Joseph and Elizabeth Putnam, who were also leaders in a kind of underground resistance movement against those who were condemning innocent neighbors. The story is threaded around Susanna's personal struggle with guilt as she discovers the deadly intent of the accusing girls and is made fearful when she attempts to reason with them. "We can name anyone. The power has been given to us by the ministers themselves. They anxiously look to us for the names." Rinaldi compellingly conveys the complexities of human failings and the courage of a large cast of characters; the appalling complicity and righteousness of ministers and magistrates, for instance, are balanced by the inclusion of members of each group who opposed the trials. A concluding note explains the fictional departures from the historical record. The author's skillful manipulation of conventions of the young-adult novel—particularly the rich exploration of being an outsider and going against the mainstream—makes this book a superb vehicle for examining the social dynamics of this legendary event.

Miriam Martinez and Marcia F. Nash

SOURCE: A review of *A Break with Charity: A Story about the Salem Witch Trials,* in *Language Arts,* Vol. 70, No. 8, December, 1993, p. 683.

It is 1692, and Susanna English, like many of the girls who live in Salem, Massachusetts, chafes under the restrictions of her rigid Puritan community. She longs to join the girls that meet daily at the parsonage to have their fortunes told by the slave Tituba. Yet when Susanna finally gains the courage to visit Tituba, she realizes, much to her dismay, that she is witnessing a hysteria that is growing out of control. As the girls in the inner circle begin to "cry out" and name people throughout the community as witches, Susanna longs to tell all that she knows but doesn't dare to for fear that her own parents will be named as witches. Finally, after great inner struggle, she overcomes her own fears and superstitions and steps forward to help end the mass hysteria that is threatening to destroy Salem. Rinaldi has woven a fascinating tale about the way in which the dark side of human nature can tear a community apart.

📖 *IN MY FATHER'S HOUSE* (1993)

Carolyn Phelan

SOURCE: A review of *In My Father's House,* in *Booklist,* Vol. 89, No. 12, February 15, 1993, pp. 1054-55.

Rinaldi notes that her novel is based on this quirk of historical coincidence: the first battle of the Civil War took place on the Manassas farm of Wilmer McLean, who eventually moved with his family to Appomattox, where the Civil War ended with Lee's surrendering to Grant in the McLeans' parlor. While some facts are known about the McLean family, the framework is bare enough to give Rinaldi full rein in creating an involving historical novel. Oscie, the narrator, begins the story as a seven-year-old girl who regards McLean suspiciously, just as any young girl might regard a prospective stepfather; by the end, she is a young woman who understands and respects him. While Oscie never sounds quite as young as seven, her transformation from child to woman is convincingly portrayed against a backdrop of the changing South before, during, and slightly after the Civil War. Rinaldi's interest in Wilmer McLean, who began by giving his farm to the cause and later profiteered in sugar, pulls the focus of the novel away from Oscie's story at times. This is, in any case, a story of many intertwining threads rather than one with a strong, central theme. Many readers will find they can't put it down.

Roger Sutton

SOURCE: A review of *In My Father's House*, in *Bulletin of the Center for Children's Books*, Vol. 46, No. 7, March, 1993, p. 223.

Rinaldi's latest historical drama is based upon an intriguing fact: the first battle of the Civil War (Manassas) was fought on the land of Will McLean; the terms of Lee's surrender to Grant were signed on the same man's table, at a house he was renting in Appomattox. This is a fabulous frame, but unfortunately, the author has attempted to work too much information about the war into a novel about McLean's family. The heroine, Oscie, is McLean's stepdaughter, and she's a classic Civil War heroine. Headstrong, heedless, brave (and if the cover is anything to go by, a looker), Oscie loves unwisely, cares for her sisters, and fights with her stepfather. Only the last relationship, fictionally developed through a series of confrontations, has any real impact. Neither Oscie's sisters nor her suitors have enough personality to sustain our attention. The view of slavery here is Margaret Mitchell-benign, with a convenient distinction made between good and bad slaveholders: "We owned slaves, yes, but our nigras were family." But the real problem here is the sprawling canvas, with the information on the progress of the war sometimes going on for paragraphs and distracting attention from the fictional focus.

Lucinda Snyder Whitehurst

SOURCE: A review of *In My Father's House*, in *School Library Journal*, Vol. 39, No. 3, March, 1993, p. 224.

Osceola Mason tells the story of her family's involvement in what some Southerners still call "The War of Northern Aggression." Rinaldi's attention to historical detail is admirable. Her use of Civil War letters and diaries gives the story a great deal of authenticity. The author's note explains which events are documented and where she used artistic license. In the "politically correct" atmosphere of the 1990s, many pitfalls await the author of a Civil War novel. Any depiction of slavery, from harsh to familial, may be considered offensive by some. Rinaldi uses the word "slaves" in a general sense; Oscie's family always says "nigras" or "darkies." The slaves' dialogue is in dialect but is not difficult to understand. The author carefully presents the varying reasons for the war, including slavery and the argument over states' rights. She also demonstrates that the North was not a human-rights utopia, with children and immigrants working long hours for low wages in unsafe factories. However, the characters seem to possess too much 20th-century perspective in their easy acceptance that the War is a lost cause and that the South must change. Rinaldi's research and her ability to present differing viewpoints cannot be faulted, but her story fails to capture the intensity of the period. Part of the problem is the focus on Oscie's often difficult relationship with her stepfather at the expense of other dramatic elements, such as her sister falling in love with a Yankee and her own romance with a Confederate soldier. Many teenage readers will lose patience with the slow-moving narrative.

Kay Parks Bushman and John H. Bushman

SOURCE: A review of *In My Father's House*, in *English Journal*, Vol. 83, No. 1, January, 1994, p. 80.

The Civil War is brought to life through the lives of the Will McLean family, especially from the point of view of Oscie, Will McLean's stepdaughter. The first battle of the Civil War—the battle of Bull Run—was fought on the McLean property. Interestingly, the final act of the War was signed in Will McLean's drawing room at Appomattox. All that takes place between these two traumatic events is graphically detailed by Rinaldi. While the war continues, a family struggle occurs as well. Oscie, a teen during this tragic time, believes the South should stay as it is. Will McLean believes the South must change if it is to be strong. This compelling historical novel brings to life the incidents and the people who lived through them in a way that no history book ever could. Readers empathize with Oscie as she listens to her stepfather; to Mary Ann, a slave she's misused; and to Miss Buttonworth, her Northern tutor. Through the relationship with these people, Oscie begins to see that the South she so admired and loved will soon be gone. The book is lengthy but demands attention. High-school students will feel the strength and power that Rinaldi brings to the work. As in most historical fiction by Rinaldi, an author's note at the end separates the fact from fiction. A must read for students of history and lovers of historical fiction.

Barbara Shepp

SOURCE: A review of *In My Father's House*, in

KLIATT: Young Adult Paperback Book Guide, Vol. 29, No. 2, March, 1995, p. 12.

This engrossing historical novel by experienced author Rinaldi follows one Virginia family from 1852 until the end of the Civil War. In one of those coincidences of history that are wondrous to discover, the family, the McLeans, played a role in both the beginning and the end of the war; the first battle (at Bull Run in Manassas) took place on their farmland, and the surrender at Appomatox was arranged between Generals Grant and Lee in their home, to which they had moved to escape the fighting. While the war itself remains in the background, as the story is told from the point of view of Oscie, Will McLean's teenage stepdaughter, the book encompasses many of the important issues and attitudes of the time. Secession, slavery, the New South, the Old South, Yankees good and bad, the horrors of war, chivalrous officers, profiteering, shortages, and romance all get their due.

Oscie McLean is a strong-willed, independent young woman who comes to maturity during the war. She is in frequent conflict with her stepfather, and her struggle to understand, accept, and even love him is a major theme, reflecting the struggle between the Old South and the New South. In addition, it is a parent-child conflict with which today's teens can easily identify. Oscie is involved in two romances, both nicely understated but compelling and believable. There are several other interesting characters: Button, a fine, wise woman from Boston who tutors Oscie and is a voice of reason and intelligence; Mary Ann, a slave whom Oscie fears and battles against until, late in the book, she learns compassion; Alex, a handsome Confederate officer, the quintessential Southern gentleman, who is Oscie's first love; Maria, Oscie's sister, who falls in love with a wounded Union soldier. These characters serve as individual examples of some of the "types" who were affected by the war.

In an author's note at the end of the story, Rinaldi describes her research process and differentiates between historical fact and the fiction she created. This should be helpful to the young reader, and adds to the experience of reading this book. A bibliography and chronology of major events in the Civil War are also included. Highly recommended for middle school and high school students.

📖 THE FIFTH OF MARCH: THE STORY OF THE BOSTON MASSACRE (1993)

Publishers Weekly

SOURCE: A review of *The Fifth of March: A Story of the Boston Massacre,* in *Publishers Weekly,* Vol. 240, No. 45, November 8, 1993, p. 78.

Historical events aren't as neat and tidy as they appear in history books, nor are they dissimilar from modern happenings (i.e., the Rodney King case), as Rinaldi ably demonstrates in this painstakingly researched tale told by a young servant in colonial Boston. Rachel is 14, bound as a nursemaid to the children of John and Abigail Adams, at whose house she sees many of the town's "movers and shakers" (one of the book's few faults is its jarringly anachronistic language). When British troops are sent to Boston to keep order, Rachel—despite her increasingly anti-Royalist sentiments—takes pity on Matthew Kilroy, the young sentry posted at the Adamses' door. Their relationship gradually blossoms, but Rachel, who has embarked on an ambitious program to educate herself and who rightly fears "getting into circumstances," refuses to demonstrate her affection in more than verbal terms. Lonely, frustrated, underpaid and reviled by the citizenry he was sent to protect, Matthew explodes during a riot on March 5, 1770, after which he and his fellows are tried for murder and manslaughter in the deaths of five colonialists. How Rachel acts according to her newly awakened social conscience and sense of self-worth makes for engrossing and educational reading. However, readers may object to Rachel's sense of guilt over Matthew's sexual frustration, and to her pronouncements on "good breeding."

Kathryn Jennings

SOURCE: A review of *The Fifth of March: A Story of the Boston Massacre,* in *Bulletin of the Center for Children's Books,* Vol. 47, No. 4, December, 1993, p. 132.

In a novel about the Boston Massacre, Rinaldi uses an historical but little-known teenage girl as her narrator. Rachel Marsh was an indentured servant and nursemaid to the children of John and Abigail Adams during the early days of the American Revolution. Because John Adams was an important lawyer in 1770, Rachel lived in one of Boston's political centers. Rinaldi's Rachel does more than stay at home and watch the children, however; she visits Henry Knox's bookstore and gets educated, she "walks out" on Sundays with a young British soldier, and she sometimes has advance knowledge of riots from her activist friend, Jane. It is Rachel's involvement with the British soldier that leads the Adamses to find her a place in another home away from Boston. For readers interested in American history, this novel serves as a telescope for the events surrounding the Boston Massacre. Unfortunately, Rinaldi is so preoccupied with historical accuracy that the plot moves slowly and the dialogue gets very long-winded. Rachel's final act of leaving her beautiful dowry at the Adamses seems heavily contrived to show her newly acquired independence. A note and bibliography give helpful background.

Kirkus Reviews

SOURCE: A review of *The Fifth of March: A Story of the Boston Massacre,* in *Kirkus Reviews,* Vol. LXI, No. 23, December 1, 1993, p. 1528.

Carefully researched and lovingly written, Rinaldi's latest presents a girl indentured to John and Abigail Adams during the tense period surrounding the 1770 Massacre.

Like the author's other protagonists, Rachel is seeking her place in a turbulent world. Inspired by Abigail Adams's gentility and intellectual achievement to educate herself, she's befriended by people involved in the increasing resistance to British authority, questions her own loyalties, and comes to accept herself as one of the new "Americans"; after meeting Matthew Kilroy, a lonely British private, she also realizes that the rowdy Bostonians aren't always right. Risking her position, she secretly "steps out" with Matthew and eventually witnesses his participation in the Massacre (which was provoked by the Patriots, as Rinaldi suggests in an excellent historical note). After John Adams successfully defends the British soldiers and ends Rachel's indenture (he deems her actions unsuitable for a nursemaid), she secures work with Philadelphia Quakers, abandons her dowry, and sets out, secure in having learned to make choices and speak up for herself. Fortuitously timed, a novel that illuminates a moment from our past that has strong parallels to recent events in Los Angeles and Somalia.

Chris Sherman

SOURCE: A review of *The Fifth of March: A Story of the Boston Massacre,* in *Booklist,* Vol. 90, No. 10, January 15, 1994, p. 925.

Rinaldi's latest historical novel, which takes place in 1770, is told from the point of view of 14-year-old Rachel Marsh, an indentured servant in the household of John Adams. Rachel feels lucky to have the position, believes she is well treated, and greatly admires Abigail and John Adams. Although not political herself, she worries about friends who support rebellion and have told her that a time will come when she will have to take a stand. It is only when she meets Matthew Kilroy, a young, argumentative British soldier who has been sent to Boston as part of a peacekeeping force, that Rachel begins to question British domination of the colonies and to see herself as an American. When Matthew is arrested for his part in the Boston Massacre, Rachel, who's convinced he's caught up in a political war not of his making, defies convention and the Adamses' wishes and visits him in jail. Although the act costs her her job, she knows she has done the right thing. Rinaldi provides a vivid picture of colonial life and the pre-Revolutionary War period, including the disagreements among various American factions and the frightening actions of mobs and British retaliation. Because the issues she raises—the role of peacekeeping forces, the use of violence to achieve political goals, and the courage required to take a stand—are as significant today as they were at the time, this will be a wonderful selection to use in language-arts and social-studies classes.

A STITCH IN TIME (first novel in the "Quilt" trilogy, 1994)

Publishers Weekly

SOURCE: A review of *A Stitch in Time,* in *Publishers Weekly,* Vol. 241, No. 4, January 24, 1994, p. 56.

The powerful symbolism of a quilt named Trust supplies a strong send-off for the first of Rinaldi's new trilogy about a Salem shipping merchant family in America's early post-revolution years. Sisters Hannah, Abby and Thankful Chelmsford, driven into separate journeys as a result of their father's cold and manipulative ways, each take a piece of the quilt; the conceit here is that only fabric taken from their most trusted friends will be added to it. Eldest sister Hannah, the narrator, stays in Salem while Abby elopes with a sea captain and fractious Thankful joins their father on a dangerous expedition to western territory. Hannah's feelings, from her doubts about her own prospects to her guilty resentment of Thankful, are fresh and contemporary, effectively contrasting with the story's archaic sex roles and adding to the richness of Rinaldi's well-researched setting. With her infectious fascination for American history and her sensitive characterizations, Rinaldi again creates an adventurous, heart-catching story that will leave readers in eager anticipation of its successors.

Carolyn Phelan

SOURCE: A review of *A Stitch in Time,* in *Booklist,* Vol. 90, No. 13, March 1, 1994, p. 1253.

Rinaldi's latest historical novel, the first of the Quilt Trilogy, takes place in Salem, Massachusetts, from 1788 to 1791. Apart from the prologue and epilogue, the story is narrated by 16-year-old Hannah, who has looked after her family since the death of her mother some years before. "You brood too much for one so young," another character tells Hannah early on, but she has a lot to brood about: her younger brother's planning to run away to sea; her sister Abby's about to elope; their younger sister Thankful blackmails them with the knowledge of the elopement; their ill-tempered father, older brother, and Thankful leave for the wild frontier; Hannah's father's partner seems likely to make unwelcome advances during their absence; and she pledges her love to Richard before he sets sail, only to have her old love, Louis, return from the frontier to ask her to care for his baby, whose Indian mother died. It's a tribute to the author's plotting and characterization that readers can keep it all straight. Dark secrets are alluded to throughout and occasionally revealed, and every so often one of the characters will underscore the analogy between the family quilt Hannah works on and the patchwork of their lives. The author tells more than she shows, though; given the many threads running through the story, it would take more than three volumes to show all. Limiting the plot and characters somewhat might have allowed for more depth. Rinaldi knows how to keep the pages turning by raising readers' curiosity, though whether they'll clamor for the sequels is an open question.

Kirkus Reviews

SOURCE: A review of *A Stitch in Time,* in *Kirkus Reviews,* Vol. LXII, No. 5, March 1, 1994, p. 309.

Set in late 18th-century Salem, Massachusetts, first of a

projected trilogy (to trace three generations) in which a quilt made by three sisters is the central motif. Hannah, the eldest, is the glue that keeps the troubled Chelmsford family from flying apart. Autocratic Father, embittered by a single infidelity by his deceased wife (whom he abused), favors bratty daughter Thankful and rejects illegitimate son Cabot. Hannah and her brother Lawrence conspire in sister Abigail's planned elopement with South Carolina sea captain Nate Videau. Hannah's own earlier romance, squelched by her father, enables her to realize her love for poor but ambitious Richard Lander. Hoping to prevent her from revealing Abby's plans, Hannah encourages their father to take Thankful to the Ohio Territory—where she is captured by Indians and ultimately chooses to remain with them. Meanwhile, each sister works on a piece of the quilt, which Hannah has decided will symbolize trusted people in their lives. Mr. Chelmsford becomes a partner in an early cotton mill; Hannah is drawn into social work on behalf of its exploited workers. Though Rinaldi's research (detailed in a note) occasionally intrudes, it also keeps the setting and flavor authentic. Characteristically for this writer, dialogue is an awkward mix of contemporary and period idiom (Videau's southern accent is particularly inconsistent). Still, the memorable characters and their historically accurate context balance the flaws, raising the story from the soap-opera level.

Deborah Stevenson

SOURCE: A review of *A Stitch in Time,* in *Bulletin of the Center for Children's Books,* Vol. 47, No. 8, April, 1994, p. 269.

It's Salem in 1788, and Hannah is the mainstay of the stormy Chelmsford family: her mother is dead, her father brutal; her one sister planning an elopement with a Southerner, her other sister willfully wicked; her younger brother hated by her father and her other brother preparing to leave for the West. The plot thickens—boy, does it thicken—when a concern headed by her father brings low-paying textile mills to town, Hannah's old flame returns from the West with a half-Indian baby, which she cares for, Hannah falls in love with a young man suspected of running a slave ship, she discovers the dark secret about her mother, her good sister seems to be lost at sea, and her father and bad sister go west, where her sister is kidnapped by Shawnee. *And* she works on a quilt. Even as a lengthy but undemanding historical sudser this has problems: the multitude of events makes the saga more sprawling than sweeping, the romances don't spark, and the villain isn't convincing. Rinaldi's historical research, documented in an author's note and bibliography, goes for naught when contemporary sentiments and phrases break the mood ("Lack of trust ruined my parents' marriage"; "The man is slime"). In *A Break with Charity,* about the Salem witch trials, Rinaldi focused with great success on an emotion-charged historical situation, making the incredible truth credible; here the events aren't really involving because there's little emotional underpinning to the story. Readers who simply like historical settings may

enjoy the early-American details. Two more books about the fate of the Chelmsford family's quilt over the generations are planned.

FINISHING BECCA: THE STORY OF PEGGY SHIPPEN AND BENEDICT ARNOLD (1994)

Janice Del Negro

SOURCE: A review of *Finishing Becca: The Story of Peggy Shippen and Benedict Arnold,* in *Booklist,* Vol. 91, No. 6, November 15, 1994, pp. 590-91.

In 1778, 14-year-old Becca Syng goes to work as the personal maid for spoiled society beauty Peggy Shippen. The British are occupying Philadelphia, and the self-absorbed Peggy is seen most often on the arm of dashing Captain Andre. By the time the British decamp, Peggy's father is on the brink of ruin. It's then Peggy meets the notorious General Benedict Arnold, and the rest is history. According to Becca, who narrates the story, it was Peggy Shippen Arnold who was responsible for her husband's betrayal of the American Revolutionary cause. The historical context is sometimes too obvious, and the word *nigra,* though a historically legitimate term, eventually becomes distracting. But Rinaldi's evocation of the rip-roaring life and devil-be-damned personality of Peggy Shippen, which forms the real core of the story, makes you want to find out more about the people and the history—and that's certainly one of the goals of good historical fiction.

Ann W. Moore

SOURCE: A review of *Finishing Becca: A Story About Peggy Shippen and Benedict Arnold,* in *School Library Journal,* Vol. 40, No. 12, December, 1994, p. 130.

In 1778, Becca Syng, 14, becomes Peggy Shippen's maid and enters another world. For over a year, she assists Peggy in her revelry, culminating in her mistress's marriage to General Benedict Arnold. Like the Arnolds, Becca is faced with decisions about loyalty: to her country, to her family and, above all, to herself. This first-person historical novel has some major problems. First, since Becca is not a direct participant in Shippen-Arnold affairs, Rinaldi continually relies on the fortuitous overhearing of conversations, chance meetings, and convenient letters to develop her plot. Too much history is crammed into dialogue, and too much confiding in animals occurs to update readers. Second, the author relies on talk, thought, and feelings at the expense of action. Consequently, the story drags. Given Becca's age and inexperience, her perceptiveness is unrealistic; her overwrought language is better suited to a Gothic romance. Finally, Shippen and Arnold are such unpleasant characters that nothing excuses Becca's enduring them for so long. Their complex personalities, apparent in adult biographies, are absent here—she's spoiled and manipulative and he's merely a selfish egotist. This one-track approach not only does these individuals a disservice, but it also becomes tedious to read.

Laura L. Lent

SOURCE: A review of *Finishing Becca: The Story of Peggy Shippen and Benedict Arnold,* in *Voice of Youth Advocates,* Vol. 17, No. 6, February, 1995, pp. 340-41.

Set in Philadelphia during the American Revolution, this riveting story revolves around two people and their very different lives—the fictitious life of Becca Syng and the real life of Peggy Shippen. Although Becca is the main character, it is easy to see that Rinaldi has created her to be Peggy Shippen's antagonist.

Becca, an impoverished teenager, lives on a farm in the Pennsylvania countryside with her mother and her stepfather, Henry Job. Because money is tight, Becca's mom has been unable to send Becca to a finishing school. Therefore, when Becca's mom is asked by the Shippens, a prominent Quaker family in Philadelphia society, if Becca would like to become their daughter's personal maid, she agrees on the condition that Becca also be taught the ways of a genteel lady—playing the harp, doing crewel, speaking French, learning proper manners, etc. Becca's employment as Peggy Shippen's personal maid makes Becca privy to the inner-workings of Philadelphia's elite during the American Revolution. At first, Becca is entranced with the lifestyles of these people; however, the more she learns about them, the more upset she becomes. She compares their self-indulgent lifestyles with those of the starving, sick men who are serving under her brother, Blair, at Valley Forge.

This wastefulness is stopped in June of 1778 when the Patriots force the British and many of the families who sympathize with them to evacuate the city. Peggy ingratiates herself with the new commander in town whose name is Benedict Arnold. Although Arnold is many years Peggy's senior, the two fall in love and get married. While in the Arnold household, Becca overhears the two of them plotting against the Americans—devising a plan to give colonial control back to the British. Unfortunately for Becca, she is caught eavesdropping and is dismissed. However, before her dismissal, Becca learns a little about Benedict Arnold's treasonous activities—piquing the reader's curiosity.

Rinaldi's intriguing approach depicting the life of Peggy Shippen through the eyes of Becca Syng will appeal to young adults with an interest in history. Not only will readers learn how average colonists like Becca and her family survived during the American Revolution in contrast to wealthier people like the Shippens, but they will also see how the Patriots (men fighting for American Independence) survived the brutal winter at Valley Forge under General George Washington. With this work, Rinaldi has added another wonderful piece of historical fiction to her "American Colonies" series.

Norma Hunter

SOURCE: A review of *Finishing Becca: A Story About Peggy Shippen and Benedict Arnold,* in *The Book Report,* Vol. 14, No. 1 May-June, 1995, pp. 41-2.

Becca's mother wants her to learn to be a gracious lady, so she sends her to work as personal servant to Peggy, daughter of the wealthy Shippen family of Philadelphia. In return for her service, Becca is taught French, needlework, music and dancing, but in watching Peggy and her suitors, she also learns about deceit, conspiracy and manipulation. Set during the Revolutionary War, this well-written book provides the feel of the time through Rinaldi's use of language from that era. Even food and drinks that were popular during that time help establish the setting. Historical figures such as Benedict Arnold and John Andre are accurately portrayed, but it is the use of Becca as the storyteller that will make this book entertaining and believable for teen readers.

THE SECRET OF SARAH REVERE (1995)

Kay E. Vandergrift

SOURCE: A review of *The Secret of Sarah Revere,* in *School Library Journal,* Vol. 41, No. 11, November, 1995, p. 122.

Once again Rinaldi has given readers a young woman's perceptions of what has too often been the all-male story of American history and politics. Paul Revere comes to life through the eyes and voice of Sarah, his 13-year-old daughter. Through the girl's observations, her father emerges as a family man, a caring friend, and a loyal patriot. Dr. Joseph Warren, an often forgotten hero of the Revolution, is warmly portrayed, as is Rachel, Revere's second wife. As Sarah comes of age against the strife of the times, she weaves critical events of American history into the everyday details of her family's life, making the characters convincing as real people. She is interested in clothing, food, and her older sister's romantic liaison, and has her own reverential crush on the handsome Dr. Warren. Because her father's activities take their toll on the family, she is also keenly aware of political and military events and secrets. Her analyses of them are painful but beautifully crafted, giving readers a sense of and a sensitivity to this period of history. The brief bibliography offers evidence of Rinaldi's scholarship, and her note discusses the process whereby she validates available historical facts but goes beyond them to interpret and draw her own conclusions in composing historical fiction.

Susan Dove Lempke

SOURCE: A review of *The Secret of Sarah Revere,* in *Booklist,* Vol. 92, No. 6, November 15, 1995, pp. 548-49.

When a man comes to interview her father, Paul Revere, Sarah recalls the eventful past two years. Historically significant goings-on, such as the Boston Tea Party and her father's famous rides, intertwine with the personal, including Sarah's wondering whether her father's new wife is betraying him with another patriot. Sarah's growth into womanhood complicates matters even further. Rinaldi's depiction of daily life in Boston rings true (readers may think twice before drinking tea), and, for the most part, her dialogue remains free of anachronistic expressions. Her technique of framing the story within Sarah's recollections creates some initial confusion, but the swift pace and credible characters combined with impeccable research make the novel an involving and informative venture into history.

Elizabeth Bush

SOURCE: A review of *The Secret of Sarah Revere,* in *Bulletin of the Center for Children's Books,* Vol. 49, No. 5, January, 1996, p. 169.

Domestic tranquility is shattered for Sarah, teenage daughter of Paul Revere, as hostilities between Colonists and Crown edge toward war. Her father and brother arrange clandestine activities for the Committees of Correspondence, old Tory friends may be conspiring with the Patriots, and the handsome widower James Warren (whom Sarah more than admires) seems to be carrying on with her stepmother. The opening battles of the Revolution drag some truths to the surface—Dr. Warren and Mrs. Revere have been part of an information web for the rebel colonists. Other truths must remain buried: Paul knows who fired the opening shot at Lexington but he's not telling; Sarah recalls her harsh accusations to Dr. Warren and muses, "I did not make it up with a dear friend before he died . . . And what's true is that I shall carry my shabby, sad secret with me forever." Rinaldi skillfully balances the dual aspects—witness at the fringe of political upheaval, and jealous, love-struck teen—of Sarah's life. From the cantankerous grandmother to the libidinous older sister, each historical footnote character has a credible role in family alliances and conflicts. Historical ambiguities are zealously preserved; a concluding note discusses the extent of Rinaldi's literary liberties and comments on the fate of each Revere child.

📖 *BROKEN DAYS* (second novel in the "Quilt" trilogy, 1996)

Journal of Adolescent and Adult Literacy

SOURCE: A review of *Broken Days,* in *Journal of Adolescent and Adult Literacy,* Vol. 39, No. 6, March, 1996, p. 514.

The second installment in the Quilt Trilogy, begun with *A Stitch in Time,* opens during a time of great unrest between the U.S. and Britain. Walking Breeze, the daughter of Thankful Chelmsford, is traded by the Native Americans and sent to her Aunt Hannah in Salem, Massachusetts. The Chelmsford family is overjoyed at the prospect

of meeting Thankful's daughter, if she is indeed who she purports to be. Ebie, however, is less than thrilled. While Ebie's father is away on business, she lives with Aunt Hannah and suffers already from a lack of familial affection. To her, the arrival of Walking Breeze means losing what little claim she has to her aunt and grandfather. She plots to destroy Walking Breeze's proof of ancestry: the quilt, divided into three parts when Hannah's sisters began their voyages.

Cyrisse Jaffee

SOURCE: A review of *Broken Days,* in *The Horn Book Magazine,* Vol. VII, No. 1, Spring, 1996, p. 75.

Rinaldi continues the story of the dysfunctional Chelmsford family in early nineteenth-century Salem, Massachusetts, who must now deal with the arrival of fourteen-year-old Walking Breeze, a half-Shawnee girl claiming to be a family member. Although well researched, the plot is somewhat confusing, and the characters are not always likable or fully realized. Fans of *A Stitch in Time* however, will enjoy the story.

📖 *KEEP SMILING THROUGH* (1996)

Elizabeth Bush

SOURCE: A review of *Keep Smiling Through,* in *Bulletin of the Center for Children's Books,* Vol. 49, No. 8, April, 1996, p. 277.

For fifth grader [Kay Hennings], the privations resulting from rationing are nothing new; World War II has merely provided her tightwad father with an excuse to be close with his money, and her stepmother is loathe to spend anything on her even in the best of times. The war does immerse [Kay] in propaganda and patriotic rhetoric, and when she is forced to do some of the family shopping with a German neighbor, she is instinctively mistrustful of the woman's warm and gracious manners. However, [Kay] discovers that her own grandfather may harbor German loyalties, and that you can't tell the good guys from the bad guys strictly on the basis of national origin. The believability of the tale is strained by the presence of the stock wicked stepmother and the overly-righteous reporter who defends German-Americans, sounding more like a 1990s ACLU lawyer than a creation of his time, but Rinaldi paints a credible portrait of a gullible young girl forced to reexamine her war-bred prejudices.

Kirkus Reviews

SOURCE: A review of *Keep Smiling Through,* in *Kirkus Reviews,* Vol. LXIV, No. 7, April 1, 1996, p. 535.

Wrapped in a WW II world of rationing and radio dramas, 10-year-old Kay learns that doing the right thing in life doesn't always mean a happy ending. Kay has become her pregnant, pampered stepmother's target for abuse: blamed for everything, slapped for minor infractions, forced to wear dresses made from feed sacks or festooned with ugly ruffles. Her stepmother's parents are kind to her, but Kay is horrified to overhear her German-born stepgrandfather discussing the old country with a local merchant, even taking a political pamphlet. After he and the merchant are assaulted by anti-German thugs, Kay tells what she heard to a reporter, making sure he knows that her grandpa was showing concern, not disloyalty. Her enraged stepmother straps her, later goes into premature labor, and gives birth to a daughter who dies in the hospital.

Writing about an era in which she lived (explained in an author's note), Rinaldi fills her story with lively period detail (from Mary Janes to Margaret O'Brien) and period attitudes, too (others know of Kay's suffering but don't try to help her). Though her characters tend to be types, or, in the evil stepmother's case, caricatures, Rinaldi allows Kay to salvage her self-respect with the information that the baby's death was the result of an equipment shortage—far from the front, she was a war casualty nonetheless. A bittersweet historical novel.

Publishers Weekly

SOURCE: A review of *Keep Smiling Through,* in *Publishers Weekly,* Vol. 243, No. 22, May 27, 1996, p. 79.

Rinaldi takes a break from early American historical fiction to explore the period of her own childhood, WWII. Expertly evoking the patriotic fervor on the home front as it permeates everything from scrap drives to popular songs, the author introduces 10-year-old Kay Hennings, the narrator, as preoccupied with justice and fighting the good fight as any of her radio heroines. Kay's family is steeped in misery of fairy-tale proportions: her stepmother takes almost sadistic pleasure in depriving Kay and her four older siblings of every semblance of comfort, and her miserly father shows more concern for his coffers than for his children. What would be melodrama in lesser hands generates tension here—how will Kay bear it, much less "keep smiling through"? Rinaldi rewards Kay with an adventure worthy of her favorite radio show, then submits her to a test of honor and loyalty. Kay passes—and learns the awful, adult lesson that "you can do the right thing and sometimes it all goes bad for you anyway." Kay's vulnerability spills across the entire novel, bathing it in poignancy and enveloping the reader in its old-fashioned, bittersweet truths.

📖 *HANG A THOUSAND TREES WITH RIBBONS: THE STORY OF PHILLIS WHEATLEY* (1996)

Kirkus Reviews

SOURCE: A review of *Hang a Thousand Trees with Rib-*

bons: The Story of Phillis Wheatly, in *Kirkus Reviews,* Vol. 64, No. 20, October 15, 1996, p. 1538.

The short and not very happy life of America's first black poet, brought to vibrant life by Rinaldi.

Keziah is kidnapped from her village in Senegal in 1761 and handed over to a notorious slave trader for transport to America. She is brought to Boston, where she is purchased by the Wheatley family, who rename her Phillis after the ship on which she arrived. Nathaniel, the son and potential heir to the substantial Wheatley estate, becomes intrigued by the slave's intellect, and teaches her to read and write, then tutoring her in the Latin and Greek classics. Phillis's gift for writing poetry impresses the Wheatleys and their guests at their frequent soirees, but no American publisher will print her work; she is sent to England, where she is published to great acclaim. She is grudgingly granted freedom upon her return to Boston, but it does not bring the happiness she expected: She is unprepared to be on her own. A disastrous marriage ends with the deaths of her children and her own death at 30, and she is buried in a pauper's grave.

A powerful portrait of an innocent who, uprooted from her world, enters another where she is allowed to rise above the average slave's lot; Rinaldi makes clear to readers that Wheatley's good fortune is a double-edged sword that destorys her. A tragic tale, beautifully written and researched.

Mike Angelotti

SOURCE: A review of *Hang a Thousand Trees with Ribbons: The Story of Phillis Wheatly,* in *The ALAN Review,* Vol. 24, No. 2, Winter, 1997, p. 27.

Here is a beautifully written story true to the historical facts of the life of Phillis Wheatley, America's first black poet. Yet its credibility rests in its imaginative treatment of Phillis Wheatley the human being, of how a young African slave might have learned to read and write American English in pre-Revolutionary-War Boston. The novel is written as Phillis Wheatley might have written a memoir covering the period in her life from ages seven through approximately twenty-one; that is, from Keziah's abduction from a Senegal rice field by her vengeful uncle's warriors to her interview with General George Washington as "free nigra woman" Phillis Wheatley. Especially moving is her description of the "middle passage" between Senegal and Boston on the slave ship *Phillis*. Complementing a study of Phillis Wheatley's poetry might be her running commentary on the significance of writing and on her writing process. Her easy conversational style should make historical detail pleasantly consumable to young readers studying the period. In fact, Ann Rinaldi's fascinating "Author's Note" discusses the interplay of fact and fiction in the story. This book has strong interdisciplinary potential. It was much enjoyed and is highly recommended.

Barbara A. Zynda

SOURCE: A review of *Hang a Thousand Trees with Ribbons: The Story of Phillis Wheatly,* in *Kliatt Young Adult Paperback Book Guide,* Vol. 31, No. 1, January, 1997, p. 10.

Rinaldi's story is another example of her wonderful historical novels. Phillis Wheatley was named after the ship that brought her as a slave from Senegal in 1761 and the wealthy family who bought her in Boston. She adores Nathaniel Wheatley, the son of the family, who teaches her reading, writing and Latin. When the family discovers her talent for writing and poetry, they encourage her. Eventually they get her work published in London, since America is not yet ready to recognize its first Negro woman poet. The book ends with the beginning of the American Revolution and Phillis's marriage to John Peters. The author adds notes about what happened to Phillis after that. Rinaldi describes both the attitudes and the events of the times. In spite of Wheatley's talent, the whites treat her like a curiosity and a pet. Her masters feel betrayed when she says she wants to be free, interpreting that as ingratitude for the comfortable life they provide. Although "good" people, they are prejudiced and patronizing, unable to understand the deep human desire to be free. What could be drier for middle school students than learning about the Stamp Act? However, reading about it as it affected the lives of real people makes it easier to understand and much more interesting. Rinaldi's message seems to be that history is what happens to people.

📖 *THE BLUE DOOR* (1996)

Carolyn Phelan

SOURCE: A review of *The Blue Door,* in *Booklist,* Vol.. 93, No. 5, November 1, 1996, p. 491.

Set in 1841, the third volume in Rinaldi's "Quilt" trilogy takes place more than 50 years after *A Stitch in Time* and about 30 years after *Broken Days.* The fabric of the series is indeed a patchwork now. Familiar bits of family history and characters are side by side with new people, places, and events. And though a few aspects are jarring, for the third book in a trilogy, *Blue Door* stands alone very well. Amanda leaves her South Carolina plantation home to visit her great-grandfather in Massachusetts. On the steamship, she changes clothes with a girl she befriends. When the ship is wrecked, she is unable to prove her identity, so she continues to Lowell and takes a mill job, using her resources to work for better conditions and to find her way back to her family. The idea of setting each book in a different generation of the same family was ambitious. Although this device is not always successful, the trilogy tells involving stories of several strong female characters, shows people at different stages in their lives, and ties together three periods in America's past.

📖 *THE SECOND BEND IN THE RIVER* (1997)

Publishers Weekly

A review of *The Second Bend in the River,* in *Publishers Weekly,* Vol. 244, No. 2, January 13, 1997, pp. 76-7.

Rinaldi crafts an elegant and moving account of the budding romance between Shawnee chief Tecumseh and a young frontier girl, set against the events leading up to the War of 1812. As usual, Rinaldi's sense of her period setting is on target—the speech and details of everyday life are arresting and accessible; the characters are multidimensional and believable; and she shows how rumors and mistrust on both sides fueled the dispute between the Indians and settlers. The real story, however, is smart, strong-willed Rebecca Galloway's admiration for and attraction to Tecumseh. Rebecca teaches Tecumseh about verb tenses and the Bible, while he reveals much about the beauty of wild things. Tecumseh's proposal of marriage, Rebecca's confusion and their final love scene will pull at all hearts that have felt the pangs of first love. Rebecca's shrewd observations make her a character to be reckoned with—and one girls on the threshold of womanhood will appreciate.

Kay Weisman

A review of *The Second Bend in the River,* in *Booklist,* Vol. 93, No. 12, February 15, 1997, p. 1016.

In 1798, seven-year-old Ohio pioneer Rebecca Galloway first meets the great Shawnee chief Tecumseh when he visits the site of his boyhood home, now the Galloway farm. Although she is initially frightened by the tall stranger, he is quite taken by "little straw-hair" and presents her with a silver bracelet. When the Galloways realize Tecumseh's agenda is peace between the whites and Indians, a family friendship ensues, one that will last more than a decade. With each of the chief's return trips to the farm, the bond between Rebecca and him deepens and matures, until he finally asks for her hand in marriage. She is torn, almost overwhelmed by the intensity of their feelings (the kind of love that "pulls each other's souls out"), but realizes her own need to stay in the white world. As she did in *The Wolf by the Ears,* Rinaldi weaves a powerfully romantic tale of two Americans from the colonial era. Her attention to period details (ranging from frontier wedding customs to garden plantings) and careful separation of fact from fiction strengthen the credibility of the story without diminishing any of its appeal.

Carrie Schadle

A review of *The Second Bend in the River,* in *School Library Journal,* Vol. 43, No. 6, June, 1997, p. 126.

Set around the turn of the 18th century, this book mixes fact, fiction, and conjecture to tell the story of Rebecca

Galloway, a young girl living in the wilds of pioneer Ohio, and the visionary Shawnee leader Tecumseh. Rinaldi skillfully imagines seven-year-old Rebecca's initial meeting with Tecumseh and relates intermittent visits up through her teenage years, leading to his asking for her hand in marriage, an offer she refuses because their worlds are too different. Along the way readers are shown the difficulties and rewards of pioneer life, and introduced to the excitement felt by settlers who took part in the process of building a nation. The Galloways are drawn as a family with high principles: Rebecca's father fought in the Revolutionary War, moved his family away from Kentucky where slavery was permitted, and championed the cause of the displaced Indians among the not always sympathetic whites. Rebecca is a strong-minded character with a believable and authentic voice. Anyone who enjoys historical fiction will find much to like about this well-written and carefully researched novel. It succeeds in presenting both the plight and frustrations of Native Americans and the exuberance of the early pioneers in a sympathetic way, although the author falls clearly on the side of those who mourn the loss of a culture destroyed by white settlers. A rewarding and satisfying read.

Additional coverage of Rinaldi's life and career is contained in the following sources published by Gale Research: *Authors and Artists for Young Adults,* Vol. 15; *Contemporary Authors,* Vol. 111; *Junior DISCovering Authors* (CD-ROM); and *Something about the Author,* Vol. 78.

Nicole St. John

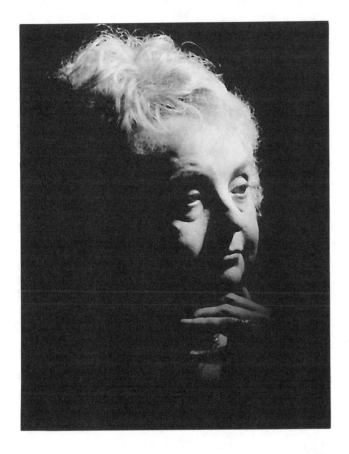

(Also writes under names Norma Johnston, Lavinia Harris, Kate Chambers, Pamela Dryden, Catherine E. Chambers, Elizabeth Bolton, and Adrian Robert) American author of fiction and nonfiction for children, young adults, and adults.

Major works include *The Keeping Days* (as Norma Johnston, 1973), *Of Time and of Seasons* (as Norma Johnston, 1975), *Timewarp Summer* (as Norma Johnston, 1983), *Carlisles All* (as Norma Johnston, 1986), *Louisa May: The World and Works of Louisa May Alcott* (as Norma Johnston, 1991).

INTRODUCTION

Writer of over seventy books, primarily for young adults, Nicole St. John demonstrates a great range of historical knowledge and an ability to evoke and immerse her readers in the settings and social mores of past eras. She is best known for creating such memorable characters as the Sterlings of the "Keeping Days" series and the Carlisles of the "Carlisle Chronicles"—large, loving, multigenerational families whose members are close-knit, but often embroiled in conflicts that will change the course of their lives. At the center of these and other of her young adult novels are strong adolescent female characters; St. John's heroines tend to be introspective and complex—creative young women who face the inevitable challenges of growing up, and, in doing so, gain insight into their own values and emerging selves. According to *Horn Book* critic Mary Burke, such novels are "nostalgic but not sentimental, flavored generously with romance, . . . [capturing] the anxieties of adolescence with its naivete and awareness." St. John writes under a variety of names: as Kate Chambers, she invented the teenage sleuth Diana Winthop, for young adults; as Elizabeth Bolton and Adrian Robert, she created mystery series for younger readers; and as Catherine Chambers, she penned the historically based "Adventures in Frontier America" series, also for younger readers. Her more recent works have included biographies of Louisa May Alcott and Harriet Beecher Stowe—both of which recall her young adult novels in their use of family anecdotes, rich dialogue, and a historical framework to chronicle her subjects' lives—and for adults she has delved into the realm of Greek mythology. St. John writes about past eras because she believes that readers can learn a great deal from their forebears' mistakes and accomplishments, and that they may be more willing to "listen" to basic truths about human nature if presented through the lens of fiction. "And so I write," she explained in *Something about the Author,* "[about finding] moments of truth; of the rites of passage in which we know we have gone irrevocably from innocence into knowledge; of the verities I believe to be unchanged in a changing world."

Biographical Information

Born in Ridgewood, New Jersey, St. John was the only child of Eugene and Majorie (Pierce) Johnston. Surrounded by several generations of relatives on both sides during her childhood, St. John later drew on family history in addition to her own life experiences to write her books. Her creative pursuits began at an early age; at three, she started ballet lessons—a passion for performance arts has continued into adulthood—and her love of writing emerged in elementary school, during which she wrote her first full-length book. Yet St. John also excelled in art and intended after high school to enroll at a New York art school to study design. It was her father's untimely death that convinced her to attend the nearby Montclair College, from which she earned a B.A., and pursue a writing career; and, with support from her mentor, writer Maud Hart Lovelace, she devoted herself to submitting her work to contests and publishers. Her first published book, *The Wishing Star* (1963), was adapted from a story she had written at age sixteen about her church youth group and the relationships among its teen members. For the next several years, she continued to publish about one book a year, also working as an editor at a religious publishing house and founding the Geneva Players theater group. The 1970s, when young adult fiction was gaining popularity, marked a pivotal change in St. John's personal and professional life: health problems that had plagued her since childhood—including arthritis and respiratory difficulties—severely limited her outside activities, and the demand for books of her genre increased. She began writing full time and has published under eight different names—Nicole St. John, Norma Johnston, Elizabeth Bolton, Catherine E. Chambers, Kate Chambers, Pamela Dryden, Lavinia Harris, and Adrian Robert—all of which were adopted from real-life ancestors. In addition to writing several mystery series for younger readers, she wrote adult books retelling stories from Greek mythology, and, in the 1990s, published biographies for young adults of Louisa May Alcott and Harriet Beecher Stowe. St. John and a group of close friends have also operated St. John Enterprises, an organization that specializes in freelance editing and ghostwriting services, and sells herb mixtures for cooking.

Major Works

The "Keeping Days" series is a group of historical novels—including *The Keeping Days, Glory in the Flower* (1974), *A Mustard Seed of Magic* (1977), *The Sanctuary Tree* (1977), *A Nice Girl Like You* (1980), and *Myself and I* (1981)—set between the turn of this century and the end of World War I, which traces the lives of the Sterling family, characters based on members of St. John's own family. In *The Keeping Days,* narrator and main character Tish Sterling aspires to be a famous writer and uses her journal to record family events and her own transformation from the self-absorption typical of adolescence to a more mature consideration of others' feelings and perspectives. A "keeping day" for Tish, and for St. John, becomes an important metaphor for such memorable moments of growth that remain with us regardless of the passage of time. St. John also uses a historical setting in *Of Time and Of Seasons*; in this novel, which takes place during the Civil War, fifteen-year-old Bridget struggles to find her place in a family whose abundant talents seem to contain mixed blessings. She wonders what her own artistic contribution might be as she witnesses the personal and societal pressures placed on her mother, a writer using a male pseudonym, her father, a well-known painter, and her twin brother, who scorns his musical abilities and wishes to join the army. When her mother leaves town on a writing assignment, Bridget assumes greater responsibility for the household and comes to value her own perceptiveness and ability to deal with others. In *Timewarp Summer,* told from the point-of-view of a teenage boy, Scott Martin devotes the summer before his last year in high school to shooting a movie with a camera given to him as a Christmas gift. Aided by his friend from childhood, Bettina, who has a crush on him, and an "older" woman, Dr. Laura Weller, with whom he starts a roman-

tic relationship, Scott completes his project and begins to see that Bettina has been his faithful and loving friend all along. *Timewarp Summer* is divided into sections with prefatory directions suggestive of a movie script, and interspersed with the actual story are edited typescripts of Scott's film. The "Carlisle Chronicles"—which includes *The Carlisles's Hope* (1986), *To Jess, With Love and Memories* (1986), and *Carlisles All*—details the lives of the multigenerational Carlisle family. Jess, a teenage girl, is the main character, and her father's job in the foreign service provides a different setting for each book. In *Carlisles All*, Jess and her family are enjoying Christmas until Mr. and Mrs. Carlisle are sent on an emergency trip to the Middle East. After being informed that the embassy housing provided for their parents has been the target of a bomb attack, the Carlisle children band together as they pray for news of their parents' safety while, due to the secret nature of the mission, they must pretend to outsiders that their family is intact and celebrating the holiday. Readers join Jess and her siblings, who meet the challenge of being home alone in a crisis with admirable composure, in wait-by-the phone suspense before the happy reunion with their parents occurs at the end. Although a biography, St. John's treatment of the life of Louisa May Alcott in *Louisa May: The World and Works of Louisa May Alcott* uses some of the same elements as her fictional novels for young adults. St. John paints an accurate and vivid picture of the way of life in New England in the late nineteenth century, and dramatizes anecdotes about family life in the Alcott household. The work discusses important influences in Alcott's life—including her parents, who were both involved in education reform and human rights issues—before moving into a more detailed account of how Alcott became the writer of such young adult books as the autobiographical *Little Women.*

Awards

St. John received awards from the New Jersey Institute of Technology in 1964 for *The Wider Heart,* in 1965 for *Ready or Not,* in 1967 for *Bridge Between,* in 1983 for *Timewarp Summer,* in 1987 for *Shadow of a Unicorn,* in 1989 for *Return to Morocco,* and in 1990 for *The Delphic Choice.* She received the Secondary Outstanding Merit Carter G. Woodson Book Award, National Council on Social Studies, 1995, for *Harriet: The Life and World of Harriet Beecher Stowe. Pride of Lions: The Story of the House of Atreus* was a *Horn Book* honor list book. Many of St. John's books have been on the New York Public Library Best Books for the Teen-Age list and numerous state honor book lists.

GENERAL COMMENTARY

Drew Stevenson

SOURCE: A review of *The Case of the Dog-Lover's*

Legacy, Danger in the Old Fort, and *The Secret of the Singing Strings,* in *School Library Journal,* Vol. 30, No. 1, December, 1983, p. 84.

Diana's daring rescue of a dog from New York City's East River makes her a media hero in ***The Case of the Dog-Lover's Legacy***. Diana, meanwhile, is determined to find out who threw the dog in the river. It turns out that, in his will, an old man left his estate, including a mystery treasure, for the care of the dog Annie. After Annie's death the fortune will be left to the person who has cared for her. Who would stand to gain the most by Annie's sudden demise? Enough people enthusiastically immerse themselves completely in the dog's plight to give this mystery an atmosphere of continuous energy. Energy, though, isn't enough to buoy up a shaky premise and a plot which takes too many far-fetched turns too often. ***Danger in the Old Fort*** takes place in San Juan, where accidents are plaguing the shooting of 17-year-old Diana's father's television production. In ***The Secret of the Singing Strings,*** Diana comes to the aid of her blind cousin, who is in danger after she overhears a plot to steal a valuable museum piece. These three books are strikingly similar to all of the Nancy Drew or Linda Craig mysteries, with all of the strengths and weaknesses associated with series fiction.

Tess McKellen

SOURCE: A review of *Frontier Dream: Life on the Great Plains and others,* in *School Library Journal,* Vol. 31, No. 5, January, 1985, pp. 72-3.

These four docu-dramas discuss various aspects of the westward movement and frontier life in the mid and late 1800s. In ***Frontier Dream,*** a Scandinavian family relocates from Omaha to the Dakota territory and struggles to make a home on the plains. ***Frontier Farmer*** relates the trials of a boy and his mother attempting to "prove" their claim to their Kansas homestead. ***Frontier Village*** follows the establishment of a tiny frontier town in Wisconsin over a four-year period. ***Wagons West*** describes a wagon train journey from Missouri to Oregon. The format is identical to that of the "Adventures in Colonial America" series, but the illustrative material is inferior, and in general the content is less engaging. As in the earlier series, there are no indexes or glossaries. However, most unfamiliar words are explained within the text. The pen-and-ink illustrations are competent commercial art, but they lack the originality and attention to detail evident in the Colonial series. Although each title focuses on the experiences of a single family, characterization is minimal. The writing is competent, the material is well organized, and much information is presented. Unfortunately there is little insight into the hardships and frustrations experienced by those crossing or living on the frontier. In general, a sense of "place" is diminished by a lack of detail about weather and physical features. ***Frontier Dream*** and ***Frontier Farmer*** are the most effective of the four titles because characters are more individualized, hardships and setbacks are described, and a feeling for

the vastness and loneliness of the Great Plains is communicated. Both titles contain brief but helpful explanations of the "great migration" of the 1860s, thus giving readers a sense of the larger picture. The lack of maps is a serious omission, as in three of the four titles westward migration is the principal focus or is peripherally significant, yet readers cannot follow the overland journeys visually. All in all, these titles represent an adequate but flawed treatment of frontier life.

Sandra L. Ricker

SOURCE: A review of *California Gold Rush: Search for Treasure, Indiana Days: Life in a Frontier Town,* and *Texas Roundup: Life on the Range,* in *School Library Journal,* Vol. 31, No. 6, February, 1985, p. 71.

These titles share the same basic format as they weave historical facts with fictitious characters. ***California Gold Rush*** tells the story of the 1848 Gold Rush by focusing on one young boy's experiences. Sometimes the historical facts seem forced into a weak plot. Although Chambers adequately describes what life was like at that time, she includes very little action. ***Indiana Days,*** set in the 1840s, tells of Kristi, a 12-year-old girl who must leave the Iowa frontier to be educated with relatives in Indiana. The book succinctly describes the life style of people at that time. ***Texas Roundup,*** an exciting tale of a cattle roundup, tells of Juan, a young Hispanic in 19th-century Texas who drives off a cattle rustler. The characterization is adequate but unexciting. The simple pen-and-ink sketches on every page of each book enhance the narratives. Vocabulary is italicized and explained through the context of the text. Large type and wide spacing make the series appealing to reluctant readers. These books are a good choice for school and public libraries that need historical fiction at low reading levels.

Nancy Kewish

SOURCE: A review of *Daniel Boone and the Wilderness Road, Flatboats on the Ohio: Westward Bound,* and *Log-Cabin Home: Pioneers in the Wilderness,* in *School Library Journal,* Vol. 31, No. 6, February, 1985, p. 72.

Stories of family life in the early 1800s. In ***Daniel Boone and the Wilderness Road,*** Grandpa Halliday tells his grandchildren about his experiences exploring with Daniel Boone and the settling of Boonesborough, Kentucky. The Sawyer family moves West by water, and an account of their travels is related in ***Flatboats on the Ohio.*** In ***Log Cabin Home,*** the Craley family moves from Virginia to Kentucky, searching for a new farm home. The format of all three is inviting, with wide margins and attractive pen-and-ink drawings on each page. Historical details are integrated into the simple story lines, providing authenticity, but the characterizations are flat, and the harsh realities of pioneer life are only lightly touched upon.

TITLE COMMENTARY

 THE WISHING STAR (written as Norma Johnston, 1963)

Virginia Kirkus' Service

SOURCE: A review of *The Wishing Star,* in *Virginia Kirkus' Service,* Vol. XXXI, No. 3, February 1, 1963, p. 126.

Resolutely turning her back on reality, Miss Johnston presents a hearts-and-flowers, turn-of-the-century soap opera for youth. Julie Forrest, the pouting teenager who holds center stage, is angry when she moves East with her family to Valleyfield, Massachusetts. Julie is wildly jealous of her exotic mother, and sets out to prove that she, too, can be the apple of the world's eye. Going enthusiastically to parties, church group meetings, and the corner drug store, Julie falls too much in love with Bill—who remains just *plain Bill* throughout the book. In the large, cardboard cast, other teenagers wander across stage: there is Kathy, plagued by an alcoholic mother; and Sue, out for a reckless, good time; and a host of boys who trail after the troubled girls. The drama takes place in 1899, but the author makes no attempt to create an appropriate atmosphere or mood.

Zena Sutherland

SOURCE: A review of *The Wishing Star,* in *Bulletin of the Center for Children's Books,* Vol. XVI, No. 10, June, 1963, pp. 162-63.

A turn-of-the-century story in which a family adapts to a New England town; Mr. Forrest is to be the first principal of the new high-school, and sixteen-year-old Julie fervently hopes that nobody will ever discover that her mother was an actress. Julie is shy, slower to fall in love than she is to make friends of her own sex; she feels overshadowed by her glamorous mother. Despite some gossip about her mother, the town accepts the Forrests; Julie becomes increasingly self-confident. The pace of the story is slow and the dialogue occasionally seems too modern, but the characters are well-developed and well-differentiated, and the values and relationships are good.

 THE WIDER HEART (written as Norma Johnston, 1964)

Virginia Kirkus' Service

SOURCE: A review of *The Wilder Heart,* in *Virginia Kirkus' Service,* Vol. XXXII, No. 5, March 1, 1964, p. 241.

This series of emotional explosions and tense withdrawals begins a few days after the death of Gillian Sheldon's father and ends less than a year later with a prospective stepfather on the doorstep. Her mother, Mimsy, is childlike (and, at times, downright childish); she is petite, unrealistic, and unable to cope with her new life. However Gillian, a seventeen year old tower of strength, attempts to run the show and mother, until she collapses—the result of emotional strain plus pneumonia. There's a cast of extremes: Kitty, the selfish snob, an intriguer of Medician proportions; Anne, a victim of loneliness who engages in minor theft; Paul, a quietly logical Harvard brain who acts as Gillian's wise adviser; Ritchie, a handsome lad out to get whatever will aid Ritchie; Lee, a self-sacrificing, happy, loyal friend, etc. It's an unrealistic "study" of delicate relationships. There's a great deal of boy-girl, girl-boy mix-ups, and an unusual amount of hand-holding and hugging among the girls that seem more like 6th grade than high school.

Zena Sutherland

SOURCE: A review of *The Wider Heart,* in *Bulletin of the Center for Children's Books,* Vol. XVIII, No. 1, September, 1964, p. 12.

When her father dies, Gillian feels responsible for her always-protected mother; she and Mimsy decide to open a shop in the old family home in a small town. The problems of making friends, adjusting to a new school, and keeping spendthrift Mimsy and the shop under control are aggravating; Gillian is further disturbed when jewelry is stolen from the store. She becomes involved in a tense and complicated situation in which the rejected girl who stole the pin is dating the boyfriend of a rival who engineered the theft. Same boyfriend is rejected by Gillian for the worthy brother of the girl next door. The book has some good developmental values in the handling of the theft, of Gillian's attitude toward the culprit, and of the problem of the individual's responsibility to his community; the characters, however, are quite stereotypical and the situations written to formula.

 READY OR NOT (written as Norma Johnston, 1965)

Virginia Kirkus' Service

SOURCE: A review of *Ready or Not,* in *Virginia Kirkus' Service,* Vol. XXXIII, No. 5, March 1, 1965, p. 242.

In the tension-and-rumor-filled months of early 1861, Carlie Benson's father, New Jersey newspaper editor, takes his wife on a trip to Washington for some first-hand reporting and on to North Carolina to visit relatives. While they are gone, the war breaks out, leaving the parents on one side of the border and their children on the other. The young Bensons face the adult problems of running the house and newspaper and fighting the town a contempt for their parents' assumed defection. Carlie, the middle sister at 15, has been waging her own battle against growing up, and suddenly finds herself without a choice. The author's theme is mature responsibility and she presents it with a fine sense of the kind of struggle it is to attain. Laura, the eldest, abandons her flightiness and shows the strength under her prettiness; Ben bridles his outspokenness to take competent charge of the newspaper; and Carlie stops having childish tantrums to find herself and her love. A delightful story, told with wisdom and skill, and if the ending is a bit too good to be true, the people are indeed believable.

Allie Beth Martin

SOURCE: A review of *Ready or Not,* in *Library Journal,* Vol. 90, No. 8, April 15, 1965, p. 80.

Overtones of *Little Women* pervade plot and characters here. Carlie Benson, her parents, family, and friends are caught in the conflict of the Civil War. The parents must remain in the South away from the New Jersey home and family for many months mysteriously leaving family responsibilities to 15-year-old Carlie and her sister and three brothers. A romantic invalid, hostile neighbors, tragedy and misunderstanding and two incipient love affairs all come into the plot. Carlie bears the major responsibility and solves all the problems. There is no real development of plot or characters. Buy where light historical fiction for girls is urgently needed.

THE BRIDGE BETWEEN (written as Norma Johnston, 1966)

Virginia Kirkus' Service

SOURCE: A review of *The Bridge Between,* in *Virginia Kirkus' Service,* Vol. XXXIV, No. 14, July 15, 1966, pp. 696-97.

"Love, understanding, compassion . . . this ability to feel with others, deep beneath the surface, this was the bridge between." Well, not too deep beneath the surface are all of Jenny's feelings as comes the Revolution to Jersey Dutch country in 1776—she wants things to stay as they are and she doesn't want to be involved in the war. But circumstances overrule her conscientious objections and her attempt to keep her home a "place of peace"; the boy it is assumed she will marry is off to fight; her father is arrested and interned; her younger brother (Jenny has been surrogate mother to all her family) comes home with a sizeable amount of Hessian gold which Jenny eventually will smuggle through to General Washington and his bedraggled, mutinous men. The infiltration here of certain morality-maturity concepts is also in the attempt to make this more worthwhile than the usual teen-aged historical although one questions whether they won't have shied away from quiltings and hymn sings to begin with. The story is better than the prose which you will have judged for yourself, above.

Sr. M. Denis, R.S.M.

SOURCE: A review of *The Bridge Between,* in *Best Sellers,* Vol. 26, No. 17, December 1, 1966, p. 340.

Jenny Demarest is the "heart of her family" and the hinge of the plot as she courageously bears the burdens of a sick mother, entangles herself in espionage and involves herself in a love affair and, finally, emerges as a mature person of 16 in this novel with a Revolutionary War setting. The style is realistic, the mood melancholy and pensive, the characters delicately portrayed amidst tragic and terrifying incidents with excellent contrast of the sensitive and the daring. This should enthrall Junior High students.

THE KEEPING DAYS (written as Norma Johnston, 1973)

Lillian N. Gerhardt

SOURCE: A review of *The Keeping Days,* in *Library Journal,* Vol. 98, No. 18, October 15, 1973, p. 3156.

It's got almost everything a family story can supply—the teenage narrator's parents quarrel and make up, her mother is resentful of an unplanned pregnancy, her father's job is threatened, her older sister is beleaguered with simultaneous marriage proposals, her older brother has a religious crisis over loss of faith, her younger siblings quarantine part of the family with nearly fatal cases of scarlet fever. The narrator, Tish, records one year of the daily lives of the active Sterling family in Yonkers, N.Y. in 1900—their conflicting/contrasting temperaments and their interactions with others at home, in school, on the job, at church. It's a big inter-generation cast; the story's well written for action and dialogue. The Sterlings care about each other, and the narrator (who takes herself and her own teen concerns seriously but not tragically) convinces readers to care, too. Although it lacks contemporaneity, current teen novels, relentlessly concentrating on one given problem, could take a lesson from this book; the Sterlings and their concerns didn't cease to exist with W.W.I.

Kirkus Reviews

SOURCE: A review of *The Keeping Days,* in *Kirkus Reviews,* Vol. XLI, No. 21, November 1, 1973, pp. 1211-12.

Fourteen year-old Tish's journal for the year 1900 manages to incorporate both a semiprecious style and a naive faith in virtue and God that are appropriate to the period. But this is not always a plus for readers who are trying to empathize with the problems of her large, troubled family or to accept the solutions proffered. Sixteen year-old Bronwyn, who has been too immature and undirected to choose among her many suitors, finally marries a middle aged friend of her father; brother Ben, a confirmed outsider, recovers from a bout of atheism after a few days of sulking; and Mama will apparently get over her disgust with housework and depression over the prospect of yet another child. Meanwhile Tish examines her own feelings and motives with unflinching honesty—admitting to being jealous of her younger sister's figure even while watching her suffering with scarlet fever, and recording her very surprising reactions to an unwelcome and inappropriate kiss ("my insides felt as though some strange flower had started to grow within me"). Tish draws a sufficient number of keepable insights from the confusing summer—to be shared by anyone who has the fortitude to survive her florid, often tacky, prose.

Mary M. Burns

SOURCE: A review of *The Keeping Days,* in *The Horn Book Magazine,* Vol. XLIX, No. 6, December, 1973, p. 591.

Turn-of-the-century Yonkers is the setting for Tish Sterling's first-person account of her experiences as the fourteen-year-old member of a lively and unpredictable family. Although somewhat reminiscent of *Little Women* both in structure and events (such as the younger sister's bout with scarlet fever), the story of the Sterlings is by no means a carbon copy of the story of the Marches; nor is Mama, relishing the role of Early Christian Martyr as she copes with a post-forty pregnancy, a latter-day version of the ever-patient, discreet Marmee. Nostalgic but not sentimental, flavored generously with romance, the novel captures the anxieties of adolescence with its naïveté and awareness. In chronicling her experiences, Tish favors a lush, dramatic style appropriate for a self-proclaimed writer whose chef-d'oeuvre is to be "a very profound book, and very sad, because it is going to make everybody realize what it's like to be sensitive and misunderstood, and how one suffers on account of people being unwittingly cruel. Only they will realize too late, for I shan't allow it to be published till I've passed on." A fresh, compelling story told with perception and spontaneity.

Denise M. Wilms

SOURCE: A review of *The Keeping Days,* in *The Booklist,* Vol. 70, No. 8, December 15, 1973, p. 446.

Given vitality by the naturalness of its fourteen-year-old narrator Tish Sterling, whose maturing is evident during the seven-month period of the story, this is a warm turn-of-the-century family tale set in Yonkers, New York. Regarding herself as the sensitive one in her family, Tish, third of six children, is quite self-centered and unable to cope with her mother's abrupt, often "Early Christian Martyr" manner, and even her mother's change-of-life pregnancy does not, at first, soften the relationship. This is also the year Tish's father is in danger of losing his job, her older sister is shuffling suitors, her brother Ben is skipping school and getting into trouble, and her twelve-year-old sister Marnie almost dies of scarlet fever. Characterizations are especially good and interrelationships well developed.

📖 *GLORY IN THE FLOWER* (written as Norma Johnston, 1974)

Kirkus Reviews

SOURCE: A review of *Glory in the Flower,* in *Kir-*

kus Reviews, Vol. XLII, No. 4, February 15, 1974, p. 192.

Even though this journal installment is subtitled "The Tears and Trials of Letitia Sterling," the effusive sentimentality of *The Keeping Days* has eased up a little. Tish is still too much of a princess to be universally popular and she reflects and upholds the starchy morality of the "nice" people in turn-of-the-century Yonkers—an ethic which today's young people might find more frightening than quaint. Morality crops up again and again when she sublimates her feelings for Ken in the Browning Society's production of *Romeo and Juliet,* and sadly, as the class slut Mary Lou Hodge acts out her role to its pregnant conclusion, though the reader will realize long before Tish does just how much pluck goes into Mary Lou's bitchy pose. And Tish's meek friend Celinda becomes a victim of the other side of morality when her embittered mother adopts religion with a vengeance. Tish also makes spasmodic attempts to conquer her great fault of self-dramatization though most of her peers will enjoy seeing it indulged by her reign as Juliet. And the purposely anachronistic style and viewpoint forms a believable context for chronicling the myriad tears and trials of the freshman class of 1901.

Lillian N. Gerhardt

SOURCE: A review of *Glory in the Flower,* in *Library Journal,* Vol. 20, No. 7, March, 1974, p. 118.

Sequel to **The Keeping Days** this continues 14-year-old Tish Sterling's diary account of her large family's life during the first six months of 1901 in Yonkers, N.Y. These two books are robust examples of the family saga, a form seldom encountered these days for older children. The birth at home of her baby sister, with Tish as midwife, the dangerous insanity of her best friend's mother, the out-of-wedlock pregnancy of a high school classmate, and the death of her grandfather are all closely reported by Tish, whose main trial and triumph in this book is her interpretation of Juliet in the high school play and the role's effect on her understanding of herself and others. As with the first book, the outstanding feature here is the total picture it offers of one girl's life—at home, at school, at church, with her girl friends and with her boyfriend. Together the two books are in refreshing contrast to the many juvenile novels with contemporary settings that overdirect all characters to a single social or emotional problem. Offering the interaction of many vivid characters of all ages and tracing attractively serious Tish's growth from self-concern to mature consideration for others, this will assuredly satisfy adolescents in search of a long read.

The Booklist

SOURCE: A review of *Glory in the Flower,* in *The Booklist,* Vol. 70, No. 14, March 15, 1974, p. 820.

This is the sequel to the author's **The Keeping Days** and

completes Tish Sterling's fourteenth year in Yonkers, New York, of 1901. Once again, Tish grows rapidly and bumpily, this time mainly under the gaze of her schoolfriends. Tish finds comfort in her large, aggressive family and derives self-importance from a turbulently developed lead role in the school's production of *Romeo and Juliet.* She uncovers the covert but insistent warmth of her girl friends, who rebel against her egotism when it runs rampant, and finds a new depth of feeling in her relationship with her friend and schoolmate Ken. Outside her immediate circle, she is indirectly involved in the amusing and tragic activities of a closely-knit neighborhood's social misfits. Despite its sentimentality and its old-fashioned aura, this book will strike a harmonious chord with today's teens; it stands in proud contrast to more trendy—and less literary—works which focus too narrowly on individual aspects of human emotion and growth.

Zena Sutherland

SOURCE: A review of *Glory in the Flower,* in *Bulletin of the Center for Children's Books,* Vol. 27, No. 11, July-August, 1974, p. 179.

Supposedly a journal kept over half a year, this makes no concession to the journal form but is told as the first person account of Tish Sterling's fourteenth year, 1901, her first year in high school. The book is primarily a school and family chronicle rather than a story with a plot: Tish has a troubled relationship with another girl, a developing affection for a boy, a crisis she handles well at home, an adjustment to her grandfather's death. The period details and dialogue are convincing, and the plot threads nicely knitted, but what the story gains in diversity it loses in focus.

📖 STRANGERS DARK AND GOLD (written as Norma Johnston, 1975)

Kirkus Reviews

SOURCE: A review of *Strangers Dark and Gold,* in *Kirkus Reviews,* Vol. XLIII, No. 5, March 1, 1975, pp. 245-46.

Strangers Dark and Gold is one of those worthy but essentially arid undertakings—a retelling of the Jason and Medea story which merely amalgamates the sources of Apollonius, Pindar and Euripides into a single coherent narrative without imposing any significant interpretation on the material. Johnston does develop the motivations of Jason and Medea, though along traditional lines—Jason as a man not cut out for the role destiny has dealt him, Medea as endowed with a more modern consciousness of her own powers for good and evil. However no other characters are portrayed in this manner, the pacing is that of myth, and the language is formal and stately—a diction that compares well to many pseudo-19th century and pseudo-biblical retellings, but still artificial. Johnston creates a Medea of impressive dignity and power, while steering clear of the gore and eroticism of John Gardner's

Jason and Medea. But the earlier episodes on the *Argo* do tend to drag on, and it's unlikely that anyone without a strong interest in classical myths will persist. As for those who are ready to appreciate Johnston's intelligent, if not very creative, handling of the sources, they will still find this work incidental to the Greek drama and poetry they could read just as easily and far more profitably.

Natalie Babbitt

SOURCE: A review of *Strangers Dark and Gold,* in *The New York Times Book Review,* May 11, 1975, p. 8.

The story of the Argonauts—of Jason and Medea and the Golden Fleeces—is at least 28 centuries old and has survived on sheer magnetism, for it has no single classic chronicler—no Homer to sing it into perpetuity—and exists in no single authorized version. It has been pruned, sterilized and squeezed into countless children's anthologies, including *Tanglewood Tales,* much of its violence and all of its passion sliced away. And yet it survives. For when left intact, it is the greatest of the myths, a brawling, bloody, delicious saga compared to which *The Odyssey* is a stroll home from Grandma's.

To my knowledge, there are only two complete versions in English. One is Robert Graves's magnificent novel, *Hercules, My Shipmate,* published in 1945. The other is brand new: Norma Johnston's *Strangers Dark and Gold,* just out this spring as a juvenile. I have never been so eager to read a book, or so anxious to like it, for it is high time the myth came out in its proper form for young people.

This much can be said outright: Johnston's scholarship seems faultless. She has spared no pains, and everything is here, every adventure, with none of the requisite gore omitted. So her book represents an enormous labor. Any complete version must perforce be long and complicated, with unpronounceable names, labyrinthine geography and tangled genealogies. Johnston does as well with all that as anyone could, and must have agonized in the process.

However, scholarship is not enough. Three things are sufficiently wrong to ruin the final effect:

First, Johnston has opted for a prose that can only be described as pulpit-archaic: "What did he see when he did look upon me?" It is full of peculiar constructions: ". . . the slight figure started and poised, motionless in flight . . . "; "Then his voice changed to that of one stunned by a great stone . . . "; "Within was wide and spacious . . . "; "It was a stillness growing mixed with fury." It is painfully overwritten: "The grotesque ghost of an ironic smile cracked the shriveled lips." All this puts great strain on the patience of the reader.

Second, Johnston's Medea is a real departure: not the shrewd, wild sorceress, god-ridden into a passion for pretty, petty Jason, but a civilized, unliberated child/woman who is high on silent suffering and low on pride and confidence. Because of this, her acts of violence are emasculated and much of the story's savage majesty is lost.

Finally, the editing is quite frankly the worst I've ever seen. There are frequent grammatical errors: "To whom can you yourself turn to, save the gods?" "Behind him on Argo's deck, no excited discussion spurred." "... child of a mother different than herself ...," "... there was to be no bartering terms." There are redundancies: "the alien stranger," "osiers and willows," "... each trying to outlast the other in endurance." There are word repetitions that ruin emphasis: "He shut the gates firm shut against the women ..." Such carelessness is unforgivable.

Graves's *Hercules, My Shipmate* was not intended for young people, but that was in the 40's. I can't see any reason why it wouldn't be perfectly acceptable for young people nowadays. If you want an Argonautica that is intact, scholarly and finely written, go to Graves.

William B. Hill, S.J.

SOURCE: A review of *Strangers Dark and Gold,* in *Best Sellers,* Vol. 35, No. 3, June, 1975, p. 60.

The story of Jason and Medea is retold in this novel. The Dark Stranger (stranger to Iolcus and Greece) is Medea, princess of Colchis and Priestess of Hecate; the Gold Stranger is Jason, who sailed in search of the Golden Fleece and won it in Colchis with the help of Medea. It is a many-times-told story; Apollonius of Rhodes composed an epic, *The Argonautica;* Pindar was perhaps the first to tell the tale; Euripides made a tragedy of the fate of Medea; in more recent years, Robert Graves' *Hercules My Shipmate* was published in 1945; Blasco-Ibanez wrote *Los Argonautos* in 1914. Myth and magic and love and hate are all woven together. For the blond Jason, when he returned to Iolcus, fell in love with a princess of Corinth and put Medea aside. It is Medea's tragedy, although she had her revenge in her anger. Norma Johnston's telling of the tale is mercifully much shorter than any translation of Apollonius; and she shows her familiarity with the epic diction. In her version, the story moves swiftly to its inevitable end.

The Booklist

SOURCE: A review of *Strangers Dark and Gold,* in *The Booklist,* Vol. 71, No. 20, June 15, 1975, p. 1070.

Based primarily on the three earliest written accounts that have survived intact to the present—those by Apollonius, Pindar, and Euripides—this retelling of the dramatic, ultimately tragic epic of Jason and Medea is written in an eloquently poetic style and is imbued with vitality. The story follows the trials and triumphs of Jason and the Argonauts in the quest for the Golden Fleece and Jason's winning of Medea—virgin priestess of Hecate and princess of Colchis—who betrayed her father and homeland

for love of Jason, only to be betrayed by her love later in life. Jason comes across as a young man not himself heroic but able to inspire others to great deeds, while Medea stands out as a courageous, indomitable woman who does what she does out of love rather than selfishness and who bears up stoically in the realization that her tragic fate is her own doing. Background notes and a glossary are appended. A rewarding reading experience for high school and good junior high readers who appreciate Greek mythology.

Zena Sutherland

SOURCE: A review of *Strangers Dark and Gold,* in *Bulletin of the Center for Children's Books,* Vol. 29, No. 1, September, 1975, p. 12.

A stirring, lyric retelling of the mythological adventures of Jason in his quests and of the tragic love of Jason and Medea is based on the three earliest accounts that have survived intact; the author discusses these in her very helpful notes and points out that the three (Apollonius, Pindar, and Euripides) were telling tales that were familiar to their audiences and that therefore they differed in details and approach. **Strangers Dark and Gold** is a synthesis of the early versions, smoothly woven, told with a high sense of narrative and written with the strength and dignity befitting an epic tale. A glossary is appended.

OF TIME AND OF SEASONS (written as Norma Johnston, 1975)

Kirkus Reviews

SOURCE: A review of *Of Time and of Seasons,* in *Kirkus Reviews,* Vol. XLIII, No. 20, October 15, 1975, pp. 1193-94.

This hothouse historical throws us into the laps of the Vandever family: father Paul is a famous Hudson River School painter; writer/mother Celia divides herself between potboilers and serious essays under the pseudonym Martin St. James; Jason is being pushed toward a career as a concert pianist; Betony writes; Jon paints; brother Joshua attends West Point . . . and eighteen-year-old Bedelia is special in another way, she hasn't really learned much since an accident at age two. Bridget does nothing else but tell this story, which gets off to a violent start when temperamental Jason shames a reluctant Josh into enlisting in the Civil War and Bedelia is "interfered with" by the no-good Culhaine boys. Fearing Jason's temper again, Betony and Bridget decide to keep the outrage a secret (Bedelia herself is stunned mute) and soon enough everyone is distracted by the arrival of two more decoratively two dimensional characters—great-grandmother Lady Sandiman who's spent the last few decades dallying in Arabia and housemaid Marrit, one of the Ramapo Mountain People. Lots more happens, including the arrival of a baby and a suitor for Bedelia and a lover for Celia. Johnston, whether in the admirable **Keeping Days** or the tortuous *Strangers Dark and Gold,* has never been a writer to leave things out. Each of the Vandevers is favored by a personal Muse and, as a group, they're so self-conscious of their own specialness that it's hard to credit them belonging to 1861 or any other time. And even their starchy energy begins to pall as it becomes obvious that this chronicle has more ingredients than one of Celia's potboilers.

Shirley M. Wilton

SOURCE: A review of *Of Time and of Seasons,* in *School Library Journal,* Vol. 22, No. 3, November, 1975, p. 91.

Much happens in the Vandever household in the nine months between March and October of 1861. The outbreak of war between the States affects the careers of both mother Celia, a well-known journalist, and father Paul, a noted painter. The older children each face a personal crisis: Joshua, the oldest son, must go to the war; Jason struggles to decide whether his destiny is a music career. Bedelia, who at 18 is still a child-like innocent, is sexually abused; and 15-year-old Bridget, narrator of the story, laments her lack of artistic talent until she discovers her ability to understand people and help them to know themselves. Johnston's smooth, consciously eloquent prose suits the period setting; however, the conventional plot situations are sometimes contrived. Johnston evokes sentimentality rather than genuine emotion, but readers of her previous novels will still enjoy the drama and romance of this lengthy literary soap opera.

The Booklist

SOURCE: A review of *Of Time and of Seasons,* in *The Booklist,* Vol. 72, No. 5, November 1, 1975, p. 368.

The Civil War is brewing, and in New Jersey Bridget and her family react to its turbulent shadow in their own individual ways. Her fifteenth year is already one of conflicting emotions as she searches for her unique place in a family overflowing with talent: her father, a famous painter; her mother, an outspoken writer using a male pseudonym; one brother, a brilliant West Point student but a reluctant soldier; her twin a musician scorning his talent and longing to join the army; and her beautiful older sister, escaping reality in a childlike mind. When her mother leaves for Washington to do on-the-scene war reporting, new responsibilities are forced on Bridget. She gropes for understanding when a town drunk misuses her sister, when her brother deserts after Bull Run, and when her feelings for Clu of the undesirable Culhaine family begin to overwhelm her. Building on the motif "to everything there is a season," Johnston puts several plots together with expressive characters and a thought-provoking conclusion. She has a remarkable ability to paint pictures with words and portray family relationships that are warm and close, yet fraught with conflict. As in *The Keeping Days* and *Glory in the Flower,* Johnston brings

perception to today's readers through characters who lived yesterday.

Virginia C. Jones

SOURCE: A review of *Of Time and of Seasons,* in *Best Sellers,* Vol. 35, No. 9, December, 1975, p. 296.

For a young girl growing up with a noted painter for a father and a brilliant writer for a mother, the environment could have been much more disasterous than it really was for Bridget. But Bridget was the mainstay and stabilizer of the family.

The Civil War arose to cause controversies between the brothers and the family, but the family love and care never slackened. Rifts between the parents occurred, however, as would be natural between two talented and artistic people. Bridget bore the brunt of whatever catastrophes befell.

The setting is a lovely old home in the Ramapo hills of North Jersey amid some fond but some "look down the nose" more conventional neighbors.

I wish more could have been said about Marrit De Groat, the invaluable "hired girl" of the "Mountain People." When I lived in the vicinity they were called "Jackson Whites." I had my "Manny." We did a lot of missionary work with them and their history, and the effects of the encroachment of civilization on them would be an interesting side story.

For want of a better word, I would call this book "packed." Beautifully so. There is hardly a moment in the lives of this family and all the characters involved that is not completely delineated. I could have wished for a few more chapters!

A STRIVING AFTER WIND (written as Norma Johnston, 1976)

Alice Corwin

SOURCE: A review of *A Striving After Wind,* in *School Library Journal,* Vol. 23, No. 1, September, 1976, p. 134.

Overly talky without saying much, this Civil War story concerns the Vandevers, an artistic, articulate family whose spokesperson in the novel is 16-year-old Bridget. Everybody from father, the artist; mother, the author; younger brother, the musician; and the three daughters are all involved in finding direction in their lives. Particularly Bridget looks for "meaning" in her platonic relationship with a 50-year-old actor. Unfortunately, there is neither action nor historical background to compensate for Johnston's stilted characterizations, reducing *Wind* to just a lot of hot air.

Kirkus Reviews

SOURCE: A review of *A Striving After Wind,* in *Kirkus Reviews,* Vol. XLIV, No. 17, September, 1, 1976, p. 982.

The continuing saga of the fervidly creative Vandevers (first met in *Of Time and of Seasons,*) has the gossipy complexity but none of the astuteness of this author's *Keeping Days* duo. Here Bridget, still typed as the only non-artist in the family, watches while, again and again, "truth hides for the sake of justice." Mentally retarded Delia, having been raped by neighborhood rowdies, is read out of church for refusing to reveal the name of her baby's father. The family keeps secret the fate of Joshua, who deserted the Union army. Mother Celia's identity as the political essayist Martin St. James is protected by the gallant lies of her former sweetheart, Lord Pagford. And Bridget neglects her loyal boyfriend Clu for clandestine afternoon teas with the aging actor, O., who teaches her Shakespeare and fires her dramatic ambitions. Bridget's notion of "justice" is family-centered and often closer to simple adolescent smugness, and for every reader vicariously stimulated by the Vandever's educational Sunday teas and intellectual exchanges, there'll be another who finds them stifling. As for the title, let's just say it's all too accurate.

Barbara Elleman

SOURCE: A review of *A Striving After Wind,* in *Booklist,* Vol. 73, No. 2, September 15, 1976, pp. 176-77.

This sequel continues the dominating theme begun in *Of Time and of Seasons*—Bridget's search for her own individual place among her talented, competitive family. The struggle for self-recognition often puts her inwardly at odds with her painter father, novelist/newspaper-writer mother, musician brother, and budding-author sister. The whole family is consistently together, however, in their concern for Josh, who has fled the Civil War battlefield into Canadian exile, and for Bedelia, their brain-injured sister, pregnant after an assault by a local drunkard. The main thrust is Bridget's confusion over her growing relationship with Clu, a local boy her age, and with a renowned actor traveling incognito whom she dubs Mr. Odysseus. Daily secret meetings with O, as she eventually calls him, lead Bridget to a wider understanding of people's emotions and an insight into their motives, but open a floodgate of conflicts in her own feelings. Johnston's gift for individualizing her characters with well-developed interrelationships is somewhat shadowed by the overload of complex situations in which they find themselves and the highly noble way they meet them. But readers will agonize along with Bridget as she attempts to sort through her life, and those liking a long story will find themselves quickly immersed and sorry to reach the end.

Zena Sutherland

SOURCE: A review of *A Striving After Wind,* in *Bulletin*

of the Center for Children's Books, Vol. 30, No. 7, March, 1977, p. 108.

In a sequel to *Of Time and of Seasons,* Bridget continues the story of her family (artist father, journalist mother writing under a masculine pseudonym, retarded sister, deserter brother, and other children) in the Civil War period. The Vandever family, as depicted by Bridget, is creative, liberal and candid, ahead of their time in many of their ideas—but Bridget wonders if all their efforts have any real meaning, and she finally concludes that "the journey was all. That, and using one's talents." Meanwhile, she has fallen out with her swain and had an intense relationship with an older man; she has grieved because her retarded sister (who had been raped) is cast out of church because she will not divulge the name of her child's father; she has been concerned about her parents' roles and her brothers', under the pressure put on them by those whose wartime patriotism is feverish. Johnston has assembled an interesting cast, but the book has too many characters, too many problems, and too much emotion to be wholly successful despite an excellent writing style.

📖 **THE SANCTUARY TREE (written as Norma Johnston, 1977)**

Kirkus Reviews

SOURCE: A review of *The Sanctuary Tree,* in *Kirkus Reviews,* Vol. XLV, No. 3, February 1, 1977, p. 98.

Sweetheart Ken Lathan moves to Pennsylvania; Gramps dies and the contents of his farmhouse are sold at auction; father's cataract operation forces her to resign from the Browning Society play; depression and fear of criticism cause her to abandon her writing: for Tish Sterling her fifteenth year is a season of loneliness, disappointment, and burdensome family responsibilities. But Johnston, in this sequel to *The Keeping Days,* is once again comfortably at home—both with the "prunes and prisms" 1901 milieu, where Sunday night socials at the Parish House are the stuff of gossip and with the bustle and ferment of an old-fashioned extended kinship. Tish is perhaps one of the more self-centered heroines around, yet her battle to preserve both privacy and ego in the face of the expectations that go with her role as eldest daughter at home is all the more empathic because Johnston never defines it in purely feminist terms. Tish passes up a chance to play Nora in *A Doll's House* in order to keep house herself, and it is a bible-quoting anonymous correspondent—and, surprisingly, sister Bronwyn's "jughead" stepson, Junius—who help Tish snap out of her melancholy. An ingenuous turn of circumstances, but one that Tish carries off with her usual panache.

Barbara Elleman

SOURCE: A review of *The Sanctuary Tree,* in *Booklist,* Vol. 73, No. 16, April 15, 1977, p. 1267.

Tish Sterling, Johnston's turn-of-the-century heroine of *The Keeping Days* and *Glory in the Flower* is now 15. Continually at odds with herself and her world, she struggles to understand her mother's insistence on breaking up and selling her grandfather's farm, her own block in the writing that has always been her refuge, her feelings when boyfriend Ken's family moves away, and the need to give up her school drama activities to take over at home during a family emergency. Tish's inner growth becomes the focal point as she prods, examines, and finally comes to realize her own hopes and to see others in a more understanding light. As usual, Johnston's plot bursts with incidents and dynamic characters, sometimes tending to the over-dramatic; but she continues, in a perceptive and thought-provoking way, to imbue her story with the problems and transitions of growing up.

Zena Sutherland

SOURCE: A review of *The Sanctuary Tree,* in *Bulletin of the Center for Children's Books,* Vol. 31, No. 1, September, 1977, p. 18.

A sequel to *The Keeping Days* and *Glory in the Flower* continues Tish's account, month by month, of her fourteenth year. The time is 1901, the story is again as much a record of family events as it is a description of her own feelings and reactions to the year's changes. Pa has an eye operation, Mama takes over running his secretarial school; older sister Bronwyn has a baby, younger sister Marnie acquires a boyfriend; Tish and Mama don't get along, especially because Tish mourns her grandfather but Mama thinks her callous; Tish's beloved moves out of town. In sum, in addition to problems within the family, Tish must adjust within a few months to new responsibilities, an apparent rift between her and her beloved Ken, having to give up a chance to star in a school play, etc. The ending is a bit on the all-ends-tied side, with Pa home recuperating, Tish's acceptance of another girl's dramatic ability, and a happy reunion with Ken, who has finally won Mama's approbation by finding a younger child who's run away. The characterization is adequate and the writing style has vitality; the dialogue is quite good, although Mama's clipped speech is not convincing: "Just had letter this morning," or, "Don't count chickens, had your chance."

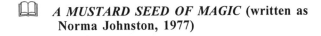 *A MUSTARD SEED OF MAGIC* (written as Norma Johnston, 1977)

Barbara Elleman

SOURCE: A review of *A Mustard Seed of Magic,* in *Booklist,* Vol. 74, No. 3, October 1, 1977, p. 298.

Set around the turn of the century, this fourth story about the Sterlings picks up just a few days after *The Sanctuary Tree* ends. With the close of the holidays, Tish's beau Ken returns to Pennsylvania, the Sterling household settles down, and Tish hopes to concentrate on her writing.

Her first excitement over her teacher's offer for critiquing sessions wears thin when she finds them more drudgery than she expected, as well as a blow to her literary pride. In addition, she finds her energies divided among other emerging problems as her parents argue about who should run their secretarial school, new controversies develop around the scandalous Mary Lou Hodge, and a sister's stepson increasingly intrudes on her time. Johnston's plotting is as inventive as ever, with twists and turns that keep the pages turning; if Tish's philosophical renderings seem a bit overblown for 15, they'll provide thoughtful content for the introspective reader.

Phyllis Milder

SOURCE: A review of *A Mustard Seed of Magic,* in *Best Sellers,* Vol. 37, No. 9, December, 1977, p. 294.

This is the latest book in a very good series about the Sterlings. Written from Tish's point of view, each book takes the reader immediately into the midst of this vibrant, slightly chaotic, sensitive and loving family of nine. Every month brings new challenges to the family unit (in the first book, for example, the mother is unhappily pregnant with baby number seven, the father may lose his job, and the children are sent to the grandparents for a while because of the family problems). The solutions never come easily and the answers each family member finds are not always right, but the Sterlings are so believable, their approach is so honest and blunt, that much is to be learned from their struggles.

In *A Mustard Seed of Magic,* Tish becomes deeply involved with Mrs. Owens, the advisor of the literary club and a personal mentor who directs Tish's creative gifts. Tish must learn to accept hard criticism and she finds this most difficult. The biggest town scandal is that Mary Lou Hodge's illegitimate baby is being raised as a member of the Hodge family. How should teenagers deal with this and Mary Lou's continued unabashed flirtatious behavior? Also, Tish's mother has been working in place of her husband who had surgery. Once liberated, Mrs. Sterling does not want to return to the home, and the parents are fighting so much that the children often cry themselves to sleep.

I highly recommend this book as well as the others in the series. In fact, I could see a value for *A Mustard Seed of Magic* in the classroom. The style is fine, smooth, and readable. Every topic from religion (too much, Christianity versus Judaism, none at all) to sex and the first boyfriend, to relations with parents and teachers, to understanding the fluctuating friendships of the teenage years is sensitively explored. What a wonderful gift this book would be for that young person beginning to grapple with the realities of adult life which now are not so far away.

Zena Sutherland

SOURCE: A review of *A Mustard Seed of Magic,* in

Bulletin of the Center for Children's Books, Vol. 31, No. 6, February, 1978, p. 97.

A continuation of the turn-of-the-century story of Tish Sterling, and of the problems and relationships in her circle of friends, teachers, and family. One teacher, Mrs. Owens, plays a major role here because sixteen-year-old Tish balks at her teacher's criticism of her writing. The discipline of Mrs. Owens' editing is effective, however; bitter at first, Tish realizes how much she has helped. Trying to help other people adjust to their problems, Tish confronts her own difficulties, getting support from her faith, her friends, and her growing insight into her own strengths and limitations. Although the many threads of the story are nicely knit, the book is weakened by a plethora of subplots. The characterization is good, the writing style adequate, occasionally jarring because of such errors as " . . . he had not yet designed to take us into his confidence."

THE SWALLOW'S SONG (written as Norma Johnston, 1978)

The Booklist

SOURCE: A review of *The Swallow's Song,* in *The Booklist,* Vol. 74, No. 15, April 1, 1978, p. 1249.

The time is 1920 and the Standishes have returned to Ocean Grove for the summer, but 16-year-old Allison finds the once comfortable atmosphere of her now senile grandmother's home completely gone and with it her own self-complacency. Angered by parental constraints, troubled by lack of familial warmth, and disturbed by her brother's increasingly irresponsible attitude, Allison gladly retreats to the rose-colored world of the wealthy Farradays. Her relationship with college-age Dirk Farraday and growing friendship with his sister Lisa make Allison privy to surprising Farraday family problems, and through her efforts to help them, she discovers personal strengths and manages to see her own family in proper perspective. Johnston, the author of several previous novels, ably maintains a feeling of the period amid convoluted plot turnings (and sometimes self-conscious dialogue) and manages important teenage themes with a grace that produces a warm afterglow.

Peggy Sullivan

SOURCE: A review of *The Swallow's Song,* in *School Library Journal,* Vol. 24, No. 9, May, 1978, p. 77.

Allison Standish's 17th summer in 1920 is spent at a New Jersey resort where, along with her family, she copes with her grandmother's increasing senility and meets the wealthy Farradays who have a profound effect on her. She admires and envies Lisa and loses her heart to Dirk but comes to realize that the Farradays have problems—including a cocaine-addicted father and a confused, flirtatious mother—that make Allison's own seem minor. There is some drama but it's too superficially resolved in

the conclusion, when the Standishes reach out more openly to one another than ever before. Johnston seems intent on showing that adolescent problems are universal but fails because the story's setting of 50-plus years ago is not fully realized: some contemporary expressions sound anachronistic in the dialogue, and some contemporary attitudes seem forced.

Hildagarde Gray

SOURCE: A review of *The Swallow's Song,* in *Best Sellers,* Vol. 38, No. 4, July, 1978, p. 135.

The Roaring Twenties carried behind its sparkling, spangled exterior the dreary decay of the idle rich, while the "other half" looked on with envy. Flappers tossed their "it girl" hair-dos, trailing wisps of scarf behind as they roared off in expensive cars completely accessoried with sheik, flask, and do-di-o-do!

At Ocean Grove, New Jersey, a community noted for its ultraconservatism, young Allison Standish feels smothered in her close family environment. Grandma exhibited senility in nocturnal rambles, so Allison's family has come to stay the summer with Granny while pondering the solution to the dilemma of old age. Escape from such stifling obligation comes for both brother Jerry and Allison when they meet the elite young on the beach. A poor little rich girl, Lisa Farraday, suffers identical depression as Grandad Farraday, who holds the purse strings, pulls them to keep Father and Mother Farraday, as well as dashing Dirk and lovely Lisa, dancing to his monetary tango. As the worlds of Lisa and Allison collide, each feels the other's world is the answer to happiness. The climax, in which liquor, drugs, philandering and jealousy bring both families to the point of disintegration, points up the value of strong family ties, a sense of responsibility, and the truth that the grass is *not* always greener over there!

Cluttered with clichés and burdened with a solve-all ending, *The Swallow's Song* still will enjoy a good following. Clean language, virtue rewarded, and a devil-may-care atmosphere make a safe story that only *sounds* wild, rather refreshing!

Zena Sutherland

SOURCE: A review of *The Swallow's Song,* in *Bulletin of the Center for Children's Books,* Vol. 32, No. 1, September, 1978, p. 11.

Allison, sixteen, begins the story with "I shall always remember the first time I ever saw Lisa Farraday." Allison has come with her family to stay with Gran, who has become senile; the summer holds little promise until she meets Lisa, daughter of a wealthy couple whose frenetic social life seems exciting compared to her own unhappy home situation. Allison is wooed by Lisa's brother, and she yearns to have the freedom Lisa and Dirk Farraday enjoy. But the more she gets to know the Farradays, the more she knows of the serious problems in the family. And so she gains perspective about her own situation. Johnston gives a vivid picture of a 1920's resort community, especially of the Fitzgerald atmosphere of the Farradays' pursuits, but the story is weakened by having a plethora of problems: Gran's senility, Dirk's use of drugs, Mr. Farraday's alcoholism, Allison's worry about her brother. A colorful canvas, but too crowded.

IF YOU LOVE ME, LET ME GO (written as Norma Johnston, 1978)

Booklist

SOURCE: A review of *If You Love Me, Let Me Go,* in *Booklist,* Vol. 75, No. 1, September 1, 1978, p. 39.

Johnston resumes the story of Allison Standish, begun in *The Swallow's Song,* with the Standishes' return to Glenwood to face new crises—financial reverses demand the closing of the family store, the physical and mental decline of Allison's grandmother continually tests family strength, Jerry's unhappiness and ultimate failure at college brings him home, and Allison is forced to reevaluate her friendship with Lisa Farrady. The novel stands best alongside its predecessor, and although the period flavor of the earlier book is less evident and the characters' philosophical insights wax a bit heavy at times, teenagers who enjoyed *The Swallow's Song* will want to follow Allison's latest progress toward self-understanding and the true meaning of love and friendship.

Cyrisse Jaffee

SOURCE: A review of *If You Love Me, Let Me Go,* in *School Library Journal,* Vol. 25, No. 2, October, 1978, p. 156.

In this sequel to *The Swallow's Song,* Allison, a teenager in the 1920s, continues to grapple with a senile grandmother, rebellious brother, and harassed, going bankrupt father and to find herself drawn once again into the glamorous, sordid world of the wealthy Farraday family. Her close friendship with Lisa Farraday undergoes a change when each experiences the need to be alone (thus the title). For a while it seems as if handsome Pat Adams will fill the gap, until Allison meets medical student Mario, to whom she is powerfully attracted despite their differences in religion and background. The relationship alleviates Allison's agonies over her confused sexual attraction to sophisticated, decadent Dick Farraday. Johnston succeeds in capturing Allison's concerns and emotions, against the background of the Roaring 20s. However, the crises in the Standish and Farraday households are unending, and the writing style is melodramatic and occasionally cliched. The lack of focus and of variation in pacing makes the story tedious and, in the conventional romantic formula, Allison's newly discovered sense of self is sublimated as soon as she meets Mario, an Italian stereotype.

Zena Sutherland

SOURCE: A review of *If You Love Me, Let Me Go,* in *Bulletin of the Center for Children's Books,* Vol. 32, No. 4, December, 1978, pp. 63-4.

In a sequel to *The Swallow's Song* Allison learns that part of love and friendship means sharing the other person. In the first book, Lisa Farraday had become a dear friend through a difficult summer. Now Allison is back home, her family still coping with a senile and erratic grandmother, when Lisa appears, announcing that her parents have separated and that she and her mother have come to Allison's small town. Lively and popular, Lisa helps Allison achieve a similar popularity, but Lisa wants to be free to have other friends, and Allison goes through a very unhappy period before she can accept the fact that this doesn't mean she's being rejected. Other threads in the story are Gran's death, following a hospital stay, and Allison's romance with a young doctor, Mario Rienzi, whom she's met at the hospital and of whom her parents disapprove. The writing style is adequate, the story and characters believable, but—as with the earlier book—the canvas is overcrowded.

Kirkus Reviews

SOURCE: A review of *If You Love Me, Let Me Go,* in *Kirkus Reviews,* Vol. XLVI, No. 23, December 1, 1978, pp. 1309-10.

A sequel to *The Swallow's Song* that's even more inane than the original—a Fifties cast spouting Seventies clichés in a Twenties setting. Allison Standish returns from her pivotal summer with the uppercrusty Farradays to small-town New Jersey, intent on being part of the high school crowd—she's now got modish trimmings on her dresses. Sure enough, Pookie and the others seem to accept her and then Lisa Farraday shows up too: her parents are in the midst of a scandalous divorce and Allison's homey home is just the antidote. Allison seems to have it made but all these other threads keep tripping her up: her Gran, now living with them, is deteriorating rapidly; her Dad's store is failing too; Harvard brother Jerry is indifferent to the family's stresses and flunking out; and an Italian Catholic orderly at Gran's hospital makes a play for Allison's Episcopalian sympathies. All those loose ends get tied up, of course, but it takes some doing—much too much. And meanwhile, a reader must suffer through lines like "The auditorium rocked with mirth" or (Lisa to Allison, never mind the circumstances) "If you do love me, let me grow." Let it go.

THE CRUCIBLE YEAR (written as Norma Johnston, 1979)

Booklist

SOURCE: A review of *The Crucible Year,* in *Booklist,* Vol. 75, No. 14, March 15, 1979, pp. 1142-43.

Although subtleties will escape teenagers unfamiliar with

Arthur Miller's play *The Crucible,* they will, nonetheless, grasp part of its significance, which Johnston weaves into her latest teenage novel using the play as a structural and thematic underpinning. Beth Newcomb finds the transition from her insulated private school world into the realm of public education easy with the help of Mollie Hanrahan, who gets her involved in a progressive humanities class where she auditions for a part in the production of Miller's play and where she gets to know Paul Brandini. But the rosy glow of high school parties, camaraderie, and first love fades as Beth involves herself in a campaign to protect a teacher from unjust dismissal due to rumors of homosexuality and becomes Paul's confidante (almost, at one point, his physical intimate) when he grapples with the shock of his father's promiscuity and doubts about his own sexual identity. For the author's following, this is likely to evoke reflections on conformity, courage, and the meaning of humanity, without—thanks to Johnston's able plotting and ability to remain at a distance from her characters—becoming too ponderous.

Karen M. Klockner

SOURCE: A review of *The Crucible Year,* in *The Horn Book Magazine,* Vol. LV, No. 2, April, 1979, p. 200.

A year in the life of Elizabeth Newcomb—a sixteen-year-old high school junior—during which events in her own life and in the lives of those closest to her turn in unexpected and confusing directions. Her humanities class performs Arthur Miller's *The Crucible,* and frightening parallels between the drama and her real life become apparent. "More and more, we lived in a *Crucible* world. We were bound together by a special intimacy, special tensions." The first-person narrative is written in a fluid style as Elizabeth looks back at people and events, and the inclusion of news clippings and journal excerpts provides a variety of perspectives. The book raises questions about sexual identity, personal integrity, stereotypes, prejudices, and religion as Elizabeth strives to gain autonomy from her overprotective mother and define values of her own. Particularly effective are descriptions of scenes on stage when her identity blends with that of the character she is portraying. The book is written as if it were an attempt to recollect and understand, not as if the author set out to write a story. As a result, the characters and relationships have a verisimilitude that is flawed only by a tendency toward melodrama.

Patt Parsells Kent

SOURCE: A review of *The Crucible Year,* in *Children's Book Review Service Inc.,* Vol. 7, No. 13, July, 1979, p. 128.

This is the touching story of teenage Elizabeth Newcomb and the adjustments she makes when she must switch from private to public school. This is an exciting change for her; she makes new friends, among them her drama teacher and Paul, a fellow cast member in "The Cruci-

ble." These new experiences take Elizabeth away from her old ideas and way of life, but when rumors spread about Paul and Mr. Cartwright, Elizabeth finds her new ideas are not so strong a part of her that she can ignore the slander. *The Crucible Year* is a very thoughtful interpretation of growth, not only Elizabeth's, but the whole community's as well.

PRIDE OF LIONS: THE STORY OF THE HOUSE OF ATREUS (written as Norma Johnston, 1979)

Booklist

SOURCE: A review of *Pride of Lions: The Story of the House of Atreus,* in *Booklist,* Vol. 76, No. 2, September 15, 1979, p. 110.

Johnston turns to Greek mythology as she did in ***Strangers Dark and Gold*** based on a legend of Jason and Medea, this time to recount the dramatic epic of the cursed House of Atreus. After establishing the mythological genealogy and setting the background, she focuses in particular on the story of Clytemnestra and Agememnon, telling of the perfidious ruler Agamemnon, who sacrificed his daughter Iphigenia to aid the cause of the Trojan War; of Queen Clytemnestra's grief and grim revenge; and of the effects on their other children, Electra and Orestes, who ultimately bring the curse of generations to a bloody finish. Events take shape through a combination of dramatic dialogue, poetry, and narrative, making the story structurally complex, but it is a powerful, evocative interpretation of a classic tale and an able exploration of conflicting human emotions, nonetheless. Background notes and a genealogy chart would have been helpful.

Paul Heins

SOURCE: A review of *Pride of Lions: the Story of the House of Atreus,* in *The Horn Book Magazine,* Vol. LVI, No. 2, April, 1980, p. 180.

In *The King of Men* Olivia Coolidge reconstructed the early life of Agamemnon in novel form; and in *A Fair Wind for Troy* Doris Gates recounted the events leading up to the Trojan War and brought her version to a climax with a dramatic retelling of the sacrifice of Iphigenia. In a more extended version of the Agamemnon story the author is especially indebted to all of the great Greek tragedians—Aeschylus, Sophocles, and Euripides. Beginning with creation according to classical mythology and briefly considering the stories of Tantalus, Pelops, and Niobe—the guilt-ridden ancestors of the house of Atreus—the reteller develops at length and in detail the horror and the power of a family saga riddled with crime: human sacrifice, murder, and matricide. The narrative so intimately concerned with the relationship between husband and wife, parents and children has been carried to its logical conclusion, exploring the meaning of vengeance, justice, and retribution and ending triumphantly with the absolution of Orestes. The story is unfolded with poetic intensity; its phraseology is steeped in memories of the King James translation of the Bible, ancient Greek poetry, and the tragedies of Shakespeare, while the passionate arguments and the staccato dialogue skillfully reflect the technique and workmanship of Athenian tragedy.

A NICE GIRL LIKE YOU (written as Norma Johnston, 1980)

Barbara Elleman

SOURCE: A review of *A Nice Girl Like You,* in *Booklist,* Vol. 76, No. 14, March 15, 1980, p. 1058.

Tish Sterling, protagonist of four other Johnston novels, the last of which was *A Mustard Seed of Magic,* is now an adult and a secondary character, relinquishing the spotlight to niece Saranne, daughter of Bronwyn and Sidney Albright. A supposed likeness to her aunt makes the similarity of the characters believable as Saranne, in the late 1920s, copes with many of the emotional turmoils her aunt underwent a generation before. Choice of local outcast Paul Hodge for a role in the school's production of *Merchant of Venice* brings several conflicts to a head: the mystery concerning Paul's birth, Saranne's awakening interest in the boy, and the garnering of her courage to act on something she believes in. Fewer extraneous subplots intervene here, making a cleaner narrative, but this also results in less coverage of minor characters. For example, why Tish did not marry Ken Latham (predicted in the other stories) is never fully explained. Set against the turmoil of World War I, the novel contains some artificiality and a few contrived incidents but also proves once again Johnston's ability to tell a story dramatically charged with suspense.

Ethel L. Heins

SOURCE: A review of *A Nice Girl Like You,* in *The Horn Book Magazine,* Vol. LVI, No. 3, June, 1980, pp. 306-07.

The prolific author now writes about a new generation of Sterlings and Albrights, the two families featured in the quartet of novels that began with *The Keeping Days.* In 1917 Sarah Anne (Saranne), known as "'that nice little Albright girl,'" lives in a small-town atmosphere in the Bronx; her father is a respected lawyer, her mother an articulate suffragette. Surrounded by her active, assertive extended family, their homes linked by a network of loyalty and concern, Saranne feels a comforting sense of warmth and security. She is acutely aware of the plight of a neighbor, Paul Hodge, a fifteen-year-old boy famed as a troublemaker, feared and ostracized by his schoolmates, but actually the innocent victim of community gossip and of his own father's unexplained hatred. Working with a high school play production, Saranne incurs the surprise and scorn of her friends when she becomes involved with "'that wild Hodge boy,'" Meanwhile, America enters the war, the emotional temperature rises, and Saranne's fa-

mous Aunt Tish, now widowed, dramatically returns with her child from England. Incidents and characters abound, all of them carefully worked into the plot; it becomes obvious that Paul has all his life been the central figure in a conspiracy of secrecy. The author is a fluent storyteller; the families are as full of vitality as ever, constantly caught up in turmoil or triumph, and the World War I setting comes through more definitively than did the turn-of-the-century background of the earlier books.

Zena Sutherland

SOURCE: A review of *A Nice Girl Like You,* in *Bulletin of the Center for Children's Books,* Vol. 33, No. 11, July-August, 1980, pp. 215-16.

Saranne, the narrator, is the daughter of Bronwyn and the niece of Tish, two of the characters in Johnston's earlier books about the Sterling and Albright families (*The Keeping Days, The Sanctuary Tree,* and others). Saranne is a quiet, dependable girl, not one to confront or dispute, but she feels that everyone at school, as well as the members of her family, has been unfair to Paul Hodge, a classmate. True, Paul is hostile and often troublesome, but Saranne feels that he is often prejudged. She knows Paul doesn't get on well with his parents, but she's impressed by the way he responds to the war-shocked apathy of her young cousin Nichola, who has come home with her mother, Aunt Tish, after the latter's British husband is killed in action in World War I. Most of Johnston's books are overcrowded with characters and incidents; this is less so, despite the almost equal emphasis on Paul's and Nichola's problems, but it is weakened by the dramatic ending: persuaded by Saranne and her Uncle Ben, Paul's sister confesses in court that she is actually Paul's mother, and that she has been silent both because of her career as a movie star and because her parents felt such shame. The writing style, the characters, and the relationships are adequately drawn, but the story line (which ends with Saranne in Paul's arms, saying "And 'nice little girl' was not an adequate term for me at all.") seems both busy and saccharine.

Margaret Mary Ptacek

SOURCE: A review of *A Nice Girl Like You,* in *Voice of Youth Advocates,* Vol. 3, No. 3, August, 1980, p. 33.

Johnston has offered us another in the series of books about the Sterlings and Albrights of West Farms, New York. The setting is just before WW I. Sarah Anne Albright is 15; like her Aunt Tish whom we first met in *The Keeping Days,* Sarah is a sensitive young girl who is always looking out for the underdog. In this case, it's Paul Hodge a rebellious classmate. The town is against Paul until Sarah starts her private campaign to improve Paul's image.

Johnston has done a superb job in creating a group of characters that we can touch and believe in. The warm intimacy of the Sterling and Albright clans is cozy but real. The cover promises a more provocative story than it delivers. I find this a flaw, but probably good business; it widens the book's appeal.

The book could be used in a YA program on the misjudgment of people and fighting against stereotypes. Yet, I feel that its main audience will be female, [with] its main merit being a good teen story.

📖 MYSELF AND I (written as Norma Johnston, 1981)

Zena Sutherland

SOURCE: A review of *Myself and I,* in *Bulletin of the Center for Children's Books,* Vol. 34, No. 8, April, 1981, p. 153.

In a sequel to *A Nice Girl Like You,* the narrator Saranne is almost sixteen and having a mild relationship with Tim, when the scapegrace Paul of the earlier book unexpectedly comes back from California. Again Saranne becomes Paul's champion; this time she also tries to help Paul discover who his father is (in the earlier book he'd learned that his movie star older "sister" was his never-married mother) and to comfort him when he finds out and is disappointed. While Johnston, in analyzing the relationship between Saranne and the troubled, dependent Paul, reaches a deeper level of characterization than in the earlier book or the still earlier stories about Saranne's family, this book has some of the same weaknesses as its predecessors: a surfeit of characters, a repeated harking back to events of earlier books, a slow development of story line.

Barbara Elleman

SOURCE: A review of *Myself and I,* in *Booklist,* Vol. 77, No. 15, April 1, 1981, p. 1105.

When Paul Hodge left for California after discovering that Mary Hayes was his mother rather than his sister (at the close of *A Nice Girl like You*), Saranne Albright thought she might never see him again. But ever restless, explosive, and often irresponsible, Paul returns to New York determined to rekindle his romance with Saranne and discover who his real father is, thinking it will bring about an answer to his problems. Saranne as well as her close-knit family are caught up in the resulting turmoil that opens old wounds when Paul and Saranne delve into past family histories. Old hurts are healed as well, but not before Saranne recognizes that Paul's dependence on her clouds her own sense of self. Johnston's World War I setting expands the story with colorful tidbits of the era. The complex problems of the Albright-Sterling-Hodge families tend sometimes to resemble "the soaps," but their problems—realistic, sensitively approached, and relevant to today—are presented with graceful and rigorous expertise. Readers may have more empathy for Tim Molloy, Saranne's would-be boyfriend, than the moody Paul

Hodge; and the conclusion, in which Paul leaves to join the army and Saranne declares her need to discover her own identity, leaves room for still another sequel in the series.

Susan Melcher

SOURCE: A review of *Myself and I,* in *Catholic Library World,* Vol. 53, No. 2 September, 1981, p. 92.

This is a continuation of the story of Paul Hodge and Sarah Anne Albright. When Paul returns, Sarah realizes she loves him and we follow an up and down year at school. Other people can see that Sarah's love is too protecting and mothering to let Paul grow. Paul only uses her love to have a shoulder to cry on. His search for his own identity by trying to find out the name of his father upsets many around him, and the answer doesn't give him satisfaction. These young lovers, Sarah and Paul, and their friends Mark and Katie show us intensity without an "R" rating. Johnston's writing style allows the reader to move along with the characters and, with Sarah, work out her feelings about Paul and struggle to help Paul understand himself. Highly recommended for grades 7-10.

Nancy E. Curran

SOURCE: A review of *Myself and I,* in *School Library Journal,* Vol. 28, No. 3, November, 1981, p. 106.

Sarah Anne Albright, a teenager during World War I, is the object of the attention of two young men, Paul and Tim. She suffers mental anguish over the trauma of Paul's return to New York and the subsequent revelation of his paternity, as well as from the physical pain resulting from a torn ligament suffered on an outing with Tim. Ultimately, Paul asks Sarah Anne to secretly marry him before he goes overseas; however, she declines and says if they are meant for each other, he'll find her when the war is over. Threaded through the narration are adult romantic entanglements including that of Paul's mother and incidents demonstrating the strong anti-German feelings prevalent during this era. For girls who clamor for still another love story and who will accept a romance that lacks a contemporary setting.

📖 THE DAYS OF THE DRAGON'S SEED (written as Norma Johnston, 1982)

Sally Estes

SOURCE: A review of *The Days of the Dragon's Seed,* in *Booklist,* Vol. 78, No. 16, April 15, 1982, p. 1086.

Drawing on Greek mythology as she did for *Pride of Lions* and *Strangers Dark and Gold* Johnston once again retains the aura of Greek tragedy as she retells the story of the royal house of Thebes—Oedipus, who murdered his father and married his mother despite a desperate attempt to escape his predicted destiny, and his daughter, Antigone, who followed him into exile and, after his death, was herself condemned to death for burying her brother. Through her command of language and characterization, Johnston carefully unfolds the tragedy, giving it an immediacy for modern-day teenagers as well as raising philosophical questions for good readers to contemplate. Background notes, a glossary, and sources appended.

Diane C. Donovan

SOURCE: A review of *The Days of the Dragon's Seed,* in *Best Sellers,* Vol. 42, No. 3, June, 1982, p. 120.

The story of Oedipus is retold here in such a manner as to make it accessible and relevant to a young adult of today.

Oedipus first realizes a discrepancy in his knowledge of his heritage when he hears rumours that his noble parents are not his true mother and father. Upon consulting an oracle during a pilgrimage, he learns that he is fated to destroy his father and marry his mother. Horror-struck at this unexpected news, he flees his country and becomes a wanderer, choosing exile over the horrible possibility of destroying those he loves.

In the course of his travels, Oedipus meets and kills an arrogant man, solves the riddle of a monster which is holding a city enslaved, and in due course marries and has children by the queen of that city, beautiful Jocasta. As the years pass, though, a blight falls upon the city, and Oedipus is driven to find the source of the corruption which plagues his newfound kingdom.

As a novel, *The Days of the Dragon's Seed* will appeal more to serious readers than to a general-interest, leisure-reading audience. However, it will hold value for students of Greek mythology who seek an easier, less lyrical language than Sophocles, in order to understand many of the philosophical and psychological conflicts inherent in the character of Oedipus.

Judith Geer

SOURCE: A review of *Days of the Dragon's Seed,* in *Voice of Youth Advocates,* Vol. 5, No. 5, December, 1982, p. 33.

Johnston's modernized prose version of the Oedipus trilogy (*Oedipus, Oedipus at Colonus* and *Antigone*) is an excellent book. She begins with a prologue concerning the myth of Cadmus who founded the Greek city of Thebes, then picks up the story a few generations later as his descendant, Oedipus, Prince of Corinth travels to the Oracle at Delphi to learn his fate. There he is told that he will kill his father and marry his mother. In spite of the goodness of his nature, Oedipus cannot escape the Oracle's predictions. When he learns the truth about his past he blinds himself and goes into self-exile at Colonus near

Athens. Although this episode is the least interesting it serves as a bridge between the tragedy of Oedipus and that of his daughter, Antigone. Johnston's writing is clear and easy to follow. A glossary and interpretive notes at the end of the story make it more valuable and its potential for classroom use, especially in junior high, is excellent.

Ruth Cline

SOURCE: A review of *The Days of the Dragon's Seed,* in *The ALAN Review,* Vol. 10, No. 2, Winter, 1983, p. 83.

The story of Oedipus is retold in a modern style appropriate for junior or senior high students. Johnston uses Sophocles' plays as her principal source, but relies on Aeschylus and Larousse as well. Much of the theatrical element is retained in her writing, making the reader aware of sights and sounds which surround the action. The story begins with Oedipus' trip to Delphi where he learns, not about his past as he had hoped, but rather a grim prediction of his future.

The novel is divided into six parts and shows the entire destruction predicted in the seed of the dragon's teeth. The author hoped to convey the *why* questions which control our lives and the *how* that is their answer. At the end, the blind old soothsayer Tiresias tells Creon, " . . . he who sins is not forever lost if he makes amends, if he is not too stubborn for repentance." But Oedipus, Antigone, and Creon were all stubborn and too late.

Many teachers who work with Greek heroes and Greek tragedy will welcome this easily read edition.

Ruth M. Stein

SOURCE: A review of *The Days of the Dragon's Seed,* in *Language Arts,* Vol. 60, No. 4, April, 1983, pp. 481-82.

Johnston combines the epics of Oedipus who unknowingly killed his father and married his mother, and of Antigone who was condemned to death for burying her brother after he had attacked his own city. The tragedies of father and daughter are well known. Johnston brings clarity and passion to the myths. She portrays larger-than-life characters with "that red thing within them that drove them to ask hard questions, and to do what they had to do, no matter the price." I just wish that red mist hadn't risen so often; when it does the reader knows someone is about to make a terrible decision with disastrous consequences. A fine book to introduce the stories to older students.

MASK FOR MY HEART (written as Pamela Dryden, 1982)

Jean S. Bolley

SOURCE: A review of *Mask for My Heart,* in *Kliatt Young*

Adult Paperback Book Guide, Vol. XVII, No. 3, Spring, 1983, p. 6.

At school Sarah McLain thinks of herself as a hermit crab, but at the hospital where she works as candy-striper she is confident, outgoing and depended on by patients and staff. She is something of a loner and has never had a boyfriend. Then while hiding behind a mask at a medieval benefit for the hospital Sarah finds herself the belle of the ball. She also captures the attention and affection of Chris, a boy from the prep school in town. Afraid that Chris won't like the real Sarah, she tries to juggle her three worlds until they meet with the inevitable crash. Although somewhat contrived, the story moves right along and this will be popular with the girls reading romances.

Patricia Berry

SOURCE: A review of *Mask for My Heart,* in *Voice of Youth Advocates,* Vol. 6, No. 2, June, 1983, p. 96.

Brainy, white, old-fashioned, shy Sarah Lucinda McClain is the daughter of Dr. Daniel J. McClain, Chief-of-Staff at Kenilworth Hospital! Sarah is bright, mousy, withdrawn, and ethical. She has a lot on the ball but wants to feel normal in the social, romantic scene. When she volunteers to work at a charity masquerade ball to help her dad raise money for a new hospital CAT scan, Sarah meets "Blue Eyes," "Prince Charming (P.C.)," a Kenilworth (private school) man, Chris Porter.

They date, she wonders if he'll call. Will she do well at the formal dance at his school, will he think she's a loser because she doesn't date others? She plays coy, she plays the field, they part, she worries a lot, they come together again. He sees her value as a human being. It is a hopeful ending.

For a middle-aged reviewer, the sexist sentiments and dripping nostalgia are sometimes overwhelming but young teenage women need to read this literature as part of their development toward adulthood and "normalcy." This kind of reading seems to reflect the experimenting with roles most young girls go through as they work at forming their own identity on the threshold of the adult, sexual, social world.

TIMEWARP SUMMER (written as Norma Johnston, 1983)

Sally Estes

SOURCE: A review of *Timewarp Summer,* in *Booklist,* Vol. 79, No. 13, March 1, 1983, p. 870.

Scott Martin, a teenager obsessed with science-fiction filmmaking; Bettina Blair, the girl next door whose passion is Scott; and Dr. Laura Weller, a 27-year-old newly divorced research scientist—three people, all vulnerable and at turning points in their lives. During the summer before Scott's senior year, the emotions of these three become entwined when Scott undertakes the making of an amateur sf movie. His single-minded, proprietary direction of the film alienates friends acting in it, and he also rides roughshod over Bettina's feelings, though the real shock comes when she realizes that Scott and Laura are having an affair. Cast in scenarios that parallel the development of the shooting script and couched in revolving third-person-viewpoint narratives, the deliberately episodic story probes interpersonal relationships via the eternal triangle given new dimension through solid characterizations—though Laura, being coolheaded on the one hand and emotionally wrecked on the other, comes across as almost too good to be true at the end, when she bolsters both Bettina and Scott before leaving town. Not easy reading, but compelling, this is suggested for readers with some maturity.

Zena Sutherland

SOURCE: A review of *Timewarp Summer,* in *Bulletin of the Center for Children's Books,* Vol. 36, No. 8, April, 1983, p. 152.

This is not a fantasy; "Timewarp" is the name of the film that Scott hopes to finish by the end of the summer; there's a second meaning, in the "time is out of joint" sense, for Scott falls in love and has an affair with an older woman, Laura. Scott's getting over a stormy love affair, Laura's getting over a divorce; the sweet girl who lives next door to Scott and has helped him with the film and is in love with him is stunned to learn of the affair. When it is all in the open, Laura leaves town and Scott, anguished, abruptly recovers enough to suddenly appreciate the girl next door, and rushes over to heal the breach. The story is told in short segments, as though for a filmscript, a device that adds nothing to the narrative flow but punctuation; the characters are believable through iteration rather than depth.

Paul Heins

SOURCE: A review of *Timewarp Summer,* in *The Horn Book Magazine,* Vol. LIX, No. 2, April, 1983, p. 171.

Scott Martin, a Milwaukee high school senior, had long had a passion for science fiction films. Encouraged by Bettina Blair, a next-door neighbor who had been his friend from early childhood, he planned to produce a movie during the summer vacation, using the camera his mother had given him for Christmas. Scott and Bettina had summer jobs at Kinefilm, and both were soon fascinated by the sophistication of Dr. Laura Weller, a woman in her twenties who was Bettina's supervisor. The boy was a perfectionist, and despite Bettina's aid in helping with the script and securing amateur actors, Scott discovered it was Laura who was able to help him solve the problems plaguing his movie. Almost inadvertently he and Laura fell in love. Bettina considered herself betrayed by both of them, but by the end of the summer Scott had to face two crucial facts. Laura, in her wisdom, refused to see him any longer, and he suddenly realized that Bettina had always been his faithful, helping, and loving companion. Divided into sections with prefatory directions suggesting a movie script, the narrative is supplemented with reproduced and edited typescripts of Scott's film. Actually cast in the form of a classical love triangle, the story succeeds in honestly portraying the emotions of three sincere people caught in the web of their shared creative activity.

Virginia Marr

SOURCE: A review of *Timewarp Summer,* in *School Library Journal,* Vol. 30, No. 1, September, 1983, pp. 135-36.

During the summer before his senior year, Scott spends his time writing and filming a sci-fi movie. He meets and becomes involved emotionally and sexually with Laura (recently divorced, a successful scientist who is older by ten years). "Afterwards, that was the way Scott Martin would always see this summer—like long shots and zoom-ins, montages, and, above all, still shots, as though all were a part of one of his beloved movies." So starts this accessible story, thanks to a deft handling of dialogue and a cinematic control of action and character that lengthens and deepens into something quite wonderful by the ongoing creation of a story within a story. Woven in are some complex issues: one's sense of responsibility to another, psychological needs and resulting relationships, the creative process itself with its exhilaration, need for group effort and its manipulation of character and, above all, the determination of what is real and what isn't, what can be changed and what can't.

Carolyn Caywood

SOURCE: A review of *Timewarp Summer,* in *Voice of Youth Advocates,* Vol. 6, No. 4, October, 1983, p. 203.

When Scott breaks up with the neurotic Julie, he devotes the summer to making an 8mm science fiction movie with the help of the girl-next-door, Bettina. His growing involvement with a divorced woman at the film studio is devastating to the faithful Bettina, but all their various passions are sorted out by the end of the summer. Much of the story is told in a script format with focus shifting from one character to another. This has a distancing effect, and, combined with the parallels the author insists on drawing between the teenagers and the older woman, it disturbs the credibility of her otherwise well-developed characters. The dull gray jacket with its pseudo science fiction illustration further confuses the intended audience of this heavy-handed romance.

GABRIEL'S GIRL (written as Norma Johnston, 1983)

Stephanie Zvirin

SOURCE: A review of *Gabriel's Girl,* in *Booklist,* Vol. 80, No. 1, September 1, 1983, p. 75.

In a notable departure from Johnston's previous works, 17-year-old Sarah Gabriel Langham flies to Spain to locate her apparently missing father, who is ostensibly there gathering material for some kind of exposé he is planning to write. Her unannounced arrival, which reveals that her father has indeed vanished, triggers all kinds of sinister goings-on. With the help of Quent Robards, a college student who claims to know her, she traces her father to London. But her penchant for asking questions backfires, jeopardizing her life and threatening her father's carefully constructed undercover operation. If some of the dialogue seems a trifle stilted or overworked, the author more than compensates with her spunky teenage heroine, scrupulous attention to plot detail, and enough clues and plot twists to propel teenage mystery/espionage fans eagerly through to the novel's conclusion.

Mary M. Burns

SOURCE: A review of *Gabriel's Girl,* in *The Horn Book Magazine,* Vol. LIX, No. 5, October, 1983, pp. 583-84.

Motherless seventeen-year-old Sarah Langham proves that she is indeed her father's daughter in a fast-paced story of suspense and international intrigue. Because Gabe Langham, a best-selling author, travels extensively, gathering material for his exposés, Sarah is unperturbed by his absences until a household emergency impels her to call him at the Spanish hotel from which he last wrote to her. Much to her dismay, she is informed that he never registered. Concern for his well-being precipitates her decision to travel to Spain and later to London and unearth the facts behind his disappearance. In a rapid series of events recalling techniques used by Alfred Hitchcock to create tension, Sarah is thrust into the center of the mystery: Her suitcase and passport are stolen; a lurking figure follows her every move; her father's friend at the American Embassy dispenses platitudes instead of information; and attempts to harm her seem coincidental with the presence of attractive, friendly Quentin Robards. Deducing that her father may be looking for information about international terrorist groups, Sarah must depend on her intelligence, investigative instinct, and ability to assess her acquaintances in order to resolve her father's problems as well as her own. Narrated by Sarah, the story derives its appeal from the panache of its heroine, the lure of distant settings, the rapidity of movement from crisis to crisis, and discreet suggestions of developing romance.

Melanie Eiger

SOURCE: A review of *Gabriel's Girl,* in *Best Sellers,* Vol. 43, No. 9, December, 1983, p. 347.

Sarah Gabriel Langham is the seventeen-year-old daughter of Gabriel Langham, a widowed investigative reporter of international renown. When their housekeeper is incapacitated, Sarah wants her father's permission to stay at home alone. She attempts to telephone him at the hotel in Spain at which he told her he would be staying, and she is told that no such person has been there. Sarah is well aware of her father's penchant for secretiveness in his work, but she also knows his reputation for courting danger. She acts upon her panic by taking off for Spain.

Thus far, as narrator of her own tale, Sarah has sounded almost timid and far too conventional to act so recklessly. Furthermore, her friend's mother would surely exert a calming influence, taking Sarah into her home for the interim, rather than facilitating this "rescue mission."

It requires an effort of will on the reader's part to overcome disbelief and continue on the journey which follows, but the promise of a lively, romantic tale of suspense keeps one optimistic. Unfortunately, events become progressively more implausible.

Sarah's search for her father involves her in a simultaneous quest for and flight from international terrorists. The consequences she suffers are far too slight for the risks she takes and the company she keeps. The confusing denouement is followed by a lengthy explanation that is as anticlimactic as it is convoluted. When Sarah and Langham are safely together again, the coolness of their reunion is the last bafflement in this puzzling book.

A final puzzlement:—as reviewer, do I classify this "Young People's Book" as A, B or C? Although *Gabriel's Girl* is not objectionable in any way, the theme of terrorism calls for parental guidance; however, my recommendation to parents of a more mature adolescent reader of romantic, suspense novels, would be to introduce her to the works of Daphne DuMaurier, or, in a more contemporary, topical vein, the novels of Helen MacInnes.

Drew Stevenson

SOURCE: A review of *Gabriel's Girl*, in *School Library Journal*, Vol. 30, No. 4, December, 1983, p. 85.

Gabriel's Girl is Sarah Langham, daughter of former (and possibly current) CIA agent turned investigative author Gabriel Langham. Sarah is accustomed to her father's globetrotting and is prepared to stay at home when he leaves for Spain on another secret project. Following an emergency, however, Sarah tries to call her father at his Spanish hotel only to be told they have never heard of him. Sarah flies to Spain to find him and ends up in a whirlwind of intrigue. Her search eventually takes her to London where persistent inquiries lead her to the heart of a network made up of ruthless men who divert legal charity funds to buy illegal weapons and explosives for terrorist organizations. It is the combined resourcefulness of father and daughter which prevents the ring from going any further. It doesn't take readers long to be caught up in Sarah's growing paranoia and fear. The breathless plot has plenty of surprises and excitement but as good as it is, it is Sarah's gritty gutsiness which really shines throughout and makes Gabe's girl some girl indeed!

THE SECRET OF THE SINGING STRINGS (written as Kate Chambers, 1983)

Zena Sutherland

SOURCE: A review of *The Secret of the Singing Strings*, in *Bulletin of the Center for Children's Books*, Vol. 37, No. 4, December, 1983, p. 64.

This is the first of a new series, with a heroine—Diana Winthrop—who is in the Nancy Drew tradition: shrewd, observant, courageous, and apparently indefatigable. Motherless, she lives in a large Manhattan house with her father, grandmother, blind cousin Jacintha, and a faithful retainer. The writing style is better than that of the Nancy Drew series, but the plot is just as weak as those in most of the Stratemeyer books: intricate, contrived, and often dependent on coincidence for its development. Here Jacintha is hit by a car, loses a valuable art work from her bag, has temporary amnesia; the valuable toy Stradivarius that has disappeared is traced, found, proves to contain an enormous emerald, and both the violin and the emerald are used in a police-supervised situation (conceived, of course, by Diana rather than the police) to trap the criminals.

Ruth Cline

SOURCE: A review of *The Secret of the Singing Strings*, in *Voice of Youth Advocates*, Vol. 6, No. 5, December, 1983, p. 278.

This new mystery series will provide "escape" reading for junior high girls searching for post-Nancy Drew excitement. Diana Winthrop is a charming 17-year-old-girl who already has quite a reputation as a detective. The cast of characters includes a busy lawyer father (now turned filmmaker), a society-conscious grandmother who is too busy with her obligations to meddle with Diana's business, the maid Lily who takes care of their physical needs, and Brad, helpful male friend who provides a "proper" romantic interest. Cousin Jacintha lives in her own apartment in their spacious New York City home. Although blind, Jacintha's remarkable sense of hearing and touch have gotten her a job with the Mannertheim Museum of Music where she is to test the authenticity of a newly acquired pochette (miniature violin), supposedly a Stradivarius. A hit-and-run accident, a valuable emerald, and connections with Italy and individuals of declining fortunes are all important to the plot. Although Diana works with the police, it is her intuition and intelligence that solve the mystery. Some similarity with the "Doris Fein" mysteries, and could lead to Agatha Christie books. Hints of future episodes will lead the reader to look for the next volume.

DANGER IN THE OLD FORT (written as Kate Chambers, 1983)

Ruth Cline

SOURCE: A review of *Danger in the Old Fort*, in *Voice*

of Youth Advocates, Vol. 6, No. 5, December, 1983, pp. 276, 278.

Diana Winthrop has been called to San Juan to fill in for a young actress who had been hurt in an accident on the set of a TV production about the history of Puerto Rico. The author of the novel, Lydian Sinclair, becomes one of Diana's friends, and the two of them plus Brad Ferriers, Diana's boyfriend, work to solve the mystery of the many delays and "accidents" that have plagued the production. The reader learns something about Puerto Rican history through the novel and also some insights into the work involved in such a massive production. Diana's father is the producer of the TV film series and he asks Diana to use her stage name, Kathleen Crawford, so she can investigate without raising the curiosity of the cast. Several characters are suspected of the sabotage because of old grudges, egos, and the nationalism of the natives, but the climax is reached when the star is thrown off his horse in a dramatic scene and is tossed on the rocks below. Blackmail, bad debts, and high insurance risks are all involved in the plot. Mystery fans will welcome this easy-reading book, especially junior high girls. Diana's wonderful intuition is too convenient, but the pace of the book will carry the reader along.

THE CASE OF THE DOG-LOVER'S LEGACY (written as Kate Chambers, 1983)

Connie Lawson

SOURCE: A review of *The Case of the Dog-Lover's Legacy,* in *Voice of Youth Advocates,* Vol. 6, No. 6, February, 1984, p. 337.

High school senior Diana Winthrop's hobby is solving mysteries. When she dives into the East River to save a dog Diana eventually discovers that the dog, Annie, was companion to wealthy, eccentric Elias Kulholland who left his hidden fortune to whomever cared for the animal until its death. In New York City, before Annie's identity is established, we meet Diana's attorney-turned-TV producer father, her acerbic but proper grandmother, her blind but spunky cousin and the Kulhollands, and the Winthrops receive some strange calls and visitors. After Annie is identified and her owner is determined the setting shifts to Marysville, N.Y. where the question of the hidden fortune remains unanswered until eight-year-old Casey Kulholland provides Diana with the missing clue. Kate Chamber's mystery is no better or worse than the series romances and horror stories that are currently flooding the market. Diana Winthrop is a diluted Nancy Drew and none of the characters are very well developed. There are looks and blushes but no overt romances in the plot. The action and violence are very carefully measured so there is just enough of the former to keep the plot moving but not enough of the latter to offend anyone. Readers looking for light mystery will enjoy this but Bethancourt's "Doris Fein" series is better written.

THE SECRETS ON BEACON HILL (written as Kate Chambers, 1984)

Kliatt Young Adult Paperback Book Guide

SOURCE: A review of *The Secrets of Beacon Hill,* in *Kliatt Young Adult Paperback Book Guide,* Vol. XVIII, No. 3, April, 1984, p. 6.

Diana is visiting her socially prominent grandmother on Beacon Hill when the theft of some valuable pearls is suspected within the family circle. Her grandmother asks her to conduct a secret investigation to solve the mystery without causing any publicity. The plot ties together exceedingly well, and should satisfy young readers who are sick of Nancy Drew mysteries and want something a bit more believable.

Debra L. Maier

SOURCE: A review of *The Secrets on Beacon Hill,* in *Voice of Youth Advocates,* Vol. 7, No. 3, August, 1984, p. 146.

Diana Winthrop is the heroine of a new mystery series which provides a bridge between Nancy Drew mysteries and adult suspense. Written at a 6th grade reading level, it is just the thing for readers who are ready to move on. In this fourth book, Diana returns to her ancestral home for her childhood friend's 18th birthday celebration. During the festivities, a priceless oriental pearl necklace is stolen. Grandmother Winthrop asks Diana to investigate when it becomes clear that the perpetrator is a member of the family. Diana traps the thief and uncovers the jewels in a pleasant mystery with emphasis on the plot rather than the characters. Sometimes the Back Bay referrals are pretentious, but the character of Diana is innocuous enough. The clues and mystery move along at a good pace and the work itself holds the attention. Diana Winthrop should find fans.

THE LEGACY OF LUCIAN VAN ZANDT (written as Kate Chambers, 1984)

Mary F. Perkins

SOURCE: A review of *The Legacy of Lucian Van Zandt,* in *Kliatt Young Adult Paperback Book Guide,* Vol. XVIII, No. 6, September, 1984, pp. 5-6.

Set in New York City, the story concerns the hunt for a possible heir amidst the threat of blackmail and rumors that the Van Zandt School would be sold to a land development concern. Plans to celebrate Founder's Day at the school send Diana searching for information that could be used as script material.

Diana, quick-witted and a sharp talker, finds herself so involved in the maze of Lucian Van Zandt's life and legacy that at times everyone seems to be guilty of something. As in most mysteries a semblance of order comes out of chaos and the inheritance is rightfully restored to the "new" cousins and the school is saved. Again good triumphs over evil and Diana decides to continue solving mysteries.

Carole A. Barham

SOURCE: A review of *The Legacy of Lucian Van Zandt,* in *Voice of Youth Advocates,* Vol. 7, No. 5, December, 1984, p. 260.

A search for information about Lucian Van Zandt, her school's long ago benefactor, for a research paper and background for a Founder's Day celebration play, leads Diana into the thick of blackmail, treacherous plots and "an urgent hunt for a mysterious heir." Using her "sixth sense" plus the skills of her lawyer/TV producer dad, her blind cousin, Jacintha, dad's "special friend," investigative reporter Lydian Sinclair, her boyfriend, Brad and others, Diana solves the mystery, uncovers the bad guy and sees to it that everyone lives happily ever after. Set in present-day New York City, Diana dashes from her brownstone home, to the New York Public Library, her private school, in always-available taxis(!) pursuing clues and solving her mysteries. Generously sprinkled with bits and pieces of earlier Diana Winthrop mysteries, this is up-to-date; well-written (assuming acceptance of the premise of a high school senior detective solving "real" mysteries—crimes); it should be popular with mystery-fan YAs.

THE GREAT RIP-OFF (written as Lavinia Harris, 1984)

Hazel Rochman

SOURCE: A review of *The Great Rip-Off,* in *Booklist,* Vol. 81, No. 10, January 15, 1985, p. 708.

Readers lured by the cover's promise of a formula romance will be disappointed. Cute little sophomore Sidney Webster is a computer whiz, and she turns detective to trace the "hacker" in the high school community who is stealing her father's important research on computers and brain waves. There is some love interest (poorly developed) between Sidney and brilliant newcomer Joshua, but the focus is on crime and detection by computer. Very lightweight, this will be intelligible to readers with a minimum of computer knowledge, and with its easy reading level, it should draw some reluctant readers away from their machines.

Dorcas Hand

SOURCE: A review of *The Great Rip-Off,* in *School Library Journal,* Vol. 31, No. 8, April, 1985, p. 97.

Light romance/mystery books appeal to readers of any age who just want to relax, and this one will be no exception. Sidney Scott Webster is a high-school computer whiz. Her father is doing advanced and highly secret research based on the premise that computers can be taught to respond to the alpha brain waves of their human operators. Arrogant Joshua J. Rivington, III, new to town, is also a computer whiz. Sidney and Josh are thrown together at the same computer terminal and work uneasily, concerned about the privacy of their own projects. And then information about Sidney's father's research begins to appear in the memory of Samantha (as this computer is known). Other local computer hackers are implicated in this plot involving transfer of information by modem and the invasion of government computer banks. The mystery develops predictably: Josh and the other hackers are proved innocent, the guilty are trapped, and Sidney and Josh discover that they actually like one another. Nothing exciting, nothing objectionable—basic escape fiction.

CARLISLE'S HOPE (written as Norma Johnston, 1986)

Publishers Weekly

SOURCE: A review of *Carlisle's Hope,* in *Publishers Weekly,* Vol. 229, No. 26, June 27, 1986, p. 96.

In one of the slimmest plots to launch a new series (The Carlisle Chronicles) this season, Jessica Carlisle is a part of an old family (and a lot of old family traditions), in whose roots she finds much comfort. Her father, who is with the foreign service, has kept the Carlisles on the move in the last few years, and Jess finds, in the family name, the stability she craves. When her Aunt Faith dies in a car accident, Jess gains access to information which proves that her father is the descendant of an adopted Carlisle, not the real stuff. She's devastated. John Henry, Aunt Faith's 10-year-old son, is temporarily living with the Carlisles while his own father is abroad. Unhappy, he goes back to his family home. His act of running away brings the Carlisles together, and Jess realizes that the boundaries of family love stretch across geography and bloodlines. While readers may find the set-up appealing— old family, foreign service, exotic characters—the plot doesn't generate any real excitement. Jess's battle cry "Up the Carlisles" is uttered far too often, and one never really cares about her problems, of lineage and otherwise.

Ilene Cooper

SOURCE: A review of *Carlisle's Hope,* in *Booklist,* Vol. 82, No. 21, July, 1986, p. 1612.

Like her Aunt Faith, fifteen-year-old Jess Carlisle is tradition loving and family oriented. When Aunt Faith dies, leaving a box of puzzling documents indicating her grandfather was adopted and not really a Carlisle, Jess uses a school genealogy project to track down the mysterious truth about her family. Too many characters crowd Johnston's narrative, and the myriad genealogical details slow it down. Nevertheless, Johnston is such a good writer their she salvages the story, especially through a subplot about Jess' orphaned cousin and another about her confused friend. Readers versed in genealogy will find this title of special interest and schools using the subject in their curriculum will want it as fictional supplement.

Joyce Adams Burner

SOURCE: A review of *Carlisle's Hope,* in *School Library Journal,* Vol. 32, No. 10, August, 1986, p. 101.

If *Carlisle's Hope* is an accurate indication, adolescent readers have a lot of enjoyment ahead in Johnston's "Carlisle Chronicles" series. The Carlisles are a large, affluent family with a strong sense of tradition. They have lived abroad and are now settled near Washington, D.C. The narration comes from 15-year-old Jess, who is devastated by the accidental death of her beloved young aunt. Falling back on the family roots she treasures, she uncovers a family secret that threatens her entire self-image. This family, although privileged, is real and warm. They interact naturally and believably, and the story flows easily. Johnston writes with a friendly grace, obviously enjoying her characters. She smoothly incorporates material on genealogies and the District of Columbia. The action moves quickly enough to sustain interest, and each episode moves surely into the next. Enjoyable, wholesome fiction that teen readers will eat up.

📖 THE WATCHER IN THE MIST (written as Norma Johnston, 1986)

Stephanie Zvirin

SOURCE: A review of *The Watcher in the Mist,* in *Booklist,* Vol. 83, No. 8, December 15, 1986, p. 641.

Romance, a tinge of the occult, and a murder mystery are the ingredients in Johnston's latest (a departure from her more substantial fiction), which aims strictly to entertain. Hired to help out Elizabeth Lancaster, a recently widowed relative planning to turn a family home into a New England inn, Cindy Clayborne arrives at Rockcove Hall to find things in complete confusion. She soon learns that the unexplained fire that has damaged the inn's kitchen is but one of a number of glitches that have troubled Elizabeth. For Cindy, it is only the beginning of a sequence of curious goings-on with supernatural undertones that lead her back to the circumstances surrounding the death of Elizabeth's husband. What the police labeled an accident seems to Cindy very possibly to have been a murder. A bit of a mishmash with suspects and tangents galore, but certainly palatable reading.

Publishers Weekly

SOURCE: A review of *The Watcher in the Mist,* in *Publishers Weekly,* Vol. 230, No. 26, December 26, 1986, p. 61.

Teenager Cindy Clayborne detects a sense of urgency in her cousin Elizabeth's plea to work at Rockcove Hall for the summer. When Cindy arrives at the newly opened seaside inn, she finds recently widowed Elizabeth besieged with worries. Local residents blame various mishaps on Rockcove Hall's ghost, The Watcher. Many of the inn's guests flee in terror. Then a local man is found dead, apparently murdered in the same fashion as Elizabeth's husband. Cindy finds a strange connection between herself and the inn's ghost, who helps her to find important clues in solving the two murders. By the story's end, Rockcove Hall's evil spirit is laid to rest, and Cindy has found a new love. Johnston, author of **"The Carlisle Chronicles,"** has written a romantic mystery that should appeal to teen girls. The sensible, spunky heroine and the evocative setting is an attraction in itself.

Doris Losey

SOURCE: A review of *The Watcher in the Mist,* in *Voice of Youth Advocates,* Vol. 9, No. 6, February, 1987, p. 285.

Seventeen year old Cindy is excited about spending the summer helping her cousin run a country inn, especially because her boyfriend will be working on a newspaper in the next town. Cindy's excitement soon turns to worry and fear as strange accidents begin to occur daily and soon take on a deadly purpose. The locals attribute these accidents to the Watcher, the ghost of an 18th century sea captain's wife, but Cindy is sure that the Watcher is only a friendly yet warning presence. Mystery, romance, supernatural happenings, and local history are skillfully combined in this fast-paced, easy reading teen novel. Recommended for all collections.

📖 CARLISLES ALL (written as Norma Johnston, 1986)

Katherine Bruner

SOURCE: A review of *Carlisles All,* in *School Library Journal,* Vol. 33, No. 8, May, 1987, p. 112.

This, the third in the series, is a smoothly written and swiftly flowing, hold-on-tight tale of adolescent adventure in the vortex of international intrigue. What begins as an idyllic Christmas together for the Carlisle clan quickly turns into an emotional and political survival saga. Dad, a U.S. Information Agency senior officer, is sent on a hurried trip to the Middle East and persuades Mom to go along. The five young Carlisles (brothers, sisters, or cousins all) are dependable enough to be left on their own. Then the TV report of a suicide car crashing into the U.S. embassy in Bashiran, killing the ambassador, sets crisis in motion. Only the kids and Jessamyn's boyfriend Greg know that their Dad was in that embassy. Fifteen-year-old Jess now plays center in the waiting game, pivoting from overseas phone calls and diplomatic visitors to solidifying the family in their public charade of enjoying the holidays as usual. Johnston's family *célèbre* handles everything with remarkable dexterity, even while revealing enough personal weaknesses and individualities to bond with readers. Teens will devour this and wait for yet the next in the series.

Leslie Chamberlin

SOURCE: A review of *Carlisles All,* in *Voice of Youth Advocates,* Vol. 10, No. 2, June, 1987, p. 85.

In this era of so much negativeness about "The Family," it is refreshing to find a teenage novel centered around a large, strong, loving family unit. This is the third title in the "The Carlisle Chronicles." Here we find neither the indigent homeless nor the emotional bankruptcy that sometimes accompanies vast wealth. What we find instead is an intriguing blend of Washington, D.C. fantasy politics, several threads of chaste teenage romance that stops short of sex, an alcoholic single mother of a friend who is confronted with her problems and checks in for rehabilitation; concerns about school work, friendship, family loyalty, patriotism, and church activities. We see that affluence is taken for granted when the kids are given $500 for groceries for an anticipated few days, with the ubiquitous home computer and other electronic gadgetry. Some of the expressions do not sound like contemporary YA argot to this reviewer's ear. It almost seems as if publishers should hire hip teenagers to read the novels and purge adult jargon. The most disconcerting is the obviously positive, frequently repeated: "Up the Carlisles!"

Here are some examples of oddly used language: things and persons as "Warm Blankets", "Does Tracy want him in or out of her hair?" "Apply a little elbow grease to let out the tension." "It was stress talking." "Underground dope", meaning inside information. Even with the political intrigue surrounding the father's apparent capture in the Middle East leading to tremendous fear about his safety, the tone of this novel is pleasantly cheerful, positive, supportive, and constructive.

SHADOW OF A UNICORN (written as Norma Johnston, 1987)

Publishers Weekly

SOURCE: A review of *Shadow of a Unicorn,* in *Publishers Weekly,* Vol. 231, No. 21, May 29, 1987, p. 80.

Sarah, orphaned when her mother dies, goes to live at Unicorn Farm with her cousin Rowena, who breeds and races thoroughbreds. The Kentucky horse farm has been hit by one disaster after another—Rowena's parents died in a fire of suspicious origins, and several horses have died under mysterious circumstances—giving rise to speculation that the place is cursed. Although frightened, Sarah and Rowena refuse to give up the farm. A large cast of potential troublemakers offers mystery buffs and horse lovers a lively story; it unfolds slowly and satisfyingly.

Johnston is especially deft in evoking the Kentucky landscape.

Hazel Rochman

SOURCE: A review of *Shadow of a Unicorn,* in *Booklist,* Vol. 83, No. 22, August, 1987, p. 1737.

When orphaned teenager Sarah is given a home on her cousin's thoroughbred horse farm, she investigates the series of catastrophes that seem to haunt the farm like a curse, including the deaths of her aunt and uncle and the continuing disease and injury among valuable horses. The mystery creates a sense of danger as the suspects increase, but the solution is unconvincing and characterization is minimal. For Johnston's following as well as horse lovers, who will enjoy the depiction of a modern breeding farm, its science and big business; a light romance adds interest.

Laura Dixon

SOURCE: A review of *Shadow of a Unicorn,* in *School Library Journal,* Vol. 34, No. 2, October, 1987, p. 140.

Arson, murder, and romance combine to create a suspenseful mystery. When her mother dies, Sarah Burton goes to live with her cousin Rowena Drake at Unicorn Farm, a horse breeding farm that has been in the family for generations. However, since Rowena has taken charge, mysterious happenings have been taking place and threaten the farm's future. Some people blame Rowena for bad management, while others claim that there is a curse on the farm. Sarah teams up with Tim, a college student working at Unicorn Farm, to investigate the strange occurences. They, of course, solve the mystery, but not until some very exciting events take place. There are a few unexplained events—how the new stable manager became involved in the sabotage and the potential involvement of Rowena's boyfriend. The ending does leave some things up in the air, but on the whole the conclusion is tied up neatly. Johnston does well at weaving tidbits of horse breeding into the story, but these inclusions aren't so overbearing as to turn off non-horse people. Mystery readers should be pleased with this offering.

Jane Van Wiemokly

SOURCE: A review of *Shadow of a Unicorn,* in *Voice of Youth Advocates,* Vol. 10, No. 4, October, 1987, p. 202.

This is what I would consider a real gothic set in contemporary Kentucky. A full moon shows through darkening clouds as 16 year old Sarah Burton runs before the paddock of a rearing horse on the melodramatic cover. Mysterious and sometimes fatal occurrences, which many believe are the result of a curse, take place at the horse farm of Sarah's cousin. Sarah has come to live there after the death of her mother expecting to find peace and serenity. Instead she finds that horses, and perhaps people, are being killed. In true gothic fashion there is a love interest, a stable groom who just might not be trustworthy. Sarah begins investigating the possible culprits to try to solve the mysteries.

The descriptions of the horses, the stables, and the horses are apt. I found myself caring more for the horses than for most of the human characters, and grieved at their helpless deaths. My main reason for this is because I found it ridiculous and irrational that not one supposedly intelligent human realized the advisability, or even simply the need, for informing the police or any other agency about the rash of catastrophes befalling the Unicorn Farm and its equine and human inhabitants. I realize that if the characters had informed the police this would not be the story it is. If the reader accepts the given premises, the story works. I could not.

THE POTTER'S WHEEL (written as Norma Johnston, 1988)

Kirkus Reviews

SOURCE: A review of *The Potter's Wheel*, in *Kirkus Reviews*, Vol. LVI, No. 4, February 15, 1988, pp. 279-80.

With this story of an eventful family reunion, Johnston turns in another well-crafted novel about the strength of family relationships.

Family matriarch Serena Van Zandt, having restored her Pennsylvania homestead (Williamsburg style), invites her family for the opening. Her charismatic personality has strongly affected her three daughters; Kay, whose reaction is to rebel, goes to England instead of coming. It falls to her only child—Laura, 16—to represent their branch of the family. Discovering that her parents are divorcing, Laura stays on after the reunion; during the rest of the summer, she learns about her cousins' strengths and weaknesses, the power of physical attraction, and her own untapped talents as a leader and administrator; she also gains better understanding of her parents' marriage, her grandmother's character, and the power of love in an extended family.

Although the theme of the search for identity and a place in the world is familiar, Laura is a strong heroine. Some of the lesser characters are predictable, and the story is slow to start; still, Johnston delivers solid entertainment and adds another memorable family to her gallery.

Catherine vanSonnenberg

SOURCE: A review of *The Potter's Wheel*, in *School Library Journal*, Vol. 34, No. 7, March, 1988, p. 214.

Sixteen-year-old Laura Blair has led a pampered and seamless life. When her mother leaves for an assignment in Europe, her often-absent architect father delivers Laura to a family reunion in Pennsylvania. There she is immersed in a round of celebrations overseen by the family's respectfully feared matriarch, Grandmother Serena (Laura's mother's mother), and attended by a collection of well-to-do cousins and aunts—all either artsy overachievers or rebels. When Laura's mother writes that she and Laura's father are divorcing, Laura is devastated. However cloyingly classy these family members may appear to readers, they do rise to Laura's aid, and with their support and her own willfulness, Laura is able to define and resolve her relationship with her parents, her self, and her future. Johnston has written around a standard coming-of-age crisis with a somewhat unusual setting and cast of characters. Until Laura's parental problem is presented and she herself is humbled to a more human (and sympathetic) character, the whole cool cast may have left readers feeling bored and uninvolved. It's only in the last third of the book that readers and the other characters are sufficiently drawn into Laura's problem that the mature resolution becomes meaningful and satisfying.

Publishers Weekly

SOURCE: A review of *The Potter's Wheel*, in *Publishers Weekly*, Vol. 233, No. 20, May 20, 1988, p. 93.

The rich texture of Johnston's writing gives this story of Laura and her kin immediacy, incorporating themes of family, self-discovery and love into a moving novel of depth and intricacy. Laura attends the family reunion at her powerful and charismatic grandmother's new home. Gran's "home" is a town newly restored to showcase art, music, antiques and memories. Laura and her cousins Sophie and Beth spend the summer with Gran, each discovering a new part of themselves and understanding better their family's complexity and instability. Sophie, with her carefree, European lifestyle, delicate Beth who conceals her desire to abandon dancing, and Laura, who discovers she is strong and more like her grandmother than she had ever expected, are some of the fully realized characters in this witty, potent offering.

Carmen Oyenque

SOURCE: A review of *The Potter's Wheel*, in *Voice of Youth Advocates*, Vol. 11, No. 2, June, 1988, p. 87.

The summer she turns 16, Laura Serena Blair's family receives a telegram from Serena Van Zandt, her maternal grandmother, inviting the family to come from Wisconsin to Pennsylvania where Gran has restored Vredezucht, the Van Zandt home village. Kay, Laura's mother who feels threatened by Serena, doesn't want to go and refuses to let Laura go alone. When Kay receives a job offer and goes to England solo, and Laura's father's work takes him to Philadelphia, Laura travels across the country with him to participate in the events at Vredezucht. During the summer Laura lives alone in the potter's house where Gran comes to work with clay when she is troubled. Laura's visit lasts through the summer which gives Laura the opportunity to know family members. Gran is wealthy, energetic, and creative and Laura finds that she shares many of Serena's qualities. Laura plans and directs a series of "living pictures" depicting scenes from the family history, befriends her reckless cousin Sophie and her fragile cousin Beth, learns to restore antique furniture, and develops inner strength to handle the breakup of her parents' marriage. Her maturity is symbolized by the creation of an urn-shaped vase which she leaves behind for Serena when she returns to Wisconsin with her father.

The attractive watercolor cover shows Serena in her traditional caftan with Laura in front of the potter's house. Readers who enjoyed Johnston's **"The Keeping Days"** and **"The Carlisle Chronicles"** will appreciate this family saga.

RIDING HOME (written as Pamela Dryden, 1988)

Zena Sutherland

SOURCE: A review of *Riding Home,* in *Bulletin of the Center for Children's Books,* Vol. 41, No. 11, July-August, 1988, p. 226.

Formula fiction is no less formulaic when it uses two standard patterns rather than one; here the success-after-obstacles horse story is combined with the rapport-after-obstacles family adjustment story. Betsy works at a stable three days a week after school and yearns for the horse her father has promised she'll have—someday. She's jealous of her new stepsister Ferris, whose interests (musical) are taken more seriously and whose academic record (both are in middle school) is enviable. Eventually a true sisterly affection develops, and it is Ferris who helps Betsy with her schoolwork and with her dreams for winning kudos as a rider. Superficial, but grist for the popular fiction fan, this has adequate style, trite situations, and shallow characterization.

RETURN TO MOROCCO (written as Norma Johnston, 1988)

Merilyn S. Burrington

SOURCE: A review of *Return to Morocco,* in *School Library Journal,* Vol. 35, No. 1, September, 1988, p. 200.

Seventeen-year-old Tori Clay's genteel grandmother invites her to accompany her on a Mediterranean cruise that she describes as a "pilgrimage back into her youth." Upon arriving in Tangier, Tori discovers that Nannie's past is like a scene from *Casablanca,* fraught with perilous, clandestine unfinished business that Nannie must confront. During World War II, while Nannie was working with the French Resistance in Morocco as an agent for the Office of Strategic Services, she uncovered shocking information that has implications on today's political scene. Tori grapples with corpses, muggings, and poisonous snakes,

but her greatest ordeal is coming to terms with the truth about Nannie and learning to forgive her. She comes to rely on C. D., a collegiate amateur photographer whose invariable Superman-like arrivals whenever catastrophe strikes create an implausible note. A suspenseful tale of international espionage in a skillfully-drawn Third World setting.

Kirkus Reviews

SOURCE: A review of *Return to Morocco,* in *Kirkus Reviews,* Vol. LVI, No. 18, September 15, 1988, p. 1405.

A contrived but suspenseful spy thriller, set in a classic location, with a squeaky-clean romance attached.

Tori Clay, 17, escapes her upcoming debut when her beloved Grandmother ("Nannie") invites her along on a Mediterranean cruise. It becomes evident that Nannie has a hidden agenda when the two explore Tangier amid deadly traps, corpses, assault, and unknown intruders. Tori sees a new side to Nannie, who kills a man with a rolled-up magazine and is shortly thereafter struck by a speeding car. With Nannie hospitalized, C.D. Mackenzie, a fellow passenger, provides Tori with a masculine arm to lean on. After an investigation festooned with remarkable coincidences, the story comes out: while working for the OSS in WW II, Nannie found and hid proof that her lover was a double agent; now, 40 years later, he's a famous French war hero and about to be Premier; he will stop at nothing to save his career. In the course of learning this, Tori has a propensity to scream, hyperventilate, or burst into hysterical laughter. She's passively willing to be led around by men until the climax, when she impulsively enters an obvious trap alone. Face to face with the bad guy, she persuades him to retire by appealing to his better nature, meanwhile gunning down the two henchmen he has left.

As usual, Johnston captures the distinctive flavor of her setting. The chemistry between Tori and C.D. will set young hearts athrob, but even Phyllis Whitney's mysteries feature spunkier heroines.

Publishers Weekly

SOURCE: A review of *Return to Morocco,* in *Publishers Weekly,* Vol. 234, No. 16, October 14, 1988, p. 79.

Tori, 17, is happy to miss her debut in favor of going with her spunky grandmother to Morocco. Nannie knows Morocco—she was a celebrated photographer there during World War II. While Nannie insists that they have come to take care of her husband's business interests, Tori senses that her grandmother is hiding something from her. Following a violent turn of events leading to Nannie's hospitalization, Tori realizes that she and her one friend, C.D., a young photographer, must figure out her grandmother's secret past before it's too late. The exotic locale and fast-paced first half of this book offer suspense and romance reminiscent of Phyllis Whitney's works, but when Tori—and her attempt to understand Nannie's other identity—becomes the main focus, the novel loses momentum. And weak characterizations make the adventure story lifeless and clichéd.

Donna Houser

SOURCE: A review of *Return to Morocco,* in *Voice of Youth Advocates,* Vol. 11, No. 5, December, 1988, p. 239.

Mystery, adventure, and a new boyfriend are in store for Tori Clay when she goes with her grandmother, Mrs. Henry (Nannie) Clay, to Morocco. Mrs. Henry Clay, known as Nance O'Neille during World War II, has seen an article in the newspaper concerning General Argenteuil. Argenteuil is running for premier of the French government, and Mrs. Clay knows him as a double agent from the War. To prevent his election, she needs a document that she had left in Morocco in the French underground's hands when she had to escape in order to save her life. Since Nannie has been pretending that this trip is to get away, Tori doesn't understand the perilous events that start happening the minute they arrive in Morocco. Nannie realizes she and her granddaughter are in serious danger, so Nannie reveals her past. Until then, the strange events do not make sense to Tori, but now that she understands about her grandmother's previous life, Tori realizes she must get the document. By then, Nannie is unable to help, but C.D., a young man from the ship that Tori and her Grandmother have come over on, is staying in Morocco and helps Tori solve the mysteries.

This is a fascinating, quick-paced story that incidentally relates some facts about Morocco and WWII. Excellent book for this genre, with a neat cover that depicts C.D. and Tori's recovery of the needed document.

WHISPER OF THE CAT (written as Norma Johnston, 1988)

Colleen Macklin

SOURCE: A review of *Whisper of the Cat,* in *Voice of Youth Advocates,* Vol. 11, No. 4, October, 1988, p. 182.

Sixteen year old Tracy chooses to live with her father when her mother accepts a job in South America. Her father has remarried and lives on an island in Georgia. Immediately upon her arrival, Tracy senses a danger and secrecy on the island. Her stepmother, Catriona, an anthropologist, is attempting to renovate the family home, a plantation with an evil history. A sadistic ancestor who carried a cat-o'-nine-tails, killed a female slave who put a curse upon Cat's family, or so the local population believes. As accident after accident occurs, and a dead body is found, the locals attribute each to the family curse, or whisper of the cat. Tracy seeks to find out what is really happening, and stumbles upon a drug dealing operation. She almost loses her life, but instead finds ro-

mance on the mysterious island. Cliche-ridden dialogue, and a familiar story line work against Johnston; but when all is said and done, she can write action-filled romance with some flair. This is a good recreational gothic for teenage girls who are looking for something more than the series romance.

THE DELPHIC CHOICE (written as Norma Johnston, 1989)

Kirkus Reviews

SOURCE: A review of *The Delphic Choice,* in *Kirkus Reviews,* Vol. LVII, No. 6, March 15, 1989, p. 465.

From a much-practiced novelist, another adventure-romance in the vein of *Return to Morocco*.

Just out of high school, Meredith has come to Istanbul to help her aunt. Felicity, through a difficult pregnancy. As she arrives, Felicity's husband—Mark, a Quaker peace-negotiator—disappears, presumably to try to free a friend taken hostage by a new Muslim terrorist group. Meredith, a self-reliant, take-charge sort, is called on to run the household and field not only reporters but cryptic messages from Mark and the terrorists who now hold Mark, and eventually to deal with the CIA. In these endeavors she has the help of the Quaker community, friendly Muslim neighbors, and an impeccable American graduate student she picked up in Delphi; the "choice" she ultimately makes (concurring with Mark's prescient instructions) is that public good has to outweigh private safety; fortunately, the consequences here are not as cruel as they can often be.

Johnston brings a real sense of place to her fast-moving story, neatly tucking in nuggets of social and political history. There are improbabilities: to save the baby, Felicity is kept in the dark about her husband, even though she's a level-headed person who later says, "Suspecting is far worse than knowing." And Meredith carries messages to the terrorists with only mild trepidation—but that's par for the genre. Light, but lively and entertaining.

Zena Sutherland

SOURCE: A review of *The Delphic Choice,* in *Bulletin of the Center for Children's Books,* Vol. 42, No. 9, May, 1989, p. 226.

Meredith, the seventeen-year-old narrator, is at Delphi when she meets Brandon (also American, also bound for Istanbul) and he explains the conflict between public and private duty that influenced oracular pronouncements in ancient Greece. Meredith's aunt Felicity is with her, and they are called back to Istanbul when Felicity's husband Mark (Quaker, peace negotiator) disappears. What follows is a taut story of increasing fear and tension as Mark becomes hostage to terrorists who also threaten Felicity and her children. There's plenty of action here, and a setting that has topical interest and some suspense; characterization is adequate if not deep, and the writing has a controlled structure despite the fact that the author has overcrowded her story with so many incidents and characters and—to a lesser extent—descriptive passages that have the aura of a travel brochure.

Linda L. Lowry

SOURCE: A review of *The Delphic Choice*, in *School Library Journal*, Vol. 35, No. 9, May, 1989, p. 126.

Seventeen-year-old Meredith Blake is spending time in Istanbul tending to her pregnant aunt's two children when she is faced with a Delphic choice—a choice between public and private duty. While acting as a hostage negotiator, her uncle is kidnapped by a terrorist organization who wants Meredith to relay messages between them and the United States government. Readers will be drawn into Meredith's dilemma as she realizes that the wrong choice could endanger many lives. While some passages are slightly didactic, Johnston weaves an adventurous story rich with the color of the Middle East. Teens will admire the intelligence and strength of the main character and will be intrigued by the excitement and mystery of the plot. Readers who have enjoyed Norma Johnston's other titles will find this one to be equally satisfying.

Stephanie Zvirin

SOURCE: A review of *The Delphic Choice*, in *Booklist*, Vol. 85, No. 17, May 1, 1989, p. 1539.

Johnston's latest spy caper again features a teenage protagonist whose aplomb in unusual situations is unquestionably top-notch. Beset with the responsibility for her bedridden aunt and the woman's children, 17-year-old Meredith suddenly finds herself faced with the disappearance of her beloved uncle, apparently kidnapped by a small group of Middle East terrorists. Despite plot potential, suspense is forced at best, and discerning genre readers are bound to notice some of the liberties Johnston has taken with logic. Still, if books with foreign settings are in demand, this one is larded with exotic trappings—from fanatical demonstrations to scenery. And Johnston has added a hint of romance for extra appeal.

📖 *THE TIME OF THE CRANES* (written as Norma Johnston, 1990)

Stephanie Zvirin

SOURCE: A review of *The Time of the Cranes*, in *Booklist*, Vol. 86, No. 15, April 1, 1990, p. 1540.

The unexpected death of her mother and taunts from students at her new school have shaken Stacy Winbrand to the point that she doubts herself, both as a performer and as a person. So she is surprised to discover that Madame

Karpova, an acting teacher with whom she lost touch long ago, believed in her enough to make her beneficiary in a will. Though grateful for Karpova's bequest, Stacy finds that her mentor's legacy burdens her with an unwanted responsibility: not only must she live up to Karpova's faith in her acting talent, but she must also find out the truth about the old woman's death—a truth that someone is trying very hard to hide. A subplot involving a nursing home scandal provides some tense moments in the narrative, but Johnston's novel is not a thriller. Rather, it is about self-acceptance and moving forward after tragedy has taken its toll, themes that Johnston handles with leisurely grace and theatrical flair.

Publishers Weekly

SOURCE: A review of *The Time of the Cranes*, in *Publishers Weekly*, Vol. 237, No. 17, April 27, 1990, p. 62.

On the day she lands the lead in the school play, Stacy learns that her former acting teacher has died. Madame Karpova has named Stacy next of kin and left her much of her estate. Madame's bequest sends Stacy into a bewildering flurry of activity: she throws herself into rehearsals (not surprisingly, her role is one in which Madame once triumphed), investigates the lame mystery surrounding Madame's death, begins her first romance and attempts to work through her feelings about her mother's recent death. And as if all that weren't enough, her widower father starts to date an actress who worked and studied with Madame. With so many issues vying for center stage, it is difficult to determine what this novel is really about. A cast of fully realized characters might be able to sort out the overabundance of plots and subplots, but this task is beyond the reach of shallow Stacy and her one-dimensional friends.

Susan F. Marcus

SOURCE: A review of *The Time of the Cranes*, in *School Library Journal*, Vol. 36, No. 5, May, 1990, p. 122.

In the two years since her mother died and she and her father moved away from New York, Stacy has rarely thought about her former drama teacher, Madame Karpova. Now in her junior year of high school, waiting anxiously to learn if she has earned a part in the school play, she is shocked to learn that Madame has died in a nursing home nearby, naming Stacy her beneficiary. With the support of her father and of Gideon, a volunteer at the nursing home, Stacy shoulders the responsibilities thrust upon her, discovering that Madame's death, allegedly a heart attack, is suspicious. Eventually, she finds out that Madame, suffering from brain cancer, took an overdose of painkillers in order to die with dignity. In the meantime, Stacy comes to terms with the deaths of both Madame and her mother and attains the breakthrough that has eluded her in her acting. Johnston sometimes bestows Stacy with a less-than-believable wisdom, but she provides a satisfying read for fans of fast-moving soap operas, acting enthusiasts, and mature readers who can grapple with the issue of elderly suicide.

Allan A. Cuseo

SOURCE: A review of *The Time of the Cranes,* in *Voice of Youth Advocates,* Vol. 13, No. 2, June, 1990, p. 105.

Stacy Winbrand, high school student, aspiring actress and former protégée of the famed Russian actress Madame Varvara Karpova, must cope with the death of her mother and her father's loss of his job. It is when Stacy learns of Madame's death at the Sunnyside Nursing Home, and that she has inherited her estate, that the mystery begins. Was Madame's death the result of brain cancer, an intentional drug overdose, or malpractice?

Johnston attempts to weave elements of Jewish and Christian traditions, Russian history, the beginnings of young love, violence, nursing home problems, hints of murder, theater lore, and grief into what is basically a warm story. Although the pace bogs down at times, the reader's interest is usually peaked. Was Madame murdered by the doctors and nurses; will Stacy and Gideon, the amateur clown, fall in love; will Stacy be a success in her school's production of Chekhov's *The Seagull;* will Stacy's father fall in love with Marianne, the famous television soap opera star? There are many holes in the plot and considerable suspension of belief is required but, similar to Bette Midler's movie remake *Stella,* Johnston pulls it off because the reader enjoys the journey. Johnston uses *The Seagull,* which established Chekhov as a major dramatist, to link some of the plot elements: Madame had starred as Nina in her youth, Marianne played Nina and is, therefore, able to coach Stacy; the play concerns an aspiring actress, and a suicide; and the theme of loss and identity is in both the play and book.

At times, Johnson's writing is poetical and the inclusions of Chekhov's words are welcome, but the novel, similar to the faded glory of Madame Karpova, is reminiscent of the YA plot-laden, character-deficient novels of the 1950s. And yet, to quote Chekhov, "How lovely it was in the old days . . . how warm, how joyful . . . Men and lions . . . starfish and tiny creatures—these and every form of life have ended . . . The cry of the cranes is heard no more in the meadows; the hum of the cockchafers is silent in the linden groves."

📖 ***THE DRAGON'S EYE* (written as Norma Johnston, 1990)**

Pat Katka

SOURCE: A review of *The Dragon's Eye,* in *School Library Journal,* Vol. 36, No. 12, December, 1990, p. 121.

As Jenny Price juggles junior-year classes, Youth for Literacy activities, and her grandfather's art showings, she makes room for one more assignment—sleuthing. Jenny vows to track down the "Eye of the Dragon," an audacious hacker who sends cryptic warnings via the school's computer system. However, before she can identify the culprit, the messages change in style and substance, suggesting that more than one dragon is tampering with the mainframe. Then Jenny discovers a link between the threatening messages and two tragic events—a football player's drug-related death and classmate Doris' attempted suicide. Jenny and Doris are believable in their actions and appearance, but occasionally these 16 year olds use expressions or make references that are inappropriate for their generation, e.g. "he's no spring chicken," and "Madame Queen" (Amos 'n' Andy). The plot is burdened with too many characters, extraneous excursions into the catering business and art world, and copious computer messages that ultimately become tedious. The jacket illustration promises a light computer caper, not a hybrid mystery/contemporary problem novel. Readers seeking a fast-paced and gripping mystery should find Johnston's ***Return to Morocco*** more satisfying.

Sue-Ellen Beauregard

SOURCE: A review of *The Dragon's Eye,* in *Booklist,* Vol. 87, No. 10, January 15, 1991, p. 1053.

Popular high school junior Jenny Price helps her widowed mother with the family catering business, is involved in a school literacy project, and has an active social calendar. Then nasty, cryptic messages start appearing on school lockers, over the computer-generated loudspeaker system, and in other public places, and her idyllic life begins to unravel. While Jenny and her friends are investigating, things turn even more sinister: her distant cousin dies during a football game, apparently the victim of a drug overdose. Could Jenny have prevented the death? Who supplied the pills? And who keeps sending those messages? The clues become confusing, but they're all eventually sorted out in this swiftly paced, if convoluted, story with an admirable protagonist who will appeal to fans of earlier Johnston novels.

Shirley Carmony

SOURCE: A review of *The Dragon's Eye,* in *Voice of Youth Advocates,* Vol. 13, No. 6, February, 1991, p. 352.

When a nasty graffiti campaign on the school lockers escalates to include embarrassing messages to several people on the school's computer network, more and more people are hurt. Doris Haywood is the initial victim of the graffiti messages, but before long, Jenny Price, the central character, also receives some of the disturbing messages. When Jenny sets out to discover the identity of the writer of the messages, the "Eye of the Dragon" (the message writer) claims to "know what you're doing" and threatens to tell. Then serious and frightening things begin to happen around Jenny, including the death of the star football player and Doris's attempted suicide. Eventually Jenny realizes the truth, that the message was initially sent to the wrong person through the computer mailbox system and the deadly consequences have been the result of someone else's guilty conscience.

The novel is indeed a suspenseful one that pulls the reader along and keeps the identity of the real culprit just out of reach until the very end. The characters are fun, and the novel utilizes some very up-to-date parts of students' lives—computer mailboxes, computerized announcements, and steroids. All in all, the novel reads quickly and is quite enjoyable.

📖 LOUISA MAY: THE WORLD AND WORKS OF LOUISA MAY ALCOTT (written as Norma Johnston, 1991)

Kirkus Reviews

SOURCE: A review of *Louisa May: The World and Works of Louisa May Alcott,* in *Kirkus Reviews,* Vol. LIX, No. 20, October 15, 1991, p. 1344.

An author of over 60 YA novels brings fine narrative skill to a sympathetic portrait of one of her greatest predecessors.

Much has been added to the record since the 1933 publication of [Cornelia] Meigs's well-researched but traditional biography, the Newbery-winning *Invincible Louisa.* Alcott's letters and journals, several collections of the "thrillers" that kept the family pot boiling, and a novel whose genesis was ruefully described in *Little Women* have been recently published; scholarly studies point out the extent to which the author's autobiographical fiction was an unrealistic reformulation of a difficult life and of a gifted but impossible family (especially her improvident philosopher father). Johnston, bless her, succeeds in reconciling the loving family in *Little Women* with the facts of Alcott's rich but extraordinarily demanding life. She posits that, though Bronson Alcott was indeed a remarkably innovative educator as well as an eminent scholar, it was her mother, Abba May Alcott, who most profoundly influenced Louisa. Pioneer social worker and sometimes, of necessity, family breadwinner, she was, like Louisa, an outstandingly courageous, independent, yet nurturing woman, deeply loved though not so unrealistically patient as "Marmee."

Good as it was, Meigs's book seemed colorless compared to Alcott's fiction. Johnston—by depicting the real life in all its complexity while showing the many links with the fiction—not only enriches understanding of Alcott's books but also paints a fascinating picture of her life. A must.

Rachel Gonsenhauser

SOURCE: A review of *Louisa May: The World and Works of Louisa May Alcott,* in *Voice of Youth Advocates,* Vol. 14, No. 5, December, 1991, p. 337.

History, anecdotes about family life, and biographical episodes in both her life and the lives of her parents make this an interesting, if a bit wordy biography of Louisa May Alcott. The book is rich with historical facts about the United States intertwined with the story of Alcott's family and how she evolved into a writer of children's books. The book begins with her parents' lives, delving too deeply into them at times, making one forget it is a story of Louisa's life. But the values and way of life she espoused were directly influenced by those of her parents, who were both involved in education and human rights. Their family was extremely close knit, and much is made of the tragedies they all suffered. In fact, Alcott modeled the March family of *Little Women* after her own family, including herself. The only disappointment I felt in reading the book was that more emphasis was not on her writings, *per se,* not much was mentioned until the end of the book. But the way of life of the late 19th century in this country is realistically depicted, and that should be of interest to anyone reading the book, which is meant for older YAs, at least grades 8-9. There are illustrations of family members and homes they lived in, and a partial listing of Louisa May Alcott's works at the close.

Carolyn Phelan

SOURCE: A review of *Louisa May: The World and Works of Louisa May Alcott,* in *Booklist,* Vol. 88, No. 8, December 15, 1991, pp. 756-57.

Those who assume that the idyllic family scene depicted in *Little Women* was a thinly veiled portrait of Louisa May Alcott's happy home life will find this biography an eye-opener. Early in the book, Johnston focuses on Louisa's remarkable parents and characterizes the Alcotts as "a dysfunctional family that achieved a miracle." Relying on recent compilations of Louisa's letters and journals, Johnston considers the physical, emotional, intellectual and social stresses on the Alcott family and how Louisa coped with them in her writing and in her life. While some readers may lack the patience to read about the biographee's parents (Louisa isn't born until chapter four), those who do will be rewarded with a fuller understanding of this complex woman. An intelligent biography that underscores the difficulties and achievements of a "celebrated American authoress."

Deborah Stevenson

SOURCE: A review of *Louisa May: The World and Works of Louisa May Alcott,* in *Bulletin of the Center for Children's Books,* Vol. 45, No. 5, January, 1992, p. 130.

This well-crafted biography is a worthy companion and a serious contrast to [Cornelia] Meigs' Newbery winner, *Invincible Louisa:* Johnston makes it clearer why Louisa *needed* to be invincible. Where Meigs' Alcott, for instance, has sadness and delicate health, Johnston's has bitter awareness of the cruelty of 19th century medical realities that robbed her of loved ones and wracked her own days with pain. The book is neither ill-natured nor depressing, however, just vividly honest in its description of Alcott's constant physical and literary labor. Johnston evokes a fascinating milieu of both everyday toil and daily contact with the makers of American intellectual history (everyone from Hawthorne to Emerson to Margaret Fuller is here), creating an absorbing portrait of interest even to readers who aren't *Little Women* fans. The style is crisp and telling ("All his life, Bronson had a gift for inspiring women to make sacrifices for his work") and bespeaks good research, although one regrets the absence of notes. Not many books convey the grinding reality of writing to make money; this one does that and provides a look at a talented and determined woman as well.

Barbara Hutcheson

SOURCE: A review of *Louisa May: The World and Works of Louisa May Alcott,* in *School Library Journal,* Vol. 38, No. 2, February, 1992, p. 114.

Johnston combines recent scholarship and her own reading and experience to present a fresh look at the author of the beloved *Little Women.* The highlights of Alcott's life are familiar. One of several daughters born to an impoverished educational visionary, she turned her hand to sewing, teaching, nursing, and finally writing to help support her struggling family. Johnston attempts to round out this picture, to balance the well-known influence Bronson Alcott had on his daughter with that of her mother and her own development as a creative individual. In so doing she presents Alcott as a richer, more complex figure, whose relevance to readers is undiminished by the passage of time. Instead of an old-fashioned sentimentalist, Alcott comes across as a woman of talent, strength, passion, and perseverance. The author sets her agenda in an introductory note, and then goes on to support her text with a wealth of primary and secondary sources, one as recent as 1991. The bibliography is annotated, although, except for [Cornelia] Meigs's classic *Invincible Louisa,* the citations are all of adult titles. Fans of *Little Women* will need little urging to read this biography, and even less to move on from it to other Alcott titles. Solidly researched, well written, respectful of readers, this will be a major addition to biography shelves.

HARRIET: THE LIFE AND WORLD OF HARRIET BEECHER STOWE (written as Norma Johnston, 1994)

Kirkus Reviews

SOURCE: A review of *Harriet: The Life and World of Harriet Beecher Stowe,* in *Kirkus Reviews,* Vol. LXII, No. 12, June 15, 1994, p. 846.

By the author of a fine Alcott biography (***Louisa May***), a perceptive portrait. Like Suzanne M. Coil (*Harriet Beecher Stowe*), Johnston has done her research thoroughly and

offers a detailed, balanced account. Johnston's narrative skills, honed in over 60 YA novels, give her an edge; her depiction of Harriet's happy marriage to the scholarly but impractical Calvin Stowe is more credible than Coil's ("despite his hypochondria, his inability to cope with crises or to earn much money," Calvin "had faith in her even when she did not herself [and] admired her mind"); her pivotal passages on the actual writing of *Uncle Tom's Cabin* are especially dramatic, while the final scenes of the aged widow wandering next door to pluck Sam Clemens's flowers, roots and all, have a touching authenticity. She also does a fine job of setting context and of showing how Harriet's Calvinist roots—particularly as manifested in the powerful Beecher clan—and other influences, radical and traditional, played roles in the development of her ideas and writing. Harriet continues to fascinate as a woman of—and also, in many ways, ahead of—her time, who did whatever she undertook with enormous competence and persistence. A dour jacket portrait does its subject scant justice.

Deborah Stevenson

SOURCE: A review of *Harriet: The Life and World of Harriet Beecher Stowe,* in *Bulletin of the Center for Children's Books,* Vol. 48, No. 2, October, 1994, pp. 50-1.

Harriet Beecher Stowe came from a charismatic and important family, rubbed shoulders with significant and famous people, and wrote a pivotal work in American history. Norma Johnston provides a detailed account of the author's life, times, and experiences, starting with the background of the Beecher family and continuing through Stowe's birth, upbringing, writing, and international fame. This book offers a more technically complete account than Jean Fritz's biography, containing an occasionally dizzying array of names and places and a great deal of useful information about Stowe's writing generally. The book is well organized, and chapters are helpfully headed by the dates covered within them; so many people (and some similarly named, particularly in the Beecher family) appear, however, that one might benefit from more frequent explanations or reminders of identity. Generally, though, the book is capable and comprehensive, providing a multitude of information about the period and its issues as well as Harriet Beecher Stowe herself. Johnston includes source acknowledgments and a bibliography but regrettably does not include specific source notes for her information (this absence in both the Fritz and Johnston biographies makes the contradictions between them particularly vexing); black-and-white photographs appear throughout the text, and an index is appended.

Kathleen Beck

SOURCE: A review of *Harriet: The Life and World of Harriet Beecher Stowe,* in *Voice of Youth Advocates,* Vol. 17, No. 4, October, 1994, p. 231.

"So you're the little woman who wrote the book that

made this great war!" Abraham Lincoln is reported to have said upon meeting Harriet Beecher Stowe. Her novel *Uncle Tom's Cabin* raised the consciousness of a nation on the issue of slavery, strengthening calls for abolition and exacerbating the tensions that led to the outbreak of the Civil War.

Quite an influence for a tiny, introverted woman who took to writing to supplement the income of her growing family. In this biography Johnston makes Stowe come to life. The brilliant, sometimes chaotic household of her famous preacher father, Lyman Beecher; the exciting years on the frontier in Cincinnati; her marriage to the widower of her best friend; and her gradual emergence from the shadow of her better-known relatives to become an international figure, all are described in lively and appealing prose. Johnston's own talents as a storyteller are strongly in evidence. She excels at illustrating Harriet's own quirky sense of humor and the gradual development of her talent as a writer. Harriet is set firmly in the social and religious context of the time. The strong influence of her father and siblings is given its due. What a surprise it must have been for them to see mousy Harriet outshine them all!

At times Johnston makes assumptions about the reader's background, describing the importance of the Unitarians in Boston society, for example, without ever explaining what a Unitarian is. Toward the end the narrative bogs down in tales of travels and names of friends. But in general this is a very readable account which may make some new friends for biographies.

REMEMBER THE LADIES: THE FIRST WOMEN'S RIGHTS CONVENTION (written as Norma Johnston, 1995)

Carolyn Phelan

SOURCE: A review of *Remember the Ladies: The First Women's Rights Convention,* in *Booklist,* Vol. 91, No. 17, May 1, 1995, p. 1570.

Focusing on the 1848 Women's Rights Convention in Seneca Falls, New York, this book offers an evenhanded account of that event. Interwoven is the life story of Elizabeth Cady Stanton and descriptions of other key participants including Lucretia Mott and Frederick Douglass. Johnston also gives readers a sense of the convention's ties, which stretched backward in time to the Declaration of Independence and forward to the passage of the Nineteenth Amendment. Johnston shows respect for young readers by sorting out fact from supposition and, in the introductory note, acknowledging the difficulties of writing history from incomplete and somewhat unreliable sources. Following a chronology of the women's rights movement though 1920, there are source notes for the

many quotations in the text. A good resource for students of women's history.

THE IMAGE GAME (written as Norma Johnston, 1995)

Sherri Forgash Ginsberg

SOURCE: A review of *The Image Game,* in *Kliatt Young Adult Paperback Book Guide,* Vol. 30, No. 3, May, 1996, p. 8.

Celia is going to be a sophomore in a New Jersey high school and would like to start off on the right foot with a relationship with Brock Peters, the school football hero. Celia's mother's best friend has a high school senior son, Zack, who is a bit nerdy but good looking. A friendship pact between Celia and Zack evolves and Celia proceeds with her new popularity plan. A local chemical company that employs Zack on a part-time basis wants to expand and the town is divided on whether this is good or bad. The high school students get involved and the story has political seriousness when ecological problems arise. At times the story moves slowly but it is skillfully told.

LOTTA'S PROGRESS (written as Norma Johnston, 1997)

Kirkus Reviews

SOURCE: A review of *Lotta's Progress,* in *Kirkus Reviews,* Vol. LXV, No. 9, May 1, 1997, pp. 722-23.

Spun off from Johnston's **Louisa May,** this tale of a German immigrant family's harsh first winter in America not only captures some of the flavor and spirit of *Little Women,* it also artfully suggests how incidents and people from Alcott's real life ended up in her novels. One of five children (with another on the way), Lotta Muller watches hard times take their toll: Her mother and little sister fall ill; Vater, unable to find steady work, takes to drink and finally disappears altogether; her brother is jailed for stealing food. Fortune smiles on the Mullers at last when a kindly passerby gives Lotta the address of Mrs. Bronson Alcott, who briskly enlists her gentle, brilliant husband and four lively daughters to take matters in hand. Sixteen-year-old "Louy" becomes Lotta's special friend, helping her to learn English in exchange for German lessons, and teaching her to value her own mind and talents. Chock full both of biographical facts and literary references (the Alcotts are so close to the Marches, and the Mullers to the Hummels, that Johnston's story and the classic may blend in some readers' minds), this book, strong enough to stand on its own, also makes an engaging prelude—or postscript—to its timeless progenitor.

Additional coverage of St. John's life and career is contained in the following sources published by Gale Research: *Authors and Artists for Young Adults,* Vol. 12; *Contemporary Authors New Revision Series,* Vol. 32; *Junior DISCovering Authors* (CD-ROM); *Something about the Author,* Vol. 89; and *Something about the Author Autobiography Series,* Vol. 7.

Diane Stanley

1943-

American author and illustrator of picture books.

Major works include *Peter the Great* (1986), *Shaka: King of the Zulus* (1988), *Good Queen Bess: The Story of Elizabeth I of England* (1990), *Bard of Avon: The Story of William Shakespeare* (1992), *Charles Dickens: The Man Who Had Great Expectations* (1993).

INTRODUCTION

A highly regarded author and illustrator, Stanley has provided pictures for the works of a number of well-known writers, including Jane Yolen and Verna Aardema, in addition to both writing and illustrating her own books for children. She is perhaps best known for her picture-book series of biographies of great figures from world history, created with her husband and coauthor, Peter Vennema. Stanley and Vennema have been praised for

the skill with which they have abridged and simplified great masses of adult material for primary graders. Stanley's earliest efforts were illustrations of traditional rhyming texts. Marjorie Lewis wrote in a review of *Fiddle-I-Fee: A Traditional American Chant* (1979) that Stanley's illustrations are "witty with details and subtleties." Stanley went on to create simple stories of her own, combining realism with fantasy, and retelling familiar folktales like the *Country Mouse and the Town Mouse* with a new twist. However, the unexpected success of her first picture book biography, *Peter the Great*, helped Stanley recognize the need for such nonfiction for younger children. Although she continues to fashion lighthearted stories for early readers, Stanley's most noteworthy accomplishment has been to make accessible to a new generation the life and times of such powerful personalities as Queen Elizabeth of England, King Shaka of the Zulus, and literary giants like William Shakespeare and Charles Dickens.

Biographical Information

Born in Texas, the only child of divorced parents, Stanley grew up among her mother's people, the Grissoms, who were articulate, artistic, and creative. Her early years were spent in New York City, where she and her mother enjoyed the city's cultural opportunities, entertained artists, musicians, and actors, and where her mother wrote and published a mystery. When her mother was diagnosed with tuberculosis, Stanley—just out of second grade— was sent to live with her aunt Nancy for several years in Texas, where she reveled in an active, carefree, out-of-doors childhood with her cousins. After her mother recovered, the two moved to La Jolla, California, where Stanley experienced the joys of acting in school plays, writing poems and stories, and reading. By her senior year in college, Stanley realized that she had a talent for drawing. A job in a hospital led to medical illustration and a year abroad as an art student in Scotland. While in Europe, she took trips whenever possible to other countries, most notably to Russia. She later discovered children's books while raising two daughters during her first marriage. After divorcing her first husband, Peter Zuromskis, Stanley moved to New York City to be near her mother, working full-time at publishing houses while pursuing a side career as an illustrator of children's books. She also became reunited during this period with Peter Vennema, whom she had known fourteen years earlier, and the two were married and moved together to Texas. After illustrating several books by other writers, Stanley began writing her own stories following the birth of her third child, a son. The success of the first of her picture book biographies, *Peter the Great*, led in turn to *Shaka: King of the Zulus*, inspired by her husband's time in South Africa and greatly aided by his help with the research. The couple's productive teamwork has continued with a series of well-received biographies.

Major Works

Peter the Great was inspired by a tape Stanley heard of Robert K. Massie's adult biography of the eccentric Russian czar. Deliberately omitting Peter's marriages and military expeditions, Stanley selected only those colorful episodes that she deemed appropriate for her young audience. She then drew on memories of her trip to Moscow and Leningrad during her college days and the Russian art, history, and literature she absorbed at that time, while carefully basing her pictures on documented sources—from painted portraits to written descriptions and photographs. Ilene Cooper referred to Stanley's artwork, which "features both Oriental and European elements," as "captivating," and Betsy Hearne wrote that Stanley's pictures "offer a visual depth that increases the impact of the book considerably." With *Shaka*, Stanley provides a thorough and accurate account of the fascinating life of the African leader. Lacking sufficient written records, she turned to oral tradition and two books by Europeans that focused on his adult years. Mary A. Bush remarked that Stanley's "competent rendering of place

and culture is the most striking feature of the book and reveals the very wide range in the illustrator's capability." For *Bard of Avon: The Story of William Shakespeare*, Stanley supplemented the meager facts available on the playwright's personal life with scenes from his famous plays. She also added a postscript providing information on words Shakespeare coined that are still in use today. *Charles Dickens: The Man Who Had Great Expectations* has been acclaimed for its simple, lucid text and Stanley's meticulously detailed drawings of nineteenth-century England.

Awards

Good Queen Bess: The Story of Elizabeth I of England and *Leonardo da Vinci* were named *Boston Globe-Horn Book* Honor Books for nonfiction in 1991 and 1996 respectively. *Peter the Great* won the Gold-en Kite Award and, like many of Stanley's subse-quent biographies, was named a Notable Children's Trade Book in the Field of Social Studies and a Notable Book by the American Library Association in the year of its publication; *All Wet! All Wet!* (1984) was designated an Outstanding Science Trade Book for Children by the Children's Book Council and the National Science Teachers Association in 1985. *Bard of Avon: The Story of William Shakespeare* was named a Notable Children's Book in the Language Arts, 1993. Stanley has also received numerous parents' choice and child-selected honors.

TITLE COMMENTARY

📖 *THE FARMER IN THE DELL* (adapted and illustrated by Diane Stanley as Diane Zuromskis, 1978)

Kirkus Reviews

SOURCE: A review of *The Farmer in the Dell*, in *Kirkus Reviews*, Vol. XLVI, No. 7, April 1, 1978, p. 370.

Enclosed in circular frames that emphasize the sense of contrivance, Zuromskis' doll-like folk figures pose for a series of frozen, token scenes from a marriage. Once wed, "the wife takes a child," and you see the couple in night clothes smiling fondly at the baby in a cradle beside their bed; next, the nurse in a rocker is feeding the baby while its dish spills over unobserved; and the dog is introduced licking up the spill as Nurse tucks Baby into the cradle. Zuromskis ends with the blond-pigtailed wife, her broom raised to strike, leading the whole menage down the road in pursuit of the cheese-stealing rat. (Oddly, all the animals are more lifelike than the yarn-haired humans.) It's the sort of nonentity that will circulate—cute and (at the level of the spilled baby food) clever enough to invite a look-through, but too one-dimensional to reward it at any level.

Publishers Weekly

SOURCE: A review of *The Farmer in the Dell,* in *Publishers Weekly,* Vol. 213, No. 14, April 3, 1978, p. 80.

Zuromskis's first book suggests that she has begun a rich career. Her delicate pastel paintings take little readers through the adventures of the legendary farmer and his family, beginning with his bachelor days, when he is shown planting seeds and tending his flocks. Then come depictions of the courtship during which "the farmer takes a wife," and scenes that become livelier on each page, what with dog taking cat, cat taking rat, rat taking cheese and the entire company chasing rat while "the cheese stands alone."

Denise M. Wilms

SOURCE: A review of *The Farmer in the Dell,* in *Booklist,* Vol. 74, No. 18, May 15, 1978, p. 1492.

You already know the text; the pictures that accompany it here are clean and cozy, each circle-bound and center-set opposite a line or verse of text. There's lots of creamy white space to be seen, and it contrasts nicely with the brown-toned, green-blue-yellow-highlighted drawings. The figures are cheerful—a boyish-looking farmer, his golden-haired wife, their cuddly but not too sweet animals—and the look is fancifully pristine. A pleasant enough confection for picturebook browsers drawn to the familiar lines they can "read" to themselves.

📖 ***FIDDLE-I-FEE: A TRADITIONAL AMERICAN CHANT* (adapted and illustrated by Diane Stanley, 1979)**

Marilyn Kaye

SOURCE: A review of *Fiddle-I-Fee,* in *Booklist,* Vol. 76, No. 7, December 1, 1979, p. 556.

In the cozy, muted color pictures, a little girl sets a table, puts on a fancy dress, and welcomes her friends to dinner to the accompaniment of a cumulative chant that begins, "Had me a cat, the cat pleased me, I fed my cat in yonders tree, Cat went fiddle-i-fee." And on it goes, as each animal joins the dinner party: hen, pig, dog, sheep, turkey, cow, horse. The slight text has an appealing lilt to it; illustrations are fanciful, with clothed and bejeweled creatures and an overall look that is dreamy and quietly silly. One warning: librarians had better be prepared to answer the inevitable question: "What's a 'yonders tree'?"

Marjorie Lewis

SOURCE: A review of *Fiddle-I-Fee: A Traditional American Chant,* in *School Library Journal,* Vol. 26, No. 5, January, 1980, p. 55.

A rousing, cumulative old folk chant about feeding all the animals in "yonders tree." Pictorial excitement mounts as a red-headed girl cooks and serves a dinner party to a variety of animal guests in a marvelous tree house one starry night. The sturdy full-color drawings are witty with details and subtleties that amplify the minimal text and manage to give each individual beast (dressed in appropriate party clothes) the attention its idiosyncrasies deserve.

Kirkus Reviews

SOURCE: A review of *Fiddle-I-Fee: A Traditional American Chant,* in *Kirkus Reviews,* Vol. XLVIII, No. 3, February 1, 1980, p. 122.

The chant on which this otherwise wordless book is built is the one beginning "Had me a cat, the cat pleased me, / I fed my cat in yonders tree, / Cat went fiddle-i-fee." And what we have here, beginning on the title-page spread, is a little blue-jeaned girl climbing up into a full-scale, furnished tree *house,* somehow cooking a party dinner (we see her mixing dough, etc.; we don't see an oven), and then going to bed in a star-flecked gown and tiara. Overleaf—presumably in her dreams—the rhyme begins with the entrance of the aforementioned cat. The other animals arrive ("Had me a sheep, the sheep pleased me," etc.), make their characteristic sounds ("Sheep went baa-baa-baa"), and depart—leaving the little girl dozing off again at the table. It's necessary to be literal because that's exactly what this is—not an imaginative extension but a reduction to implausibility.

Virginia Haviland

SOURCE: A review of *Fiddle-I-Fee: A Traditional American Chant,* in *The Horn Book Magazine,* Vol. LVI, No. 2, April, 1980, p. 165.

A jolly cumulative rhyme is accompanied by lively four-color illustrations depicting the growing company of pleasantly anthropomorphic animal characters and a little girl with red hair and freckles, who is preparing for a party. The verso of the title page reproduces her hand-printed invitation: "You are invited to dinner tonight (very fancy) at my place (upstairs)." Printed on following pages are lines from the catchy song: "Had me a cat, the cat pleased me / I fed my cat in yonders tree / Cat went fiddle-i-fee." Unfortunately, the music for the folk song is not included.

📖 ***THE MAN WHOSE NAME WAS NOT THOMAS* (written by M. Jean Craig, 1981)**

Publishers Weekly

SOURCE: A review of *The Man Whose Name Was Not Thomas,* in *Publishers Weekly,* Vol. 219, No. 19, May 8, 1981, p. 254.

Stanley's bonny, minutely detailed pictures in soft colors illustrate Craig's new story, what could be called a triumph of negativism. As the text describes an old-fashioned country lad whose name is *not* Thomas or dozens of others (not even *John*) and tells all the things he isn't and doesn't want, the paintings give clues to what he is and does want. He wants, more than anything, to marry and to live with his wife *not* in the tiny corner of his shop but in a proper house. He does *not* want someone he can't love, but luckily he finds a lass he does love and who loves him and would be happy in the house he is building. So giggly readers have a perky story and a rousing guessing game and the merriment of finding out, at last, that the groom (*not* Thomas) is none other than Ferdinand Jeremiah Murgatroyd Alexander Fitzgerald Maximilian Abraham Cristoforo Ladislaw Plunkett.

Barbara Elleman

SOURCE: A review of *The Man Whose Name Was Not Thomas,* in *Booklist,* Vol. 78, No. 2, September 15, 1981, p. 102.

Thomas is not this young man's name, but neither is Richard, Charles, or John. And he isn't a fisherman, a carpenter, or a blacksmith. What he does, how he builds a house, whom he chooses for his wife, and which day he is to be married are all part of this guessing game-story that is cleverly linked through picture and text. Illustrations, glowingly rendered in full color, have intrusively heavy decorative borders in places, but the rich shades and folktale styling work together for a pleasing effect.

Nancy Palmer

SOURCE: A review of *The Man Whose Name Was Not Thomas,* in *School Library Journal,* Vol. 28, No. 2, October, 1981, p. 127.

Everything we know about the title character's name, abode, career, courting and marriage comes from the text's listing of what is *not* true about his life and from the richly colored and artfully simple pictures of what *is* true. When we are told, on the left-hand page, that " . . . He did not weave cloth or mend shoes. He was not a farmer or a bricklayer or a fisherman. He was something else," that something else appears on the facing page: we see non-Thomas putting a cake into his bakery oven. Creatively composed and intriguingly bordered illustrations itemize the negatives and surround the text, while the "answer" picture is straightforwardly and squarely framed. Children will enjoy guessing and discovering from the pictures just what, indeed, is going on in these pieces of non-Thomas' life. There is almost no action as he works and weds the woman down the lane, but the folk-tale structure, the medieval cast to the illustrations and the warmth of the happy ending make this an attractive choice.

Zena Sutherland

SOURCE: A review of *The Man Whose Name Was Not Thomas,* in *Bulletin of the Center for Children's Books,* Vol. 35, No. 3, November, 1981, p. 43.

Deftly bucolic paintings, nicely framed and decorated, illustrate a tale that is negatively told, as the title is, in large part by a statement of what didn't happen, or wasn't chosen. The man who was not named Thomas (or several other names) had a job that wasn't farming or bricklaying or weaving; he didn't want to marry someone with green hair or a woman who never laughed aloud, and when he went courting he didn't wear a torn jacket or a sweater with a hole in the elbow—and so on. The story ends with a snug new house built, the man making a magnificent wedding cake and marrying the woman he loved. All of what isn't said in the text is shown in the pictures (so that readers can see the man's a baker) and the many names the man does have are revealed during the wedding ceremony. Amusing, different, sunny, and nicely told.

PETROSINELLA, A NEAPOLITAN RAPUNZEL (written by Giambattista Basile, 1981; revised edition with text adapted by Stanley, 1995)

Patricia Dooley

SOURCE: A review of *Petrosinella: A Neapolitan Rapunzel,* in *School Library Journal,* Vol. 28, No. 1, September, 1981, p. 104.

This tale of Petrosinella ("parsley") predates the Grimms' "Rapunzel" (or "rampion") by 200 years and provides the same memorable elements: the pregnant woman's longing, the promise exacted by a witch, the high tower without door or stair, the heroine's long hair, the young prince. It omits Rapunzel's singing, the prince's cruel blinding, the cutting off of Rapunzel's hair and all mention of the twins she bears in Grimm. But it introduces some distinctive features of its own, chiefly three magic acorns that Petrosinella uses to escape forever, with her lover, from the ogress (who is eaten by a wolf). The tale is adorned by some lovely, detailed illustrations on a generous, folio scale (9"x12"). The heroine is beautiful, the ogress hideous (she has an equally scarifying chum) and the colors glowing (especially a deep green and a bright indigo, found on every page), with the enameled sheen of manuscript illuminations. The tale does not have all the smoothness and style of later, more heavily edited fairy tales, but its basic appeal is considerably heightened by Stanley's art.

Natalie Babbit

SOURCE: A review of *Petrosinella: A Neapolitan Rapunzel,* in *The New York Times Book Review,* February 7, 1982, p. 27.

At first glance this picture book will remind you of Nancy Ekholm Burkert's *Snow White,* but it differs in several important ways. For one thing its strong, plain colors, general design and sometimes peculiar perspective are modeled—successfully, I think—on medieval Books of Hours. For another, although *Petrosinella* lacks the luminosity and mystery of Mrs. Burkert's work, as well as her flawless craftsmanship, it is somewhat more accessible. And while there is more space given to text, so that the book is not so overwhelmed by its pictures, it has a rather formal appearance, which it owes largely to its handsome roomy layout.

The story is a version of *Rapunzel,* which is more complex and longer than that tale, with two ogresses instead of one witch, and escape from the tower by means of three magic acorns. These, thrown one by one at the pursuing ogresses at the end, impede their progress and finally consume them altogether, allowing for the obligatory happy ending—marriage to the prince. The language is as formal as the layout, and therefore perfectly suitable.

The difficulty with this book—and many of its cousins—is that it is finally a small robust story in a large romantic package. The pictures are often beautiful, but they lack the blood and thunder one's own imagination could supply if the story was simply read aloud from a thinly illustrated collection like the one I had as a child. The old fairy tales are full of violence and horror; that is part of their therapeutic charm. But the work of modern illustrators has a tendency to take out the sting and immediacy—to render them somehow remote—by imposing on them the very weight and beauty of the artwork. We might do better if we let them work their own magic instead of using them so often as vehicles to exercise our virtuosity.

Kirkus Reviews

SOURCE: A review of *Petrosinella: A Neapolitan Rapunzel,* in *Kirkus Reviews,* Vol. LXIII, No. 10, May 15, 1995, p. 716.

[*The following review is of the 1995 edition, in which Stanley adapted the text.*]

Stanley combines her 1981 illustrations for this tale with a new, less-contrived, more modern-sounding retelling.

Parsley (Petrosinella) is forcibly abducted by an ogress, and years later takes an active role in making her escape, using three magic acorns to throw off pursuit. This is a softer, less violent version than some Rapunzels—the prince isn't blinded, for one thing, nor are the lovers separated—and the paintings reflect that: Against neat, richly colored backgrounds, gracefully posed figures seem to float slightly over stone pavements; Parsley's massive, honey-colored locks flow airily behind her; and the ogress's gruesome death is not only partially concealed around a bend in the road, but visually counterweighted by a bunny creeping cautiously from under a tree. An elegant alternative to the Brothers Grimm.

📖 *SLEEPING UGLY* (written by Jane Yolen, 1981)

Nancy Palmer

SOURCE: A review of *Sleeping Ugly,* in *School Library Journal,* Vol. 28, No. 4, December, 1981, p. 75.

In Jane Yolen's clever turn on a traditional tale, Miserella (beautiful but mean—the princess you love to hate) loses out to Plain Jane (kind to animals and old ladies) in the post-hundred-year-sleep-kiss contest and becomes *Sleeping Ugly*—ugly on the inside that is. The old fairy who engineers this bit of justice gets an apartment (complete with TV antenna) for her pains, and Miserella, still unkissed, still sleeping, stands in Jane and Prince Jojo's cottage as a part-time coat rack. Diane Stanley's expressive illustrations, jumping from once upon a time to right now, add an intriguing perspective to the tale's witty text and humorous play with fairytale conventions.

Zena Sutherland

SOURCE: A review of *Sleeping Ugly,* in *Bulletin of the Center for Children's Books,* Vol. 35, No. 5, January, 1982, pp. 99-100.

[Jane] Yolen pokes fun at the patterned sleeping-princess story in a tale that's written with brisk simplicity and humor; although the parody seems at times forced, it is amusing, it has plenty of action, and it's easy to read. Beautiful but nasty, Princess Miserella is lost in the wood, repeatedly insults a fairy who has taken her to the cottage of homely but kind Jane, and loses her chance of getting home when the fairy awards Jane three wishes. After the second wish, all three fall into the traditional century of sleep; the young man who comes across them is smitten at the sight of the beautiful princess, but decides he should practice his wake-up kisses on the fairy and Jane. Jane, waking, is in turn smitten and sighs that she wishes he loved her. This is, of course, wish number three. Love and marriage lead to almost all living happily ever after: they keep the princess asleep, using her as a conversation piece to entertain their friends—or sometimes prop her up in the hallway to hold extra coats. Two-color illustrations alternate with black and white drawings, their static quality relieved by humorous details.

Denise M. Wilms

SOURCE: A review of *Sleeping Ugly,* in *Booklist,* Vol. 78, No. 10, January 15, 1982, p. 656.

This comic fairy tale bears scant resemblance to its implied namesake. What it does have is a princess named Miserella who is beautiful to look at but nasty on the inside, and a peasant Plain Jane who's homely to look at but has the virtue of a saint. The crux comes when Miserella's snippy talk brings an enchanted sleep on herself, Jane, and an attending fairy godmother. Miserella gets her comeuppance when the prince charming who stumbles on them years later kisses the godmother and Jane first and never makes it to Miserella. The moral: "Let sleeping princesses lie / or lying princesses sleep, / whichever seems wisest." With black-and-white and two-color drawings that have some very funny moments.

THE MONTH BROTHERS: A SLAVIC TALE
(retold by Samuel Marshak, 1983)

Kirkus Reviews

SOURCE: A review of *The Month Brothers: A Slavic Tale,* in *Kirkus Reviews,* Vol. LI, No. 2, January 15, 1983, p. 61.

The tale is a marvelous one, seldom found in such a direct and pure version: a cruelly-used stepdaughter, sent into the forest in January to pick snowdrops for her stepsister's birthday, finds twelve men—three of them old, three middle-aged, three young, three mere boys—gathered around a fire. At her explanation of what she's looking for and why, the youngest of the twelve says to an elder: "Brother January, let me take your place for just an hour." But to keep the months in order, "shaggy February" makes a quick appearance before young March takes over, and the snowdrifts give way to snowdrops. On the little girl's arrival home, however, her stepmother scolds her for not asking for something valuable out-of-season— like strawberries and pears. The haughty stepsister sets out, and is struck down and frozen to death for her effrontery; the stepmother, going to search for her, is frozen to death too. ("And that's how both of them remained in the forest to wait for the summer.") At the close the stepdaughter, grown and a mother, is in a luxuriant, all-season garden where, say her neighbors, she has "all the months of the year as her guests." In [Thomas P.] Whitney's accomplished translation, the tale is also so well told that even Diane Stanley's posey, awkward pictures don't harm it—and the snow does have a frigid, tingling, all-enveloping feel.

Karla Kuskin

SOURCE: A review of *The Month-Brothers: A Slavic Tale,* in *The New York Times Book Review,* March 20, 1983, p. 30.

Take an oppressed orphan, her wicked stepmother and stepsister, the impossible quest the two send her off on and a wintry, magical forest, and you have the basic ingredients of a classic folk tale.

This new version of *The Month-Brothers* is set in Czechoslovakia. The wicked stepmother dispatches her unloved stepdaughter into the freezing January woods to pick snowdrops. Everybody knows there are no snowdrops in January woods. But there are 12 unusual men, and the child makes their acquaintance. "They were all beautifully dressed—some in silver, some in gold, some in green

velvet." And because she is a deserving girl, the 12 undertake to help her.

January cedes some of his time to February, who cedes some of his time to March. Though March is only a boy, it is he who clears the snow from the forest floor, producing a carpet of snowdrops. The tale does not stop there. A generous helping of revenge is added to sweeten the ending. When the greedy stepsister makes her own, very aggressive visit to the Months, she is not only turned away but, with her awful parent, meets an icy doom.

Diane Stanley's meticulous watercolors glow from the wide-bordered pages of this big picture book. Her brush dwells appreciatively on details of multi-patterned costumes, textures and landscapes.

But despite the careful rendering of swirling wind and snow, there is little real feeling of motion or energy beneath the handsome surfaces. And there is little animation in the characters posed in set tableaus. Both text and illustration could have used more spontaneous grace to bring this book fully to life.

Paul Heins

SOURCE: A review of *The Month-Brothers: A Slavic Tale,* in *The Horn Book Magazine,* Vol. LX, No. 2, April, 1983, p. 161.

A Czechoslovakian folk tale retold by the Russian writer [Samuel Marshak] for children has been profusely illustrated with full-page pictures and oval vignettes. Sent by her stepmother into the forest during a January blizzard to pick snowdrops for her disagreeable stepsister's birthday, a hard-worked little girl discovered twelve magnificently dressed men around a bonfire. They were the rulers of the months, and January and February gave March the gift of an hour so that the girl could find the flowers. Needless to say, when the surly stepsister later tried to browbeat the months into giving her vegetables and fruits, she failed miserably. Meticulously drawn with intricately textured surfaces, the richly colored pictures suggest the art of Nancy Ekholm Burkert. Most effective is the contrast between the realistic scenes of the lonely girl in the forest and those of the group of the sumptuously clad month-brothers. Unfortunately, the final idyllic scene of the grown-up heroine with her own children is sentimental and visually anticlimactic.

Ilene Cooper

SOURCE: A review of *The Month-Brothers: A Slavic Tale,* in *Booklist,* Vol. 79, No. 16, April 15, 1983, p. 1096.

This story translated from the Russian [by Thomas P. Whitney] and set in Bohemia has all the traditional elements of folklore. A lovely young girl serves her wicked stepmother and layabout stepsister. When she is sent out in the middle of January to pick some snowdrops for her sister's birthday, she feels she is going into the woods to die. Instead, she meets the 12 month brothers, who decide to befriend her; they make March come for an hour so that she can find the flowers. Upon her return, the step-mother and -sister learn what has transpired and decide there will be profit in summer-on-command so they can pick fruits and vegetables to sell. The stepsister's arro-gant attitude provokes the brothers' wrath, and she freez-es in the woods as does her mother, who ventures out to find her. Stanley's artwork makes use of vivid coloring and subtle contrasts of light and dark. But as the artist showed in *Petrosinella,* her strong suit is design and pat-terning. Both the month brothers' elaborate costumes and the simple texturing of the snow amply illustrate this. Therefore, it is disappointing that her characters' faces are so bland and curiously devoid of emotion. The collo-quial retelling is a bit informal for the handsome pictures, but in the main, folktale lovers will find this a striking rendition.

Sonia W. Thomas

SOURCE: "Innovatively Illustrated," in *The Christian Science Monitor,* May 4, 1984, p. B5.

[The Month-Brothers] is a wicked-stepmother tale—this one is set in Bohemia. Diane Stanley's delightfully au-thentic full-page illustrations accompany the story.

It is said that long ago a girl was sent out into a midwin-ter snowstorm to gather Snowdrops (flowers) for her pam-pered stepsister's birthday. The quest seems hopeless, but the girl obeys. She comes upon a group of 12 men and boys in a clearing in the woods who represent the months of the year. When they hear the girl's sad story they decide to help her. They set aside the usual sequence of the months and instantly March appears and the ground is covered with Snowdrops. The girl gathers the flowers and takes them home.

When the greedy stepmother hears the remarkable story, she sends her own daughter out into the snow to ask the Month Brothers for delicious sweet tasting fruits from the summer months. Time passes and the stepmother goes out to look for her daughter and they both perish in the cold.

Naturally, the stepdaughter lives a long happy life at the edge of the forest surrounded by a wonderful garden which bears fruit earlier than any other place. And it is said, "That woman has all the months of the year as her guests."

Yes, that's the way folk tales end.

📖 *THE CONVERSATION CLUB* (1983)

Ilene Cooper

SOURCE: A review of *The Conversation Club,* in *Booklist,* Vol. 80, No. 2, September 15, 1983, p. 173.

A cozy little story with pictures to match. Peter Field-mouse, new in town, is welcomed by another mouse who invites him to join the Conversation Club. At the first meeting Peter sees that the club lives up to its name. There's plenty of conversation, all right, it's just that everyone converses at once. So Peter decides to form his own group, the Listening Club. When the mice troop to Peter's house, they don't quite know what to expect, but they soon find the sound of just one voice talking can be wonderful. Stanley has illustrated other books including *Petrosinella,* but this is her first outing as an author. The story is a bit wordy but gets its mild message across. The text is bolstered by delicate drawings, some in jewel-toned colors and others in penciled sketches. As in other books, her patterning and design work are visual delights.

Nancy C. Hammond

SOURCE: A review of *The Conversation Club,* in *The Horn Book Magazine,* Vol. LIX, No. 6, December, 1983, pp. 705-06.

When Peter Fieldmouse moves into his new home, he is welcomed with gifts and an invitation to join the neigh-borhood Conversation Club. Overwhelmed by the reputed expertise of the members and pressed for his own special-ty, Peter tentatively suggests, "'Couldn't I just listen?'" and is immediately deemed a listening expert. At his first meeting the mouse discovers that his specialty is unique; the club members talk simultaneously. He is assaulted by a cacophonous babble: "'In the opening game you add some parsley stir the crocuses which resemble the sound of shrieking in our solar system.'" Besieged, Peter devel-ops a headache and an alternative—a listening club. With an instant membership it eventually provides a forum where each member's expertise is appreciated—and heard. Despite a prosaic beginning, the humorous story unfolds lightly and smoothly. The small scenes of mice in their cozy, wallpapered homes are framed in tiny, decorative prints and glow with the luminous hues of Easter eggs.

Pamela Warren Stebbins

SOURCE: A review of *The Conversation Club,* in *School Library Journal,* Vol. 30, No. 4, December, 1983, pp. 60-1.

Quiet, thoughtful Peter, new mouse in the neighborhood, is invited to join a conversation club, whose members are Charlie, a gardening expert; Sam, the expert on cooking; Pearl, who tells ghost stories; Nancy, the expert on sports and Fay, who talks on space. Peter is amazed to find everyone talks at the same time and leaves with a head-ache. Peter, then, starts a new club, "a listening club." There a quiet thoughtful mood is established through de-scriptions of the sounds of a snowstorm. Once settled, the members are quiet, but each one is reminded of some-thing to say. Peter changes the rules of his club to enable each member to talk, but one at a time. The evolution of the club, while predictable, seems natural. The book's quiet tone is set by descriptions of nature sounds: the wind, leaves falling, snowstorms, etc., and by the blues and purples of the color illustrations. The illustrations, in alternating spreads of color and black and white, are appealing and well drawn. The small format of the book welcomes readers into Peter's miniature world.

📖 *ALL WET! ALL WET!* (written by James Skofield, 1984)

Kirkus Reviews

SOURCE: A review of *All Wet! All Wet!*, in *Kirkus Reviews,* Vol. LII, Nos. 1-5, March 1, 1984, p. J9-J10.

Not a felicitous title. Not, for sure, a novel theme. But more is afoot here than at first appears when we see a little boy, with umbrella, slicker, and boots, gently padding, one rainy dawn, toward the woods. He will be at most a passive observer (unmentioned in the text, perhaps a surrogate for the child-audience)—as, in an entrancing cutaway, the fox and rabbits take to their burrows; as, in one of [James] Skofield's happiest lines, "the silent fish hear the sound of rain upon their roof." There is a spot of action, part of nature's give and take: undeterred by the rain, Skunk "comes upon Quail's unprotected nest . . . snatches up an egg and shuffles on." We see the "soft, star-nosed mole" burrow underground too, while Quail searches vainly for her egg and Skunk, sated, falls asleep. "The storm trails off . . . light breaks through." Other plants and animals are noted, responding. The generalized pictures, all smooth slopes and rounded tree trunks, ignore some of this: Stanley is more a conjurer of mood than a captor of the actual. But her star-nosed mole, "blink[ing] up at the sky," is as surely imagined as Skofield's star, "blink[ing] back at her." The occasional crystalline image, the happenings that naturally happen, make this more than another rainy-day reprise, if not a surpassing entity.

Zena Sutherland

SOURCE: A review of *All Wet! All Wet!,* in *Bulletin of the Center for Children's Books,* Vol. 37, No. 10, June, 1984, p. 192.

A small child spends a rainy day in the woods observing the animals: a skunk stealing eggs from a quail, a river hawk diving for fish, deer drinking at the river's edge. The text is slight but gently poetic ("Below and blind, the soft, star-nosed mole swims through dark and damp, deep-rooted, fragrant earth") with nice balance and structure. (When the rain ends and night comes we see the mole emerge and blink at a star.) Stanley's detailed, quiet, and softly colored illustrations fulfill the mood. The child does not appear in the text, only in the pictures, watching, and serving as a visual metaphor that fuses pictures, text, and reader.

Ilene Cooper

SOURCE: A review of *All Wet! All Wet!*, in *Booklist,* Vol. 80, No. 20, June 15, 1984, p. 1486.

In this quiet story, a small boy spends a rainy day walking through the forest. As the child experiences the sights and sounds of the rain-soaked woods, so do the animals and birds who make their homes there. The story has a dualistic quality—the text is written from the animals' point of view with no mention of the boy. The blond child, decked out in yellow slicker and boots, is seen only in the soft-hued pictures. [James] Skofield paints some lovely word pictures, with phrases such as "spiders, sitting like black stars, motionless, at the hub of diamond webs" integral to the story's dreamy quality. Stanley's artwork carries out the mood in subdued tones of blue, yellow, and green. Her forest dwellers are effectively drawn, and children will especially enjoy the pictures that show rabbits and moles in their burrows. An atmospheric wedding of words and art.

Kate M. Flanagan

SOURCE: A review of *All Wet! All Wet!,* in *The Horn Book Magazine,* Vol. LX, No. 4, August, 1984, pp. 460-61.

Meticulously detailed, softly colored illustrations show the wonders to be found on a rainy day. A small boy sets off with his umbrella on a wet morning, stopping here and there to observe the insects, animals, and plants he encounters. The text describes in hushed tones the actions of the animals as they seek shelter from the storm. A mother fox heads for her den, rabbits snuggle in their burrow, and "in the wood, a quail calls, 'All wet! All wet!'" The poetic text is balanced by carefully rendered illustrations accurately depicting the various occupants of the woods. Several cross-sectional drawings even show animals as they huddle in their homes beneath the ground. And one can forgive the illustrator's artistic license in showing the small boy uncomfortably close to a skunk. The book presents an idyllic look at nature, from rainy dawn to clear, star-filled night; a reverent appreciation of the treasures to be discovered all around us.

Kathleen Evans Daly

SOURCE: A review of *All Wet! All Wet!,* in *School Library Journal,* Vol. 31, No. 2, October, 1984, p. 151.

The simple rhythm of a rainy day is recounted in this gentle, evocative book. How the woodland creatures are affected by the rainy day is the focus of the story, told in a poetic style spare of extraneous words and with a minimum of anthropomorphism. Fox, rabbits, fish and others are present, with Quail acting as a sort of one-creature Greek chorus. It's only in the illustrations, and not in the text, that a small boy who is observing the wildlife appears. Stanley's gray, green, yellow and blue drawings are well-wed with the text, and one depends upon the other: the text tells of the creatures' doings, but the wet woodland scenes are filled with wildlife in action and show the child as observer. *All Wet! All Wet!* should have a long-lasting place in picture book collections.

📖 *BIRDSONG LULLABY* (1985)

Dana Whitney Pinizzotto

SOURCE: A review of *Birdsong Lullaby,* in *School Library Journal,* Vol. 32, No. 2, October, 1985, p. 163.

Romantics of every age will delight in this dialogue between an imaginative daughter and her mother. "If I were a bird . . . ," begins the daughter. The conversation continues from fancy to fancy: "I could play in our birdbath"; "I could see what kind of pajamas kings wear"; "I could catch all the lost balloons and give them back to children." The luminous quality of Stanley's drawings perfectly illustrate the text. There is magic in these thought pictures, from the King's bunny slippers and a mist-shrouded mountain lake to the girl-bird with p.j.'s and feathered wings. The text is more than just a vehicle for these visual treats: the mother's enviable, nurturing responses demonstrate encouragement, acceptance and true delight in sharing the little girl's visions. When bedtime arrives, Momma suggests that maybe there will be a dream about it, and that it will seem very real. The concluding illustration reveals an open, double-hung window filled with light from a full moon and many stars, a single feather left on the sill and a tiny bird-person flying into the distance. Uplifting!

Ilene Cooper

SOURCE: A review of *Birdsong Lullaby,* in *Booklist,* Vol. 82, No. 3, October 1, 1985, p. 270.

A young girl wonders to her mother what it would be like to be a bird, setting the stage for a lyrical bedtime fantasy. Sprouting wings, the pajama-clad child peeks in windows, eats cake in her mother's birdbath, catches stray balloons, and sails through the air touching clouds. The poetic, first-person narrative is matched by Stanley's dreamy, softly colored illustrations. The careful attention to detailing, the airborne perspectives, and the delicate birds that flit in and out of the pictures add to the story's magical quality. A splendid sleepy-time story.

Zena Sutherland

SOURCE: A review of *Birdsong Lullaby,* in *Bulletin of the Center for Children's Books,* Vol. 39, No. 7, March, 1986, p. 138.

In a mother-daughter bedtime exchange, a little girl describes her fantasy of flying, with each suggested scene developed graphically in fine-line pastel illustrations of a winged child in pajamas hovering over landscapes or peeking into windows. At one point the little girl suggests, "I could catch all the lost balloons and give them back to children," to which Mama responds, "What a pretty idea!" That's really all the book is, a pretty idea, but it is one that many children indulge in, and for that reason they will enjoy both the views and the last page, with a feather suggesting the narrator's flight out the open window into her dream.

📖 *A COUNTRY TALE* (1985)

Denise M. Wilms

SOURCE: A review of *A Country Tale,* in *Booklist,* Vol. 82, No. 4, October 15, 1985, p. 341.

Stanley offers a primly didactic story of two dear cat friends, Cleo and Lucy, whose relationship undergoes a severe strain when Cleo becomes enamoured of the aristocratic Mrs. Snickers' life-style. Cleo meets the wealthy woman when the regally dressed feline is out looking for someone to help with her trunks. Mrs. Snickers' apparent interest in her flatters Cleo, who seems unbothered that her poorly dressed friend Lucy is ignored. Cleo responds by adopting a few airs and trying to cultivate a friendship with Mrs. Snickers. When the lady returns to the city, Cleo pays a visit, but finds herself totally out of place. To make matters worse, she is robbed and beset with bad luck. Home again, she's sadder but wiser about the truth of true friendship. Stanley's accompanying pictures are sumptuous, full-color drawings replete with nuance and detail. Her cat figures, with their disconcertingly intense faces and Victorian garb, move through tidy English-looking landscapes that seem unblemished by any hint of strife. Her interiors are carefully detailed too, whether they be humble or otherwise. In fact, the illustrations are the major reason for the book's impact. The story itself has a somewhat abstract conclusion but the richness of the pictures makes it easy to overlook any last minute weaknesses.

Zena Sutherland

SOURCE: A review of *A Country Tale,* in *Bulletin of the Center for Children's Books,* Vol. 39, No. 6, February, 1986, p. 118.

An elegant book that spoofs elegance, this gets away with an old-fashioned air because the subject is durably relevant. Two close country friends, Cleo and Lucy, are affected by the arrival of wealthy, snobbish Mrs. Snickers from the city. The grand dame succeeds in making Cleo feel discontented with her lot and in completely rejecting Lucy, who has enough good sense to ride out Cleo's temporary attack of fashion and eventually help her back to her old self. The characters are meticulously drawn cats, each whisker and patch of fur fine-lined. The expressions are both feline and typically human, as in Cleo's careful imitation of Mrs. Snickers' pout. Colors are sometimes sharply patterned and then again, subtly blended. Children will recognize a playground situation in this pastoral, Victorian setting.

Janet Hickman

SOURCE: A review of *A Country Tale*, in *Language Arts*, Vol. 63, No. 2, February, 1986, pp. 193-94.

Cleo and Lucy, nineteenth century cats in an appropriately romantic setting, are dear friends. Lucy is domestic and true-hearted, but Cleo's head is turned by a fancy summer visitor from the city, Mrs. Snickers. Cleo changes her clothes and her habits to suit the newcomer and neglects her old friend. When the season ends, Cleo pays Mrs. Snickers a visit in the city and finds herself both uncomfortable and unwanted. A series of misfortunes on the way home leaves Cleo without her new finery and not even certain who she is, until Lucy sets her straight.

This variant of the familiar be-yourself theme is made special by the quality of its illustrations. Full color pictures show the sweep of English country lawns, charming cottages, billowing skirts, and carefully appointed interiors, plus the delicate faces of cats registering human emotions without distorting their animal features. Painstaking work with pen and brush created the rich textures and subtle shadings that make each illustration lifelike. "Lovely" and "charming" are both words that apply, but the pictures are also slyly funny. The sumptuously-dressed city cats are parodies of an unbending upper class, and the paintings on their walls are also parodies, including a "nude" with fur.

From Leonardo da Vinci, *written and illustrated by Diane Stanley.*

📖 *THE GOOD-LUCK PENCIL* (1986)

Ilene Cooper

SOURCE: A review of *The Good-Luck Pencil*, in *Booklist*, Vol. 82, No. 17, May 1, 1986, p. 1317.

On the day Mary Ann forgets to do her math homework, she finds a pencil on the ground that swiftly completes her assignment. Math is suddenly not only easy for Mary Ann, but all day long terrific words and pictures seem to flow from her good-luck pencil. That night, Mary Ann has to write a composition about her family. Thinking they are hopelessly dull, she starts off on a different tack and before long is describing her mother as a world-famous ballerina, her father as an astronaut, and her home as a big mansion. When she puts her good-luck pencil down, she is amazed to find that she is actually living in the huge house she described. Life there is not quite what it seems, however, and after a few dreadful experiences (such as being forced by her swimming coach to do 100 laps in her gigantic pool), Mary Ann realizes that reality can be better than fantasy. She promptly dashes off a new, truer composition that lands her back home, much to her relief. The magic pencil goes into the wastepaper basket, where it can't do any more harm. Stanley's story feeds right into a child's make-believe world. . . .

Joan Hamilton Bowman

SOURCE: A review of *The Good-Luck Pencil*, in *School Library Journal*, Vol. 32, No. 10, August, 1986, p. 88.

An imaginative and entertaining story about Mary Ann, a school-age cherub, who discovers an ordinary pencil that exhibits extraordinary powers. Mary Ann agonizes over an assignment to write a composition about her seemingly dull, commonplace family. Good-luck pencil to the rescue, as out of its point flows a tale of the family about which Mary Ann has often fantasized. Subsequently, Mary Ann is transported to this world that her pencil has conceived. Here, she discovers that the incredible life which she envisioned is not what she expected. Scribbling out this composition, Mary Ann replaces it with one about the real world in which she dwells, for this world of love, security and serenity is quite extraordinary after all. . . . The combination of reality and fantasy will satisfy children, as will the resolution of the conflict between the two.

📖 *PETER THE GREAT* (1986)

Kirkus Reviews

SOURCE: A review of *Peter the Great*, in *Kirkus*

Reviews, Vol. LIV, No. 17, September 1, 1986, p. 1379.

Despite its brevity, a carefully balanced biography of the tsar (1672-1725) who opened communication between Russia and the rest of Europe.

Stanley emphasizes the events in Peter's life most likely to interest children—e.g., the war games he played at 13, with an army of boys and real guns, and his trip "in disguise" to learn ship carpentry in Holland (even without his retinue of 250, his 6'7" height would have betrayed him). But she also makes his contradictory character and importance clear: an innovator who not only collected technology all over Europe but also made hands-on acquaintance with it; a reformer who built schools, roads, and vineyards, funded by merciless taxation; a visionary who planned one of the world's most beautiful cities in order to have a base for his new navy, yet a tyrant who did it at deplorable human cost. Still, he made important steps toward treating women as social equals, "changed Russia forever," and was mourned at his death.

Stanley's jewel-like pictures give vivid impressions of Russian landscapes and interiors, dwelling on rich ornament and avoiding visual reference to poverty or the other miseries with which the period was fraught. Like Fritz's brief biographies of famous Americans, this is an excellent introduction to an important figure.

Betsy Hearne

SOURCE: A review of *Peter the Great,* in *Bulletin of the Center for Children's Books,* Vol. 40, No. 2, October, 1986, pp. 37-8.

Peter the Great, although a riveting figure, is an unusual choice of subjects for a picture-book biography. However, Stanley has compressed a good deal of complex information into a compact text while managing to convey some sense of Peter's wildly unique personality and contributions to Russian history. Her illustrations, rhythmical in coloration and patterning, offer a visual depth that increases the impact of the book considerably. Except for the inevitable odd generalization or two (" . . . the Russians never could tell one European from another"), this offers an intriguing perspective on a rare meeting of an implacable force for progress with an immoveable object of traditional society.

Ilene Cooper

SOURCE: A review of *Peter the Great,* in *Booklist,* Vol. 83, No. 3, October 1, 1986, p. 275.

Jean Fritz led the way with accessible biographies for children. Now, Stanley follows firmly in the tradition with her handsome full-color paintings an added bonus. She captures readers' attention right from the start as she describes how Peter, at age 13, would startle the country-

side by playing war games. Much of the focus is on Peter as a young boy when the luxury that accompanied his station is juxtaposed with a compelling belief that honors in life should be earned. In simple yet graceful language, Peter's effort to modernize Russia and bring it closer to Europe is carefully described as is the controversy surrounding many of his social reforms. On every page are full-color pictures reminiscent of a primitive style, rendered in gouache. The captivating artwork, which features both Oriental and European elements, demands a second and third look. Stanley's thorough research is evident in her source list at the book's beginning. The genre will profit if this is just the first of her forays into biography.

Janice M. Del Negro

SOURCE: A review of *Peter the Great,* in *School Library Journal,* Vol. 33, No. 3, November, 1986, p. 83.

This profusely illustrated biography has a moderate amount of good-sized text and at least one illustration on every two-page spread. Stanley's fine illustrations of Tsar Peter and his Russia are vivid and uncluttered, yet still give a sense of the ornate formality of the royal surroundings and attire. That Stanley concentrates on the extraordinary achievements of Peter the Great is not surprising, but the omission of some basic biographical data is a problem. Peter's ascent to the throne is presented as without difficulty, when it was actually a struggle for power among Peter, his half-brother Ivan, and his half-sister Sophia. The bitter upheavals caused by Peter's attempt to reform the church and limit its influence is reduced to the Tsar taxing long beards at court; his desire to establish Russia as a seapower is based on a pleasant sailing experience, instead of the military defeat at Azov that made Peter acknowledge his nation's lack of adequate sea vessels and ports. Peter's accomplishments are highlighted, while the measures he took to achieve such sweeping reforms are given scant attention. Incidents—Peter's childhood, his love of sailing, traveling across Europe in disguise—are described in an effort to make this complex historical figure accessible to the primary/middle grade age group, and in this Stanley is successful. A more balanced portrayal—with Peter the Great as less a saint of progress and more the ambitious ruler—is yet to come.

Jean Fritz

SOURCE: "The Wedding Gift Had Tusks," in *The New York Times Book Review,* November 9, 1986, p. 58.

Diane Stanley's biography **Peter the Great** stays close to the historical record and turns out to be the strongest story of all. It would be hard to invent a hero like Peter the Great (1672-1725), and Ms. Stanley, in direct, informal prose, has the good sense not to embellish his extraordinary life and to let it speak for itself.

Czar from the time he was 10 years old, Peter always got

what he wanted. If as a boy he wanted (and got) trained monkeys, dancing bears and a staff of dwarfs, as a man he wanted (and got) a new Russia with a beautiful new city, a navy and new customs to match those of the rest of Europe. No more old-fashioned beards on men; no more hiding away of women. But lots more taxes. Someone had to pay for the Czar's extravagant ideas. Many of course suffered; many died in Peter's war with Sweden and in the teams of forced labor used to build St. Petersburg. But if in this account much of the fury is missing from Peter's whirlwind life, it is because the author has chosen to concentrate instead on the 6-foot-7-inch reformer's boundless imagination and energy.

Diane Stanley's exquisite illustrations hang like framed pictures on her pages. Some are small and exact, without an extraneous detail; others are full-page, minutely decorated, elaborate, jewel-like. They establish Peter the Great's Russian background, an element indispensable not only to Peter but to anyone trying to picture his story.

Mary A. Bush

SOURCE: A review of *Peter the Great,* in *The Horn Book Magazine,* Vol. LXII, No. 1, January-February, 1987, pp. 76-7.

Curious, energetic, headstrong—these characteristics are clear throughout Diane Stanley's personable sketch of the life of Tsar Peter Alexeevich from his boyhood games of war, in which real weapons were used, through adult years filled with travel, industrial expansion, and far-reaching changes of social custom. The organizing theme in the simple, abbreviated account is Peter's role in "bringing Russia into the modern world," and there is an emphasis on his fascination with things European which drove him to abolish much of the isolationism which had kept Russia from moving forward. Although the tone is generally adulatory, the author admits to some of Peter's excesses—the heavy burdens of taxation, the loss of lives in his construction projects, the abruptness of social change. While there is minimal fictionalizing, aside from a small amount of reconstructed conversation, the selectivity exercised in this introductory biography is both faithful to the personal qualities of Peter and misleading about one major aspect of his life. There is unaccountably no mention that Peter ever married or had children, though he is clearly accompanied by a crowned consort in one picture, and two grieving women are shown at the bedside in the death scene. To be sure, this material is complicated and probably difficult to contain in the compact structure and tight focus of the text. The book is exceptionally well served by Stanley's warmly colored and richly detailed illustrations, which are at once pretty and humorous. The palette and costume are similar to those executed by the illustrator in Samuel Marshak's retelling of *The Month Brothers,* but in this book they are set in smaller, crisper scenes which are both elegant and informative. A very welcome extension of her work in picture books, Stanley's illustrated, biographical story is conceptually strong and very well executed.

CAPTAIN WHIZ-BANG (1987)

Kirkus Reviews

SOURCE: A review of *Captain Whiz-Bang,* in *Kirkus Reviews,* Vol. LV, No. 17, September 1, 1987, pp. 1325-26.

A cat is named for Captain Whiz-Bang, a comic-strip hero, and lives up to the honor in this gentle story about growing up and going through different stages of life.

The changing fashions in clothing, furnishings and cars is one of the most charming aspects of this book, at least for the adult. Running from the late 1920's to the 1940's: in the opening pages the mother has marcelled waves, and toward the end the no-longer-little girl marries a man in navy uniform. Captain Whiz-Bang has brought amusement as a kitten, glory as the young winner in the Elm Street Cat Olympics, and companionship when the girl has reached the status of a dignified young lady. The book closes with his meeting the girl's daughter, who is delighted with a loving, purring, no-longer-active lap cat. The illustrations are done in the softened colors of happily remembered scenes—bright Christmas trees and pastel skies in happy summers. The cover is composed of panels from "Captain Whiz-Bang's" Sunday supplement showing a thrilling episode in which he saves his girlfriend from Dr. Blood.

For children who are curious about what their grandparent's childhood lives were like, this is a delight for sharing.

Ilene Cooper

SOURCE: A review of *Captain Whiz-Bang,* in *Booklist,* Vol. 84, No. 5, November 1, 1987, p. 485.

In this quiet story, Stanley describes the life of Captain Whiz-Bang, a black-and-white cat who arrives at Annie's house on Christmas morning. Annie knows this is no ordinary cat and names him after a hero in the funny papers; Whiz-Bang lives up to his name, winning races, climbing trees, and spending some quiet, dreamy times with his young mistress. As Annie grows up, Whiz-Bang just grows older, wheezing when he runs and getting fat. Once Annie is off and married, Whiz-Bang finds his place on the windowsill and stays there until the exciting Christmas day when Annie comes back with her own family. Annie's tenderhearted daughter is immediately taken with Whiz-Bang—once a running and jumping cat, he's now a purring and gentle one, and hers to love. Although adults may best appreciate the story's poignancy, children will certainly respond to its warmth and gentleness. The story begins in the 1930s, and Stanley carries out the Captain Whiz-Bang theme with cover art that depicts the comic strip. The rest of the white-bordered pictures have the soft focus of long-ago snapshots. This is obviously a very personal story, but one whose tender mood will have high appeal.

Eleanor K. MacDonald

SOURCE: A review of *Captain Whiz-Bang,* in *School Library Journal,* Vol. 34, No. 4, December, 1987, p. 77.

Annie could tell right away that her Christmas kitten would be big, strong, and fast so she named him after Captain Whiz-Bang, a favorite comic book character. They become constant companions and Whiz-Bang, true to her prediction, can climb trees, chase dogs, and win the Elm Street Cat Olympics hands down. The years pass, and Annie grows up, gets married, and goes away, while Whiz-Bang becomes an older, fatter, sleepier cat. Then one Christmas Annie returns with her own little girl, who holds him, rocks him, and gently sings. "It was the second best Christmas Captain Whiz-Bang had ever had." While the visual setting of the story is late '30s into the '40s, and is faintly tinged with nostalgia, this story combines a timeless tale of old age and lasting friendship with an original and unsentimental approach. The softly colored illustrations and the text are neatly separated and framed on the page, echoing the comic book motif. While the illustrations are fairly realistic, the story moves forward in direct steps, not unlike a comic book, with lots of visual reinforcement to the action. This fresh and appealing book manages to convey without excess sentiment the grace that love can bring to old age.

The Reading Teacher

SOURCE: A review of *Captain Whizbang,* in *The Reading Teacher,* Vol. 41, No. 7, March, 1988, p. 723.

Stanley, in **Captain Whizbang** (all ages), has chosen to portray a cat's lifespan. Her sensitive drawings, complete with details of costume and settings of an earlier American era, lend nostalgia and loss without being maudlin. The warm colors are balanced by the softened edges of the figures just as the story of a beloved pet is tinged with sadness at our understanding of its mortality. Said one friend upon reading this book, "I cried and I don't even like cats!"

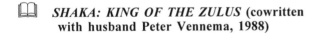 *SHAKA: KING OF THE ZULUS* (cowritten with husband Peter Vennema, 1988)

Kirkus Reviews

SOURCE: A review of *Shaka: King of the Zulus,* in *Kirkus Reviews,* Vol. LVI, No. 18, September 15, 1988, p. 1408.

Like Stanley's *Peter the Great,* a beautifully illustrated picture-book biography with a careful text of some substance.

Shaka (or Chaka, 1787-1828) is in some ways an inspirational figure: a minor chief's son who was ostracized after his father returned him and his mother to her village, he became a warrior and gifted strategist, a leader who, as

king, commanded 40,000 troops. In 1824, he made friends with the English; and, like the Native Americans, he made the mistake of signing away a large part of his country to them. The authors point out that Shaka's tactics were unacceptable by today's standards—"he ruled through force and fear"—and that he had an unusually strong bond with his mother; he never married, and at her death imposed his grief on his people to such an extent that it provoked his own assassination. The authors conclude by lauding him for military genius, boldness, and imagination.

An attractive introduction to an important figure in the history of South Africa's largest ethnic group.

Betsy Hearne

SOURCE: A review of *Shaka: King of the Zulus,* in *Bulletin of the Center for Children's Books,* Vol. 42, No. 3, November, 1988, p. 85.

Like her middle-grade picture book biography **Peter the Great,** this recounts the life of a major historical figure whose complexities have been subject to much historical investigation. Outcast as a boy, Shaka is driven to prove himself as a warrior, eventually becoming chief of a clan that he builds from obscurity to dominance in a vast empire. Each double spread, with formally coordinated text and full-page pictures, focuses on an important scene in his rise to power. At least twice, his violence and cruelty are explained in context of the times, and his mental instability is suggested, along with his military genius. The format is decorative, with traditional design motifs and illustrations dominated by browns and tans. Although the human figures seem stiff and sometimes glamorized, the rounded shapes and smooth lines render panoramic the movement of the subject, his warriors, and their landscape.

Susan Faust

SOURCE: "Information That Entertains," in *The Christian Science Monitor,* November 4, 1988, pp. B1, B6.

A fine example of illustrated biography is the newly published **Shaka, King of the Zulus,** by Diane Stanley and Peter Vennema, illustrated by Diane Stanley. As in an earlier book about Peter the Great, author-illustrator Stanley delivers spectacular art along with a tight and textured tale. Here, veld-tone paintings, bordered in typical Zula beadwork, help to present the dramatic life of a unique 19th-century African warrior-king. Shaka rose to unimaginable power that eventually corrupted, and in this rendition his story is told with restraint and respect.

Peter F. Neumeyer

SOURCE: "His Soldiers Dared Not Flinch," in *The New York Times Book Review,* November 13, 1988, p. 56.

The story of Shaka is an epic: it is the chronicle of the

founding of a nation. In this judicious, coolly written, stunningly illustrated book the emphasis is on just those dramatic highlights in the life that would, for me, as a boy, have remained unforgettable—scenes that would fill my dreams for decades: how the brave Zulu youngster, redeeming himself from earlier disgrace, confronts a leopard single-handed with a spear; how the shrewd, youthful warrior invents a new, short thrusting spear and a sort of judo maneuver with the shield that makes the more or less desultory clan warfare lethal—as revolutionary an innovation for combat in Africa, perhaps, as the invention of the stirrup for European warfare. We see the young king drilling his soldiers in formation, see them toughen their feet by dancing barefoot on thorns and read that soldiers who flinched were killed on the spot.

Shaka (1787-1828), a genius in warfare, was almost superhuman in stature—heroic, commanding, tyrannical, dispassionately cruel and—by any standards we may apply—quite mad at the end.

Early 18th-century Zulu social organization may shed some light on the psychology of this monumental hero—his lust for increase, his rage to prove his prowess, his symbiosis with his mother. Zulu family structures were immense, extended and extraordinarily complex. Polygamy was the norm, and children, who were nursed for three or four years, were emotionally closely tied to their mothers. They lived with them in modest or, in the case of royalty, immense compounds. These kraals, which housed the people and enclosed the cattle, determined wealth and indicated status, were in large part the cause for endless wars and ceaseless migration.

Shaka, who was conceived under marginally incestuous circumstances, and his mother were only reluctantly taken into the kraal of his father, the king. For a momentary lapse in skill or courage, little Shaka, together with his mother, was sent into exile. For years their life was a burden, but the bond between them strengthened. Strong, matured, the boy returned to his paternal clan, distinguishing himself by individual and dramatic acts of prowess.

Increasingly, Shaka joined in military forays, gave his counsel in meetings with elders. At his father's death he became chief. He displayed strength and power as he captured thousands of men whom he brought back to swell the ranks of the formidable Zulu warriors. He forbade them to marry until they had acquitted themselves in battle. (Although he had a harem of 1,200 women, Shaka himself left no offspring.)

As the 12 years of his rule passed, Shaka assimilated hundreds of thousands from the clans he conquered, and sent whole populations into exile starvation and desolation as his rule, his demands, his ravages increased. When, in 1827, his beloved mother died, 7,000 mourners were incited to murder one another, until the rivers were swollen with their corpses. Shaka commanded that the world grieve with him, that all milk be poured on the ground, that no crops be planted for a year—an edict that would have meant starvation for his people had he not been

talked out of such a suicidal measure in the third month. Overstepping one time too many the bounds of what one can ask of even the most loyal troops, Shaka was assassinated by two of his half brothers soon thereafter. *Sic semper . . .*

Diane Stanley and Peter Vennema have culled the massive amount of historical material that exists about this strange and fascinating figure. Their text is lucid; the incidents are tactfully within the scope and decorum of a children's book but representative and true to the facts. They have made a valid but selective interpretation for young readers of a potentially controversial subject—the founding of a nation by a hero who was a scourge.

Above all, the book is gorgeous. Ms. Stanley demonstrated her flair for exceptional illustrated biography of larger-than-life figures with **Peter the Great**. Here her work is accurate in the smallest detail: Zulu artifacts, the singular design of Shaka's great shield, even the straw hat worn by a visiting Englishman. The massed ranks of warriors are a visual pageant suggesting genuine epic scale. The rhythm of the illustrations—shields ranged in phalanx, herds of white cattle passing, even the orange background behind them—makes each page not only a realistic representation but also an artistic composition. And over all there hovers the misty greenish-yellow hue of the great, unforgiving land—a yellow reflected even in the beautiful text pages with their delicate margins of distinctively Zulu bead design.

From a minor clan of 1,500 souls and 350 warriors, Shaka built a nation of more than two million Zulus, shaping the greatest fighting force ever seen on the African continent. Today, 160 years after his death, more than six million descendants of the Zulus inhabit South Africa—they are the largest ethnic group, black or white, in the land. *Shaka: King of the Zulus* is a thrilling introduction to the Zulu people and a remarkable chapter in African history.

Mary A. Bush

SOURCE: A review of *Shaka: King of the Zulus,* in *The Horn Book Magazine,* Vol. LXV, No. 1, January-February, 1989, pp. 93-4.

The handsome volume marks an impressive extension of Diane Stanley's work in the area of picture book biography. Like **Peter the Great** the new book is a chronological sketch of the life of a very dramatic historical figure; the events and significance of Shaka's life are recounted in an abbreviated but informative fashion. His violent rule in the 1820s was a powerful force in the history of the Zulus, pulling disparate clans into a conquering nation for a brief moment in time. The authors mention Shaka's brutal practices, acknowledging them in their historical context. The early life of Shaka and his military might are emphasized in the paintings in umber tones set on buff colored pages. The pictures are all full-page illustrations or half-page double-spreads, allowing for numerous details and wide vistas. Bands of beads woven in varied patterns run beneath pictures or along the side of pages of text, adding a decorative motif. The competent rendering of place and culture is the most striking feature of the book and reveals the very wide range in the illustrator's capability. Stanley favors massed groupings of people, sometimes using them in stylized patterns and in the closer scenes depicting the figures as distinct individuals. There is texture, warmth, energy, and careful attention to costume. Shaka's rule was cut short by assassination, and his reign witnessed the arrival of white Europeans, whom he received amicably. The brief-lived cohesiveness of the Zulu nation did not fare as well after Shaka's death, and the white role in southern Africa increased. Shaka is treated as a figure who left a heritage of pride to the Zulus; his story has been developed more fully elsewhere, and this compelling introduction invites further reading.

Anne Lundin

SOURCE: A review of *Shaka: King of the Zulus,* in *The Five Owls,* Vol. III, No. 4, March-April, 1989, p. 59.

In 1787, an infant America congregated in Philadelphia to create a new order, a Constitution. In the same year, in a small village on the hillsides of southern Africa, a child was born who would also shape a new nation and would make a name for himself among the great warrior heroes. This is Shaka, the father of the Zulu Nation. Despite the enormous significance of this legendary hero, American children are only beginning to learn the names of those who shaped Africa, the ancestral home of many Americans.

Shaka is the son of the chief of the Zulus, a small clan, one among many in southern Africa. Shaka's job in the tribe is to guard the sheep and cattle, their livelihood, the neglect of which leads to his banishment along with his mother, who injudiciously intervened. Ostracized, the boy and his mother live like nomads before finding a new home where Shaka grows into boyhood in dreams of glory.

Shaka is soon recognized as a young military genius. After he slays his first leopard, he masters the secret of battle: the right weapons, steps, and strategies to succeed. He is given responsibility over soldiers who are forced to submit to his monastic order and single-minded obsession. His instincts are always those of a guerilla fighter, walking barefoot over thorns to improve his leopard-leap, his dance of death.

Shaka's drive to conquer forges a new nation out of the once tiny Zulu clan. He turns the conquered into converts, unifying disparate tribes by sword and shield. Surprisingly, he cooperates with the English settlers who save his life and threaten his shores. His loyalties are intense, diabolical, his mother's death pushing him into madness and mass destruction. The authors view his excesses within an historical perspective of "a cruel age, when wars of conquest were considered glorious and kings held the

power of life and death over their subjects." His enemies finally overpower him, slaying him with the swords he had designed for death.

Stanley and Vennema bring to life a complex hero who shatters our expectations of noble savages or sacrificial lambs. As in Stanley's biography ***Peter the Great,*** the authors present the full humanity of their subject with a new level of integrity. Shaka has all the power and mystery of an Aeneas or a Beowulf, a figure larger than life. The authors bring to this epic figure ambiguities of motive, tangled emotions, fears and longings, all on a level of great simplicity.

The epic of Shaka is brilliantly depicted through the panorama of the picture book, where the visual images tell a different story than the massive historical record—a touching, delicate grandeur to a ruthless warrior. Stanley's details of costume, weaponry, and landscape are true to history and to biography for young readers. Stanley shows Shaka constructing clay figures instead of tending sheep and shields us from the bloodshed of innocent victims in harm's way. Each page develops a significant episode in Shaka's rise to power, with reproductions of beadwork on each page in ornamental praise.

Kathleen T. Horning

SOURCE: A review of *Shaka: King of the Zulus,* in *School Library Journal,* Vol. 35, No. 10, June, 1989, p. 101.

Stanley uses a style and format similar to that of ***Peter the Great*** in this picture book biography of Shaka, the notorious military leader who, between 1816 and 1828, united over 100 tribes and clans into the powerful Zulu nation of southern Africa. The concise, clearly written text focuses on the details of Shaka's life and his military accomplishments. The book's overall tone is one of respect and admiration, although the authors do not gloss over Shaka's violent, sometimes sadistic, strategies. To the authors' credit, Shaka and the peoples of southern Africa remain central to the story throughout a description of their first contact with Europeans. Unfortunately, there is little, if any, variety or diversity in the faces of the dozens of black Africans pictured in the illustrations, while four white Europeans are easily distinguished from one another. The text is well-documented with an extensive bibliography of sources; however, its requisite simplicity, together with the pastoral beauty of the full-color illustrations, serves to romanticize Shaka and his times. Still, as an introduction for a young audience, it suffices.

📖 *FORTUNE* (1990)

Kirkus Reviews

SOURCE: A review of *Fortune,* in *Kirkus Reviews,* Vol. LVIII, No. 3, February 1, 1990, p. 185.

A poor peasant makes good with a tiger named Fortune in this exotic original tale of Persian enchantment.

Omar has no assets beyond the money in his purse when he heads to market to pursue a living. Should he find a way to sustain a wife, he plans to return to his farm and his childhood friend and betrothed, Sunny. His one purchase is a sad-eyed, dancing tiger; with the tiger to exhibit, Omar travels from village to village and becomes wealthy. In search of a woman worthier of his fortune than Sunny, Omar finds a princess, but she mourns her own lost love. After Omar unintentionally restores her to happiness, he gets another chance with Sunny, bringing this deft story to a gratifying close.

Stanley continues to defy categorization with her art. Here, her ornately studied illustrations pay tribute to oriental miniatures of the past. Ablaze with color, intricate geometric shapes and lavish adornment of the page provide striking accompaniment to each twist of the tale, right down to that happy ending. Folk-tale fans, welcome.

Denise Wilms

SOURCE: A review of *Fortune,* in *Booklist,* Vol. 86, No. 12, February 15, 1990, p. 1172.

For a poor farmer's son, Omar does remarkably well: a dancing tiger acquired at a village market makes him a rich man, and his travels in search of a princess to marry lead to yet more good fortune, even if a lesson in humility is a painful part of the bargain. When Omar first acquires wealth, he leaves behind his sweetheart, who is but a poor farm girl; now that Omar is successful, he wishes to marry a princess. But the princess he wants is in love with another—a man who has disappeared through an enchantment. It is Omar who inadvertently brings the two together in a way that breaks an evil witch's spell. He then realizes his foolishness and returns home to seek his sweetheart's forgiveness and to marry her. Though the folktale-like story is set in Persia, there is no mention of its background. The straightforward telling and intriguing plot will easily entertain listeners, who will find the art suits the story. Ornate scenes full of decorative patterning and slight stylization characteristic of Middle Eastern art fill the pages. Visually rich and conceptually intriguing, this will hold an audience well.

Marcia Hupp

SOURCE: A review of *Fortune,* in *School Library Journal,* Vol. 36, No. 4, April, 1990, pp. 97-8.

Omar, a poor and not very clever farmer, must seek his fortune before he and Sunny, his much more sensible betrothed, can marry. In a market town nearby, a strange woman sells him a dancing tiger he names Fortune, and in no time at all, Omar's fortune is made. Now, dazzled by his own success, Omar fancies himself too grand to marry a commoner. But there is enchantment at work here, and when Omar decides to seek a princess for a bride, he sets in motion a chain of events that leaves him humbled but happily wed to Sunny. This original tale has a traditional spirit that is enhanced by extravagant illustrations in the Persian manuscript style. Jeweled tones shimmer against a parchment background; graceful, mannered figures pose amidst a profusion of ornamental detail. Stanley's lavish paintings and textual embellishments complement and extend a tale with all the enchantment and wit of *The Arabian Nights.*

Roger Sutton

SOURCE: A review of *Fortune,* in *Bulletin of the Center for Children's Books,* Vol. 43, No. 9, May, 1990, p. 228.

With no source note to the contrary, this seems to be an original story in the "folk-like" tradition. A young Persian man goes off to seek his fortune, which he finds in the form of a docile, dancing tiger offered to him by a mysterious woman. Omar makes his fortune by exhibiting Fortune (as he names the tiger), and disdaining his girl-next-door first love ("I'm sure you can see that it can never work out between us") seeks the hand of a princess. The solution, in which all are restored to their various high and humble places, involves both an interior tale and a "Beauty and the Beast" switch on the part of the tiger, conclusions which seem contrived rather than inevitable. The illustrations are an ornate tribute to the traditions of Persian miniatures, with elaborate borders and patterns framing iconographically stylized figures. While the rich colors and intricate designs have an innate eye appeal, the hyper-stylization may keep some young lookers-on at an emotional distance.

Margaret M. Burns

SOURCE: A review of *Fortune,* in *The Horn Book Magazine,* Vol. LXVI, No. 5, September-October, 1990, p. 598.

Although no source is given to authenticate its origins, this handsomely embellished story of luck, love, and enchantment certainly has the style and pacing characteristic of a masterfully retold folk narrative. The setting is the Persia of long ago when magic was still possible. A poor young man, betrothed to a farmer's daughter named Sunny, takes her advice and sets forth to find his fortune, which by a nice twist of fate turns out to be a dancing tiger. Thanks to the talents of this obedient beast, Omar becomes wealthy, but, given his new status, begins to question the suitability of his liaison with Sunny. Relying on her good nature, he breaks their engagement and once again sets forth, riding on Fortune the tiger to find a bride of high degree. Nor do his instincts fail him, for he indeed finds a princess, mourning her lost love, who seems most suitable in person, wealth, and station. But fate once again intervenes, leaving Omar to ponder his intentions and reconsider his decision to abandon the faithful Sunny, who, it is clear, is far more wise and clever than he.

The illustrations, echoing the delicacy and meticulous detail of Persian miniatures, are a sparkling accompaniment to the vibrant text.

Sam Swope

SOURCE: A review of *Fortune,* in *The New York Times Book Review,* October 28, 1990, p. 32.

Imagine you meet a big, slimy frog who gazes at you with mournful eyes. Would you kiss it? Now imagine a witch turns you into a frog: there you are, able to love but unlovable, always a frog until kissed. Who will save you? This complex metaphor, ripe with spiritual, sexual and psychological meaning, sits at the heart of great transformation tales such as *The Frog Prince* and *Beauty and the Beast.* These stories, full of moral imperative, ask the uncomfortable question: What should we do—ignore the suffering soul within the hideous body, or press our lips against the frog's moist mouth? The obvious answer requires the kind of courage children understand: You have to kiss the frog. (Unsettlingly, you might even find you like it.)

Both *Fortune* by Diane Stanley and *The Clay Flute* by Mats Rehnman tell transformation tales. Coincidentally, both of these writer-illustrators were inspired by Persian miniatures, and their handsome books are full of intricate, colorful images that will appeal to children and adults. The sentimental stories Ms. Stanley and Mr. Rehnman tell, however, disappoint—we feel we've read them before, and their setting in long-ago Persia seems arbitrary, as though chosen to justify the illustrations.

The formal, restrained and elegantly complex illustrations in *Fortune* match a formal, restrained and confusingly complex text. Omar, a peasant lad engaged to a neighbor girl named Sunny, goes to the city to make some money. By chance he becomes the owner of Fortune, a docile, dancing tiger. While Omar plays the flute, Fortune dances, and their act is so successful that Omar is soon too rich for Sunny. Nothing but a princess will suit him now, and off he goes in search of one, allowing Fortune to lead him.

Before long he hears of Shirin, a "weeping princess" whose fiancé mysteriously vanished the day before her wedding. Omar, deciding he must have Shirin, kidnaps her with the clever lie that his tiger will take her to her lost prince. The princess is so grateful that she kisses Fortune, who turns out to have been her enchanted fiancé.

I suppose we are to understand that all is "fortune"; without question the kiss is not an act of will. Ms. Stanley's tiger, with his hat and sad dance, is more pathetic than frightening, and by emasculating the beast the story robs the princess of her courage.

As for Omar, his selfish lie would, in other tales, have been the act of a scheming witch: "Come with me, my pretty!" But the narrator of "Fortune" indulges Omar,

dismissing his deceit as just "a little lie," and the happy reunion he unintentionally brings about is rewarded by "great lands and a splendid house and more wealth than he could ever spend." To complete the happy ending. Omar abruptly realizes his folly and marries Sunny.

In most stories, as in life, self-knowledge comes through suffering. Ms. Stanley, whose other books include *Shaka: King of the Zulus* and *Captain Whiz-Bang* here offers a good-natured tale, but it suggests with troubling ease that it doesn't matter how we behave; if we trust to fortune, everything comes right in the end. No price must be paid. Flying in the face of life, this is a story determined to be happy.

GOOD QUEEN BESS: THE STORY OF ELIZABETH I OF ENGLAND (cowritten with husband Peter Vennema, 1990)

Kirkus Reviews

SOURCE: A review of *Good Queen Bess: The Story of Elizabeth I of England,* in *Kirkus Reviews,* Vol. LVIII, No. 16, August 15, 1990, p. 1174.

Appropriately for their audience, the authors only hint at the darker side of Elizabeth's reign. They include a simplified but accurate explanation of the English Reformation and its immediate consequences; a discussion of the Queen's political astuteness, its roots in her troubled childhood, and how she made being a woman an asset; a fair account of her vexed dealings with Mary, Queen of Scots; and illuminating details of interest to children—such as summers "on progress," when Elizabeth escaped the plague and "stopped in little villages . . . received humble gifts . . . and won the hearts of her people."

As in the authors' *Peter the Great,* Stanley's carefully researched, beautifully detailed illustrations take up even more space than the text. Combining 20th-century realism with the decorative, more formal style of 16th-century painting, they add both drama and a visual sense of history. An admirably clear, attractive summary.

Denise Wilms

SOURCE: A review of *Good Queen Bess: The Story of Elizabeth I of England,* in *Booklist,* Vol. 87, No. 1, September 1, 1990, p. 50.

This biography of Queen Elizabeth I does an excellent job of describing the context of her life so that reasons for many of her actions become clear. The resulting depth is a pleasant surprise and will give the book a wide audience. Stanley's illustrations fill the pages, showing Elizabeth in all of her glory throughout her long life. The text, meanwhile, informs on many aspects of Elizabeth's life: her childhood, how she became queen, what the political climates were that shaped her strategies and decision making, and who the key players were in her life, including the man she would have liked to marry but couldn't. The authors are admiring of Elizabeth, and readers will be too; the account leaves no doubt about why this monarch's name labels an entire era.

Betsy Hearne

SOURCE: A review of *Good Queen Bess: The Story of Elizabeth I of England,* in *Bulletin of the Center for Children's Books,* Vol. 44, No. 2, October, 1990, p. 46.

This compressed history of Elizabeth I's life and times benefits from a combination of selective text and elaborated art. Stanley's formal, full-color illustrations on every page showcase the principal characters with precise detail and pure, tightly patterned hues. The personal and the politic are companionably balanced, as are background information and specific incident. Despite the picture book format, older elementary-grade readers who are the real target audience can be persuaded to read this by the sophisticated pictorial style and the uncondescending narrative, as was the case with Stanley's biography of Peter the Great. A brief introduction explains the European context of religious tension between Catholics and Protestants during the Reformation, and a bibliography lists a dozen other books—nine adult and three juvenile—on Elizabeth I.

Amy Kellman

SOURCE: A review of *Good Queen Bess: The Story of Elizabeth I of England,* in *School Library Journal,* Vol. 36, No. 12, December, 1990, p. 120.

That most wise and wily queen of England, Elizabeth I, is the subject of this picture biography. The handsome illustrations, exemplified by the visualization of those small English boats set afire and launched to face the Spanish Armada, are worthy of their subject. Although the format suggests a picture-book audience, this biography needs to be introduced to older readers who have the background to appreciate and understand this woman who dominated and named an age, and of whom the authors write, "When it came to a clash of wills, the two houses of Parliament and all her councillors were no match for Elizabeth." The text is clearly written, explaining the main events and key decisions of Elizabeth's life and reign. For readers wanting more depth, a short bibliography of mostly adult titles ends the book.

Mary A. Bush

SOURCE: A review of *Good Queen Bess: The Story of Elizabeth I of England,* in *The Horn Book Magazine,* Vol. LXVII, No. 1, January-February, 1991, p. 91.

"'She is only a woman, only mistress of half an island, and yet she makes herself feared by Spain, by France, by the Empire, by all!'" These grudging words of respect from a political enemy, Pope Sixtus, epitomize the major issues of womanhood and political power which marked all of Elizabeth's long life and reign. She is certainly viewed as much more than "'only a woman'" in this admiring and admirably distilled presentation. Complexities of politics and personality are necessarily simplified for this slim, handsome volume, but their substance is remarkably well conveyed. Diane Stanley and Peter Vennema have proven adept at encapsulating the elements of a complete life and conveying historical flavor in their previous picture-book biography, *Shaka, King of the Zulus.* Stanley has drawn widely on paintings from the Elizabethan period for costume details, artistic style, and shades of color. Her gouache scenes of court life are nearly luminous, shaded in softened tones of red, blue, green, and tan, with black robes and gowns adding emphasis. On every page there is a painting, sometimes filling the whole page or often placed above a segment of text. The continuous narrative is a careful survey of Elizabeth's character and accomplishments. The great monarch's intelligence, astute judgment, kindness, sociability, and love of the arts are emphasized. The story tells of her birth to King Henry VIII and Anne Boleyn, her betrayal by Queen Mary of Scotland, her reluctance to marry or name a successor, and her defeat of the Spanish Armada. The beautifully developed synthesis is a fascinating introduction to one of history's most influential figures.

Marianne Partridge

SOURCE: A review of *Good Queen Bess: The Story of Elizabeth I of England,* in *The New York Times Book Review,* March 17, 1991, p. 26.

For the simple reason that Elizabeth Tudor was not born a boy, her father killed her mother and declared the child a bastard. Shunned and ignored for most of her childhood, in fear for her life throughout her adolescence, Elizabeth never the less grew up to become England's most brilliant and compassionate ruler.

Certainly the woman who could triumph over this unhappy background would be an exemplary role model for anyone growing up in our own unsettled time, and this was clearly the purpose behind Diane Stanley and Peter Vennema's handsome illustrated biography, *Good Queen Bess.*

In plain language and with detailed illustrations, the book accurately describes the history, costume and culture of the Elizabethan era. Sadly, however, it does little to capture the spirit of this extraordinary queen.

Though the first third of Elizabeth's life was preparation for the perils of the throne she assumed in 1558 at the age of 25, this book devotes little space to her childhood. In all fairness, the authors accept the basic interpretation of Elizabeth's early life put forth by most historians. She survived so well, they say, because she was the product of systematic neglect. Describing the time shortly after the birth of her half brother, Edward, they write that she "was no longer so important now that England had a prince. She did not live at court with her father, but grew up at the Palace of Hatfield, where she had her own governess, servants, and teachers."

This delightful picture not only distorts the facts somewhat but also leaves us without any sense of the child. Elizabeth always lived in a household of her own; she seldom saw her mother, Anne Boleyn, before her beheading in 1536; she saw her father, Henry VIII, even less, except at court occasions, many of which were designed to honor her brother, the Prince of Wales. Raised by a beloved nurse until she was 5, Elizabeth spent the next seven years with a string of governesses and a few fine tutors.

At age 10, because of an unrecorded incident that displeased her father, Elizabeth was sent away from court in disgrace. Generally this type of childhood does not result in a great sense of self-esteem, but by the time she was 15, two years after her father's death, she was able to withstand treachery and outwit the feared Protector, the Duke of Somerset, who was trying to involve her in a plot against Edward VI. Those who had witnessed Elizabeth practicing her signature over and over again until she had perfected it at the age of 11 would not have been surprised at her sense of destiny. What is surprising is that so little of this confidence is described in a book for young readers. Her whole childhood is dealt with in three short paragraphs.

Though the authors do an admirable job of wading through the messy details of Bloody Mary Tudor's reign, they fail to convey the genius with which Elizabeth eluded the entrapment of her enemies. The majority of the tale, devoted to Elizabeth's reign, continues on as a well-researched story of her magnificent statecraft, but the grandeur never materializes.

Perhaps the book's most disturbing failure is also its most striking feature: the numerous and elaborate illustrations, all based on contemporary court portraits and engravings. It is hardly fair comment to complain that these illustrations lack the passion of Holbein's drawings, which so influenced Tudor portraiture, but by adopting the formal style of court artists Ms. Stanley—whose other books include **Shaka, King of the Zulus,** also written with her husband, Peter Vennema, and **Peter the Great**—carefully conveys the pageantry of royal life without reflecting any of its liveliness.

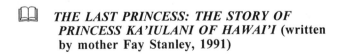

THE LAST PRINCESS: THE STORY OF PRINCESS KA'IULANI OF HAWAI'I (written by mother Fay Stanley, 1991)

Roger Sutton

SOURCE: A review of *The Last Princess: The Story of Princess Ka'iulani Hawai'i,* in *Bulletin of the Center for Children's Books,* Vol. 44, No. 7, March, 1991, p. 178.

Although the eleven-year-old Princess Ka'iulani was heir to the throne of Hawai'i, her mother had a deathbed vision of Ka'iulani's future: "You will go far away from your land and your people and be gone a very long time. You will never marry and you will never rule Hawai'i." These prophecies would all eventually come true, but not before Princess Ka'iulani, at the age of seventeen, convinced President Cleveland of the United States to block his country's annexation of her kingdom. (It would, however, occur after Cleveland left office.) Ka'iulani makes a strong focus for this usually glossed-over piece of American history, and readers will be enlightened by Ka'iulani's quiet determination in standing up to colonialism. The tone of the text is sometimes adulatory and the depictions of Ka'iulani are facially inexpressive, but both the text and the full-page facing illustrations have intensity and dignity. Larger, bolder, and simpler than her pictures for **Good Queen Bess,** Stanley's portraits of Ka'iulani use strong patterns and have an almost ceremonial—if somewhat mannered—composition.

Ann Stell

SOURCE: A review of *The Last Princess: The Story of Princess Ka'iulani of Hawai'i,* in *School Library Jouranl,* Vol. 37, No. 3, March, 1991, pp. 208-09.

Diane Stanley's newest picture biography with a text by her mother is the story of Princess Ka'iulani of Hawai'i. Expected to one day become queen, she is sent to England to be educated, only to have the *haoles* (foreigners) threaten her family's right to rule. Although her courageous plea to President Grover Cleveland postponed the end of Hawaii's independence, the islands were annexed by the United States in 1897. The beautiful Princess Ka'iulani died only 2 years later at the age of 23. As with Stanley's other biographies, readers are transported into another very believable world. The full-page paintings are stunning, reflecting the beauty of the islands and the handsome, racially mixed people who live there. Although her style evolves and adapts somewhat to her material, the book has an unmistakably Stanley look. A helpful note on the Hawaiian language and an extensive bibliography complete this visual treat.

Ilene Cooper

SOURCE: A review of *The Last Princess: The Story of Princess Ka'iulani of Hawai'i,* in *Booklist,* Vol. 87, No. 14, March 15, 1991, p. 1504.

In her previous illustrated biography, Stanley introduced Queen Elizabeth I to readers. Here, she looks again at a member of royalty, but quite a different figure—the last princess of Hawaii. Ka'iulani, the first heir born to the royal family, led an idyllic childhood in beautiful Oahu, surrounded by a loving family, until her mother died. On her deathbed Princess Likelike foresaw three things for her child: "You will go far away from your land and your people and be gone a very long time. You will never marry and you will never rule Hawai'i." Ka'iulani would spend many years studying abroad in England, preparing for her reign, but true to her mother's prediction, she never became queen. Though she fought tirelessly and even spoke personally to President Grover Cleveland, Ka'iulani was not able to persevere against American interests that wanted the U.S. to annex the islands. Not long after Annexation Day, August 12, 1898, Ka'iulani was caught in a downpour, became ill, and died at age 23. Fay Stanley's prose is occasionally stiff, but this bittersweet drama will certainly capture the reader's imagination. Diane Stanley's moving full-color paintings expressively re-create the human emotion of the story. It's all here: grieving Ka'iulani's last visit with her mother, the compelling scene when Queen Lili'uokalani is told American marines have marched into Honolulu, the despair Ka'iulani feels after the annexation. Biography that tells its story and touches the heart.

Kirkus Reviews

SOURCE: A review of *The Last Princess: The Story of Princess Ka'iulani of Hawai'i,* in *Kirkus Reviews,* Vol. LIX, No. 7, April 1, 1991, p. 476.

Third in line for the throne when she was born in 1875 to the younger sister of Princess (later Queen) Lili'uokalani and the Scottish Archibald Cleghorn, Ka'iulani's short life was dominated by the dissolution of the Hawaiian monarchy. Her happy childhood came to an end when her mother died in 1887; she was sent to school in England, where it took weeks for her to learn that American Marines had forced her aunt to give up the throne. At 17, Ka'iulani traveled to Washington to intervene for her people, but—despite a sympathetic hearing from President Cleveland—to little avail; back in Hawaii by the time of formal annexation, she caught pneumonia a few months later, dying at 23.

The artist's mother reports this brief life with simple dignity; but most compelling here are Diane Stanley's well-researched, jewel-bright paintings, her carefully delineated figures, stiff as old photos, deployed against a wealth of pattern and landscape. Attractive; informative.

Ann A. Flowers

SOURCE: A review of *The Last Princess: The Story of Princess Ka'iulani of Hawai'i,* in *The Horn Book Magazine,* Vol. LXVII, No. 5, September-October, 1991, p. 616.

The little-known story of the Crown Princess of Hawaii, who tried to save her country from annexation by the United States, is a sad one. The niece of King Kalakaua and Queen Lili'uokalani, the last royal ruler of Hawaii, she was trained from infancy for her future role. After her mother's death, Princess Ka'iulani was sent to England for her education and, while there, was warned by her uncle, the king, to "'be on guard against certain enemies

I do not feel free to name in writing.'" Suddenly, the king was dead, and Queen Lili'uokalani, who succeeded him, was overthrown. Although shy, the princess attempted to save her country from annexation by appealing to President Cleveland, and believed that she had succeeded. But all attempts failed, and Princess Ka'iulani, deeply loved by her people for her courage and dignity, died in despair at the age of twenty-three. The princess's story sheds new light on long-forgotten history; the vibrant, handsome gouache illustrations establish the lush Hawaiian background and provide historic detail.

SIEGFRIED (1991)

Dorothy Hamilton and Jane Marino

SOURCE: A review of *Siegfried,* in *School Library Journal,* Vol. 37, No. 10, October, 1991, p. 33.

A delightful story, more about a cat than Christmas, but a cat not to be missed. Siegfried, an old and pampered feline, has his peaceful life shattered one Christmas day when his family receives a cuckoo clock as a gift. It is ticking and tocking away when—right in the middle of a lovely nap—Siegfried is startled by a "Bong! Bong!" and the appearance of a tiny yellow bird who jumps out and calls out "Cuckoo, Cuckoo." This feline is outraged; he is angry; he is obsessed. The story of his revenge and triumph over his tormentor is done with the humor and style befitting an animal with such a self-assured personality.

Publishers Weekly

SOURCE: A review of *Siegfried,* in *Publishers Weekly,* Vol. 238, No. 46, October 18, 1991, p. 60.

Siegfried is an old, happy feline, "living contentedly in his cozy world" with his family, the equally old and contented Mr. and Mrs. Fritz. A Christmas visit from the Fritzes' adult children, however, disrupts Siegfried's well-ordered world, as a gift cuckoo clock brings an unwelcome guest into the house. The territorial cat realizes he must defend the household from this flighty invader, a bright yellow bird who pops out on the hour and calls the beleaguered calico a rude name. Told entirely from Siegfried's point of view, Stanley's comical caper perfectly captures Siegfried's sense of righteous indignation—though the humor is occasionally overly sophisticated. Readers do not have to be cat lovers to be captivated by the frantic gyrations of this put-upon puss, who takes several years off his age in his vigorous pursuit.

BARD OF AVON: THE STORY OF WILLIAM SHAKESPEARE (cowritten with husband Peter Vennema, 1992)

Kirkus Reviews

SOURCE: A review of *Bard of Avon: The Story of Wil-

liam Shakespeare, in *Kirkus Reviews,* Vol. LX, No. 14, July 15, 1992, p. 926.

The authors of several handsomely illustrated historical biographies take on an unusually demanding subject with intelligence, scrupulous regard for the historical record, and a wise eye to the interests of their audience. Emphasizing how little is known for sure about Shakespeare, they phrase their straightforward text to make admirably clear the boundaries of fact and the bases for plausible conjecture, often commenting on what, interestingly, is *not* known ("No one knows when he left [Stratford for London] or under what circumstances"). Summarizing the most significant events, they illuminate them with well chosen, often intriguing details and tell as much about the Elizabethan theater as about the playwright. Stanley's elegant illustrations are especially well suited to the topic; she uses details of Tudor architecture and costume to richly decorative effect, while her artfully structured compositions and somewhat stylized figures harmonize well with the theatrical topic. An excellent "Postscript" discusses the evolution of Shakespeare's English, his own inventions (e.g., "majestic," "leapfrog," "gloomy") and the continuing ubiquity of his vivid descriptions. Outstanding.

Carolyn Phelan

SOURCE: A review of *Bard of Avon: The Story of William Shakespeare,* in *Booklist,* Vol. 89, No. 1, September 1, 1992, p. 55.

Similar in approach to Stanley's previous picture-book biographies, *Shaka, King of the Zulus* and *Good Queen Bess,* this handsome volume presents the life of Shakespeare. Writing even a brief biography of the bard can be tricky, since little is known of his life. The author deals with this problem in a commendably straightforward fashion; in the introduction, she discusses the meager sources available and states, "we have tried to show how historians investigate a life lived long ago." The text points out when a fact is conjectural or controversial. Would that other biographers, for adults as well as children, were as forthright in their presentation! Besides following Shakespeare's story through the well-written text and intriguing illustrations, readers will learn something of the Elizabethans and, particularly, their theaters. While the book's layout is somewhat static, with text on the left-hand pages and pictures on the right, there's a quiet vivacity in the art itself, which ranges from portraits of famous actors and political figures, to dramatic scenes of the players and their audiences, to domestic pictures of Shakespeare at home in Stratford. Stanley's finesse with the decorative elements of painting makes each illustration a pleasure and the whole book visually satisfying. Accessible to a wide age range, this is a fine introduction for anyone beginning to read Shakespeare.

Sally Margolis

SOURCE: A review of *Bard of Avon: The Story of Wil-*

From Rumpelstiltskin's Daughter, *written and illustrated by Diane Stanley.*

liam Shakespeare, in *School Library Journal,* Vol. 38, No. 11, November, 1992, p. 114.

This is a wonderful book. A fine companion biography to *Good Queen Bess,* this life of Shakespeare builds on the methods developed in *Bess* and *Shaka, King of the Zulus.* Using the few facts known about their subject, Stanley and Vennema manage a full-bodied portrait of a life and time without resorting to fictionalizing or sloppy speculation. In fact, the book starts with an appealing invitation to examine the historical research process. And, without wasting words in pedantic explanation, it keeps readers on a firm footing regarding the scholarly basis of any assertion. In the course of a brief text, the authors manage to touch not only upon the life but also upon important aspects of many of the major plays. There is even a tantalizing postscript with introductory glimpses of the development of the English language. As with their previous works, the authors provide a short but meaty bibliography. Stanley's distinctive full-color gouache paintings are clearly her own, and just as clearly planted firmly in archival research. They reinforce and expand the text with humor and movement. As icing on the cake, the generous open space and attractive page decoration rival the production given *Shaka.* Books like these need only be displayed to attract readers. And once opened, they keep their promise. Lucky kids!

Ann A. Flowers

SOURCE: A review of *Bard of Avon: The Story of William Shakespeare,* in *The Horn Book Magazine,* Vol. LXVIII, No. 6, November-December, 1992, pp. 737-38.

The few facts available about William Shakespeare would seem to limit sharply any reasonable recounting of his life. But, as the authors remark, "like detectives, historians gather all the known facts together until a pattern begins to appear," and they are scrupulous in reporting only verifiable facts and justified inferences. A remarkably rounded picture of Shakespeare's life and the period in which he lived is presented—more detailed in the time during which he was an actor and playwright—together with a thoughtful attempt to relate circumstances in his personal life to the content of his plays. Especially interesting is the description of the actors of the time and what can be inferred about their acting style by the roles that were created for them. The text is splendidly supported by the illustrations, which are stylized, yet recognizable, and present a clear view of life in the late sixteenth century. A discerning, knowledgeable biography, rising far above the ordinary.

Deborah Stevenson

SOURCE: A review of *Bard of Avon: The Story of William Shakespeare,* in *Bulletin of the Center for Children's Books,* Vol. 46, No. 4, December, 1992, p. 123.

Stanley and Vennema, co-creators of picture-book biographies of *Good Queen Bess* and *Shaka, King of the Zulus,* here take on—and quite successfully—the Immortal Bard. The authors makes a clear distinction between the little actually known about William Shakespeare's life and their speculation based on general knowledge of the Elizabethan era ("We don't know what play they performed. Perhaps they did *Ralph Roister Doister,* a funny play with characters named Matthew Merrygreek and Margery Mumblecrust") as it traces the actor-playwright's life from country childhood through London dramatic life, then back to his final rural days. While biography is sometimes sweepingly implicated as a force in Shakespeare's writing (about his last plays, the authors say "There is a gentle quality about them, and a love of the countryside, which suggests that William Shakespeare had found peace in the village of his childhood"), the discussion of the place of his individual works and drama in general is succinct, understandable, and peppered with interesting facts—kids will enjoy hearing about the theft of an entire theatre and the playwright's famous bequest of the second-best bed to his wife. Illustrations run to earth tones and a slightly flat, stylized look that gives them a period flavor; they offer a good idea of theatre life, although it looks un-Elizabethanly clean and tidy (it's also difficult to discern in group scenes which man, if any, is Shakespeare). A highly readable and informative postscript about spelling and language is included, as is a bibliography.

M. Jean Greenlaw

SOURCE: A review of *Bard of Avon: The Story of William Shakespeare,* in *The New Advocate,* Vol. 6, No. 1, winter, 1993, p. 81.

It is amazing how the authors have included so much fascinating information about Shakespeare, his time period, and the development of theaters in this relatively short illustrated biography. Of greatest interest to me was the information about the motivation behind many of the plays and that many of them were crafted to show off the best talents of the actors. The text is facile and Stanley's naive folk art style is both attractive and informative. A postscript on spelling and the many phrases in common use today that Shakespeare coined could make a splendid basis for creative classroom study. A bibliography is appended. I have enjoyed many previous books by Stanley, but this is the best!

MOE THE DOG IN TROPICAL PARADISE (1992)

Roger Sutton

SOURCE: A review of *Moe the Dog in Tropical Paradise,* in *Bulletin of the Center for Children's Books,* Vol. 46, No. 3, November, 1992, p. 89.

For readers too sophisticated for Margaret Bloy Graham's Harry, but not yet ready for Maira Kalman's ultra-hip Max, Moe the Dog and his pal Arlene might make for some diverting new friends. Moe and Arlene, dogs in an otherwise human world, are *cold.* Free for a week's vacation (in January) from their jobs with the Frozen Cow Ice Cream company, Moe and Arlene look for ways to keep warm, but the cinema is showing *Polar Voyage* and *Whales of the Arctic* and a trip to Tahiti costs too much. Arlene goes home discouraged (and cold), and Max does the same, but a hot bath gives him an even hotter idea, and after a trip to the attic, the art store, the grocery, and the building supply, he creates his own tropical paradise and invites Arlene over for a swim. Stanley's storytelling has a casual swing that's just right for this tale of two against the ice. . . .

Kirkus Reviews

SOURCE: A review of *Moe the Dog in Tropical Paradise,* in *Kirkus Reviews,* Vol. LX, No. 22, November 15, 1992, p. 1449.

A couple of illustrators with wide-ranging talents . . . form a new comedy team. Weary of winter, friends Moe and Arlene yearn for the tropics, but travel prices are out of sight. Undaunted, Moe sets to work and builds a beach in his own house, complete with sand, pool, gorgeous palm-studded backdrop, bananas, and pineapples. Summoned to bring her swim suit, Arlene is surprised and enchanted, and the two spend a blissful vacation. Next year, Egypt: "We'll save the sand." . . . [Elise] Primavera captures the canine friends' warmth and energy while imaginatively elaborating Stanley's lighthearted tale about making do, with panache. Just the story to share on a bleak wintry day—or to spark creative play.

Publishers Weekly

SOURCE: A review of *Moe the Dog in Tropical Paradise,* in *Publishers Weekly,* Vol. 239, No. 51, November 23, 1992, p. 62.

This blithesome tale of canine ingenuity offers midwinter warmth to those who begin thinking of island getaways even before the first snowflakes fall. While blizzard-like conditions prevail, scruffy mutt Moe and his springer spaniel pal Arlene work in the Frozen Cow Ice Cream Company's nippy climes. Given a week's vacation, they ponder an escape to Tahiti but can't afford plane fares; Arlene resigns herself to frostbite but Moe gets a better idea. With deck chairs, a wading pool, a few pineapples and some paint, he transforms his home into a beach where palm trees flourish and no one gets sunburned. In a debonair departure from her weightier, generally biographical topics, Stanley keeps tongue firmly in cheek with her low-key, deceptively matter-of-fact prose. . . . Anthropomorphic Moe rapidly adjusts from disgruntled working class hound to laid-back and friendly beachcomber. Although dumping sand on the living room floor may be a bit extreme, this happy-go-lucky narrative suggests that life can indeed be a beach.

Kathleen Odean

SOURCE: A review of *Moe the Dog in Tropical Paradise,* in *School Library Journal,* Vol. 39, No. 1, January, 1993, p. 86.

Moe the dog and his friend Arlene have a week's vacation in January but can't afford to go somewhere warm. Moe makes a tropical paradise in his house by painting backdrops of palm trees, filling a small pool, setting up lawn chairs in the imported sand, and wearing sunglasses. He invites a surprised Arlene to join him. . . . Humorous touches appear throughout, such as Moe's vacation reading, which includes *Old Yeller* and *101 Dalmations.* Overall, though, this is a one-joke book stretched out over 32 pages. . . .

📖 CHARLES DICKENS: THE MAN WHO HAD GREAT EXPECTATIONS (cowritten with husband Peter Vennema, 1993)

Kirkus Reviews

SOURCE: A review of *Charles Dickens: The Man Who Had Great Expectations,* in *Kirkus Reviews,* Vol. LXI, No. 13, July 1, 1993, p. 866-67.

The authors follow their splendid *Bard of Avon* with an equally handsome book on the beloved novelist. Dickens's troubled, well-documented life has plenty to interest children—the early vicissitudes depicted in *David Copperfield,* his championship of needy children, the reception of his books and dramatic readings in the US (where he was "horrified by the hideous institution of slavery"). Nicely shaping their lucid, accessible narrative, the authors begin with Dickens's boyhood dream of living in Gad's Hill (his actual home in his last years) and temper a discreet account of his unfortunate marriage with first-love Maria Beadnell's comical reappearance—plump, middle-aged, and tiresomely persistent. While linking the biographical facts to the fiction, they focus on the life itself; it makes a lively, entertaining story for children who enjoy *A Christmas Carol* in its various guises. As in *Bard,* Stanley uses an elegantly muted palette and delicately stylized figures, bringing decorative period patterns to her beautifully structured compositions; full-bleed art draws readers into the appealing scenes, while b&w text-page vignettes recall Victorian engravings. A must.

Ann W. Moore

SOURCE: A review of *Charles Dickens: The Man Who Had Great Expectations,* in *School Library Journal,* Vol. 39, No. 8, August, 1993, pp. 183-84.

This picture-book biography of the great English novelist is attractive and appealing. Stanley's full-color, full-page gouache paintings are expressive and inviting; the abbreviated text covers all of the major events in Dickens's life. One wonders, though, why an entire page is given to his reacquaintance with his first love, Maria Beadnell, and why his last love, actress Ellen Ternan, is omitted. Dickens's ill-health as a child and the famous story of him, at 12, leading a friend to the wrong house out of embarrassment are also excluded. Stanley and Vennema only partially list the author's works in their bibliography. They merely cite, by title, those mentioned in the text. They also leave out Dickens's birthdate and place—the first thing students look for!—and misspell Ebenezer Scrooge's name. Despite its flaws, *Charles Dickens* is interesting and readable, and should inspire children to delve into his novels. But what children? As in their other books, Stanley and Vennema have created a biography that functions visually and textually on quite different levels. Younger children, while entranced by the pictures, won't understand much of the text—and most won't know or care who Dickens is. Older children who can read his books and are curious about his life will be turned off by the volume's size and appearance. Consequently, the task of placing this biography in the right hands will fall on librarians.

Bill Ott

SOURCE: "Should We Tell the Kids?" in *Booklist,* Vol. 90, No. 1, September 1, 1993, p. 56.

Writing literary biography for children is no picnic. Authors, after all, don't usually lead very exciting lives, at least on the surface, especially when compared to the sports heroes, pop-music idols, and other contemporary celebrities who capture most kids' imaginations. Diane Stanley and Peter Vennema recognize the demands of their audience as well as any authors in their specialized field. In *Bard of Avon*, *Booklist*'s 1992 Top of the List winner for nonfiction, and now in *Charles Dickens*, they have picked their subjects carefully: Shakespeare offered the opportunity for an engaging history lesson on the early days of theater, and Dickens, already familiar to many kids through *A Christmas Carol*, boasts a life almost as melodramatic as his novels. Stanley and Vennema make the most of their material, telling Dickens' story succinctly but with a flair for the dramatic, emphasizing the happy childhood turned nightmare when young Charles' father was sent to debtors prison, and Charles was forced to quit school and toil in a blacking factory.

Stanley's illustrations are every bit as striking here as they were in *Bard*. The full-color, full-bleed gouache paintings are rich with Victorian detail, whether it's a pub full of well-fed, fancily dressed gentlemen chuckling as they read *Pickwick Papers*, or the solitary Dickens making his melancholy way through the moonlit streets of London. Though her colors are soft, almost muted, Stanley's renderings of busy street scenes or crowded drawing rooms still capture the sense of unbridled energy that Dickens felt so keenly in Victorian England. The attempt to incorporate Dickens' characters, his imaginary children, into the artwork, though a daring experiment, is only partially successful. Stanley should be applauded for the concept, as it effectively mimics the way Dickens' creations became a vivid part of their author's life, often more real than many of the people around him. On the page, however, the characters, drawn in hazy silvers or pale blues, look like the kind of cliched ghosts who haunt Mrs. Muir or Topper—hardly an appropriate fate for Fagin or Uriah Heep.

In general, it's only when Stanley or Vennema bump up against Dickens' dark side that they stumble. Writing about Shakespeare, of whom we know relatively little, the problem of what to say and what not to say was rarely an issue. With Dickens, about whom we know much, the problem is thorny indeed. Stanley and Vennema mention Dickens' failed marriage and his seeming preference for his wife's sister (concluding only that things might have been better if Mrs. Dickens had been a more accomplished housekeeper), but they ignore altogether the presence in Dickens' life of actress Ellen Ternan, with whom the novelist shared a strange, secret, possibly asexual relationship that lasted nearly 15 years. Why expunge Ternan from Dickens' life in the same way that propriety-conscious adult biographers banished her from their work for generations? Not, surely, to spare impressionable minds the "ugliness' of an extramarital relationship—not in an era when children's fiction routinely deals with sexual issues and with "alternative" families of every kind. Whatever the motive, the effect of ignoring the most important person in the second half of Dickens' life is to distort the emotional reality of that life. For example, Dickens' last

years at Gad's Hill Place, portrayed here as the final realization of young Charles' great expectations, were in fact a stressful, crazed period of jumping between lives, of secret train rides between Gad's Hill and Ternan's home in London. Certainly one doesn't expect a nuanced exploration of complex relationships in a 48-page biography for children, but one doesn't expect a sanitized life either.

Meshing the subject with the audience is perhaps the trickiest part of all writing, and it's never more tricky than in children's biography. Stanley and Vennema err by locking Ellen Ternan in the closet, a very Victorian fate, incidentally, right out of *Jane Eyre*, but they succeed in making of Dickens' life a legitimate contender for the attention of kids with Michael Jordan on their minds.

Deborah Stevenson

SOURCE: A review of *Charles Dickens: The Man Who Had Great Expectations*, in *Bulletin of the Center for Children's Books*, Vol. 47, No. 3, November, 1993, pp. 101-02.

The latest in Stanley and Vennema's series of picture-book biographies, this volume depicts the life and career of the famous Victorian writer. The book describes the best of times and the worst of times, from Dickens' childhood to his fantastic adult popularity; it explores the personal (Dickens' unhappy marriage) while remaining conservative (there's no mention of Dickens' possible extramarital involvements), and it mentions the high points of Dickens' literary career and fame rather than merely listing his prolific output, although some explanation of the serial publication of the novels should have appeared. The final authorial summation is more sentimental than is usual for this team, but Dickens can have that effect. The illustrations, with Stanley's signature flattened and stylized figures and historically convincing if too-clean streets, are distant enough to be intriguing but human enough to be engaging, particularly the comic portrait of middle-aged Maria Beadnell making eyes at Mr. Dickens. This is a good introduction to an unnecessarily daunting literary figure—you might want to use it in conjunction with a readaloud of *A Christmas Carol* or another short piece.

Mary Lou Burket

SOURCE: A review of *Charles Dickens: The Man Who Had Great Expectations*, in *The Five Owls*, Vol. VIII, No. 2, November-December, 1993, pp. 36-7.

Much as they did in the excellent *Bard of Avon: The Story of William Shakespeare*, Diane Stanley and Peter Vennema have compressed the life of a major English writer into an engaging picture book. A streamlined text and large pictures that reduce the need for description work efficiently together.

In Stanley's illustration of Charles Dickens's unhappy

marriage ("one of the worst mistakes he ever made"), the couple appear at their dining room table where Charles is sawing away at a burned and shriveled roast. Information is suggested about their relationships (tense and distant), their household (poorly managed), their class (upper middle), and the period (gas lamps, long dress). Not only do we see how people lived in Dickens's day, we see how Dickens himself lived.

This is one of the advantages of art over photography: the pictures tell us what the artist wants to tell us. Nothing is extraneous, and nothing is left out.

As all the world knows, reversals of fortune are the stuff of Dickens's fiction. They also shaped his life. While the authors are somewhat reticent about the pressures and conflicts that drove Dickens, they talk a lot about what happened to him—and what he caused to happen. We learn about his rapid success, his trips to the United States, his famous readings. Most interesting of all is his childhood, shattered by the father who "spent more money than he made."

While *Bard of Avon* seems to me the more shapely and better integrated of the two biographies, there's no doubt that the creator of Scrooge and Oliver Twist is a more likely subject for children. Both books combine the power of "it really happened" with a touch of "let's imagine."

Ann A. Flowers

SOURCE: A review of *Charles Dickens: The Man Who Had Great Expectations,* in *The Horn Book Magazine,* Vol. LXIX, No. 6, November-December, 1993, pp. 756-57.

A fine pictorial biography of Dickens brings his life before the young reader's eyes and does justice to his brilliance and creativity. The authors present Dickens's life as the source material of his famous works with great success, dwelling upon his unhappy experiences as a child and his hard-working youth. Dickens had the unusual opportunity of experiencing how both the extremely poor and the extremely well-to-do lived in the Victorian era. The stories of his achieving his lifelong dream of owning Gad's Hill Place and the ludicrous reappearance in his later life of an early, lost love lend humor and personal feeling to the biography of a giant among authors. Dickens's fame brought him gratification and also unwanted attention, especially on his two trips to the United States, and he drove himself to his death through overwork. His blazing personality—he called himself "The Sparkler"—and his hard work and driving ambition are apparent in the illustrations, which frequently re-create well-known and recorded incidents of his life; the subdued and neutral colors foster the feeling for the period. It is unfortunate that the misspelling of the name Ebenezer—as *Ebineezer*—Scrooge, one of his most famous characters, mars this excellent work.

THE GENTLEMAN AND THE KITCHEN MAID (1994)

Carolyn Phelan

SOURCE: A review of *The Gentleman and the Kitchen Maid,* in *Booklist,* Vol. 90, No. 10, January 15, 1994, pp. 939-40.

In a museum gallery, a young artist copies the Dutch portrait of a young gentleman and becomes aware of what the other portraits in the room have been gossiping about for some time: the gentleman has fallen in love with the kitchen maid whose painting hangs on the opposite wall, and she with him. When the maid's portrait is moved to another gallery the next day, the artist sets things right as only she can—by painting the two together and hanging the picture on the wall of her apartment, where the other subjects of her paintings are more broad-minded than the talking pictures in the museum and their conversation more stimulating. There are so many reasons why this picture book shouldn't work, from the static gallery as setting to the romantic device as motive. But in fact, this fanciful plot works quite well, given children's inclination to see almost any painting as narrative art. Stanley's deft writing sweeps the story along without undo sentimentality, and [Dennis] Nolan's sensitive watercolor illustrations make each portrait in the museum a definite character in the story. An original.

Kirkus Reviews

SOURCE: A review of *The Gentleman and the Kitchen Maid,* in *Kirkus Reviews,* Vol. LXII, No. 6, March 15, 1994, p. 405.

Scene: an elegant museum exhibit where a dapper gentleman (by Frans Hals or Rembrandt?) has long gazed affectionately from his frame at a wholesome lass with a basket of apples (typical Vermeer). Prim burghers in the room's other paintings disparage the inappropriate attachment, but an art student is intrigued. Remarking on their plight, she copies both lovers into a single new composition from which they can look happily into her room at home, where the other paintings are "quite modern and open-minded." Just in time, too: in the museum, the kitchen maid has been moved, leaving her detractors to turn their disdain on a rowdy group scene. The disarming tale brings the 17th-century art to life in an original manner. . . .

Joanne Schott

SOURCE: "Innovative Renovations," in *Quill & Quire,* Vol. 60, No. 4, April, 1994, p. 42.

Imagination, art, and fantasy combine in this story as a young art student brings two unusual lovers together. Paintings of the kitchen maid and the young gentleman have for years hung across from each other in the gallery where Rusty comes to learn by copying the work of Dutch masters. They have fallen in love. The duchess, the stern gentleman in black, and the bearded old man in the gallery's other paintings make no secret about their disapproval of the unsuitability of the match.

Rusty approves, though, as she copies the young gentleman and follows his gaze to the painting of the kitchen maid, who looks back at him with a smile. She notices a sadness in his eyes the next day, however, for the museum staff has moved the maid to another room. Rusty paints hurriedly, leaving out the background, and hastens to the room around the corner. When she hangs her copy of the two lovers united in one painting, the pictures on *her* walls are quite open-minded.

This light-hearted fantasy-romance and the clever solution to thwarted love make a delightful story. In the gallery setting, it takes little suspension of disbelief to accept that paintings talk to each another and express decided opinions.

Shirley Wilton

SOURCE: A review of *The Gentleman and the Kitchen Maid,* in *School Library Journal,* Vol. 40, No. 8, August, 1994, p. 146.

Stanley's imaginative tale, brought to life by [Dennis] Nolan's realistic illustrations, unfolds in a spacious, unnamed museum among a collection of paintings that appear to be by 17th-century Dutch masters. At night, portraits in the styles of Rembrandt, Hals, and others converse and gossip over the romantic feelings of the aristocratic gentleman in one canvas, whose gaze falls steadily on the painting of a kitchen maid across the room. During the day, all is quiet while visitors roam the hall and art students, like the young red-haired woman named Rusty, copy the famous paintings. Rusty notices on a return visit that the gentleman has lost his merry look, and that the kitchen maid has been removed to another gallery. Her solution is ingenious. She copies the maid on the same canvas as the gentleman and, back home on her own apartment walls, the two are forever bound in the same frame, locked in a mutual gaze of affection. This light-hearted story is deftly told and handsomely illustrated. More believable in its fantasy than the elaborate *Rembrandt's Beret* by Johnny Alcorn, it serves the same purpose of adding a dimension of familiarity and human interest to the sometimes intimidating atmosphere of a great art museum.

📖 *CLEOPATRA* (cowritten with husband Peter Vennema, 1994)

Kirkus Reviews

SOURCE: A review of *Cleopatra,* in *Kirkus Reviews,* Vol. LXII, No. 16, August 15, 1994, p. 1140.

Cleopatra was a Greek-descended Egyptian queen near the turn of the first millennium. While Julius Caesar was trying to unite the world under Rome, Cleopatra was harboring similar hopes for Alexandria. When the rulers met, however, they fell in love and attempted to conquer the world together. Cleopatra stayed with Caesar until his death in 44 B.C., and afterwards she began the affair with Mark Antony that would continue until both their deaths. As the authors state in a prefatory note, the sources about Cleopatra—other than Plutarch—are patchy and often negative, having been written by her enemies, and the only pictures we have of her are from the coins minted during her rule. Stanley and Vennema use these sources to try to give an accurate account of Cleopatra's life. In striving for accuracy, however, the authors sacrifice the romance of the story. Stanley's drawings, on the other hand, are exquisitely wrought with vivid color and fine mosaic detail.

Stanley and Vennema's latest illustrated biography is a beautifully decorated, dull account of one of the most powerful women rulers of all time.

Carolyn Phelan

SOURCE: A review of *Cleopatra,* in *Booklist,* Vol. 91, No. 2, September 15, 1994, p. 133.

Using their distinctive picture book biography format made popular in their volumes on Shaka, Shakespeare, and Dickens, Stanley and Vennema present the life of a legend, Cleopatra. The artwork includes full-page paintings of dramatic scenes as well as impressive painted mosaics that make up the jacket art, title page, and the background for the text. The story concerns Cleopatra's life from the age of 18, when she became the queen of Egypt (51 B.C.), through her liaisons with Julius Caesar and Mark Antony, and her struggle to bring back Egypt's former glory, to her death at the age of 39. One of the most impressive qualities of this beautiful book is its recognition of the problems of researching and writing history. Not only does a note introduce Plutarch as the main source, but it also discusses why Plutarch's account may not be entirely reliable. Even in the text, the authors point out areas of doubt or inconsistency. Taken simply as a story, the book has a sumptuous setting, heroic characters, name recognition, high drama, and a tragic ending. An intriguing portrait.

Deborah Stevenson

SOURCE: A review of *Cleopatra,* in *Bulletin of the Center for Children's Books,* Vol. 48, No. 2, October, 1994, pp. 67-8.

The talented picture-book-biography team of Stanley and Vennema here take on one of their most romantic subjects: the famed Cleopatra. The text describes her life and its dramas, including her return to power in Egypt with the help of Julius Caesar, her long affair with him, her union with Mark Antony, her questionable behavior in the naval battle that Rome waged against Egypt, and, finally, her memorable suicide after her capture and Antony's death. 2000-year-old anecdotes being hard to come by, there is less a sense of the character of this subject than in the authors' other works; nonetheless, the book does a good job of expanding a legendary figure into an important historical personage and placing her into context of both past and present. Stanley's flat, stylized art is sometimes a little too flat here, and the colors sometimes lack shading and subtlety, but the historical research shows through in the details, including the decor, tilework, and even Cleopatra's face. The tile-style cover portrait and the subject will lure readers, who will find out more about the lady than most people know.

Carolyn Noah

SOURCE: A review of *Cleopatra,* in *School Library Journal,* Vol. 40, No. 10, October, 1994, p. 140.

"It is traditionally believed that Cleopatra dazzled Caesar with her great beauty. Instead, it was the power of her intelligence and personality that drew him to her." In this lively, well-crafted biography, Stanley and Vennema brush the cobwebs from the popularly held portrait of Cleopatra to reveal a vital, warm, and politically adroit ruler. Lucid writing combines with carefully selected anecdotes, often attributed to the Greek historian Plutarch, to create an engaging narrative. The young queen's marriage to her brother Ptolemy XIII is placed in the context of practices of the rulers of the day. A "Note on Ancient Sources" and a map precede the text; an epilogue, pronunciation guide, and a brief bibliography are appended. Stanley's stunning, full-color gouache artwork is arresting in its large, well-composed images executed in flat Greek style. The palette is as rich and sumptuous as the court at Alexandria. Cover art and endpapers simulate period mosaics; the text is set against a faux-tile backdrop that reinforces the book's design and illustration. The figures of Cleopatra, Julius Caesar, and Mark Antony stride powerfully across scenes of Egypt and the Roman Empire. Finally, Cleopatra emerges as a savvy, astute, and complex leader who followed both her heart and mind.

Mary Breasted

SOURCE: "The Queen and the Mathematician," in *The New York Times Book Review,* November 13, 1994, p. 50.

Children are natural believers in the great-man theory of history. They can scarcely grasp history in any other terms, unless the teacher says there will be costumes. Maybe the amorphous mass of time and humanity that preceded them is so discouragingly irrelevant to their sense of self-importance and so gloomily full of the implication that someday they, like all the others here before them, will die that they would rather not think about it at all.

Provide them, however, with a fabulous hero or a deliciously horrible villain capable of being portrayed in a simple drama and period dress, and they are ready to look at any era. The trick is to get them to think of the past not as a place where dead people live, but rather as the great backstage to the theater of now.

Classical history is thus especially well suited to children, limited as it is to the deeds of the great and famous few, whose apparel, hairdos and weaponry are blessedly easy to put together out of old sheets, ribbons and cardboard.

Cleopatra, by the husband-wife team of Diane Stanley and Peter Vennema, has glorious illustrations done by Ms. Stanley, who clearly loved depicting the lavish artistry of Cleopatra's barge and the luxurious details of her daily life. A feast for the eyes, the book is unfortunately marred by the resentful tone of the text. The driving energy is feminist and angrily defensive in Cleopatra's behalf, which rather weakens the authors' laudable efforts to set the record straight about this extraordinary woman.

We learn from them, for instance, that Cleopatra was a Greek, not an Egyptian, although she is of course famous for having been Queen of Egypt. The poisonous asp that Cleopatra is thought to have put to her breast to kill herself after her lover Mark Antony had fallen on his sword may just be popular legend, the authors say. (I am so glad Shakespeare did not know this. He made such gorgeous use of the sexual connotations an asp offers.)

It is good to have the errors of popular assumption corrected, but the authors have bent the spirit of correction too far in several places to serve the shape of their speculations. They say Cleopatra's "enemies" wrote her story in the past, yet they don't mind quoting Plutarch as if he is to be trusted when he writes flatteringly about her charms and her force of personality. Then they dismiss as uninformed his descriptions of Cleopatra's embarrassing flight from the scene of the battle at Actium, when she took her fleet of ships off at full sail, deserting Antony in the heat of the battle he and Cleopatra had with Octavian. The authors don't mind speculating at this point, without any reference to sources, that Cleopatra was doing the bidding of Antony's generals, in other words secretly helping Antony. But when Antony leaves the scene of the battle himself, they pronounce his action "much more difficult to explain."

The authors portray Antony's subsequent sorrowful withdrawal as evidence of extreme "self-pity," while Cleopatra's conduct is presented as proof of her "amazing powers of recovery." Similarly, Julius Caesar's murder, which came about in part because of his involvement with Cleopatra, is described as her tragedy, not his. Antony's suicide also is depicted as Cleopatra's great loss, not Antony's. Indeed, the authors make his final demise sound like a pleasurable escape: he "found peace in death," while "Cleopatra's trials were not yet over." In other words, the rat deserted her for his sword.

I would recommend this *Cleopatra* with heavy caution. Children need to know that history is always a subjective narrative, but they can take only so much uncertainty about whose version is right before they turn off. They want facts to be facts.

Ann A. Flowers

SOURCE: A review of *Cleopatra,* in *The Horn Book Magazine,* Vol. LXX, No. 6, November-December, 1994, pp. 747-48.

In another splendidly illustrated biography for younger readers, Diane Stanley and Peter Vennema have succeeded brilliantly in bringing the power and magnificence of Cleopatra and her world to life. The book begins with a preface giving careful background information on a complex episode in ancient history, notes on the original sources and their reliability, and a map of the ancient world in 51 B.C. The authors point out that Cleopatra, in spite of her reputation, was not beautiful by our standards and that she was really a Macedonian Greek rather than of Egyptian blood. She is presented as a woman of great ambition, intelligence, vigor, and fascination. In her attempts to return Egypt to its former position of power and to regain its empire, she gained both the love and the political and military support of first Julius Caesar and then Mark Antony, the two greatest leaders of the Roman world. Although her spectacular career ended in defeat and suicide, her overwhelming personality assured her enduring fame. Her compelling story is told in a simple, straightforward text, often focusing on episodes and details of interest to young readers, and carefully pointing out still unsolved ambiguities in the source materials. The dramatic story is given life and excitement by the dazzling illustrations, with massive architecture, rich mosaic designs, noble columns both Egyptian and Roman, Cleopatra's golden barge, Caesar's assassination, and the sometimes brooding, sometimes vivacious, but always extraordinary Cleopatra herself.

📖 *WOE IS MOE* (1995)

Publishers Weekly

SOURCE: A review of *Woe Is Moe,* in *Publishers Weekly,* Vol. 242, No. 11, March 13, 1995, p. 69.

Moe the dog gave his friend Arlene a faux beach in Stanley and [Elise] Primavera's infectiously upbeat *Moe the Dog in Tropical Paradise;* now it's Arlene's turn to surprise Moe. This time, the shaggy brown protagonist invents a slogan for the ice-cream company where he and Arlene work ("Golly wow! Try Frozen Cow! It's the cat's meow!")—and snags a big promotion. Success quickly spoils him—he's so busy hyping product and strutting in his money-green suit that he doesn't have time to meet Arlene at the Happy-All Chinese restaurant; the message on Moe's answering machine, which announces, "If you're calling to request an interview, press 'two' *now,*" emphasizes the distance between him and his best pal. So, with a series of fortune-cookie messages, the lonely Arlene leads Moe on a treasure hunt to the Happy-All, where he

discovers that money is no substitute for friendship. The familiar moral receives a winning treatment in Stanley's skilled hands. . . .

Stephanie Zvirin

SOURCE: A review of *Woe Is Moe,* in *Booklist,* Vol. 91, No. 14, March 15, 1995, p. 1338.

Devoted dog friends first encountered in the delightful ***Moe the Dog in Tropical Paradise*** are back in another entertaining friendship story. Here, Moe's creativity earns him a chance to escape the drudgery at the Frozen Cow ice-cream factory where he and his friend Arlene work. The perks of his new job are great, but the responsibilities strain the friendship. "Woe is Moe" until Arlene comes up with a solution that brings the buddies back together. Stanley's comic view of the modern work ethic is presented simply enough that most kids will catch on, but even those who don't will grasp the friendship message. . . . Not as spunky as ***Tropical Paradise,*** but still lots of wacky fun.

Karen James

SOURCE: A review of *Woe Is Moe,* in *School Library Journal,* Vol. 41, No. 6, June, 1995, p. 96.

Moe and Arlene, two canine friends, work at the Frozen Cow ice-cream factory. They hate their jobs, since Frozen Cow is the worst ice cream ever made, but at least they get to work together. At the end of the week, they share simple pleasures, eating at Mr. Chang's Happy-All Chinese restaurant, going to the movies, and watching the night sky from a park bench. When Moe wins a Frozen Cow slogan contest and is appointed vice president in charge of advertising, things change. He no longer has time to spend with his pal. Despite his new jet-setting lifestyle, he is lonely—until Arlene, who has left the factory to become the fortune-cookie baker at Happy-All, takes the initiative to reestablish their friendship. While there may be a moral here for baby-boomers on the fast track, Stanley wisely sticks to simply telling the story, using the same clear, unembellished prose that is so successful in her nonfiction titles. . . . On one level, this is a story about the importance of friendship; it could also be a useful discussion-starter for exploring ideas about values.

📖 *THE TRUE ADVENTURE OF DANIEL HALL* (1995)

Kirkus Reviews

SOURCE: A review of *The True Adventures of Daniel Hall,* in *Kirkus Reviews,* Vol. LXIV, No. 14, July 15, 1995, p. 1030.

Stanley retells the wild adventures of Daniel Hall, seaman

from New Bedford, Mass. The year is 1856 and Daniel, at the ripe old age of 14, ships out aboard the whaler *Condor*. The voyage is scheduled to last three years, but Daniel cuts his journey short when he flees the ship (and the brutal ministrations of the sadistic captain) while on the chilly eastern coast of Siberia. With a little help from the Yakut people, Daniel survives eight months of mean winter, and is ultimately returned to New Bedford on another whaler. In less adept hands, this would have been but another cruel tale, but Stanley's nimble touch keeps melodrama at bay, provides intriguing glimpses into whaling life, and renders lovely, age-worn pastel illustrations that look as though they were lifted from 19th-century cameos. An example of her care is the inset maps that appear on a number of the pages to show Daniel's location at a given time. A book as quick on its feet and as engaging, as real, as its young hero.

Patricia Manning

SOURCE: A review of *The True Adventure of Daniel Hall,* in *School Library Journal,* Vol. 41, No. 9, September, 1995, p. 216.

Using an 1861 autobiographical work by Hall called *Arctic Rovings,* Stanley has provided modern readers with a brief look at an exciting, true adventure. Rejecting a clerking career, Daniel, 14, signed on a New Bedford, MA, whaling ship for a perilous three-year voyage. Though accepting of hard work and uncomfortable conditions, the teen innocently incurred his captain's ill will. Suffering mental and physical abuse, he and a young companion deserted on the bleak Siberian shore, where they endured a brutal winter and were aided by inmates of a prison colony. They were rescued in the spring and Daniel was eventually reunited with his widower father. An afterword completes what is known about Hall's later life. Dramatic pastel illustrations complement the composed text, giving young readers visual images of towering masts, snarling wolf packs, and harpooned whales spouting blood. The large format may prove a tad off-putting to some older readers who would truly be amazed at Daniel's adventures, but should please youngsters looking for a nifty piece of nonfiction to whet their imaginations.

Janice Del Negro

SOURCE: A review of *The True Adventure of Daniel Hall,* in *Booklist,* Vol. 92, No. 2, September 15, 1995, p. 157.

It is nineteenth-century New England, and 14-year-old Daniel Hall wants to go to sea. With the reluctant blessings of his father, he signs on for a three-year term on the whaling ship *Condor*. Daniel gladly endures cramped quarters, grueling work, and storms at sea, only to be so badly mistreated by the captain that he and a friend jump ship in the Siberian wilderness. An adaptation of *Arctic Rovings; or, The Adventures of a New Bedford Boy on Sea and Land,* this short picture-book biography is an

easy booktalk with a guaranteed audience. Stanley's watercolor illustrations include enough maps, sailing ships, whales, and wolves to please even the most demanding adventure lovers; the elegant design and accessible format will attract reluctant readers, while the well-written, absorbing content will keep them happily involved.

Elizabeth Bush

SOURCE: A review of *The True Adventure of Daniel Hall,* in *Bulletin of the Center for Children's Books,* Vol. 49, No. 3, November, 1995, p. 106.

Independent readers and even some younger listeners will find plenty of action in this fact-based account of a fifteen-year-old's first voyage on a whaling ship. Surviving stormy seas and perilously exciting whale hunts, Daniel is finally broken in body and spirit by the vicious attacks of Captain Whiteside. He and a mate abandon ship on the Siberian coast, only to face illness, hard labor, wolves, and bears before eventual rescue. The text, substantial for a picture book, sails right along, and Stanley does a fine job of putting nineteenth-century attitudes toward whaling into perspective. Her signature artwork is somewhat over-tidy for this rough-edged story. The deck that "became a slippery mess of grease and gore" as the whale carcass is processed could merit a Good Housekeeping seal, and Daniel's cabin in Oudski is portrayed as a spacious and comfortable hideaway. In itself, the overall design is crisp and appealing; atop each text page a medallion features an image from Daniel's adventures or a map that shows how heartbreakingly far from home Daniel is at that point. A postscript relates the demise of Captain Whiteside's career, the few known facts concerning Daniel's later years, and the source from which the tale is drawn.

Elizabeth S. Watson

SOURCE: A review of *The True Adventure of Daniel Hall,* in *The Horn Book Magazine,* Vol. LXXI, No. 6, November-December, 1995, p. 758.

Contributing to her fine repertoire of books featuring lesser-known historical figures, the author tells of a fourteen-year-old seaman named Daniel Hall, who left his New Bedford, Massachusetts, home in 1856 on a whaling voyage that would last for four years. Daniel was a good sailor but unfortunately incurred the wrath of the captain, who began to harass him unmercifully, using any excuse to beat the boy. How Daniel survived to finally achieve vindication against the cruel captain makes a wonderful adventure expertly illustrated by the artist's spectacularly rich pastel illustrations. Because Daniel eventually deserted the ship on the coast of Siberia, the book has chilled forest landscapes as well as magnificent seascapes, in addition to its beautifully graphic renderings of riggings and ship interiors. Each double-page spread includes a full-page painting on the left and a small insert on the right above the block of text. The inserts contain maps that help the reader to keep track of Daniel's journey or small details of the larger paintings. For all the readers who ask for "adventure stories," this one—based on a longer work by Daniel Hall himself—will hit the spot.

☐ *ELENA (1996)*

Elizabeth Bush

SOURCE: A review of *Elena,* in *Bulletin of the Center for Children's Books,* Vol. 49, No. 7, March, 1996, p. 243.

Stanley reimagines events from the family history of her mother's friend, fictitiously renamed Elena here, who fled from Mexico to California during the Mexican Civil War. Despite the tale's complicated and personal pedigree, there is much here to intrigue young readers—military occupation, threat of abduction by the rebel army, deathbed prophecies fulfilled. However, readers must wade through a prelude of details about Elena's early life before they hit the drama. Although these details are intended to establish Elena's strength of character, her childhood pursuit of education and teenage defiance of her father are never directly linked to the decisions she makes as a widow to remove her children from their war-ravaged country. Subject matter which should appeal to a middle-school audience is delivered in clipped sentences and simplified vocabulary more appropriate to younger readers. Historical notes and an introduction to the "real" Elena's family are included.

Hazel Rochman

SOURCE: A review of *Elena,* in *Booklist,* Vol. 92, No. 15, April 1, 1996, p. 1366.

Based on true events, this story is set around the time of the Mexican Revolution. Growing up in a wealthy home in the mountains of Jalisco, Mexico, Elena rejects the traditional passive woman's role prescribed for her. She learns to read and to do math, and later she overcomes her father's opposition and insists on marrying the man she wants. Her husband dies, and when civil war breaks out, she finds the strength to take her family on a dangerous journey across the border to the U.S. The story is told in the voice of Elena's daughter, who becomes a "real" American but knows that her independent mother always feels caught between Mexico and California. Stanley is a fine biographer for the middle grades. This is her first fiction book, and it reads almost as a short outline for a novel or as family folklore. We are told about Elena's conflicts, but there's little character development. The setting and the events are the drama.

Publishers Weekly

SOURCE: A review of *Elena,* in *Publishers Weekly,* Vol. 243, No. 18, April 29, 1996, p. 73.

Author and illustrator of numerous acclaimed picture-book biographies, Stanley turns her talents to preserving a more personal history, the experiences of a friend of her mother's. The sheltered daughter of a prosperous Mexican family, Elena has aspirations higher than those of her four sisters. While they concentrate on singing and embroidery, Elena studies secretly with a priest and learns to love books and "master the magic of numbers." Later, she refuses her father's attempts to marry her to a landowner's son and is finally given permission to marry her true love. Years later, during the Mexican Revolution, her determination stands her in good stead; widowed, she and her children escape from their beloved but pitifully ravaged country to carve a new life in California. Stanley's spare, graceful prose shapes a credible portrait of a person of singular insight and courage. Given the narrative's dearth of young characters and solitary focus on a grown woman, mature young adults and adults rather than middle-graders will be the most appreciative audience for this book. The format, however, may be problematic: the brevity of the text, printed in large type on small pages, could leave bookstore browsers wondering whether they're getting enough book for the buck.

☐ *LEONARDO DA VINCI* (1996)

Publishers Weekly

SOURCE: A review of *Leonardo da Vinci,* in *Publishers Weekly,* Vol. 243, No. 28, July 8, 1996, p. 84.

Adding this Renaissance genius to the illustrious lineup of individuals whose lives she and Peter Vennema have chronicled, among them Cleopatra, Charles Dickens and William Shakespeare, Stanley produces her most stunning pictorial biography to date. Drawing from a range of sources, including her subject's extensive notebooks, Stanley's conversational narrative describes Leonardo da Vinci's astoundingly far-reaching and varied achievements. Young readers will come to appreciate both da Vinci's universally renowned accomplishments as a painter and the breadth of his scientific experimentation and research. While her text is thoroughly intriguing, even more impressive is the artistic challenge Stanley takes on and triumphantly meets: her paintings not only portray the period particulars and likenesses of da Vinci, his patrons and colleagues, but successfully incorporate, in seamless collages, miniature reproductions of such celebrated masterpieces as *The Last Supper* and the *Mona Lisa.* These exquisite reproductions, as well as sepia-toned spot art taken from da Vinci's notebooks, sit uncommonly well within Stanley's own paintings, educating the reader about da Vinci's masterpieces as a natural part of the visual storytelling. A virtuosic work.

Kirkus Reviews

SOURCE: A review of *Leonardo da Vinci,* in *Kirkus Reviews,* Vol. LXIV, No. 14, July 15, 1996, p. 1056.

Stanley goes to great lengths to portray Leonardo da Vinci

as a real person, explaining how his genius often went unrecognized by the generations that followed his. His out-of-wedlock birth prevented him from entering upper-class professions (law, medicine, or banking), so Leonardo became an artist by trade. He had difficulty completing the arduous task of painting: His restlessness comes across through the hundreds of inventions and ideas recorded in his notebooks, at least a third of which, readers may be surprised to learn, have been lost. In fact, much of what Leonardo is known for is incomplete or lost: A giant bronze statue of Francesco Sforza on horseback was never made, and the experimental paint Leonardo used for *The Last Supper* began peeling not long after the painting's completion.

Stanley's large, accessible art mirrors the mood of the Renaissance. Insets help readers see what the text describes, and a thorough bibliography provides sources for more information. More than Leonardo's genius, this book captures the caprice time and fate plays on even the gifted, so that what readers finally admire in Leonardo are not his creations, but his ideas.

Deborah Stevenson

SOURCE: A review of *Leonardo da Vinci*, in *Bulletin of the Center for Children's Books*, Vol. 50, No. 1, September, 1996, p. 32.

Stanley, sometimes aided by her husband Peter Vennema, has capably biographized historical figures ranging from Cleopatra to Peter the Great; here she turns to one of the greatest minds and most celebrated painters of the millennium. She not only explores Leonardo's life and achievements but also the Florentine culture that both offered Leonardo opportunities and circumscribed them. Her descriptions of various artistic processes (the casting of sculptures, the elaborate preparations for an oil painting) are clear and concise, and they gain interest from their relevance to Leonardo's character (the artist several times failed to carry a work through to completion, suggesting a greater interest in planning than finishing) and to real-life exigencies (Leonardo's patron used his bronze supply for cannon rather than to mold Leonardo's planned statue of a horse). Though she keeps speculation to a minimum, Stanley conveys a sense of Leonardo as a man—audacious, arrogant, brilliant, and thoughtful—by judicious inclusion of his own writings and the words of those responding to him and to his work. (She doesn't, however, address the question of Leonardo's sexual orientation, though she does refer to his close relationships with several young male artists.) Stanley's mixed-media art uses muted colors and her usual flat and distanced style; it's doubtful that Renaissance Italy was as tidy as it looks here, but the art conveys a different world and also offers a dramatic contrast to the genuine da Vinci art that is not only reproduced in vignettes but also included appropriately within the narrative scenes. Without being overstuffed, oversimplified, or over the heads of the audience, this makes it elegantly clear what Leonardo accomplished and why his fame

endures. A historical postscript and a bibliography are included.

📖 *SAVING SWEETNESS* (1996)

Ursula Adams

SOURCE: A review of *Saving Sweetness,* in *Children's Book Review Service,* Vol. 25, No. 7, February, 1997, p. 79.

It's the sheriff's job to return Sweetness to the orphanage from where she ran away. He also must protect her from the mean outlaw Coyote Pete. Sweetness cleverly escapes the sheriff several times and in an interesting twist saves the sheriff from Coyote Pete. The kind-hearted sheriff ultimately adopts her and the other orphans thus rescuing them from the nasty Mrs. Sump. Told from the sheriff's point of view, the book is written in old Western dialect and includes many humorous sayings.

Martha Davis Beck

SOURCE: A review of *Saving Sweetness,* in *The Five Owls,* Vol. XI, No. 4, April, 1997, p. 84.

With the plight of neglected children a persistent sore spot in our consciousness—and a frequent serious theme in children's books—this comic tale of a resourceful runaway orphan is sweet medicine. Written by the versatile Diane Stanley, **Saving Sweetness** is set in the Wild West and features a cast of types. The story's tone and the unambiguous character of its players are conveyed in colorful rural vernacular by the narrator, the kindhearted sheriff in the dusty Texas outpost where the action is set.

Sweetness is the name of the "ittiest bittiest" resident of an orphanage run by mean old Mrs. Sump, a woman "nasty enough to scare night into day." She disciplines the children by having them scrub the floor with toothbrushes. When Sweetness runs away, the sheriff is called into pursuit, to rescue her from the desert and the likely clutches of the outlaw Coyote Pete, a character "as mean as an acre of rattlesnakes."

The humor builds as the sheriff, an absentminded fellow, neglects to bring food or water along on his sojourn through the desert, and is repeatedly "saved" by the tyke he is seeking. She appears first with a canteen of water; later she toasts marshmallows for him on a fire; finally she knocks out Coyote Pete with a large rock, just as he is about to shoot the sheriff. Through all this, the sheriff appears not to realize who's doing the rescuing. But Sweetness has the last word: she convinces the sheriff to become her Pa. . . .

Saving Sweetness is a tall tale shrunk down to a modest size, just right for relating the plight of a plucky little girl, and for tickling the funny bones of readers in the mood for a Wild West yarn.

📖 *RUMPELSTILTSKIN'S DAUGHTER* (1997)

Kirkus Reviews

SOURCE: A review of *Rumpelstiltskin's Daughter,* in *Kirkus Reviews,* Vol. LXV, No. 4, February 15, 1997, p. 306.

A feminist revision of Rumpelstiltskin, in which the small man and the miller's daughter marry and raise a daughter, Hope, who finds herself in the same room of straw her mother once faced. She tricks the king out of his selfish ways, by making him provide for his subjects, who then raise golden wheat in the fields, and dress in golden wool knit clothes. The king realizes that generosity brings far more wealth than mere gold can; Hope becomes the country's prime minister. Stanley plugs in quips and fast plot maneuvers to keep this tale hopping, but it's the detailed, humorous illustrations that will entice readers, for she slightly alters her familiar style to encompass the comic pitch. Those who like Babette Cole's send-ups will find plenty of giggles in this reworking.

Publishers Weekly

SOURCE: A review of *Rumpelstiltskin's Daughter,* in *Publishers Weekly,* Vol. 244, No. 7, February 17, 1997, p. 219.

Stanley blazes a new path for herself in this effervescent revisionist fairy tale, and the results are as stunning as her best picture-book biographies (**Leonardo da Vinci; Bard of Avon**). Here she brings her meticulous illustrator's eye for detail to bear upon a fantasy kingdom that exists somewhere between Versailles and high farce, projecting an ornately imagined setting for a tale that scores a few serious points as it pokes fun at a nursery room favorite. This miller's daughter can't imagine why anyone would want to marry the money-loving king, and she feels grateful for the short little man who has saved her life by spinning straw into gold. When he bargains for her firstborn child, she is only too glad to counter-offer with a proposal of marriage ("I like your ideas on parenting, you'd make a good provider, and I have a weakness for short men"). Sixteen years later, the couple's daughter proves equally independent-minded when the king approaches *her*. The art is even more winning than the story: the king's palace is filled with famous works of art, e.g., the Mona Lisa, all featuring the vain monarch in place of their actual subjects; spreads spoof the *Très Riches Heures*—and the prevailing loony lavishness will tickle those who don't get the visual allusions. A 24-karat prize.

Ellen J. Brooks

SOURCE: A review of *Rumpelstiltskin's Daughter,* in *Children's Book Review Service,* Vol. 25, No. 10, May, 1997, p. 117.

It's the classic story of Rumpelstiltskin, but with a new twist and a more contemporary tone. The miller's daughter develops a fondness for Rumpelstiltskin, admitting her weakness for short men and admiring his ideas about parenting and his ability to be a good provider. The two marry and have a beautiful, clever daughter. Their daughter is a feminist at heart, and as the story unfolds, life in the kingdom improves and the king learns a few lessons. An engaging and imaginative story that will spark interest and discussion. The colored pencil and collage illustrations are rich in detail and feeling.

Additional coverage of Stanley's life and career is contained in the following sources published by Gale Research: *Contemporary Authors New Revision Series,* Vol. 32; *Something about the Author,* Vol. 80; and *Something about the Author Autobiography Series,* Vol. 15.

Hans Wilhelm

1945-

German author and illustrator of picture books and non-fiction.

Major works include *The Trapp Family Book* (1983), *Tales from the Land Under My Table* (1983), *A New Home, A New Friend* (1985), *I'll Always Love You* (1985), *Let's Be Friends Again!* (1986).

INTRODUCTION

Praised for his entertaining, instructive books for children, Wilhelm has written and illustrated both realistic and fanciful stories for primary graders around the world. He has also provided pictures for the works of other writers for children, including Eve Merriam, Joseph Rosenbloom, and Jean Marzollo. In his family stories, Wilhelm focuses on childhood experiences like the death of a dog or a move to a new home, treating sensitive subjects with honesty and tenderness. His appealing works of fantasy frequently center on endearing animal characters such as the clever young dragon Boland and Franklin, a uniquely tidy pig. Perhaps Wilhelm's most memorable character is the big, white, shaggy dog Waldo, who first appeared in *A New Home, A New Friend* and returned for several more adventures. The popular "Waldo" has also lent his image to toys, calendars, cards, book clubs, and even a television show. Wilhelm's art, characteristically consisting of watercolors with pen and ink, has been variously described as warm, humorous, bright, and affectionate. Wilhelm is also noted for *The Trapp Family Book*, his biography of the family portrayed in the film *Sound of Music*.

Biographical Information

Born in postwar Germany, Wilhelm grew up in the countryside where he vented his feelings and frustrations through drawing and secretly reading American magazines about Mickey Mouse and Prince Valiant. Following in his banker father's footsteps, however, he prepared for a career as a businessman with proper college credentials and a commercial apprenticeship. In the evenings he enrolled in art courses for his own pleasure. At the age of nineteen, Wilhelm astounded his parents by announcing that, upon graduation, he intended to move to South Africa. For ten years, he worked in Johannesburg as a sales manager of magnetic tapes, enjoying his freedom and independence, the natural beauty of the country, and opportunities for travel and cultural pursuits, including painting. Through his friendship with a fellow German, Helme Heine, Wilhelm found his artistic urges rekindled. As the political climate in South Africa worsened, Wilhelm—an outspoken critic of apartheid—sold all his possessions and

set off for the next several years across Australia, Asia, the United States, and Europe, looking for a place to settle down. When his idea for a book of cartoons on the Chinese horoscope met with success in England and was published, he subsequently moved to New York to begin his lifelong dream of writing and illustrating books for children.

Major Works

Tales from the Land Under My Table, Wilhelm's first published collection of children's stories, consists of four tales about a covetous giant and a clever stranger, a grumpy king and his jester, a battle between cabbages and cucumbers, and a bird who yearned to be beautiful. The first of the popular Waldo books, *A New Home, A New Friend*, tells of Michael, who dreads moving and having to leave behind all of his friends, only to discover the new place isn't so bad after he makes a new friend, an irresistible, tall, white dog with a bushy tail. One of Wilhelm's most highly praised books, *I'll Always Love You*, was based on the author's own dog, Elfie. In this sensitive story, a young boy grieves over the death of the family pet, recalling happy memories while finding comfort in knowing he had told the dog he loved her every night. In a sequel, *Let's Be Friends Again!,* a brother explodes when his young sister lets his pet turtle go, but subsequently forgives her—highlighting a theme critics encounter infrequently in children's books. A departure from Wilhelm's realistic and fanciful stories, *The Trapp Family Book* is a biography of the intrepid governess Maria and her life with Baron von Trapp and his gifted children, all immortalized in the Julie Andrews musical, *Sound of Music.*

Awards

The Trapp Family Book was named Best Book of the Year by the West German publication *Eltern* in 1983, and *Tales from the Land Under My Table* was selected one of *Time* magazine's Best Children's Books that same year. *A New Home, A New Friend* received a Children's Book Award from the International Reading Association in 1986, while *Let's Be Friends Again!* was chosen one of the Child Study Association of America's Children's Books of the Year in 1987. *I'll Always Love You* received a *Books Can Develop Empathy* award in 1990.

TITLE COMMENTARY

📖 *TALES FROM THE LAND UNDER MY TABLE* (1983)

Elaine Edelman

SOURCE: A review of *Tales from the Land Under My Table,* in *The New York Times Book Review,* December 11, 1983, p. 44.

The opening sentence of the first of these four short fables—"A long time ago there lived a cruel and greedy king named King Cabbage"—sets the tone for the book.

Hans Wilhelm claims it's under his dinner table that he dreamed up the small, good creatures who, without too much trouble, outwit evil forces to prove again that Little is not Insignificant.

Life's endless power struggle, as Mr. Wilhelm tells it, wears a silly grin and is chewable by milk-teeth. Take King Cabbage's attempt to conquer all the other vegetables, which is only finally foiled by a tiny, nameless worm. This worm is no David gunning for Goliath; he merely happens to live inside a cucumber the king has gobbled. And he's only doing his natural thing as he eats his way out of the king who has eaten him, freeing himself and finishing off King Cabbage. There's also a terrible giant brought low by a clever pussycat and a small gray bird named Harold who has trouble with self-esteem. When Harold trades his native talent (singing) for bright feathers so he can look like the other birds, the identity lesson gets heavy.

We don't come to know the folks in these tiny sitcoms well enough to love them dearly, but Mr. Wilhelm's way with his paintbrush is bright and so full of sweetness it nearly doesn't matter. His friendly farmyard and vegetable creatures cavort so gaily through their titanic struggles, they almost persuade us about wishes and horses—that even the littlest among us may learn to harness both.

Maria Salvadore

SOURCE: A review of *Tales from the Land Under My Table,* in *School Library Journal,* Vol. 30, No. 6, February, 1984, p. 64.

Four original tales are presented from the ***Land Under My Table,*** where "we can dream up stories, have magical adventures, and meet all sorts of wonderful creatures." **"King Cabbage"** is the story of a leafy tyrant who meets a well-deserved end from a tiny, hungry worm. One unnecessary bit of gore is an unfortunate inclusion: King Cabbage leads his rotund cabbage troops with a blood-dripping sword held firmly in his hand. In **"Giant Mountain,"** a bright cat outwits a homely, thieving giant and returns the animal-villagers' wealth to them. **"The Little Gray Bird"** is dissatisfied with his plain appearance until he learns the price of freedom. In the final story Maurice, a mouse, serves as King Lester's court jester. When a song is needed for visiting royalty, Maurice's feathered friends rally around him to create "The Song." The stories are clichéd and a bit didactic but light and brief. Expressive, colorful, cartoon-like creatures fill the pages, adding humor and movement.

📖 *THE TRAPP FAMILY BOOK* (1983)

E. Colwell

SOURCE: A review of *The Trapp Family Book,* in *The Junior Bookshelf,* Vol. 48, No. 3, June, 1984, p. 135.

This is the story of the *real* family Trapp, made famous by the musical *The Sound of Music.* It is difficult to dissociate the real people from the actors who took their parts and it comes as a double shock, therefore, to see them depicted as burlesque and comic figures in the coloured drawings. The true story of the family's escape from enemy-occupied Austria is indeed stranger than the fictitious one and the aftermath is a tribute to their courage and talent. Their last concert was given almost thirty years ago, and the members of the Trapp family are scattered far and wide, but their name has not been forgotten as an example of what happened to one family in a time of war.

📖 *BLACKBERRY INK* (written by Eve Merriam, 1985)

Publishers Weekly

SOURCE: A review of *Blackberry Ink,* in *Publishers*

Weekly, Vol. 227, No. 20, May 17, 1985, pp. 117-18.

Wilhelm's colorful pictures, full of beans, match the spirit in Merriam's new collection of poems. Suggested by topics familiar to small children, the pithy verses lift off with a paean to berry-picking: "Look at my mouth, / It's huckleberry purple. / Look at my tongue, / It's blackberry ink." Dizzy Bella is one of the types kids will love to laugh at, seeing her striding through a storm with a new umbrella she won't use. Closed tight, the umbrella is tucked under Bella's arm while her socks grow soggy, her glasses get foggy, until "All she could speak was a weak *kachoo*! / But Bella's umbrella / Stayed nice and new." A pizza with everything, a hole in a pocket, a cat's tongue, a night light, snow and lots of other things are transformed into rollicking amusements by the poet and illustrator.

Carolyn Phelan

SOURCE: A review of *Blackberry Ink,* in *Booklist,* Vol. 81, No. 21, July, 1985, p. 1558.

An agreeable collection of . . . light poems for reading aloud, this has the look and appeal of a picture book. The teddy bear dripping with blackberry juice on the cover reappears throughout the book, providing unity to the poems, which are linked by tone rather than by subject. Merriam is playing with words here, bouncing rhythms and juggling rhymes. There's the feel of an insouciant child on a very familiar playground, and indeed some of the poems bounce along like jump-rope rhymes. While not as technically proficient as the verse, the watercolor illustrations are a good match in humor, verve, and innocent enjoyment. The bouyancy of the artist's conception and the clean, open look of the pages add to the book's appeal. Merriam is a poet sure of her craft and capable of committing nonsense with style.

Susan Scheps

SOURCE: A review of *Blackberry Ink,* in *School Library Journal,* Vol. 32, No. 1, September, 1985, p. 122.

These . . . simple poems touch everyday objects and occurrences—elusive butterflies, seasonal happenings, favorite foods, bedtime routine, animal antics and more. They overflow with descriptive rhythms and rhymes both pure and nonsensical. The smiling teddy on the cover appears throughout the pages in the midst of charming watercolor illustrations featuring delightfully devilish children and whimsical animals. Merriam's poems are great fun to read. They may even make children want to grab a pen (and some blackberry ink?) and write a few of their own! Sure to tickle small funnybones everywhere and to provide many moments of pleasure.

A NEW HOME, A NEW FRIEND (1985)

Publishers Weekly

SOURCE: A review of *A New Home, a New Friend,* in *Publishers Weekly,* Vol. 227, No. 24, June 14, 1985, p. 73.

Wilhelm contributes sparkle and fun to Meritales, designed for reading aloud to the tinies. The hero and best friend of Michael is Waldo, a huge dog who knows it's scary to move far from home into a strange, big, empty house. Michael trusts his mother who assures him that the new place will be fine, once they settle in. But it sure is quiet and gloomy right now. In the backyard, though, Michael meets Waldo. The poor dog is sad; he needs a bath and love that he gets and returns, helping Michael to unpack his things and make his room inviting with familiar toys and books. Then the two companions have a high old time, exploring the house which is now home, thanks to Waldo. Color-filled pictures illustrate this Meritale and a sequel, *Don't Give Up, Josephine!*

I'LL ALWAYS LOVE YOU (1985)

Ilene Cooper

SOURCE: A review of *I'll Always Love You,* in *Booklist,* Vol. 82, No. 5, November 1, 1985, p. 415.

The narrator is a young boy who loves Elfie—"the best dog in the whole world." The soft watercolor illustrations show some of the good times the boy and Elfie have together, playing knights, enjoying a birthday, and dressing up. Although everyone in the family loves Elfie, the boy is the only one who tells her. As the years go by, Elfie gets rounder as the boy gets taller. She has less and less energy and soon cannot even climb the stairs. The vet says she is just getting old but that does not make the boy love her less. One day Elfie does not wake up. The family grieves, and the boy, who has always told Elfie how much he loves her, finds solace in the fact. Though someone offers the boy a new pet, he knows he is not ready for it. But when he is, he will always remember to say, "I love you." Wilhelm's sweet message is an important one for children (as well as adults!). This will be a good book to use with children who have suffered the recent death of a pet or those with an aging animal. The pictures have a piquant charm of their own and convey both humor and sorrow.

Pat Pearl

SOURCE: A review of *I'll Always Love You,* in *School Library Journal,* Vol. 32, No. 4, December, 1985, p. 84.

In this gentle, moving story, Elfie, a dachshund, and her special boy progress happily through life together. When she is young, Elfie is full of pep and pranks; but as her master grows taller and taller, Elfie grows fatter and slow-

Five little monsters
By the light of the moon
Stirring pudding with
A wooden pudding spoon.
The first one says,
"It mustn't be runny."
The second one says,
"That would make it taste funny."
The third one says,
"It mustn't be lumpy."
The fourth one says,
"That would make me grumpy."
The fifth one smiles,
Hums a little tune,
And licks all the drippings
From the wooden pudding spoon. ✧

From Blackberry Ink, *written by Eve Merriam. Illustrated by Hans Wilhelm.*

er. One morning Elfie does not wake up. The family grieves and buries her, and the boy refuses a new puppy. He is not yet ready for another pet; but when he is, he will tell that one, as he told Elsie every night, "I'll always love you." The watercolor illustrations, tender and warm in color and mood and cozily rounded in form, suit the simple text perfectly. Elsie's gradual change from a lively mischief-maker to a portly old dog is treated with a sweet humor. [Judith] Viorst's *The Tenth Good Thing About Barney* and [Miriam] Cohen's *Jim's Dog Muffins* also treat the loss of a beloved pet with great understanding, but anyone who has or ever had an old dog in the family will be especially touched by this book.

Zena Sutherland

SOURCE: A review of *I'll Always Love You*, in *Bulletin of the Center for Children's Books*, Vol. 39, No. 5, January, 1986, p. 100.

"This is a story about Elfie—the best dog in the whole world." Since pets are often a child's introduction to the wonders of birth and the sadness of death, the young narrator's account is most appropriate for sharing with listeners bound to experience the aging of their animals. Gentle, appealing watercolors and a brief text unfold the friendship of a puppy, Elfie, and his boy as they both learn to pee in the right place, romp, rest, and dream

together. When Elfie gets older and rounder, his boy must carry her up the stairs to bed, yet never forgets to say "I'll always love you" every night. That's what makes it easier in the end, when Elfie dies in her sleep, and that's what will leave children with a renewed commitment to all creatures small. Wilhelm displays a graphic sense of dogginess in scenes of Elfie's mischief and amusing reluctance to move out of comfortable positions as time wears on. Like [Judith] Viorst's *Tenth Good Thing About Barney* and its successors, this will have an assured spot in family reading.

Janet Hickman

SOURCE: A review of *I'll Always Love You*, in *Language Arts*, Vol. 63, No. 1, January, 1986, p. 90.

In this story a little boy remembers his dog Elfie, who has died. In the best tradition of books that help children deal with the death of a pet, this one focuses on the good times yet doesn't ignore the grief. The whole family " . . . buried Elfie together. We all cried and hugged each other." The little boy turns down his neighbor's offer of a new puppy. What helps him most is " . . . to remember that I had told her every night, 'I'll always love you.'"

The warmth, humor, and real affection in the illustrations balance the somber topic. Elfie and her boy are babies together and grow up together, Elfie growing rounder while the boy grows taller. Their play and Elfie's escapades are pictured in soft watercolors, often against a white background that accentuates the dog's plump lines. Special appeal lies in the range of Elfie's canine expressions, from blissful sleep to the fierce determination of digging in mother's flower garden. An eloquent back view shows boy and dog sharing his coat against an autumn wind. This is a book that can help children rehearse or rethink losses of their own as it encourages them to share stories of the pets that they will always love.

Jill Bennett

SOURCE: A review of *I'll Always Love You,* in *Books for Keeps,* No. 42, January, 1987, p. 7.

A touching but not over sentimental story in words and pictures of a boy and his relationship with his dog. It works on several levels; as well as showing the fun of having a dog and the amusing mishaps that can occur, the book also deals with the inevitable growing old and death of a pet. The first person narrative style is most effective in conveying the love of boy for dog and the importance to the narrator of having expressed that love out loud. The author's own paintings of the ever more rotund Elfie and her master and family bring just the right touch of humour and sensitivity.

📖 *LET'S BE FRIENDS AGAIN!* (1986)

Kirkus Reviews

SOURCE: A review of *Let's Be Friends Again!,* in *Kirkus Reviews,* Vol. LIV, No. 14, July 15, 1986, p. 1122.

According to the author, this story should help the growing child reinforce his "natural, loving instinct to forgive."

A small boy tells how his little sister let his pet turtle loose in a pond, thinking it needed more exercise. Furious, he wants to kill her. He goes to his room and imagines ways to punish her, taking out his anger by crying, punching his pillow, and making himself sick. At last he knows what to do: he takes his sister's hand and says, "By the way, the thing about the turtle is OK. I'm not angry anymore." Then, hand in hand, they go to buy two hamsters, one for him and one for her. Soft watercolor illustrations are sweet, but have a greeting-card quality with a smiling boy, girl, dog and frog, and a rosy sunset for the finale. Unconvincing.

Publishers Weekly

SOURCE: A review of *Let's Be Friends Again!,* in *Publishers Weekly,* Vol. 230, No. 8, August 22, 1986, p. 96.

Let's Be Friends Again takes sibling conflict seriously,

presenting an undiluted portrait of a boy's rage at his younger sister. Wilhelm makes the sister's transgression substantial: she decides to give her brother's pet turtle some exercise by setting him free in the pond. When the boy finds out what she's done, he exclaims: "I was madder than I'd ever been before. I could have killed her right there and then." He doesn't kill her, but he imagines various gruesome punishments that he feels would befit a turtle-liberating sister. Finally, he lets off steam by pounding on his pillow. His anger dissipated, he is able to be friendly with his sister again. This valuable book will help children understand that anger is a normal, manageable emotion.

Virginia Opocensky

SOURCE: A review of *Let's Be Friends Again!,* in *School Library Journal,* Vol. 33, No. 4, December, 1986, pp. 96-7.

Little sisters are a mixed blessing, according to this young narrator. But the last straw is when she decides that his turtle needs more exercise and turns it loose in a pond. The boy fantasizes about all sorts of ways to punish his sister. He punches his pillow and screams until he feels better. Finally, he is ready to make friends with her again, and off they go hand-in-hand to buy a hamster for each of them. Wilhelm's simply told story will strike a chord of understanding among preschoolers who have siblings. The watercolor illustrations, unframed on broad white pages with a few words, are expressive in their simplicity, helping to convey the message of forgive and forget. This is a pleasant addition to the sibling rivalry list, presenting a slightly different aspect of the subject. . . .

📖 *PIRATES AHOY!* (1987; British edition as *Pigs Ahoy!,* 1990)

Jill Bennett

SOURCE: A review of *Pigs Ahoy!,* in *The School Librarian,* Vol. 38, No. 4, November, 1990, p. 142.

Pigs ahoy! is . . . straightforward. Fletcher relieves the boredom of his farmyard friends when he finds an old wagon which quickly becomes a 'rumbly bumbly pirate ship' as they trundle down the road. Great fun is had by all as the 'pirates' commandeer a school bus, a fire engine, drop in to a circus and take to the air before ending up back in the farmyard. The joyful exhuberance of the animals as they cavort about the countryside is made abundantly clear in Hans Wilhelm's watercolours which extend the few well-chosen words used to tell the story.

📖 *THE FUNNIEST DINOSAUR BOOK EVER!* (written by Joseph Rosenbloom, 1987)

Publishers Weekly

SOURCE: A review of *The Funniest Dinosaur Book Ever!,*

in *Publishers Weekly,* Vol. 232, No. 26, December 25, 1987, p. 73.

Take almost any elephant joke, substitute the word "dinosaur," and that's the source for most of the little ditties in this book. But that doesn't mean they aren't just the kinds of worn-out jokes that seem to appeal to children most: "When a dinosaur goes into a restaurant, where does it sit? Anywhere it wants." However, there are a couple indigenous to the breed, especially one about the mixing of Tyrannosaurus Rex with a cowboy hat. (What do you get? Tyrannosaurus Tex!) Wilhelm's pictures—of giggling beasts, shivering bones and children telling jokes to each other—are by far the freshest part of this package.

Ilene Cooper

SOURCE: A review of *The Funniest Dinosaur Book Ever!,* in *Booklist,* Vol. 84, No. 10, January 15, 1988, pp. 866, 868.

Rosenbloom, who seems to have more jokes up his sleeve than there are stars in the sky, provides a compilation featuring one of kids' favorite subjects, dinosaurs. The funnies here are simple efforts, easily understandable (and repeatable) by young comedians. They are placed strategically across two-page spreads, filling the pages with expressive dinosaurs and extending the humor. The art, in full color, is several notches above that often seen in joke books; this title should easily find a place on library shelves.

OH, WHAT A MESS (1988; British edition as *Franklin and the Messy Pigs,* 1990)

Publishers Weekly

SOURCE: A review of *Oh, What a Mess,* in *Publishers Weekly,* Vol. 233, No. 19, May 13, 1988, p. 273.

Franklin's family lives in, well, a pigsty. As a meticulously neat piglet, Franklin finds his family's slovenly ways a great embarrassment, and he dares not encourage visitors. At school, his brothers' unruly antics further humiliate him. All this changes when Franklin wins first prize for his painting of a rainbow. His father chooses the perfect spot to hang the picture, but Franklin asks him if he could first wash the wall. The entire family dives into a housecleaning spree and the result is a home worthy of Franklin's masterpiece. Friends even visit, and the family enjoys staying clean (except for an occasional mud bath). Wilhelm's book plunges right to the center of the concerns of children who sometimes feel like the odd member out among the people in their families. His text and watercolors capture the charms of this porcine clan both before and after their radical reformation.

Ilene Cooper

SOURCE: A review of *Oh, What a Mess,* in *Booklist,* Vol. 84, No. 19, June 1, 1988, p. 1680.

Young Franklin is the only neat pig in a family of, well, pigs. They are dirty and smelly even by porcine standards, and Franklin is embarrassed by the whole crew. One day in school, Franklin paints an award-winning picture of a rainbow and takes it home to show the family. To his surprise, they love his work and want to hang it on a wall. But the picture doesn't look very good against the filthy backdrop. Hesitantly, Franklin suggests washing the wall; the sight of the pretty wallpaper underneath prompts the family to do a major cleanup of the house and themselves. This very appealing story is illustrated with pictures that have more than a passing resemblance to the artwork of Helme Heine. Wilhelm's pictures have the same robust charm and feature a jaunty crew of pigs who are pink, fat, and amusing. Fun for story hours.

Betsy Hearne

SOURCE: A review of *Oh, What a Mess,* in *Bulletin of the Center for Children's Books,* Vol. 41, No. 11, July-August, 1988, p. 242.

Franklin's family is a swinish lot that lazes about in a pen so filthy that he's embarrassed to ask any of his friends over or even acknowledge his siblings at school. Then Franklin wins a painting contest with a picture of a rainbow so beautiful that it reforms his father into washing the wall on which it hangs. That inspires Grandfather to change the straw, Mother to wash the curtains, etc., until the whole house with its inhabitants is hospitably clean—except for the occasional mud bath. Though not as natural a winner as Wilhelm's *I'll Always Love You,* this moral tale has lots of fun in it. What's puzzling is the illustration, which is either a tribute to Helme Heine or such an exact imitation that it could be termed blatant plagiarism. Not only are the pigs, chickens, and mice perfectly reflective of Heine's characters, but the colors and style of watercolor painting, the humorous postures, and even the theme of the relation of art and life are signature Heine. Children will not care—it's a dilemma for professionals to note and consider.

Ruth Semrau

SOURCE: A review of *Oh, What a Mess,* in *School Library Journal,* Vol. 35, No. 4, December, 1988, p. 95.

Franklin is a pig who appreciates cleanliness, promptness, and similar conservative values. His family, however, lack these characteristics. They are traditional pigs who don't mind a lot of dirt. When Franklin wins a contest at school with his picture of a rainbow, he not-so-subtly suggests that the prize-winning picture deserves a better setting and thereby he inspires his piggy folks to clean up and mend their swinish ways. How did Franklin learn to be such an insufferable little prig? Certainly not from his family. What are readers to make of parents who suddenly "come to realize" that they ought not to be lazy and dirty? Wilhelm's carefree watercolors of short fat pigs who look blissfully untroubled in their pigginess contradict the carping tone of the text.

Jill Bennett

SOURCE: A review of *Franklin and the Messy Pigs,* in *Books for Keeps,* No. 63, July, 1990, p. 9.

Young Franklin pig isn't like the other members of his family: he is clean and likes things neat and tidy, but his home and family are a total mess. That is until Franklin's prize-winning painting causes them to see the error of their ways—literally.

An amusing tale, but the real delight is in the pictures depicting fastidious Franklin in all his pinkness in stark contrast to his filthy family; these really say more than the words.

Audrey Laski

SOURCE: A review of *Franklin and the Messy Pigs,* in *The School Librarian,* Vol. 38, No. 3, August, 1990, p. 106.

Morality tales about tidiness usually have the central character as the messy one needing to change. Hans Wilhelm takes a different line, making his hero the one clean and tidy person in a family 'simply too dirty and smelly—even for pigs'. He manages to make Franklin an attractive character, not a prig, and actually links his cleanliness to creativity; it is when Franklin paints a prize-winning picture that his family get carried away by a new urge for cleaning up and discover the delights of the bubble bath. The illustrations are vigorous cartoons, the author drawing Franklin's virtuous activities and his brothers' mucky ones with equal relish. There is a wonderfully grandiose family portrait which Franklin is seen painting, towards the end of the book, which speaks volumes about art and life.

📖 *TYRONE THE HORRIBLE* (1988)

Kirkus Reviews

SOURCE: A review of *Tyrone the Horrible,* in *Kirkus Reviews,* Vol. LVI, No. 15, August 1, 1988, p. 1160.

If children's problems are to be dramatized with animal characters, what better surrogate for coming to terms with the local bully than dinosaurs? Boland is a cute, roly-poly little dinosaur; his problem—who is about twice as tall—looks a good deal like a tyrannosaurus (though he's apparently a vegetarian). Boland tries to stay out of Tyrone's way, but he still gets punched and teased and has snacks stolen. Trying to be friendly backfires; fighting back is disastrous; and although friend "Stego" suggests that he may just have to learn to live with the unbeatable Tyrone, Boland has one more, successful idea: the next

snitched snack proves to be made of hot pepper. Although unexceptional, Wilhelm's dinosaurs are appealing, and his story addresses a universal problem in a common-sense way.

Publishers Weekly

SOURCE: A review of *Tyrone the Horrible,* in *Publishers Weekly,* Vol. 234, No. 9, August 26, 1988, p. 88.

Wilhelm uses dinosaurs to explicate his very modern tale about a young dinosaur named Boland who finally outsmarts the bully that had terrorized the swamp. Boland seems to be the special target of Tyrone the Horrible; day after day, he is victimized. He tries to avoid trouble, tries pleasing Tyrone, tries fighting back, but nothing works. Finally, Boland laces a sandwich with red pepper and gets a wonderfully satisfying reaction when Tyrone gobbles it up! Preschool and early elementary youngsters will certainly identify with Boland's problem. Wilhelm's arresting, attractive watercolors fill the pages. Knowledgeable dinosaur fans may have a quibble: Tyrone is clearly a tyrannosaurus (and therefore carnivorous), yet he is shown as a plant eater. But as a story of a bully about to meet his match, this one will have joyful appeal for kids.

Ilene Cooper

SOURCE: A review of *Tyrone the Horrible,* in *Booklist,* Vol. 85, No. 1, September 1, 1988, p. 86.

Wilhelm combines two popular topics, dinosaurs and bullies, into an effective tale. Boland, a little dinosaur, is having problems with Tyrone, a *Tyrannosaurus rex*-like character who's making Boland's life a prehistoric misery, so Boland asks his friends for advice on how to deal with his nemesis. One suggests being nice to Tyrone, but that only results in an ice cream cone being dumped on Boland's head. Another counsels ignoring the bully, which only gets Boland's tail stomped. Finally, Boland decides to fight back; when Tyrone takes Boland's sandwich, he finds a hot, peppery surprise awaiting him. The chunky artwork does not show much finesse, but its elementary shapes do have cartoon-quality appeal. Certainly, it's hard not to like Boland (and to boo the nasty Tyrone). When Tyrone gets his comeuppance, preschool audiences will cheer.

📖 *MORE BUNNY TROUBLE* (1989)

Publishers Weekly

SOURCE: A review of *More Bunny Trouble,* in *Publishers Weekly,* Vol. 234, No. 24, December 9, 1988, p. 64.

Ralph and Emily, two bunnies, first appeared in Wilhelm's ***Bunny Trouble***. In this new book, Ralph is told to watch his baby sister Emily. But he pays more attention to the Easter eggs he is painting than to his sibling. When Ralph looks up, Emily has disappeared. Ralph runs to his mother, who calls together all the rabbits to search for Emily, but in vain. Ralph's own ingenuity provides the means for Emily to be found, much to the chagrin of a resident fox who was hoping to eat her for dinner. Although readers will experience relief at Emily's safe homecoming, the plot itself is rather trite, and resolved too easily to generate any emotional tension. However, Wilhelm's watercolor illustrations are quite pleasing.

Carolyn Phelan

SOURCE: A review of *More Bunny Trouble,* in *Booklist,* Vol. 85, No. 13, March 1, 1989, p. 1198.

Tapped to watch his little sister bunny while Mama works, Ralph reluctantly stops playing soccer and sits with Emily, alternately punching her and painting Easter eggs patterned like soccer balls. Absorbed in his brushwork, he doesn't notice when baby Emily, enchanted by new sights and smells, crawls into the meadow and out of sight. All the neighborhood rabbits join the search party, racing to find Emily before the lurking fox catches her or sunset dims their chances. Ralph redeems himself when his idea of forming a chain leads them to his sleeping sister. The bright spring colors and broadly caricatured faces of Wilhelm's watercolors will appeal to many children. A likable picture book set in the Easter season, but with minimal connection to the holiday.

Kirkus Reviews

SOURCE: A review of *More Bunny Trouble,* in *Kirkus Reviews,* Vol. LVII, No. 5, March 1, 1989, p. 386.

Ralph—of **Bunny Trouble**—thinks his baby sister, Emily, is overrated: "She cried a lot and was always wet." He tends to do things like poking her, not really hard, but hard enough to make Emily cry. Left to watch her, he's too busy decorating eggs (making them look like soccer balls) to notice her wander off after a passing butterfly, but her absence does elicit his concern; in fact, it's Ralph who organizes the searchers into a long line, holding paws, to comb the tall grass and eventually find his sister. Wilhelm unabashedly depicts his rabbits in a popular, expressive, cartoon-like style, but his spacious, skillfully painted settings betray the fact that his talent goes beyond caricature. Although the plot here is predictable, the telling is lively and should amuse beginning readers.

Lee Bock

SOURCE: A review of *More Bunny Trouble,* in *School Library Journal,* Vol. 35, No. 9, May, 1989, p. 94.

As in **Bunny Trouble,** the bunnies in this sequel should have real kid appeal. Ralph bungles his babysitting responsibilities by letting baby bunny sister crawl away into tall, fox-infested grass while he blithely paints Easter eggs.

Ralph comes up with the solution to find her—in the nick of time—and "From then on, Ralph watched his favorite sister very carefully." Pastels dominate, appropriate for the Easter theme of the story. It is didactic, but gently so, and if the writing isn't masterful, the cartoonlike illustrations and the holiday link will make this a likely choice.

SCHNITZEL'S FIRST CHRISTMAS (1989)

Susan Helper

SOURCE: A review of *Schnitzel's First Christmas,* in *School Library Journal,* Vol. 35, No. 14, October, 1989, p. 45.

Schnitzel, a dog, is enjoying his first winter until Gruff, the cat, explains that he had better be thinking about what he wants Santa to bring him. Schnitzel knows that he has everything—enough chew toys and plenty of squirrels to chase. Even after he asks other animals for suggestions, Schnitzel can't come up with anything he wants. Santa, surprised to find someone who wants nothing, leaves a package anyway. Inside is Pretzel, a new doggy companion who will become Schnitzel's best friend. Cheerful colored pencil and watercolor illustrations keep the story moving. A bit didactic, but not unbearable.

Children's Book Review Service

SOURCE: A review of *Schnitzel's First Christmas,* in *Children's Book Review Service,* Vol. 18, No. 6, Winter, 1990, p. 66.

Schnitzel's First Christmas is a heartwarming story of the preparation of the Christmas holiday from the eyes of a young puppy. He learns it is a time for wishing, but in the process of trying to think what he could wish for, he discovers he has everything he could want. Santa surprises him at the end of the story, even though he hadn't made a wish. The soft and playful illustrations are especially delightful! Children should enjoy this new view of the Christmas season and learn something special about the spirit of the holiday.

A COOL KID—LIKE ME! (1990)

Ellen Mandel

SOURCE: A review of *A Cool Kid—Like Me!,* in *Booklist,* Vol. 87, No. 2, September 15, 1990, p. 176.

Often left alone by parents preoccupied with themselves and their work, the youngster telling this story confides that his mom and dad really don't know him very well. They think he's self-assured and cool, but his grandma understands that he's still a little boy with doubts and insecurities. Before she leaves on a vacation, Grandma gives him a teddy bear. His parents are aghast: "He's too old for that. . . . He's already into computers." But teddy does the trick, helping the boy through those dark nights and enabling him to be "as cool as he could be." With softly painted illustrations as sensitive as the message, this unusual story gives kids license to be kids, and it reminds everyone that cuddly toys still have their place, even in a high-tech world.

Lauralyn Persson

SOURCE: A review of *A Cool Kid—Like Me!,* in *School Library Journal,* Vol. 36, No. 12, December, 1990, p. 90.

A refreshingly honest picture book, told in the first person by an only child. His busy, emotionally distant parents treat him as if he were a third adult in the household, but he does get love and attention from his grandmother. When Grandma leaves for a long vacation, she gives the boy a teddy bear, to whom he can confide his nighttime fears of being laughed at, of not having a best friend, of his parents arguing. The story ends on an upbeat note, with his apprehensions subsiding in the daylight, and his grandmother's return. Wilhelm conveys plenty of emotion in a brief text, and the illustrations beautifully enhance both meaning and mood of the story. Especially effective is a picture showing the child leaning against a wall, framed on each side by the shadow of an angry parent. Picture books depicting more dramatic problems have become fairly commonplace, but not many approach the subject of a middle-class family in which a child may be ignored or misunderstood. A sympathetic look at how life can be in an imperfect, human world, where both young and old can thrive by building support systems.

Judith Sharman

SOURCE: A review of *A Cool Kid—Like Me!,* in *Books for Keeps,* No. 71, November, 1991, p. 8.

This is an extremely disturbing book—for the parent. The children in my class seemed to take it at face value and it was widely borrowed. The general consensus was that they found it reassuring that even a 'cool kid' shared their concerns. The cool kid is popular, knows he has talents and apparently takes most things in his stride. His parents are blithely unaware of his innermost worries and fears and only his grandmother truly relates to him. The book pulls no punches and depicts a particular set of family relationships with devastating honesty that left this parent feeling very distressed!

Clare Kelly

SOURCE: A review of *A Cool Kid—Like Me!,* in *The School Librarian,* Vol. 39, No. 4, November, 1991, p. 143.

The value of this book is in the message it gives to children, boys in particular, that you don't have to be tough to be cool. The hero of the story prides himself on his 'coolness' yet secretly suffers the familiar childhood fears and anxieties about the dark, friendship, desertion, and so on. With parents who are always preoccupied, he finds a sympathetic ear in his grandma who is 'the only one I would let hug me'. When Grandma goes on holiday, she leaves a replacement in the form of a teddy who fills the gap perfectly until she returns. A rather sad story, with a sympathetic tone, which will connect with many children who feel obliged to be 'tough' despite their tender years.

📖 *TYRONE THE DOUBLE DIRTY ROTTEN CHEATER* (1991; British edition as *Tyrone the Dirty Rotten Cheat*)

Publishers Weekly

SOURCE: A review of *Tyrone the Double Dirty Rotten Cheater,* in *Publishers Weekly,* Vol. 238, No. 1, January 4, 1991, pp. 71-2.

The prolific Wilhelm introduced his benignly naughty dinosaur in *Tyrone the Horrible,* and kids who loved to hate him in that lively tale will do the same here. Boland and his dinosaur pals are not overjoyed when Tyrone tags along on a week-long camping trip to Swamp Island. Living up to his reputation as a troublemaker, the unscrupulous Tyrone cheats at every game and ends up winning all the prizes. Children will cheer when the sneaky dinosaur unsuccessfully tries to steal Boland's buried treasure and instead gets his just deserts. As always, Wilhelm knows what will tickle the funny bones of young readers; they will snicker at Tyrone's dreadful behavior, shifty eyes and caustic tongue.

Leone McDermott

SOURCE: A review of *Tyrone the Double Dirty Rotten Cheater,* in *Booklist,* Vol. 87, No. 11, February 11, 1991, p. 1133.

Tyrone the Horrible is a dinosaur-kid bully. When Boland, a little dinosaur, and his friends go camping on Swamp Island, Tyrone is there to spoil the fun. He cheats at every game from meteorite bowling to the dinosaur egg race, and when he gets caught, he threatens Boland. But Tyrone outsmarts himself when he eavesdrops on Boland's plans for a secret treasure hunt and winds up with bee stings instead of a prize. Every child who's feared a bully will empathize with Boland's outrage and enjoy watching Tyrone, rotten to the core, get his just deserts. Wilhelm's colorful, cartoonlike illustrations, though not always executed with the greatest of care, are humorous and vital, with lots of focus on Tyrone's sly glee as he pulls off yet another dirty trick.

Nancy A. Gifford

SOURCE: A review of *Tyrone the Double Dirty Rotten*

From Tyrone the Horrible, *written and illustrated by Hans Wilhelm.*

Cheater, in *School Library Journal,* Vol. 37, No. 7, July, 1991, p. 65.

Tyrone the Horrible returns to fine tune his aggression towards Boland and the other small dinosaurs by cheating at every game while camping on Swamp Island. Even catching Tyrone in the act doesn't help, since he lies and is too big and mean to challenge. Finally Boland calls a secret meeting about a hidden treasure. Naturally Tyrone overhears and goes after the treasure himself, with some surprising results. Large, colorful illustrations of dinosaurs are sure to attract young readers, even though the creatures are given all-too-human personalities. While ostensibly about dealing with cheaters, there are no constructive suggestions given and readers won't be convinced that a lesson has been learned by the bully. This offering proves that Tyrone is just as horrible as he was in his previous story, which was pretty horrible in its own right.

Cliff Moon

SOURCE: A review of *Tyrone the Dirty Rotten Cheat,* in *The School Librarian,* Vol. 39, No. 3, August, 1991, p. 100.

These dinosaurs are people in prehistoric clothing and Tyrone himself is the villain of the piece. He cheats and lies himself into winning all the games and prizes until he accidentally disturbs a swarm of bees and gets his comeuppance. How much more satisfying it would have been

if Boland and his friends could have engineered his downfall. Still, children will enjoy spotting Tyrone's tricks as and when they are prefaced in the somewhat stark but energetic illustrations.

Judith Sharman

SOURCE: A review of *Tyrone the Dirty Rotten Cheat,* in *Books for Keeps,* No. 75, July, 1992, p. 9.

This book was greeted like an old friend. It's proved very popular and is now well thumbed and a bit grubby—an extremely good sign!

It may be churlish of me but I'm disappointed that Hans Wilhelm stuck with Tyrone and didn't create another dinosaur villain. True, he does, once again, get his comeuppance but I couldn't shake off my depression that some of the satisfaction and power of the previous book, *Tyrone the Horrible,* has now been lost. Tyrone's bullying had been brilliantly and graphically defeated by Boland's ingenuity and to find him not only thriving but still persecuting Boland in this book somehow defeats the whole object.

Chris Lutrario

SOURCE: A review of *Tyrone the Terrible* and *Tyrone the Dirty Rotten Cheat,* in *Books for Keeps,* No. 76, September, 1992, p. 24.

[*The following excerpt presents criticism of* Tyrone the Horrible *and* Tyrone the Dirty Rotten Cheat.]

Tyrone the Horrible and *Tyrone the Dirty Rotten Cheat* introduce us to 'the world's first big bully'—a Tyrannosaurus Rex, inevitably. Little Boland tries all sorts of strategies to prevent Tyrone from making his life a misery: avoidance, making friends, nonchalance, fighting. Nothing works. So Boland tricks Tyrone into eating a 'double-thick-red-hot-pepper-sandwich' and disturbing a nest of bees. There's a natural satisfaction in seeing a bully get his just deserts, but there's an unpleasant edge of violence here. The problem of how to stop a bully without using force crops up again and again, in books as in life.

📖 *SCHNITZEL IS LOST* (1991; British edition as *Ruffles Is Lost*)

Alexandra Marris

SOURCE: A review of *Schnitzel Is Lost,* in *School Library Journal,* Vol. 37, No. 10, October, 1991, p. 106.

A slight, sentimental story. When the garden gate is left open, Schnitzel the puppy goes exploring. He ignores his friend's warnings and chases a leaf until he gets lost. Pursued by a large dog, he accidentally boards a bus. He jumps out at the first stop and finds himself home again, safe and sound. There are some disturbing aspects to this simple escapade. Schnitzel violates major safety precautions that most adults try to instill in young children. First, he runs off by himself without asking or telling anyone where he is going. Second, he tries to cross a busy street and is almost hit by a car. Third, when he discovers that he is lost, he runs helter-skelter and becomes even more disoriented. The book fails as a cautionary tale since the pup does make it home again—but only through unlikely circumstance and luck—not through any intelligent efforts of his own. Wilhelm's bright, colorful, watercolor-washed cartoons, outlined in pencil and crayon, convey a sense of energetic movement. Expressive faces on the puppies will appeal to some, but for the most part, they are coy and overly cute.

Moira Small

SOURCE: A review of *Ruffles Is Lost,* in *Books for Keeps,* No. 71, November, 1991, p. 6.

A charming story about two small dogs: one adventurous, the other timid. Ruffles, the adventurous one, finds the gate open and sets off to explore. Scruff follows cautiously. Soon they become separated—Scruff returns home but Ruffles is lost. He's nearly run over by a car, gets chased by a larger dog and eventually (but accidentally) arrives home in a bus.

A very useful story to inform and help children understand about their world—it gives cheerful, but clear warnings of danger, as well as being entertaining with detailed illustrations and lively text.

Julie Cosaro

SOURCE: A review of *Schnitzel Is Lost,* in *Booklist,* Vol. 88, No. 5, November 1, 1991, p. 534.

When Schnitzel (the adventurous dog) and Pretzel (his reticent friend) run out of their backyard through an open gate, Schnitzel chases a falling leaf down the street and gets lost. Nearly run over by a car and pursued by a German shepherd who upsets a café, a produce stand, and a street painter, Schnitzel finally escapes onto a bus that safely returns him home—relieved but with no regrets. The autumn-hued wash-and-crayon paintings portray the mayhem in the European town from the little lost dog's perspective. Breezy and affectionate, this tale by the author of the *Waldo* books should appeal to more than the "lost children" listed as a subject heading.

📖   ***THE BREMEN TOWN MUSICIANS* (written by the Brothers Grimm, retold and illustrated by Hans Wilhelm, 1992)**

Publishers Weekly

SOURCE: A review of *The Bremen Town Musicians,* in

Publishers Weekly, Vol. 239, No. 7, February 3, 1992, p. 80.

The trademark lighthearted, somewhat cartoony watercolors by Wilhelm, himself a Bremen native, imbues this blithe retelling with a timeless, fairy-tale setting. A better choice for young readers than P. K. Page's version of the story, Wilhelm's book offers a shorter text, at once pithy and descriptive. The child-appealing prose is studded with such distinctive phrases as a depiction of the forlorn cat, whom the donkey and the dog find by the roadside, "looking as dismal as three wet days." When the feisty quartet interrupts a group of robbers in a thatched-roof cottage counting their money as they enjoy a feast, observant readers will notice that these bad guys look quite a bit like the animals' former owners. This is just one of the quixotic twists that make Wilhelm's spirited rendition so refreshing.

Carolyn Noah

SOURCE: A review of *The Bremen Town Musicians,* in *School Library Journal,* Vol. 38, No. 4, April, 1992, pp. 105-06.

An insouciant text and vibrant full-color illustrations make this retelling of the Grimm Brothers' classic a rollicking performance. Cat meets donkey in an unforgettable exchange: "Now then, what is the matter with you, old Whiskerwiper?" asks the donkey. "Who can be cheerful when his life is in danger?" replies the cat. Somehow this menagerie succeeds. Because of the simple language, heavy on dialogue, the book will interest even the most reticent audiences and early readers. Wilhelm's musicians are loopy and lovable. His thieves are greedy and dumb, and best of all, strangely resemble the musicians' former owners. All are irresistibly executed in bright, amusing watercolors, and the whole-page design adds energy to the tale. It's satisfying to the final double-page spread, which shows the animal friends snuggled peaceably by the cottage fire, books at hand. Compared to Josef Palacek's version for older audiences, this one is more satisfying, warm, and filled with good humor.

Kirkus Reviews

SOURCE: A review of *The Bremen Town Musicians,* in *Kirkus Reviews,* Vol. LX, No. 7, April 1, 1992, p. 474.

A Bremen native follows the Grimms in his straightforward, accessible retelling, providing lively watercolor illustrations that depict the characters in an appealing cartoon style and varying multiple vignettes with cinematic double spreads. There are many editions of this popular story, but Wilhelm's visual narration has unusual panache, making it a good choice for collections that can use one more.

Carolyn Phelan

SOURCE: A review of *The Bremen Town Musi-*

cians, in *Booklist,* Vol. 88, No. 16, April 15, 1992, p. 1534.

If there was ever an illustrator who could consider this story his birthright, it's Hans Wilhelm, who was born in Bremen and grew up with the tale. While his text stays close to the original, the illustrations tie it together more tightly than usual: the cruel owners who threatened their donkey, dog, cat, and rooster reappear as the robbers, whom the animals frighten away. The dramatic characterizations, broad humor, and large scale of these watercolor illustrations will make this a popular version for reading aloud to groups of children as well as to individuals.

THE BOY WHO WASN'T THERE (1993)

Publishers Weekly

SOURCE: A review of *The Boy Who Wasn't There,* in *Publishers Weekly,* Vol. 240, No. 45, November 8, 1993, p. 76.

Wilhelm's polished, classic watercolors and a stylized typeface intensify the invitingly nostalgic flavor of this tale set "many years ago." On a rocky New England beach, lonely Sarah is visited by a ghost-like boy, who tells her that she will soon have a best friend. On another day, the same figure returns and announces that he needs Sarah's help. Instructing her to bring her favorite toys, a pair of puppets, the boy takes her to a rundown house, where an anxious mother hovers over her feverish daughter, Angela. The puppets spring to life, putting on a show that revives and cures the child. When Sarah explains to the mother that she was led to the house by the boy whose picture is framed by Angela's bed, the girl learns his identity. He is Angela's brother, who had disappeared two years before, swept out to sea trying to save another boy who was washed away by a wave. Broken into three brief chapters, this quietly dramatic "mystery" is a beguiling choice for beginning readers.

Kirkus Reviews

SOURCE: A review of *The Boy Who Wasn't There,* in *Kirkus Reviews,* Vol. LXI, No. 23, December 1, 1993, p. 1532.

To introduce a favorite genre, a three-chapter ghost story—appropriately set on the bleak and desolate New England coast in a long-ago December. Lonely Sarah, home from boarding school for Christmas, has no one to play with but her puppets. She's brooding on the windy beach when a boy—quite a translucent boy, in Wilhelm's picture, with no footprints—suddenly materializes and predicts that she'll soon have a friend. Later, he appears in her house and takes her to a nearby cottage, where she finds a grieving mother, an ill child who recovers when she sees the puppets and the girl who brought them, and a photo of the mysterious boy—the woman's son—drowned two years ago in trying to save a friend who'd

been washed into the sea. The plot is pretty basic, but it gains atmosphere in the telling and in Wilhelm's sweeping, dramatically impressionistic paintings. An enjoyable addition.

Children's Book Review Service

SOURCE: A review of *The Boy Who Wasn't There,* in *Children's Book Review Service,* Vol. 22, No. 8, March, 1994, p. 94.

Hans Wilhelm sensitively and believably portrays the encounter between a lonely girl and a mysterious boy who has the power to disappear. The boy guides her to bring joy into the life of a sick girl, and the two become lifelong friends. Mr. Wilhelm has discovered a new venue that will expand his audience from the loyal readers of his classic tales to include older children. Imaginative illustrations enhance this memorable book.

Susan Hepler

SOURCE: A review of *The Boy Who Wasn't There,* in *School Library Journal,* Vol. 40, No. 3, March, 1994, p. 212.

Set on the New England coast in the 19th century, this three-part mystical story tries to do too much. Sarah, brooding on the shore with her hand puppets, wishes she had a friend. A strange boy appears, reassures her that she will make one, and then disappears. Just before Christmas, he reappears and begs her to come with him to entertain a sick child. She does, and her efforts break the girl's fever. Sarah explains that she was brought there by a boy—the one in the picture by the bed. While alert readers will suspect all along that he is a ghost, Sarah doesn't until the third part, when Angela's mother tells how her son, Allan, died saving another boy. An epilogue assures readers that Sarah and Angela became friends, went to college (improbable in the 1800s, but not impossible), got married, and each named her first son Allan. Wilhelm's text, with its undeveloped characters, jerky plot, and unsatisfyingly quick ending, does not command readers' attention. His dramatic watercolor landscapes and bold use of color don't save this well-intentioned ghost story from too much telling and not enough showing.

HIGGLE-WIGGLE: HAPPY RHYMES (written by Eve Merriam, 1994)

Publishers Weekly

SOURCE: A review of *Higgle Wiggle: Happy Rhymes,* in *Publishers Weekly,* Vol. 241, No. 10, March 7, 1994, pp. 71-2.

Fans of *Blackberry Ink* will delight in Merriam and Wilhelm's second collection of bouncy, joyful poems for preschoolers. Merriam's appealing verses contain a wealth of rhythms, rhymes and action: a pair of boots go "clomping / stomping along"; a child describes a cat that "slithered and stretched . . . quivered and prowled"; and a bath which begins with "slipple slapple slubble" ends when the water "guggle uggle gluggle[s]" down the drain. Wilhelm sprinkles his stark white pages with a garden of children and winsome stuffed animals (a plump Piglet-like charmer appears frequently with his teddy bear). Perfect for counting and finger rhymes or group activities, these sunny verses will offer youngest readers an easy entry into the joy of wordplay and imagination. Whether they are about mashed potatoes ("mashed potato clouds, / mashed potato moon, / scoop it all up / with a giant's spoon") or about dancing ("dance out of bed, / dance on the floor, / dance down the hallway, / dance out the door"), these short poems reflect a world of mirth and merriment.

Hazel Rochman

SOURCE: A review of *Higgle Wiggle: Happy Rhymes,* in *Booklist,* Vol. 90, No. 15, April 1, 1994, p. 1457.

Tickle rhymes, wiggle rhymes, snuggle words, messy words: these nonsense verses are for and about the lap audience. The sound and feel and action of words will appeal to the youngest child, whether it's the physical pleasure of mashed potatoes, the clink clank clunk of keys, or the funny chant of "banana banana." Sound is meaning ("in a gurgle a glop / in a slippity slop"), and repetition and rhyme are a joyful lure to the pleasure of story. In the middle of the splutter and mess, there's also the hush of secrets ("Don't tell anyone / not even me"). The late Merriam has left children a joyful gift, and Wilhelm's watercolors of pigs, toddlers, toys, and animals express the exuberance of the verse.

Kirkus Reviews

SOURCE: A review of *Higgle Wiggle: Happy Rhymes,* in *Kirkus Reviews,* Vol. LXI, No. 8, April 15, 1994, p. 560.

"Happy" is the right word for these 25 deftly constructed poems about childhood pleasures: sounds, making faces ("How to Be Angry": "Scrunch your eyebrows / up to your hair, / pull on your chin / and glare glare glare . . . "), animals, weather, food, riddles, counting, day's end. The ebullient rhymes and onomatopoeia are perfect for tuning young ears for reading readiness ("Bath Time" ends with "Water down the drain . . . guggle uggle gluggle / Gurgle / urgle / *gug*"—Merriam's made-up words for sounds are always apt). Buoyant with humor and sketched with unassuming ease, Wilhelm's watercolors are actually crafted with great care. An expressive pink piglet that appears in most spreads lends unity to the whole, while even a simple vignette—like a rubber duck watching the last of the bathwater glug down the drain—can suggest a whole story. Nifty.

Betsy Hearne

SOURCE: A review of *Higgle Wiggle: Happy Rhymes,* in *Bulletin of the Center for Children's Books,* Vol. 47, No. 11, July-August, 1994, p. 368.

These twenty-five posthumously published poems are cheery in content and neat in rhyme, with physical movement suggested by frequent repetition: "Dance out of bed, / dance on the floor, / dance down the hallway, / dance out the door." Adults can use many of the verses to set kids into motion, but the collection doesn't really sparkle with the verbal surprise for which Merriam is famous. "How to Be Angry," for instance, is fun to do ("Puff out your cheeks, / puff puff puff, / then take a deep breath / and huff huff huff") but too mild to exert any real tonal force or contrast. Wilhelm's illustrations emphasize pastel colors and merry expressions, adding to the toddler-time gaiety without much variation so that a certain monotony sets in despite the sprightly pace. Overall, it's a book that will please those with a poetic sweet tooth and will provide plenty of potential for action with toddler groups.

THE ROYAL RAVEN (1996)

Kirkus Reviews

SOURCE: A review of *The Royal Raven,* in *Kirkus Reviews,* Vol. LXIV, No. 1, January 1, 1996, p. 75.

A perhaps familiar story, related with a dose of irony and illustrated with dazzling special effects. Crawford the Raven feels that he's special, but looks like any other raven; a witch transforms him into "a spectacular creature" leading to his move to the king's palace, where he is promptly caged. To gain his freedom, he yanks out his feathers, and returns to his friends in the forest, plucked but happy. Perfectly timed wisecracks are hatched whenever the story permits; Wilhelm uses his characteristically understated humor that reveals itself best in slightly skewed expressions or the deadpan use of familiar idioms. If the text is understated, the illustrations take the opposite tack. The main feature of these big, colorful watercolors are the raven's glittering gold feathers; similar in effect to the fins on Marcus Pfister's *Rainbow Fish,* these plump the book with real live magic.

Mary Jane Dubner

SOURCE: A review of *The Royal Raven,* in *Children's Book Review Service,* Vol. 24, No. 8, March, 1996, p. 90.

Crawford wants to look different from an ordinary raven. After several attempts, he visits an old woman known for her magical powers. Crawford is transformed into a dazzling creature who is captured when he ventures into the royal garden. Beauty, attention and a terrific home engulf Crawford. He eventually loses his razzle-dazzle and accepts himself. The "dazzling" pictures complement the tale and magnify the underlying message. An outstanding book for gaining a positive self-image—a classic for the home and classroom.

Susan Dove Lempke

SOURCE: A review of *The Royal Raven,* in *Booklist,* Vol. 92, No. 14, March 15, 1996, p. 1269.

Crawford the raven, who feels special inside, can't understand why he looks so ordinary. After unsuccessfully trying a variety of adornments, he persuades an old woman "known for her special powers" to give him some "razzle dazzle." She does, and his feathers explode off the page in shiny, gold holographic sparkles. Comparison to Pfister's phenomenally popular 1993 book *Rainbow Fish* is inevitable, with this book subject to some of the same criticism because of its similar theme: being special is a bad thing. Crawford's downfall is skipped over too quickly, making his fall from grace at the royal palace seem unbelievable and contrived, but Wilhelm's watercolors are as winning as ever. A book that will rarely be left on the shelf.

Publishers Weekly

SOURCE: A review of *The Royal Raven,* in *Publishers Weekly,* Vol. 243, No. 13, March 25, 1996, pp. 82-3.

Convinced that he's "special," Crawford the raven is disgruntled with his ordinary appearance. After making several funny, futile attempts to change, the frustrated bird entreats a woman with magical powers to give him "some color, some flash, some razzle dazzle." Wilhelm has her pull this off masterfully, as holographic gold foil and splashes of blazing color transform Crawford's plumage into a sparkling, kid-thrilling sight. After making an ill-fated attempt at hobnobbing with the royal family, the cocky creature is banished to a cage in the palace garden, where he grows increasingly despondent until finally realizing he must lose his unnatural grandeur in order to regain his freedom. Though the shimmering feathers are obvious scene-stealers, Wilhelm's bustling, double-page watercolor art glitters even where there is no gold. As an extra treat, Wilhelm hides a tiny ladybug on each spread.

Additional coverage of Wilhelm's life and career is contained in the following sources published by Gale Research: *Contemporary Authors New Revision Series,* Vol. 48; *Something about the Author,* Vol. 58; and *Something about the Author Autobiography Series,* Vol. 21.

John (Brian) Yeoman

1934-

English author of picture books.

Major works include *The Bear's Water Picnic* (1970), *The Wild Washerwomen: A New Folk Tale* (1979), *Rumbelow's Dance* (1983), *Our Village: Poems* (1988), *The Singing Tortoise: And Other Animal Fables* (1994).

INTRODUCTION

A notable writer of children's literature, John Yeoman is particularly well-known as the author of collaborative picture books that combine his droll texts with the comical art of illustrator Quentin Blake. Praised for charming and inventive animal narratives, he is also cited for the whimsically rhymed verse of such works as his *Mother Hubbard* books, volumes that prompted a *Junior Bookshelf* critic to declare of Yeoman and Blake, "There is no better partnership today." Among his other well-received works are the poetic and effervescent *Rumbelow's Dance* and his inventive *The Do-It-Yourself House that Jack Built* (1994), which a reviewer for *The School Librarian* called "an absolute delight. . . . This will be a favourite family book for years and the nursery rhyme will never be the same again." Yeoman's talents also range into folklore, with retellings—among them *The Singing Tortoise: And Other Animal Fables*—and such freshly imagined works as *The Wild Washerwomen: A New Folk Tale*. Overall, his books are considered a delightful synthesis of childhood happiness, blending the best of animal tales, nursery rhyme verse, juvenile absurdity, and child-like humor.

Biographical Information

Yeoman was born in Forest Gate, London, England, in 1934. He attended Downing College, Cambridge, and later the London University Institute of Education. In 1960 he took a job as an English instructor at the Watford Boys' Grammar School, and that same year published his first children's book, *A Drink of Water, and Other Stories*. The book was followed by *The Boy Who Sprouted Antlers* in 1961. Yeoman then took an extended hiatus from children's literature and began translating technical books from Russian into English. In 1962 he transferred to the Lycee Francais de Londres in London, and was eventually named head of the school's English department in 1969. Soon, Yeoman revived his career as a children's writer with the publication of *Alphabet Soup* (1969). He followed this volume with several more stories and books of poetry for young people, each time teaming with illustrator Quentin Blake. Still based in London, Yeoman continues to write and publish fiction for children full-time and since 1961 has produced more than twenty humorous picture books.

Major Works

Yeoman's works for children represent a broad range from nursery rhyme verse to short narrative picture books to longer stories for somewhat older readers. Among his earliest books, *Alphabet Soup* is an amusing collection of rhymes on the ABC theme. *Sixes and Sevens* (1971) takes counting as its subject and follows a fellow named Barnaby as he transports his numbered—and sometimes antagonistic—living cargo down a river on his way to the village of Limber Lea. Yeoman explores the comic pleasures of the animal narrative in *The Bear's Winter House* (1969). Settling down to hibernate for the winter, a bear endeavors to sleep in his cozy lodge but is thwarted by the arrival of a host of other animals seeking shelter from the cold. Yeoman employs a similar theme in *The Bear's Water Picnic*. This time the bear attempts to take his friends hedgehog, hen, pig, and squirrel on his raft for a picnic, but finds the serenity broken by some noisy frogs. Nevertheless, when the raft becomes stuck, these seemingly bothersome amphibians come to the rescue. *Featherbrains* (1993), another of Yeoman's animal stories, details the misadventures of Flossie and Bessie, two hens content to remain within the safety of their henhouse until they are accidentally released into the dangerous world outside. Another of Yeoman's unique volumes, *The Singing Tortoise: And Other Animal Fables,* contains eleven stories from around the globe—*pourquoi* and cautionary tales, trickster narratives, and some playfully familiar yarns, such as a Cinderella-style story from the Zuni culture.

Amusing books about humans make up a significant portion of Yeoman's literary repertoire as well, and include the slight but comically subversive *The Wild Washerwomen: A New Folk Tale*. Dottie, Lottie, Molly, Dolly, Winnie, Minnie, and Ernestine, a group of overworked washerwomen from a bygone era, terrorize passers-by, their fellow villagers, and the cruel laundry-owner Mr. Balthazar Tight. Their rampage ends when they happen upon seven eligible woodcutters whom they promptly marry. Yeoman makes a return to verse in *Rumbelow's Dance*. In this work the diminutive and infectiously optimistic Rumbelow cheers a host of downcast animals and people with his joyful dance and happy song as he makes his way to his grandparents' house. Rhymed verse is also at the heart of Yeoman's quartet of *Old Mother Hubbard's Dog* books (all published in 1989) and *Our Village: Poems*. The latter contains twenty-one short poetic vignettes which describe the eccentric inhabitants of a quaint little village. *The Do-It-Yourself House that Jack Built* adds another dimension to this familiar nursery rhyme by offering the often absurd observations of differing characters in the story. *The Puffin Book of Improbable Records* (1975) represents something of a departure for Yeoman, but with the same comic intent of his other books. A parody of record books such as *The Guinness Book of World Records, Improbable Records* features such ridiculous entries as one concerning a potato that bore the unmistakable likeness of Queen Victoria and which was occasionally used by the monarch as a stand-in during particularly boring royal functions.

Awards

The Wild Washerwomen: A New Folk Tale was cited as a highly commended title by the Greenaway Award selection committee in 1979. *Rumbelow's Dance* was named runner-up for the Kurt Maschler Award in 1982.

TITLE COMMENTARY

📖 *THE BEAR'S WINTER HOUSE* (1969)

The Times Literary Supplement

SOURCE: "Modern Baby's Bookshelf," in *The Times Literary Supplement,* No. 3536, December 4, 1969, p. 1397.

[Quentin Blake's] innocent paintings perfectly set off John Yeoman's *The Bear's Winter House,* a charming little tale about a nice, quiet bear whose attempts to hibernate are thwarted by jolly, live-wire pig and his party-loving playmates—a squirrel, a hen and a hedgehog. The patient agony of the bear, as the hen sits singing on his head, is a sight to see.

The Junior Bookshelf

SOURCE: A review of *The Bear's Winter House,* in *The Junior Bookshelf,* Vol. 34, No. 1, February, 1970, p. 23.

This is a charming modern folktale, fully involving young listeners or readers in sympathy for the bear whose foresight protects him from the cold, only to be kept awake by the improvident friends whom he has kind-heartedly allowed into his winter house. Being a spirited animal, he does something about this, but even had the text been less amusing and satisfying, this would have been an outstanding picture book, made memorable by Quentin Blake's clean fresh illustrations with their economy of line, the delicate autumn colours enlivened by touches of violet and windswept blue and the pinkness of the pig.

Gary M. Ormond

SOURCE: A review of *The Bear's Winter House,* in *Library Journal,* Vol. 95, No. 12, June 15, 1970, p. 2305.

Hints of "The Little Red Hen" pervade this adequate tale of a kindly bear. Determined to spend a warm and comfortable winter, the bear constructs (according to blueprint) a house, unaided by his scoffing friends. But the bitter winter weather eventually drives the hen, pig, squirrel and hedgehog to seek shelter with him. The hospitable bear suffers through months of fun and games with his riotous friends, who show no inclination to sleep. Spring's return finds the weary host dismantling his house and sneaking away to rebuild—in a more remote spot. The crayon and watercolor illustrations [by Quentin Blake] are superior to the text and deftly characterize the carefree animals, as well as the hapless bear; the depictions of the seasons are particularly evocative: e.g., the heavy, dark and dreary winter clouds. Young readers can manage the text, which would also make a passable readaloud.

Julie Eccleshare

SOURCE: A review of *The Bear's Winter House,* in *British Book News Children's Books,* June, 1987, p. 6.

John Yeoman's charming bear needs a house for the winter. All the other animals laugh as he follows the detailed instructions for a house built of logs and branches lined with moss. They won't help with the building, even though he offers them a share of the shelter if they do. Then winter comes. The wind howls. Bear is warm and cosy but the squirrel, hedgehog, pig and hen shiver in their winter quarters. Kind bear takes them all in and they proceed to shatter his peaceful slumber. When spring comes they are up and off but bear settles down to catch up on the winter sleep he has missed. Both John Yeoman's text and Quentin Blake's illustrations are subtle and affectionate.

📖 *ALPHABET SOUP* (1969)

Pat Garrett

SOURCE: A review of *Alphabet Soup,* in *Children's Book Review,* Vol. I, No. 2, April, 1971, p. vii.

This is the latest variation on the 'A was an archer who shot at a frog' rhyme. With this clever version by John Yeoman 'A is for Actor who's learning his part'. The rhymes are witty and lively, and the drawings [by Quentin Blake] droll and amusing in three colours, blue, red and black.

📖 *THE BEAR'S WATER PICNIC* (1970)

Margery Fisher

SOURCE: A review of *The Bear's Water Picnic,* in *Growing Point,* Vol. 9, No. 6, December, 1970, p. 1645.

The bear takes his friends squirrel, hedgehog, hen and pig

for a picnic on a raft but the party is disturbed by the noisy comments of inquisitive frogs; these, however, prove useful when the raft goes aground on a mud bank. Quentin Blake's comic spiky pictures, with their happy, bright colours, strike just the right note for the comedy.

Kirkus Reviews

SOURCE: A review of *The Bear's Water Picnic,* in *Kirkus Reviews,* Vol. XXXIX, No. 3, January 15, 1971, p. 50.

Down a forest path come the pig, the squirrel, the hedgehog and the hen "looking very smart"; waiting at the lake's edge is the bear, with a picnic basket, an extra straw hat for the pig, and—"after they had all said hello to each other"—a newly-made raft: on a freshly minted spring day, could there be a better start for a picnic? And all goes well, with something apt for everyone (acorns for the pig, dead beetles for the hedgehog, etc.) until, poling away from a noisy chorus of frogs, they go aground on a sandbank. No one can or will swim for help, but the frogs, hailed, pitch in to make an enormous wave. Afloat again, they welcome the frogs—who welcome not their food but the flies attracted to it. Now, when the frogs sing their "awrk, awrk" song, the hen clucks, the hedgehog wheezes, the squirrel chatters, the pig snorts, the bear booms. Uncommonly fitting with an edge of affability and no slack.

The New York Times Book Review

SOURCE: "With a Hop and a Croak," in *The New York Times Book Review,* May 2, 1971, p. 8.

This is really a story about a bunch of other animals—a bear and a pig, a squirrel, a hen and a hedgehog. The story is about a picnic that these animals have, on a raft in a lake. There are frogs in the story and they are even responsible for the happy ending, but it isn't like this is a significant contribution to the body of frog literature. It's a simple story told in a friendly way with the happy illustrations of Quentin Blake. But it's not something that a frog would get all excited about.

Virginia Haviland

SOURCE: A review of *The Bear's Water Picnic,* in *The Horn Book Magazine,* Vol. XLVII, No. 4, August, 1971, p. 376.

A picnic by raft is organized by an infectiously convivial bear who provides for hedgehog, pig, hen, and squirrel their most toothsome foods and all the usual accoutrements of picnicking, down to individually monogrammed napkins. But bear could no more foresee the hazards of water-picnicking than the blithe company could imagine how the noisy frogs would save their day. The gay spirits of the party and the humor of the episodes are caught by the artist [Quentin Blake], who matches the clean preci-

sion of the prose telling in ink-line drawings with delicate colored overlays. The choreographic community of frogs (their graceful leaping in concert could, of course, raise the water level where needed) is remarkable.

Denise M. Wilms

SOURCE: A review of *The Bear's Water Picnic,* in *Booklist,* Vol. 84, No. 1, September 1, 1987, p. 75.

When a pig, a squirrel, a hedgehog, and a hen join their friend the bear for a pleasant picnic aboard a raft that bear has constructed, the day promises to be a blissful one. However, the animals' peaceful sojourn is interrupted by a chorus of frogs on a cluster of lily pads. The frogs want to join in the picnic but can't stop croaking, so the animals pole to a quieter part of the lake. The raft unexpectedly runs aground, however, and the animals are unable to extricate themselves; it's the frogs who come to the rescue, resulting in a fine new friendship between the two groups. The story has an amiable quality that makes it satisfying despite its rather sedate plot. Providing a boost are [Quentin] Blake's comical line-and-wash drawings; the artist's quick pen and eye for the nonsensical never fail to amuse. A beguiling bit of whimsy.

SIXES AND SEVENS (1971)

Jeff Jackson

SOURCE: A review of *Sixes and Sevens,* in *Children's Book Review,* Vol. I, No. 2, April, 1971, p. 48.

Barnaby takes a raft trip up river collecting an assortment of passengers en route. With the aid of a large tin trunk, that surrenders more objects than Harpo's bottomless drawers, to counter every eventuality, the voyage is a resounding, repeat resounding, success. Despite Quentin Blake's irresistible, funny water-colours and names to conjure with, such as Dorothea Gurdon, Eliza Distaff; localities named Pollard Weir, Couchgrass Common and so forth; the story remains a disappointment in that its ending lacks any element of surprise. Still, better to travel in hope etc . . . Yes, sixes and sevens.

Margery Fisher

SOURCE: A review of *Sixes and Sevens,* in *Growing Point,* Vol. 10, No. 2, July, 1971, p. 1775.

A sequential narrative drifting down river with Barnaby as he carries goods on a raft to Limber Lea. One kitten at Harmer's Landing, two mice at Long-acre Bottom . . . and so on to "Ten grasshoppers, bright and gay at Sandy Elbow". The stowing of the freight provides amusing crises to suit Quentin Blake's vivacious line and there are bonuses such as practice in counting and a fine wit in the choice of names for places and clients. A book to be savoured slowly.

C. Martin

SOURCE: A review of *Sixes and Sevens,* in *The Junior Bookshelf,* Vol. 35, No. 4, August, 1971, pp. 220-21.

Another wonderful book from this happy collaboration, in which the calm organisation shown in the text is seen against the mounting chaos portrayed in [Quentin Blake's] pictures. Barnaby takes a cargo from each village in turn as he punts his raft along the river, one kitten, then two mice, three schoolmistresses, up to ten grasshoppers at the penultimate stop. Each mutually antagonistic load is provided for by something out of the large brown trunk which Mother gave him, a sock to put the kitten in so that it won't attack the mice, who in their turn are found a jam jar so as not to be obnoxious to the next cargo. The text is delightful, breaking into rhyme on each page when the new passengers are introduced, whilst the bedlam on board is done with the artist's usual humour and skill; in fact he is better than ever, witness the rainy scene with its dripping skies and flat grey river, the three schoolmistresses, "stiff as twigs", holding up their obviously inadequate umbrellas. At the end of the journey ten cheerful people collect their several consignments and the young reader has learnt to count up to ten. Or if he hasn't, at least he has enjoyed his travels.

Aileen Howard

SOURCE: A review of *Sixes and Sevens,* in *The Booklist,* Vol. 68, No. 9, January 1, 1972, p. 396.

There is much to look at and laugh at in this delightful counting book. As Barnaby poles his raft up the river to Limber Lea he picks up as cargo and passengers 1 kitten, 2 mice, 3 schoolmistresses, 4 schoolboys, and so on to 9 frogs and 10 grasshoppers. Although he has a boxful of such things as drainpipes (to contain the 8 snakes) to help keep the situation in hand, bedlam prevails. Repetition and rhyme enhance the text and humor and action abound in the watercolor illustrations [by Quentin Blake] which gaily picture the mounting confusion on the raft.

Virginia Haviland

SOURCE: A review of *Sixes and Sevens,* in *The Horn Book Magazine,* Vol. XLVIII, No. 1, February, 1972, p. 43.

Nonsense in a blithe number book. One kitten, two mice, three schoolmistresses, . . . nine frogs, and ten grasshoppers become a company of incongruous passengers for young Barnaby's river-raft pick-up service downstream to Limber Lea. The fun is developed by means of rhymes with chantable lines, wonderfully absurd names, and amusing water-color scenes [by Quentin Blake]. Barnaby's passenger list, Lear-like in exaggeration, increases until upon its arrival at Limber Lea the raft bears a congested, writhing, jumping lot of creatures ready for "ten cheerful people / who had come to collect"

them. An extra element of the absurd, which creates continuity from episode to episode, is Barnaby's big box. The listener soon begins to realize that it will provide equipment for any newcomer and ensure peace and amity on the raft. "The snakes can stay in the drainpipes from here to Limber Lea," says Barnaby in his relaxed resourcefulness.

Judith Sharman

SOURCE: A review of *Sixes and Sevens,* in *Books for Keeps,* No. 52, September, 1988, p. 7.

This zany number book collaboration between Yeoman and [Quentin] Blake is tremendously successful. Verse and illustration complement each other with delicious absurdity. As Barnaby sails on his raft down to Limber Lea, he picks up an extraordinary collection of creatures and people. It is only by ingenuity and with the aid of the amazing contents of his red box that all arrive almost intact at their destination.

MOUSE TROUBLE (1972)

Marcus Crouch

SOURCE: A review of *Mouse Trouble,* in *The Junior Bookshelf,* Vol. 36, No. 6, December, 1972, pp. 362-63.

Mouse Trouble has an original story and a lively and resourceful presentation. The humour, exquisitely matched between words and pictures, has just that quality of sober absurdity which children particularly love. What other author-artist team would think of mice and a cat ganging up against the miller? The lively and musical text and the swift scribbly drawings are dropped upon the page with an expertise which could teach lessons to many more self-conscious artists in this medium.

Kirkus Reviews

SOURCE: A review of *Mouse Trouble,* in *Kirkus Reviews,* Vol. XLI, No. 1, January 1, 1973, p. 3.

John Yeoman pulls off an unlikely cat and mice story with disarming *eclat,* and Quentin Blake's comfortably untidy line and water color pictures are just as accomplished. The scene is a lovingly particularized rundown windmill infested with capering mice who finally drive the miller to buy a cat. But the ineffectual tabby provides the mice with so much fun and exercise that they foil the now disgruntled miller's attempt to drown him—the natural enemies then coexisting harmoniously in the mill "and playing endless games of cat and mice." Blake's ebullient profusion of mice—sliding down the grain chute, revolving on the old millstone, or congregating in the pockets of hung up aprons—and his frazzled tabby match the fluent telling with their own brisk mobility.

Publishers Weekly

SOURCE: A review of *Mouse Trouble,* in *Publishers Weekly,* Vol. 203, No. 9, February 26, 1973, p. 123.

Here, [Yeoman and Quentin Blake] have an original and droll creation about a grumpy miller who, pestered by hundreds of mice, buys a tabby cat. But the miller is so mean that he won't feed the cat, which becomes too weak to chase the lively mice. They are affectionate rodents and feel sorry for their feckless enemy so they let him pretend to catch them and invent games for him to play. Everyone is happy until the miller discovers more mice than ever in his place; then, he makes up his mind to drown the tabby. How the mice save the day and themselves makes a merry tale and pictures.

Zena Sutherland

SOURCE: A review of *Mouse Trouble,* in *Bulletin of the Center for Children's Books,* Vol. 26, No. 9, May, 1973, p. 148.

A nonsensical story has a frail plot, depending for its appeal on the incongruity of the situation, the satisfactions of outwitting a curmudgeon, and the lively illustrations of hundreds of amiable mice. The mice live in a mill, detested by the miller, who obtains a large cat. The miller is "so mean" that he mistreats the cat, who is apathetic; the mice decide to make life more pleasant for the cat, so they pretend to fear him. The cat is happier, but he catches no mice, so he is tied in a sack by the miller. The compassionate mice replace the cat with objects of suitable weight after extracting a promise that there will be no mouse-catching if the cat's life is spared. The miller throws the sack in the river—and the cat thereafter lives in secret content at the top of the mill, playing happy games of cat and mouse. Mildly amusing, but the story has little punch and a very weak ending.

📖 *BEATRICE AND VANESSA* (1974)

Marcus Crouch

SOURCE: A review of *Beatrice and Vanessa,* in *The Junior Bookshelf,* Vol. 39, No. 1, February, 1975, pp. 24-5.

No partners give such exquisite pleasure today—mainly, one suspects, by giving pleasure to themselves—as the [John Yeoman-Quentin Blake] team. Their new book is about another happy partnership, that between the ewe Beatrice and the nanny-goat Vanessa. The story of their adventures on holiday owes something to folk tale, but the treatment is entirely individual. The hilarious narrative is handled in deadpan fashion. I love it, and so will many children.

Kirkus Reviews

SOURCE: A review of *Beatrice and Vanessa,* in *Kirkus Reviews,* Vol. XLIII, No. 8, April 15, 1975, p. 450.

Beatrice the ewe and Vanessa the nanny-goat, who have spent 40 years nattering together at the same gate, decide to take a vacation—and as they have nothing of their own to pack they borrow from the farmhouse an old shopping bag and a wolf head hung with balloons (seems the farmers are sleeping off a party). Employing both their wits and their unusual baggage, the two animals save themselves from a pack of lean, hungry wolves and a fat bear who has them up a tree (a nice touch of gentle absurdity), and go home. But now as they continue their conver-sation at the gate, "they really have got something to talk about." This is not much more remarkable than the old friends' everyday lives, but Quentin Blake's amiable sketches have an easy-going air that complements the unpretentious telling.

Publishers Weekly

SOURCE: A review of *Beatrice and Vanessa,* in *Publishers Weekly,* Vol. 207, No. 19, May 12, 1975, p. 66.

A ewe and a nanny goat, both well past middle age, are the plucky heroines of this lively adventure, set in a dark forest. Beatrice and Vanessa find farm life dull, after many long years, and decide to take a vacation. Setting off with only a stuffed wolf's head and a string of balloons, they encounter a ferocious bear and a pack of hungry wolves. The story is a real cliffhanger, with our heroines (Vanessa is especially clever) outwitting their pursuers at the very last moment. The story is a treat and so are Quentin Blake's wash drawings.

Anita Silvey

SOURCE: A review of *Beatrice and Vanessa,* in *The Horn Book Magazine,* Vol. LI, No. 3, June, 1975, p. 259.

Beatrice, a ewe, and Vanessa, a nanny-goat, "for as long as they could remember . . . had nibbled the same grass, ambled slowly round the same farm buildings, rubbed their sides against the same tree, and stood nattering together with their chins resting on the same gate." But eventually the boredom grew oppressive, and they ventured from their everyday abode into the forest. A little short on brains, Beatrice had to rely on Vanessa to frighten away a pack of wolves and a furry, but nevertheless ferocious, bear. After all the excitement, their adventures ended as peacefully as they had begun—only now they really had "something to talk about" at their favorite gate. The story is less inventive and less interesting than *Mouse Trouble* and *Sixes and Sevens,* but the illustrations are marked by the vivacity and high spirits that always characterize Quentin Blake's work.

The Booklist

SOURCE: A review of *Beatrice and Vanessa,* in *The Booklist,* Vol. 71, No. 20, June 15, 1975, p. 1078.

Two dear old friends, Beatrice, a timid ewe, and Vanessa,

a sensible nannygoat, find barnyard life dull and decide to take a holiday. Their problem of what to pack is solved when they tiptoe in and "borrow" from the farmhouse. The wolf-head trophy, clutch of balloons left over from last night's party, and roomy totebag that they make off with are unlikely baggage but turn out to be just the items to ward off a nasty wolf pack and fearsome bear. [Quentin] Blake's deft, scattered lines form animals that fit the story's whimsical absurdity perfectly. The zesty, energetic humor displayed in such exaggerations as the wolves' rolling red tongues or the complete disarray of their flight will not be lost on young audiences, who will also enjoy savoring the civilized demeanor of the two pasture chums.

Zena Sutherland

SOURCE: A review of *Beatrice and Vanessa*, in *Bulletin of the Center for Children's Books*, Vol. 29, No. 3, November, 1975, p. 56.

Amicable companions for many years, Vanessa the nanny goat and Beatrice the ewe decide that their lives are dull and they need a vacation. Since they have nothing of their own to pack, they borrow some balloons left from a party, a shopping bag, and a stuffed wolf's head and go off. The stuffed head frightens off a pack of hungry wolves; the balloons, popping, convince a predatory bear that guns are being fired. Beatrice and Vanessa go home. A slight plot, weakened by the coincidence of the packed objects, but there's a mildly silly air about the whole thing that is not unappealing, and the raffish line and dulcet hues of [Quentin Blake's] illustrations (watercolor with pen and ink) echo nicely the mildness and the silliness.

THE PUFFIN BOOK OF IMPROBABLE RECORDS (with Quentin Blake, 1975; reprinted as *The Improbable Book of Records*, 1976)

Anita Silvey

SOURCE: A review of *The Improbable Book of Records*, in *The Horn Book Magazine*, Vol. LII, No. 5, October, 1976, pp. 489-90.

This spoof on the *Guiness Book of World Records* requires no familiarity with the original; it should amuse even the uninitiated. From the first piece of information—that the book "is the only one to be issued to all the U.S. Marines as part of their survival kit on account of the high nutritional value of its paper and printing ink"—and from the accompanying illustration of the compilers measuring an octopus's tentacle, it becomes clear that the author-artist team [of Quentin Blake and John Yeoman] has produced another zany creation. The inventiveness of the records is almost less brilliant than the way they are visually depicted; the artist has worked out all the intricacies of a man balancing twenty-eight bananas on his nose and the subtle qualities of a potato bearing a striking resemblance to Queen Victoria. (Incidentally, the authors

inform us that this tuber "stood in for Her Majesty at a number of rather boring royal functions.") Every improbable record is wonderfully absurd; each picture, even more madcap; and the entire creation, delightful.

Marjorie Lewis

SOURCE: A review of *The Improbable Book of Records*, in *School Library Journal*, Vol. 23, No. 2, October, 1976, p. 104.

For addicts of Guinness and Ripley—a witty spoof that attempts to appeal to both sides of the Atlantic but is really weighted on the side of the British. Americans will miss the humor of "the longest football fan's scarf" (over 7.2 miles and begun as a sock) or the sausage served for school dinner 8,947 times and returned uneaten, and few will even know what a "conker" is. [Quentin] Blake's colorful drawings are deliciously demented, and the combined wit of Blake and Yeoman is most marvelously evident in inventive names for their record holders (Eliza Widdershins, Adam Senilitude). But, like Hoban's *How Tom Beat Captain Najork and His Hired Sportsmen*, also illustrated by Blake, the humor is so parochial that the audience for this will be very, very limited. The picture-book set or even those in the lower elementary grades will not find this their cup of tea.

THE YOUNG PERFORMING HORSE (1977)

Margery Fisher

SOURCE: A review of *The Young Performing Horse*, in *Growing Point*, Vol. 16, No. 9, April, 1978, p. 3297.

Vicky and Bertie (significantly named), sent to market to buy a horse to take them to school, are tempted by a curious spotted creature who prefers sandwiches to hay and who helps them finally to fame and fortune in the Victorian theatre, with a command performance before the Queen, who is "highly amused" by a Red Riding Hood Ballet. This diverting good-luck tale is illustrated in serenely shadowed, muted colour, with the element of parody and satire nicely balanced against a fantasy perfectly adapted to youthful aspirations. A jewel of a book.

Marcus Crouch

SOURCE: A review of *The Young Performing Horse*, in *The Junior Bookshelf*, Vol. 42, No. 3, June, 1978, p. 136.

Quentin Blake calls for detailed study and for many re-readings. This is not to say that **The Young Performing Horse** is not hilarious from the word go, just that it gets better with each repetition. The action moves from an idyllic countryside to theatreland in Victorian London and a command performance at Buckingham Palace. For once the widowed Queen was amused, and so was Prince Teddy, a fat boy in kilt. If not a laugh a line, there is certainly at least one laugh to the square inch of this enchanting book.

Publishers Weekly

SOURCE: A review of *The Young Performing Horse,* in *Publishers Weekly,* Vol. 215, No. 16, April 16, 1979, p. 76.

[Quentin] Blake's exuberant cartoons in full color multiply the joys in Yeoman's fanciful tale. Vicky and Bertie Priddy buy a small horse to carry them from their farm home to school. The amiable animal is so intelligent that the teacher welcomes him in the classroom and he learns lessons with the children, even performs in their square dances. Then come hard times; the Priddy crops fail and so the tearful parents send Vicky, Bertie and the performing horse to London to seek their fortunes as thespians. The trio become world famous, with the horse as star of the acts at Mr. Crumble's Theatre. Their hungry times end when they give a command performance for the Queen. The book too is a gala performance, but it would help young Americans if details such as the price of the horse (two guineas) and others were explained.

Jane Bickel

SOURCE: A review of *The Young Performing Horse,* in *School Library Journal,* Vol. 26, No. 1, September, 1979, p. 125.

The team of Yeoman and Blake (**Mouse Trouble,** 1973) again gives a zany tale distinctive treatment. A twin brother and sister purchase a **Young Performing Horse** to give them rides to school. The horse does beautifully in class—learning sums, spelling, and folkdancing. When hard times befall the family, the children and their talented pet go to London to seek a fortune on the stage. Of course, they become such celebrities that the Queen commands a performance. The romp is enhanced by [Quentin] Blake's playful line-and-wash cartoons in bright colors. The hero is winning and the scenes of children's theater suitably boisterous.

📖 THE WILD WASHERWOMEN: A NEW FOLK TALE (1979)

Paul Heins

SOURCE: A review of *The Wild Washerwomen: A New Folk Tale,* in *The Horn Book Magazine,* Vol. LVI, No. 1, February, 1980, pp. 50-1.

Told in the manner of a folk tale, the story tells how seven washerwomen—Dottie, Lottie, Molly, Dolly, Winnie, Minnie, and Ernestine—worked hard washing mountains of dirty laundry in the river. Finally, disgruntled with their job, they went berserk, splashing passers-by with muddy water, raising havoc in the marketplace, steal-ing fruit in orchards, and generally making themselves the terror of neighboring villages. But meeting their match in seven woodcutters who lived in the forest, they all married and settled down to a happy life of clothes-washing and woodcutting. The preposterous, joyful narrative and the expressive caricaturing of the slapdash line drawings washed with color [by Quentin Blake] are perfectly balanced; story and pictures move from page to page in a hilarious progress, the illustrations continuously echoing and expanding the often understated humor of the text.

Barbara Elleman

SOURCE: A review of *The Wild Washerwomen: A New Folk Tale,* in *Booklist,* Vol. 76, No. 11, February 1, 1980, p. 774.

Mr. Balthazar Tight, a mean old laundry owner, keeps his seven washerwomen working day and night until one day, fed up with "filthy sheets, grubby hankies, horrid socks, grimy nightshirts, messy tablecloths, and ghastly towels," they decide to revolt. They shove the clothes in Mr. Tight's face, grab an empty goat cart, and, leaving chaos in their wake, race through the marketplace. When the ladies see seven extremely dirty woodcutters, their instincts take over and they rowdily plunge the men into the water for scrubbing. Whereupon seven woodcutters take seven brides—and all live happily ever after. This rollicking romp is visualized in scrawly lines awash in a mélange of colors that effectively convey the boisterous spree with great spirit and style.

Zena Sutherland

SOURCE: A review of *The Wild Washerwomen,* in *Bulletin of the Center for Children's Books,* Vol. 33, No. 7, March, 1980, pp. 143-44.

This isn't a very substantial story, but it's told with such abandon and illustrated with such vigor and humor that it's an engaging tall tale. [Quentin] Blake's scrawly, energetic line takes full advantage of the harum-scarum plot and its excesses, as the seven washerwomen rebel against their hard-driving employer and go on a rampage that includes upsetting market carts, bashing hats in a hat shop, spraying passersby with mud as their goat-cart careens through the town pond, etc. Seven woodcutters hear of the rampage, try to teach the obstreperous women a lesson and end by being scrubbed, soaked, pounded, rinsed, wrung out, and put in the sun to dry like laundry. As any reader might foretell, they all pair off, and then the seven woodcutters' wives live bucolically ever after. Not sensible, but fun.

Mary B. Nickerson

SOURCE: A review of *The Wild Washerwomen,* in *School Library Journal,* Vol. 26, No. 7, March, 1980, p. 127.

Good grief, are we still having to deal with this sort of

thing? Seven washerwomen rebel against their employer, make off with a goat cart, and rampage through the countryside, overturning market stalls, stealing food, ringing churchbells. (A dissatisfied, assertive woman will go out of control.) There are several jaunty illustrations of the women beating up men, bending their rifles, dunking them in rain barrels. Eventually seven burly woodcutters hear about the women and, after dirtying themselves to look as frightening as possible, encounter them on a woodland path. One of the women cries, "Come on girls, remember you're washerwomen!" and the men are washed and wooed. (All those women really wanted was. . . .) The last picture is of the men, women, and their babies all sharing tasks together—a sop to liberation and a patently illogical one at that. Alas, the story is happily illustrated with giddy and well-designed watercolors, so children might be attracted to it, and artfully paced so they might remember it. Let's hope this talented English team will thump a different drum next time around.

Gabrielle Maunder

SOURCE: A review of *The Wild Washerwomen,* in *The School Librarian,* Vol. 28, No. 2, June, 1980, p. 143.

All conservatives and all men be warned that this book is both subversive and Militant Lib. As soon as it is placed in a library it will provoke a queue of eager readers. How could anyone resist a fairy tale about seven washerwomen, called Dottie, Lottie, Molly, Dolly, Winnie, Minnie and Ernestine, who take up the cudgels against the exploitation of the laundry owner, Mr Balthazar Tight? Having found freedom, they go on the rampage in the local town and behave in the most reprehensible way, to the consternation of the local population. All ends happily, with seven weddings and a 'Seven brides for seven brothers' romp. A most exhilarating book. The pace is fast and furious, the pictures crammed with [Quentin] Blake's spiky-fingered females and unkempt dogs. I loved every moment.

RUMBELOW'S DANCE (1983)

Candida Lycett Green

SOURCE: "Prancing Along," in *The Times Literary Supplement,* No. 4156, November 26, 1982, p. 1306.

The text of *Rumbelow's Dance,* is the sort of thing young children love to hear and old parents get bored with reading. Like the woman who can't get her pig home from market, Rumbelow performs in reverse. A repetitive verse grows longer and longer with each page as Rumbelow collects a wild and motley crew along his way through water colour woods until he has a mad procession dancing and prancing behind him into town. They all tumble in a gaggle of arms and legs onto the door-step of Rumbelow's grandparents and end up dancing market day away. It is the perfect medium for [Quentin] Blake to display his range of rural lads, lasses and animals and a

happy one for John Yeoman, who once he's written the first verse, is away.

For four to seven year olds I would recommend it because it is light and merry and happy and, perhaps best of all, has no hidden political message. The illustrations are superbly funny though the text is less so. My four year old son should, in the end, be the ultimate judge, and he, when I'd finished reading it to him said, "That was good that."

Marcus Crouch

SOURCE: A review of *Rumbelow's Dance,* in *The Junior Bookshelf,* Vol. 47, No. 1, February, 1983, p. 10.

It would be absurd to offer any criticism of **Rumbelow's Dance**. There is no better partnership today than Yeoman and Blake. Word and drawing seem to have come about through a single creative act. The story is a memorable variant on the cumulative folk-tale. Rumbelow, who appears to be about two feet tall but cheerful and energetic, goes to visit his grandparents. He dances away, and meets in succession a number of gloomy characters, human and animal. These succumb to Rumbelow's optimism and join in the dance. By the time Rumbelow reaches his grandparents' house he has enough companions to fill it; happily there is tea and cakes for all. Most attention will inevitably be directed to the pictures, which show Quentin Blake at his inventive best, but do look closely at the words. John Yeoman applies the repetitive formula—repetition with variation—with the greatest skill and gusto. There is not a syllable too many nor a word out of tune. How good to see such fun and unaffected popular appeal coming out of a work based firmly on fine craftmanship and sound observation.

Margery Fisher

SOURCE: A review of *Rumbelow's Dance,* in *Growing Point,* Vol. 21, No. 6, March, 1983, p. 4049.

Folk-tale cumulation provides the shape for an entrancing and pointed look at a child's talent for improvising and for spontaneous enjoyment. Off to visit grandparents, small Rumbelow attaches to himself a farmer with a lazy pig, a tinker with a heavy pack, an organ-grinder with a recalcitrant monkey and other burdened travellers, whose troubles are lightened by the gay dance that ends with generous hospitality from the old couple, skipping almost as lightly as their grandson. The pictures follow the text with dash and vigour and with a visual rhythm and movement which exactly match the jigging progress of the text.

THE HERMIT AND THE BEAR (1984)

Margery Fisher

SOURCE: A review of *The Hermit and the Bear,* in

Growing Point, Vol. 23, No. 4, November, 1984, p. 4355.

After fifteen years waiting for his advertisement for a pupil to bring results, the Hermit takes on a Bear which happens to be passing—a pupil whose eagerness to master the principles of cookery, masonry, punting and boxing is gratifying in principle but destructive in practice. Fortunately the last lesson in the curriculum, Community Work, gives enormous pleasure to the local Darby and Joan Club on their annual outing, even if a good deal of tea is spilled in the process, and the elegantly correct Prize Giving (with a decorative sash labelled 'Miss Hastings Old Town 1947' added to a decorative scroll) leads to the newly qualified Bear being taken on as 'Assistant Tutor, to share light house-work duties'. The author has multiplied incongruities with the help of Quentin Blake's quaintly veracious drawings, to make an entertaining bit of drollery with a certain emotional bite underneath.

John Mole

SOURCE: "Space to Dance," in *The Times Literary Supplement,* No. 4258, November 9, 1984, p. 1294.

An example of routine Quentin Blake, the jobbing illustrator, can be found in John Yeoman's *The Hermit and the Bear*. This is the pleasantly written tale of a clumsy, literal-minded bruin, and of the attempts of a dotty, long-suffering hermit to educate him in practical matters and the ways of civilization. Everything that can possibly go wrong does, but in the end the pupil receives his diploma for having achieved "a much higher average attainment than we could reasonably have expected of him".

Marcus Crouch

SOURCE: A review of *The Hermit and the Bear,* in *The Junior Bookshelf,* Vol. 48, No. 6, December, 1984, pp. 259-60.

In the world of the picture-book the firm of Yeoman and Blake is well ahead of most of its competitors. The balance between picture and text, and the harmony between artist and writer, are near perfection. But now John Yeoman has become more ambitious. Instead of 32 pages we have 112, many of them without benefit of Quentin Blake's inimitable drawings, and no colour. This puts rather more strain on the writer than he is at present capable of sustaining. It is a funny book—no book with Mr. Blake's famous bear in it could be otherwise—but not funny enough. For more than half of its length the writer seems to be feeling his way, labouring over the jokes and underlining them in case they get missed. Then suddenly he finds himself and the book ends in a most agreeable frolic.

The hermit takes Bear as his pupil and gives him instruction in a number of practical skills. The bear, in a sense,

passes his tests. It is a great idea, and might have come off better in picture-book form. Mr. Blake is a master of line and his bear is irresistibly funny always, but he seems to miss colour and the text restricts him for most of the book to only two characters. Nice as the book is, it does less than justice to both contributors, for opposing reasons.

Marcus Crouch

SOURCE: A review of *The Hermit and the Bear,* in *The School Librarian,* Vol. 33, No. 2, June, 1985, p. 132.

Quentin Blake and John Yeoman are well known and much loved as one of the most successful partnerships in the making of the picture book. But ***The Hermit and the Bear*** is not a picture book, but a long story with a sadly limited number of line illustrations. Mr Yeoman is, in fact, trying to break out, and on the evidence of this book I wish he wouldn't. There are some nice touches in the story of how the hermit attempts to educate a stupid but resilient bear, and of course Mr Blake is infinitely resourceful and accomplished; but many of the jokes are heavily laboured, as if the reader is assumed to be as dim as the bear. A good idea has managed to find the wrong form for its expression. Let us hope that these two fine craftsmen will go back to what they do supremely well.

OUR VILLAGE: POEMS (1988)

Publishers Weekly

SOURCE: A review of *Our Village,* in *Publishers Weekly,* Vol. 234, No. 9, August 26, 1988, p. 88.

Yeoman and [Quentin] Blake create an entire village, from the maps on the endpapers to the poems within the pages, which introduce both people and places: a washer woman "pegs the washing up to dry, / like brightly colored kites," and "Headache, nosebleed, / Cough or flu—Dr. Potts / Knows what to do." A gardener grows oversized plants, but he is the smallest man in town; a tailor is too busy to notice how much his own clothing needs to be replaced or patched. And a pond in winter has "a coating of ice like a great windowpane." The characters frolic on the pages, in Blake's looselined, flowing art. And the result of both poems and pictures is a strong sense of place, where readers will meet town eccentrics and ordinary folk, tumbling through the book, busy with their lives.

Ellen Fader

SOURCE: A review of *Our Village,* in *The Horn Book Magazine,* Vol. LXV, No. 1, January-February, 1989, pp. 62-3.

The baker, Mr. Crumb, and the black-smith, Mr. Smutts,

are but a few of the intriguing residents readers meet during a visit to *Our Village*. Absent-minded Dotty Lou relies on her cows to stop her from falling in the river; Samuel Flowerbutts grows onions the size of footballs; and the Podgsons's General Store is so cluttered with stock that a half an hour is required to find a ball of string. [Quentin] Blake's characteristic watercolor and ink drawings artlessly evoke a simpler time, when children swam in ponds, skated at night by the light of the moon, and were entertained by Mr. Mandolini and his sad dancing bear. Endpapers enticingly picture, in spring and winter, the places described in each verse. Yeoman's twenty-one poems vary in length and rhythm, adding diversity and interest to the collection. Enjoyably free of nostalgia yet resonant with a warm and relaxed feeling that draws the reader wholly into another time and place, *Our Village* is a perfect book for adventurers and armchair travelers alike.

Ruth K. MacDonald

SOURCE: A review of *Our Village,* in *School Library Journal,* Vol. 35, No. 7, March, 1989, p. 175.

This book is introduced only by a poem on the front flap. Inside the cover, there is a map of *Our Village,* but otherwise, there are no titles to the poems, nor any indicators as to where this village is or in which period the poems are supposed to be set. The poems are funny, but not great poetry; frequently the lines are filled out by an inventive repetition of words, as though the poet were at a loss for an appropriate iamb or alternative. The pictures are cartoon-like and full of motion and humor, but the historical detail with which the poems are frequently concerned do not appear in them. The result is a volume with some occasionally entertaining character vignettes and some interesting illustrations, but the two do not merge into an artistic whole, so the volume seems without purpose or vision.

Marcus Crouch

SOURCE: A review of *Our Village,* in *The Junior Bookshelf,* Vol. 53, No. 2, April, 1989, p. 64.

The tried and proven partnership of Yeoman and Blake is here again, and again proves an unbeatable formula for a really funny picture-book. In loosely woven, shrewdly observant verses John Yeoman introduces the odd, readily recognised characters who make up his village community. Quentin Blake adds his inimitable colour and wit. Pictorial end-papers lay out the topographical outline; then we meet in order Mr. Crumb the baker, Mr. Puce the postman, Mr. Arkwright who rides a penny-farthing, Miss Thynne the teacher, and all the other unconventional inhabitants of this enchanting place. As ever Mr. Blake packs every corner of his designs with very funny and appropriate detail. The book has a cumulative effect. Great stuff.

📖 *OLD MOTHER HUBBARD'S DOG DRESSES UP* (1989), *OLD MOTHER HUBBARD'S DOG LEARNS TO PLAY* (1989), *OLD MOTHER HUBBARD'S DOG NEEDS A DOCTOR* (1989), *OLD MOTHER HUBBARD'S DOG TAKES UP SPORT* (1989)

Publishers Weekly

SOURCE: A review of *Old Mother Hubbard's Dog Dresses Up* and others, in *Publishers Weekly,* Vol. 237, No. 32, August 10, 1990, p. 442.

There four fetching farces chronicle various canine capers of this celebrated pet. The eccentric and delightfully dotty Mother Hubbard frets as her dog outsmarts and frazzles his poor mistress at every turn. When she criticizes his coat, the playful dog dresses up first as Lord Nelson, then a clown and a knight in full armor. When chided for reading too much, the wily animal tries out a variety of instruments, leaving the frustrated old dame with pillows clamped over her ears. While some of the idiomatic phrases require a certain facility on the reader's part, the overall richness of language and vibrant humor stand out. The notable pen-and-ink and watercolor illustrations sparkle with sass and vitality, as they keep perfect tempo with the marvelously bouncing verse.

Lee Beasley

SOURCE: A review of *Old Mother Hubbard's Dog Dresses Up* and others, in *Children's Book Review Service,* Vol. 19, No. 2, October, 1990, p. 18.

Old Mother Hubbard does what many adults do when they see their children sitting around reading. She thinks her dog should be doing something instead of enjoying his book. He takes her suggestions literally and his zany activities drive her to distraction. These four little books with their rhyming texts will keep youngsters thinking up other activities. The sprightly and comical illustrations add to the humor.

Carolyn Phelan

SOURCE: A review of *Old Mother Hubbard's Dog Dresses Up* and others, in *Booklist,* Vol. 87, No. 8, December 15, 1990, p. 863.

In each book Dame Hubbard offers her insouciant hound some motherly advice. In response, the dog stops reading in his comfortable chair and takes up the suggestion with high spirits, dramatic flair, and comical excess that drive the old woman to distraction. While the verses follow the nursery rhyme's familiar rhyming pattern, Yeoman's sassy lines are original. [Quentin] Blake's line drawings, bright with watercolor washes, are well suited to the text in every way. In fact, much of the comic effect comes from the facial expressions and body language of the two main characters. While the bindings are not substantial, neither is the price. Good books to choose for short, snappy story-hour fillers, these are certain to please kids who like their humor on the silly side and don't mind watching a spunky little fellow run circles around his "mother."

Ellen Fader

SOURCE: A review of *Old Mother Hubbard's Dog Dresses Up* and others, in *School Library Journal,* Vol. 37, No. 2, February, 1991, pp. 76-7.

Old Mother Hubbard, dissatisfied with her dog's behavior, prompts him to get exercise, take pride in his coat, and learn to play instead of sitting around reading. When, with the indefatigable energy of the typical toddler, he heeds her suggestions, he exhausts her by getting involved in every imaginable situation from blowing the rugs off the floor with his trombone to using her piglets to practice the shot put and stealing the legs off the bed while dressed up as a burglar. It is not pleasure in the language or witty wordplay that will generate smiles here; the books' appeal lies in the dog's irreverent behavior, which will intrigue children. [Quentin] Blake's familiar energetic black-line and watercolor illustrations are perfectly paired with these brief rhymes, reinforcing the silly unpredictability of each.

Miriam Martinez and Marcia F. Nash

SOURCE: A review of *Old Mother Hubbard's Dog Learns to Play,* in *Language Arts,* Vol. 69, No. 1, January, 1992, p. 64.

Old Mother Hubbard's dog has always been full of surprises. (Remember how she found the dog quite dead on returning from her trip to the baker? And then, when she went to the undertaker to buy him a coffin, she returned to find him laughing!) Given that history, perhaps Old Mother Hubbard should have thought twice before telling her dog, who sat engrossed in a book, that he really should learn to play, for reading is bad for the eyes. Well, the dog made every attempt to learn to play—musical instruments, that is. The dog took up instrument after instrument, and each attempt, much to Old Mother Hubbard's chagrin, was equally disastrous. We suspect that in the midst of this hilarity, there is a lesson for Old Mother Hubbard about the values of reading.

📖 *FEATHERBRAINS* (1993)

Ann Darnton

SOURCE: A review of *Featherbrains,* in *The School Librarian,* Vol. 41, No. 3, August, 1993, p. 112.

Flossie and Bessie are battery hens condemned—and perfectly happy to be so condemned—to a stifling and regimented life in a long shed which they share with twenty thousand other hens. Each day they perform the same

actions, repeat the same stock phrases and, in Bessie's case, dream the same delightful dream in which she is a hen living in a long shed with twenty thousand other hens. All this changes one Thursday morning when Jackdaw accidently frees Flossie and Bessie and introduces them to the pleasures of the outside world. With the assistance of Quentin Blake's typically pointed and observant illustrations, John Yeoman tells the amusing story of the two hens' attempts to come to terms both with the freedom of choice and with the dangers which inevitably accompany such freedom.

This book will give much pleasure to Key Stage 1 readers; however, it would be well worth using with older children too. This isn't simply a book about factory farming. Its story provides a metaphor for our own modern life-style dominated by over-heated houses, vitamin-enriched convenience foods, and lack of exercise and consequently will provide an amusing but perceptive starting point for discussion across the primary range.

Jill Bennett

SOURCE: A review of *Featherbrains,* in *Books for Keeps,* No. 87, July, 1994, p. 7.

Flossie and Bessie are accidentally released by Jack(daw) from their battery cage. At first they find the world outside strange—how can you walk on the ground when there's no wire to hold on to?—and want to go back to their 20,000 companions in the battery shed. But with the help of the worldly-wise Jack, they discover what it's like to be real chickens.

John Yeoman uses humour and irony in this entertaining exposé of factory farming, egged on by Quentin Blake, whose scruffy and naïve hens are a treat to behold.

Alan Horsfield

SOURCE: A review of *Featherbrains,* in *Magpies,* Vol. 9, No. 3, July, 1994, p. 30.

The title **Featherbrains** immediately captures the intent of this tightly constructed adventure. Two battery hens are lured from their safe, fully automated shed into the wide world outside by a jackdaw. They are tentative and not sure they are going to like it. Their subsequent encounters provide a number of amusing misadventures. The hens' efforts to interpret the real world with their experience from the laying shed come close to causing disaster.

The text is clear and the story, with the aid of the illustrations, flows effortlessly. The repetition created by Flossie and Bessie's inane discussions is not forced or contrived. It completely suits their serious, naive simplicity.

Quentin Blake's scratchy line drawings complement the character and antics of the two escaped hens and the topsy-turvy world in which they discover that there is life outside the laying shed. Blake captures the ridiculous and absurd. It is very easy to visualise two confused battery hens trying to find security in a discarded shopping trolley.

Reading this book to a class group, I found that a large percentage of the children had no real concept of battery hens. Recommended reading, especially for those with an off-beat sense of humour.

📖 THE FAMILY ALBUM (1993)

Marcus Crouch

SOURCE: A review of *The Family Album,* in *The Junior Bookshelf,* Vol. 58, No. 1, February, 1994, p. 17.

[John Yeoman's] loose-rhythmed lines lurch along in the best tradition of doggerel. Who cares? He introduces us to a typically eccentric family—'Our lot really are a remarkable crowd'—and provides a series of photo-opportunities for Quentin Blake at his most exuberant and assured. His swift spidery lines fill every nook and cranny of the page. Great fun, shrewd observation, yet not an unkind word or line anywhere.

Gill Roberts

SOURCE: A review of *The Family Album,* in *Books for Keeps,* No. 95, November, 1995, p. 9.

> 'Granpa beckons us over and quick as can be
> We all snuggle down on the squashy settee.'

This provided a family history session which honestly left a class of six- and seven-year-olds (plus me, of course) chuckling long after the downright raucous laughter had waned.

There's Cousin Charlie who's 'only just ten' and has 'lived in the kitchen since goodness knows when' not to mention super-powered-bike-mad Annabelle Jane, disguise artists Uncle Ignatius and Auntie Diane, Great Uncle Bertie (who thinks he's a budgie), Uncle Marvello and Auntie Shazam (alias Eric and Pam), Baby Cedric super crawler, tardy Cousin Ted, paint-potty Cousin Lucy and many more. . . .

A brilliant book, brilliantly illustrated, which defies anyone to keep a straight face. No classroom, staffroom, home or library should be without it.

📖 THE SINGING TORTOISE AND OTHER ANIMAL FOLK TALES (1994)

Margaret Clark

SOURCE: A review of *The Singing Tortoise,* in *Books for Keeps,* No. 83, November, 1993, p. 32.

The eleven tales retold by John Yeoman in *The Singing Tortoise* come from all over the world, were unknown to me (no expert) and are characterised by a strict morality. Make the most of your wits and you will win; break a promise and you will lose; greed and jealousy lead to disaster. The retelling is crisp; Quentin Blake's illustrations are typically cheerful; the production (in an attractive, almost square format) is exemplary.

Marcus Crouch

SOURCE: A review of *The Singing Tortoise and Other Animal Folk Tales,* in *The Junior Bookshelf,* Vol. 58, No. 1, February, 1994, p. 25.

The new Orchard Book makes an immediate and pleasing impression. Fourteen familiar—but not too well-known—folk tales from around the world are presented in satisfactory versions, without gimmicks and in good colloquial prose as well suited to oral presentation as to reading. Each tale has a generous share of colourful, appropriate and often witty illustrations, and a common decorative motif brings the book into a harmonious whole. The book makes an ideal present for the whole family where it should have a long and profitable life.

Although the new Yeoman/Blake book is cheaper, smaller and less obviously 'special'. I am inclined to rate it even more highly. There is a greater degree of inner harmony which comes from the long and close partnership of writer and artist. John Yeoman's collection of eleven animal-fables is suffused with his very individual humour. The stories are told with the utmost simplicity and economy, qualities which must appeal to the oral story-teller, which children will welcome, and which make them the perfect vehicle for Quentin Blake's deceptively simple drawings. Mr. Blake's repertoire of animals is already familiar, so that we inevitably identify, for example, the high spirited ravens who make a fool of the coyote in one of these tales with Mortimer. The artist draws upon his stock-in-trade, but he still reanimates it afresh in each new context. These designs are full of life as of humour. I cannot forecast a long life for this book. It will be worn to ribbons by many eager young readers.

Publishers Weekly

SOURCE: A review of *The Singing Tortoise: And Other Animal Folktales,* in *Publishers Weekly,* Vol. 241, No. 20, May 16, 1994, p. 64.

Thoughtful editing, careful pacing and animated tones make this collection of 11 folktales a worthy addition to the genre. While each story has a cautionary tone, it is neatly balanced by Yeoman's humorous, playful style and [Quentin] Blake's inimitably puckish art. His loose, spirited illustrations, color and black-and-white, capture the mood of the various follies described in the texts, from a jackal who outwits a hungry crocodile to a turkey incarnation of Cinderella to an ingenious rabbit who saves his burrow from greedy elephants by pretending to be the moon. The animals here are alternately greedy and boastful, wise and resourceful; not all of them earn happy endings. A final chapter supplies a brief background on each tale, explaining that most were recorded in the late 19th or early 20th century, and identifying sources as far-flung as Tibet, Ghana, Papua New Guinea and Spain.

Betsy Hearne

SOURCE: A review of *The Singing Tortoise and Other Animal Folktales,* in *Bulletin of the Center for Children's Books,* Vol. 47, No. 10, June, 1994, p. 340.

Eleven stories from almost as many traditions get handsome treatment here, with Yeoman providing dexterous adaptations and [Quentin] Blake providing jaunty pen-and-wash illustrations. Unfortunately, nobody has provided source notes ("*The Impudent Little Bird* flew in from Spain" just doesn't qualify), so all we know are the countries from which these came, named in an afterword and marked by red Xs on a blank world map that will leave most kids mystified. The stories themselves are a mix of familiar (the Zuni "Turkey Girl") and less commonly anthologized (the Hindi "Ranee and the Cobra"), and Yeoman has, to his credit, never happified endings of the more poignant selections such as Ghana's "Singing Tortoise," where a man is beheaded for breaking a promise. A brisk style gives proper folkloric distance on such incidents, and Blake's sly, adroitly drawn caricatures of human and animal alike lighten any weighty moral lessons that happen to attend or even generate these ancient tales. Despite the lack of citations, this is a volume that children will find attractive and easy to read independently.

Sheilamae O'Hara

SOURCE: A review of *The Singing Tortoise and Other Animal Folktales,* in *Booklist,* Vol. 90, Nos. 19 & 20, June 1 & June 15, 1994, p. 1814.

Yeoman has collected folktales from throughout the world and retells them with wit, including several trickster tales and others in which the protagonist is punished severely for betraying a secret or failing to keep a pledge. In "The Ranee and the Cobra," a woman gives birth to twin foxes while a fox delivers two girls. No explanation is given for these unlikely events, and when the girls grow up and marry well, they are ashamed to tell their husbands of their unusual parentage. One kills her mother while the other conceals the body and pretends that her parents are wealthy jungle people. The murderess is suitably punished, but the liar is aided in her deception by a cobra with magic powers. In "Animal Language," a man is about to reveal a fatal secret to his wife when a rooster warns, "If he's as big a fool as that the world won't miss him. I've got over a hundred wives and if I find a tasty grain of corn in the yard I cluck-cluck-cluck until they all come

running, and then I eat it myself. Just to show who's boss." Quite the proper cautionary tale. Many stories are humorous, and [Quentin] Blake's illustrations are droll—but feminist readers beware.

Kirkus Reviews

SOURCE: A review of *The Singing Tortoise: And Other Animal Folktales,* in *Kirkus Reviews,* Vol. LXII, No. 12, June 15, 1994, p. 854.

With origins as far-flung as Papua New Guinea, Africa's Gold Coast, and Spain, 11 tales ranging from simple stories of the weak outwitting the strong ("The Cat and the Mice" from Tibet; "The Rabbit and the Elephants" from India) and trickster and *pourquoi* tales to complex stories of boons granted by animals to humans ("Animal Language" from Serbia) and the promises made (or broken) in return (the Zuñi Pueblo's "The Turkey Girl" is a Cinderella cognate with an unhappy ending). Western animal stereotypes are often inverted here: Elephants are foolish or timorous; turkeys have magical powers; snakes are magnanimous and just; a turtle is a thief. Recast in a uniform literary style, the stories lack the immediacy of colloquial storytelling but are nonetheless effective when read aloud. The "twittery mice" of *Mouse Trouble* (an earlier Yeoman/Blake collaboration), the tortoise from *Esio Trot,* and other comical creatures make welcome returns in [Quentin] Blake's dashing illustrations. A note comments on the tales' places of origin without citing specific sources.

Kathleen Odean

SOURCE: A review of *The Singing Tortoise: And Other Animal Folktales,* in *School Library Journal,* Vol. 40, No. 7, July, 1994, p. 98.

A disappointing collection of 11 animal folktales from around the world. The notes unfortunately do not cite specific sources, but mention country and culture of origin. Although Yeoman explains that the best way to enjoy the tales is to tell them aloud, his retellings do not have the sound of oral literature. Instead, they rely heavily on adverbs, adjectives, and complex sentences. A comparison between his version of the title story and Harold Courlander and George Herzog's in *The Cow-Tail Switch and Other West African Stories* (1988) illustrates Yeoman's more literary style. Whereas Courlander writes simply: "Time passed. People began to say angry things to Ama," Yeoman's text is much wordier: "Gradually, faint whispers began to run through the crowd; and then they turned into discontented muttering, which finally gave way to an outburst of anger and scorn." Nor do [Quentin] Blake's characteristically lively illustrations suit an international folktale collection. They minimize rather than highlight the differences among cultures, while their humorous quality lends the wrong tone to the more serious tales.

THE DO-IT-YOURSELF HOUSE THAT JACK BUILT (1994)

Marcus Crouch

SOURCE: A review of *The Do-It-Yourself House That Jack Built,* in *The Junior Bookshelf,* Vol. 59, No. 2, April, 1995, p. 64.

The firm of Yeoman and Blake set up their workshop on the site of jack's traditional house. On each verso page is the familiar text which poses more questions than it answers. On the recto are the solutions to many puzzles which have troubled children and, still more, their parents. Why, for example, was the bridegroom 'tattered and torn'? Quentin Blake explains. When Jack and a team of untrained helpers, each contributing an excess of enthusiasm to an abundance of incompetence, are at work there are bound to be accidents. The tattered man is one casualty. More seriously the rat is another. The cat was not really to blame, his hammer just happened to slip when the rat was below clearing up all that malt. No wonder the cat was worried by the dog's prediction that 'he'll come back to haunt you'. The Yeoman-Blake logic informs every opening. There is every reason why Jack's house should turn out so oddly. A glorious frolic.

Ann G. Hay

SOURCE: A review of *The Do-It-Yourself House That Jack Built,* in *The School Librarian,* Vol. 43, No. 2, May, 1995, p. 62.

This is an absolute delight. The verse of the nursery rhyme appears on the left-hand page; opposite is a typically zany illustration, with each character's observations on the situation. Children will love the daftness of it, the reading-aloud adult will appreciate the lovely touches—the dog 'worried the cat' by making him feel guilty for having caused the accidental death of the rat, the maiden is 'all forlorn' because they won't let her use the power drill. This will be a favourite family book for years and the nursery rhyme will never be the same again. I hope this pair will tackle more traditional verses in the same way. 5 to 65 (with teenage gap).

Additional coverage of Yeoman's life and career is contained in the following sources published by Gale Research: *Contemporary Authors,* Vol. 106, and *Something about the Author,* Vol. 80.

Lisbeth Zwerger

1954-

Austrian illustrator of picture books.

The Gift of the Magi (1982), *Little Red Cap* (1983), *The Nightingale* (1984), *A Christmas Carol* (1988), *Dwarf-Nose* (1994).

INTRODUCTION

Internationally acclaimed illustrator of picture books for children and winner of the coveted Hans Christian Andersen award, Lisbeth Zwerger is praised for her thoughtful and witty interpretations of classic tales by authors such as the Grimm Brothers, Charles Dickens, O. Henry, and Oscar Wilde. Readers and critics alike appreciate her imaginative and expressive watercolor paintings that offer new dimensions to old works. Typically working with warm, muted colors, Zwerger's spacious yet balanced compositions support and enhance the text. Moreover, she successfully captures the mood of the characters within her illustrations and often includes historical overtones from the era of each tale. Her fine lines against a soft wash offer a visual sophistication which the illustrator admits has taken her great pains to perfect. Equally chal-

lenging for Zwerger is finding the right story to illustrate. The artist once commented: "When I look for a story, it has to contain all the right ingredients: for a start, it has to be the right length; I like it to have a main character who is both comical and touching; it has to interest me (of course); it has to be the sort of story that my type of illustrations fit; and last but not least, it has to have no sexist morals." The artist maintains, however, that having such firm criteria allows her to do what she enjoys most: reading and drawing.

Biographical Information

Born in Vienna, Austria, in 1954, Zwerger was surrounded by artistic people. Her father, a graphic artist, and her mother, a lover of fashion design, encouraged Zwerger and her sister to sketch. Although Zwerger liked to illustrate, she didn't care for school. As a matter of fact, she hated it. It was not until she enrolled in a Vienna university for art that she found any pleasure in learning. Even then she was disappointed that the classes didn't focus more on illustration. Discouraged, she eventually dropped out and stopped illustrating. Some time later her English boyfriend (now her husband), John Rowe, introduced Zwerger to Arthur Rackham's illustrations. Rackham's use of color and line inspired Zwerger to illustrate again. Rowe taught her how to use a two-color technique, which she used to create scenes from stories by classic authors, such as E. T. A. Hoffmann, Hans Christian Andersen, and others. Eventually, Friedrich Neugebauer, the owner of a small publishing company, liked her drawings for Hoffmann's *The Strange Child* and asked her to prepare more illustrations for that story. The project became Zwerger's first published picture book in 1977. Since then, Neugebauer and his son Michael have continued to publish her work. She has won numerous awards for her illustrations, and has traveled twice through the United States and to Japan in recognition of her work.

Major Works

The Gift of the Magi, a classic short story by O. Henry, tells the tale of a poor young couple who sell their most prized possessions to buy each other Christmas gifts. While this story generally attracts teen and adult readers, Zwerger's softly colored, delicate drawings attract younger readers as well. In *Little Red Cap,* a fairy tale by the Grimm Brothers similar to *Little Red Riding Hood,* a young girl and her grandmother are eaten by a hungry wolf at Grandma's house, then rescued by a nearby hunter. Here, Zwerger is noted for realistically capturing the human and animal characteristics of each character. Hans Christian Andersen's *The Nightingale* describes how a Chinese emperor banishes a real nightingale for a mechanical one made of jewels. Years later, when the emperor is near death, the faithful bird returns to help him. Unlike her other works, Zwerger wielded pastel coloration to capture the flavor of Chinese art. In Charles Dickens's classic holiday tale *A Christmas Carol,* Zwerger again returned to her signature muted watercolors and fine lines, but added an oversized page design to create a striking illustrative book. *Dwarf-Nose,* a fairy tale originally written in 1827 by Wilhelm Hauff, contains a number of watercolor characters painted in a surrealistic style. An aging fairy changes the main character, Jacob, into a squirrel after he is rude to her. She forces him to work at her home until he escapes seven years later. Upon returning home the boy finds he has turned into a hunched-back dwarf with a hooked nose. Eventually, the evil spell is broken and Jacob returns back to his old self.

Awards

Hansel and Gretel was named a Notable Book of 1980 by the American Library Association, while *The Gift of the Magi, The Legend of Rosepetal,* and *Little Red Cap* were named *New York Times* Best Illustrated Books of the Year in 1982, 1983, and 1985, respectively. Zwerger received the Golden Apple at the International Biennial of Illustration at Bratislava in 1985 for her illustrations in *The Selfish Giant,* and then in 1990 Zwerger received the prestigious Hans Christian Andersen Award for Illustration.

AUTHOR'S COMMENTARY

Bookbird

SOURCE: "Lisbeth Zwerger," in *Bookbird,* No. 2, 1984, pp. 10-12.

Lisbeth Zwerger is a young illustrator of extraordinary skill and depth. She was born in Vienna in May 1954, where she attended the Academy of Art, and where she lives and works today. In a few years, she has risen to the first rank among internationally known and respected illustrators of children's literature. Lisbeth Zwerger's first book, ***Das fremde Kind*** (***The Strange Child***), was published in 1977. Between then and now, she has twice won a Plaque at the International Biennial of Illustration at Bratislava, been honored three times for Graphic Excellence at the Bologna International Children's Book Fair, and had two books chosen by *The New York Times* among the Best Illustrated Books of the Year. Europe's premier book-arts museum, the Klingspor, honored Ms. Zwerger in 1983 with a one person show of her illustrations. Her nomination for the 1984 Hans Christian Andersen Award only confirms what has been apparent from the start: Lisbeth Zwerger is among the very finest illustrators of children's literature in the world today.

This is what Lisbeth Zwerger has to say about her work: "I think I've always been interested in illustration, but it wasn't always easy to stick to my aim, especially during the period I attended college. I was often told, or rather warned, of the difficulties involved with finding work, and criticized for not being 'modern' enough, which naturally left me feeling totally confused, not really knowing what direction my work should take. In fact, I almost stopped drawing completely, limiting myself to the occasional black and white ink drawing.

"One day my boyfriend showed me a book illustrated by Arthur Rackham and suddenly something seemed to 'click,' my doubts vanished and I felt inspired to illustrate again.

"After seeing Rackham's work I became more and more involved with English illustration and writing: Heath Robinson, Dulac, Beatrix Potter, and Shepard, whose beautiful drawings for 'Winnie the Pooh' I find show the perfect balance literature and illustration are capable of reaching. In fact, English children's literature in general contains a magical mood for me, something I can't seem to find anywhere else.

"At first I continued to work only in black and white because of a lack of nerve to use colour. My boyfriend showed me a basic two colour technique which helped me over the first awkward steps, as I attempted to illustrate several stories for my own pleasure.

"At that time, I was less concerned with content and tended to illustrate favourite stories from my childhood, stories such as 'Snow White' and 'Cinderella' that I might think twice about now. In fact, it wasn't long before the question of which story to illustrate began to be a serious problem for me. So many of the classic fairytales contain messages from a very harshly moralistic point of view.

"Content is still my biggest problem when looking for suitable stories to illustrate. In fact, I have to look upon them as pieces of literature rather than good messages for children. So far I haven't found the ideal story.

"Therefore, I'm mainly concerned that the stories I choose contain the right ingredients, such as a comical side, a likeable main character, etc. Of course, I'm very lucky that my publisher allows me the greatest freedom to choose whatever story I wish to illustrate. Without this liberty I would probably find it impossible to express myself through illustration."

TITLE COMMENTARY

📖 ***HANSEL AND GRETEL* (written by Jakob and Wilhelm K. Grimm, 1980)**

Zena Sutherland

SOURCE: A review of *Hansel and Gretel,* in *Bulletin of*

the Center for Children's Books, Vol. 33, No. 9, May, 1980, p. 173.

In a picture book format, a new translation of a familiar story adheres closely to the original but is smoothly and discriminatingly simplified. The illustrations, by an eminent Austrian illustrator, are in ink and wash; save for an occasional background detail, the backgrounds are in blended earth tones. The figures are strongly defined, but delicately tinted and detailed, and they are prominent in full-color pages with effectively simple composition.

Paul Heins

SOURCE: A review of *Hansel and Gretel,* in *The Horn Book Magazine,* Vol. LVI, No. 3, June, 1980, pp. 286-87.

Like Charles Scribner's version of "Hansel and Gretel" the translation is well-cadenced and fluent—as all good storytelling should be; but the newer retelling has the further merit of keeping closer to the vivid, strongly realistic diction of the original. The illustrations, however, are somewhat unconventional in their quiet but sensitive approach to the familiar story. Avoiding any trace of eeriness or melodrama, the paintings employ muted, full-color tonalities; and although the witch is bloated and amorphous, the artistic concentration on the reactions of Hansel and Gretel makes for a feeling of originality as well as of intimacy.

Ruth M. McConnell

SOURCE: A review of *Hansel and Gretel,* in *School Library Journal,* Vol. 26, No. 10, August, 1980, p. 64.

A finely crafted treatment of the popular folktale, with a direct text and more somber artwork that will tend to attract an older audience than the version illustrated by Adrienne Adams. The spare, serviceable text does not make concessions to the picture-book age group by making a rhymed couplet of the witch's plaint ("Nibble, nibble, munch, munch. / Who is gnawing on my house?") nor of the children's response to witch or duck and marks no break between story and its tag-ending. The young Austrian illustrator has done 11 pleasing line-and-wash paintings in low-key color and shrouded backgrounds. Five include the witch, giving her a goblin aspect with a billowing robe from which bony limbs project and a skull-like face with red eyes. The sure sketches have nice details—the children's hungry, expectant faces at the witch's table, or the hag's clutch at the oven doorjamb as Gretel shoves determinedly.

THE SEVEN RAVENS (written by Jakob and Wilhelm K. Grimm, 1981)

Patricia Dooley

SOURCE: A review of *The Seven Ravens,* in *School Library Journal,* Vol. 27, No. 8, April, 1981, p. 113.

A sensitive translation [by Elizabeth D. Crawford] of this brief and moving tale and delicate, 19th-Century style illustrations in subtle, muted colors combine to make this a book of quiet and memorable beauty. The story tells of a little girl whose birth is the innocent occasion of her brothers' transformation into ravens. When she learns of their existence, she walks "to the very ends of the earth" and must flee from both sun and moon to find them and undo the spell. The sober hues of the book suit this tale of staunch moral courage, but it also has a happy ending and an admirable heroine. The rosy-cheeked boys lighten the beginning and ending with their lively figures, and the few other faces that appear, like the cups and plates, the chairs and the girl's kerchief, are satisfyingly homely. The gentle washes of color, the spare design and the graceful, unstudied line balance the harsh world of the text, where sons are cursed by a father's merely impatient word.

Michele Slung

SOURCE: "Thrice Told Tales," in *The New York Times Book Review,* April 26, 1981, pp. 55, 66.

Austrian artist Lisbeth Zwerger, in deciding to breathe new life into *The Seven Ravens,* has lit upon a selection from Grimm's "Nursery and Household Tales" that has so far not suffered from overexposure. It is one of those tales of arbitrary transformation, in which words uttered in anger trigger metamorphosis. Here seven brothers are changed into "seven coal-black ravens" after they fail to return from fetching water for their sister's christening quickly enough to satisfy their father.

Their sister, feeling herself responsible, sets out to undo the terrible magic, a quest that takes her far from home, past the sun, the moon and the stars. Her purity of purpose sustains her on the mission, and of course she succeeds in lifting the spell.

Miss Zwerger is a lyrically witty artist; there is smooth movement in her warmly hued pictures, as well as visual sophistication. Arthur Rackham has obviously influenced her style, but Miss Zwerger's is a simpler, less eye-aching version. If one or two of the drawings are insipid, the overall effect is hauntingly lovely, particularly the illustration in which the stars are seen sitting on their stools. I also very much like some of the amusing detail, such as the bonnets worn by a pair of bunnies. The translation, by Elizabeth D. Crawford, is felicitous and true to the original, in which the young girl cuts off her finger to use as a key. (Some versions bowdlerize this typically Grimm bit and have the girl substitute a drumstick or a piece of wood for the lost key.)

Margery Fisher

SOURCE: A review of *The Seven Ravens,* in *Growing Point,* Vol. 20, No. 3, September, 1981, p. 3948.

The suave illustrations, somewhat resembling Rackham in their drab browns and blues and in the puppet-like figures, concentrate on the domestic element of this familiar tale; the loyal devotion of the daughter who saves her enchanted brothers is far more important than the slight element of magic in the personification of Sun and Stars and the strange manner of her success. The very simple text brings the book within a listening range of five or six, while the deep implications of the story are there for older children to catch.

📖 **THE SWINEHERD (written by Hans Christian Andersen, 1982)**

Ruth M. McConnell

SOURCE: A review of *The Swineherd,* in *School Library Journal,* Vol. 28, No. 7, March, 1982, pp. 127-28.

The mockingly satiric Andersen tale receives rather a gently comic treatment by the Austrian illustrator. With all heads or glances averted, the court rejects the simple but princely gifts, the princess her suitor, and the swineherd/prince his bride in this tale of assumptions and guises. Only the animals are pictured acting naturally—and they are admonished by the fairytale-like humans. In format, brown line and wash similar to her illustrations for the Grimm Brothers' **Seven Ravens,** her tableaux have more charm than bite, though their treatment—like the prince with the box of hats choosing a role to disclose the princess' light-mindedness—is imaginative. The original translation is well done, in a text that grades four and up can enjoy reading.

Mary M. Burns

SOURCE: A review of *The Swineherd,* in *The Horn Book Magazine,* Vol. LVIII, No. 3, June, 1982, pp. 277-78.

Because human nature remains essentially the same, the story of the proud princess whose folly cost her a kingdom and a bridegroom is as relevant today as it was more than a century ago—perhaps because of its multidimensional structure which transforms a comic opera situation into a commentary on society's foibles. The translation, vigorous and fresh, retains the acerbic tone as well as Andersen's characteristic storytelling style. The illustrations, while developing characters and action, also emphasize the tale's suitability for adaptation to the theater and recall its having been produced as a play in nineteenth-century Germany. The artist's expressive line captures the vapid pettiness of the princess and her ladies, the stalwart qualities of the rejected suitor, and the bumbling but honest reactions of the emperor. Less somber than her earlier work, the pictures are both comic and earthy, quite appropriate for a modest, semirural court.

📖 **THE GIFT OF THE MAGI (written by O. Henry, 1982)**

Zena Sutherland

SOURCE: A review of *The Gift of the Magi,* in *Bulletin of the Center for Children's Books,* Vol. 36, No. 3, November, 1982, p. 48.

Zwerger's romantic drawings in the Rackham tradition are softly-colored and gentle, appropriate for the subject of O. Henry's story and given full scope by the oversize pages. The story itself, however, both in style and subject, seems less appropriate for young readers than for the adult audience for which it was written. Published early in the century, the tale of a poor young couple who sacrifice their dearest possessions to buy each other Christmas gifts is still touching albeit sentimental.

Thomas Lask

SOURCE: "Old Friends Return," in *The New York Times Book Review,* November 14, 1982, p. 49-50, 52.

In spite of its prevailing popularity, O. Henry's **The Gift of the Magi,** in which a loving wife sells her tresses to buy a watch fob and chain for her husband, who in turn sells his watch to buy a comb for his wife, is no more than an anecdote, without much literary merit. But Lisbeth Zwerger has made up for it with her beautifully wrought illustrations, delicate, uncluttered and splendidly composed. And in a field where too many illustrations seem to have been largely influenced by 19th-century Romantic German art, she supplies a contemporary feel and tone.

Kicki Moxon Browne

SOURCE: "Young and Very Young," in *Times Literary Supplement,* No. 4169, February 25, 1983, p. 185.

O. Henry's short stories are not by themselves readily accessible to preteenage children. His urbane jests and consciously waggish style are an acquired taste, even in such a simple and optimistic tale as **The Gift of the Magi** with its message that sacrifice in love is in itself godly and wise, however messy the outcome. But the sheer allure of this picture-book presentation could make it attractive to children as young as eight or nine. It is a remarkably beautiful book because of its very shape (unusually tall and slender), its smooth thick pages, its elaborately executed manuscript text, but above all because of Lisbeth Zwerger's exquisite illustrations in muted shades of grey and green. The oblique style of the pictures subtly mirrors the story; as O. Henry delicately skates round the issues avoiding head-on confrontations and deliberately understating the dramatic climaxes, so Zwerger's characters are forever turning away, avoiding our eyes (save in the reflection of a mirror) or disappearing round corners or through doors. This book is obviously not for very young children, but I would push it determinedly in the direction of many older children who might consider themselves too old for picture books.

THE NUTCRACKER AND THE MOUSE KING (1983; original German edition as *Nussknacker und Mausekönig,* written by E. T. A. Hoffmann, 1979)

Zena Sutherland

SOURCE: A review of *The Nutcracker and the Mouse King,* in *Bulletin of the Center for Children's Books,* Vol. 37, No. 2, October, 1983, p. 30.

Soft paintings in subdued colors are beautifully detailed, their romantic air tempered by the quiet humor of figures that have spindly shanks or fantastic qualities. Unlike many of the "Nutcracker" books on the market, this is based not on the ballet but on the original story on which the ballet is based. Published in 1819 under the title *Nussknacker und Mausekönig,* the story has been shortened and simplified very smoothly by the adaptor-translator: the story of a small girl, Marie, whose fantasy adventures are spurred by the marvelous nutcracker made by her ingenious godfather as a Christmas gift.

Thomas Lask

SOURCE: "Still Classic," in *The New York Times Book Review,* November 13, 1983, p. 41, 53.

Partly through Tchaikovsky's music, partly through the ballet by Ivanov and its subsequent modifications, the story of *The Nutcracker* has had wide currency. Yet both the music and ballet center on only a small part of E. T. A. Hoffmann's story. Now Anthea Bell has provided a much fuller, though still not complete, version of **The Nutcracker,** with all sorts of turnings and twistings in the plot. I'm not sure a young reader won't get lost in this narrative maze and yearn for the briefer version familiar from the stage. Lisbeth Zwerger, who will be remembered for her superb work in last year's *Gift of the Magi,* has supplied a series of warm but more conventional illustrations.

LITTLE RED CAP (written by Jakob and Wilhelm K. Grimm, 1983)

John L. Ward and Marian Nitti Fox

SOURCE: "A Look at Some Outstanding Illustrated Books for Children," in *Children's Literature Association Quarterly,* Vol. 9, No. 1, Spring, 1984, pp. 19-21.

A recent edition of **Little Red Cap,** the Grimm Brothers' version of *Little Red Riding Hood,* illustrated by Lisbeth Zwerger, also uses the format of facing text and pictures and ranks with [Chris Van Allsburg's] *Jumanji* as one of the most beautiful and effective books we examined. In this work the illustrations are watercolors, in which a few notes of heightened color (notably the red cap of the title) are set off against primarily warm, monochromatic washes. Although exquisitely designed as coherent entities, the

pictures create a sense of continuity and openness that contrasts sharply with Van Allsburg's closed spaces. This effect is created by allowing the picture to fill the whole surface of the page, by setting the figures and a few necessary environmental details within a space otherwise defined only by a light, washed-in tone, by the greater amount of unoccupied space, and by the visible traces of the preliminary underdrawing. The presence of the warm tone, filling much of the space in the pictures and overflowing the edges of the page, assists in creating a sense of spatial continuity. As in *Jumanji,* spatial perspectives are carefully utilized to situate the viewer in an effective relationship to the event; but whereas Van Allsburg's space emphasizes tangible volumes and eminence of form, Zwerger's space emphasizes continuity and fluidity of spatial movement. In one illustration the viewer, together with the wolf in the foreground, observes Little Red Cap approach from the distance. A picture of great economy and subtlety, it creates a sense of the girl's unwary approach and the wolf's calculation. Zwerger's pictures (like Van Allsburg's, but in a totally different style) permit the viewer to be aware of the properties of the medium and of the formal decisions without letting them distract from the narrative. The choices seem right—*surprisingly* right—rather than merely drawing attention to themselves. The artist's drawing is marked by the ease with which she captures the poses and gestures of figures in space and by a compelling dramatic sense that effectively and improbably mixes poignance and wit. The muted colors, understated description, and generally serious expressions of the characters give the story a quietly lyrical, almost sad flavor that is played off against shrewdly humorous touches that do not conflict with, but subtly modify the overall mood. An example is Zwerger's picture of the grandmother being helped from the wolf's belly by the huntsman. This grotesque undertaking is performed with complete sobriety but is depicted with considerable low-keyed wit.

Jane Doonan

SOURCE: "Two Artists Telling Tales: Chihiro Iwasaki & Lisbeth Zwerger," in *Signal,* No. 44, May, 1984, pp. 93-102.

In it [*Little Red-Cap*] Lisbeth Zwerger appears to have found a satisfactory visual equivalent for a folk tale. If we think for a moment about the characteristic narrative methods, we understand that their formal opening and closing sentiments, patterns, and other devices create a larger-than-life atmosphere and lead the child through an experience which is about the truth but not about the real. A picture-book artist is faced with the necessity of creating her own visual 'Once upon a time', and Lisbeth Zwerger has done just this. The text is placed low on each left-hand page, with plenty of space above it, while the illustrations lie on the opposing right-hand page, being full plates with bled edges. As one turns the pages, the formal sequence of text page and opposing full plate sets up an orderly framework to contain events.

Fairly and squarely meeting the villain of the piece, Lisbeth Zwerger invites us to think about the wolf right from the beginning of the book, where he cavorts triumphantly on the title page in Gran's nightgown. Are we to be taken in by him, just as Red-Cap was? Our first view of him in the story illustration shows him in a dominating position, close up, lower right in the picture plane, speculatively watching Red-Cap's small figure leaving the light and entering the sepia gloom of his territory. His pose is human, sitting paw on hip; his concave belly, the bushy tail maintaining his balance, the pricked ears with their soft inner hairs, and his sharp muzzle remind us that he is, first and foremost, a hungry, predatory animal. The next illustration shows him up on his hind legs, winsomely seducing Red-Cap from her purpose. Once she is absorbed in gathering flowers, he is off on all fours, tongue lolling.

In contrast, the next views of him are almost too humorous. Four sequences on one page show him, belly full of Gran, struggling to get her nightgown over his head, then puzzling out whether to put his ears inside or outside her nightcap. Cleverly, by selecting to illustrate this business, Zwerger saves the 'bed scene' for the more interesting and crucial one with Red-Cap, delays our seeing the old lady until a much more dramatic moment, and gives form to a visually entertaining interlude. It is worth noticing that only three of the four poses are human; the fourth makes it clear that, under the white cambric flounces, there is an animal poised to act.

Our viewpoint is from behind and to the left of the wolf, when he attacks Red-Cap. He leaps diagonally, away from us and towards the child's figure, as she stands between the bed curtains, still trying to reconcile that voice and that appearance with her grandmother's. She has a puzzled look on her face; we are left to imagine the wolf's mask. The tumbled bedding receives summary treatment, allowing our attention to be held by the wolf's powerful, flexed hind quarters.

Over the page, replete with both Red-Cap and Grandmother, the wolf snores in bed, jaw slack, belly domed. The woodcutter stands beside a chest of drawers, scissors in left hand, needlebox beneath his right hand. The pose suggests that he dare not take his eyes off the wolf for a second. His dog sniffs Red-Cap's scent on a fallen, creamy flower in the middle of the floor. This visual echo is a pertinent reminder of how Red-Cap allowed herself to be tempted in the first place. The danger of the moment has been caught through the emphasis on the actions of the woodcutter and his dog.

Our penultimate view of the wolf is a close-up, flat on his back, slit from chest to lower belly. The woodcutter heaves Grandmother free; Red-Cap, already released, stands tucked close to her rescuer, watching. The illustration is extraordinary. A strong sense of movement comes through the use of diagonal forms. It is a dramatic demonstration of how the eye may pass from one form to the other—grandmother's right arm, head, her left arm, the woodcutter's heaving hands, his braced torso, then on down the

From The Gift of the Magi, *written by O. Henry. Illustrated by Lisbeth Zwerger.*

curve of his back, to Red-Cap, whose glance directs the eye still lower to a shadow which leads across the pillow to the wolf's heavy body. The characters are linked spatially and emotionally, demonstrating how a visual form may be found for frightening material which is truthful, forceful, but not melodramatic; Zwerger presents it almost prosaically, ordinary people doing extraordinary things. Pose, colour and setting all play their parts.

If we look at the poses of the figures, we see that Zwerger has the gift of bringing into being real people in particular moments through a knowledge of the way they sit, stand, and make familiar gestures. In the first illustration Red-Cap stands patiently in front of her seated mother. The mother leans forward, concentrating on tying a bow with Red-Cap's apron ribbons. Beneath her spreading skirts it is possible to understand how her knees are spread to support the forward tilt of her upper torso. When Red-Cap gathers flowers, it is not with a smile-and-a-song and an audience of squirrels and bunnies, but with her total attention. She holds the flowers out in front of her, the skin between her thumb and forefinger stretched to encompass their stems, and she judges whether she has sufficient for a generous bunch. 'Only when she had as many as she could carry did she continue on her way,' says the 1812 text. Zwerger amplifies the picture-book adaptation.

In the final plate Red-Cap, Granny and the Woodcutter celebrate. Intent on keeping the balance of the custard on the dish, Red-Cap moves forward carefully. Granny spreads her lap and eyes the food with the expectation and anticipation of the very old, for whom it represents so much pleasure. The woodcutter grasps the wine bottle in one hand and the corkscrew in the other, and takes the strain of the pull right through to his toes. Each of them is concerned with his or her own experience.

As for the colour, washes of ochre, umber, and olive are used for the shadowy world which Red-Cap experiences. Subtle stripes, checks, floral and tiny geometric patterns introduce variety on the clothing and all look as if vegetable dyed. Colour is used emotively, as when Red-Cap meets the wolf, for it is colour rather than density of trees which suggests the shadowy wood. The relatively saturated red of her cap is the only bright hue in the book, and serves to draw our attention to her and counterbalance the attractions of the wolf.

In contrast to the realism of the figures, settings are reduced to a minimum. Lines to denote walls or floor areas are usually missing. Zwerger is not concerned with providing anything more than the barest illusion of space. When she does give form to an object it is for a purpose, and will yield meaning. For example, while Red-Cap is being prepared for her journey, the family's cat has leapt on to the table and stuck his nose into Red-Cap's basket, reminding us that it is natural for hungry animals to be attracted to food, and over the page another hungry animal will be repeating the activity. Again, outside the grandmother's cottage stands her refuse bin, and only a few vegetables and long grasses grow in her garden. They are stark reminders that sick old ladies cannot walk far or cultivate their gardens fully.

The composition of this same painting shows that Zwerger can find a visual equivalent for the feelings of apprehension which are touched on in the text and which are more strongly expressed in the original version. The little fenced garden is set at an oblique angle, high, to the left of the picture plane. The facade of the cottage is set to the right in opposition. They do not meet at the centre though, and space flows on beyond them. The middle and lower third of the picture plane are unworked, save for the palest sepia wash. The cottage door is ajar, with impenetrable darkness behind. Little Red-Cap hovers, back towards us, on the doorstep. Only one foot is on the step, as she leans forward, left arm bracing her body, right arm pushing on the door. She is looking small and vulnerable, partly because she is exposed in so much open space and partly because she is depicted on the same scale as in the earlier picture, when she is shown entering the wood. Her perky apron ties are prominent, reminding us of the earlier scene when she makes her promise to her mother. We want to haul her back by them, away from the cottage where we know that the wolf is waiting once again, but we cannot. We are rendered helpless by the great expanse of empty foreground which separates us from her. She is too far away.

Finally, the psychological attraction of wolves we all meet, whether inside or outside ourselves, is honestly portrayed. If you do not feel the attraction of giving in to the wolf, just as Red-Cap did, then the point of the tale is lost. The wolf is ruthless, wily, and finally overcome. He pops up again on the endpapers though, reminding us that overcoming a wolf is a temporary measure.

Zwerger's treatment of the wolf gives rise to interesting speculation. As I said at the beginning, a work of art is a cultural object and carries coded messages about the ideas and values of its time. The brothers Grimm give us a story which warns children about the dangers of their own sexuality, and Zwerger does not play down the sexual undertones. The image of the wolf is a sensual one; we see his exposed soft lower belly, his strong thighs. But his prominence on the cover, title page and endpapers, the entertaining sequence in which he dresses up, reveal an ambivalence in the artist's intention. The very wood he inhabits is surprisingly neutral in tone. Zwerger seems to reflect the present-day conflicts which surround changing attitudes to sensuality. Her tone is less repressive than that of the brothers Grimm, that's for sure.

Although so different in style, Lisbeth Zwerger and Chihiro Iwasaki [illustrator of *The Red Shoes*] have qualities in common. Neither attempts to create the illusion of the real world, preferring to suggest the feelings of it. The work of both is free of superfluous details: every form carries literary meaning, none is mere decoration. This is a rare quality in folk- and fairy-tale picture books. It encourages speculation and also brings a beautiful economy to the page. Both artists do much more than make pictorial comment on the written word, though Iwasaki tells us more about herself than about Andersen. Lisbeth Zwerger, achieving the delicate balance between content and form, comes very close to creating an exceptional picture book, offering a genuinely expressive, highly personal interpretation for us to experience.

📖 *THE SELFISH GIANT* (written by Oscar Wilde, 1984)

Ann A. Flowers

SOURCE: A review of *The Selfish Giant,* in *The Horn Book Magazine,* Vol. LX, No. 4, August, 1984, p. 463.

The familiar, touching tale gains a new dimension by means of the lovely illustrations. Cool, clear, lambent watercolors show children—sometimes lively, sometimes unhappy—and particularly the poignant figure of the little boy. Pictured as no more than a very tall man, the giant looks sad and uncertain; perhaps he is meant to appear merely as an adult observed through a child's eyes. One particularly affecting, yet not sentimental, illustration shows him shabby and pensive, looking into the garden from a room almost entirely bare. The restrained colors echo the delicate style of the story, while the tall, narrow shape of the volume in this case emphasizes the height of the giant. Altogether, a beautiful book with exquisite, graceful illustrations to match a classic tale.

📖 *THE STRANGE CHILD* (1984; original German edition as *Das fremde Kind,* written by E. T. A. Hoffmann, 1977)

Selma G. Lanes

SOURCE: A review of *The Strange Child,* in *The New York Times Book Review,* December 2, 1984, p. 53.

In her brief (seven-year) career, Lisbeth Zwerger, an Austrian artist, has only illustrated time-tested works: stories by O. Henry, the Grimms, Oscar Wilde, Hans Christian Andersen. Her first illustrated book, E. T. A. Hoffmann's *The Strange Child,* is now available here in a new translation-adaptation by the British writer Anthea Bell. A strange and dreamy tale of 1817, it is an extended metaphysical fantasy contrasting the joys of childhood in the world of nature with the workaday drudgery of lessons and cultivated life in society. Hoffmann's elegiac tone is matched by Miss Zwerger's gray-background mood pictures. Her children are oddly melancholy and disassociated, as if they are actors in someone else's dream. Miss Bell's choppy, idiosyncratic adaptation seems well suited to the material. While unlikely to be every child's cup of tea, it exudes an undeniable, if indefinable, force.

Zena Sutherland

SOURCE: A review of *The Strange Child,* in *Bulletin of the Center for Children's Books,* Vol. 38, No. 5, January, 1985, p. 87.

Newly translated, a story first published in 1817 is shortened here and smoothly retold—but it is still a laboriously fantastic story that, whether read alone or aloud, is heavy going. Two children receive a visit from their better-educated cousins, reject the gifts the cousins have brought, and are solaced by a mysterious child who plays with them in the woods and makes them happy. Sent a tutor by their cousins' father, the children immediately dislike Master Inkspot. Indeed, he proves to be an evil spirit in disguise, and he is bested by other magical creatures. Later the children's father dies, and the strange child they had played with reappears to comfort them and their mother. Realism and fantasy don't quite mesh, unfortunately. This was the first book illustrated by Zwerger, and it is typical (although not polished) of her later work: misty tones, a subdued palette, figures that are often elongated and sharp-featured.

Ethel R. Twitchell

SOURCE: A review of *The Strange Child,* in *The Horn Book Magazine,* Vol. LXI, No. 2, March-April, 1985, pp. 177-78.

Heavy-handed fantasy and a lack of unity diminish the impact of a less familiar story by the creator of *The Nutcracker* [E. T. A. Hoffmann]. Amiable parents have allowed their son and daughter to run wild in the woods; the two children are overjoyed by the appearance of a mysterious child who conjures up dazzling and magical games for their entertainment. But overbearing cousins find the children woefully uneducated and foist a harsh tutor on them, bringing the woodland idyll to a halt. The tutor, in reality, is the evil Pepser, a dire enemy of the strange child's mother—who just happens to be the queen of the fairies. Pepser is eventually dispatched by the children's father; their father dies; the impoverished family must move in with relatives; and the strange child, entreating the children to love her, claims she will keep them from harm. Compensating for the ambiguous and unconvincing text are handsome illustrations which capture the enchantment of the mysterious playmate with a romantic and melancholy sensitivity. But they, too, by not always clearly indicating what is going on, add further to the book's enigmatic and ultimately unsatisfying quality.

Nancy Schmidtmann

SOURCE: A review of *The Strange Child,* in *School Library Journal,* Vol. 31, No. 8, April, 1985, p. 88.

The title suits this tale that combines folk elements with allegorical hints and modern psychodrama. Christlieb and Felix, children of a provincial nobleman, feel like country bumpkins when their sophisticated city cousins visit and bring toys as gifts. They realize they don't know how to play with toys, destroy them and return to Nature's more familiar playthings. A strange child appears to them in the forest, plays with them and helps them realize that the creatures of Nature are more wonderful than toys. A wicked tutor (in reality, Pepser, King of the Gnomes) arrives; in the shape of a giant fly, he sets out to destroy the strange child. He fails, but the strange child is gone, returning only after their father's death, when the children are wandering, homeless and destitute, through the forest. He comforts them, promises good fortune and vows to remain with them forever in their dreams. The story is flawed by an incongruous blend of the mystical and the modern. It is neither folk tale nor pure fantasy. The translation [by Anthea Bell] does not flow naturally; it is frequently awkward and heavy. Each section is distractingly outlined in the margin. The dream-like illustrations in earth-tone watercolors show elongated figures in ballet-like poses and expertly capture the mood of the story. This book, by the author of *The Nutcracker* [E. T. A. Hoffmann], is a curiosity, but it is of questionable interest for children's library collections.

📖 *THE NIGHTINGALE* (written by Hans Christian Andersen, 1984)

Selma G. Lanes

SOURCE: A review of *The Nightingale,* in *The New York Times Book Review,* December 2, 1984, p. 53.

. . . [Felicitously] translated by Miss [Anthea] Bell and illustrated by Miss Zwerger is Hans Christian Andersen's *The Nightingale*. Here, the artist's increasing experience shows. Gone is the labored background wash. Sure, well-delineated characters move with authority across beautifully composed pages. All picture elements are pleasing, no detail is extraneous, and there is never an upstaging of text. Like the Emperor's mechanical-toy nightingale, however, they achieve the highest perfection of craft yet lack, somehow, the breath of life.

Hayden E. Atwood

SOURCE: A review of *The Nightingale*, in *School Library Journal*, Vol. 31, No. 6, February, 1985, p. 61.

[Hans Christian] Andersen's story of the nightingale whose beautiful singing was able to rescue the Chinese Emperor from Death is given another single-edition treatment. [Anthea] Bell's translation is essentially the same as others preceding it, but Zwerger's superb illustrations set the book apart. Full-page illustrations in soft and muted cool colors with simple and direct character outlines evoke the sparseness and delicate beauty associated with Chinese art. Other illustrated versions, such as Nancy Ekholm Burkert's, while colorful and evocative of the Oriental mood, seem bold and heavy by comparison.

Ethel L. Heins

SOURCE: A review of *The Nightingale*, in *The Horn Book Magazine*, Vol. LXI, No. 2, March-April, 1985, p. 172.

A faithful rendering of the famous narrative [by Hans Christian Andersen] into well-cadenced storytelling prose is presented in a format similar to that of the artist's editions of other Andersen tales—*Thumbeline* and *The Swineherd*—as well as of her three stories from the Brothers Grimm. The symbolic tale of devotion and forgiveness, of the genuine versus the artificial, is illustrated with a reticence rare in Central European picture books. Rather than overwhelming the implicit drama of the text, the paintings are understated and, as in the artist's other work, emphasize characterization more than action or setting. And instead of the rich palette of *The Nutcracker* or the warm, muted tones of her previous folk-tale illustration, Lisbeth Zwerger has employed much pastel coloration, giving the book a luminous Oriental delicacy rather than an exotic splendor.

Karla Kuskin

SOURCE: A review of *The Nightingale*, in *The New York Times Book Review*, November 3, 1985, pp. 32-3.

In feathery, pale shades and a sure sepia line Lisbeth Zwerger, the young Austrian artist of increasing renown, makes *The Nightingale* her own. She peoples an everyday Chinese court with distinct individuals who convince

us of the truth of the tale. The kitchen maid who leads the Lord-in-Waiting to the nightingale is a plump child stacking dishes. The self-important Lord-in-Waiting is accompanied everywhere by his self-important Pekingese. And Death, his hair rising from his fearful head like white flames, is a specter in the flesh. Miss Zwerger is self-assured and uses her gifts modestly. Her final full page is a triumph of understatement. She captures the moment just before the mourning ministers meet the Emperor they believe to be dead. As they approach weeping, he stands, half-hidden by a curtain, his body inclined in a slight bow, the smallest exultant smile on his serene face.

THE LEGEND OF ROSEPETAL (1985; original German edition as *Das Märchen von Rosenblättchen*, written by Clemens Brentano, 1978)

Judith Gloyer

SOURCE: A review of *The Legend of Rosepetal*, in *School Library Journal*, Vol. 32, No. 2, October, 1985, p. 169.

[Clemens] Brentano's Romanticist fairy tale seems to include every fairy tale device imaginable in conjunction with heavy dollops of symbolism, death and cruelty. There is one bizarre or cruel turn after another with no purpose. Perhaps one could make a case that it shows that one can survive child abuse. Almost half of the story concerns Rosepetal's vain and selfish mother. Rosepetal finally arrives on the scene only to be killed when her jealous mother accidentally drives a sharp comb into her head. Not to fear—Rosepetal is preserved within seven glass coffins. After her mother's death, she awakens to a cruel foster mother. Now she is threatened with drowning and hit daily so that her "face was all black and blue, as if she had been eating blueberries." Sensitive souls will flee before an odd light tone is added at the end. Rosepetal marries a handsome prince and is sent a little prince by Heaven, who has related this hair-raising tale for a piece of gingerbread. Zwerger uses the same flowing line embellished with rich pattern found in *The Nutcracker and the Mouse King* and *Gift of the Magi,* but her colors are much darker in keeping with the tone of this work. Brentano's text, as translated by Bell, is skillfully written, and the many strands of the tale are tied together. However it is highly stylized and rather overwhelming. A book for historical or research collections.

E. Colwell

SOURCE: A review of *The Legend of Rosepetal*, in *The Junior Bookshelf*, Vol. 49, No. 4. August, 1985, p. 172.

An odd story [by Clemens Brentano] from 'the heart of German Romanticism' in which several folk tale themes appear. A Princess has two passions in her life, roses and her beautiful long hair which keeps six 'braiding maids' busy all day. She tells a Prince who asks for her hand that she is as likely to marry him as 'a rosebush is to marry a pumpkin'. This unlikely union does happen, however, for her rejected suitor becomes a rose bush for her sake and in a confusion of enchantment and symbolism, a baby girl appears in a pumpkin. But Rosepetal dies through her mother's fault and is enclosed in seven glass coffins. After some years she comes to life again, is treated like a Cinderella by her aunt but rescued to marry happily.

This is a comparative simplification of an incredibly complicated plot, too involved and strange surely for children of the usual age for fairy tales.

This volume is one of a series of lavishly produced fairy tales. It is attractively illustrated in harmonising shades of brown and yellow and the decorative flowing lines of the design on the pages is a delight. The faces of the characters, angular like those of carved wooden puppets, seem disappointing.

It seems likely that this story may be of more interest to the folklorist than to children.

THUMBELINE (written by Hans Christian Andersen, 1985)

Karla Kuskin

SOURCE: A review of *Thumbeline,* in *The New York Times Book Review,* November 3, 1985, p. 35.

Fairy tales let us believe the impossible. Lisbeth Zwerger depicts magical occurrences with a deft simplicity that imbues them with truth. Her output this season also includes *The Legend of Rosepetal.* Her *Thumbeline,* a graceful girl, bends over a sick bird twice her size, with real love and sadness. We are convinced by animals in mufflers and velvet coats and find their human hands and slippered feet unsurprising. The ghost of a benevolent Arthur Rackham hovers over the windblown line and warm earthtones of these pages. The final picture is lit by a bright white flower, a throne for Thumbeline and her prince. Although the words describe her as wearing his crown, that detail is absent. Some child will point this out to you.

John Cech

SOURCE: A review of *Thumbeline,* in *The Christian Science Monitor,* November 11, 1985, p. B6.

Lisbeth Zwerger's version of Andersen's **Thumbeline,** with a new translation by Anthea Bell, is one of the most elegant of all the Andersen remakes this season. Zwerger has the ability to make credible Andersen's fantasy world of the tiny girl, caught in the dark underworld of moles and field mice and spiders, who finally, through her kindness, long-suffering, and pluck, manages to escape to find her true love—not in the mole's house, but on a daisy petal, with the prince of the flowers. In looking at Zwerger's work, one thinks of Rackham and other 19th-century masters of illustration. But the sensitivity and grace of

these illustrations are all her own, and she gives of both qualities fully in her recreation of this story.

THE DELIVERERS OF THEIR COUNTRY (written by Edith Nesbit, 1985)

Ethel L. Heins

SOURCE: A review of *The Deliverers of Their Country,* in *The Horn Book Magazine,* Vol. LXII, No. 2, March-April, 1986, p. 195.

E. Nesbit's stories of dragons first appeared in England in the *Strand Magazine* at the turn of the century and were soon collected in *The Book of Dragons.* Later another story was discovered, and long after the author's death came her *Complete Book of Dragons.* Nesbit could present everyday people caught up in supernatural situations just as naturally as she permits the realistic details of everyday life to obtrude into her world of fantasy. And her sense of the comic, free of adult condescension, is always inherent in her characters, her events, and her lucid, engaging style. After Effie got something in her eye—it seemed to be a tiny dragonlike insect—increasingly larger specimens were discovered, and soon a plague of "winged lizards" overspread the land. But green, scaly, winged dragons they were, "and they breathed fire and smoke, as all proper dragons must." So Effie and her brother Harry, resourceful children, decided to rid the country of the pestilential creatures; in the church they found the tomb of St. George and, seeking his help, woke up the marble effigy. But affable though he was, he felt unequal to a task of such magnitude: "'I was always for a fair fight—one man one dragon, was my motto.'" So, instead, he gave the children some expert, efficacious dragon-killing advice. As in some of Lisbeth Zwerger's previous works utilizing the picture book format, the illustrations fare better than does the sizable text, which is set out in long, unbroken pages of type. In her calm, uncluttered full-page pictures the illustrator subtly captures the Edwardian ambiance of the story. She deals masterfully with negative space, leaving the viewer's imagination free to savor her cool, delicate colors and to discern her droll humor, which precisely reflects the author's disarming absurdity.

Susan H. Patron

SOURCE: A review of *The Deliverers of Their Country,* in *School Library Journal,* Vol. 32, No. 8, April, 1986, p. 91.

First published in *Strand Magazine* in 1899, this story appeared in [Edith] Nesbit's *The Complete Book of Dragons* with pen-and-ink illustrations by Erik Blegvad. Two children save England from being overrun by dragons. Captured by a large child-eating dragon and taken to a cave, they discover the "Universal Tap-room." They half turn off the tap labeled "Sunshine" and turn *on* the ones called "Fair to moderate" and "Showery" since dragons cannot survive in such weather, "and both taps stuck . . . which accounts for our climate." This single-story edition features large-size pages printed on fine quality paper and 11 beautifully composed watercolors. Zwerger's illustrations enhance the story, which is probably best read to a child who can sit close enough to the reader to examine the pale, evocative pictures closely. Text covers each entire facing page and could be intimidating, thus the book's best use is as a read-aloud. British terminology is generally understood in context, and the turn-of-the-century costuming adds interest. Nesbit's humor and distinctive clear style carry the story briskly along, while Zwerger's illustrations lend it great charm.

Margery Fisher

SOURCE: A review of *The Deliverers of Their Country*, in *Growing Point*, Vol. 25, No. 1, May, 1986, p. 4636.

"The ones this size did not eat people only lettuces, but they always scorched the sheets and pillow cases dreadfully." Who but Edith Nesbit could carry off such a bizarre combination of the ordinary and the sinister? When Edwardian England is plagued by multi-sized dragons rising from asbestos nests in the fields, Effie and Harry consult the effigy of St. George in the local church and bravely put his advice into practice; predictably, their elders are less grateful than they might be, distrusting children with such unusual powers. A blithely absurd, shrewdly comic tale presented in picture-book format with wash and line pictures elegantly and precisely placing the characters in a suitably historic setting to match traditional views of the dragons.

Julia Briggs

SOURCE: "Revenants and Revivals," in *Times Literary Supplement*, No. 4346, July 18, 1986, p. 798.

Lisbeth Zwerger has produced a delightful picture book using [Edith] Nesbit's *The Deliverers of Their Country* (from her *Book of Dragons*). Here each page of the (authentic) text faces a full-page, delicately coloured illustration, animated by a sense of movement, space and evocative period detail—there are even faint reminiscences of the drawings of the Edwardian Punch artist, Phil May. Lisbeth Zwerger's work has undergone an impressive process of change and development. From the outset she has used rich and subtle watercolour tones to create a vivid atmosphere, but the line work in her early illustrations tended to be decorative rather than informative. In this book, her drawings reveal with a new economy her grasp of structure, architecture and gesture. Not since her original illustrator, H. R. Millar, has E. Nesbit been so well served.

📖 *THE CANTERVILLE GHOST* (written by Oscar Wilde, 1985)

Publishers Weekly

SOURCE: A review of *The Canterville Ghost*, in *Pub-*

lishers Weekly, Vol. 230, No. 22, November 28, 1986, p. 75.

There is nothing as creamy as the prose of Oscar Wilde—spoofing both Brits and Yanks, ethereal and earthly—in one of the most famously funny ghost stories of all time. Is it for children? A resounding yes; doubters are challenged to read the descriptions of the Otis twins' pranks on the hapless Canterville haunt and see if they can keep a straight face. Zwerger has illuminated the story with special zeal—as "Reckless Rupert, or the Headless Earl," her ghost's head looks gloomily toward his trunk, seeming to suspect that even this splendid get-up won't have any effect on the skeptical Americans inhabiting his home. Virginia's pity on the ghost—his salvation—is told in every picture as she turns away from the scenes of his failed tricks and later as a married woman, lays flowers on his grave where he finally rests. A hilarious story, and a truly spirited blend of words and pictures.

Barbara Chatton

SOURCE: A review of *The Canterville Ghost*, in *School Library Journal*, Vol. 33, No. 5, January, 1987, pp. 85-6.

Lovers of Oscar Wilde's stories will delight in this new illustrated version of *The Canterville Ghost* if the picture book format does not keep them from finding it. Wilde's story of an American family who moves into Canterville Chase and annoys a weary ghost with their lack of belief in him is a wry commentary on the ways of British nobility and of their hard-headed American cousins. Like many of Wilde's tales, this one is filled with sophisticated allusions to his social and political milieu, but ends as sentimental romance. Zwerger's wry pictures high-light this tone beautifully. Her toothless ghost is round and comical, as would suit a ghost whom no one fears, and her heroine, Virginia, is young and sweetly boyish. All of the illustrations are set against misty gray watercolor backgrounds except for the climactic scene, echoed on the front cover, in which the tiny huntsmen on the wallpaper call out to Virginia to "Go Back." This will make a fine read-aloud for audiences of secondary students who are prepared to savor Wilde's ironic humor and Zwerger's delicate watercolors.

📖 *A CHRISTMAS CAROL* (written by Charles Dickens, 1988)

Publishers Weekly

SOURCE: A review of *A Christmas Carol*, in *Publishers Weekly*, Vol. 234, No. 11, September 9, 1988, p. 138.

A well-loved holiday story, Dickens's slim tale has been opened up on the oversize pages of this new version, similar in format to Zwerger's treatment of *The Gift of the Magi*. Expanses of white space around and between lines of text give the volume a clean-looking design, which sets off the artist's charm-filled, airy water-colors. And that design is of key importance to the unabridged text, for the book appears accessible to readers just out of the picture book age. This is a fine collector's edition as well; Zwerger has chosen not to represent the three spirits of Christmas, but merely hints at their presence in her pictures. That grounds the story of Scrooge's night firmly in the realm of the almost-real and the possible, and renders his transformation a fully believable phenomenon.

Susan Hepler

SOURCE: "December Holiday Book Round Up," in *School Library Journal,* Vol. 35, No. 2, October, 1988, pp. 32-8.

In an oversized format . . . and with illustrations similar to her illustrations for O. Henry's *Gift of the Magi,* Zwerger gives her own distinctive depiction of Dickens' complete text. Muted watercolors, varying view-points, uncluttered interiors, and a slightly humorous rendering of characters tend to distance viewers. In contrast, [Trina Schart] Hyman's dramatic depiction of characters, events, and settings and a straight-on viewpoint seem more involving. However, Zwerger more than triples the illustrations found in Hyman's book—a plus for young listeners and lookers. The text appears to crowd the page, as very little white space has been left as a border. While neither version shows to great advantage at story hours, both belong on your Christmas list for the family read-aloud shelf this holiday season.

Mary M. Burns

SOURCE: A review of *A Christmas Carol,* in *The Horn Book Magazine,* Vol. LXIV, No. 6, November-December, 1988, pp. 762-63.

It is as difficult to imagine Christmas without Scrooge and Tiny Tim as it is to envision Christmas without Santa Claus, for Dickens's tale has become a part of our holiday lore. Yet there is something reassuring about the perennial fascination with a particular subject; the story has enduring and universal appeal as well as the artistry of an author who could touch our sensibilities without becoming mired in sentimentality. The complete text has been embellished with Lisbeth Zwerger's distinctive and cannily interpretive illustrations. As always, her sense of color is impeccable. She suggests light without ever becoming garish and darkness without becoming muddy. Her use of fine line is particularly remarkable, recalling the genius of the great nineteenth-century illustrators yet retaining her own distinctively fluid, economical style. While each picture is a gem, the image of Scrooge approaching a deserted graveyard, accompanied by the Ghost of Christmas Yet to Come, is as dramatic and memorable a piece of visual storytelling as one is likely to encounter. The oversized format belies the contents, for the book is an illustrated story rather than a picture book. Because the volume is an unabridged version, the pages—without

pictorial material, with rather narrow top and bottom margins, less-than-generous leading, and light print—are, on first glance, somewhat daunting. Further, the elongated design, although striking, may make the book difficult to maneuver for ordinary reading purposes. However, most of these seeming flaws can be turned to advantage for oral interpretation: the size is well suited for a lectern; the lengthy runs of text mean fewer pages to turn; and the slimness of the volume allows it to lie flat. Certainly, the production is unique—a fine addition to holiday collections.

AESOP'S FABLES (written by Aesop, 1989)

Denise Wilms

SOURCE: A review of *Aesop's Fables,* in *Booklist,* Vol. 86, No. 6, November 15, 1989, p. 655.

Zwerger's restrained watercolor paintings feature her customary spacious compositions and flushes of watery color to create appealing visual interpretations of 12 familiar Aesop stories. All but one will be understood by children. The odd one, "The Man and the Satyr," with the moral "I cannot be friends with a man who blows hot and cold with the same breath" is likely to confuse in its present context. Among the more successful selections are "Town Mouse and Country Mouse," "The Fox and the Grapes," and "The Milkmaid and Her Pail." A pleasant choice where picture-book Aesops are in demand.

Denise Anton Wright

SOURCE: A review of *Aesop's Fables,* in *School Library Journal,* Vol. 35, No. 16, December, 1989, p. 92.

Just when it appears as if every possible interpretation of the fables attributed to Aesop has been done, the acclaimed Zwerger produces a thoughtful version that is filled with wit and wisdom. Twelve fables are retold with an economy of language, stressing the universal truth behind each moral. There's a satisfying blend of well-known favorites such as "Town Mouse and Country Mouse" and "The Hare and the Tortoise," rounded out with selections usually overlooked in most collections. Opposite each fable is a colored-ink and wash illustration. Utilizing a somber range of browns, grays, and blues, Zwerger periodically includes a dash of bright red to catch viewers' eyes. The luminous colors make her use of the white space even more noticeable. The illustrations seem to be inspired by Winslow Homer in both their composition and restrained use of color. The characters—both animal and human—are executed in a fairly realistic manner which accommodates Zwerger's impish sense of humor. The balance between each page of text and its accompanying illustration is pleasing, with the book's overall effect being one of a leisurely journey through the reasons for human behavior. A fine addition to larger collections desiring another interpretation of Aesop's fables.

From A Christmas Carol, *written by Charles Dickens. Illustrated by Lisbeth Zwerger.*

Zena Sutherland

SOURCE: A review of *Aesop's Fables,* in *Bulletin of the Center for Children's Books,* Vol. 43, No. 6, February, 1990, p. 129.

Lisbeth Zwerger's delicate line and economical composition, her restraint in use of color, and the humor in the animals' faces make this edition of the fables a pleasure to look at. Zwerger has chosen a dozen fables to illustrate, some as popular as "The Fox and the Grapes," others ("The Man and the Satyr") less well known. The retellings and the moral tags may be more fully comprehensible to the reader in the middle grades, but this can also be used for reading aloud to younger children.

📖 *THE MERRY PRANKS OF TILL EULENSPIEGEL* (retold by Heinz Janisch, 1990)

Publishers Weekly

SOURCE: A review of *The Merry Pranks of Till Eulenspiegel,* in *Publishers Weekly,* Vol. 237, No. 46, November 16, 1990, p. 56.

Hans Christian Andersen Medalist Zwerger cunningly il-lustrates 11 folktales about the famous German prank-ster—from Till's triple dunking at his baptism, to his funeral, at which he leaves a last trick for his mourners. Both art and text are distinctly quaint and European. Although the stories are told colloquially, as if by a villager who knew Eulenspiegel well, there is a forced merriment to the narrator's intrusions: "'What a crazy fellow!' folks say when they hear of Till's merry pranks," he too frequently tells the reader. However, Zwerger's bright paintings, bordered by gaily patterned, thin ribbons, are tightly designed and populated by a rich panoply of German peasants and kings, who laugh with Eulenspiegel even as they are being duped.

John Mole

SOURCE: "Thereby Hangs a Picture," in *Times Educational Supplement,* No. 1267, February 15, 1991, p. 31.

The spirits of Walter Crane and Heath Robinson would approve of Lisbeth Zwerger's quaintly mischievous, thickly populated illustrations for *Till Eulenspiegel*. As befits the remorseless sequence of merry pranks, everyone is shown as either gaping with amazement or wearing a knowing look. There are lots of funny hats and pointed shoes, and the escapades of this ever-popular, rather tediously whimsical subversive who thrives on proving that figures of speech should be taken literally are engagingly recounted.

Ethel L. Heins

SOURCE: A review of *The Merry Pranks of Till Eulenspiegel,* in *The Horn Book Magazine,* Vol. LXVII, No. 2, March-April, 1991, p. 210.

Few, if any, stories for children about the celebrated rogue remain in print; most adults familiar with Till Eulenspiegel—Till Owlglass—have probably learned of him through Richard Strauss's well-known orchestral tone poem. Yet after the invention of printing, stories about the fourteenth-century German peasant clown spread throughout Germany and the Low Countries, first through chapbooks and then through collections, novels, and poetry. As in much folklore, the German narratives are full of earthy, satiric humor; they tell how the townspeople are befooled by the trickster—the personification of peasant cleverness outwitting dull, bourgeois complacency. The eleven newly translated tales—terse, brisk, and full of sprightly word play—reveal a cheerful, boisterous mischief-maker whose antics are reflected in spirited paintings, medieval in costume and setting, by the winner of the 1990 Hans Christian Andersen Medal. More and more, in her recent books Lisbeth Zwerger displays a mastery of composition; here each story, complete on a single page, is embellished with a deft little drawing and illustrated not with the muted watercolors of her earlier work but with a rich, often brilliant palette for dramatic contrast and emphasis.

Elizabeth Hormann

SOURCE: A review of *The Merry Pranks of Till Eulenspiegel,* in *The School Librarian,* Vol. 39, No. 2, May, 1991, p. 58.

Till Eulenspiegel is a popular figure in German folklore, a master prankster who bests his betters and enjoys narrow escapes. Anthea Bell has translated eleven of his adventures from cradle to grave. Lisbeth Zwerger has provided bright colourful illustrations to accompany each of them. At his best, Till pulls the legs of his stuffy betters or takes advantage of their gullibility. Invariably he comes out on top, but it is sometimes a near thing. 'Till bakes owls and monkeys,' 'Till comes to the sea' and 'Till makes green into blue' show him to best advantage.

But some of the tales are terribly tame—or fall flat altogether—and the language is a bit beyond the picture book crowd to which the book is geared. The result is very uneven—a nicely illustrated collection that should be a classic piece of humour, but somehow isn't quite. As a picture book it may get a lot of wear for Lisbeth Zwerger's very appealing illustrations, but only a few of the tales are lively enough to make the 'most requested story' list. Perhaps a reworking would make Till Eulenspiegel's charms more apparent to an English readership.

Carolyn Noah

SOURCE: A review of *The Merry Pranks of Till Eulenspiegel,* in *School Library Journal,* Vol. 37, No. 6, June, 1991, p. 94.

In 11 single-page vignettes, Till Eulenspiegel captures the imaginations of another generation of children. Recounted are his three baptisms, Till on the tightrope, baking owls and monkeys, and other lesser-known prankster tales. [Anthea] Bell's elegant translations are full of meaning, and can be read aloud to young listeners with enjoyment, while older children will howl at the double entendres that characterize these traditional stories. Missing, however, is any folkloric background, and only intrepid hunters will discover from the CIP that Till is of German origin. Zwerger's illustrations relay impish human expressions wonderfully, but overall her delicate, wispy pictures fail to snatch the vivacious energy of the practical joker. Handsome individual borders emphasize the contained quality of the watercolors, but are a visual treat in themselves. While these tellings may be the only ones available for this audience, older readers will also enjoy Jay Williams's *The Wicked Tricks of Tyl Uilenspiegel,* which sports more dynamic art by Friso Henstra.

📖 *DWARF NOSE* (written by Wilhelm Hauff, 1994)

D. A. Young

SOURCE: A review of *Dwarf Nose,* in *The Junior Bookshelf,* Vol. 58, No. 6. December, 1994, p. 203.

Wilhelm Hauff died in 1827 a few days before his 25th birthday. In that short time he had produced no less than thirty volumes of writing. He is perhaps best known for his finely crafted fairy tales which tend to be rooted in reality rather than the romanticism more popular with his contemporaries. *Dwarf Nose* is one of the stories from *The Sheikh of Alexandria and His Slaves.*

Jacob's mother sold fruit and vegetables in the market. One day a troublesome old woman customer so upset his mother that Jacob told her in no uncertain terms that she was a pest. Nevertheless he was persuaded to carry her purchases home for her. He thought that the sack contained his mother's cabbages but the old woman drew out human heads! Jacob was bewitched into the shape of a dwarf with a nose as long as his arm. He spends seven years in the kitchens of the witch then she turns him loose. How his cooking skills win his return to normality makes an intriguing story which ends up happily with Jacob back with his parents, taller and, we hope, wiser.

The illustrations are brilliantly inventive adding much to the pleasure of the reading. Lisbeth Zwerger has a considerable reputation as a book illustrator and received the Hans Christian Andersen Lifetime Achievement Award in 1990.

Kirkus Reviews

SOURCE: A review of *Dwarf Nose,* in *Kirkus Reviews,* Vol. LXIII, No. 24, December 15, 1994, p. 1564.

A beautifully crafted fairy tale, in which young Jacob, the son of poor parents living in a large German town, has a run-in with the bad fairy Herbwise, a hideous enchantress. Herbwise changes Jacob into a miserable hunchbacked dwarf with a megacolossal schnozzle. Trials and tribulations follow, not the least of which is the wretched treatment Jacob receives from the townsfolk, even his mother and father, who refuse to believe his protestations that he is their son. A bit of luck brings Jacob (by then a renowned cook) together with Mimi, a girl cast by a spell into a goose, and the rare herb sneezewell, found flowering under a chestnut tree by the light of a full moon. Part of a linked series of tales, this is a wondrous story, full of drama and magic, holding the townsfolk's petty, malicious behavior up to sharp light. Zwerger's paintings, with their ancient feel and their tranced quality, situate the story four-square in its own strange land.

The world of fairy tales was made a whole lot poorer when [Wilhelm] Hauff died in 1827, at only 25 years old.

Susan Scheps

SOURCE: A review of *Dwarf Nose,* in *School Library Journal,* Vol. 41, No. 1, January, 1995, p. 118.

An odd, rather lengthy German fairy tale, written in 1827. When a boy insults an elderly fairy, she changes him into a squirrel and makes him work in her household, run by guinea pigs and squirrels, for seven years. At the end of that time, he is transformed into a hunchbacked, long-nosed dwarf. Spurned by his parents and chased by the townspeople, he uses his skills as a chef (learned from his time in the fairy's service) to obtain work in the Duke's kitchen. With the help of an enchanted goose (really a wizard's daughter), he reverses the spells, and all ends happily. *Dwarf Long-Nose,* translated by Doris Orgel and illustrated by Maurice Sendak, has a nicer flow to the language and a more eye-pleasing format; [Anthea] Bell's translation is capable, but stiff, and unlike the people in many of Zwerger's earlier books, the main characters here are painted in a somewhat surrealistic style. A dear illustration of the animals in the old fairy's house and a scene in the Duke's kitchen soften the appropriately grotesque tenor of the book. Libraries that do not own the earlier version may want to consider this new one.

Christine Heppermann

SOURCE: A review of *Dwarf Nose,* in *The Five Owls,* Vol. IX, No. 3, February, 1995, p. 62.

Social satire succeeds as children's literature only at the hands of a better-than-average storyteller. This lively original fairy tale, first published in Germany in 1827, takes frequent gentle jabs at bourgeois society that children obviously will not catch. But, happily, Wilhelm Hauff could work with fanciful as well as satirical details: guinea pigs wearing nutshells for shoes, a wicked fairy with teeth so rotten she must eat bread made of sunbeams, a dwarf whose long nose whacks against furniture. Aided by Lisbeth Zwerger's elegant, spirited watercolors, the odd chain of events Hauff presents, first and foremost, makes a good story.

Appearance weighs heavily in ***Dwarf Nose***. Jacob might have had more patience with the difficult customer, later revealed to be the fairy Herbwise, who picks over his mother's attractively arranged wares at the market, if not for her red eyes, incredibly long nose, and neck "thin as a cabbage stalk." Herbwise predicts quick-tempered Jacob will one day sport a schnoz similar to her own and, it appears, the customer is always right. After a seven-year stint as a squirrel on the enchantress's all-rodent domestic staff, Jacob escapes her home only to find himself changed into a much maligned, barrel-chested, hook-nosed dwarf.

Done primarily in warm, dry tones, Zwerger's illustrations artfully intersperse with the substantial blocks of text. Her most energetic paintings depict the more bizarre characters.

She literally interprets Hauff's claim that Herbwise moves "as if she had wheels on her legs," showing the spidery-limbed crone rolling to and fro, her sack dress billowing up to reveal spoked feet. Shifts in perspective give readers a taste of how big and mocking the world must seem to the deformed Jacob.

Utility can take you farther than beauty, Jacob discovers when the culinary secrets he learned as a squirrel land him a respected position as Assistant Master Cook to the Duke. Poking fun at this middle-class value, Hauff mischievously twists the traditional fairy tale ending. Yes, Jacob turns back into his old handsome self, but no, he does not run off with the beautiful maiden. He returns to his parents, buys a shop with his earnings and gifts, and becomes rich and happy. How very practical and grown-up of him! A little something for everyone, Hauff seems to say, child or adult.

Prue Goodwin

SOURCE: A review of *Dwarf Nose,* in *The School Librarian,* Vol. 43, No. 1, February, 1995, p. 17.

It is always pleasing to see books from North-South, as we get so few examples of children's books in translation. It is also delightful to see more of Lisbeth Zwerger's illustrations. If for no other reasons, **Dwarf Nose** is a very welcome addition to a folktale collection. The "feel" of the pages is enticing before you reach the story; however, this is not an easy read.

The story itself involves the complexity of plot common to early nineteenth-century fairy tales. The eponymous hero is kidnapped, changed in shape, spends years under a spell, is rejected by his parents, serves the Duke as a cook, buys a talking goose, seeks a magic herb, and so on. All good stuff, but quite a tough read even for an able primary pupil, especially as the typography is not very inviting. Line length and print density are a little off-putting. The illustrations, however, are outstanding and they, and the quality of production, make reading this book well worth the effort. It is a text more for the student of folk tales than the child looking for a stimulating read, though I am sure many youngsters would enjoy hearing this tale read aloud.

Kay Weisman

SOURCE: A review of *Dwarf Nose,* in *Booklist,* Vol. 91, No. 17, May 5, 1995, p. 1573.

A new translation of [Wilhelm] Hauff's 1827 fairy tale tells the story of Jacob, a young boy kidnapped by an old woman. He insults her, and in return, she transforms him into an ugly dwarf with a long nose. When he finally escapes, he goes unrecognized by his parents and is forced to work as a cook for a duke until a young girl who has been turned into a goose helps him undo the spell. He reciprocates by helping her regain her true form. Zwerger's Old World-style watercolor paintings mesh nicely with the classic text, and combined with high quality paper, they make for an elegant book. Most intriguing are the fanciful illustrations; for example, the one featuring the young goose/girl can be viewed from multiple perspectives. Although the story may seem somewhat verbose to modern listeners, it will be popular with fairy tale fans and belongs in larger collections.

CHRISTIAN MORGENSTERN: LULLABIES, LYRICS AND GALLOWS SONGS (translated from the German by Anthea Bell, 1995)

Sally R. Dow

SOURCE: A review of *Christian Morgenstern: Lullabies, Lyrics and Gallows Songs,* in *School Library Journal,* Vol. 41, No. 5, May, 1995, p. 102.

These nonsense poems and lyric verses by the late 19th-century German poet have been compared to works by Edward Lear and Lewis Carroll for their imagination and playfulness. The translator has tried to retain original rhyme schemes and meter, substituting English equivalents for invented names and puns when necessary. An example of concrete (wordless) poetry defined by design, and another consisting of pure sound (described by the poet as "phonetic rhapsody") have been left intact. Layout is attractive, with ample space allowed by the placing of only one poem per page, often with full-page, full-color illustrations opposite. A mixture of type faces— from large, bold letters to small, softer ones—lends diversity. Gentle, finely drawn watercolors capture the selections' dry, witty humor. These offbeat poems demand more than one reading. The book will be of most interest to libraries seeking to add to poetry collections from around the world.

Deborah Stevenson

SOURCE: A review of *Christian Morgenstern: Lullabies, Lyrics and Gallows Songs,* in *Bulletin of the Center for Children's Books,* Vol. 49, No. 1, September, 1995, p. 23.

Christian Morgenstern, according to a combination of flap copy and mid-book translator's note, was a turn-of-the-century German poet who wrote lyric verses and nonsense poetry. The lullabies and lyrics are sweet but slender, generally more pretty than resonant ("In Winter Time," about fish thinking a pebble atop the ice is food, and "Lullaby," about a shorn and chilly sheep, are the most memorable). The "Gallows Songs"—nonsense poems— have more zing to them, offering some droll and dark turns on gentle childhood verse ("At dawn the moonsheep will be dead / its fleece all white, the sun all red"— "Dream of the Moonsheep"). While translation of such things can be difficult (two of the poems in the "Gallows Songs" section, in fact, are in their original untranslatable nonsense form) Bell does nonsense proud in poems such as "Gruesong" ("The Flidderflopped gloameth / through igglywangled wole . . .") and "Suggestions to Nature for New Species" ("The Oxsparrow / the Chameleoduck / the Lionworm / the Toadle . . ."). Zwerger's watercolors

sometimes fill the square page and sometimes simply offer a decorative comment on a poem, never overwhelming the poems but sometimes unwontedly conventionalizing the gallows songs. While the book's merits sometimes seem to lie more in attractive design than in poetic concept, and it's a pity that there's no compact biographical note on Morgenstern in the book itself (and no explanation of the piquant term "Gallows Songs"), it's still intriguing to see some poetry with a difference.

LITTLE HOBBIN (written by Theodor Storm, 1996)

Susan Scheps

SOURCE: A review of *Little Hobbin,* in *School Library Journal,* Vol. 42, No. 1, January, 1996, p. 96.

This odd cautionary tale written in 1849 has been abbreviated and illustrated. Hobbin, a fearless, demanding little boy, is unable to get his fill of being wheeled around in his crib. He makes a sail out of his nightshirt when his mother falls asleep and rolls up the walls and over the ceiling, up a moonbeam, through the keyhole, up and down the nighttime streets, through the dark forest, ". . . over the moors to the world's end, and straight on into the sky." When the moon and stars disappear, the sun throws the boy into the sea, where his small bed sinks: ". . . that's when you and I came to the rescue and picked up little Hobbin in our boat. If we hadn't saved him, he might well have drowned." Zwerger's soft paintings reflect the dreamlike quality of the story. While this fantastic bedtime tale might cause some children to chuckle, it lacks the substance and charm of Nancy Willard's *Nightgown of the Sullen Moon* and the delightful detail of Maurice Sendak's *In the Night Kitchen,* both of which have less text per page and more illustrations.

Julie Corsaro

SOURCE: A review of *Little Hobbin,* in *Booklist,* Vol. 92, No. 11, February 1, 1996, p. 940.

Zwerger's delicate watercolors add a mesmerizing quality to this little known lullaby by [Theodor] Storm, a nineteenth-century German poet. It tells of Little Hobbin who goes on a nocturnal journey in his baby bed. Although it remains to be seen whether this smoothly translated, rather romantic tale will appeal to modern sensibilities, the pictures are sure to please. Zwerger's elegant style is familiar, but she manages to suffuse her softly colored images with freshness and vitality—her personified moon is the perfect blend of grandfatherly compassion and lunar texture. This ranks among her best work.

Additional coverage of Zwerger's life and career is contained in the following sources published by Gale Research: *Major Authors and Illustrators for Children and Young Adults; Something about the Author,* Vol. 66; and *Something about the Author Autobiography Series,* Vol. 13.

CUMULATIVE INDEXES

How to Use This Index

The main reference

> **Baum, L(yman) Frank**
> 1856-1919 .... **15**

lists all author entries in this and previous volumes of *Children's Literature Review*.

The cross-references

> See also CA 103; 108; DLB 22; JRDA;
> MAICYA; MTCW; SATA 18; TCLC 7

list all author entries in the following Gale biographical and literary sources:

AAYA = *Authors & Artists for Young Adults*
AITN = *Authors in the News*
BLC = *Black Literature Criticism*
BW = *Black Writers*
CA = *Contemporary Authors*
CAAS = *Contemporary Authors Autobiography Series*
CABS = *Contemporary Authors Bibliographical Series*
CANR = *Contemporary Authors New Revision Series*
CAP = *Contemporary Authors Permanent Series*
CDALB = *Concise Dictionary of American Literary Biography*
CLC = *Contemporary Literary Criticism*
CLR = *Children's Literature Review*
CMLC = *Classical and Medieval Literature Criticism*
DAB = *DISCovering Authors: British*
DAC = *DISCovering Authors: Canadian*
DAM = *DISCovering Authors Modules*
    DRAM: dramatists module
    MST: most-studied authors module
    MULT: multicultural authors module
    NOV: novelists module
    POET: poets module
    POP: popular/genre writers module

DC = *Drama Criticism*
DLB = *Dictionary of Literary Biography*
DLBD = *Dictionary of Literary Biography Documentary Series*
DLBY = *Dictionary of Literary Biography Yearbook*
HW = *Hispanic Writers*
JRDA = *Junior DISCovering Authors*
LC = *Literature Criticism from 1400 to 1800*
MAICYA = *Major Authors and Illustrators for Children and Young Adults*
MTCW = *Major 20th-Century Writers*
NCLC = *Nineteenth-Century Literature Criticism*
PC = *Poetry Criticism*
SAAS = *Something about the Author Autobiography Series*
SATA = *Something about the Author*
SSC = *Short Story Criticism*
TCLC = *Twentieth-Century Literary Criticism*
WLC = *World Literature Criticism, 1500 to the Present*
YABC = *Yesterday's Authors of Books for Children*

CUMULATIVE INDEX TO AUTHORS

CUMULATIVE INDEX TO NATIONALITIES

AMERICAN

Aardema, Verna **17**
Adkins, Jan **7**
Adler, Irving **27**
Adoff, Arnold **7**
Alcott, Louisa May **1, 38**
Alexander, Lloyd (Chudley) **1, 5**
Aliki **9**
Anglund, Joan Walsh **1**
Armstrong, William H(oward) **1**
Arnosky, James Edward **15**
Aruego, Jose (Espiritu) **5**
Ashabranner, Brent (Kenneth) **28**
Asimov, Isaac **12**
Atwater, Florence (Hasseltine Carroll) **19**
Atwater, Richard (Tupper) **19**
Avi **24**
Aylesworth, Thomas G(ibbons) **6**
Babbitt, Natalie (Zane Moore) **2**
Bacon, Martha Sherman **3**
Bang, Molly Garrett **8**
Baum, L(yman) Frank **15**
Baylor, Byrd **3**
Bellairs, John (A.) **37**
Bemelmans, Ludwig **6**
Benary-Isbert, Margot **12**
Bendick, Jeanne **5**
Berenstain, Jan(ice) **19**
Berenstain, Stan(ley) **19**
Berger, Melvin H. **32**
Bess, Clayton **39**
Bethancourt, T. Ernesto **3**
Block, Francesca (Lia) **33**
Blos, Joan W(insor) **18**
Blumberg, Rhoda **21**
Blume, Judy (Sussman) **2, 15**
Bond, Nancy (Barbara) **11**
Bontemps, Arna(ud Wendell) **6**
Bova, Ben(jamin William) **3**

Brancato, Robin F(idler) **32**
Branley, Franklyn M(ansfield) **13**
Brett, Jan (Churchill) **27**
Bridgers, Sue Ellen **18**
Brink, Carol Ryrie **30**
Brooks, Bruce **25**
Brooks, Gwendolyn **27**
Brown, Marcia **12**
Brown, Marc (Tolon) **29**
Brown, Margaret Wise **10**
Bruchac, Joseph III **46**
Bryan, Ashley F. **18**
Bunting, Eve **28**
Burnett, Frances (Eliza) Hodgson **24**
Burton, Virginia Lee **11**
Byars, Betsy (Cromer) **1, 16**
Caines, Jeannette (Franklin) **24**
Calhoun, Mary **42**
Cameron, Eleanor (Frances) **1**
Carle, Eric **10**
Carter, Alden R(ichardson) **22**
Cassedy, Sylvia **26**
Charlip, Remy **8**
Childress, Alice **14**
Christopher, Matt(hew F.) **33**
Ciardi, John (Anthony) **19**
Clark, Ann Nolan **16**
Cleary, Beverly (Atlee Bunn) **2, 8**
Cleaver, Bill **6**
Cleaver, Vera **6**
Clifton, (Thelma) Lucille **5**
Coatsworth, Elizabeth (Jane) **2**
Cobb, Vicki **2**
Cohen, Daniel (E.) **3, 43**
Cole, Brock **18**
Cole, Joanna **5, 40**
Collier, James L(incoln) **3**
Colum, Padraic **36**
Conford, Ellen **10**

Conrad, Pam **18**
Cooney, Barbara **23**
Corbett, Scott **1**
Cormier, Robert (Edmund) **12**
Cox, Palmer **24**
Creech, Sharon **42**
Crews, Donald **7**
Crutcher, Chris(topher C.) **28**
Curry, Jane L(ouise) **31**
Danziger, Paula **20**
d'Aulaire, Edgar Parin **21**
d'Aulaire, Ingri (Mortenson Parin) **21**
Day, Alexandra **22**
de Angeli, Marguerite (Lofft) **1**
DeClements, Barthe **23**
DeJong, Meindert **1**
Denslow, W(Illiam) W(allace) **15**
dePaola, Tomie **4, 24**
Dillon, Diane **44**
Dillon, Leo **44**
Disch, Thomas M(ichael) **18**
Domanska, Janina **40**
Donovan, John **3**
Dorros, Arthur (M.) **42**
Dr. Seuss **1, 9**
Duncan, Lois **29**
Duvoisin, Roger Antoine **23**
Eager, Edward McMaken **43**
Ehlert, Lois (Jane) **28**
Emberley, Barbara A(nne) **5**
Emberley, Ed(ward Randolph) **5**
Engdahl, Sylvia Louise **2**
Enright, Elizabeth **4**
Epstein, Beryl (M. Williams) **26**
Epstein, Samuel **26**
Estes, Eleanor **2**
Ets, Marie Hall **33**
Feelings, Muriel (Grey) **5**
Feelings, Tom **5**

CUMULATIVE INDEX TO TITLES

Title Index

Title Index

Title Index

Title Index

Die Zweite Revolution (Goebbels)
   See *Die Zweite Revolution*

Title Index

ISBN 0-7876-1140-9

90000